WEST HAM UNITED

FROM GREENWOOD TO REDKNAPP

– Match by Match –

BOOKS BY CLIVE LEATHERDALE

Football
WEST HAM: FROM GREENWOOD TO REDKNAPP – MATCH BY MATCH
WIMBLEDON: FROM SOUTHERN LEAGUE TO PREMIERSHIP – A COMPLETE RECORD
ABERDEEN: THE EUROPEAN ERA – A COMPLETE RECORD
THE ABERDEEN FOOTBALL COMPANION
ENGLAND: THE QUEST FOR THE WORLD CUP – A COMPLETE RECORD
SCOTLAND: THE QUEST FOR THE WORLD CUP – A COMPLETE RECORD
IRELAND: THE QUEST FOR THE WORLD CUP – A COMPLETE RECORD
THE BOOK OF FOOTBALL (*as editor*)

Dracula and Vampirism
DRACULA: THE NOVEL & THE LEGEND
A STUDY OF BRAM STOKER'S GOTHIC MASTERPIECE
THE ORIGINS OF DRACULA
THE BACKGROUND TO BRAM STOKER'S GOTHIC MASTERPIECE
THE JEWEL OF SEVEN STARS (*as editor*)
CALMET'S TREATISE ON VAMPIRES AND REVENANTS (*as editor*)

International Relations
BRITAIN AND SAUDI ARABIA 1925-1939: THE IMPERIAL OASIS

Far Eastern Travel
THE VIRGIN WHORE AND OTHER CHINESE CHARACTERS
TIANANMEN, TRAVELS AND TRAUMAS
TO DREAM OF PIGS: TRAVELS IN SOUTH AND NORTH KOREA

Education
SO YOU WANT TO TEACH ENGLISH TO FOREIGNERS

WEST HAM UNITED

FROM GREENWOOD TO REDKNAPP

– Match by Match –

CLIVE LEATHERDALE

Desert Island Books

First Published
in 1998 by
DESERT ISLAND BOOKS
89 Park Street, Westcliff-on-Sea, Essex SS0 7PD
United Kingdom

British Library Cataloguing-in-Publication Data
A catalogue record for this book is available from the British Library

ISBN 1-874287-19-8

Printed in Great Britain
by
Biddles Ltd, Guildford

PHOTOGRAPH CREDITS
The publishers wish to acknowledge with thanks West Ham United FC, John Helliar, the South Essex Recorder Newspaper Group, and Steve Bacon for the provision of photographs for this book

Preface

1965 was a crucial year in my life, just as it was for my club, West Ham. It was the year I signed as an apprentice professional for the club and it was the year when the Hammers gained international acclaim when they beat Munich 1860 2-0 to win the European Cup-Winners' Cup at Wembley.

The sheer quality of that performance really did signal the start of an exciting era for West Ham, when they became recognised wherever they played. It gained them a reputation that was the envy of many, and certainly owed its origin to the coaching beliefs of Ron Greenwood, who had assumed control a few years earlier.

He always encouraged players to maximise their potential by enjoying their football, and always emphasised the importance of providing entertainment for the supporters who paid our wages. Bobby Moore, Geoff Hurst and Martin Peters were three magnificent examples of his methods, and key members of England's memorable World Cup success in 1966.

Ron's influence has been in place ever since, with John Lyall carrying forward that same emphasis on skill. He managed our FA Cup successes in 1975 and 1980 – even teaching me sufficient heading skills to score that winner against Arsenal! I retired myself in 1984, and in 19 memorable years under Ron and John I can honestly say I still enjoyed my training sessions at the end, as much as those at the beginning.

John left in 1989, with Lou Macari, Billy Bonds and Harry Redknapp the subsequent managers. The tradition of skill and exciting attacking play is one they have all tried to retain, although the escalating finances of the modern game makes equality so much harder. But West Ham must never change that philosophy because their supporters cannot remember anything less.

Long may it continue.

Trevor Brooking

Author's Note

Most football histories focus on the important. There are hundreds of published accounts of West Ham's FA Cup triumphs at Wembley, but not a sentence about some run of the mill League fixture at Coventry or a League Cup-tie at Plymouth.

It is to redress this imbalance that this book is aimed, to shed light on every game, not just those that grabbed the headlines. I first adopted this approach in the early 1980s with a book that covered England's World Cup quest from 1950, recording and reporting every fixture. I kept to the same format with later volumes on Scotland and Ireland's World Cup quests.

My books on Wimbledon FC and Aberdeen FC were divided into two halves, a chronological narrative followed by a match by match section. With a club as big as West Ham, however, I felt there was little I could add by way of general history. What was lacking was the minuscule detail of every game played, and which I hope now to have rectified. Please bear in mind that until recently there were no videos to check what sports writers scribbled down at the time, often in haste, and without the benefit of slow-motion replays to verify what was written.

There is no place here for friendly matches or short-lived tournaments – the Watney Cup, the Texaco Cup, The Anglo-Italian Cup, the Simod Cup, and the like. This book concentrates on the League, the League Cup, FA Cup, the Charity Shield and the European Cup-Winners' Cup. Although Ron Greenwood was appointed at the tail end of the 1960-61 season, this book takes up the story from 1961-62.

The fifty-word summaries are, I hope, more than just match reports. I have used them to relate what was happening off the pitch as well as on it, transfer talk, or simple gossip. Where possible I have taken coverage from the national rather than local press, the neutral rather than the partisan, in the belief that this is what most supporters would prefer.

Needless to say, a project such as this entails endless checking. I could not have done it alone and would like to thank those who in various ways have assisted me. Gary Firmager, editor of the fanzine 'Over Land and Sea', and Tony Fowles of 'The Ultimate Dream' endorsed the book. Lorraine Gunn in the club office is constantly cheerful and helpful. Peter Stewart promoted the book in the match programme and Steve Bacon willingly provided photographs at short notice. Hammers fan Paul Brand designed the dust jacket. Leigh Edwards and Donal Cullen went through every word of the manuscript, pointing out errors and ambiguities. So did John Northcutt, co-author of the Breedon history of West Ham.

Above all I must thank John Helliar, whose family have been associated with West Ham virtually since the club was founded. His father, Jack Helliar, edited and printed the match programme from World War II to 1983. John Helliar – official Hammers historian and press relations officer – kindly put at my disposal his vast personal archives, without which this book would have been much delayed.

CLIVE LEATHERDALE

GUIDE TO SEASONAL SUMMARIES

Col 1: Match number (for league fixtures); Round (for cup-ties).
e.g. 2:1 means 'Second round; first leg.'
e.g. 4R means 'Fourth round replay.'

Col 2: Date of the fixture and whether Home (H), Away (A), or Neutral (N).

Col 3: Opposition.

Col 4: Attendances. Home gates appear in roman; Away gates in *italics*.
Figures in **bold** indicate the largest and smallest gates, at home and away.
Average home and away attendances appear after the final league match.

Col 5: Respective league positions of West Ham and their opponents after the match.
West Ham's position appears on the top line in roman.
Their opponents' position appears on the second line in *italics*.
For cup-ties, the division and position of opponents is provided.
e.g. *2:12* means the opposition are twelfth in Division 2.

Col 6: The top line shows the result: W(in), D(raw), or L(ose).
The second line shows West Ham's cumulative points total.

Col 7: The match score, West Ham's given first.
Scores in **bold** indicate West Ham's biggest league win and heaviest defeat.

Col 8: The half-time score, West Ham's given first.

Col 9: The top lines shows West Ham's scorers and times of goals in roman.
The second line shows opponents' scorers and times of goals in *italics*.
A 'p' after the time of a goal denotes a penalty; 'og' an own-goal.
The third line gives the name of the match referee.

Team line-ups: West Ham line-ups appear on the top line, irrespective of whether they are home or away. Opposition teams appear on the second line in *italics*.
Players of either side who are sent off are marked !
West Ham players making their league debuts are displayed in **bold**.

Substitutes: Names of substitutes appear only if they actually took the field.
A player substituted is marked *
A second player substituted is marked ^
A third player substituted is marked "
These marks do not indicate the sequence of substitutions.

N.B. For clarity, all information appearing in *italics* relates to opposing teams.

No	Date		Att	Pos	Pt	F-A	H-T	Scorers, Times, and Referees	1	2	3	4	5	6	7	8	9	10	11
1	H	MANCHESTER U			D	1-1	1-1	Dick 37	**Leslie**	Kirkup	Bond	Malcolm	Brown	Moore	Scott	Woosnam	Sealey	Dick	Musgrove
	19/8		32,628		1			*Stiles 18*	*Gregg*	*Brennan*	*Cantwell*	*Stiles*	*Foulkes*	*Setters*	*Quixall*	*Viollet*	*Herd*	*Pearson*	*Charlton*
								Ref: M Fussey	Ron Greenwood misses the season's opening game because of a terrible head cold. Both sides entertained the crowd with fast, neat play. Man U also welcomed David Herd, a £30,000 signing from Arsenal. Viollet's lob was turned in by Stiles, then Sealey squared for Dick to tap in.										
2	A	TOTTENHAM			D	2-2	1-1	Woosnam 40, Musgrove 54	Leslie	Kirkup	Bond	Malcolm	Brown	Moore	Scott	Woosnam	Sealey	Dick	Musgrove
	23/8		***50,214***		2			*Dyson 7, 80*	*Brown*	*Baker*	*Henry*	*Blanchflower*	*Norman*	*Marchi*	*Jones*	*Collins*	*Smith*	*Allen*	*Dyson*
								Ref: E Jennings	A Wednesday night game. Double-winning Spurs' new floodlights draw gasps from the crowd when they are switched on. Phil Woosnam signs a new contract seven hours before kick-off. Both Scottish goalies played blinders. Both Terry Dyson's goals went in off a goal-post.										
3	A	WOLVES		14	L	2-3	1-1	Musgrove 19, Sealey 87	Leslie	Kirkup	Bond	Malcolm	Brown	Moore	Scott	Woosnam	Sealey	Dick	Musgrove
	26/8		*25,471*	*11*	2			*Murray 33, 63, Deeley 57*	*Finlayson*	*Stuart*	*Harris*	*Clamp*	*Slater*	*Flowers*	*Deeley*	*Mason*	*Murray*	*Broadbent*	*Hinton*
								Ref: J Cattlin	Wolves' debutants Alan Hinton and John Harris inspired the home side to their first win, aided by a fluke goal. Hinton's corner was completely miskicked by Norman Deeley, the ball spinning in an arc past Leslie, leaving the keeper beating his fists into the ground and muttering darkly.										
4	H	TOTTENHAM			W	2-1	1-0	Scott 40, Sealey 77	Leslie	Kirkup	Bond	Malcolm	Brown	Moore	Scott	Woosnam	Sealey	Dick	Musgrove
	28/8		**36,348**		4			*Allen 64*	*Brown*	*Baker*	*Henry*	*Blanchflower*	*Norman*	*Marchi*	*Jones*	*Smith J*	*Smith R*	*Allen*	*Dyson*
								Ref: R Smith	Upton Park's £30,000 new floodlights are switched on. The hot, humid conditions made many fans faint and the St John's Ambulance men were kept busy. Following 19-year-old Alan Sealey's wonder goal the crowd chanted 'We want six'. Sealey had previously missed two sitters.										
5	H	NOTT'M FOREST		7	W	3-2	1-1	Scott 42, Sealey 46, Musgrove 65	Leslie	Kirkup	Bond	Malcolm	Brown	Moore	Scott	Woosnam	Sealey	Dick	Musgrove
	2/9		23,000	*6*	6			*Addison 45, 69*	*Grummitt*	*Palmer*	*Gray*	*Whitefoot*	*McKinlay*	*Iley*	*Burton*	*Addison*	*Vowden*	*Quigley*	*Le Flem*
								Ref: L Callaghan	Forest's first league defeat was not an occasion to savour. Compared to the Spurs fiesta, this was an error-strewn game. Musgrove made it 3-1, going past two defenders before scoring in off a post. After Addison replied with a swirling 35-yarder, Forest pressed hard for an equaliser.										
6	A	BLACKPOOL			L	0-2	0-1		Leslie	Kirkup	Bond	Hurst	Brown	Moore	Woosnam	**Boyce**	Sealey	Dick	Scott
	4/9		*19,838*		6			*Horne 38, Hill 54*	*West*	*Armfield*	*Martin*	*Hauser*	*Gratrix*	*Durie*	*Hill*	*Peterson*	*Charnley*	*Parry*	*Horne*
								Ref: K Collinge	West Ham had no punch near goal, but nevertheless looked in little danger themselves until they were undone by a freak goal. Des Horne threaded a pass forward. No one moved and it trundled past Lawrie Leslie into the net. Andy Hill's 20-yarder secured Blackpool's second win.										
7	A	ASTON VILLA		6	W	4-2	0-0	Dick 47, 64, Scott 62, Sealey 74	Leslie	Kirkup	Bond	Hurst	Brown	Moore	Scott	Woosnam	Sealey	Dick	**Crawford**
	9/9		*32,000*	*17*	8			*Crowe 46, McParland 58*	*Sidebottom*	*Neal*	*Lee*	*Crowe*	*Dugdale*	*Deakin*	*McEwan*	*Baker*	*McParland*	*O'Neill*	*Burrows*
								Ref: G Hartley	Villa were desperately unlucky to lose this. They led 2-1 through McParland, the best goal of the game, when keeper Geoff Sidebottom handed Hammers two goals on a plate. First he lost Moore's high lob to let Dick equalise. Then he let Dick's shot bounce out of his hands into the net.										
8	H	CHELSEA		5	W	2-1	2-0	Dick 7, Musgrove 24	Leslie	Kirkup	Bond	Hurst	Brown	Moore	Scott	Woosnam	Sealey	Dick	Musgrove
	16/9		27,000	*15*	10			*Bridges 58*	*Bonetti*	*Sillett J*	*Harris*	*Docherty*	*Scott*	*Mortimore*	*Brabrook*	*Blunstone*	*Bridges*	*Tambling*	*Harrison*
								Ref: L Hamer	Violence on the pitch and in the crowd. Woosnam had already gone off for treatment following Docherty's concrete tackle, then Tambling's boot opened up Leslie's head. The ball broke to Bridges. Irate fans invaded the pitch as Leslie was carried off. Bobby Moore went into goal.										
9	H	BLACKPOOL			D	2-2	0-0	Musgrove 49, Boyce 65	Rhodes	Kirkup	Bond	Hurst	Brown	Moore	Scott	Boyce	Sealey	Dick	Musgrove
	18/9		26,000		11			*Hauser 86, Parry 88*	*West*	*Armfield*	*Martin*	*Hauser*	*Gratrix*	*Durie*	*Hill*	*Crawford*	*Charnley*	*Parry*	*Perry*
								Ref: J Taylor	West Ham might have been three goals up had not the referee disallowed acting skipper, John Bond's, 40-yarder for a foul on the keeper. Blackpool's South African Peter Hauser sparked a heart-breaking finish, heading Pool's first goal, then crossing for Parry's equalising header.										
10	A	SHEFFIELD UTD		3	W	**4-1**	2-0	Dick 13, 88, Musgrove 41, Sealey 87	Rhodes	Kirkup	Bond	Hurst	Brown	Moore	Scott	Woosnam	Sealey	Dick	Musgrove
	23/9		*21,034*	*17*	13			*Pace 90*	*Hodgkinson*	*Coldwell*	*Shaw G*	*Richardson*	*Shaw L*	*Summers*	*Allchurch*	*Russell*	*Pace*	*Kettleborough*	*Simpson*
								Ref: A Jobling	The Bramall Lane crowd were entertained beforehand by the Regimental Band of the Coldstream Guards, then tormented by West Ham once play began, then infuriated when the ref disallowed Kettleborough's effort which would have made it 2-1. Three goals in the last three minutes.										

No	H/A	Opponents / Date	Att	Pos	Pts	Res	HT	Scorers, Times, Referees	1	2	3	4	5	6	7	8	9	10	11
11	H	LEICESTER		2	W	**4-1**	4-0	Sealey 4, Dick 14, 37, Woosnam 38	Leslie	Kirkup	Bond	Hurst	Brown	Moore	Scott	Woosnam	Sealey	Dick	Musgrove
		30/9	26,746	*16*	15			*McLintock 80*	*Banks*	*Chalmers*	*Norman*	*McLintock*	*King*	*Appleton*	*Riley*	*Keyworth*	*McIlmoyle*	*Wills*	*Mitten*
								Ref: P Bye	Matt Gillies' Leicester are sunk under a torrent of first-half goals. Woosnam scored one and made three. The first goal came when Woosnam's shot hit Banks' legs and Sealey crashed home the rebound. This was John Dick's 300th league game, and only Burnley are above West Ham.										
12	A	IPSWICH		3	L	2-4	0-0	Sealey 71, Musgrove 87	Leslie	Kirkup	Bond	Hurst	Brown	Moore	Scott	Woosnam	Sealey	Dick	Musgrove
		7/10	*28,051*	*4*	15			*Crawford 57, 67, Phillips 66, 73*	*Bailey*	*Carberry*	*Compson*	*Baxter*	*Nelson*	*Elsworthy*	*Stephenson*	*Moran*	*Crawford*	*Phillips*	*Leadbetter*
								Ref: P Brandwood	Almost an hour passed without a goal, then six came in a rush. Alf Ramsey's Ipswich are the only team to have beaten leaders Burnley. Lawrie Leslie, wearing a jockey's cap against the sun, dived over Ted Phillips' first goal. West Ham had tried to sign the burly Phillips last season.										
13	H	BURNLEY		2	W	2-1	2-1	Crawford 3, Dick 6	Leslie	Kirkup	Bond	Malcolm	Brown	Moore	Crawford	Boyce	Sealey	Dick	Musgrove
		14/10	32,234	*1*	17			*Harris 27*	*Blacklaw*	*Angus*	*Elder*	*Adamson*	*Cummings*	*Miller*	*Towers*	*McIlroy*	*Lochhead*	*Robson*	*Harris*
								Ref: E Jennings	West Ham win this clash of the titans without Woosnam, playing for Wales. Burnley were minus Pointer and Connelly, playing for England. Ian Crawford, appearing for the first time on the right wing, scored first. Dick hit a 20-yarder. Harris scored off a post; Towers then hit the bar.										
14	A	FULHAM		2	L	0-2	0-1		Leslie	Kirkup	Bond	Malcolm	Brown	Moore	Crawford	Woosnam	Sealey	Dick	Musgrove
		21/10	*32,275*	*5*	17			*Mullery 14, Leggat 63*	*Macedo*	*Cohen*	*Langley*	*Mullery*	*Dodgin*	*Lowe*	*Leggat*	*Metchick*	*Cook*	*Haynes*	*Chamberlain*
								Ref: H Richards	A local derby played in a commendable spirit. The Fulham midfield of Johnny Haynes, Lowe, and young Alan Mullery destroyed West Ham. Mullery headed in George Cohen's cross and Haynes then chipped a free-kick onto Graham Leggat's head. This result lifts Fulham up to fifth.										
15	H	SHEFFIELD WED		6	L	2-3	1-2	Bond 29p, Dick 89	Leslie	Kirkup	Bond	Malcolm	Brown	Moore	Crawford	Woosnam	Sealey	Dick	Musgrove
		28/10	26,463	*7*	17			*Griffin 19, 84, Megson 38*	*Springett*	*Johnson*	*Megson*	*McAnearney*	*Swan*	*Kay*	*Finney*	*Griffin*	*Ellis*	*Fantham*	*Dobson*
								Ref: J Kelly	Monsoon conditions help Vic Buckingham's Owls inflict West Ham's first home defeat. Wednesday's Ron Springett and Swan both played for England in midweek. Griffin thumped in Kay's free-kick for the first goal which was soon cancelled out when Kay felled Musgrove in the box.										
16	A	MANCHESTER C		4	W	5-3	1-3	Dick 20, 75, Musgrove 54, [Sealey 55, 58]	Leslie	Kirkup	Bond	Hurst	Brown	Moore !	Crawford	Woosnam	Sealey	Dick	Musgrove
		4/11	*18,839*	*12*	19			*Dobing 6, 15, 25*	*Trautmann*	*Betts*	*Sear*	*Kennedy*	*Ewing*	*Oakes*	*Baker*	*Dobing*	*Barlow*	*Hayes*	*Wagstaffe*
								Ref: K Tuck	City's Peter Dobing, signed from Blackburn, scored a first-half hat-trick that few will remember in view of the second-half transformation. Seconds from time Bobby Moore fouled Dave Wagstaffe and was sent off, though no one knew it until the ref confirmed it after the match.										
17	H	WEST BROM		3	D	3-3	3-1	Musgrove 16, Sealey 17, Bond 25p	Leslie	Kirkup	Bond	Hurst	Brown	Moore	Crawford	Woosnam	Sealey	Dick	Musgrove
		11/11	**18,000**	*14*	20			*Jackson 32, Howe 54p, Kevan 70*	*Millington*	*Howe*	*Williams*	*Robson*	*Jones*	*Drury*	*Jackson*	*Burnside*	*Smith*	*Kevan*	*Clark*
								Ref: W Crossley	The exact opposite of last week's turnaround, as this time West Ham squander a three-goal lead. Albion boss Archie Macaulay can't believe his eyes. England's Don Howe conceded one penalty, fouling Musgrove, which made it 3-0, then scored from the spot after Smith was fouled.										
18	A	BIRMINGHAM		5	L	0-4	0-0	*[Bloomfield 89]*	Leslie	Kirkup	Bond	Hurst	Brown	Moore	Crawford	Woosnam	Sealey	Dick	Musgrove
		18/11	*20,645*	*18*	20			*Auld 58, Orritt 59, Harris 69p,*	*Schofield*	*Lynn*	*Sissons*	*Hennessey*	*Smith*	*Beard*	*Hellawell*	*Bloomfield*	*Harris*	*Orritt*	*Auld*
								Ref: J Finney	Bertie Auld, so often barracked at St Andrews, masterminded this surprise thrashing, heading in Hellawell's cross for the first goal. Orritt's goal was also a header, while Harris's penalty was awarded for a push by Bond. Strange to say, West Ham had started the match in fine fettle.										
19	H	EVERTON		4	W	3-1	0-1	Dick 57, 62, Crawford 88	Leslie	Kirkup	Bond	Hurst	Brown	Moore	Crawford	Woosnam	**Tindall**	Dick	Musgrove
		25/11	27,100	*3*	22			*Vernon 28*	*Dunlop*	*Parker*	*Thomson*	*Gabriel*	*Labone*	*Harris*	*Bingham*	*Collins*	*Young*	*Vernon*	*Fell*
								Ref: D Howell	Tindall has a quiet debut, closely marshalled by Brian Labone. Leslie was stranded in no man's land when Vernon put Everton ahead, but West Ham levelled when Dunlop fisted out Musgrove's cross to Dick. For once it was not the Hammers who lacked bite, but fancy-boys Everton.										
20	A	ARSENAL		6	D	2-2	1-2	Tindall 2, 90	Leslie	Kirkup	Bond	Hurst	Brown	Moore	Crawford	Woosnam	Tindall	Dick	Musgrove
		2/12	*47,206*	*7*	23			*Strong 36, Skirton 40*	*Kelsey*	*Bacuzzi*	*McCullough*	*Clamp*	*Brown*	*Groves*	*MacLeod*	*Ward*	*Strong*	*Eastham*	*Skirton*
								Ref: K Burns	Ron Tindall's last-minute header from Bond's cross cruelly denied Arsenal their first win over West Ham since World War II. It would have been academic had man-of-the-match George Eastham shot under rather than over the bar from close in. He had made both Arsenal goals.										
21	H	BOLTON		5	W	1-0	0-0	Woosnam 72	Leslie	Kirkup	Bond	Hurst	Brown	Bovington	Crawford	Woosnam	Sealey	Dick	Musgrove
		9/12	19,472	*12*	25				*Hopkinson*	*Harris*	*Farrimond*	*Threlfall*	*Edwards*	*Rimmer*	*Holden*	*Stevens*	*McAdams*	*Hill*	*Pilkington*
								Ref: J Loynton	A maul in the mud. This best-forgotten game was rescued by Woosnam who somehow kept his balance when shoved in the back by Threlfall. He accepted a return pass from Sealey and dribbled round two defenders to score the winner. Moore missed the match through suspension.										

LEAGUE DIVISION 1 | Manager: Ron Greenwood | SEASON 1961-62

No	Date			Att	Pos	Pt	F-A	H-T	Scorers, Times, and Referees	1	2	3	4	5	6	7	8	9	10	11
22		A	MANCHESTER U		4	W	2-1	0-1	Dick 75, 85	Leslie	Kirkup	Bond	Hurst	Brown	Moore	Crawford	Woosnam	Tindall	Dick	Musgrove
	16/12			*29,472*	*20*	27			*Herd 18*	*Gaskell*	*Brennan*	*Dunne*	*Nicholson*	*Foulkes*	*Setters*	*Chisnall*	*Giles*	*Herd*	*Lawton*	*Charlton*
									Ref: L Callaghan	Moore returns after his one-match suspension and helps to heap more trouble on lowly Man U. Herd put them ahead with defenders appealing for offside. Poor visibility caused the floodlights to be switched on early. John Dick thundered the equaliser, then converted Musgrove's pass.										
23		H	WOLVES			W	4-2	2-1	Musgrove 1, Hurst 4, 78, 81	Leslie	Kirkup	Bond	Hurst	Brown	Moore	Crawford	Woosnam	Tindall	Dick	Musgrove
	18/12			21,261		29			*Murray 9, 53*	*Finlayson*	*Stuart*	*Kelly*	*Kirkham*	*Slater*	*Flowers*	*Wharton*	*Durandt*	*Murray*	*Broadbent*	*Hinton*
									Ref: D Smith	Wrote Norman Giller afterwards: 'I have always been a Moore fan. Now I rate him with the late, great Duncan Edwards.' Wolves were sent spinning to their seventh straight defeat at Upton Park by a goal inside 14 seconds. Musgrove's cross-shot was the quickest goal of the season.										
24		H	BLACKBURN		5	L	2-3	2-3	Tindall 10, Dick 12	Leslie	Kirkup	Bond	Hurst	Brown	Moore	Crawford	Woosnam	Tindall	Dick	Musgrove
	26/12			22,250	*16*	29			*Byrom 19, 21, 35,*	*Else*	*Taylor*	*Newton*	*Clayton*	*Woods*	*McEvoy*	*Douglas*	*Lawther*	*Pickering*	*Byrom*	*Ratcliffe*
									Ref: W Clements	An icy morning frolic that ends with Blackburn notching their second away win of the season. They owe a huge debt to John Byrom, who bags his first ever league hat-trick. He fittingly had the last kick of the game. Had Hammers won they would have been top of the table till tea-time.										
25		A	NOTT'M FOREST		5	L	0-3	0-2		Leslie	Kirkup	Bond	Hurst	Brown	Moore	Crawford	Woosnam	Tindall	Dick	Musgrove
	13/1			*20,359*	*16*	29			*Gray 16, Julians 44, 88*	*Grummitt*	*Palmer*	*Gray*	*Iley*	*McKinlay*	*Quigley*	*Hockey*	*Booth*	*Julians*	*Addison*	*Le Flem*
									Ref: L Tirebuck	At 36, Billy Gray is the oldest player on view, yet his shot from 25 yards beats Leslie all ends up. The keeper later moaned: 'I've never seen anything like it. I had the shot covered but the wind caught the ball and it seemed to go all ways.' West Ham haven't won here in 26 visits.										
26		H	ASTON VILLA		5	W	2-0	2-0	Woosnam 2, Dick 18	Leslie	Kirkup	Bond	Bovington	Brown	Moore	Scott	Woosnam	Sealey	Dick	Musgrove
	20/1			20,000	*12*	31				*Sims*	*Lee*	*Aitken*	*Crowe*	*Sleeuwenhoek*	*Deakin*	*McEwan*	*McMorran*	*Dougan*	*Wylie*	*Burrows*
									Ref: P Rhodes	Alan Deakin commits a quick foul, Tony Scott flights the free-kick, and Woosnam heads West Ham in front. The lead was doubled when Sims came out for Musgrove's centre but missed it. Villa look completely clueless in attack, which enables West Ham to hang on comfortably.										
27		A	CHELSEA		4	W	1-0	1-0	Moore 34	Leslie	Kirkup	Bond	Bovington	Brown	Moore	Scott	Woosnam	Sealey	Tindall	Musgrove
	3/2			*34,258*	*21*	33				*Bonetti*	*Shellito*	*Butler*	*Malcolm*	*Scott*	*Bradbury*	*Brabrook*	*Shaw*	*Moore*	*Tambling*	*Blunstone*
									Ref: E Crawford	Chelsea will finish bottom, and won't thank Moore for his peach of a goal that inflicts yet another defeat. When Moore shaped to collect from Woosnam, everyone expected him to pass. Instead he let fly on the volley. When Chelsea's Scott fouled Tindall, Bond fired the penalty wide.										
28		H	SHEFFIELD UTD		5	L	1-2	0-1	Woosnam 88	Leslie	Kirkup	Bond	Bovington	Brown	Moore	Scott	Woosnam	Sealey	Dick	Musgrove
	10/2			21,829	*6*	33			*Pace 41, 74*	*Hodgkinson*	*Coldwell*	*Shaw G*	*Richardson*	*Shaw J*	*Summers*	*Allchurch*	*Kettleborough*	*Pace*	*Russell*	*Simpson*
									Ref: R Mann	All West Ham's early season gloss has disappeared. The Blades have gone 13 games without defeat and in Derek Pace have one of the stars of the moment. Walter Winterbottom must have admired his volley which opened the scoring. At the death, Woosnam scored, then hit the bar.										
29		A	LEICESTER		4	D	2-2	1-1	Woosnam 36, Dick 88	Leslie	Kirkup	Bond	Bovington	Brown	Moore	Scott	Woosnam	Sealey	Dick	Musgrove
	17/2			*21,312*	*9*	34			*Keyworth 1, 51*	*Banks*	*Chalmers*	*Norman*	*White*	*King*	*Appleton*	*Riley*	*Walsh*	*Keyworth*	*Gibson*	*Stringfellow*
									Ref: J Parkinson	Stringfellow centres in the first minute and Keyworth heads in. Leicester are pegged back by Woosnam's thumping 20-yard volley. Another Keyworth header, this time from Gibson's cross, restores the lead. Moore then heads down to Dick lurking near the goal line to make it 2-2.										
30		H	IPSWICH		4	D	2-2	1-1	Dick 6, Kirkup 46	Leslie	Kirkup	Bond	Bovington	Brown	Moore	Scott	Boyce	Sealey	Dick	Musgrove
	24/2			27,760	*3*	35			*Leadbetter 20, Phillips 78p*	*Bailey*	*Carberry*	*Compton*	*Baxter*	*Nelson*	*Elsworthy*	*Stephenson*	*Moran*	*Crawford*	*Phillips*	*Leadbetter*
									Ref: P Brandwood	West Ham needed to win to overtake Alf Ramsey's high-flying Ipswich. Woosnam missed the game with a twisted knee sustained in training. Just after half-time Kirkup's 30-yard effort spun through Bailey's hands over the line. Musgrove then handled in the box to concede a penalty.										
31		A	BURNLEY		5	L	**0-6**	0-3	*[Pointer 44, Elder 85]*	Leslie	Kirkup	Lyall	Bovington	Brown	Moore	Scott	Woosnam	Sealey	Dick	Musgrove
	3/3			*24,279*	*1*	35			*Robson 1, 76, Towers 24, 73,*	*Blacklaw*	*Angus*	*Elder*	*Adamson*	*Cummings*	*Miller*	*Connelly*	*McIlroy*	*Pointer*	*Robson*	*Towers*
									Ref: J Powell	This massacre by the league leaders widens the gap between them to seven points. Burnley have now scored 51 goals in 13 home games, an average of almost four a game. 'We want eight' roared the crowd. Lyall made his comeback and Moore kept up a running battle with the ref.										

No	H/A Date	Opponent Att	Pos	Res Pts	F-A	H-T	Scorers, Times, and Referees	1	2	3	4	5	6	7	8	9	10	11
32	A	SHEFFIELD WED	5	D	0-0	0-0		Leslie	Kirkup	Bond	Hurst	Brown	Moore	Sealey	Woosnam	**Byrne**	Tindall	Musgrove
	17/3	*31,403*	*8*	36				*Springett*	*Johnson*	*Megson*	*Hardy*	*Swan*	*Kay*	*Finney*	*Dobson*	*Young*	*Fantham*	*Holliday*
							Ref: H Richards	Johnnie Byrne makes his debut after signing from Crystal Palace for £65,000. His impact is negligible as Springett enjoys a 90-minute holiday. The action was all at the other end, where Leslie's acrobatics, two goal-line clearances by Joe Kirkup, and a post from Dobson, earned a point.										
33	H	MANCHESTER C	6	L	0-4	0-2		Leslie	Kirkup	Bond	Hurst	Brown	Moore	Woodley	Woosnam	Byrne	Tindall	Musgrove
	24/3	25,808	*11*	36			*Hayes 17, Dobing 36, 56, 81*	*Trautmann*	*Kennedy*	*Sear*	*Benson*	*Leivers*	*Oakes*	*Young*	*Dobing*	*Barlow*	*Hayes*	*Wagstaffe*
							Ref: A Sparling	Peter Dobing scores a simple hat-trick as West Ham's slide continues. It is his third of the season and second against the Hammers. Not the ideal match for Derek Woodley to come in on the wing. The result might have been different had Woosnam's 5th-minute effort not hit a post.										
34	A	BLACKBURN	6	L	0-1	0-1		Leslie	Kirkup	Bond	Hurst	Brown	Moore	Woodley	Woosnam	Byrne	Tindall	Musgrove
	28/3	**8,800**	*10*	36			*Byrom 13*	*Else*	*Taylor*	*Newton*	*Clayton*	*England*	*McGrath*	*Douglas*	*Lawther*	*Pickering*	*Byrom*	*Haverty*
							Ref: D Carr	John Byrom, Rovers' 17-year-old starlet who sunk West Ham with a Boxing Day hat-trick, scores the crucial goal in yet another defeat. In driving sleet and snow, Leslie fumbles Clayton's 20-yard effort and Byrom pounces. Centre-half Mike England marks Byrne out of the game.										
35	A	WEST BROM	6	W	1-0	1-0	Musgrove 23	Leslie	Kirkup	Bond	Hurst	Brown	Moore	Woodley	Woosnam	Byrne	Tindall	Musgrove
	31/3	*18,000*	*13*	38				*Millington*	*Howe*	*Williams G*	*Robson*	*Jones*	*Drury*	*Jackson*	*Hope*	*Smith*	*Kevan*	*Clark*
							Ref: W Crossley	Greenwood's team adopt hit and run tactics, with nine Hammers defending for most of this one-sided match, and constantly after they scored. The only goal came when Jones miscued in attempting to clear Kirkup's through ball, which runs to Musgrove. Drury hit the bar for Albion.										
36	H	BIRMINGHAM	6	D	2-2	0-0	Musgrove 55, 75	Leslie	Kirkup	Bond	Hurst	Brown	Moore	Woodley	Byrne	Sealey	Tindall	Musgrove
	6/4	22,548	*10*	39			*Bloomfield 59, Lynn 60*	*Schofield*	*Lynn*	*Sissons*	*Hennessey*	*Smith*	*Beard*	*Hellawell*	*Bloomfield*	*Harris*	*Leek*	*Auld*
							Ref: K Collinge	A Friday night match. Musgrove's two goals temporarily silence the Upton Park boo-boys. All Johnnie Byrne achieved was to be lectured by the ref after a flare-up with Bloomfield. Considering Stan Lynn limped out on the wing for 88 minutes, City were effectively playing with 10.										
37	A	EVERTON	7	L	0-3	0-1		Leslie	Kirkup	Bond	Hurst	Brown	Moore	Woosnam	Tindall	Byrne	Dick	Musgrove
	14/4	*45,171*	*3*	39			*Stevens 41, Vernon 47, Temple 73*	*Dunlop*	*Meagan*	*Thomson*	*Gabriel*	*Labone*	*Harris*	*Bingham*	*Stevens*	*Young*	*Vernon*	*Temple*
							Ref: H Wilson	Everton extend their unbeaten home record to 15 games. New boy Stevens had squandered three simple chances before lobbing Leslie from the edge of the box. At 2-0 Thompson handled, but John Bond fired his penalty straight at Dunlop, the ball wedging between the keeper's ankles.										
38	H	CARDIFF	6	W	**4-1**	1-0	Baker 15 (og), Sealey 53, Crawford 68, [Byrne 83]	Leslie	Kirkup	Lyall	**Peters**	Lansdowne	Moore	Scott	Byrne	Sealey	Dick	Crawford
	20/4	25,459	*21*	41			*Pickerell 58*	*John*	*Stitfall*	*Milne*	*Baker*	*Rankmore*	*Hole*	*McCarthy*	*King*	*Charles*	*Durban*	*Pickerell*
							Ref: H Horner	Greenwood drops six players, among them Woosnam, Bond, and Hurst. Moore is made captain. Cardiff were dreadful, typified by Baker's hilarious own-goal. Byrne almost scored when hitting the bar, from which Sealey netted, then from a tight angle scored his first for West Ham.										
39	H	ARSENAL	6	D	3-3	1-1	Scott 16, Dick 75, Lansdowne 84	Leslie	Kirkup	Lyall	Peters	Lansdowne	Moore	Scott	Byrne	Sealey	Dick	Crawford
	21/4	31,912	*8*	42			*MacLeod 42, Clapton 60, Strong 70*	*Kelsey*	*Magill*	*McCullough*	*Brown*	*Neill*	*Petts*	*Clapton*	*Griffiths*	*Strong*	*Eastham*	*MacLeod*
							Ref: J Mitchell	Had Arsenal won it would have lifted them above West Ham. Early in the second half Lawrie Leslie's hand was stamped on. John Lyall went in goal while Leslie played out time on the right wing. Leslie sped past two men to force a corner from which Billy Lansdowne equalised.										
40	A	CARDIFF	7	L	0-3	0-2		**Rhodes**	Bond	Peters	Hurst	Brown	Moore	Musgrove	Woosnam	Sealey	Byrne	Crawford
	23/4	*11,200*	*21*	42			*Ward 5, 37, Tapscott 73*	*Vearncombe*	*Stitfall*	*Milne*	*Hole*	*Rankmore*	*Baker*	*King P*	*Tapscott*	*Ward*	*Durban*	*Pickerell*
							Ref: E Norman	Stand-in keeper Rhodes dislocates a shoulder. This time it is Peters who goes in goal. There is almost half an hour still to play, yet Peters saves three powerful shots before being beaten by Tapscott. The loudest cheer came at half-time when Cardiff fans heard that Fulham were losing.										
41	A	BOLTON	10	L	0-1	0-0		**Dickie**	Kirkup	Lyall	Peters	Lansdowne	Moore	Scott	Byrne	Sealey	Dick	Crawford
	28/4	*17,333*	*11*	42			*Holden 89*	*Hopkinson*	*Hartle*	*Farrimond*	*Hatton*	*Edwards*	*Rimmer*	*Holden*	*Hill*	*Davies*	*McGarry*	*Pilkington*
							Ref: E Jennings	West Ham play three different keepers in three games. Alan Dickie is only 17 and he is denied a clean-sheet in the last minute when Wyn Davies harasses Peters into an error and Holden's 25-yard effort flies in off a post. That at least gave spectators something to talk about.										
42	H	FULHAM	8	W	4-2	2-1	Dick 32, 39, Crawford 46, 68	Dickie	Kirkup	**Burkett**	Peters	Lansdowne	Moore	Scott	Byrne	Sealey	Dick	Crawford
	30/4	22,000	*20*	44			*Langley 36p, Henderson 65*	*Macedo*	*Cohen*	*Langley*	*Mullery*	*Dodgin*	*Lowe*	*Leggat*	*Henderson*	*Cook*	*Haynes*	*O'Connell*
	Home Average 25,515	Away 26,531					Ref: R Mann	Fulham are already assured of another season in the top division. Although Cardiff are only two points behind, their goal-average is far inferior. The left-footed Dick put West Ham ahead when shooting with his right. Moore fisted out Henderson's drive to concede the penalty.										

LEAGUE DIVISION 1 (CUP-TIES) Manager: Ron Greenwood SEASON 1961-62

League Cup				F-A	H-T	Scorers, Times, and Referees	1	2	3	4	5	6	7	8	9	10	11
1 H PLYMOUTH	6	W		3-2	1-1	Crawford 31, 83, Woosnam 65	Rhodes	Kirkup	Bond	Hurst	Brown	Moore	Scott	Woosnam	Sealey	Dick	Crawford
11/9	12,170	*2:5*				*Maloy 39, Williams 68*	*MacLaren*	*Robertson*	*Fulton*	*Williams*	*Newman*	*Casey*	*Anderson*	*Carter*	*Kirby*	*McAnearney*	*Maloy*
						Ref: K Burns	Lucky West Ham. Ian Crawford, a £7,000 signing from Hearts, scores first and last in this five-goal fiesta. His first, a fierce shot, was hardly merited by his team-mates on the balance of play. His last, sparing West Ham the indignity of a replay, was set up by a cross from Tony Scott.										
2 H ASTON VILLA	3	L		1-3	1-2	Musgrove 26	Leslie	Kirkup	Bond	Hurst	Brown	Moore	Scott	Woosnam	Sealey	Dick	Musgrove
9/10	17,775	*14*				*McParland 35, Burrows 44, Bond 83 (og)*	*Sidebottom*	*Neal*	*Aitken*	*Tindall*	*Sleeuwenhoek*	*McMorran*	*McEwan*	*Baker*	*McParland*	*Wylie*	*Burrows*
						Ref: G Roper	Villa are defending the League Cup with the youngest side in their history. Six of their players are under 21. The crucial moments came when Villa were hanging on to a 2-1 lead. Both Dick and Sealey hit Sidebottom's crossbar before John Bond turned Burrows' cross into his own net.										

FA Cup				F-A	H-T	Scorers, Times, and Referees	1	2	3	4	5	6	7	8	9	10	11
3 A PLYMOUTH	5	L		0-3	0-1		Leslie	Kirkup	Bond	Hurst	Brown	Moore	Crawford	Woosnam	Tindall	Dick	Musgrove
3/1	*26,915*	*2:5*				*Carter 13, Williams 56, Maloy 85*	*MacLaren*	*Robertson*	*Fulton*	*Williams*	*Fincham*	*Newman*	*Anderson*	*Carter*	*Kirby*	*McAnearney*	*Maloy*
						Ref: D Smith	Second Division Plymouth gain revenge for their League Cup defeat. Early on they were indebted to their huge keeper MacLaren, but once Carter headed in Maloy's corner West Ham struggled. Williams had another Plymouth 'goal' disallowed before scoring No 2 from 25 yards.										

		Home					Away					
	P	W	D	L	F	A	W	D	L	F	A	Pts
1 Ipswich	42	17	2	2	58	28	7	6	8	35	39	56
2 Burnley	42	14	4	3	57	26	7	7	7	44	41	53
3 Tottenham	42	14	4	3	59	34	7	6	8	29	35	52
4 Everton	42	17	2	2	64	21	3	9	9	24	33	51
5 Sheffield Utd	42	13	5	3	37	23	6	4	11	24	46	47
6 Sheffield Wed	42	14	4	3	47	23	6	2	13	25	35	46
7 Aston Villa	42	13	5	3	45	20	5	3	13	20	36	44
8 WEST HAM	42	11	6	4	49	37	6	4	11	27	45	44
9 West Brom	42	10	7	4	50	23	5	6	10	33	44	43
10 Arsenal	42	9	6	6	39	31	7	5	9	32	41	43
11 Bolton	42	11	7	3	35	22	5	3	13	27	44	42
12 Manchester C	42	11	3	7	46	38	6	4	11	32	43	41
13 Blackpool	42	10	4	7	41	30	5	7	9	29	45	41
14 Leicester	42	12	2	7	38	27	5	4	12	34	44	40
15 Manchester U	42	10	3	8	44	31	5	6	10	28	44	39
16 Blackburn	42	10	6	5	33	22	4	5	12	17	36	39
17 Birmingham	42	9	6	6	37	35	5	4	12	28	46	38
18 Wolves	42	8	7	6	38	34	5	3	13	35	52	36
19 Nott'm Forest	42	12	4	5	39	23	1	6	14	24	56	36
20 Fulham	42	8	3	10	38	34	5	4	12	28	40	33
21 Cardiff	42	6	9	6	30	33	3	5	13	20	48	32
22 Chelsea	42	7	7	7	34	29	2	3	16	29	65	28
	924	246	106	110	958	624	110	106	246	624	958	924

Odds & ends

Double wins: (2) Aston Villa, Chelsea.
Double losses: (1) Blackburn.

Won from behind: (3) Villa (a), Man C (a), Man U (a).
Lost from in front: (3) Wolves (a), Blackburn (h), Villa LC (h).

High spots: Three straight wins in December leaving the Hammers 4th.

Low spots: Seven games without a win in February and March.
Losing to Second Division Plymouth Argyle in the FA Cup.
Losing 0-6 at Burnley.

West Ham faced Plymouth in both domestic cups.

Hammer of the Year: Lawrie Leslie.
Ever-presents: (0).
Hat-tricks: (0).
Leading scorer: (23) John Dick.

	Appearances			Goals			
	Lge	LC	FAC	Lge	LC	FAC	Tot
Bond, John	**37**	2	1	**2**			**2**
Bovington, Eddie	**7**						
Boyce, Ronnie	**4**			**1**			**1**
Brown, Ken	**38**	2	1				
Burkett, Jackie	**1**						
Byrne, Johnny	**11**			**1**			**1**
Crawford, Ian	**19**	1	1	**5**	2		**7**
Dick, John	**35**	2	1	**23**			**23**
Dickie, Alan	**2**						
Hurst, Geoff	**24**	2	1	**1**			**1**
Kirkup, Joe	**41**	2	1	**1**			**1**
Lansdowne, Billy	**4**			**1**			**1**
Leslie, Lawrie	**37**	1	1				
Lyall, John	**4**						
Malcolm, Andy	**8**						
Moore, Bobby	**41**	2	1	**3**			**3**
Musgrove, Malcolm	**36**	1	1	**13**	1		**14**
Peters, Martin	**5**						
Rhodes, Brian	**3**	1					
Scott, Tony	**22**	2		**4**			**4**
Sealey, Alan	**32**	2		**11**			**11**
Tindall, Ron	**13**		1	**3**			**3**
Woodley, Derek	**4**						
Woosnam, Phil	**34**	2	1	**6**	1		**7**
(own-goals)				**1**			**1**
24 players used	**462**	**22**	**11**	**76**	**4**		**80**

No	Date		Att	Pos	Pt	F-A	H-T	Scorers, Times, and Referees	1	2	3	4	5	6	7	8	9	10	11
1	A	ASTON VILLA			L	1-3	0-2	Byrne 78	Leslie	Kirkup	Peters	Hurst	Lansdowne	Moore	Crawford	Boyce	Byrne	Dick	Musgrove
	18/8		*37,000*		–			*Dougan 1, McEwan 3, Thomson 46*	*Sims*	*Lee*	*Aitken*	*Crowe*	*Sleeuwenhoek*	*Deakin*	*McEwan*	*Baker*	*Dougan*	*Thomson*	*Burrows*
								Ref: R Windle	Hammers did the double over Villa last season, but three minutes into this they are 0-2 down. Baker, Dougan and McEwan all hit Leslie's post in the second half. When West Ham delayed their reappearance, Dougan entertained the crowd by playing with claret and blue balloons.										
2	H	WOLVES			L	1-4	0-1	Musgrove 86	Leslie	Kirkup	Lyall	Peters	Brown	Moore	Crawford	Woosnam	Byrne	Dick	Musgrove
	20/8		30,020		–			*Crowe 37, Wharton 61, Farmer 62, 85*	*Davies*	*Showell*	*Thomson*	*Goodwin*	*Woodfield*	*Flowers*	*Wharton*	*Crowe*	*Farmer*	*Murray*	*Hinton*
								Ref: J Cooke	Stan Cullis's Wolves – average age 21 – scored eight in their first match and four in this, their second. Their pace and power brush West Ham aside like gossamer. Wolves' first three goals were all driven in from 25 yards or more, securing their first win at Upton Park in four years.										
3	H	TOTTENHAM		22	L	**1-6**	0-2	Woosnam 83 *[Jones 62, White 74]*	Leslie	Kirkup	Lyall	Peters	Brown	Moore	Crawford	Woosnam	Sealey	Byrne	Musgrove
	25/8		30,517	*4*	–			*Lyall 10 (og), Medwin 14, Greaves 54,58,*	*Brown*	*Baker*	*Henry*	*Blanchflower*	*Norman*	*Mackay*	*Medwin*	*White*	*Allen*	*Greaves*	*Jones*
								Ref: K Burns	The FA Cup-holders inflict yet more misery on West Ham, yet manager Bill Nicholson winced as his team squandered another half-dozen easy chances. Goal of the match was Spurs' third, finished by Greaves after bewildering interplay. Lyall began the rout, turning in Allen's cross.										
4	A	WOLVES		22	D	0-0	0-0		Leslie	Kirkup	Burkett	Peters	Brown	Moore	**Dear**	Woosnam	Sealey	Byrne	Crawford
	29/8		*32,000*	*1*	1				*Davies*	*Showell*	*Thomson*	*Goodwin*	*Woodfield*	*Flowers*	*Wharton*	*Crowe*	*Farmer*	*Murray*	*Hinton*
								Ref: R Johnson	This looked a home-banker for top v bottom. Wolves had scored 14 in three matches, West Ham had conceded 13. Only once was Leslie beaten, but Moore flung himself to jab Crowe's effort away. After the break Hammers even pressed forward and Davies saved from Woosnam.										
5	A	LEYTON ORIENT		22	L	0-2	0-2		Leslie	Kirkup	Burkett	Peters	Brown	Moore	Dear	Woosnam	Sealey	Byrne	Crawford
	1/9		*23,918*	*18*	1			*Dunmore 6, Graham 40*	*Robertson*	*Charlton*	*Lewis*	*Lucas*	*Bishop*	*Lea*	*Deeley*	*Bolland*	*Dunmore*	*Graham*	*McDonald*
								Ref: J Pickles	West Ham need to beat winless, promoted Orient, but quickly fall behind to Dunmore's header from Deeley's corner. Graham ran 20 yards before firing the second goal. Several fans fainted in the heat. Off the field Upton Park is disrupted by pay squabbles, now apparently settled.										
6	H	LIVERPOOL		20	W	1-0	1-0	Scott 5	Leslie	Bond	Burkett	Peters	Brown	Moore	Scott	Woosnam	Byrne	Hurst	Musgrove
	3/9		22,262	*9*	3				*Furnell*	*Byrne*	*Moran*	*Milne*	*Yeats*	*Ferns*	*Callaghan*	*Hunt*	*St John*	*Melia*	*A'Court*
								Ref: H Hackney	The unexpected always happens. Bill Shankly's promoted Liverpool are going well, but are undone by a team determined to restore its pride. Roger Hunt hit Leslie's post in the third minute. Had it gone in, who knows what would have happened. Within minutes Scott volleyed home.										
7	A	MANCHESTER C		19	W	**6-1**	4-1	Musgrove 27, 70, Scott 37, Byrne 40,	Leslie	Bond	Burkett	Peters	Brown	Moore	Scott	Woosnam	Byrne	Hurst	Musgrove
	8/1		*25,000*	*22*	5			*Barlow 28* [Peters 43, Hurst 80]	*Trautmann !*	*Betts*	*Kennedy*	*Benson*	*Leivers*	*Oakes*	*Barlow*	*Dobing*	*Harley*	*Young*	*Hayes*
								Ref: K Stokes	Another bizarre result, this time against the team which replaces West Ham at the bottom. When Musgrove put Hammers 5-1 up, City keeper Trautmann insisted he was offside. He booted the ball into the ref's back and was sent off for the second time in his career. Oakes went in goal.										
8	A	LIVERPOOL		19	L	1-2	0-1	Byrne 50	Leslie	Bond	Burkett	Peters	Brown	Moore	Scott	Woosnam	Byrne	Hurst	Musgrove
	12/9		*39,261*	*10*	5			*St John 39, 86*	*Furnell*	*Byrne*	*Moran*	*Milne*	*Yeats*	*Leishman*	*Callaghan*	*Hunt*	*St John*	*Melia*	*A'Court*
								Ref: R Smith	Revenge for Shankly, but it was barely merited. Liverpool keeper Furnell's long throw-out set up Ian St John's first goal. Furnell then allowed deep-lying Byrne's shot to slip through his hands for the equaliser. Near the end Yeats headed against the bar and St John forced the ball in.										
9	H	BLACKPOOL		18	D	2-2	1-2	Musgrove 32, Scott 84	Leslie	Bond	Burkett	Peters	Brown	Moore	Scott	Woosnam	Byrne	Hurst	Musgrove
	14/9		24,000	*13*	6			*McPhee 20, 33*	*Waiters*	*Armfield*	*Martin*	*Crawford*	*James*	*Durie*	*Watt*	*Green*	*Charnley*	*McPhee*	*Horne*
									Ronnie Stuart's Blackpool enjoyed two gift goals in the Friday night fixture. Peters and Brown made a mess of a clearance for the first goal, and Brown's clearance bounced off Charnley for the second. Musgrove's 25-yarder was followed by Tony Scott bagging the second equaliser.										
10	A	BLACKBURN		15	W	4-0	1-0	Hurst 35, Musgrove 62, Byrne 88, [Peters 90]	Leslie	Bond	Burkett	Peters	Brown	Moore	Scott	Woosnam	Byrne	Hurst	Musgrove
	22/9		*15,400*	*20*	8				*Else*	*Taylor*	*Bray*	*Clayton*	*Woods*	*Newton*	*Douglas*	*Ferguson*	*Pickering*	*Byrom*	*Harrison*
								Ref: W Downey	At start of play, both teams had identical records. 90 minutes later West Ham's revival had pitched Rovers to the bottom. Blackburn pressed strongly at first and Pickering came close, but the tide had turned by the time Hurst headed in. Two late goals distorted the balance of play.										

No	Venue / Date	Opponent / Att	Pos	Res / Pts	F-A	H-T	Scorers, Times, and Referees	1	2	3	4	5	6	7	8	9	10	11
11	H	SHEFFIELD UTD	13	D	1-1	0-1	Scott 64	Leslie	Bond	Burkett	Peters	Brown	Moore	Scott	Woosnam	Byrne	Hurst	Musgrove
	29/9	22,707	*8*	9			*Shaw G 22p*	*Hodgkinson*	*Coldwell*	*Shaw G*	*Richardson*	*Shaw J*	*Summers*	*Allchurch*	*Kettleborough*	*Pace*	*Hodgson*	*Hartle*
							Ref: R Spittle	Blades' manager John Harris was aggrieved about Scott's equaliser, from Bond's booming cross, which might have been offside. West Ham had gone behind when Moore toppled Allchurch, and Graham Shaw fired the penalty in off the bar. Thereafter Alan Hodgkinson stood defiant.										
12	H	BIRMINGHAM	11	W	5-0	2-0	Hurst 3, Byrne 18, 49, Musgrove 52, [Brown 87]	Leslie	Bond	Burkett	Peters	Brown	Moore	Scott	Woosnam	Byrne	Hurst	Musgrove
	6/10	21,039	*22*	11				*Withers*	*Foster*	*Lynn*	*Hennessey*	*Smith*	*Beard*	*Hellawell*	*Bullock*	*Harris*	*Leek*	*Auld*
							Ref: H New	Hammers squeeze into the top half after this demolition. Birmingham have now lost all seven away games, conceded 21 goals and scored none. Walter Winterbottom watched Hurst, enjoying the switch to centre-forward, and Byrne grab important goals. Brown hit his first league goal.										
13	A	ARSENAL	10	D	1-1	0-1	Scott 58	Leslie	Bond	Burkett	Peters	Brown	Moore	Scott	Woosnam	Byrne	Hurst	Musgrove
	13/10	***49,597***	*15*	12			*Baker 20*	*McClelland*	*Magill*	*McCullough*	*Neill*	*Brown*	*Snedden*	*MacLeod*	*Strong*	*Baker*	*Eastham*	*Skirton*
							Ref: A Sparling	Billy Wright's Arsenal have adopted Wolves' up-and-under tactics. They score first through £70,000 signing Joe Baker, after Leslie spilled McLeod's effort, but are denied their first post-war win over West Ham when Byrne's pass set up Scott's leveller. A petty, niggling match.										
14	H	BURNLEY		D	1-1	1-1	Hurst 1	Leslie	Bond	Burkett	Peters	Brown	Moore	**Brabrook**	Woosnam	Byrne	Hurst	Musgrove
	22/10	**34,612**		13			*Robson 40*	*Blacklaw*	*Angus*	*Elder*	*Adamson*	*Talbut*	*Miller*	*Connelly*	*Lochhead*	*Towers*	*Robson*	*Harris*
							Ref: J Osborne	Peter Brabrook, a £35,000 signing from Chelsea, took 40 seconds to project the cross from which Hurst netted. Burnley had flown down, but got caught in traffic, arriving 10 minutes before kick-off. Jimmy Adamson's 400th league game was rewarded by Jimmy Robson's equaliser.										
15	A	MANCHESTER U	14	L	1-3	1-2	Musgrove 29	Leslie	Burkett	Lyall	Peters	Brown	Moore	Brabrook	Woosnam	Sealey	Byrne	Musgrove
	27/10	*29,204*	*20*	13			*Quixall 17p, 41, Law 79*	*Gregg*	*Brennan*	*Cantwell*	*Stiles*	*Foulkes*	*Setters*	*Giles*	*Quixall*	*Herd*	*Law*	*Charlton*
							Ref: D Howell	Man U climb off the bottom with this important win. Leslie sent Nobby Stiles spinning inside the box and Albert Quixall netted the penalty. Following Musgrove's equaliser, Sealey missed an open goal and Brabrook hit the bar. Leslie pushed out Giles' centre to the lurking Quixall.										
16	H	BOLTON	16	L	1-2	1-1	Moore 45	Leslie	Bond	Burkett	Peters	Brown	Moore	Brabrook	Woosnam	Byrne	Hurst	Musgrove
	3/11	19,866	*14*	13			*McGarry 10, 62*	*Hopkinson*	*Hartle*	*Farrimond*	*Stanley*	*Edwards*	*Rimmer*	*Lee*	*Hill*	*Davies*	*McGarry*	*Pilkington*
							Ref: G Pullin	Bolton's first away win enables them to leapfrog over West Ham, who played as though 20 lateral passes were better than one forward one. Just after he fumbled a cross to enable McGarry to restore Bolton's lead, Leslie collided with Rimmer and broke his left leg. Peters deputised.										
17	A	LEICESTER	17	L	0-2	0-1		Dickie	Bond	Burkett	Peters	Brown	Moore	Brabrook	Boyce	Byrne	Hurst	Musgrove
	10/11	*21,064*	*4*	13			*Stringfellow 25, McLintock 58*	*Banks*	*Chalmers*	*Norman*	*McLintock*	*King*	*Appleton*	*Cheesebrough*	*Heath*	*Keyworth*	*Gibson*	*Stringfellow*
							Ref: H Richards	On a murky day high-flying Leicester maintain their unbeaten home record. Scottish signing David Gibson looked a class apart. Young keeper Dickie was beaten by Stringfellow's header and McLintock's thumping volley from 25 yards. Hurst and Byrne missed inviting chances.										
18	H	FULHAM	17	D	2-2	0-0	Hurst 57, Peters 85p	Dickie	Kirkup	Burkett	Peters	Brown	Moore	Brabrook	Boyce	Sealey	Hurst	Scott
	17/11	17,668	*21*	14			*Leggat 55, Langley 78*	*Macedo*	*Cohen*	*Langley*	*Robson*	*Lampe*	*Lowe*	*Leggat*	*Metchick*	*Brown*	*Henderson*	*O'Connell*
							Ref: J Finney	A wretched first half was followed by a stirring second. Henderson's cheeky back-pass set up a goal for Leggat. Brabrook's cross gave a tap-in equaliser for Hurst. Fulham skipper Langley thumped a shot into the corner before Leggat's arm kept out Ronnie Boyce's goal-bound effort.										
19	A	SHEFFIELD WED	18	W	3-1	3-1	Brabrook 2, Peters 27p, Scott 40	**Standen**	Kirkup	Burkett	Peters	Brown	Moore	Brabrook	Boyce	Sealey	Hurst	Scott
	24/11	*23,764*	*8*	16			*Fantham 24*	*Springett*	*Johnson*	*Birks*	*McAnearney*	*Swan*	*Kay*	*Finney*	*Wilkinson*	*Layne*	*Fantham*	*Holliday*
							Ref: J Cattlin	Jim Standen, signed for £7,000, helps inflict Wednesday's second home defeat. Hurst dummies Brabrook's cross, which beats Ron Springett. The Owls' keeper brought down Sealey for Peters to restore the lead from the spot. Tony Scott's left-footer sealed the win before half-time.										
20	H	WEST BROM	16	D	2-2	0-0	Moore 52, Hurst 85	Standen	Kirkup	Burkett	Peters	Brown	Moore	Brabrook	Boyce	Sealey	Hurst	Scott
	1/12	20,680	*13*	17			*Smith 56, 79*	*Potter*	*Howe*	*Williams*	*Cram*	*Jones*	*Drury*	*Jackson*	*Fenton*	*Smith*	*Kevan*	*Clark*
							Ref: K Dagnall	A replica of the last home game, with Fulham – a drab first half, followed by four shared goals in the second. Moore's header from Boyce's free-kick was overturned by Keith Smith's two close-range goals. A miscued defensive header enabled Hurst to volley the late point-saver.										
21	A	EVERTON	17	D	1-1	1-1	Brabrook 17	Standen	Kirkup	Burkett	Peters	Brown	Moore	Brabrook	Boyce	Sealey	Byrne	Scott
	8/12	*38,701*	*1*	18			*Stevens 5*	*West*	*Parker*	*Meagan*	*Gabriel*	*Labone*	*Harris*	*Bingham*	*Stevens*	*Young*	*Vernon*	*Veall*
							Ref: A Luty	Harry Catterick's Everton pace-setters, unbeaten at home, would have won as expected but for an incredible last-minute miss by Alex Young, who blazed over an empty net from two yards. Young was booed by the Goodison crowd at the final whistle. Both early goals were messy.										

No	Date		Att	Pos	Pt	F-A	H-T	Scorers, Times, and Referees	1	2	3	4	5	6	7	8	9	10	11
22	H	ASTON VILLA		14	D	1-1	1-0	Peters 43	Standen	Kirkup	Burkett	Peters	Brown	Moore	Brabrook	Boyce	Sealey	Byrne	Scott
	15/12		21,532	*5*	19			*Thomson 63*	*Sidebottom*	*Fraser*	*Aitken*	*Crowe*	*Sleeuwenhoek*	*Deakin*	*McEwan*	*Thomson*	*Dougan*	*Woosnam*	*Burrows*
								Ref: T Dawes	Phil Woosnam returns to Upton Park as a Villa player and is marked tightly. In heavy conditions Peters drives a spot-kick over the bar after Aitken handles, but makes amends when converting Brabrook's pass. Bobby Thomson's first-timer earned Villa's fourth away draw in a row.										
23	A	TOTTENHAM		14	D	4-4	1-2	Peters 30, Kirkup 54, Boyce 66, Scott 73	Standen	Kirkup	Burkett	Peters	Brown	Moore	Brabrook	Boyce	Sealey	Byrne	Scott
	22/12		*44,106*	*2*	20			*Smith J 8, Mackay 20, 55, 89*	*Brown*	*Baker*	*Henry*	*Smith J*	*Marchi*	*Mackay*	*Medwin*	*White*	*Smith R*	*Greaves*	*Jones*
								Ref: E Norman	John Smith, ex-Hammer, scores for Spurs in his first game of the season. Inspired by Peters, West Ham turn a 0-2 deficit into a 4-3 lead, only to be pegged back in the last moments when pocket battleship Dave Mackay secured his hat-trick with Jim Standen frozen to his goal-line.										
24	A	NOTT'M FOREST		11	W	4-3	1-2	McKinlay 7 (og), Byrne 50, B'brook 54, 84	Standen	Kirkup	Burkett	Peters	Brown	Moore	Brabrook	Boyce	Sealey	Byrne	Scott
	29/12		*18,587*	*8*	22			*Vowden 24, Addison 30, Palmer 49*	*Grummitt*	*Baird*	*Gray*	*Whitefoot*	*McKinlay*	*Palmer*	*Hockey*	*Quigley*	*Addison*	*Vowden*	*Le Flem*
								Ref: A Atherton	A snow-covered pitch was barely fit to play on. Not even the tonic of Bob McKinlay turning Scott's cross into his own net could prevent West Ham stumbling to what appeared to be a crushing defeat. Byrne's switch to centre-forward turned the tide. Boyce made both Brabrook's goals.										
25	A	SHEFFIELD UTD		10	W	2-0	1-0	Boyce 34, Sealey 77	Standen	Kirkup	Burkett	Bovington	Brown	Moore	Brabrook	Boyce	Sealey	Byrne	Scott
	16/2		*18,176*	*12*	24				*Hodgkinson*	*Coldwell*	*Shaw G*	*Richardson*	*Shaw J*	*Summers*	*Allchurch*	*Kettleborough*	*Pace*	*Hodgson*	*Simpson*
								Ref: C Duxbury	Six weeks have been frozen off. The icy pitch causes Standen and others to come out after half-time wearing canvas boots with rubber soles. The change helped earn West Ham's fifth away win, bettered only by Everton and Wolves. Boyce scored off a post; Sealey headed the second.										
26	H	ARSENAL		12	L	0-4	0-2	*[Strong 78]*	Standen	Kirkup	Burkett	Bovington	Brown	Moore	Brabrook	Boyce	Sealey	Byrne	Scott
	2/3		31,967	*8*	24			*McCullough 27, Baker 38, 55,*	*McClelland*	*Magill*	*McCullough*	*Barnwell*	*Brown*	*Sneddon*	*McLeod*	*Strong*	*Baker*	*Eastham*	*Anderson*
								Ref: D Smith	West Ham's dreadful home form continues. Billy McCullough was allowed to run 40 yards before hitting a shot that bounced, skidded and long-hopped past Standen. Joe Baker volleyed the best goal of the game, which saw as many chances created by the hosts as by the Gunners.										
27	A	BURNLEY		10	D	1-1	0-0	Byrne 86	Standen	Kirkup	Burkett	Bovington	Brown	Moore	Brabrook	Boyce	Sealey	Byrne	Scott
	9/3		*17,287*	*5*	25			*Pointer 59*	*Blacklaw*	*Angus*	*Elder*	*Adamson*	*Talbot*	*Miller*	*Connelly*	*Pointer*	*Lochhead*	*Robson*	*Harris*
								Ref: A Luty	Burnley have lost at home just once, but supporters are so angry at the sale of McIlroy to Stoke that they stay away in droves. Greenwood adopts ultra-defensive tactics and is perhaps fortunate to escape with a point when Alan Sealey's cross hits Byrne and deflects into the net.										
28	H	MANCHESTER U		11	W	3-1	1-0	Brown 36, Sealey 78, Brennan 89 (og)	Rhodes	Kirkup	Burkett	Bovington	Brown	Moore	Brabrook	Boyce	Sealey	Hurst	Scott
	18/3		28,950	*15*	27			*Herd 76*	*Gregg*	*Brennan*	*Cantwell*	*Crerand*	*Foulkes*	*Setters*	*Giles*	*Stiles*	*Herd*	*Law*	*Charlton*
								Ref: A Moore	West Ham's first home league win in five months comes against wealthy Man U, whose team cost a huge £250,000. Ken Brown bundled in Sealey's free-kick. Herd hit the bar before heading the equaliser, but Bovington then passed over Foulkes' head for Hurst to restore the lead.										
29	A	BOLTON		11	L	0-3	0-0		Rhodes	Kirkup	Burkett	Bovington	Brown	Moore	Brabrook	Boyce	Sealey	Hurst	Scott
	23/3		*19,071*	*16*	27			*Russell 50, Lee 62, Butler 67*	*Hopkinson*	*Hartle*	*Farrimond*	*Stanley*	*Edwards*	*Rimmer*	*Lee*	*Russell*	*Davies*	*Hill*	*Butler*
								Ref: J Finney	Bolton's Billy Russell, just 18, outjumped Brian Rhodes to score on his debut and send West Ham spinning to defeat. Two other 18-year-olds, Francis Lee and Dennis Butler, added further goals. The Hammers seemed preoccupied by the looming FA Cup quarter-final with Liverpool.										
30	H	SHEFFIELD WED			W	2-0	1-0	Hurst 14, Byrne 66p	Standen	Kirkup	Burkett	Peters	Brown	Moore	Brabrook	Boyce	Hurst	Byrne	Scott
	30/3		22,408		29				*Springett*	*Johnson*	*Megson*	*McAnearney*	*Swan*	*Young*	*Finney*	*Quinn*	*Wilkinson*	*Fantham*	*Dobson*
								Ref: H New	Alf Ramsey watched this mediocre match, in which West Ham looked to have a 'Liverpool' hangover. Wednesday's defence was so bad that they gave the Hammers every encouragement. England's Peter Swan fluffed a clearance to let in Hurst, then handled for Byrne's penalty.										
31	A	FULHAM		13	L	0-2	0-0		Standen	Kirkup	Burkett	Bovington	Brown	Peters	Brabrook	Boyce	Sealey	Byrne	Scott
	6/4		*26,861*	*10*	29			*Cook 47, Key 88*	*Macedo*	*Cohen*	*Langley*	*Mullery*	*Lowe*	*Robson*	*Key*	*Leggat*	*Cook*	*Brown*	*O'Connell*
								Ref: P Brandwood	Fulham soar into the top half with their eighth win in a row. Ken Brown deputised as West Ham captain in the absence of Moore, on England duty against Scotland. Leggat squared to Cook for the first goal, whereupon Tony Scott missed a hat-trick of inviting chances to equalise.										

No	Venue	Opponent	Pos	Res	F-A	H-T	Scorers, Times, and Referees	1	2	3	4	5	6	7	8	9	10	11
32	H	IPSWICH	13	L	1-3	1-1	Scott 8	Standen	Kirkup	Burkett	Peters	Brown	Moore	Brabrook	Boyce	Hurst	Byrne	Scott
	12/4	23,170	*18*	29			*Moran 44, Phillips 50, Crawford 75*	*Bailey*	*Carberry*	*Compton*	*Baxter*	*Nelson*	*Elsworthy*	*Stephenson*	*Moran*	*Crawford*	*Phillips*	*Leadbetter*
							Ref: P Bye	Lowly Ipswich have waved goodbye to their league title, but they pick up two vital points. Hammers fell behind following a bizarre blunder by Standen, who caught Phillips' header from Stephenson's cross, then dropped it over the line. 'It's a disgrace,' yelled angry fans at directors.										
33	H	LEICESTER	13	W	2-0	1-0	Sealey 19, 62	Standen	Kirkup	Burkett	Bovington	Brown	Moore	Sealey	Boyce	Hurst	Peters	Brabrook
	13/4	25,689	*2*	31				*Banks*	*Sjoberg*	*Norman*	*McLintock*	*King*	*Appleton*	*Riley*	*Cross*	*Keyworth*	*Gibson*	*Stringfellow*
							Ref: G Hartley	Leicester are knocked off the top after an unbeaten run of 16 games, as West Ham do a good turn to London rivals Spurs, who lead the pack. Greenwood reshuffled his team and was rewarded by Sealey doubling his goal tally for the season. Standen did not have one hard shot to save.										
34	A	IPSWICH	11	W	3-2	1-1	Brabrook 41, Peters 54, Hurst 75	Standen	Kirkup	Burkett	Bovington	Brown	Moore	Sealey	Boyce	Hurst	Peters	Brabrook
	15/4	*21,971*	*18*	33			*Crawford 20, Stephenson 53*	*Bailey*	*Carberry*	*Compton*	*Baxter*	*Nelson*	*Elsworthy*	*Stephenson*	*Moran*	*Crawford*	*Phillips*	*Leadbetter*
							Ref: K Stokes	Ipswich have not won at home since December, though they twice took the lead in this topsy-turvy match. First, Standen dropped a free-kick for Crawford to pounce, then Moore miskicked to let in Stephenson. Emergency centre-forward Hurst hit the winner from Moore's cross.										
35	A	WEST BROM	11	L	0-1	0-1		Standen	Kirkup	Burkett	Bovington	Brown	Moore	Sealey	Boyce	Hurst	Peters	Brabrook
	20/4	***11,600***	*16*	33			*Jackson 17*	*Potter*	*Howe*	*Williams*	*Cram*	*Jones*	*Bradley*	*Foggo*	*Jackson*	*Fenton*	*Hope*	*Carter*
							Ref: J Cattlin	Albion's new manager Jimmy Hagan smiles as Alec Jackson latched on to Hope's through pass to lash the ball past Standen from 25 yards. West Brom had lost their last four and relegation looms. They are grateful that Hurst is off form and Hammers manage just one shot on target.										
36	H	NOTT'M FOREST		W	4-1	1-1	Hurst 12, 61p, Peters 66, Moore 79	Standen	Kirkup	Burkett	Peters	Brown	Moore	Scott	Boyce	Sealey	Hurst	Brabrook
	22/4	18,179		35			*Julians 38*	*Grummitt*	*Grant*	*Wilson*	*Baird*	*McKinlay*	*Winfield*	*Hockey*	*Cobb*	*Julians*	*Addison*	*Quigley*
							Ref: C Woan	Geoff Hurst scrambled his first goal, after Grummitt spilled his first effort, then in the absence of the injured Byrne took two penalties in two minutes. The first, after McKinlay fouled Sealey, he put away; the second, after Baird handled, Hurst drove wide, spurning his hat-trick.										
37	H	EVERTON	11	L	1-2	1-2	Meagan 18 (og)	Standen	Kirkup	Burkett	Peters	Brown	Moore	Sealey	Boyce	Byrne	Hurst	Brabrook
	27/4	28,461	*1*	35			*Vernon 31, Temple 44*	*Dunlop*	*Parker*	*Meagan*	*Gabriel*	*Labone*	*Kay*	*Scott*	*Stevens*	*Young*	*Vernon*	*Temple*
							Ref: N Matthews	Harry Catterick's pace-setters recovered after full-back Meagan inexplicably prodded Brabrook's cross into his own goal and go on to their first victory in London this season. They also claim revenge for their FA Cup defeat, playing negative possession tactics after half-time.										
38	A	BIRMINGHAM	11	L	2-3	2-1	Scott 23, Hurst 34	Standen	Kirkup	Burkett	Peters	Brown	Moore	Scott	Boyce	Sealey	Hurst	Brabrook
	1/5	*14,392*	*21*	35			*Auld 40, Hennessey 60, Harris 75*	*Withers*	*Lynn*	*Green*	*Hennessey*	*Smith*	*Beard*	*Hellawell*	*Bloomfield*	*Harris*	*Leek*	*Auld*
							Ref: J Thacker	Gil Merrick's relegation-haunted Birmingham win their first home fixture since October, and do it the hard way, coming back from two goals down. Greenwood had reverted to the team which dumped Forest 4-1, which meant the axe for Byrne. Hennessey inspired City's fight-back.										
39	H	BLACKBURN	14	L	0-1	0-1		Leslie	Kirkup	Lyall	Peters	Moore	**Charles**	Scott	Boyce	**Britt**	**Sissons**	Brabrook
	4/5	18,898	*11*	35			*Pickering 44*	*Else*	*Bray*	*Newton*	*Clayton*	*Woods*	*England*	*Douglas*	*McEvoy*	*Pickering*	*Byrom*	*Harrison*
							Ref: E Jennings	The time is right to throw in the kids, and Greenwood throws in three of them. It did not produce a winning formula. Bryan Douglas fed Fred Pickering, who dribbled round Leslie, returning after his broken leg. In the second half Bobby Moore switched to the forward line, to no avail.										
40	H	LEYTON ORIENT	14	W	2-0	1-0	Brabrook 17, Scott 84	Leslie	Bond	Burkett	Peters	Brown	Moore	Brabrook	Boyce	Sealey	Byrne	Scott
	11/5	16,745	*22*	37				*Pinner*	*Charlton*	*Taylor*	*Lucas*	*Bishop*	*Lea*	*Mason*	*Gibbs*	*Musgrove*	*Bolland*	*Elwood*
							Ref: G McCabe	Orient will make a speedy return to Division 2. Greenwood dumps his kids as quickly as he had introduced them. Malcolm Musgrove, who left Upton Park for Orient, missed the chances that could have earned an away win. Brabrook's header and Scott's overhead kick win the points.										
41	A	BLACKPOOL		D	0-0	0-0		Leslie	Bond	Burkett	Peters	Brown	Moore	Brabrook	Boyce	Sealey	Hurst	Byrne
	13/5	*12,434*		38				*Waiters*	*Thompson*	*Martin*	*McPhee*	*Gratrix*	*Cranston*	*Lea*	*Quinn*	*Charnley*	*Crawford*	*Parry*
							Ref: K Tuck	Both sides are locked together in mid-table. Blackpool, minus skipper Jim Armfield, bring down the curtain on their season with this lifeless, goal-less draw. When Byrne did beat Waiters, Barry Martin was on hand to clear off the line. Leslie saved well from Charnley and Crawford.										
42	H	MANCHESTER C	12	W	**6-1**	4-0	Hurst 4, 8, Sealey 28, 82, Boyce 33, [Brabrook 53]	Leslie	Bond	Burkett	Bovington	Brown	Moore	Brabrook	Boyce	Sealey	Hurst	Dear
	18/5	**16,600**	*21*	40			*Oakes 83*	*Dowd*	*Kennedy*	*Sear*	*Oakes*	*Leivers*	*Gray*	*Young*	*Dobing*	*Harley*	*Hayes*	*Wagstaffe*
	Home	Away					Ref: S Yates	To stay up, City need to win massively and hope Birmingham lose massively. Instead, West Ham repeat the score by which they won at Maine Road, and in the process City concede their 100th goal. Moore's errant back-pass led to Oakes' consolation. West Ham now play in New York.										
Average	23,593	25,657																

LEAGUE DIVISION 1 (CUP-TIES) Manager: Ron Greenwood SEASON 1962-63

League Cup					F-A	H-T	Scorers, Times, and Referees	1	2	3	4	5	6	7	8	9	10	11
1	H	PLYMOUTH	15	W	6-0	4-0	Peters 3, Byrne 18, 30, 38p,	Leslie	Bond	Burkett	Peters	Brown	Moore	Scott	Boyce	Byrne	Hurst	Musgrove
	26/9		9,714 *2:12*				[Musgrove 51, Hurst 58]	*MacLaren*	*Roberts*	*Fulton*	*Williams*	*Wyatt*	*Newman*	*Corbett*	*Jackson*	*Garden*	*Thorne*	*Anderson*
							Ref: E Jennings	These teams also met in both last season's cups with one 'rubber' apiece. But Plymouth are sunk by Byrne's 20-minute hat-trick – two headers and a penalty after Fulton had fisted over Scott's lob. Injury-ravaged Plymouth were finished from the moment Peters headed in Scott's corner.										
2	A	ROTHERHAM	10	L	1-3	0-1	Hurst 52	Leslie	Bond	Burkett	Bovington	Brown	Peters	Scott	Woosnam	Byrne	Hurst	Musgrove
	16/10		*11,581 2:14*				*Kirkman 44, Waterhouse, 64, Weston 80*	*Ironside*	*Jackson*	*Morgan*	*Lambert*	*Madden*	*Waterhouse*	*Weston*	*Kirkman*	*Bennett*	*Houghton*	*Taylor*
							Ref: F Cowan	The last time these teams met was in Division 2 in 1958, when West Ham won 8-0. Rotherham have a fine record in the League Cup, and went ahead when Kirkman beat Burkett in the air and evaded Leslie. Hurst's header was followed by a missed penalty, when Houghton shot wide.										

FA Cup																		
3	H	FULHAM	12	D	0-0	0-0		Standen	Kirkup	Burkett	Bovington	Brown	Moore	Brabrook	Boyce	Sealey	Byrne	Scott
	4/2		21,000 *21*					*Macedo*	*Cohen*	*Langley*	*Mullery*	*Lowe*	*Robson*	*Leggat*	*Cook*	*Brown*	*Henderson*	*Stratton*
							Ref: A Holland	The weather postponed the original tie, but the pitch is still snow-bound as the worst winter in memory tightens its grip. Fulham chairman Tommy Trinder was delighted with a draw, though Byrne might have sealed a home win when he broke through but was thwarted by Macedo.										
3R	A	FULHAM	10	W	2-1	1-0	Boyce 14, Byrne 72p	Standen	Kirkup	Burkett	Bovington	Brown	Moore	Brabrook	Boyce	Sealey	Byrne	Scott
	20/2		*20,000 21*				*Robson 86*	*Macedo*	*Cohen*	*Langley*	*Mullery*	*Lowe*	*Robson*	*Key*	*Cook*	*Brown*	*Haynes*	*Metchick*
							Ref: A Holland	A replay in a snowstorm. Boyce fired in off a post from 25 yards. In the second half Boyce was fouled taking the ball round Lowe and Byrne sent Macedo the wrong way from the spot. Future England boss Bobby Robson set up a frantic climax, then Standen saved well from Haynes.										
4	H	SWANSEA	10	W	1-0	1-0	Boyce 36	Standen	Kirkup	Burkett	Bovington	Brown	Moore	Brabrook	Boyce	Sealey	Byrne	Scott
	4/3		25,924 *2:15*					*Dwyer*	*Evans*	*Griffiths*	*Hughes*	*Johnson*	*Saunders*	*Jones*	*Thomas*	*Todd*	*Reynolds*	*Morgan*
							Ref: A Moore	Only in the corners is there any grass. Otherwise the pitch is mud, mud, glorious mud. Byrne back-heeled man-of-the-match Brabrook's near-post cross and Ron Boyce netted to give Hammers their first home win since early October. Byrne later hit a post and the ball stuck in the mud.										
5	H	EVERTON	10	W	1-0	0-0	Byrne 60p	Standen	Kirkup	Burkett	Bovington	Brown	Moore	Brabrook	Boyce	Sealey	Byrne	Scott
	16/3		31,770 *3*					*West*	*Parker*	*Meagan*	*Gabriel*	*Labone*	*Kay*	*Bingham*	*Stevens*	*Young*	*Vernon*	*Morrissey*
							Ref: J Finney	Everton had won three previous cup-ties with West Ham by the same score, 2-1. Hammers were outplayed in the first half, but the tie turned when Stevens tried to check Moore and handled. Four policemen were called upon to eject an irate Everton fan who dashed onto the pitch.										
QF	A	LIVERPOOL	11	L	0-1	0-0		Standen	Kirkup	Burkett	Peters	Brown	Moore	Brabrook	Boyce	Sealey	Byrne	Scott
	30/3		*49,036 4*				*Hunt 81*	*Lawrence*	*Byrne*	*Moran*	*Milne*	*Yeats*	*Stevenson*	*Callaghan*	*Hunt*	*St John*	*Melia*	*Lewis*
							Ref: W Clements	Unlucky West Ham silenced the Kop for long stretches of this match. West Ham's adventurous 4-2-4 had Shankly's team at sixes and sevens, but Hunt, who had earlier hit the post, slid in Melia's pass from a tight angle. Sealey ought to have scored when heading straight at Lawrence.										

		Home					Away					
	P	W	D	L	F	A	W	D	L	F	A	Pts
1 Everton	42	14	7	0	48	17	11	4	6	36	25	61
2 Tottenham	42	14	6	1	72	28	9	3	9	39	34	55
3 Burnley	42	14	4	3	41	17	8	6	7	37	40	54
4 Leicester	42	14	6	1	53	23	6	6	9	26	30	52
5 Wolves	42	11	6	4	51	25	9	4	8	42	40	50
6 Sheffield Wed	42	10	5	6	38	26	9	5	7	39	37	48
7 Arsenal	42	11	4	6	44	33	7	6	8	42	44	46
8 Liverpool	42	13	3	5	45	22	4	7	10	26	37	44
9 Nott'm Forest	42	12	4	5	39	28	5	6	10	28	41	44
10 Sheffield Utd	42	11	7	3	33	20	5	5	11	25	40	44
11 Blackburn	42	11	4	6	55	34	4	8	9	24	37	42
12 WEST HAM	42	8	6	7	39	34	6	6	9	34	35	40
13 Blackpool	42	8	7	6	34	27	5	7	9	24	37	40
14 West Brom	42	11	1	9	40	37	5	6	10	31	42	39
15 Aston Villa	42	12	2	7	38	23	3	6	12	24	45	38
16 Fulham	42	8	6	7	28	30	6	4	11	22	41	38
17 Ipswich	42	5	8	8	34	39	7	3	11	25	39	35
18 Bolton	42	13	3	5	35	18	2	2	17	20	57	35
19 Manchester U	42	6	6	9	36	38	6	4	11	31	43	34
20 Birmingham	42	6	8	7	40	40	4	5	12	23	50	33
21 Manchester C	42	7	5	9	30	45	3	6	12	28	57	31
22 Leyton Orient	42	4	5	12	22	37	2	4	15	15	44	21
	924	223	113	126	895	641	126	113	223	641	895	924

Odds & ends

Double wins: (3) Manchester C, Sheffield Wed, Nott'm Forest.
Double losses: (1) Bolton.

Won from behind: (2) Nott'm Forest (a), Ipswich (a).
Lost from in front: (2) Everton (h), Birmingham (h).

High spots: Beating Manchester City 6-1 home and away.
Six unbeaten games in September and October, climbing up to 10th.

Low spots: Losing three league games in a row *three* times, in August, in October-November, and April-May.
Losing to Second Division Rotherham in the League Cup.

West Ham faced Plymouth in three successive cup competitions – in League Cup and FA Cup in 1961-62 and the League Cup in 1962-63.

Hammer of the Year: Bobby Moore.
Ever-presents: (0).
Hat-tricks: (1) Johnny Byrne.
Leading scorer: (15) Geoff Hurst.

	Appearances			Goals			
	Lge	LC	FAC	**Lge**	LC	FAC	**Tot**
Bond, John	**14**	2					
Bovington, Eddie	**10**	1	4				
Boyce, Ronnie	**27**	1	5	**3**		2	**5**
Brabrook, Peter	**29**		5	**7**			**7**
Britt, Martin	**1**						
Brown, Ken	**40**	2	5	**2**			**2**
Burkett, Jackie	**38**	2	5				
Byrne, Johnny	**30**	2	5	**9**	3	2	**14**
Charles, John	**1**						
Crawford, Ian	**5**						
Dear, Brian	**3**						
Dick, John	**2**						
Dickie, Alan	**2**						
Hurst, Geoff	**27**	2		**13**	2		**15**
Kirkup, Joe	**27**		5	**1**			**1**
Lansdowne, Billy	**1**						
Leslie, Lawrie	**20**	2					
Lyall, John	**4**						
Moore, Bobby	**41**	1	5	**3**			**3**
Musgrove, Malcolm	**15**	2		**7**	1		**8**
Peters, Martin	**36**	2	1	**8**	1		**9**
Rhodes, Brian	**2**						
Scott, Tony	**27**	2	5	**10**			**10**
Sealey, Alan	**26**		5	**6**			**6**
Sissons, John	**1**						
Standen, Jim	**18**		5				
Woosnam, Phil	**15**	1		**1**			**1**
(own-goals)				**3**			**3**
27 players used	**462**	**22**	**55**	**73**	**7**	**4**	**84**

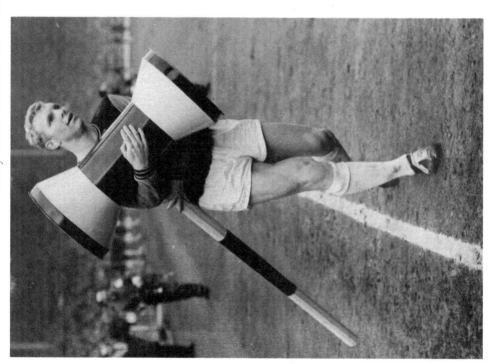

Bobby Moore celebrates with a hammer and a pinta after the 1964 FA Cup final

West Ham physio Bill Jenkins holds the 1964 FA Cup

No	Date	Att	Pos	Pt	F-A	H-T	Scorers, Times, and Referees	1	2	3	4	5	6	7	8	9	10	11
1	A CHELSEA			D	0-0	0-0		Standen	Kirkup	Burkett	Peters	Brown	Moore	Brabrook	Boyce	Byrne	Hurst	Scott
	24/8	*46,298*		1				*Bonetti*	*Shellito*	*McCreadie*	*Venables*	*Mortimore*	*Harris*	*Murray*	*Tambling*	*Mulholland*	*Moore G*	*Blunstone*
							Ref: K Seddon	West Ham's summer tournament in New York, which they won, has robbed them of new-season freshness. Harris curtailed Byrne by fair means or foul, but otherwise there was little of note. Promoted Chelsea were delighted with a draw. The ref's father played in three Cup finals.										
2	H BLACKPOOL			W	3-1	2-0	Peters 22, Boyce 35, Brabook 72	Standen	Kirkup	Burkett	Peters	Brown	Moore	Brabrook	Boyce	Byrne	Hurst	Scott
	26/8	25,533		3			*Charnley 87*	*Waiters*	*Armfield*	*Martin*	*McPhee*	*Gratrix*	*Cranston*	*Lea*	*Quinn*	*Charnley*	*Parry*	*Horne*
							Ref: D Howell	The score might not suggest it, but this was a rout. Byrne was unstoppable, and had two shots cleared off the line. Moore earned rave reviews. Boyce and Scott played a one-two to set up Peters' opener; Boyce ghosted past four defenders to add a second; and Brabrook curled the third.										
3	H IPSWICH			D	2-2	1-0	Byrne 41, Boyce 61	Standen	Kirkup	Burkett	Peters	Brown	Moore	Brabrook	Boyce	Byrne	Hurst	Scott
	30/8	27,599		4			*Baxter 55, Phillips 73*	*Bailey*	*Bolton*	*Compton*	*Baxter*	*Nelson*	*Elsworthy*	*Stephenson*	*Moran*	*Crawford*	*Phillips*	*Blackwood*
							Ref: G Roper	Twice West Ham led. If they had hung on they would have gone top. But they were undone by Ted Phillips, whose shooting had been timed at 67 mph with his right foot, 64 with his left. First he pulled an indirect free-kick back to Baxter; then blasted a shot that stuck in the stanchion.										
4	A BLACKPOOL		1	W	1-0	0-0	Byrne 57p	Standen	Kirkup	Burkett	Peters	Brown	Moore	Brabrook	Boyce	Byrne	Hurst	Scott
	2/9	*18,407*	*18*	6				*Waiters*	*Armfield*	*Martin*	*McPhee*	*Gratrix*	*Durie*	*Lea*	*Quinn*	*Charnley*	*Parry*	*Horne*
							Ref: R Harper	This game serves as a reminder of how negative and defensive West Ham could be in these years. They scored with their only chance of the match, from the spot, after Horne had brought Byrne down, and provoked the home crowd to boos and slow-handclaps. Leslie Lea hit the bar.										
5	H SHEFFIELD UTD		5	L	2-3	2-2	Byrne 34, Boyce 42	Standen	Kirkup	Burkett	Peters	Brown	Moore	Brabrook	Boyce	Byrne	Hurst	Scott
	7/9	23,837	*13*	6			*Wagstaff 4, Allchurch 8, 63*	*Hodgkinson*	*Coldwell*	*Shaw B*	*Richardson*	*Shaw J*	*Summers*	*Allchurch*	*Kettleborough*	*Pace*	*Wagstaff*	*Simpson*
							Ref: S Yates	Hammers are toppled off their perch by Blades' first win of the season. When Allchurch let fly from 20 yards to make it 0-2 few would have bet on Hammers' revival. Byrne's header and Boyce's speed of foot made it 2-2. Jim Standen flapped at a cross to gift Allchurch the winner.										
6	H NOTT'M FOREST			L	0-2	0-2		Standen	Kirkup	Burkett	Peters	Brown	Moore	Brabrook	Boyce	Byrne	Sealey	Hurst
	9/9	26,200		6			*Addison 34, Palmer 44*	*Grummitt*	*Wilson*	*Mochan*	*Palmer*	*McKinlay*	*Winfield*	*Hockey*	*Addison*	*Wignall*	*Quigley*	*Le Flem*
							Ref: J Osborne	Forest boss Johnny Carey suspended Calvin Palmer, then restored him, and Palmer plays a leading role in putting dreadful West Ham to the sword. Colin Addison was unmarked when hooking in Trevor Hockey's cross, and Palmer outjumped the limping Brown for the killer goal.										
7	A LIVERPOOL		9	W	2-1	2-0	Peters 11, Hurst 34	Standen	Kirkup	Burkett	Peters	**Bickles**	Moore	Brabrook	Boyce	Byrne	Hurst	Dear
	14/9	*45,495*	*11*	8			*Hunt 64*	*Furnell*	*Byrne G*	*Moran*	*Milne*	*Yeats*	*Ferns*	*Callaghan*	*Hunt*	*St John*	*Melia*	*Thompson*
							Ref: V James	Shankly's Liverpool have now lost all three home games. Peters' cool finish, from Moore's pass, and Hurst's lob established what ought to have been an unassailable lead. On the hour Moore handled, but Standen saved from Ron Moran. Roger Hunt beat three players to make it 2-1.										
8	A NOTT'M FOREST		11	L	1-3	0-1	Byrne 80	Standen	Kirkup	Burkett	Peters	Bickles	Moore	Brabrook	Boyce	Byrne	Hurst	Dear
	17/9	*25,369*	*2*	8			*Le Flem 26, Wignall 60, Addison 67*	*Grummitt*	*Wilson*	*Mochan*	*Whitefoot*	*McKinlay*	*Winfield*	*Hockey*	*Addison*	*Wignall*	*Quigley*	*Le Flem*
							Ref: J Mitchell	Forest's fourth successive win leaves Jim Standen with the cheers of the home crowd ringing in his ears. He alone prevented a rout. Byrne was forced to play deep to help out. Le Flem shot into the roof of the net and Wignall headed in Mochan's free-kick to leave West Ham in disarray.										
9	H ASTON VILLA		13	L	0-1	0-1		Standen	Kirkup	Burkett	Bovington	Moore	Peters	Brabrook	Boyce	Byrne	Hurst	Dear
	21/9	20,346	*12*	8			*Burrows 11*	*Sims*	*Wright*	*Lee*	*Crowe*	*Sleeuwenhoek*	*Deakin*	*McEwan*	*Baker*	*Hateley*	*Woosnam*	*Burrows*
							Ref: T Dawes	Joe Mercer's Villa, watched by Alf Ramsey, leap-frog over West Ham with this win. Moore looked wasted at centre-half and was given the runaround by big Tony Hateley, who also teed-up Harry Burrows' winner. Ex-Hammer Phil Woosnam came in for some rough treatment.										
10	A TOTTENHAM		15	L	0-3	0-2		Standen	Kirkup	Burkett	Bovington	Brown	Moore	Sealey	Boyce	Peters	Byrne	Scott
	28/9	***50,886***	*4*	8			*Jones 27, Mackay 39, Brown 61 (og)*	*Brown*	*Hopkins*	*Henry*	*Blanchflower*	*Norman*	*Mackay*	*Jones*	*White*	*Smith*	*Greaves*	*Dyson*
							Ref: E Crawford	Spurs maintain their 100% home record with ease, orchestrated by 37-year-old Danny Blanchflower. West Ham looked in dire need of a striker. Cliff Jones' header and Mackay's dipping drive – both set up by John White – were followed by Brown's blunder from Dyson's cross.										

No Date	Venue	Opponent / Att	Pos	Res / Pts	F-A	H-T	Scorers, Times, and Referees	1	2	3	4	5	6	7	8	9	10	11
11	H	WOLVES	18	D	1-1	0-0	Byrne 76	Standen	Kirkup	Burkett	Bovington	Brown	Moore	Sealey	Boyce	Peters	Byrne	Scott
5/10		21,409	*15*	9			*Hinton 50*	*Davies*	*Thomson*	*Harris*	*Goodwin*	*Woodfield*	*Flowers*	*Wharton*	*Crowe*	*Crawford*	*Broadbent*	*Hinton*
							Ref: R Tinkler	After a disjointed start this match livened up. By the close it might have finished five goals apiece. Greenwood experimented by playing Peters at centre-forward, which failed dismally. Stan Cullis's team went in front with Hinton's 18-yarder, but were pegged back by Byrne's header.										
12	H	BURNLEY	18	D	1-1	0-1	Sealey 62	Standen	Kirkup	Burkett	Bovington	Brown	Moore	Sealey	Boyce	Peters	Byrne	Scott
7/10		21,372	*10*	10			*Harris 17*	*Blacklaw*	*Angus*	*Joyce*	*Adamson*	*Talbut*	*Miller*	*Price*	*Bellamy*	*Lochhead*	*Harris*	*Connelly*
							Ref: H New	Hammers found themselves trailing for the fifth home game in a row when Gordon Harris lashed Lochhead's pass beyond Standen from 18 yards. Alan Sealey, the man the crowd love to hate, crowned a marvellous personal performance by smashing the equaliser from similar range.										
13	A	SHEFFIELD WED	16	L	0-3	0-0		Standen	Kirkup	Burkett	Bovington	Brown	Peters	Brabrook	Boyce	Sealey	Sissons	Scott
12/10		*23,503*	12	10			*Dobson 57, Pearson 62, Holliday 81*	*Springett*	*Hill*	*Megson*	*McAnearney*	*Swan*	*Young*	*Finney*	*Pearson*	*Layne*	*Dobson*	*Holliday*
							Ref: W Downey	Byrne is recovering from a car crash. West Ham had the edge when they fell behind, although Wednesday had gone closest when Layne hit the angle. Dobson turned Young's pass beyond Standen, then Man U import Mark Pearson fired a second from 18 yards for his first home goal.										
14	H	EVERTON	14	W	4-2	2-2	Boyce 27, Hurst 42, Brabrook 76, 84	Standen	Bond	Burkett	Peters	Brown	Moore	Sealey	Boyce	Britt	Hurst	Brabrook
19/10		25,163	*9*	12			*Kay 5, Rees 31*	*West*	*Parker*	*Harris*	*Gabriel*	*Labone*	*Kay*	*Scott*	*Stevens*	*Rees*	*Vernon*	*Temple*
							Ref: K Burns	West Ham's second home win was a long time coming. It was unexpected too, as they went 1-2 down to the defending champions to a goal by debutant Barry Rees. The goal that put West Ham in front was struck by Peter Brabrook but flew off Gabriel and over Gordon West's hands.										
15	A	MANCHESTER U	13	W	1-0	1-0	Britt 36	Standen	Bond	Burkett	Peters	Brown	Moore	Sealey	Boyce	Britt	Hurst	Brabrook
26/10		*42,120*	*2*	14				*Gregg*	*Dunne*	*Cantwell*	*Crerand*	*Foulkes*	*Setters*	*Moir*	*Chisnall*	*Herd*	*Law*	*Charlton*
							Ref: J Thacker	Man U were welcomed onto the pitch by the majorettes, but lost their league leadership and their 100% home record to Martin Britt's goal. Hurst had hit the bar, only for the ball to bounce into Gregg's arms. West Ham were down to 10 after an hour when Sealey went off injured.										
16	H	WEST BROM	13	W	4-2	1-2	Simpson 2 (og), Hurst 65p, 70, [Brabrook 88]	Standen	Bond	Burkett	Peters	Brown	Moore	Sealey	Boyce	Britt	Hurst	Brabrook
2/11		22,888	*11*	16			*Foggo 5, Cram 12*	*Potter*	*Howe*	*Williams*	*Fraser*	*Jones*	*Simpson*	*Foggo*	*Macready*	*Cram*	*Jackson*	*Clark*
							Ref: J Cooke	Albion's coach broke down on the M1 and they had to finish their journey crammed into a van. Their mood was not helped when Simpson ran Hurst's shot into his own net after it came back off a post. Geoff Hurst made it 2-2 from the spot after the ball bounced against Cram's hand.										
17	A	ARSENAL	13	D	3-3	1-2	Byrne 1, 53, Peters 75	Standen	Bond	Burkett	Peters	Brown	Moore	Sealey	Boyce	Byrne	Hurst	Brabrook
9/11		*52,742*	*2*	17			*McLeod 5, Eastham 31, Anderson 55*	*Wilson*	*Magill*	*McCullough*	*Brown L*	*Ure*	*Barnwell*	*McLeod*	*Strong*	*Baker*	*Eastham*	*Anderson*
							Ref: A Jobling	It takes Byrne 12 seconds of his come-back match to head past flat-footed Bob Wilson. Arsenal have not beaten West Ham at home since the war, when whisky was 12s 6d a bottle, but they stormed back to lead twice. Peters' 25-yard screamer ensures that the proud record continues.										
18	H	LEICESTER	13	D	2-2	2-1	Britt 24, Hurst 41	Standen	Bond	Burkett	Peters	Brown	Moore	Sealey	Boyce	Britt	Hurst	Brabrook
16/11		23,073	*11*	18			*Stringfellow 20, Keyworth 56*	*Banks*	*Chalmers*	*Norman*	*McLintock*	*King*	*Appleton*	*Riley*	*Cross*	*Keyworth*	*Gibson*	*Stringfellow*
							Ref: J Mitchell	Mike Stringfellow's cross-cum-shot was deflected into his own net by Standen. Britt flicked an equaliser, and Hurst bulleted Sealey's corner past Banks. Leicester had lost on their last four visits to Upton Park, but bucked the trend when Keyworth hooked in Gibson's knock-down.										
19	A	BOLTON	12	D	1-1	0-0	Hurst 52	Standen	Bond	Burkett	Peters	Brown	Moore	Sealey	Boyce	Britt	Hurst	Brabrook
23/11		***10,864***	*21*	19			*Lee 89p*	*Hopkinson*	*Hartle*	*Farrimond*	*Hatton*	*Hulme*	*Lennard*	*Davison*	*Bromley*	*Davies*	*Deakin*	*Lee*
							Ref: A Sparling	Bolton have won only once at home; their gates have plummeted. West Ham lost Sealey after five minutes with a fractured ankle and thereafter erected an eight-man barricade. Brabrook set up Hurst's breakaway goal, but Francis Lee netted from the spot after Peters tripped Deakin.										
20	H	FULHAM	13	D	1-1	0-1	Moore 71	Standen	Bond	Burkett	Peters	Brown	Moore	Byrne	Boyce	Britt	Hurst	Brabrook
30/11		23,715	*18*	20			*Leggat 10*	*Macedo*	*Cohen*	*Drake*	*Mullery*	*Keetch*	*Robson*	*Key*	*Cook*	*Leggat*	*Haynes*	*Howfield*
							Ref: J Bullough	Fulham had only scored three goals in 10 away games, so Leggat's shot from a tight angle, under the eyes of Alf Ramsey, provoked ecstatic celebrations among the white shirts. Moore levelled following a half-cleared corner. Hurst hit the bar twice. Byrne looked lost out on the wing.										
21	A	BIRMINGHAM	14	L	1-2	0-1	Britt 64	Standen	Bond	Burkett	Peters	Brown	Moore	Brabrook	Boyce	Britt	Hurst	Byrne
7/12		*15,357*	*20*	20			*Auld 28, Lynn 75p*	*Withers*	*Lynn*	*Green*	*Hennessey*	*Smith*	*Beard*	*Hellawell*	*Bloomfield*	*Thomson*	*Leek*	*Auld*
							Ref: F Cowan	Birmingham inflict West Ham's first defeat in 10 games in league and cup. Standen half-saved Bertie Auld's shot, which climaxed a spell of intense City pressure. Britt headed in Peters' cross at the far post, but Brown then flattened Mike Hellawell. Stan Lynn netted from the spot.										

No Date	Att	Pos	Pt	F-A	H-T	Scorers, Times, and Referees	1	2	3	4	5	6	7	8	9	10	11
22 H CHELSEA		13	D	2-2	0-2	Byrne 65, 67	Standen	Bond	Burkett	Peters	Brown	Moore	Scott	Boyce	Byrne	Hurst	Brabrook
14/12	21,950	*11*	21			*Blunstone 15, Tambling 40*	*Bonetti*	*Hinton*	*McCreadie*	*Harris R*	*Mortimore*	*Upton*	*Murray*	*Tambling*	*Bridges*	*Venables*	*Blunstone*
						Ref: J Taylor	Tommy Docherty's Chelsea extend their unbeaten sequence to six. A headed goal by tiny Blunstone, followed by a 30-yarder by Tambling, looks like earning a win, but Tambling's withdrawal on a stretcher – torn ligaments – reduces Chelsea to 10 men and Byrne takes advantage.										
23 A IPSWICH		13	L	2-3	1-0	Byrne 22p, Brabrook 57	Standen	Bond	Burkett	Peters	Brown	Moore	Brabrook	Boyce	Byrne	Hurst	Sissons
20/12	*11,765*	*22*	21			*Blackwood 62, Moran 67, Baker 75*	*Bailey*	*Davin*	*Compton*	*Baxter*	*Bolton*	*Dougan*	*Broadfoot*	*Moran*	*Baker*	*Hegan*	*Blackwood*
						Ref: R Spittle	Ipswich's second win of the season cannot lift them off the bottom. West Ham had led 2-0, courtesy of an iffy penalty awarded when the ball struck Joe Davin on the arm, and Brabrook's cross deceiving Bailey. Then the Hammers fell apart, and worse will follow in their next match.										
24 H BLACKBURN		16	L	**2-8**	1-4	Byrne 10, 60 *[McEvoy 35, 65, 78,]*	Standen	Bond	Burkett	Peters	Brown	Moore	Brabrook	Boyce	Byrne	Hurst	Sissons
26/12	20,500	*1*	21			*Pickering 5, 55, 89, Douglas 29,*	*Else*	*Bray*	*Newton*	*Clayton*	*England*	*McGrath*	*Ferguson*	*McEvoy*	*Pickering*	*Douglas*	*Harrison*
						Ref: J Osborne *[Ferguson 40]*	Days don't come blacker than this. West Ham lose back-to-back matches against the bottom and top clubs. This marks the biggest away win in Division 1 for eight years, it was Rovers' biggest ever away win. Star of the show was Bryan Douglas. Byrne was denied a hat-trick by the bar.										
25 A BLACKBURN		16	W	3-1	1-1	Hurst 16, Byrne 58, 65	Standen	Bond	Burkett	Bovington	Brown	Moore	Brabrook	Boyce	Byrne	Hurst	Sissons
28/12	*28,990*	*1*	23			*McEvoy 31*	*Else*	*Bray*	*Newton*	*Clayton*	*England*	*McGrath*	*Ferguson*	*McEvoy*	*Pickering*	*Douglas*	*Harrison*
						Ref: J Carr	Who would have bet on this extraordinary result? On a sodden pitch Rovers' first defeat in 11 games is a tactical triumph for Greenwood, who brings in tough-tackling Bovington for Peters, to man-mark Douglas, plus Sissons out wide. Byrne, with two more goals, likes playing Rovers.										
26 A SHEFFIELD UTD		17	L	1-2	0-1	Sissons 82	Standen	Bond	Burkett	Bovington	Brown	Moore	Brabrook	Boyce	Byrne	Hurst	Sissons
11/1	*18,733*	*10*	23			*Pace 25, Wagstaff 54*	*Hodgkinson*	*Coldwell*	*Shaw B*	*Richardson*	*Shaw J*	*Summers*	*Allchurch*	*Jones*	*Pace*	*Wagstaff*	*Hartle*
						Ref: Dagnall	The only reason lowly Hammers are not terrified of relegation is because Bolton and Ipswich are so far adrift. The Blades complete the double over the Hammers; indeed, they let them off lightly. In addition to the goals, Jones struck Standen's crossbar. Pace might have had a hat-trick.										
27 H LIVERPOOL		15	W	1-0	1-0	Byrne 28	Standen	Bond	Burkett	Bovington	Brown	Moore	Brabrook	Boyce	Byrne	Hurst	Sissons
18/1	25,546	*3*	25				*Lawrence*	*Thomson*	*Byrne G*	*Milne*	*Lawler*	*Stevenson*	*Callaghan*	*Hunt*	*Arrowsmith*	*St John*	*Thompson*
						Ref: J Finney	West Ham's second league win 11 games is a tribute to Byrne, who pivoted to score a sweet goal, and the defence, who withstood continuous bombardment throughout the second half. Callaghan hit a post, and in the final seconds Standen pulled off the save of the match from Hunt.										
28 A ASTON VILLA		15	D	2-2	1-1	Hurst 25, 66	Standen	Bond	Burkett	Bovington	Brown	Moore	Brabrook	Boyce	Byrne	Hurst	Sissons
1/2	*16,850*	*17*	26			*Burrows 10, Woosnam 49*	*Sidebottom*	*Wright*	*Aitken*	*Tindall*	*Sleeuwenhoek*	*Deakin*	*McEwan*	*Wylie*	*Hateley*	*Woosnam*	*Burrows*
						Ref: Crossley	Early in the second half, with Villa leading 2-1, Moore crash-tackled Tony Hateley, forcing his withdrawal. Though no foul was given, Moore was booed thereafter. Villa couldn't hang on with 10 men and it was not long before Hurst sprinted 30 yards to head in Brabrook's centre.										
29 H TOTTENHAM		14	W	4-0	2-0	Hurst 20, Sissons 31, Boyce 70,	Standen	Bond	Burkett	Bovington	Brown	Moore	Brabrook	Boyce	Byrne	Hurst	Sissons
8/2	**36,934**	*1*	28			[Byrne 84]	*Hollowbread*	*Baker*	*Hopkins*	*Beal*	*Norman*	*Marchi*	*Jones*	*White*	*Smith*	*Greaves*	*Dyson*
						Ref: P Brandwood	Successive defeats by Chelsea and West Ham have dampened Spurs' title chances. It is rare for Bill Nicholson's team to be given such a runaround. Geoff Hurst almost scored in the second minute, soon hit a post, and then tucked away Peter Brabrook's cross for the first goal.										
30 A WOLVES		14	W	2-0	1-0	Hurst 25, Byrne 67	Standen	Kirkup	Bond	Bovington	Peters	Moore	Brabrook	Boyce	Byrne	Hurst	Sissons
17/2	*14,000*	*15*	30				*Davies*	*Showell*	*Thomson*	*Broadbent*	*Woodfield*	*Flowers*	*Wharton*	*Knowles*	*Crawford*	*Crowe*	*Le Flem*
						Ref: P Bye	This Monday night fixture sees hot-shot Hurst take his recent tally to 10 goals in six games, scoring at the second attempt after the keeper had parried the first. Sissons set up the second goal, smashed in by Byrne. Wolves' sorties were soaked up by Hammers' 'funnel' defensive system.										
31 H SHEFFIELD WED		14	W	4-3	2-1	Byrne 17, 45, 65p, Hurst 51	Standen	Bond	Burkett	Bovington	Brown	Moore	Brabrook	Boyce	Byrne	Hurst	Sissons
22/2	24,578	*7*	32			*Finney 26, Dobson 75, Fantham 87*	*Springett*	*Hill*	*Megson*	*McAnearney*	*Swan*	*Young*	*Finney*	*Pearson*	*Layne*	*Fantham*	*Dobson*
						Ref: D Smith	Not quite the ding-dong struggle the score suggests, as West Ham led 4-1 until the closing stages. Byrne had completed his hat-trick from the spot after Megson brought down Brabrook. West Ham still can't climb the table, being the lowest on goal-average of five clubs on 32 points.										

No	Venue / Date	Opponents / Att	Pos	Res / Pts	F-A	H-T	Scorers, Times, and Referees	1	2	3	4	5	6	7	8	9	10	11
32	A	BURNLEY		L	1-3	0-2	Byrne 85	Standen	Kirkup	Burkett	Bovington	Peters	Moore	Sealey	Boyce	Byrne	Hurst	Brabrook
	3/3	*14,328*		32			*Harris 5, Robson 39, 46*	*Blacklaw*	*Angus*	*Elder*	*O'Neil*	*Talbut*	*Miller*	*Morgan*	*Robson*	*Lochhead*	*Harris*	*Connelly*
							Ref: V James	Burnley gain quick revenge for their Cup exit. Greenwood left out key players, but that could not prevent cup vendettas being played out. Gordon Harris treated John Bond to a left hook on Saturday, and Bobby Moore to a vicious foul today. Hurst twice drove against a goal-post.										
33	H	MANCHESTER U	14	L	0-2	0-0		Standen	Bond	Burkett	Bovington	Brown	Moore	Brabrook	Boyce	Byrne	Hurst	Sissons
	7/3	27,177	*5*	32			*Sadler 72, Herd 86*	*Gaskell*	*Brennan*	*Dunne*	*Crerand*	*Tranter*	*Stiles*	*Anderson*	*Chisnall*	*Sadler*	*Herd*	*Moir*
							Ref: W Clements	These teams meet soon in the FA Cup semi-finals and West Ham are all at sea. Nevertheless they might have escaped with a draw but for John Bond's silly back-pass that let in David Sadler. West Ham pressed forward, leaving gaps that David Herd exploited when racing clear for No 2.										
34	A	LEICESTER	15	D	2-2	1-2	Hugo 31, Burkett 81	Standen	Bond	Burkett	Bovington	Brown	Peters	Sealey	Boyce	Hurst	**Hugo**	Brabrook
	18/3	*11,980*	*9*	33			*Gibson 6, Keyworth 37*	*Heyes*	*Sjoberg*	*Appleton*	*McLintock*	*King*	*Cross*	*Hodgson*	*Heath*	*Keyworth*	*Gibson*	*Stringfellow*
							Ref: L Hamer	West Ham have reached one final, and shortly face Leicester with the chance of another. Greenwood rests key players for this unimportant league fixture. Roger Hugo scores on his debut and nearly bags a late winner. Burkett also scores his first ever league goal in a late flourish.										
35	H	ARSENAL	15	D	1-1	0-1	Hurst 74	Standen	Bond	Burkett	Bovington	Brown	Moore	Brabrook	Boyce	Byrne	Hurst	Sissons
	21/3	28,170	*8*	34			*Skirton 35*	*Furnell*	*Magill*	*McCullough*	*Neill*	*Ure*	*Simpson*	*Skirton*	*Court*	*Radford*	*Eastham*	*Anderson*
							Ref: R Spittle	With an eye on Wembley, Hammers fans don't take kindly to the rough treatment meted out to Byrne by Ian Ure – once nudging Budgie over a barrier. Skirton headed in Eastham's free-kick. It might have become 0-2 when Burkett fouled Skirton, but Standen saved Eastham's penalty.										
36	H	STOKE	14	W	4-1	2-1	Moore 4, Byrne 14, Boyce 69, [Brabrook 71]	Dickie	Bond	Burkett	Bovington	Brown	Moore	Brabrook	Boyce	Byrne	Hurst	Sealey
	27/3	29,484	*19*	36			*Dobing 29*	*Leslie*	*Asprey*	*Allen*	*Palmer*	*Kinnell*	*Skeels*	*Dobing*	*Viollet*	*Ritchie*	*McIlroy*	*Bebbington*
							Ref: T Dawes	Stoke beat Ipswich 9-1 in their previous match. Ex-Hammer Lawrie Leslie is made skipper for the day, but is quickly caught out of position as Moore heads in Bond's free-kick. A mesmerising four-man move was climaxed by Byrne's goal. Dobing beat Alan Dickie from 30 yards.										
37	A	WEST BROM	12	W	1-0	0-0	Hugo 72	Dickie	Kirkup	Burkett	Peters	Brown	Moore	Brabrook	Boyce	Byrne	Hugo	Sealey
	28/3	*16,000*	*10*	38				*Potter*	*Howe*	*Williams G*	*Fraser*	*Jones*	*Simpson*	*Foggo*	*Fenton*	*Kaye*	*Jackson*	*Clark*
							Ref: V Batty	Both teams appeared to be going through the motions, so much so that it came as a surprise that either team should score. Happiest player was ex-ground staff lad Roger Hugo, who took Hurst's place and grabbed his second goal in two games. Hugo wouldn't mind the slight deflection.										
38	A	STOKE	12	L	0-3	0-0		Dickie	Kirkup	Bond	Bovington	Brown	Peters	Sealey	Boyce	Byrne	Hurst	Hugo
	31/3	*24,900*	*19*	38			*Palmer 46, McIlroy 61, Dobing 85*	*Leslie*	*Stuart*	*Allen*	*Palmer*	*Kinnell*	*Skeels*	*Dobing*	*Viollet*	*Ritchie*	*McIlroy*	*Bebbington*
							Ref: N Matthews	Tony Waddington's Stoke desperately needed these points, and this is as good a time as any to face West Ham. Preston boss Jimmy Milne must have gone away scratching his head. The nearest Hammers came to scoring was when Skeels headed out Byrne's lob after 75 minutes.										
39	H	BOLTON	14	L	2-3	2-2	Sealey 25, Byrne 38	Standen	Bond	Burkett	Bovington	Peters	Moore	Brabrook	**Bennett**	Byrne	Hurst	Sealey
	4/4	**19,398**	*21*	38			*Taylor 36, Lee 40, Bromley 77*	*Hopkinson*	*Hartle*	*Farrimond*	*Rimmer*	*Edwards*	*Lennard*	*Davison*	*Bromley*	*Lee*	*Hill*	*Taylor*
							Ref: K Burns	Desperate Bolton resort to time-wasting, jeered by the fans, but it paid off. Mistakes by Moore and Bond, both irritatingly casual, cost two goals. Moore, of all people, was dispossessed in the box by Taylor. Bromley looked offside when receiving Francis Lee's pass for the winner.										
40	A	FULHAM	15	L	0-2	0-1		Standen	Bond	Burkett	Bovington	Brown	Peters	Brabrook	Boyce	Britt	Hurst	Sissons
	11/4	*22,020*	*14*	38			*Keetch 30, Haynes 73*	*Macedo*	*Mealand*	*Langley*	*Robson*	*Keetch*	*Callaghan*	*Earle*	*Metchick*	*Leggat*	*Haynes*	*O'Connell*
							Ref: J Lowry	Fulham climb above West Ham with this win. Three losses in a row is hardly the way to prepare for Wembley. Bond headed off the line, only for Keetch to head it back in. Haynes clinched matters with a belter from 25 yards. Metchick was offside but deemed not interfering with play.										
41	H	BIRMINGHAM	14	W	**5-0**	2-0	Brabrook 4, 53, Hurst 35, Sissons 58, [Byrne 63]	Standen	Kirkup	Burkett	Bovington	Brown	Moore	Brabrook	Boyce	Byrne	Hurst	Sissons
	17/4	22,106	*21*	40				*Schofield*	*Lynn*	*Martin*	*Hennessey*	*Smith*	*Thomson*	*Hellawell*	*Bloomfield*	*Leek*	*Thwaites*	*Auld*
							Ref: R Tinkler	This result leaves Birmingham three points behind Bolton with two to play. They were down to 10 men for most of the match when Hennessey smashed a clearance into the face of team-mate Smith, who departed with concussion. It was only 1-0 at the time. City will survive, yet again.										
42	A	EVERTON	14	L	0-2	0-1		Standen	Bond	Burkett	Bovington	Brown	Peters	Brabrook	Boyce	Britt	Hurst	Sealey
	25/4	*33,090*	*3*	40			*Pickering 35, 75*	*Rankin*	*Brown*	*Meagan*	*Gabriel*	*Labone*	*Harris*	*Scott*	*Stevens*	*Pickering*	*Vernon*	*Temple*
	Home	Away					Ref: D Corbett	Fred Pickering cheekily yells 'leave it' to Martin Peters, who, thinking it is a team-mate, does so. Pickering scored. Everton were in no mood for kid gloves, and Pickering missed the chance for the simplest of hat-tricks. Moore and Byrne were omitted so they could spy on Preston.										
	Average 24,618	25,890																

League Cup					F-A	H-T	Scorers, Times, and Referees	1	2	3	4	5	6	7	8	9	10	11
2	H	LEYTON ORIENT	13	W	2-1	2-1	Scott 23, Byrne 43	Standen	Kirkup	Burkett	Bovington	Bickles	Moore	Sealey	Boyce	Peters	Byrne	Scott
25/9		11,800 *2:16*					*Bolland 9*	*Davies*	*Charlton*	*Lewis*	*Lucas*	*Bishop*	*Lea*	*Deeley*	*Mason*	*Bolland*	*Ward*	*Musgrove*
							Ref: J Cooke	Orient deserved better than to lose. They controlled the midfield and Gordon Bolland tortured Dave Bickles throughout, as when taking the ball round Standen for the first goal. Scott headed the equaliser and Byrne netted the winner at the fourth attempt after rounding Reg Davies.										
3	A	ASTON VILLA	16	W	2-0	0-0	Bond 68, Britt 75	Standen	Bond	Burkett	Peters	Brown	Moore	Sealey	Boyce	Britt	Hurst	Brabrook
16/10		*11,194 19*						*Sims*	*Wright*	*Aitken*	*Crowe*	*Sleeuwenhoek*	*Tindall*	*Baker*	*Wylie*	*Hateley*	*Woosnam*	*Burrows*
							Ref: V O'Callaghan	Struggling Villa have lost five out of six home fixtures, so this result is no great shock, though Villa had won at Upton Park in the league. Villa were the first winners of the League Cup in 1961, and were finalists again in 1963. Ex-Hammer Phil Woosnam does his bit to inspire victory.										
4	A	SWINDON	13	D	3-3	2-2	Hurst 20, Brabrook 27, Boyce 47	Standen	Bond	Burkett	Peters	Brown	Charles	Sealey	Boyce	Britt	Hurst	Brabrook
4/11		*12,050 2:14*					*Rogers 36, Smith 39, McPherson 83*	*Turner*	*Dawson*	*Trollope*	*Morgan*	*McPherson*	*Woodruff*	*French*	*Hunt*	*Smith*	*Summerbee*	*Rogers*
							Ref: E Jennings	Division 2 Swindon boast an up-and-coming star in 17-year-old Don Rogers, and he begins Swindon's fight-back in the Wiltshire mud. Centre-half McPherson came close to scoring before he finally did so in a late melee. Moore had been left out as he plays for England the next day.										
4R	H	SWINDON	12	W	4-1	1-0	Hurst 1, Brabrook 50, Byrne 67,	Standen	Bond	Burkett	Charles	Brown	Moore	Scott	Boyce	Byrne	Hurst	Brabrook
25/11		15,778 *2:14*					*Rogers 62* [Scott 84]	*Turner*	*Morgan*	*Trollope*	*Sproates*	*Hallett*	*Woodruff*	*French*	*Summerbee*	*Smith*	*Smart*	*Rogers*
							Ref: J Taylor	Bert Head's Swindon babes saw their plans wrecked inside 40 seconds when Bobby Woodruff's mis-kick allowed Hurst to smash the opener. The tie stayed alive until Byrne headed against the bar and Brabrook flung himself to convert the rebound. Spies again looked at Don Rogers.										
QF	H	WORKINGTON	13	W	6-0	4-0	Byrne 12, 41, 52, Boyce 20, Hurst 38,	Standen	Bond	Burkett	Bovington	Brown	Moore	Brabrook	Boyce	Byrne	Hurst	Scott
16/12		10,160 *4:3*					[Scott 50]	*Ower*	*Johnston*	*Lumsden*	*Furphy*	*Brown*	*Burkinshaw*	*Middlemass*	*Timmins*	*Carr*	*Moran*	*Martin*
							Ref: R Tinkler	Fourth Division versus First produces a predictable outcome. The show began to roll once Byrne put away Hurst's cross, at which point Workington player-manager Ken Furphy's tactical masterplan became redundant. The crowd ended up cheering Workington's few attacks.										
SF	A	LEICESTER	15	L	3-4	1-3	Hurst 30, 70, Sealey 82 *[McLintock 50]*	Standen	Bond	Burkett	Peters	Brown	Moore	Sealey	Boyce	Byrne	Hurst	Brabrook
1	5/2	*14,087 9*					*Keyworth 5, Roberts 13, Stringellow 19,*	*Banks*	*Sjoberg*	*Norman*	*McLintock*	*King*	*Appleton*	*Hodgson*	*Roberts*	*Keyworth*	*Gibson*	*Stringfellow*
							Ref: E Crawford	Three goals down after 19 minutes of this first-leg semi-final, and 1-4 after 69 minutes, West Ham seemed doomed to miss out on a final with Stoke. But Hurst's sixth goal in three games, shrugging off King's tackle, followed by Sealey scoring on his come-back, keeps the dream alive.										
SF	H	LEICESTER	15	L	0-2	0-1		Standen	Bond	Burkett	Bovington	Brown	Moore	Brabrook	Boyce	Byrne	Hurst	Sissons
2	23/3	27,393 *9*					*McLintock 33, Gibson 71*	*Banks*	*Sjoberg*	*Norman*	*McLintock*	*King*	*Appleton*	*Hodgson*	*Cross*	*Roberts*	*Gibson*	*Stringfellow*
							Ref: J Finney (Hammers lose 3-6 on aggregate)	Leicester deny West Ham the chance of being the first club to claim both domestic cups in one season. This was a stirring cup-tie, with Banks inspired on his come-back after a five-week injury. When Roberts swung over a free-kick for McLintock to belt into the net, it looked all over.										

FA Cup																		
3	H	CHARLTON	16	W	3-0	2-0	Hurst 10, Brabrook 25, Sissons 89	Standen	Bond	Burkett	Bovington	Brown	Moore	Brabrook	Boyce	Byrne	Hurst	Sissons
4/1		34,155 *2:4*						*Rose*	*Stocks*	*Kinsey*	*Bailey*	*Haydock*	*Tocknell*	*Kenning*	*Matthews*	*Firmani*	*Edwards*	*Glover*
							Ref: J Osborne	The last match at the Boleyn ended 2-8, but memories are erased by this all-so-easy win over Division 2 Charlton. Byrne's dummy set up Hurst's opener, and man-of-the-match Byrne made the second goal too. Eddie Firmani missed what few opportunities came Charlton's way.										
4	A	LEYTON ORIENT	17	D	1-1	1-1	Brabrook 43	Standen	Bond	Burkett	Bovington	Brown	Moore	Brabrook	Boyce	Byrne	Hurst	Sissons
25/1		*34,345 2:16*					*Deeley 2*	*Pinner*	*Charlton*	*Lewis*	*Lucas*	*Bishop*	*Lea*	*Deeley*	*Dunmore*	*Gregory*	*Bolland*	*Musgrove*
							Ref: T Dawes	Norman Deeley headed Gregory's corner past Standen for a quick-fire opening, and Orient might have scored more goals during their early dominance. Sissons dummied his way past Charlton to lay on the equaliser for Brabrook. Near the end both sides seemed to settle for the draw.										
4R	H	LEYTON ORIENT	17	W	3-0	3-0	Hurst 6, 8, Byrne 15	Standen	Bond	Burkett	Bovington	Brown	Moore	Brabrook	Boyce	Byrne	Hurst	Sissons
29/1		35,383 *2:16*						*Pinner*	*Charlton*	*Lewis*	*Lucas*	*Bishop*	*Lea*	*Deeley*	*Bolland*	*Gregory*	*Dunmore*	*Musgrove*
							Ref: T Dawes	Late-comers entering the ground were astonished to find the game wrapped up. Thereafter the 22 players seemed happy to indulge in a friendly kick-about. On 51 minutes Pinner felled Hurst in the box and helped him to his feet. Hurst repaid the gesture by having his spot-kick saved.										

Rd	Venue	Opponent	Pos	Res	FT	HT	Scorers											
5	A	SWINDON	14	W	3-1	1-1	Hurst 11, 77, Byrne 73	Standen	Bond	Burkett	Bovington	Brown	Moore	Brabrook	Boyce	Byrne	Hurst	Sissons
15/2		28,582 *2:14*					*McPherson 34*	*Turner*	*Wollen*	*Trollope*	*Morgan*	*McPherson*	*Woodruff*	*Summerbee*	*Atkins*	*Stevens*	*D'arcy*	*Rogers*
							Ref: J Mitchell	West Ham face Orient and Swindon in both cups in the same season. Hammers drew 3-3 here in the League Cup, but this time are prepared for Don Rogers' magic. With a replay looking increasingly likely, Brabrook fires in two crosses and Byrne and Hurst connect with them both.										
QF	H	BURNLEY	14	W	3-2	0-1	Sissons 57, Byrne 60, 68	Standen	Bond	Burkett	Bovington	Brown	Moore	Brabrook	Boyce	Byrne	Hurst	Sissons
29/2		36,651 *11*					*Connelly 13, Pointer 80*	*Blacklaw*	*Angus*	*Elder*	*O'Neil*	*Talbut*	*Miller*	*Morgan*	*Pointer*	*Lochhead*	*Harris*	*Connelly*
							Ref: E Jennings	John Connelly skips past three tackles to put Burnley in front. Sissons screwed the ball goalwards from the by-line and Elder helped it over the line for the equaliser. Byrne's awesome volley, under the eyes of Alf Ramsey, put West Ham ahead. Byrne's next goal was hotly contested.										
SF	N	MANCHESTER U	14	W	3-1	0-0	Boyce 56, 63, Hurst 80	Standen	Bond	Burkett	Bovington	Brown	Moore	Brabrook	Boyce	Byrne	Hurst	Sissons
14/3		*65,000* *5*					*Law 78*	*Gaskell*	*Brennan*	*Dunne*	*Crerand*	*Foulkes*	*Setters*	*Herd*	*Chisnall*	*Charlton*	*Law*	*Best*
		(at Hillsborough)					Ref: K Stokes	West Ham reach their first FA Cup final since 1923, overturning last week's league defeat on a mud-heap of a pitch. Ron Boyce let rip from 25 yards past the stranded Gaskell, then added another from a short-corner. Law lunged feet-first into Standen. Moore was a Trojan in defence.										
F	N	PRESTON	14	W	3-2	1-2	Sissons 12, Hurst 52, Boyce 90	Standen	Bond	Burkett	Bovington	Brown	Moore	Brabrook	Boyce	Byrne	Hurst	Sissons
2/5		*100,000* *2:3*					*Holden 10, Dawson 40*	*Kelly*	*Ross*	*Smith*	*Lawton*	*Singleton*	*Kendall*	*Wilson*	*Ashworth*	*Dawson*	*Spavin*	*Holden*
		(at Wembley)					Ref: A Holland	The facts show Second Division Preston had 23 goal attempts to West Ham's 16. Outplayed in the first half, Hammers dug deep and were rewarded, first, when Kelly prods Hurst's header over the line, and then in injury-time when Boyce heads the winner from Brabrook's cross.										

		Home					Away					
	P	W	D	L	F	A	W	D	L	F	A	Pts
1 Liverpool	42	16	0	5	60	18	10	5	6	32	27	57
2 Manchester U	42	15	3	3	54	19	8	4	9	36	43	53
3 Everton	42	14	4	3	53	26	7	6	8	31	38	52
4 Tottenham	42	13	3	5	54	31	9	4	8	43	50	51
5 Chelsea	42	12	3	6	36	24	8	7	6	36	32	50
6 Sheffield Wed	42	15	3	3	50	24	4	8	9	34	43	49
7 Blackburn	42	10	4	7	44	28	8	6	7	45	37	46
8 Arsenal	42	10	7	4	56	37	7	4	10	34	45	45
9 Burnley	42	14	3	4	46	23	3	7	11	25	41	44
10 West Brom	42	9	6	6	43	35	7	5	9	27	26	43
11 Leicester	42	9	4	8	33	27	7	7	7	28	31	43
12 Sheffield Utd	42	10	6	5	35	22	6	5	10	26	42	43
13 Nott'm Forest	42	9	5	7	34	24	7	4	10	30	44	41
14 WEST HAM	42	8	7	6	45	38	6	5	10	24	36	40
15 Fulham	42	11	8	2	45	23	2	5	14	13	42	39
16 Wolves	42	6	9	6	36	34	6	6	9	34	46	39
17 Stoke	42	9	6	6	49	33	5	4	12	28	45	38
18 Blackpool	42	8	6	7	26	29	5	3	13	26	44	35
19 Aston Villa	42	8	6	7	35	29	3	6	12	27	42	34
20 Birmingham	42	7	7	7	33	32	4	0	17	21	60	29
21 Bolton	42	6	5	10	30	35	4	3	14	18	45	28
22 Ipswich	42	9	3	9	38	45	0	4	17	18	76	25
	924	228	108	126	935	636	126	108	228	636	935	924

Odds & ends

Double wins: (3) Blackpool, Liverpool, WBA.
Double losses: (2) Sheffield Utd, Nott'm Forest.

Won from behind: (5) Everton (h), WBA (h), Orient LC (h), Burnley FAC (h), Preston FAC (n).
Lost from in front: (2) Ipswich (a), Bolton (h).

High spots: Winning FA Cup.
Reaching semi-final of League Cup.
Seven unbeaten league games in October and November.

Low spots: Losing 2-8 at home to Blackburn.
Eight successive league games without a win in November-December.

Two days after losing 2-8 at home to Blackburn, West Ham won 3-1 at Ewood Park.
West Ham faced both Leyton O and Swindon in *both* domestic cups.
The Hammers scored 39 goals in the two cup competitions.

Hammer of the Year: Johnny Byrne.
Ever-presents: (0).
Hat-tricks: (2) Johnny Byrne (2).
Leading scorer: (33) Johnny Byrne.

	Appearances			Goals			
	Lge	LC	FAC	Lge	LC	FAC	Tot
Bennett, Peter	**1**						
Bickles, Dave	**2**	1					
Bond, John	**26**	6	7		1		**1**
Bovington, Eddie	**22**	3	7				
Boyce, Ronnie	**41**	7	7	**6**	2	3	**11**
Brabrook, Peter	**38**	6	7	**8**	2	2	**12**
Britt, Martin	**9**	2		**3**	1		**4**
Brown, Ken	**36**	6	7				
Burkett, Jackie	**40**	7	7	**1**			**1**
Byrne, Johnny	**33**	5	7	**24**	5	4	**33**
Charles, John		2					
Dear, Brian	**3**						
Dickie, Alan	**3**						
Hugo, Roger	**3**			**2**			**2**
Hurst, Geoff	**37**	6	7	**14**	5	7	**26**
Kirkup, Joe	**18**	1					
Moore, Bobby	**37**	6	7	**2**			**2**
Peters, Martin	**32**	4		**3**			**3**
Scott, Tony	**10**	3			3		**3**
Sealey, Alan	**18**	4		**2**	1		**3**
Sissons, John	**14**	1	7	**3**		3	**6**
Standen, Jim	**39**	7	7				
(own-goals)				**1**			**1**
22 players used	**462**	**77**	**77**	**69**	**20**	**19**	**108**

No	Date	Opponent	Att	Pos	Pt	F-A	H-T	Scorers, Times, and Referees	1	2	3	4	5	6	7	8	9	10	11
1	A	FULHAM			W	2-1	1-0	Byrne 18, Sissons 65	Standen	Bond	Burkett	Bovington	Brown	Moore	Brabrook	Boyce	Byrne	Hurst	Sissons
	22/8		*31,200*		2			*Metchick 60*	*Macedo*	*Cohen*	*Langley*	*Robson*	*Keetch*	*Callaghan*	*Earle*	*Metchick*	*Leggat*	*Haynes*	*O'Connell*
								Ref: P Rhodes	Johnny Byrne and Johnny Haynes were the respective men of the match. Byrne started and finished Hammers' first league goal of the season. Metchick levelled when swinging an aimless boot to send the ball in off a post. Tony Macedo then parried Hurst's shot out to John Sissons.										
2	H	MANCHESTER U			W	3-1	2-0	Byrne 4, Sissons 19, Hurst 85	Standen	Bond	Burkett	Bovington	Brown	Moore	Brabrook	Boyce	Byrne	Hurst	Sissons
	24/8		**37,070**		4			*Law 79*	*Gaskell*	*Brennan*	*Dunne*	*Setters*	*Foulkes*	*Stiles*	*Connelly*	*Charlton*	*Herd*	*Law*	*Best*
								Ref: K Burns	A full house on this Monday evening. Man U play the last half-hour with 10 men after Maurice Setters is carried off after Boyce's studs sliced through his boot. Byrne scored after Sissons' shot was blocked. Sissons then lobbed a second. Dennis Law's header set up a furious climax.										
3	H	NOTT'M FOREST			L	2-3	1-1	Byrne 14p, Sissons 71	Standen	Bond	Burkett	Bovington	Brown	Moore	Brabrook	Boyce	Byrne	Hurst	Sissons
	28/8		26,760		4			*Barnwell 36, 58, Hinton 73*	*Grummitt*	*Wilson*	*Grant*	*Newton*	*McKinlay*	*Whitefoot*	*Crowe*	*Addison*	*Wignall*	*Barnwell*	*Hinton*
								Ref: N Burtenshaw	Hammers' bogey team do it again. This Friday night cracker saw a harsh penalty given against McKinlay, whereupon broken glass rained onto the pitch from Forest fans. John Barnwell scored twice but was lucky to be still on the pitch, having shoved the referee during the penalty row.										
4	A	MANCHESTER U		14	L	1-3	1-2	Stiles 6 (og)	Standen	Bond	Burkett	Bovington	Brown	Moore	Brabrook	Boyce	Byrne	Hurst	Sissons
	2/9		*45,123*	*12*	4			*Connelly 1, Law 28, Best 53*	*Gaskell*	*Brennan*	*Dunne*	*Crerand*	*Foulkes*	*Stiles*	*Connelly*	*Charlton*	*Sadler*	*Law*	*Best*
								Ref: H Wilson	Man U chalk up their first win of the season, helped by a 45-second goal by Connelly after Best had dummied Bond, not once but twice. Stiles then turned Byrne's cross past Gaskell, but that only made Man U turn up the heat. They created chances galore but only took two of them.										
5	A	STOKE		17	L	1-3	1-1	Byrne 14	Standen	Bond	Burkett	Bovington	Brown	Moore	Brabrook	Boyce	Byrne	Hurst	Sissons
	5/9		*26,420*	*9*	4			*Viollet 38, Dobing 46, Bebbington 63*	*Leslie*	*Asprey*	*Allen*	*Palmer*	*Kinnell*	*Skeels*	*Dobing*	*Viollet*	*Ritchie*	*McIlroy*	*Bebbington*
								Ref: K Seddon	Tony Waddington's Stoke had lost their previous two home games, trailed to Byrne's shot in off the bar, and finished this match with nine fit men. Moore had a poor game. Standen was at fault with at least one goal. Dobing scored from a tight angle; Bebbington had an easy header.										
6	H	WOLVES			W	5-0	3-0	Hurst 27, 80, Byrne 33, Sissons 43,	Standen	Bond	Burkett	Bovington	Peters	Moore	Sealey	Boyce	Byrne	Hurst	Sissons
	7/9		26,879	*21*	6			[Moore 47]	*Davies*	*Thomson*	*Harris*	*Goodwin*	*Flowers*	*Woodruff*	*Broadbent*	*Kirkham*	*Crawford*	*Melia*	*Wharton*
								Ref: N Matthews	Greenwood drops Brown and Brabrook. Wolves' boss Stan Cullis is absent through illness, which was probably made worse when he heard the score. So casual did West Ham become at 4-0 that the crowd jeered and slow-handclapped them. Greenwood defended the fans' right to do so.										
7	H	TOTTENHAM			W	3-2	1-0	Byrne 23, 78, 87	Standen	Bond	Burkett	Bovington	Peters	Moore	Sealey	Boyce	Byrne	Hurst	Sissons
	12/9		36,730		8			*Greaves 57, 71p*	*Jennings*	*Knowles*	*Henry*	*Mullery*	*Norman*	*Beal*	*Robertson*	*Jones*	*Saul*	*Greaves*	*Dyson*
								Ref: G McCabe	Two penalties within a minute shape the destiny of this match. Greaves put Spurs ahead after Standen brought down Cliff Jones, then Knowles shoved Sealey at the other end, only for Jennings to catch Byrne's spot-kick. Even that could not deny Byrne a hat-trick, juggling a late winner.										
8	A	WOLVES		12	L	3-4	1-2	Brabrook 39, Harris 51 (og), Byrne 61p	Standen	Bond	Burkett	Bovington	Peters	Moore	Sealey	Boyce	Byrne	Hurst	Brabrook
	14/9		*16,000*	*22*	8			*Crawford 3, 77, Knowles 34, Harris 87*	*Davies*	*Thomson*	*Harris*	*Goodwin*	*Showell*	*Woodruff*	*Thompson*	*Knowles*	*Crawford*	*Broadbent*	*Wharton*
								Ref: F Schofield	Wolves' first win can't lift them off the bottom but it can exact revenge for the thrashing at Upton Park. Standen, who in the summer helped Worcestershire win the cricket county championship, spilled two 'googlie' crosses by Harris. Woodruff pushed Hurst to concede the penalty.										
9	A	BURNLEY		13	L	2-3	1-2	Byrne 21, Boyce 79	Standen	Bond	Burkett	Bovington	Peters	Moore	Sealey	Boyce	Byrne	Hurst	Sissons
	19/9		*13,541*	*19*	8			*Pointer 16, Lochhead 34, Towers 77*	*Blacklaw*	*Angus*	*Elder*	*Walker*	*Miller*	*O'Neil*	*Morgan*	*Pointer*	*Lochhead*	*Robson*	*Towers*
								Ref: H Hackney	Burnley, like Wolves before them, win their first game of the season at West Ham's expense. Alf Ramsey watches as Ray Pointer, returning after a seven-month lay-off, shot the first goal and crossed for the second. Boyce made it 2-3, then squandered an easy chance to make it 3-3.										
10	H	SHEFFIELD UTD		12	W	3-1	3-1	Byrne 11, 40p, Sissons 34	Standen	Bond	Peters	Bovington	Brown	Moore	Brabrook	Boyce	Byrne	Hurst	Sissons
	26/9		22,526	*5*	10			*Docherty 3*	*Hodgkinson*	*Badger*	*Shaw G*	*Richardson*	*Shaw J*	*Matthewson*	*Docherty*	*Kettleborough*	*Jones*	*Birchenall*	*Hartle*
								Ref: L Callaghan	High-flying Blades go in front through John Docherty's neat dummy and shot. Byrne celebrates fathering a daughter by scoring twice, one of them from the spot after being brought down by Richardson. Key to the overall outcome was three astonishing misses by Blades' Birchenall.										

No	Venue	Opponent / Date	Att	Pos	Res / Pts	FT	HT	Scorers											
11	A	EVERTON		12	D	1-1	0-0	Byrne 52	Standen	Bond	Burkett	Bovington	Brown	Peters	Brabrook	Boyce	Byrne	Hurst	Sissons
		3/10	*45,430*	*4*	11			*Harris 89*	*Rankin*	*Parker*	*Brown*	*Stevens*	*Labone*	*Harris*	*Scott*	*Harvey*	*Gabriel*	*Temple*	*Morrissey*
								Ref: J Taylor	Only seconds separate West Ham from their first win at Goodison for five years, and Everton from their first home defeat of the season, when Temple's pass sets up Harris's equaliser. Rankin had got both hands to Byrne's rocket, but couldn't keep it out. Then Hammers shut up shop.										
12	H	ASTON VILLA		8	W	3-0	1-0	Byrne 39, Boyce 67, Peters 89	Standen	Bond	Peters	Bovington	Brown	Moore	Brabrook	Boyce	Byrne	Hurst	Sissons
		10/10	20,600	*21*	13				*Sidebottom*	*Wright*	*Aitken*	*Tindall*	*Sleeuwenhoek*	*Lee*	*McLeod*	*Pountney*	*Hateley*	*Wylie*	*Burrows*
								Ref: J Cattlin	Villa never look like adding to their solitary away point, though it took Hammers a while to shrug off their Gantoise hangover. Villa are under acting manager Dick Taylor, but he is as helpless as his players as Hurst sets up a goal on a plate for Byrne. Boyce hooked in the second goal.										
13	A	LIVERPOOL		11	D	2-2	1-2	Hurst 23, 64	Standen	Bond	Peters	Bovington	Brown	Moore	Brabrook	Boyce	Byrne	Hurst	Sissons
		17/10	*36,029*	*17*	14			*St John 7, Hunt 27*	*Lawrence*	*Byrne G*	*Moran*	*Milne*	*Lawler*	*Stevenson*	*Callaghan*	*Hunt*	*St John*	*Graham*	*Thompson*
								Ref: K Burns	A repeat of the Charity Shield score. The champions can't get their act together in the league, and can't even hang on despite twice going in front. Hurst's close-in header levelled the first goal, a scramble on the line preceded the second, with Lawrence claiming Hurst had fouled him.										
14	H	SHEFFIELD WED		14	L	1-2	0-1	Brabrook 84	Standen	Bond	Peters	Bovington	Brown	Moore	Brabrook	Boyce	Byrne	Hurst	Sissons
		24/10	22,800	*7*	14			*Fantham 14, Quinn 85*	*Springett*	*Hill*	*Megson*	*Eustace*	*Mobley*	*Young*	*Finney*	*Quinn*	*Wilkinson*	*Fantham*	*Dobson*
								Ref: W Handley	Alan Brown's Owls arrived still looking for their first away win, having scored fewer away goals – three – than any other team. Yet they were leading in this match for 70 minutes until Brabrook unleashed a swirler from 30 yards. Straight from the kick-off Quinn netted from 10 yards.										
15	A	BLACKPOOL		12	W	2-1	1-0	Hurst 25, Brabrook 81	Standen	Bond	Peters	Bovington	Brown	Moore	Brabrook	Boyce	Hurst	Sissons	Scott
		31/10	*14,383*	*9*	16			*Green 83*	*Waiters*	*Armfield*	*Thompson*	*Rowe*	*James*	*Green*	*Oates*	*Ball*	*Charnley*	*Fisher*	*Horne*
								Ref: M Fussey	Blackpool's first home defeat was harsh, given the pressure they had exerted. Sissons prised open the defence for Hurst's goal, with Hammers thereafter defending in growing numbers. Alan Ball bored his way through many times and almost won a penalty before Brabrook's header.										
16	H	BLACKBURN		12	D	1-1	0-1	Sissons 63	Standen	Bond	Burkett	Bovington	Brown	Peters	Brabrook	Boyce	Byrne	Hurst	Sissons
		7/11	22,725	*5*	17			*Byrom 23*	*Else*	*Newton*	*Joyce*	*Clayton*	*England*	*McGrath*	*Ferguson*	*McEvoy*	*Byrom*	*Douglas*	*Harrison*
								Ref: D Smith	Rovers had won on their previous three visits to Upton Park, the last of which by 8-2. John Byrom, in particular, can't stop scoring against the Hammers and Alf Ramsey watches as he slams home Douglas's square pass. Sissons' left foot brought the equaliser from Boyce's nod-down.										
17	A	ARSENAL		7	W	3-0	1-0	Hurst 37, Byrne 60, Peters 64	Standen	Bond	Burkett	Bovington	Brown	Peters	Sealey	Boyce	Byrne	Hurst	Sissons
		14/11	*36,026*	*12*	19				*Burns*	*Howe*	*McCullough*	*McLintock*	*Neill*	*Court*	*Skirton*	*Radford*	*Baker*	*Eastham*	*Armstrong*
								Ref: K Dagnall	Seventh is the highest so far for West Ham, though they remain nine points behind leaders Man U. Arsenal missed the injured Ure, and Hurst took advantage with a flick that was turned into his own net by David Court. Peters played so well that the injured Moore wasn't missed at all.										
18	H	LEEDS		6	W	3-1	3-0	Kirkup 16, Byrne 20, Peters 35	Standen	Kirkup	Burkett	Bovington	Brown	Peters	Sealey	Boyce	Byrne	Hurst	Sissons
		21/11	28,150	*3*	21			*Belfitt 52*	*Sprake*	*Reaney*	*Bell*	*Bremner*	*Charlton*	*Hunter*	*Giles*	*Storrie*	*Belfitt*	*Collins*	*Henderson*
								Ref: J Lowry	Leeds had won their last seven, so crash to earth with a mighty bump. Kirkup, playing his first league game of the season, raced up to net from Boyce's centre. Byrne walked the ball in for No 2 after beating Sprake to Sissons' pass. Bremner hit the bar before Belfitt pulled a goal back.										
19	A	CHELSEA		6	W	3-0	3-0	Sealey 8, Peters 24, Hurst 38	Standen	Bond	Burkett	Bovington	Brown	Peters	Sealey	Boyce	Byrne	Hurst	Sissons
		28/11	*44,204*	*2*	23				*Bonetti*	*Hinton*	*McCreadie*	*Hollins*	*Mortimore*	*Harris*	*Murray*	*Graham*	*Bridges*	*Venables*	*Tambling*
								Ref: P Brandwood	Chelsea boss Tommy Docherty offered no excuses for his high-flyers' heaviest defeat so far, not even the fact that they hit the woodwork three times, or the fact that Hollins was carried off 10 minutes from time. West Ham are the only team to have scored in every match they've played.										
20	H	LEICESTER		6	D	0-0	0-0		Standen	Bond	Burkett	Bovington	Brown	Peters	Sealey	Boyce	Byrne	Hurst	Sissons
		5/12	**20,515**	*8*	24				*Banks*	*Sjoberg*	*Norman*	*Roberts*	*King*	*McDermott*	*Hodgson*	*Cross*	*Goodfellow*	*Gibson*	*Stringfellow*
								Ref: J Osborne	Here is an irony. Leicester have one of the worst defences in the division, conceding 44 goals in 20 games, but they become the first team to defy Hurst, Byrne *et al*. A wet, miserable afternoon was enjoyed mostly by Gordon Banks. Sissons and Byrne hit the bar in the same move.										
21	H	FULHAM		4	W	2-0	1-0	Byrne 10, 60	Standen	Bond	Burkett	Bovington	Brown	Peters	Brabrook	Boyce	Byrne	Hurst	Sissons
		12/12	21,985	*17*	26				*Macedo*	*Mealand*	*Langley*	*Robson*	*Keetch*	*Brown*	*Howfield*	*Callaghan*	*Marsh*	*Haynes*	*Chamberlain*
								Ref: D Lyden	Fourth place is the highest West Ham will reach this season. Matches like this, following a tiring European journey, are often lost, and Fulham had two 'goals' disallowed. Byrne, however, takes his tally to 19. Hammers are now just seven points behind the leaders with a game in hand.										

No	Date		Att	Pos	Pt	F-A	H-T	Scorers, Times, and Referees	1	2	3	4	5	6	7	8	9	10	11
22	A	NOTT'M FOREST		4	L	2-3	1-2	Byrne 33, Hurst 68	Standen	Bond	Burkett	Bovington	Brown	Peters	Brabrook	Boyce	Byrne	Hurst	Sissons
	19/12		*20,009*	*5*	26			*Hindkley 39, Quigley 42, Chapman 60*	*Grummitt*	*Hindley*	*Mochan*	*Newton*	*McKinlay*	*Whitefoot*	*Crowe*	*Quigley*	*Chapman*	*Barnwell*	*Storey-Moore*
								Ref: E Crawford	John Carey's Forest, without two international forwards – Wignall and Hinton – overtake West Ham, who placed too much of a burden on the overworked Johnnie Byrne. Hurst's 20-yarder to make it 2-3 did not spark a ferocious finale. In fact Hammers failed to create another chance.										
23	A	BIRMINGHAM		7	L	1-2	0-1	Hurst 90	Standen	Bond	Burkett	Bovington	Brown	Peters	Brabrook	Boyce	Byrne	Hurst	Sissons
	26/12		*23,324*	*19*	26			*Lynn 36, Thwaites 74*	*Schofield*	*Lynn*	*Green*	*Hennessey*	*Foster*	*Beard*	*Jackson*	*Sharples*	*Thomson*	*Vowden*	*Thwaites*
								Ref: K Stokes	The score flattered West Ham in this dress-rehearsal for the first defence of the FA Cup. City coach Joe Mallett came up with perfect tactics, pushing his full-backs up. Stan Lynn's goal, skidding through Standen's frozen fingers, confirmed him as the league's top scoring full-back.										
24	H	BIRMINGHAM		5	W	2-1	1-1	Byrne 30p, Kirkup 71	Standen	Kirkup	Peters	Bovington	Brown	Boyce	Sealey	Hurst	Byrne	Sissons	Scott
	28/12		23,800	*19*	28			*Sharples 10*	*Schofield*	*Lynn*	*Martin*	*Hennessey*	*Foster*	*Beard*	*Jackson*	*Sharples*	*Vowden*	*Auld*	*Thwaites*
								Ref: R Tinkler	City's five-game unbeaten run ends, despite Sharples' glancing header from Jackson's free-kick. Hammers looked ill at ease in rubber boots and gloves, and needed a penalty to square things when Auld stopped Hurst's header with his arm. Kirkup scored the winner at the near post.										
25	H	STOKE		7	L	0-1	0-1		Standen	Kirkup	Bond	Bovington	Brown	Peters	Brabrook	Boyce	Byrne	Hurst	Sissons
	2/1		23,913	*15*	28			*Viollet 39*	*Leslie*	*Asprey*	*Allen*	*Setters*	*Kinnell*	*Skeels*	*Palmer*	*Viollet*	*Ritchie*	*McIlroy*	*Dobing*
								Ref: E Jennings	Byrne couldn't shake off his markers, Hurst's best effort came back off a post, and big, strong John Ritchie charged Brown out of the way to nod down to Viollet, who scored. That summed up this match. West Ham resorted to long balls down the middle and hardly created a chance.										
26	A	TOTTENHAM		7	L	2-3	1-1	Byrne 17, Sissons 48	Standen	Bond	Peters	Bovington	Brown	Boyce	Sealey	Hurst	Byrne	Sissons	Scott
	16/1		***50,000***	*4*	28			*Greaves 7, 49, Dyson 62*	*Brown*	*Knowles*	*Henry*	*Mullery*	*Norman*	*Clayton*	*Robertson*	*Greaves*	*Gilzean*	*Jones*	*Dyson*
								Ref: W Clements	West Ham have won at Arsenal, Chelsea and Fulham, but were denied on a ground where only two teams have escaped with so much as a draw. When Byrne set up a goal for Sissons, an away win looked likely. But within seconds, Alan Mullery's shot flew in off Greaves' knee.										
27	H	BURNLEY		5	W	3-2	2-2	Boyce 18, Bond 44, Byrne 61	Standen	Bond	Peters	Bovington	Brown	Boyce	Sealey	Hurst	Byrne	Sissons	Scott
	23/1		25,490	*15*	30			*Lochhead 31, Irvine 38*	*Blacklaw*	*Smith*	*Angus*	*O'Neil*	*Talbut*	*Miller*	*Morgan*	*Lochhead*	*Irvine*	*Harris*	*Towers*
								Ref: N Burtenshaw	Four of the five goals were directly attributable to unforced defensive errors. The exception was the first, thumped in by Boyce from 20 yards. Bond was at fault for both Burnley goals, and was much relieved when Blacklaw dropped Sissons' drive, which fell to Byrne to win the game.										
28	A	SHEFFIELD UTD			L	1-2	1-1	Sealey 4	Standen	Kirkup	Bond	Bovington	Brown	Peters	Sealey	Boyce	Byrne	Hurst	Sissons
	6/2		*16,265*		30			*Jones 2, Birchenall 72*	*Hodgkinson*	*Badger*	*Shaw G*	*Richardson*	*Shaw J*	*Matthewson*	*Woodward*	*Kettleborough*	*Jones*	*Birchenall*	*Hartle*
								Ref: K Walker	West Ham applauded Blades' Joe Shaw on to the pitch for this, his 600th league appearance, and then played so aimlessly that he was given no one to mark. Mick Jones' header was cancelled out by Sealey scoring from Sissons' pass. Birchenall headed the winner from Hartle's corner.										
29	H	EVERTON		10	L	0-1	0-0		Standen	Bond	Peters	Bovington	Brown	Moore	Sealey	Boyce	Byrne	Hurst	Sissons
	13/2		25,163	*9*	30			*Temple 82*	*West*	*Wright*	*Wilson*	*Gabriel*	*Labone*	*Stevens*	*Scott*	*Harvey*	*Pickering*	*Vernon*	*Temple*
								Ref: G Roper	Moore returned for his first match since October but cannot prevent yet another defeat. That, however, is the fault of the forwards, who missed chances galore before Derek Temple took Harvey's pass to sprint away down the left, outstrip a bare defence and slide the ball past Standen.										
30	A	SUNDERLAND		11	L	2-3	0-1	Byrne 70, Hurst 78	Standen	Bond	Peters	Bovington	Brown	Moore	Sealey	Boyce	Byrne	Hurst	Sissons
	20/2		*32,885*	*20*	30			*Hood 34, Sharkey 84, 89*	*McLaughlan*	*Parke*	*Ashurst*	*Harvey*	*Hurley*	*McNab*	*Usher*	*Herd*	*Hood*	*Sharkey*	*Mulhall*
								Ref: J Bullough	West Ham stumble to their fifth successive away defeat, a result which lifts Sunderland out of the relegation places. Byrne's hook, followed by Hurst's rifling 20-yarder, the best goal of the game, had silenced the Roker faithful. Then Parke centred and Nick Sharkey scored on the turn.										
31	H	LIVERPOOL		10	W	2-1	0-1	Presland 48, Hurst 53	Standen	Kirkup	**Presland**	Bovington	Moore	Peters	Brabrook	Boyce	Byrne	Hurst	Sissons
	27/2		25,750	*6*	32			*Hunt 22*	*Lawrence*	*Lawler*	*Byrne G*	*Milne*	*Smith*	*Stevenson*	*Graham*	*Hunt*	*St John*	*Arrowsmith*	*Wallace*
								Ref: H New	Liverpool's 21-match unbeaten run comes to an end, and so does Hammers' run of defeats. West Ham have become something of a bogey team for Bill Shankly's outfit. Eddie Presland will always remember his debut: his shot from 30 yards brushed Smith and deceived Lawrence.										

No	Venue	Opponent	Pos	Res	Pts	F-A	H-T	Scorers, Times, Referees	1	2	3	4	5	6	7	8	9	10	11
32	A	SHEFFIELD WED	10	L		0-2	0-0		Standen	Kirkup	Presland	Bovington	Moore	Peters	Brabrook	Boyce	Byrne	Hurst	Sissons
6/3		*14,931*	*8*		32			*Mobley 48, Hickton 72*	*Springett*	*Hill*	*Megson*	*Eustace*	*Mobley*	*Smith*	*Finney*	*Quinn*	*Hickton*	*Fantham*	*Dobson*
								Ref: F Schofield	A poor game, and Wednesday's opening goal was both poor and dubious. Mobley's header from Finney's corner was stopped on the line by Kirkup. Standen picked it up to find the ref signalling that it had crossed the line. Hickton's later header couldn't assuage West Ham's anger.										
33	H	SUNDERLAND	12	L		2-3	1-2	Dear 10, 59	Standen	Kirkup	Presland	Bovington	Moore	Peters	Brabrook	Boyce	Hurst	Dear	Sissons
13/3		23,360	*18*		32			*Harvey 38, Herd 44, 61*	*McLaughlan*	*Parke*	*Ashurst*	*Harvey*	*Hurley*	*McNab*	*Hellawell*	*Herd*	*Hood*	*Sharkey*	*Mulhall*
								Ref: L Hamer	George Hardwick's lowly Sunderland secure the double over West Ham with their second away win of the season. With Lausanne looming, Greenwood left out Byrne, then lost Bovington in the third minute with an injured knee. Dear's first game of the season earned him two goals.										
34	A	BLACKBURN	13	L		**0-4**	0-2		Standen	Kirkup	Bovington	Charles	Brown	Moore	Sealey	Boyce	Hurst	Dear	Scott
20/3		***8,990***	*9*		32			*Byrom 33, 58, 62, Douglas 43p*	*Jones*	*Wilson*	*Joyce*	*Clayton*	*England*	*Sharples*	*Ferguson*	*Newton*	*Byrom*	*Douglas*	*Bradshaw*
								Ref: J Carr	Rovers' smallest gate for years watched this emphatic win. Byrom bagged his second recent hat-trick against Hammers, below par following their trip to Lausanne. It might have been different: Sealey and Scott both hit the woodwork at 0-0. Presland tripped Ferguson for the penalty.										
35	H	ARSENAL	11	W		2-1	0-0	Hurst 82, Byrne 87p	Standen	Kirkup	Peters	Boyce	Brown	Moore	Sealey	Hurst	Byrne	Dear	Sissons
27/3		24,000	*10*		34			*Baker 72*	*Burns*	*Howe*	*McCullough*	*McLintock*	*Ure*	*Neill*	*Tawse*	*Radford*	*Baker*	*Eastham*	*Armstrong*
								Ref: J Finney	Arsenal boss Billy Wright moaned afterwards about the cruelty of football. With time running out, Sissons fired against the bar and Hurst leapt to head past Burns. Then Ian Ure, booed roundly by those with memories of his rough handling of Byrne last season, under-hit a back-pass.										
36	A	ASTON VILLA	10	W		3-2	0-2	Hurst 50, Byrne 58, Dear 63	Standen	Kirkup	Burkett	Peters	Bickles	Moore	Sealey	Hurst	Byrne	Dear	Sissons
31/3		*19,900*	*20*		36			*Hateley 29, Aitken 30*	*Withers*	*Lee*	*Aitken*	*Wylie*	*Pountney*	*Deakin*	*Baker*	*Chatterley*	*Hateley*	*Woosnam*	*MacLeod*
								Ref: M Fussey	This famous fightback doesn't do Villa's relegation worries any good. Ex-Hammer Phil Woosnam engineered two Villa goals inside a minute, moments after Byrne had hit a post. Hurst's 25-yarder dipped under the bar, Byrne headed the equaliser, and Dear turned in Byrne's cross.										
37	A	LEEDS	10	L		1-2	0-0	Dear 66	Standen	Kirkup	Burkett	Peters	Brown	Moore	Sealey	Hurst	Byrne	Dear	Boyce
3/4		*41,918*	*2*		36			*Peacock 64, Bremner 80*	*Sprake*	*Reaney*	*Bell*	*Bremner*	*Charlton*	*Hunter*	*Giles*	*Storrie*	*Peacock*	*Collins*	*Cooper*
								Ref: E Norman	Wembley-bound Leeds are pressing hard for the double, yet they should have been turned over by West Ham who seemed determined to fluff all the chances they created. Peacock's header was answered by Sprake, who dropped Byrne's cross. Bremner scrambled home Hunter's cross.										
38	H	CHELSEA		W		3-2	3-0	Hurst 4, 25, Sissons 19	Standen	Kirkup	Burkett	Peters	Brown	Moore	Sealey	Boyce	Hurst	Dear	Sissons
12/4		33,288			38			*Venables 54, Bridges 69*	*Bonetti*	*Hinton*	*Harris*	*Hollins*	*Mortimore*	*Boyle*	*Murray*	*Graham*	*Bridges*	*Venables*	*Tambling*
								Ref: R Tinkler	Title-chasing Chelsea do a Zaragoza and nearly come back from the dead. Bonetti was partly to blame for Hammers' first two goals, failing to hold shots by Peters and Sealey respectively. Bonetti also got a touch to Hurst's second goal, from 25 yards. Revenge for the FA Cup defeat.										
39	H	WEST BROM	7	W		**6-1**	2-1	Peters 30, Dear 44, 53, 56, 59, 64	Standen	Kirkup	Burkett	Peters	Bickles	Moore	Brabrook	Boyce	Hurst	Dear	Sissons
16/4		27,706	*14*		40			*Astle 45*	*Potter*	*Cram*	*Williams*	*Howshall*	*Jones*	*Fraser*	*Foggo*	*Astle*	*Kaye*	*Hope*	*Clarke*
								Ref: D Smith	Brian Dear's five-goal haul in 20 minutes is unequalled in First Division football. He only played because Byrne was injured, and though he overtook John Dick's four against Rotherham, he only equalled the feat of Torquay's Robin Stubbs, who hit five against Newport in 1963.										
40	A	LEICESTER	8	L		0-1	0-1		Standen	Bond	Burkett	Peters	Brown	Moore	Sealey	Boyce	Hurst	Dear	Scott
17/4		*15,880*	*16*		40			*Gibson 40*	*Banks*	*Walker*	*Norman*	*Cross*	*Sjoberg*	*Appleton*	*Hodgson*	*Sweenie*	*Roberts*	*Gibson*	*Goodfellow*
								Ref: C Cooke	Standen palmed Gibson's shot into the net, whereupon Boyce hit a post. There was little else to report upon in the first half. After 77 minutes Boyce turned Scott's cross past Banks, but when the ref gave offside Moore was booked for dissent. Boyce also hit the underside of the bar.										
41	A	WEST BROM		L		2-4	0-3	Hurst 49, Boyce 85	Standen	Kirkup	Peters	**Dawkins**	Brown	Moore	Bennett	Boyce	Hurst	Dear	Sissons
19/4		*14,000*			40			*Foggo 8, Astle 14, Brown 33, 60*	*Potter*	*Cram*	*Williams G*	*Howshall*	*Jones*	*Fraser*	*Foggo*	*Astle*	*Crawford*	*Hope*	*Brown*
								Ref: Seddon	Unfazed by an Arctic blizzard, Albion gain revenge for the 6-1 blitz inflicted on them on Friday. Two quick goals, both from corners, and both of which were wind-assisted, gave West Ham a mountain to climb. The crucial period came at 1-3 when Dear and Boyce had goals disallowed.										
42	H	BLACKPOOL		W		2-1	0-1	Brown 47, Dear 79	Standen	Kirkup	Burkett	Boyce	Brown	Moore	Sealey	Brabrook	Hurst	Dear	Sissons
23/4		22,762			42			*Moir 6*	*Waiters*	*Armfield*	*Rowe*	*McPhee*	*James*	*Green*	*Lea*	*Ball*	*Charnley*	*Robson*	*Moir*
	Home	Away						Ref: G Martin	Ken Brown headed his second goal in a 13-year Hammers career. That Brian Dear should score was rather more predictable: his conversion of Sissons' cross was his 14th goal in 13 games. The game had started badly, Moir dispossessing Boyce and scoring. Now for Zaragoza in Spain.										
Average	25,808	26,974																	

Charity Shield			F-A	H-T	Scorers, Times, and Referees	1	2	3	4	5	6	7	8	9	10	11
A LIVERPOOL		D	2-2	1-1	Byrne 41, Hurst 84	Standen	Bond	Burkett	Bovington	Brown	Moore	Brabrook	Boyce	Byrne	Hurst	Sissons
15/8	*40,000*				*Wallace 28, Byrne 49*	*Lawrence*	*Byrne G*	*Moran*	*Milne*	*Yeats*	*Stevenson*	*Callaghan*	*Hunt*	*Arrowsmith**	*Wallace*	*Thompson*
					Ref: K Stokes	The Charity Shield is played at Anfield, not Wembley. Though substitutes have not yet been introduced in the league, Liverpool bring on Phil Chisnall for the injured Arrowsmith after 10 minutes. When Lawrence spilled Brabrook's cross to Hurst, it was totally against the run of play.										

League Cup				F-A	H-T	Scorers, Times, and Referees	1	2	3	4	5	6	7	8	9	10	11
2 A SUNDERLAND		12	L	1-4	0-4	Brabrook 55 *[Usher 38]*	Standen	Bond	Burkett	Bovington	Brown	Peters	Brabrook	Boyce	Byrne	Hurst	Sissons
30/9	*22,382*	*15*				*Mulhall 3, Mitchinson 9, Sharkey 12,*	*McLaughlan*	*Irwin*	*Ashurst*	*Harvey*	*Hurley*	*McNab*	*Usher*	*Herd*	*Sharkey*	*Mitchinson*	*Mulhall*
						Ref: P Rhodes	Accusations are made after this flop that West Ham aren't interested in the League Cup, and the sooner they are out of it the better. Moore was rested in preparation for Saturday's England game. Sunderland won despite playing with 10 men for 43 minutes, McNab's knee taking him off.										

FA Cup				F-A	H-T	Scorers, Times, and Referees	1	2	3	4	5	6	7	8	9	10	11
3 H BIRMINGHAM		7	W	4-2	1-2	Byrne 41, Hurst 52, 70, Sissons 89	Standen	Bond	Peters	Bovington	Brown	Boyce	Sealey	Hurst	Byrne	Sissons	Scott
9/1	31,056	*19*				*Thwaites 7, Jackson 27*	*Schofield*	*Lynn*	*Green*	*Hennessey*	*Foster*	*Beard*	*Jackson*	*Sharples*	*Vowden*	*Auld*	*Thwaites*
						Ref: L Callaghan	The third meeting between these sides in two weeks looks to have turned decisively City's way when Jackson scores direct from a corner to make it 0-2. The turning point came when Sissons drew Schofield from his goal and chipped to Byrne. Sealey squared for Hurst's equaliser.										
4 H CHELSEA		5	L	0-1	0-1		Standen	Kirkup	Bond	Bovington	Brown	Peters	Sealey	Boyce	Byrne	Sissons	Scott
30/1	37,000	*2*				*Tambling 10*	*Bonetti*	*Hinton*	*Harris*	*Hollins*	*Mortimore*	*Boyle*	*Murray*	*Graham*	*Bridges*	*Venables*	*Tambling*
						Ref: D Smith	A minute's silence for the death of Sir Winston Churchill. West Ham's grip on the Cup is prised open when Standen parries Venables' effort, the ball running loose. The longer the match went on the more players Chelsea pulled back. West Ham hadn't the wit to find a way through.										

European Cup-Winners' Cup				F-A	H-T	Scorers, Times, and Referees	1	2	3	4	5	6	7	8	9	10	11
1:1 A LA GANTOISE		13	W	1-0	0-0	Boyce 52	Standen	Bond	Peters	Bovington	Brown	Moore	Sealey	Boyce	Byrne	Hurst	Sissons
23/9 (Belgium)	*18,000*	*10*					*Seghers A*	*Devreese*	*De Nayer*	*Delmulle*	*De Baets*	*Mahieu*	*Ghellynck*	*Seghers U*	*Lambert*	*Mayama*	*Storme*
							The Buffaloes of Ghent, the first Belgian team to compete in this competition, are undone when their 40-year-old keeper dithered at Sealey's corner and was beaten by Boyce's slow-motion header. The hosts defended in numbers, reversing the normal pattern for European games.										
1:2 H LA GANTOISE		12	D	1-1	1-1	Byrne 43	Dickie	Bond	Peters	Bovington	Brown	Moore	Brabrook	Boyce	Byrne	Hurst	Sissons
7/10	24,000					*Peters 32 (og)*	*Seghers A*	*Van de Velde*	*Devreese*	*Mahieu*	*Denayer*	*Mayama*	*Ghellynck*	*Seghers U*	*Lambert*	*Bula*	*Storme*
						Ref: E Olsen (Norway) (Hammers win 2-1 on aggregate)	Hammers fans pay record receipts to see this decrepit performance that drives them to jeers and slow-handclaps. Though needing to score, the part-timers sat back as in the first leg. Peters jabbed a back-pass beyond the advancing Dickie. John Sissons' cross set up Byrne's life-saver.										
2:1 H SPARTAK PRAGUE		6	W	2-0	0-0	Bond 58, Sealey 82	Standen	Bond	Burkett	Bovington	Brown	Peters	Sealey	Boyce	Byrne	Hurst	Sissons
25/11 (Czech)	27,590						*Kramerius*	*Gura*	*Taborsky*	*Vojta*	*Kos*	*Steiningel*	*Dyba*	*Mraz*	*Kvasnak*	*Kraus*	*Masek*
						Ref: J de Mendibil (Spain)	The white-clad Czechs survived a tepid first-half only to be roasted in the second. John Bond hit a scorcher from 25 yards for his first goal in three years. Four times the Czechs booted the ball out of the ground to waste time. Alan Sealey hit the far post before poaching the rebound.										
2:2 A SPARTAK PRAGUE		6	L	1-2	1-0	Sissons 14	Standen	Bond	Burkett	Bovington	Brown	Peters	Sealey	Boyce	Byrne	Hurst	Sissons
9/12	*45,000*					*Mraz 73, 88*	*Kramerius*	*Gura*	*Kos*	*Taborsky*	*Tichy*	*Vojta*	*Dyba*	*Mraz*	*Kvasnak*	*Kraus*	*Masek*
						Ref: Dinov (Bulgaria) (Hammers win 3-2 on aggregate)	When 19-year-old Sissons side-stepped Taborsky to make it 3-0 overall, that should have been that. But Bond's handball concedes a penalty for Masek, which Standen saves. It was Standen who let the Czechs back in, pushing Taborsky's shot on to the bar then losing his footing.										

Rd		Opponent	Att	Pos	Res	F-A	H-T	Scorers, Times, and Referees											
QF 1	A 16/3	LAUSANNE (Switz)	*20,000*	12	W	2-1	1-0	Dear 21, Byrne 53 *Hosp 80* Ref: Schiller (Austria)	Standen *Kunzi*	Kirkup *Grobety*	Peters *Hunziker*	Boyce *Duerr*	Brown *Tacchella*	Moore *Schneiter*	Sealey *Eschmann*	Hurst *Kerkhoffs*	Byrne *Armbruster*	Dear *Hosp*	Sissons *Hertig*
									Hammers survived when Armbruster struck the bar to go ahead through Dear – on his European baptism – when Kunzi failed to hold Ronnie Boyce's free-kick. Johnny Byrne's solo goal further deflated Karl Rappan's Lausanne, who had seven Swiss internationals in their ranks.										
QF 2	H 23/3	LAUSANNE	31,780	13	W	4-3	2-1	Tacchella 42 (og), Dear 43, 89, Peters 59 *Kerkhoffs 37, Hertig 48, Eschmann 80* Ref: P Roomer (Hammers win 6-4 on aggregate)	Standen *Kunzi*	Kirkup *Grobety*	Peters *Hunziker*	Boyce *Schneiter*	Brown *Tacchella*	Moore *Durr*	Sealey *Eschmann*	Hurst *Kerkhoffs*	Byrne *Armbruster*	Dear *Hosp*	Sissons *Hertig*
									This thrilling cup-tie only swung decisively West Ham's way in the final minute, when Dear smashed the goal which finally sunk Lausanne. Kerkhoff's header put the cat among the pigeons until Tacchella turned Sealey's cross into his own net. Eschmann's overhead kick was a gem.										
SF 1	H 7/4	REAL ZARAGOZA (Spain)	35,000 *3*	10	W	2-1	2-0	Dear 9, Byrne 24 *Canario 55* Ref: R Lacoste (France)	Standen *Yarza*	Kirkup *Cortizo*	Burkett *Reija*	Peters *Isasi*	Brown *Santamaria*	Moore *Violeta*	Boyce *Canario*	Dear *Santos*	Byrne *Marcelino*	Hurst *Enderiz*	Sissons *Lapetra*
									Brian Dear heads his eighth goal in eight games. When Byrne takes a pass on his chest and volleys in from 18 yards the Boleyn is in raptures. But for the second half West Ham line up with nine defenders and Zaragoza twist them this way and that. Boos rained down on the Hammers.										
SF 2	A 28/4	REAL ZARAGOZA	*28,000*	9	D	1-1	0-1	Sissons 54 *Lapetra 24* Ref: L Horn (Holland) (Hammers win 3-2 on aggregate)	Standen *Yarza*	Kirkup *Cortizo*	Burkett *Reija*	Peters *Enderiz*	Brown *Santamaria*	Moore *Violeta*	Boyce *Canario*	Sealey *Santos*	Hurst *Marcelino*	Dear *Villa*	Sissons *Lapetra*
									Zaragoza are convinced the ref cost them a place in the final by denying them three penalties. West Ham conceded 19 fouls in the first half alone. Lapetra pounced when Standen blocked Marcelino's header. Sissons converted Dear's pass. Now for Turin or TSV Munich in the final.										
F	N 19/5	TSV MUNICH 1860 (W Germ) (At Wembley)	*100,000*	9	W	2-0	0-0	Sealey 69, 71 Ref: I Zsolt (Hungary)	Standen *Radenkovic*	Kirkup *Wagner*	Burkett *Kohlars*	Peters *Bena*	Brown *Reich*	Moore *Luttrop*	Sealey *Heiss*	Boyce *Kuppers*	Hurst *Brunnenmeier*	Dear *Grosser*	Sissons *Rebele*
									West Ham's greatest moment. Sealey celebrates his marriage last week by firing his first goal from an impossible angle and his second when Moore's free-kick wasn't cleared. Luckless Sissons struck the post and the bar. Even the ref said it was a wonderfully clean game to control.										

			Home					Away					
	P	W	D	L	F	A	W	D	L	F	A	Pts
1 Manchester U	42	16	4	1	52	13	10	5	6	37	26	61
2 Leeds	42	16	3	2	53	23	10	6	5	30	29	61
3 Chelsea	42	15	2	4	48	19	9	6	6	41	35	56
4 Everton	42	9	10	2	37	22	8	5	8	32	38	49
5 Nott'm Forest	42	10	7	4	45	33	7	6	8	26	34	47
6 Tottenham	42	18	3	0	65	20	1	4	16	22	51	45
7 Liverpool	42	12	5	4	42	33	5	5	11	25	40	44
8 Sheffield Wed	42	13	5	3	37	15	3	6	12	20	40	43
9 WEST HAM	42	14	2	5	48	25	5	2	14	34	46	42
10 Blackburn	42	12	2	7	46	33	4	8	9	37	46	42
11 Stoke	42	11	4	6	40	27	5	6	10	27	39	42
12 Burnley	42	9	9	3	39	26	7	1	13	31	44	42
13 Arsenal	42	11	5	5	42	31	6	2	13	27	44	41
14 West Brom	42	10	5	6	45	25	3	8	10	25	40	39
15 Sunderland	42	12	6	3	45	26	2	3	16	19	48	37
16 Aston Villa	42	14	1	6	36	24	2	4	15	21	58	37
17 Blackpool	42	9	7	5	41	28	3	4	14	26	50	35
18 Leicester	42	9	6	6	43	36	2	7	12	26	49	35
19 Sheffield Utd	42	7	5	9	30	29	5	6	10	20	35	35
20 Fulham	42	10	5	6	44	32	1	7	13	16	46	34
21 Wolves	42	8	2	11	33	36	5	2	14	26	53	30
22 Birmingham	42	6	8	7	36	40	2	3	16	28	56	27
	924	251	106	105	947	596	105	106	251	596	947	924

Odds & ends

Double wins: (5) Fulham, Aston Villa, Blackpool, Arsenal, Chelsea.
Double losses: (4) Nott'm Forest, Stoke, Sheff Wed, Sunderland.

Won from behind: (10) Spurs (h), Sheff U (h), Birmingham (h), Burnley (h), Liverpool (h), Arsenal (h), Villa (a), Blackpool (h), Birmingham FAC (h), Zaragoza (CWC).
Lost from in front: (6) Nott'm F (h&a), Stoke (a), Wolves (a), Spurs (a), Sunderland (h).

High spots: Winning the European Cup-Winners' Cup.
West Ham did the league double over *three* London clubs.
Run of seven unbeaten league games, October to December, up to 4th.

Low spots: Early exits from both domestic cups.
Terrible league sequence of 10 defeats in 13 games, Dec to March.

Hammer of the Year: Martin Peters.
Ever-presents: (0) (Standen and Hurst missed one European game).
Hat-tricks: (1) Brian Dear.
Leading scorer: (29) Johnny Byrne.

	Appearances				Goals				
	Lge	LC	FAC	Eur	Lge	LC	FAC	Eur	Tot
Bennett, Peter	**1**								
Bickles, Dave	**2**								
Bond, John	**29**	1	2	4	**1**			1	**2**
Bovington, Eddie	**33**	1	2	4					
Boyce, Ronnie	**41**	1	2	9	**4**			1	**5**
Brabrook, Peter	**22**	1		1	**3**	1			**4**
Brown, Ken	**33**	1	2	9	**1**				**1**
Burkett, Jackie	**24**	1		5					
Byrne, Johnny	**34**	1	2	7	**25**		1	3	**29**
Charles, John	**1**								
Dawkins, Trevor	**1**								
Dear, Brian	**10**			5	**10**			4	**14**
Dickie, Alan				1					
Hurst, Geoff	**42**	1	1	9	**17**		2		**19**
Kirkup, Joe	**15**		1	5	**2**				**2**
Moore, Bobby	**28**			7	**1**				**1**
Peters, Martin	**35**	1	2	9	**5**			1	**6**
Presland, Eddie	**4**				**1**				**1**
Scott, Tony	**6**		2						
Sealey, Alan	**21**		2	7	**2**			1	**3**
Sissons, John	**38**	1	2	9	**8**		1	4	**13**
Standen, Jim	**42**	1	2	8					
(own-goals)					**2**			1	**3**
22 players used	**462**	**11**	**22**	**99**	**82**	**1**	**4**	**16**	**103**

LEAGUE DIVISION 1 — Manager: Ron Greenwood — SEASON 1965-66

No	Date		Att	Pos	Pt	F-A	H-T	Scorers, Times, and Referees	1	2	3	4	5	6	7	8	9	10	11	12 sub used
1	A	WEST BROM			L	0-3	0-2		Standen	Kirkup	Burkett	Peters	Bovington	Moore	Brabrook	Boyce	Hurst	Bennett	Sissons	
	21/8		*19,900*		–			*Ckark 2, 89, Astle 37*	*Potter*	*Cram*	*Williams G*	*Lovett*	*Jones*	*Fraser*	*Foggo*	*Astle*	*Kaye*	*Hope*	*Clark*	
								Ref: I Callaghan	West Ham won't live on past glories, even if they are only a few weeks old. Clive Clark brought them down to earth in 90 seconds, capitalising on a rebound. WBA needed no luck with their second goal, Fraser feeding a perfect pass to Astle. Kay hit a post, the ball bouncing to Standen.											
2	H	SUNDERLAND			D	1-1	1-1	Peters 4	Dickie	Kirkup	Burkett	Peters	Bickles	Moore	**Redknapp**	Boyce	Byrne	Hurst	Sissons	
	23/8		34,700		1			*Herd 29*	*McLaughlan*	*Irwin*	*Ashurst*	*Harvey*	*Hurley*	*Baxter*	*Hellawell*	*Herd*	*O'Hare*	*McNab*	*Mulhall*	
								Ref: T Dawes	All eyes are on Sunderland's 'Slim' Jim Baxter, signed from Rangers, and he is instrumental in forging the equaliser. Martin Peters had headed in Redknapp's corner, having already headed over another corner. Little was seen of Baxter after half-time as Sunderland funnelled back.											
3	H	LEEDS		14	W	2-1	1-1	Peters 44, Hurst 83	Standen	Kirkup	Burkett*	Bovington	Bickles	Moore	Redknapp	Peters	Byrne	Hurst	Sissons	Bennett
	28/8		27,900	*4*	3			*Peacock 13*	*Sprake*	*Reaney*	*Bell*	*Bremner*	*Charlton*	*Hunter*	*Weston*	*Lorimer*	*Peacock*	*Giles*	*Cooper*	
								Ref: R Aldous	Leeds drop their first points, West Ham notch their first win, and Peter Bennett comes on after 53 minutes as their first ever league substitute. The woodwork was hit twice, first when Sprake allowed Redknapps's cross to pass through his hands; then from Lorimer's ballistic drive.											
4	A	SUNDERLAND		17	L	1-2	1-0		Standen	Kirkup	Presland	Bovington	Bickles	Moore	Redknapp	Peters	Byrne	Hurst	Sissons	
	1/9		*48,626*	*6*	3			*Mulhall 52, McNab 73*	*McLaughlan*	*Irwin*	*Ashurst*	*Harvey*	*Hurley*	*Baxter*	*Hellawell*	*Herd*	*O'Hare*	*McNab*	*Mulhall*	
								Ref: S Kayley	Charlie Hurley mistimed an interception to let in Hurst, but then it all started to go wrong. Hurley redeemed himself with a 30-yarder that was blocked and fell to Mulhall. Jim McNab then sprinted 30 yard to head the winner from Hellawell's cross. Hammers hit the woodwork twice.											
5	A	SHEFFIELD UTD		18	L	3-5	1-3	Hurst 29, Kirkup 53, Byrne 60	Standen	Kirkup	Presland	Bovington	Bickles	Moore	Brabrook	Peters	Byrne	Hurst	Sissons	
	4/9		*15,796*	*4*	3			*Birch' 9, Docherty 15, K'borough 40,*	*Hodgkinson*	*Badger*	*Mallender*	*Munks*	*Shaw J*	*Matthewson*	*Docherty*	*Kettleborough*	*Jones*	*Birchenall*	*Reece*	
								Ref: K Seddon *[Jones 77, 85]*	Blades had only scored three goals before today, yet bag their biggest total since returning to Division 1 in 1961. Byrne's exquisite touch to make it 3-3 looked to have sealed a famous fight-back, but a header, followed by a hooked goal from Mick Jones, condemned West Ham.											
6	H	LIVERPOOL			L	1-5	0-4	Peters 53	Standen	Kirkup	Burkett	Peters	Bickles	Moore	Brabrook	Boyce	Byrne	Hurst	Scott	
	6/9		32,144		3			*Milne 11, Callaghan 25, Hunt 43, 45, 46*	*Lawrence*	*Lawler*	*Byrne*	*Milne*	*Yeats*	*Stevenson*	*Callaghan*	*Hunt*	*St John*	*Smith*	*Thompson*	
								Ref: N Burtenshaw	A three-minute hat-trick, straddling half-time, by Roger Hunt put the nail in West Ham's coffin. Liverpool had come to regard the Hammers as a bogey side, but Milne was somehow left unmarked to drive in St John's pull-back. Upton Park rose to applaud Shankly's marvels at the end.											
7	H	LEICESTER		20	L	2-5	2-2	Hurst 24, 28p *[Goodfellow 83]*	Standen	Kirkup	Burkett	Bovington	Brown	Moore	Redknapp	Peters	Hurst	Sissons	Scott	
	11/9		21,400	*15*	3			*Dougan 31, 74, Sinclair 34, 47,*	*Hayes*	*Walker*	*Norman*	*Roberts*	*Sjoberg*	*Cross*	*Sinclair*	*Gibson*	*Dougan*	*Goodfellow*	*Stringfellow*	
								Ref: J Osborne	Leicester's first away win brings a hat-trick of five-goal thrashings. This was unexpected, since when Norman handled, Hurst's penalty made it 2-0. 'We want five!' the crowd chanted, not knowing they were to get them. Hammers have the worst defensive record in the Football League.											
8	A	LIVERPOOL		20	D	1-1	1-0	Hurst 37	Dickie	Kirkup	Burkett	Bovington	Charles	Moore	Bennett	Peters	Hurst	Boyce	Sissons	
	15/9		*44,397*	*6*	4			*Strong 63*	*Lawrence*	*Lawler**	*Byrne G*	*Milne*	*Yeats*	*Stevenson*	*Callaghan*	*Hunt*	*St John*	*Smith*	*Thompson*	*Strong*
								Ref: R Windle	On a filthy night it was odds-on another five-goal thrashing, which Greenwood counters by playing almost his whole team in their own penalty box. Hurst rammed in Peters' cross in a rare attacking sortie, but Liverpool's first ever league substitute, Geoff Strong, headed the equaliser.											
9	A	BLACKBURN		18	W	2-1	1-1	Peters 33, 88	Dickie	Kirkup	Burkett	Bovington	Charles	Moore	Bennett	Peters	Hurst	Boyce	Sissons	
	18/9		***10,178***	*22*	6			*Jones 36*	*Else*	*Newton*	*Wilson*	*Clayton*	*Mulvaney*	*Sharples*	*Ferguson*	*McEvoy*	*Jones*	*Byrom*	*Horrey*	
								Ref: N Callender	If Hammers are going to beat anyone, it would have to be Rovers, whom they send to the bottom. West Ham again packed their defence and won unworthily when Peters headed Kirkup's corner past Else. The public address system announced Hammers' substitute as Harry 'Redcap'.											
10	H	BLACKPOOL		18	D	1-1	0-0	Hurst 89	Dickie	Kirkup	Burkett	Bovington	Charles	Moore	Bennett	Peters	Byrne	Hurst	Sissons	
	25/9		21,000	*19*	7			*Charnley 77*	*Waiters*	*Thompson*	*Craven*	*Fisher*	*James*	*Green*	*Moir*	*Ball*	*Charnley*	*Lea*	*Horne*	
								Ref: P Rhodes	No one can say the ball isn't running kindly for West Ham. Yet again they salvage the game in the last seconds, when Waiters saved thrillingly from Byrne, only to deflect the ball to Hurst. The players looked so embarrassed they don't celebrate. Ray Charnley had scored off a post.											

No	H/A	Opponent	Pos	Res	FT	HT	Scorers, Times, and Referees	1	2	3	4	5	6	7	8	9	10	11	12 sub used
11	A	FULHAM	19	L	0-3	0-0		Dickie	**Burnett**	Charles	Peters	Brown	Bovington	Bennett	**Bloomfield**	Byrne	Hurst	Sissons	
2/10		*22,310*	*18*	7			*Charles 53 (og), Haynes 77, Leggat 86*	*Macedo*	*Nicholls*	*Mealand*	*Robson*	*Dempsey*	*Keetch*	*Key*	*O'Connell*	*Leggat*	*Haynes*	*Dyson*	
							Ref: D Smith	Before kick-off the announcer sought a spare linesman. Dickie shaped to collect O'Connell's cross, only for Charles to intervene and lob it in. Haynes added a fierce shot to set up a bizarre finale. With the ref looking elsewhere, Dickie hit a goal-kick to Leggat, who thumped it back in.											
12	A	NOTT'M FOREST	20	L	**0-5**	0-3	*[Addison 50, Wilson 88]*	Standen	Kirkup	Charles*	Peters	Bovington	Moore	Redknapp	Bloomfield	Hurst	Bennett	Brabrook	Bickles
9/10		*19,262*	*15*	7			*Hinton 32, Wignall 44, Moore 45,*	*Grummitt*	*Hindley*	*Mochan*	*Newton*	*McKinlay*	*Whitefoot*	*Storey-Moore*	*Addison*	*Wignall*	*Barnwell*	*Hinton*	
							Ref: J Mitchell	Hammers' fourth five-goal drubbing in 12 games. Forest had unleashed 14 shots before going in front, a 25-yarder from Hinton. Although Charles was injured, Greenwood delayed critically in sending on a sub. Kirkup's back-pass landed at the feet of Wignall, who hit the second.											
13	H	SHEFFIELD WED	20	W	4-2	1-2	Sissons 35, Britt 53, 70, Peters 78	Standen	Burnett	Charles	Bovington	Brown	Moore	Brabrook	Peters	Britt	Hurst	Sissons	
16/10		20,690	*19*	9			*Brown 16 (og), Wilkinson 44*	*Springett*	*Smith*	*Megson*	*Eustace*	*Mobley*	*Young*	*Wilkinson*	*Quinn*	*Hickson*	*Fantham*	*Dobson*	
							Ref: J Lowry	Howard Wilkinson did his best to defeat the Hammers. Standen saved his header, but Brown ran the ball into the net. After Sissons hit back from a rebound, Wilkinson chipped a fine goal. Britt, in his first league game of the season, netted a rebound, then headed in to make it 2-3.											
14	A	NORTHAMPTON	20	L	1-2	0-1	Brown 49	Standen	Burnett	Charles	Peters	Brown	Moore	Brabrook	Bloomfield	Britt	Hurst	Sissons	
23/10		*15,367*	*21*	9			*Foley 29p, Leek 80*	*Harvey*	*Foley*	*Cockcroft*	*Leck*	*Carr*	*Kiernan*	*Best*	*Leek*	*Hunt*	*Lines*	*Robson*	
							Ref: D Payne	Promoted Cobblers win their first match at the 14th attempt. Burnett fouled Hunt and skipper Theo Foley scored from the spot. Moore refused to shake Foley's hand at the final whistle. Brown headed an equaliser, but Leek's back-heeled winner provoked pitch celebrations at the end.											
15	H	STOKE	19	D	0-0	0-0		Standen	Burnett	Charles	Bovington	Brown	Moore	Brabrook	Peters	Britt	Hurst	Sissons	
30/10		21,545	*10*	10				*Irvine*	*Palmer*	*Skeels*	*Kinnell*	*Setters*	*Bloor*	*Bridgwood*	*Viollet*	*Dobing*	*Vernon**	*Burrows*	*McIlroy*
							Ref: G Powell	West Ham's first league clean-sheet wasn't difficult, considering Stoke had little wish to score after Vernon went off after six minutes. The nearest the crowd came to seeing a goal came in the seventh minute. Moore's pass found Brabrook, whose header hit the inside of a post.											
16	A	BURNLEY	21	L	1-3	1-1	Britt 40	Standen	Burnett	Charles	Bovington	Brown	Moore	Brabrook	Peters	Britt	Hurst	Sissons	
6/11		*16,802*	*1*	10			*Irvine 37, 86, Lochhead 76*	*Blacklaw*	*Angus*	*Elder*	*O'Neill*	*Merrington*	*Miller*	*Morgan*	*Lochhead*	*Irvine*	*Harris*	*Coates*	
							Ref: H Hackney	Burnley replace Leeds at the top. Bob Lord's team cost just £1,500 to assemble. For a long time it looked as if Martin Britt's header, allied to sterling defence, would be enough for West Ham to earn a draw, but Lochhead, back from suspension, seized on rebound to fire the killer goal.											
17	H	CHELSEA	20	W	2-1	1-0	Brabrook 32, Peters 49	Standen	Burnett	Charles	Bovington	Brown	Moore	Brabrook	Peters	Britt	Hurst	Sissons	
13/11		31,540	*10*	12			*Tambling 61*	*Bonetti*	*Shellito*	*Hinton*	*Hollins*	*Young*	*Boyle*	*Fascione*	*Graham*	*Osgood*	*Murray*	*Tambling*	
							Ref: K Walker	Chelsea had lost just once in seven away games, so this is an upset to set before Alf Ramsey. Martin Peters must be giving up hope of being called up for England, and he plays a blinder. Both Hammers goals were headers. Tambling forced the ball home to spark a frantic last period.											
18	A	ARSENAL	20	L	2-3	1-1	Hurst 41, Peters 89	Standen	Burnett*	Charles	Bovington	Brown	Moore	Brabrook	Peters	Britt	Hurst	Sissons	Bloomfield
20/11		*35,855*	*7*	12			*Skirton 24, 80, Baker 46*	*Burns*	*Howe*	*Storey*	*McLintock*	*Neill*	*Court*	*Skirton*	*Sammels**	*Baker*	*Eastham*	*Armstrong*	*Walley*
							Ref: E Wallace	Swampy Highbury sees Arsenal finally wreck West Ham's 32-year jinx over them. If only the Hammers had been more alert at the start of the second half. Sub Walley sent Joe Baker clear and he netted despite running away from goal. Skirton fired the killer goal off Standen's hands.											
19	H	EVERTON	19	W	3-0	1-0	Sissons 36, 82, Brabrook 88	Standen	Kirkup	Charles	Bovington	Brown	Moore	Brabrook	Peters	Byrne	Hurst	Sissons	
27/11		21,920	*12*	14				*Rankin*	*Wright*	*Wilson*	*Harvey*	*Labone*	*Harris*	*Temple*	*Young*	*Pickering*	*Stevens*	*Morrissey*	
							Ref: G Roper	Everton have scored just once in five games. Byrne returned for his first league game in two months and was roughly treated by Labone. Byrne crossed for Sissons to head the first goal. Kirkup handled in the box without the ref seeing, then Sissons hit his second from Brabrook's cross.											
20	A	MANCHESTER U	17	D	0-0	0-0		Standen	Kirkup	Charles	Bovington	Brown	Moore	Brabrook	Peters	Byrne	Hurst	Sissons	
4/12		*32,924*	*8*	15				*Dunne P*	*Dunne A*	*Cantwell*	*Crerand*	*Foulkes*	*Stiles*	*Best*	*Law*	*Charlton*	*Herd*	*Connelly*	
							Ref: K Burns	Man U are still unbeaten at home, but had either of Byrne's shots that struck the woodwork in the 7th and 77th minutes gone in, that might have changed. Former Hammer Noel Cantwell was playing his 100th league game for Man U. West Ham's tactics were 'blanket defence'.											
21	H	NEWCASTLE	17	W	4-3	3-0	Hurst 5, 18, 72, Brabrook 16	Standen	Kirkup	Charles	Bovington	Brown	Moore	Brabrook	Peters	Byrne	Hurst	Sissons	
11/12		23,758	*20*	17			*Bennett 61, Iley 67, Robson 84*	*Marshall*	*Craig*	*Clark*	*Moncur*	*McGrath*	*Iley*	*Napier*	*Bennett*	*Thompson*	*Hilley*	*Robson*	
							Ref: F Nicholson	West Ham were coasting at half-time; hanging on desperately by the end. Geoff Hurst, having scored early with his left foot and with his head, was called upon to settle nerves with a crashing shot, after Bennett's header and Iley's 30-yarder, in off the bar, threatened the unthinkable.											

No	Date		Att	Pos	Pt	F-A	H-T	Scorers, Times, and Referees	1	2	3	4	5	6	7	8	9	10	11	12 sub used
22	A	SHEFFIELD WED		17	D	0-0	0-0		Standen	Kirkup	Charles	Bovington	Brown	Moore	Brabrook	Peters	Byrne	Hurst	Sissons	
	18/12		*12,996*	*15*	18				*Springett*	*Hill*	*Smith*	*Eustace*	*Mobley*	*Young*	*Usher*	*Fantham*	*McCalliog*	*Hickton*	*Dobson*	
								Ref: J Cattlin	Wednesday have the meanest home defence in the division, which partly explains why West Ham fail to score. Thick mud and a greasy ball help neither side, especially the Owls, whose nimble wingers were too easily brushed off the ball. The Owls did get the ball into the net twice.											
23	H	NOTT'M FOREST		17	L	0-3	0-2		Standen	Kirkup	Charles	Bovington	Brown	Moore	Brabrook	Peters	Byrne	Hurst	Sissons	
	1/1		*25,131*	*12*	18			*Addison 15, Hinton 34, Bovington 75 (og)*	*Grummitt*	*Hindley*	*Newton*	*Hennessey*	*McKinlay*	*Whitefoot*	*Crowe*	*Addison*	*Wignall*	*Barnwell*	*Hinton*	
								Ref: G Martin	West Ham's game at Villa Park was abandoned after half an hour. Against Forest, Hammers were hit by Colin Addison's fierce shot from Wignall's pass. The result brings Forest their first away win of the season, and under Johnny Carey their sixth straight win over West Ham.											
24	A	NEWCASTLE		17	L	1-2	0-1	Byrne 90	Standen	Kirkup	Charles	Bovington	Brown	Moore	Brabrook	Peters	Byrne	Hurst	Sissons	
	8/1		*31,600*	*19*	18			*Bennett 42, Suddick 63*	*Marshall*	*Craig*	*Burton*	*Moncur*	*McGrath*	*Iley*	*Hilley*	*Suddick*	*Bennett*	*Kettleborough*	*Robson*	
								Ref: E Norman	Newcastle's first win in nine games is down to new signing Keith Kettleborough from Sheffield United, who supplied the passes from which Bennett headed the first goal and Suddick the second. Though West Ham are without five of the CWC team, this was a doddle for Newcastle.											
25	A	EVERTON		17	D	2-2	1-0	Hurst 10, Peters 78	Standen	Burnett	Burkett	Bovington	Brown	Moore	Brabrook	Peters	Britt	Hurst	Dear	
	11/1		*29,915*	*13*	19			*Scott 51, Pickering 85*	*Barnett*	*Wright*	*Wilson*	*Harvey*	*Labone*	*Harris*	*Scott*	*Hurst*	*Pickering*	*Young*	*Temple*	
								Ref: R Harper	Allowing Everton to come back twice was bad enough, but it could have been worse had Fred Pickering not fired over from the spot in the 70th minute, after Burkett fouled Wright. Controversy surrounded West Ham's second goal, scored by Peters after Britt had clattered into Barnett.											
26	H	NORTHAMPTON		17	D	1-1	1-1	Hurst 37p	Standen	Burnett	Burkett	Bovington	Brown	Moore	Brabrook	Peters	Britt	Hurst	Dear	
	15/1		21,000	*20*	20			*Brown 14*	*Coe*	*Foley*	*Everitt*	*Carr*	*Branston*	*Kiernan*	*Broadfoot*	*Moore G*	*Brown*	*Hall*	*Lines*	
								Ref: P Walters	West Ham have now dropped three points to Dave Bowen's Northampton and not many teams do that. Bowen complained that his team had hit 15 goal-posts so far. Jim Hall made it 16 early in this match. Brown's angled header for the Cobblers was cancelled out when Everitt handled.											
27	H	WEST BROM		17	W	4-0	3-0	Sissons 18, Peters 31, Hurst 35, 68p	Standen	Burnett	Burkett	Bovington	Brown	Moore	Brabrook	Peters	Britt	Hurst	Sissons	
	29/1		25,500	*9*	22				*Potter*	*Crawford*	*Williams*	*Lovett*	*Jones*	*Fraser*	*Kryzwicki*	*Brown*	*Kaye*	*Hope*	*Clark*	
								Ref: H Davies	A dress rehearsal for the League Cup final, if West Ham get past Cardiff. Albion's forwards average more than two goals a game, so keeping them quiet was some feat. Sissons got the crucial first goal with WBA defenders appealing for offside. Britt was fouled for Hurst's penalty.											
28	A	LEEDS		18	L	**0-5**	0-2	*[Lorimer 73]*	Standen	Burnett	Burkett	Bovington	Brown	Moore	Brabrook	Peters	Britt	Hurst	Sissons	
	5/2		*33,312*	*4*	22			*Hunter 18, 77, Storrie 42, Bremner 72,*	*Sprake*	*Reaney**	*Bell*	*Bremner*	*Charlton*	*Hunter*	*Storrie*	*Lorimer*	*Belfitt*	*Giles*	*O'Grady*	*Madeley*
								Ref: J Parkinson	It isn't often that Norman Hunter scores twice in one game, but he found West Ham at their most obliging. Leeds showed fewer adverse affects from a rough match with Valencia than Hammers did from their Cardiff fiesta. When Hunter hit the fifth in the mud, the crowd chanted 'easy'.											
29	A	ASTON VILLA			W	2-1	1-0	Hurst 40, Sissons 63	Standen	Burnett	Burkett	Bovington	Brown	Moore	Brabrook	Peters	Hurst	Bloomfield	Sissons	
	7/2		*13,440*		24			*Hateley 75p*	*Withers*	*Wright*	*Aitken*	*Tindall*	*Sleeuw'hoek*	*Pountney*	*MacLeod*	*Hamilton**	*Hateley*	*Woosnam*	*Scott*	*Chatterley*
									Geoff Hurst's 31st of the season keeps him as England's leading goal-getter. Not even the driving rain or the ever-present black dog could deny West Ham this win. Tony Hateley's penalty after Brown had handled hardly ruffled Hammers' feathers. Villa were jeered by their supporters.											
30	H	SHEFFIELD UTD		14	W	**4-0**	3-0	Matthewson 8 (og), Brabrook 23, [Hurst 33, Peters 73]	Standen	Burnett	Burkett	Peters	Brown	Moore	Brabrook	Boyce	Byrne	Hurst	Sissons	
	19/2		21,220	*10*	26				*Hodgkinson*	*Badger*	*Mallender*	*Matthewson*	*Shaw*	*Wagstaff B*	*Woodward*	*Wagstaff A*	*Jones*	*Birchenall*	*Reece*	
								Ref: N Burtenshaw	Greenwood is spying in Germany and misses Reg Matthewson's bizarre own-goal, shepherding the ball back towards his keeper, who slipped and fell flat on his face. Moore sent Brabrook away for the second. Alan Birchenall and Mick Jones missed countless chances for the Blades.											
31	H	ASTON VILLA		14	W	4-2	2-0	Burkett 4, Byrne 9, Brabrook 74, [Hurst 84]	Standen	Burnett	Burkett	Peters	Brown	Bovington	Brabrook	Boyce	Byrne	Hurst	Dear	
	5/3		22,058	*13*	28			*MacLeod 51, Hateley 87*	*Withers*	*Wright*	*Aitken*	*Tindall*	*Sleeuw'hoek*	*Deakin*	*MacLeod*	*Hamilton*	*Hateley*	*Woosnam*	*Scott*	
								Ref: D Wells	This win lifts West Ham 10 points clear of Blackburn in 21st position. The contest was effectively over once Villa missed two early chances and Hammers took two of theirs. Withers was at fault for the first, letting Burkett's wild shot from near the touchline squirm through his arms.											

32	H	BLACKBURN 12/3	18,566	13 22	W 30	4-1	0-1	Dear 65, Brabrook 66, Hurst 69, [Burkett 83] McEvoy 25 Ref: P Baldwin	Standen Else	Charles Wilson	Burkett Joyce	Bovington Newton	Brown England	Moore Sharples	Brabrook Ferguson	Bloomfield Jones	Hurst McEvoy	Dear Byrom	Sissons Harrison	
									How doomed Rovers knocked Hammers out of the FA Cup is, on this evidence, a mystery. But the jeers turned to cheers as three goals in four minutes sends Rovers to the bottom. Dear headed the first. The second came instantly, when Brabrook's shot was cleared from behind the line.											
33	A	BLACKPOOL 19/3	10,559	13 19	L 30	1-2	0-2	Boyce 52 Charnley 29, Ball 42 Ref: D Corbett	Standen Waiters	Burnett Prentis	Burkett Thompson	Peters Fisher	Brown James	Moore Green*	Dear Lea	Bloomfield Ball	Byrne Charnley	Boyce Waddell	Sissons Oates	McPhee
									A precious win for struggling Blackpool, which has schoolboys dancing on the pitch at the final whistle. Alan Ball set up Charnley's goal, then scored himself when racing through a spread-eagled defence. Moore led the fight-back by moving up into attack, setting up Boyce's riposte.											
34	H	FULHAM 26/3	18,977	13 21	L 30	1-3	0-1	Hurst 76 Earle 43, Barrett 46, Leggat 64 Ref: E Wallace	Standen McClelland	Burnett Cohen	Burkett Nicholls	Peters Robson	Bovington Dempsey	Moore Brown	Brabrook Earle	Bloomfield Leggat	Hurst Haynes	Boyce Pearson	Sissons Barrett	
									Vic Buckingham's Fulham have now won their last four and leave out new signing Allan Clarke. 'Easy, easy,' chant their fans at the end, rubbing salt into West Ham's League Cup wounds. Standen saved, then spilled Earle's shot; Haynes sent Barrett away for Fulham's second.											
35	H	BURNLEY 2/4	**17,635**	12 2	D 31	1-1	0-0	Brabrook 60 Irvine 75 Ref: R Tinkler	Standen Blacklaw	Burnett Angus	Charles Elder	Dawkins O'Neil	Boyce Miller	Peters Todd	Redknapp Morgan	Bloomfield Lochhead	Byrne Irvine	Dear Harris	Brabrook Coates	
									This draw leaves Burnley seven points behind leaders Liverpool with just seven games left. Without Moore, Brown and Hurst, Hammers play cautiously, shutting up shop after Brabrook netted, Redknapp's corner having been only partially cleared. Irvine heads in off Standen's arm.											
36	A	TOTTENHAM 8/4	**50,188**	12 6	W 33	4-1	2-1	Byrne 22, Hurst 24, Redknapp 47, [Boyce 75] Gilzean 16 Ref: M Fussey	Standen Brown	Burnett Kinnear	Charles Knowles	Bovington Mullery	Bickles Hoy	Peters Mackay	Redknapp Robertson	Boyce Greaves	Byrne Saul	Hurst Gilzean	Sissons Possee	
									Moore watches disgruntled from the stand. Mullery stamps on Byrne as he lies on the ground. Gilzean headed Spurs' 54th home goal, the most in Division 1. Peters set up Byrne's leveller, then keeper Brown makes three howlers, spilling a long ball and being beaten by two distant shots.											
37	A	CHELSEA 9/4	35,958	12 4	L 33	2-6	0-4	Harris 81 (og), Bennett 88 [Harris 80] Graham 5, 48, V'ables 7p, T'bling 14, 27, Ref: R Spittle	Standen Bonetti	Burnett Kirkup	Burkett McCreadie	Dawkins Hollins	Bickles Hinton	Moore Harris	Brabrook Bridges	Bloomfield Graham	Bennett Osgood	Dear Venables	Sissons Tambling	
									Two goals in a minute, one at either end, by Harris was just one of many oddities. It was Chelsea's first home win over Hammers in five years. Chelsea signed Joe Kirkup from Hammers last month and make him captain. Brabrook skippered West Ham. Dawkins handled for the penalty.											
38	H	ARSENAL 16/4	26,022	12 16	W 35	2-1	2-1	Byrne 13p, Brabrook 41 Baldwin 19 Ref: P Brandwood	Standen Furnell	Burnett Court	Charles Storey	Peters McLintock	Bickles Ure	Moore Neill	Brabrook Skirton	Boyce Radford	Byrne Baldwin	Hurst Eastham	Sissons Armstrong	
									Twice in the first 80 seconds West Ham hit the bar. They must have thought their luck was out, but Terry Neill tripped Hurst in full flight and Byrne netted the penalty. Tommy Baldwin beat Standen in a race to the ball to equalise, before Brabrook headed in Dennis Burnett's free-kick.											
39	H	TOTTENHAM 25/4	32,321	12 9	W 37	2-0	1-0	Byrne 4p, 82p Ref: J Osborne	Standen Jennings	Burnett Kinnear	Charles Knowles	Peters Mullery	Bickles Brown	Moore Beal	Brabrook Greaves	Boyce Clayton	Byrne Gilzean	Hurst Mackay	Sissons Possee	
									Two Byrne penalties topped and tailed this convincing win. Beal rugby-tackled Byrne for the first offence, Joe Kinnear punched out from under the bar for the second. Hammer of the Year Hurst hit the inside of a post, while England rival Greaves missed a sitter from two yards.											
40	H	MANCHESTER U 30/4	**36,416**	12 7	W 39	3-2	2-0	Hurst 28, 73, Byrne 42p Cantwell 63, Aston 78 Ref: P Bye	Standen Gregg	Burnett Brennan	Charles Dunne*	Peters Crerand	Bickles Cantwell	Moore Stiles	Brabrook Connelly	Boyce Law	Byrne Sadler	Hurst Charlton	Sissons Aston	Herd
									Alf Ramsey casts his eye over six players contesting places for England's match with Yugoslavia. Cantwell was hissed by the Chicken Run for writing an article slagging off West Ham. Brennan brought down Peters for Byrne's third penalty in five days. Bottles were thrown by 'fans'.											
41	A	STOKE 7/5	15,670	12 10	L 39	0-1	0-1	 Bridgwood 21 Ref: H Richards	Standen Farmer	Burnett Skeels	Charles Bentley	Peters Palmer	Bickles Kinnell	Moore Bloor	Brabrook Bernard	Boyce Bridgwood	Byrne Ritchie	Hurst Dobing	Sissons Bebbington	
									Gerry Bridgwood capitalised on Standen's mistake for the only goal. Otherwise Standen played well. Peters came nearest for Hammers, firing a free-kick against the bar. Bobby Moore looks very ordinary, and at a giveaway asking price of £80,000 seems certain to be on the move soon.											
42	A	LEICESTER 9/5	16,066	12 6	L 39	1-2	1-2	Byrne 13 Sinclair 8, Dougan 20 Ref: C Cooke	Standen Banks	Burnett Walker	Charles Norman	Bovington Roberts	Bickles Cross	Peters Appleton	Brabrook Sinclair	Boyce Goodfellow	Byrne Douglas	Hurst Gibson	Sissons Stringfellow	
Home Average 24,831		Away 25,291							Jackie Sinclair's left-foot bags his 24th goal of the season for Leicester. It came out from the stanchion so fast that some players thought it had hit the bar. Byrne headed in off a post, but Dougan replied with his 20th of the season. The following week John Bond enjoyed a testimonial.											

League Cup						F-A	H-T	Scorers, Times, and Referees	1	2	3	4	5	6	7	8	9	10	11	12 sub used
2	A	BRISTOL ROV	18	D		3-3	3-2	Hurst 2, 26, Byrne 30	Dickie	Kirkup	Burkett	Bovington	Charles	Moore	Bennett	Peters	Hurst	Byrne	Sissons	
21/9		*18,354*	*3:6*					*Brown 19, Petts 42, Jarman 59*	*Hall*	*Hillard*	*Jones G*	*Petts*	*Stone*	*Mabbutt*	*Jarman*	*Brown*	*Biggs*	*Jones R*	*Munro*	
								Ref: E Jennings	3-1 up after half an hour, West Ham looked set for Round 3 at the expense of their Third Division opponents. Petts' long-range drive closed the gap, and Jarman whipped in Jones' cross to erase it. From then on it could have gone either way. Martin Peters inadvertently hit his own post.											
2R	H	BRISTOL ROV	18	W		3-2	2-0	Byrne 29, 80, Hurst 43	Dickie	Kirkup	Burkett	Bovington	Brown	Charles	Bennett	Peters	Hurst	Byrne	Sissons	
29/9		13,160	*3:6*					*Petts 52, Jones 55*	*Hall*	*Hillard*	*Jones*	*Petts*	*Stone*	*Mabbutt*	*Jarman*	*Brown*	*Biggs*	*Jones*	*Munro*	
								Ref: G Roper	As in the first game, West Ham had only to hang on to a two-goal lead to progress, but as at Eastville, this proved beyond them. Bovington's miscued free-kick was cut out to bring the scores level. Biggs and Brown might have put Rovers in front before Hurst set up Byrne's second.											
3	H	MANSFIELD	20	W		4-0	1-0	Hurst 19, 89, Brabrook 54, Burnett 82	Standen	Burnett	Charles	Bovington	Brown	Moore	Brabrook	Peters	Britt	Hurst	Sissons	
13/10		11,590	*3:3*						*Treharne*	*Nelson*	*Humble*	*Hall*	*Gill*	*Morris*	*Gregson*	*Macready*	*Middleton*	*Cheesebrough*	*Scanlon*	
								Ref: N Burtenshaw	Third Division Mansfield never threatened the Hammers, but for too long there was only one goal in it – Geoff Hurst heading in Peters' cross. West Ham were content to play walking-pace football, and were relieved to see Peter Brabrook's shot hit the bar and the post before going in.											
4	A	ROTHERHAM	21	W		2-1	1-0	Moore 23, Hurst 65	Standen	Burnett	Charles	Bovington	Brown	Moore	Brabrook	Peters	Britt	Hurst	Sissons	
3/11		*13,902*	*2:7*					*Galley 70*	*Jones*	*Wilcockson*	*Clish*	*Casper*	*Madden*	*Tiler*	*Lyons*	*Chappel*	*Galley*	*Williams*	*Pring*	
								Ref: J Pickles	As always, the underdogs claimed misfortune. Clish hit a post just after Hurst scored, and in the last minute Brown headed Galley's header off the line. Rotherham are unbeaten at home in Division 2, and enjoy this competition so much that only once have they failed to reach Round 4.											
QF	A	GRIMSBY	20	D		2-2	1-1	Charles 32, Hurst 71	Standen	Burnett	Charles	Bovington	Brown	Moore	Brabrook	Peters	Hurst	Britt	Sissons	
17/11		*16,281*	*3:2*					*Tees 11, Green 65*	*Wright*	*Dobson*	*Taylor*	*Davidson*	*Jobling*	*Clifton*	*Collins*	*Tees*	*Green*	*Foster*	*Hill*	
								Ref: P Rhodes	The Division 3 pacesetters have already accounted for Crystal Palace, Bolton and Preston, and Matt Tees is the leading scorer in the Football League. Grimsby led twice, but were pegged back first by Charles' flukey lob, then by Hurst's scrambled shot. When to squeeze in the replay?											
QF	H	GRIMSBY	17	W		1-0	0-0	Hurst 79	Standen	Kirkup	Charles	Bovington	Brown	Moore	Brabrook	Peters	Byrne	Hurst	Sissons	
R	15/12	17,500	*3:2*						*Wright*	*Thompson*	*Taylor*	*Davidson*	*Jobling*	*Clifton*	*Collins*	*Tees*	*Green*	*Foster*	*Hill*	
								Ref: W Clements	The ref's advantage rule decided this protracted cup-tie. Future England boss Graham Taylor tried to crash-tackle Brabrook as the winger broke down the touchline. Brabrook wriggled free, his limbs in one piece, and crossed for Hurst to maintain his record of scoring in every round.											
SF	H	CARDIFF	17	W		5-2	2-0	Bovington 6, Byrne 42, Brabrook 65,	Standen	Kirkup	Charles	Bovington	Brown	Moore	Brabrook	Peters	Byrne	Hurst	Sissons	
1	20/12	19,980	*2:13*					*Andrews 86, 88* [Sissons 75, Hurst 89]	*Wilson*	*Harrington*	*Rodrigues*	*Hole*	*Murray*	*Houston*	*Farrell*	*Harkin*	*Andrews*	*Williams*	*King*	
								Ref: R Tinkler	Four goals down, Cardiff hadn't a prayer for the second leg. Two quick goals changed all that, but Hurst took advantage of a kind bounce to restore what should be an unassailable lead. Worst of the countless misses was by Brabrook, who faced with an empty goal passed to Peters.											
SF	A	CARDIFF	17	W		5-1	2-0	Hurst 5, 47, Peters 28, 64, Burnett 82	Standen	Burnett	Burkett	Bovington	Brown	Moore	Brabrook	Peters	Britt	Hurst	Sissons	
2	2/2	*14,315*	*2:13*					*Johnston 68*	*Davies*	*Coldrick*	*Yorath*	*Hole*	*Murray*	*Williams*	*Lewis*	*Johnston*	*Andrews*	*King*	*Farrell*	
								Ref: W Clements (Hammers win 10-3 on aggregate)	Cardiff boss Jimmy Scoular was up-beat before the start, but when Hurst quickly rammed in Brabrook's corner the tie was dead and West Ham can look forward to their third consecutive cup final. Shortly after Johnston scored for Cardiff he missed a penalty after Brown had fouled him.											
F:1	H	WEST BROM	14	W		2-1	0-0	Moore 72, Byrne 90	Standen	Burnett	Burkett	Peters	Brown	Moore	Brabrook	Boyce	Byrne	Hurst	Dear	
9/3		28,323	*7*					*Astle 59*	*Potter*	*Cram*	*Fairfax*	*Fraser*	*Campbell*	*Williams*	*Brown*	*Astle*	*Kaye*	*Lovett*	*Clark*	
								Ref: D Smith	Two freak goals rescue West Ham, leaving Albion players forlorn. Astle scored on his comeback after injury. Moore's goal was a cross, not a shot, while out of form Johnny Byrne had his name booed when it was announced. WBA players insisted Byrne fouled Potter before scoring.											
F:2	A	WEST BROM	13	L		1-4	0-4	Peters 75 *[Williams 34]*	Standen	Burnett	Peters	Bovington	Brown	Moore	Brabrook	Boyce	Byrne	Hurst	Sissons	
23/3		31,925	*8*					*Kaye 10, Brown 17, Clark 27,*	*Potter*	*Cram*	*Fairfax*	*Fraser*	*Campbell*	*Williams*	*Brown*	*Astle*	*Kaye*	*Hope*	*Clark*	
								Ref: J Mitchell (Hammers lose 3-5 on aggregate)	West Ham won't be in next season's Fairs Cup, though they may retain the Cup-Winners' Cup. They were swept aside on a night when all they could offer was high balls to Hurst and Byrne. Kaye netted on the half-volley, Brown with a lob, Clark with a header, Williams from 30 yards.											

FA Cup

<table>
<tr><td>3</td><td>A</td><td>OLDHAM</td><td>17</td><td>D</td><td>2-2</td><td>1-1</td><td>Burnett 10, Hurst 70</td><td>Standen</td><td>Burnett</td><td>Burkett</td><td>Bovington</td><td>Brown</td><td>Moore</td><td>Brabrook</td><td>Peters</td><td>Byrne</td><td>Hurst</td><td>Dear</td></tr>
<tr><td></td><td>22/1</td><td></td><td>25,035 3:20</td><td></td><td></td><td></td><td>Bloor 36, Quixall 77</td><td>Bollands</td><td>Frizzell</td><td>Ledger</td><td>Stevens</td><td>Asprey</td><td>Lawson</td><td>Towers</td><td>Blore</td><td>Large</td><td>Quixall</td><td>Dearden</td></tr>
<tr><td></td><td></td><td></td><td></td><td></td><td></td><td></td><td>Ref: H Davey</td><td colspan="11">Fans of the Third Division strugglers pointed to a penalty miss which cost their team dear. It came in 14 minutes when Burkett fouled Towers. Standen saved Quixall's kick. West Ham's first goal was a freak, an 80-yard hurried clearance by Burkett that bounced over Bollands' head.</td></tr>
<tr><td>3R</td><td>H</td><td>OLDHAM</td><td>17</td><td>W</td><td>2-1</td><td>1-1</td><td>Hurst 20, Brabrook 70</td><td>Standen</td><td>Burnett</td><td>Burkett</td><td>Bovington</td><td>Brown</td><td>Moore</td><td>Brabrook</td><td>Peters</td><td>Byrne</td><td>Hurst</td><td>Sissons</td></tr>
<tr><td></td><td>24/1</td><td></td><td>35,330 3:20</td><td></td><td></td><td></td><td>Pennington 3</td><td>Bollands</td><td>Frizzell</td><td>Ledger</td><td>Stevens</td><td>Asprey</td><td>Bowie</td><td>Pennington</td><td>Blore</td><td>Large</td><td>Towers</td><td>Dearden</td></tr>
<tr><td></td><td></td><td></td><td></td><td></td><td></td><td></td><td>Ref: H Davey</td><td colspan="11">Greenwood was livid after this win, which was hard on gutsy Grimbsy. The biggest home crowd of the season was mortified by what they saw from Euro champs. Pennington's free-kick sailed over Standen's head. Hurst equalised on the turn and Peter Brabrook headed the winner.</td></tr>
<tr><td>4</td><td>H</td><td>BLACKBURN</td><td>18</td><td>D</td><td>3-3</td><td>1-2</td><td>Bloomfield 25, Sissons 58, Hurst 83</td><td>Standen</td><td>Burnett</td><td>Burkett</td><td>Bovington</td><td>Brown</td><td>Moore</td><td>Brabrook</td><td>Peters</td><td>Hurst</td><td>Bloomfield</td><td>Sissons</td></tr>
<tr><td></td><td>12/2</td><td></td><td>32,350 21</td><td></td><td></td><td></td><td>Byrom 8, 37, 71</td><td>Else</td><td>Wilson</td><td>Newton</td><td>Clayton</td><td>England</td><td>Joyce</td><td>Ferguson</td><td>Byrom</td><td>McEvoy</td><td>Douglas</td><td>Harrison</td></tr>
<tr><td></td><td></td><td></td><td></td><td></td><td></td><td></td><td>Ref: E Crawford</td><td colspan="11">After just 12 minutes Douglas is crocked by Bovington and reduced to a virtual passenger, but even against 10 fit men West Ham struggle to impose themselves. They are also up against John Byrom, who bags his third hat-trick against the Hammers. Peters sets up Hurst's late goal.</td></tr>
<tr><td>4R</td><td>A</td><td>BLACKBURN</td><td>18</td><td>L</td><td>1-4</td><td>1-4</td><td>Hurst 15</td><td>Standen</td><td>Burnett</td><td>Burkett</td><td>Bovington</td><td>Boyce</td><td>Moore</td><td>Brabrook</td><td>Peters</td><td>Hurst</td><td>Bloomfield</td><td>Byrne</td></tr>
<tr><td></td><td>16/2</td><td></td><td>25,547 21</td><td></td><td></td><td></td><td>McEvoy 14, 41, 44, Byrom 34</td><td>Else</td><td>Wilson</td><td>Newton</td><td>Clayton</td><td>England</td><td>Joyce</td><td>Darling</td><td>Byrom</td><td>McEvoy</td><td>Ferguson</td><td>Harrison</td></tr>
<tr><td></td><td></td><td></td><td></td><td></td><td></td><td></td><td>Ref: E Crawford</td><td colspan="11">Tonsillitis causes the withdrawal of Ken Brown, and for some reason Greenwood hands the No 5 shirt to Ron Boyce, for his first game in five months. Moore had a stinker, and Rovers' superiority was etched in the fact that in addition to their goals they hit the woodwork four times.</td></tr>
</table>

European Cup-Winners' Cup		F-A	H-T	Scorers, Times, and Referees	1	2	3	4	5	6	7	8	9	10	11	12 sub used
2:1 H OLYMPIAKOS	20 W	4-0	2-0	Hurst 24, 43, Byrne 56, Brabrook 72	Standen	Kirkup	Charles	Bovington	Brown	Moore	Brabrook	Peters	Byrne	Hurst	Sissons	
24/11 (Greece) 27,250					*Fronimidis*	*Plessas*	*Pavlidis*	*Polychronou*	*Stefanakos*	*Zanderoglou*	*Vassiliou*	*Sideris*	*Gaitantzis*	*Yuysos*	*Botinos*	
				Ref: K Keller (Switzerland)	Long before the end, the graceless Greeks were kicking and hacking anything in claret and blue. Hurst latched onto Moore's pass to crack the first goal, and further goals followed at regular intervals. Hurst and Brabrook added headers, while Byrne capitalised on the keeper's mistake.											
2:2 A OLYMPIAKOS	19 D	2-2	1-0	Peters 28, 53	Standen	Kirkup	Charles	Bovington	Brown	Moore	Brabrook	Peters	Byrne	Hurst	Sissons	
1/12 *40,000*				*Bovington 56 (og), Polychroniou 80p*	*Fronimidis*	*Plessas*	*Milisis*	*Polychroniou*	*Stefanakos*	*Gaitantzis*	*Vassiliou*	*Aganian*	*Yuysos*	*Papazoglou*	*Botinos*	
				Ref: Bachramov (Russia) (Hammers win 6-2 on aggregate)	The Soviet ref is the linesman who will flag Hurst's goal okay in the World Cup final. Injuries diverted Peters to centre-forward, in which position he scored twice, first with a deflection, then a header. Bovington lobbed an own-goal, and Brown's foul was punished by a penalty.											
QF H MAGDEBURG	14 W	1-0	0-0	Byrne 46	Standen	Burnett	Burkett	Peters	Brown	Moore	Brabrook	Boyce	Byrne	Hurst	Sissons	
1 2/3 (E Germ) 30,620					*Blochwitz*	*Wiedemann*	*Busch*	*Zapf*	*Kubisch*	*Fronzeck*	*Klingbiel*	*Segger*	*Geschke*	*Seguin*	*Stocker*	
				Ref: J Tricot (France)	Ernst Kuemmel's team predictably defended in depth; what was less predictable was the array of chances wasted by the Hammers, who have it all to do in the away leg. The one goal came when Hurst back-headed to Byrne, who flashed a shot under the bar. No 'Bubbles' song this time.											
QF A MAGDEBURG	14 D	1-1	0-0	Sissons 79	Standen	Burnett	Burkett	Bovington	Brown	Moore	Brabrook	Boyce	Hurst	Peters	Sissons	
2 16/3 *35,000*				*Walter 78*	*Blochwitz*	*Wiedemann*	*Zapf*	*Kubisch*	*Fronzeck*	*Hirshmann*	*Klingbiel*	*Sparwasser*	*Walter*	*Seguin*	*Stocker*	
				Ref: Lauraux (Belgium) (Hammers win 2-1 on aggregate)	Sissons' instant equaliser in the Ernst Grube stadium silenced the home roars in their throats. Hirshmann had hit Standen's post in the opening minute and Sparwasser blasted over from two yards. West Ham ventured into Magdeburg's penalty area only three times in the whole match.											
SF H BOR DORTMUND	12 L	1-2	0-0	Peters 53	Standen	Brown	Charles	Peters	Boyce	Moore	Brabrook	Bloomfield	Byrne	Hurst	Dear	
1 5/4 (W Germ) 28,130				*Emmerich 86, 87*	*Tilkowski*	*Cyliax*	*Redder*	*Kurrat*	*Paul*	*Assauer*	*Libuda*	*Schmidt*	*Held*	*Sturm*	*Emmerich*	
				Ref: J de Mendibil (Spain)	West Ham avoid Liverpool and Celtic, the other semi-finalists. Byrne replaces Moore, who wants away, as captain. Hurst will encounter Hans Tilkowski in the World Cup final, and Emmerich too, who takes his Cup-Winners' Cup tally to 12, but these are his first with his right foot.											
SF A BOR DORTMUND	12 L	1-3	1-2	Byrne 43	Standen	Bovington	Charles	Peters	Brown	Moore	Brabrook	Boyce	Byrne	Hurst	Bloomfield	
2 13/4 *35,000*				*Emmerich 1, 29, Cyliax 87*	*Tilkowski*	*Cyliax*	*Redder*	*Kurrat*	*Paul*	*Assauer*	*Libuda*	*Schmidt*	*Held*	*Sturm*	*Emmerich*	
				Ref: Campanai (Italy) (Hammers lose 2-5 on aggregate)	The away-goals rule means West Ham must win 2-0 or 3-1. Having lost 2-6 on Saturday, this is unlikely, especially once Emmerich scores within 20 seconds, hitting the bar with his first effort, the net with his second. Emmerich scored again from a free-kick. Byrne headed a goal.											

	Home						Away					
	P	W	D	L	F	A	W	D	L	F	A	Pts
1 Liverpool	42	17	2	2	52	15	9	7	5	27	19	61
2 Leeds	42	14	4	3	49	15	9	5	7	30	23	55
3 Burnley	42	15	3	3	45	20	9	4	8	34	27	55
4 Manchester U	42	12	8	1	50	20	6	7	8	34	39	51
5 Chelsea	42	11	4	6	30	21	11	3	7	35	32	51
6 West Brom	42	11	6	4	58	34	8	6	7	33	35	50
7 Leicester	42	12	4	5	40	28	9	3	9	40	37	49
8 Tottenham	42	11	6	4	55	37	5	6	10	20	29	44
9 Sheffield Utd	42	11	6	4	37	25	5	5	11	19	34	43
10 Stoke	42	12	6	3	42	22	3	6	12	23	42	42
11 Everton	42	12	6	3	39	19	3	5	13	17	43	41
12 WEST HAM	42	12	5	4	46	33	3	4	14	24	50	39
13 Blackpool	42	9	5	7	36	29	5	4	12	19	36	37
14 Arsenal	42	8	8	5	36	31	4	5	12	26	44	37
15 Newcastle	42	10	5	6	26	20	4	4	13	24	43	37
16 Aston Villa	42	10	3	8	39	34	5	3	13	30	46	36
17 Sheffield Wed	42	11	6	4	35	18	3	2	16	21	48	36
18 Nott'm Forest	42	11	3	7	31	26	3	5	13	25	46	36
19 Sunderland	42	13	2	6	36	28	1	6	14	15	44	36
20 Fulham	42	9	4	8	34	37	5	3	13	33	48	35
21 Northampton	42	8	6	7	31	32	2	7	12	24	60	33
22 Blackburn	42	6	1	14	30	36	2	3	16	27	52	20
	924	245	103	114	877	580	114	103	245	580	877	924

Odds & ends

Double wins: (3) Blackburn, Aston Villa, Spurs.
Double losses: (3) Leicester, Fulham, Nott'm Forest.

Won from behind: (5) Leeds (h), Sheff W (h), Blackburn (h), Spurs (a), Oldham FAC (h).
Lost from in front: (4) Sunderland (a), Leicester (h), WBA LC, Dortmund (CWC).

High spots: Reaching semi-final of League Cup.
Reaching semi-final of Cup-Winners' Cup.
Scoring four goals in three games in a row.
Winning four league games in a row in February and March.

Low spots: Coming so close, but not winning anything.
Conceding five goals in three games in a row, dropping to 20th.

Hammer of the Year: Geoff Hurst.
Ever-presents: (0).
Hat-tricks: (1) Geoff Hurst.
Leading scorer: (40) Geoff Hurst.

	Appearances								Goals				
	Lge	*Sub*	LC	*Sub*	FAC	*Sub*	Eur	Sub	**Lge**	LC	FAC	Eur	**Tot**
Bennett, Peter	**7**	*1*	2						**1**				**1**
Bickles, Dave	**12**	*1*											
Bloomfield, Jimmy	**9**	*1*			2		2				1		**1**
Bovington, Eddie	**31**		9		4		4			1			**1**
Boyce, Ronnie	**16**		2		1		4		**2**				**2**
Brabrook, Peter	**32**		8		4		6		**8**	2	1	1	**12**
Britt, Martin	**10**		4						**3**				**3**
Brown, Ken	**23**		9		3		6		**1**				**1**
Burkett, Jackie	**19**		4		4		2		**2**				**2**
Burnett, Dennis	**24**		6		4		2			2	1		**3**
Byrne, Johnny	**23**		6		3		5		**9**	5		3	**17**
Charles, John	**25**		7				4			1			**1**
Dawkins, Trevor	**2**												
Dear, Brian	**7**		1		1		1		**1**				**1**
Dickie, Alan	**5**		2										
Hurst, Geoff	**39**		10		4		6		**23**	11	4	2	**40**
Kirkup, Joe	**17**		4				2		**1**				**1**
Moore, Bobby	**37**		9		4		6			2			**2**
Peters, Martin	**40**		10		4		6		**11**	3		3	**17**
Presland, Eddie	**2**												
Redknapp, Harry	**7**								**1**				**1**
Scott, Tony	**2**												
Sissons, John	**36**		9		2		4		**5**	1	1	1	**8**
Standen, Jim	**37**		8		4		6						
(own-goals)									**2**				**2**
24 players used	**462**	***3***	**110**		**44**		**66**		**70**	**28**	**8**	**10**	**116**

John Sissons, Ronnie Boyce and Geoff Hurst with the 1964 FA Cup

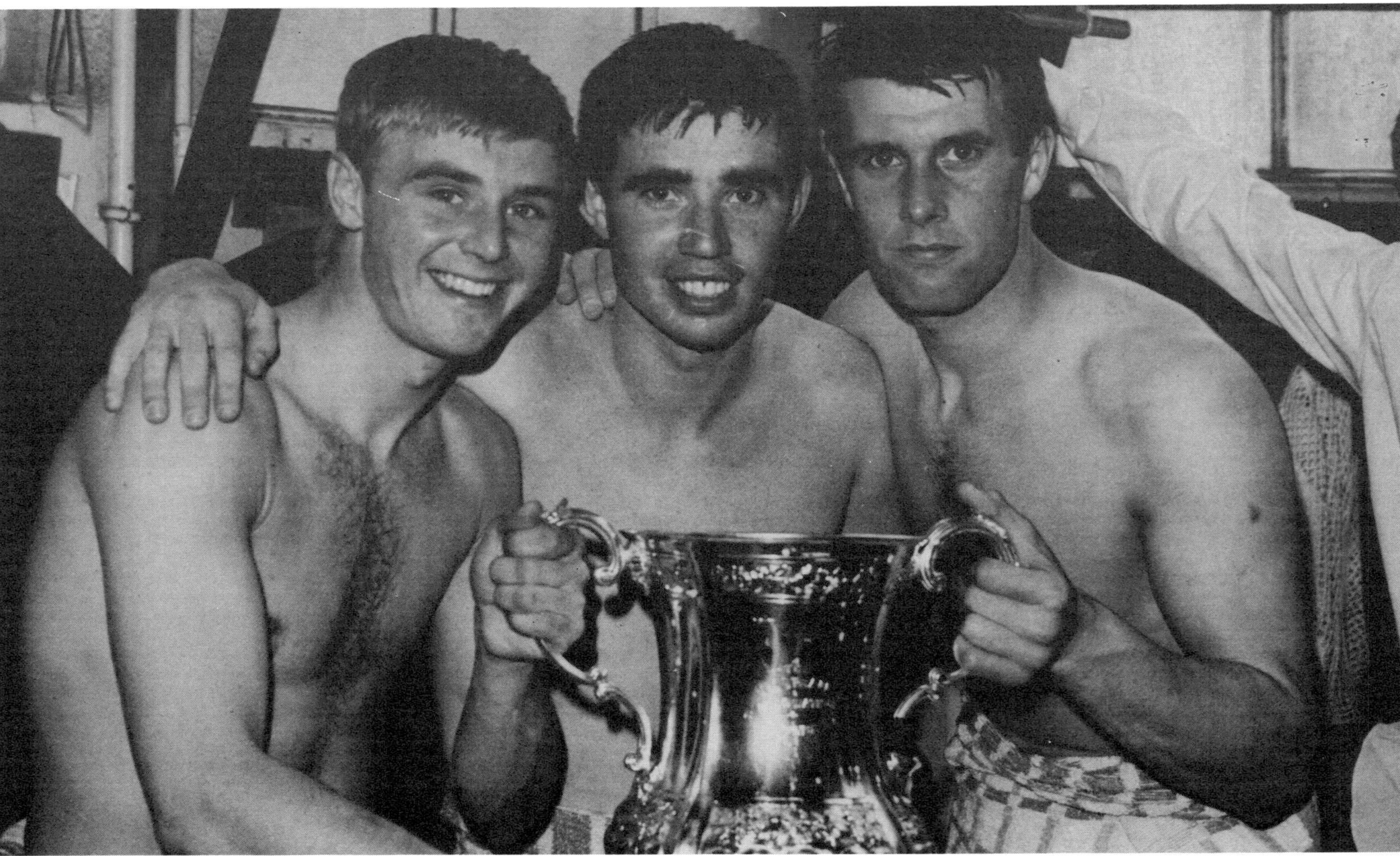

Booby Moore, with the Team Trophy, and Eusebio, the BBC Sportsman of 1966

LEAGUE DIVISION 1 Manager: Ron Greenwood SEASON 1966-67

No	Date		Att	Pos	Pt	F-A	H-T	Scorers, Times, and Referees	1	2	3	4	5	6	7	8	9	10	11	12 sub used
1	H	CHELSEA			L	1-2	0-1	Boyce 57	Standen	Burnett	Charles	Peters	Moore	Bovington	Brabrook	Boyce	Byrne	Hurst	Sissons	
	20/8		36,126		–			*Hollins 38, Cooke 72*	*Bonetti*	*Kirkup*	*McCreadie*	*Hollins*	*Hinton*	*Harris*	*Boyle*	*Graham*	*Osgood*	*Cooke*	*Tambling*	
								Ref: K Dagnall	West Ham's World Cup-winning trio take the field ahead of the rest and receive a tumultuous reception. This match was a tale of two keepers. Jim Standen was out of position, letting Cooke score into an empty goal. Bonetti was so brilliant, Greenwood is rumoured to be making a bid.											
2	A	ARSENAL			L	1-2	1-2	Byrne 42	Standen	Burnett	Charles	Peters	Moore	Bovington	Brabrook	Boyce	Byrne	Hurst	Sissons	
	23/8		*40,533*		–			*Baldwin 4, Radford 37*	*Furnell*	*Court*	*Storey*	*McLintock*	*Ure*	*Neill*	*Skirton**	*Baldwin*	*Radford*	*Sammels*	*Armstrong*	*Simpson*
								Ref: R Prichard	Arsenal's coach Dave Sexton ordered an early blitz of high balls into the box. He is rewarded when Baldwin follows up after Radford had hit the bar. Eyes were cast on Standen who had already missed one cross. West Ham had chances, notably when Hurst hit the underside of the bar.											
3	A	LEICESTER		20	L	4-5	0-2	Brabrook 48, 56, Hurst 62, 89	Standen	Burnett	Charles	Peters	Moore	Bovington	Brabrook	Boyce	Byrne	Hurst	Sissons	
	27/8		*26,850*	*11*	–			*Dougan 18, Sinclair 30, 49, 79, Good' 61*	*Banks*	*Rodrigues*	*Norman*	*Roberts*	*Sjoberg*	*Cross*	*Sinclair*	*Goodfellow*	*Dougan*	*Gibson*	*Stringfellow*	
								Ref: R Egan	Believe it or not, Hammers are playing well, and might have been three up before Derek Dougan netted from close range. The second half saw seven goals, three by Scotsman Jackie Sinclair. A great run by Roberts set up Sinclair's third goal. Banks couldn't hold Brabrook's first goal.											
4	H	ARSENAL		20	D	2-2	1-1	Moore 34, Brabrook 61	Standen	Burnett	Charles	Peters	Moore	Bovington	Brabrook	Boyce	Byrne	Hurst	Sissons	
	29/8		34,964	2	1			*McLintock 30, Sammels 89*	*Furnell*	*Simpson*	*Storey*	*McLIntock*	*Ure*	*Neill*	*Coakley*	*McGill*	*Baldwin*	*Sammels*	*Armstrong*	
								Ref: E Jennings	West Ham's cockiness at the end denied them their first win. On a rain-swept night they had recovered from Standen - rooted to his line - being beaten by Frank McLintock. West Ham replied with Moore's 30-yard dipper and Brabrook's glancing header. Sammels netted from 20 yards.											
5	H	LIVERPOOL		19	D	1-1	1-0	Hurst 6	Standen	Burnett	Charles	Peters	Bickles*	Moore	Brabrook	Boyce	Byrne	Hurst	Sissons	Bennett
	3/9		33,000	*10*	2			*Strong 89*	*Lawrence*	*Lawler*	*Smith*	*Yeats*	*Milne*	*St John*	*Stevenson*	*Callaghan*	*Strong*	*Hunt*	*Thompson*	
								Ref: D Corbett	Play was held up in the second half so that broken glass flung by Liverpool fans could be swept from the goalmouth. Shankly's offside tactics did not go down well. Hurst's close-range header looked like bringing West Ham their first win until Geoff Strong headed in a late corner-kick.											
6	A	MANCHESTER C		17	W	4-1	3-0	Hurst 20, 63, Boyce 33, Sissons 43	Standen	Burnett	Charles	Peters	Brown	Moore	Brabrook	Boyce	Byrne	Hurst	Sissons	
	7/9		*31,989*	*15*	4			*Bell 64*	*Dowd*	*Book*	*Kennedy*	*Pardoe*	*Heslop*	*Oakes*	*Connor*	*Bell*	*Summerbee*	*Crossan*	*Young*	
								Ref: K Burns	City's first home defeat was as comprehensive as the score suggests. 'West Ham, with three World Cup men in their side, often played as if they had 11,' wrote one paper. Hurst and Boyce made a goal for each other, and Sissons sealed the points when thumping home Peters' cross.											
7	H	STOKE			D	1-1	1-0	Hurst 21	Standen	Burnett	Burkett	Peters	Brown	Moore	Brabrook	Bovington	Byrne	Hurst	Sissons	
	10/9		33,293		5			*Dobing 72*	*Farmer*	*Palmer*	*Skeels*	*Viollet*	*Setters*	*Philpott*	*Bridgwood*	*Dobing*	*Ritchie*	*Eastham*	*Burrows*	
								Ref: D Brady	West Ham take their first point off Stoke since City returned to Division 1. Stoke had just beaten Man U 3-0, but under the gaze of Alf Ramsey looked to be heading for defeat once Hurst's effort ricocheted in off both Farmer and Skeels. Peter Dobing levelled form Bridgwood's cross.											
8	A	SHEFFIELD WED		14	W	2-0	1-0	Boyce 26, Byrne 60	Standen	Burnett	Charles	Peters	Brown	Moore	Brabrook	Boyce	Byrne	Hurst	Sissons	
	17/9		*29,171*	*5*	7				*Springett*	*Smith*	*Megson*	*Eustace*	*Ellis*	*Young*	*Pugh*	*Fantham*	*McCalliog*	*Ford*	*Quinn*	
								Ref: R Bickerstaffe	The Owls' first defeat is down to Jim Standen and maybe to the angry West Ham team. Wednesday boss Allan Brown protested about a colour clash, and West Ham played in the second half in all white. Boyce dribbled round Ellis and Springett for his goal. Byrne's was a diving header.											
9	H	SOUTHAMPTON		14	D	2-2	1-2	Hurst 27, Peters 46	Standen	Burnett	Charles	Peters	Brown	Moore	Brabrook*	Boyce	Byrne	Hurst	Sissons	**Howe**
	24/9		32,301	*13*	8			*Chivers 17, Davies 44*	*MacLaren*	*Webb*	*Hollywood*	*Wimshurst*	*Knapp*	*Walker*	*Paine*	*Chivers*	*Davies*	*Melia*	*Sydenham*	
								Ref: R Johnson	Ted Bates' newly promoted Saints have only lost once away from home, and Ron Davies is a handful in the air for any defence. His goal followed a huge punt downfield by keeper MacLaren. Peters levelled through a packed goalmouth. Brabrook was subbed because of a cut eye.											
10	A	SUNDERLAND		12	W	4-2	2-1	Byrne 18p, 79, Hurst 35, Peters 86	Standen	Burnett	Charles	Peters	Brown	Moore	Brabrook	Boyce	Byrne	Hurst	Sissons	
	1/10		*29,227*	*19*	10			*Martin 6, Sharkey 78*	*Montgomery*	*Irwin*	*Ashurst*	*Herd*	*Harvey*	*McNab*	*Gauden*	*Sharkey*	*Martin*	*Baxter*	*Mulhall*	
								Ref: K Walker	West Ham's third away win leaves them in the bottom half. Byrne levelled Martin's early header with a twice-taken penalty when Montgomery flattened Hurst. The keeper saved Byrne's first attempt. Sharkey's lobbed equaliser was immediately countered by Byrne, from Hurst's pass.											

No	Venue	Opponent	Pos	Res	F-A	H-T	Scorers, Times, Referees	1	2	3	4	5	6	7	8	9	10	11	12 sub used
11	H	EVERTON	14	L	2-3	1-1	Peters 29, Hurst 63	Standen	Burnett	Charles	Peters	Brown	Moore	Brabrook	Boyce	Byrne	Hurst	Sissons	
8/10		32,784	*10*	10			*Young 25, Temple 49, 69*	*West*	*Wright*	*Wilson*	*Gabriel*	*Labone*	*Harvey*	*Scott**	*Ball*	*Young*	*Temple*	*Morrissey*	*Brown*
							Ref: M Fussey	Hammers' first defeat since August is watched by Alf Ramsey. The winning goal was a triumph for man-of-the-match Alan Ball, who actually made a mug of Moore when setting up Derek Temple. Minutes earlier Hurst had made it 2-2, reacting first when West saved from Peters.											
12	A	FULHAM	15	L	2-4	1-2	Byrne 19, Hurst 82	Standen	Burnett	Charles	Peters	Bickles	Moore	Brabrook	Boyce	Byrne	Hurst	Sissons	
15/10		*34,826*	*18*	10			*Earle 10, Burnett 43 (og), Clarke 53, 62*	*McClelland*	*Cohen*	*Dempsey*	*Robson*	*Callaghan*	*Conway*	*Haynes*	*Brown*	*Earle*	*Clarke*	*Barrett*	
							Ref: R Baldwin	Fulham's first home win makes a mockery of West Ham's imposing away form. Last season Charles's own-goal sunk the Hammers at Craven Cottage; this time it's Burnett, deflecting Haynes' wayward shot past Standen. Allan Clarke takes his Fulham tally to 11 goals from five games.											
13	H	NOTT'M FOREST		W	3-1	2-0	Hurst 17, 28, Bovington 73	Standen	Burnett	Burkett	Bovington	Brown	Moore	Brabrook	Boyce	Bennett	Hurst	Peters	
26/10		23,000		12			*Moore 87*	*Grummitt*	*Hindley*	*Winfield*	*Hennessey*	*McKinlay*	*Newton*	*Crowe*	*Barnwell*	*Storey-Moore*	*Wignall*	*Hinton*	
							Ref: H New	It's late October and at last West Ham win at home. They do it without Byrne and Sissons, both dropped. Without Baker, ill with tonsillitis, Forest looked light in attack. They still wove their pretty patterns but were cut to shreds by Hurst's diving header. His 15th goal soon followed.											
14	A	SHEFFIELD UTD	14	L	1-3	0-2	Peters 48	Standen	Burnett	Burkett*	Bovington	Brown	Moore	Brabrook	Boyce	Bennett	Hurst	Peters	Sissons
29/10		*20,579*	*10*	12			*Wagstaff T 41, Woodward 42, [Burnett 60 og]*	*Hodgkinson*	*Coldwell*	*Mallender*	*Munks*	*Matthewson*	*Wagstaff B*	*Woodward*	*Wagstaff T*	*Bell*	*Fenoughty*	*Reece*	
							Ref: C Cooke	Alan Hodgkinson is skipper on his 400th appearance for the Blades. It was a black day for two Hammers in particular. Jackie Burkett clashed heads with 6ft 3in Bell and suffered concussion. With Hammers pushing forward, Bell then pressured Burnett to turn the ball into his own net.											
15	H	FULHAM	13	W	**6-1**	1-1	Hurst 29, 67, 71, 87, Peters 61, 80	Standen	Bovington	Charles	Peters	Brown	Moore	Brabrook	Boyce	Byrne	Hurst	Sissons	
5/11		22,260	*21*	14			*Callaghan 19*	*McClelland*	*Cohen*	*Dempsey*	*Robson*	*Callaghan*	*Conway*	*Haynes*	*Brown*	*Earle*	*Clarke*	*Barrett*	
							Ref: D Wells	When Johnny Haynes squared to Callaghan for Fulham's goal, the thousands who stayed away seemed vindicated. West Ham's response was sparked by the recalled Byrne, though he did not score. Hurst completed his hat-trick from 20 yards, and added a fourth from Brabrook's cross.											
16	A	TOTTENHAM	11	W	4-3	3-2	Byrne 7, Brab'k 29, Sissons 32, Hurst 78	Standen	Bovington	Charles	Peters	Brown	Moore	Brabrook	Boyce	Byrne	Hurst	Sissons	
12/11		*51,157*	*8*	16			*Greaves 24p, Venables 33, Gilzean 61*	*Jennings*	*Beal*	*Knowles*	*Mullery*	*England*	*Mackay*	*Robertson*	*Greaves*	*Gilzean*	*Venables*	*Jones*	
							Ref: R Tinkler	17 goals in a week for fantastic Hammers. The final outcome owed much to Jimmy Greaves, who hit the bar in the first minute, netted from the spot when brought down by Bovington, then missed his first ever penalty for Spurs when Moore handled. Spurs hit the woodwork three times.											
17	H	NEWCASTLE	8	W	3-0	1-0	Peters 11, Byrne 59p, Hurst 85	Standen	Bovington	Charles	Peters	Brown*	Moore	Brabrook	Boyce	Byrne	Hurst	Sissons	Burnett
19/11		31,285	*21*	18				*McFaul*	*Clark*	*Guthrie*	*Burton*	*Moncur*	*Iley*	*Robson*	*Bennett*	*Davies*	*Suddick*	*Allen*	
							Ref: E Wallace	Lowly Newcastle have scored just 12 goals all season. Within 30 seconds they were within a whisker of their 13th, but Wyn Davies headed narrowly wide. Peters scored No 1 from an acute angle, and Byrne No 2 from the spot after Bobby Moncur toppled man-of-the-match Boyce.											
18	A	LEEDS	11	L	1-2	1-1	Hurst 4	Standen	Bovington	Charles	Peters	Bickles	Moore	Brabrook	Boyce	Byrne	Hurst	Sissons	
26/11		*37,382*	*10*	18			*Johanneson 11, Giles 81*	*Sprake*	*Reaney*	*Charlton*	*Hunter*	*Bell*	*Bremner*	*Giles*	*O'Grady*	*Lorimer*	*Greenhoff*	*Johanneson*	
							Ref: J Taylor	Leeds gain revenge for the seven-goal League Cup massacre, though Hurst's shot – deflected in off Bell – had given Hammers the perfect start. Albert Johanneson headed in Peter Lorimer's cross and Giles blasted a late winner. Byrne shaved Gary Sprake's crossbar in the dying seconds.											
19	H	WEST BROM	10	W	3-0	2-0	Redknapp 14, Peters 35p, Dear 85	Standen	Burnett	Charles	Bovington	Bickles	Moore	Redknapp	Boyce	Dear	Peters	Sealey	
3/12		22,961	*20*	20				*Sheppard*	*Cram*	*Fairfax*	*Lovett*	*Jones*	*Fraser*	*Foggo*	*Brown*	*Kaye*	*Hope*	*Clark*	
							Ref: P Bye	A £25,000 price tag has been placed on Brian Dear, who crowns his recall by blasting a spectacular goal from 25 yards. He also provided the cross from which Harry Redknapp drove in the first goal. The penalty was the result of Clive Clark whipping Burnett's legs from under him.											
20	A	BURNLEY	11	L	2-4	2-2	Hurst 21, 42	Standen	Burnett	Charles	Bovington	Bickles	Moore	Peters	Boyce	Byrne	Hurst	Sissons	
10/12		***19,509***	*6*	20			*Irvine 8, 77, O'Neill 11, Lochhead 58*	*Blacklaw*	*Angus*	*Miller*	*Todd*	*Elder*	*O'Neil*	*Harris*	*Morgan*	*Lochhead*	*Irvine*	*Latcham*	
							Ref: V James	Burnley are the most prolific home side in Division 1, West Ham the most prolific away, so this thriller was always on the cards. Standen was at fault for the second goal, missing a cross, but in the last minute saved Irvine's penalty after Charles had fouled man-of-the match Morgan.											
21	A	CHELSEA	11	D	5-5	2-1	Brab' 24, Peters 29, Sis' 55, 58, Byrne 60p	Standen	Bovington	Charles*	Peters	Brown	Moore	Brabrook	Boyce	Byrne	Hurst	Sissons	Burnett
17/12		*47,805*	*2*	21			*Baldwin 40, Hateley 51, Cooke 54*	*Bonetti*	*Kirkup*	*McCreadie*	*Hollins*	*Hinton*	*Harris*	*Boyle*	*Baldwin*	*Hateley*	*Cooke*	*Tambling*	
							Ref: H Richards *[Tambling 80p, 89]*	Chelsea have won only three times at home. West Ham led 2-0 and 5-3, but are pegged back by two goals by Tambling, which gives him a new Chelsea record of 129. Moore fouled Hateley for the penalty, then Tambling put away Cooke's cross. Best of the goals was Cooke's volley.											

LEAGUE DIVISION 1 — Manager: Ron Greenwood — SEASON 1966-67

No	Date		Att	Pos	Pt	F-A	H-T	Scorers, Times, and Referees	1	2	3	4	5	6	7	8	9	10	11	12 sub used
22	A	BLACKPOOL		10	W	4-1	2-0	Hurst 8, Dear 18, Byrne 80, Sissons 87	Standen	Bovington	Burnett	Peters	Brown	Moore	Dear	Boyce	Byrne	Hurst	Sissons	
	26/12		*26,901*	*22*	23			*Charnley 66p*	*Waiters*	*Armfield*	*Hughes*	*McPhee*	*James*	*Green*	*Skirton*	*Robsosn*	*Charnley*	*Suddick*	*Moir*	
								Ref: K Stokes	Hammers flew up to Blackpool, with Dear taking the place of Brabrook, who had stomach trouble. Not even a debut for Alan Suddick can conceal the gulf between the sides. Peters made early goals for Hurst and Dear, but Brown's foul on Charnley in the box rekindled the contest.											
23	H	BLACKPOOL		7	W	4-0	1-0	Byrne 14, Moore 80, Hurst 87, Peters 89	**Macklew'rth**	Bovington	Burnett	Peters	Brown	Moore	Brabrook	Dear	Byrne	Hurst	Sissons	
	27/12		29,300	*22*	25				*Waiters*	*Thompson*	*Hughes*	*Fisher*	*James*	*McPhee*	*Skirton*	*Robson*	*Charnley*	*Suddick*	*Lea*	
								Ref: J Yates	Harry Redknapp is given the day off for his engagement party. Three late goals distorted the balance of play. For over an hour only Byrne's shot on the turn separated the sides. Blackpool were pressing hard when Moore fired in from 30 yards, a candidate for goal of the season.											
24	H	LEICESTER		10	L	0-1	0-0		Standen	Burnett	Charles*	Peters	Brown	Moore	Brabrook	Bovington	Byrne	Hurst	Sissons	Burkett
	31/12		34,168	*9*	25			*Sinclair 74*	*Banks*	*Rodrigues*	*Norman*	*Roberts*	*Sjoberg*	*Nish*	*Sinclair*	*Sweenie*	*Dougan*	*Gibson*	*Stringfellow*	
								Ref: P Walters	West Ham were the last Division 1 side to have scored in every match, but after 28 matches Gordon Banks has the final word. John Charles' error presented the chance for Jackie Sinclair. Hurst played deeper than usual. When Banks was beaten, defenders twice cleared off the line.											
25	A	LIVERPOOL		11	L	0-2	0-2		Standen	Burnett	Burkett	Peters	Brown	Moore	Brabrook	Bovington	Byrne	Hurst	Sissons	
	7/1		*48,518*	*1*	25			*Thompson 34, 40*	*Lawrence*	*Lawler*	*Milne*	*Smith*	*Yeats*	*Stevenson*	*Callaghan*	*Hunt*	*St John*	*Strong*	*Thompson*	
								Ref: J Carr	Bobby Moore OBE cannot prevent leaders Liverpool maintaining their unbeaten home record. In fact this was a totally one-sided affair, and but for Standen's agility the margin of defeat would have been greater. Peter Thompson fired in the first from 20 yards, then added a solo goal.											
26	A	STOKE		12	D	1-1	1-0	Hurst 7	Standen	Burnett	Charles	Peters*	Brown	Moore	Brabrook	Boyce	Byrne	Hurst	Sissons	Dear
	14/1		*27,274*	*4*	26			*Burrows 59*	*Farmer*	*Palmer*	*Skeels*	*Viollet**	*Bloor*	*Allen*	*Bridgwood*	*Philpott*	*Vernon*	*Eastham*	*Burrows*	*Bernard*
								Ref G Hill	Stoke confirm their reputation as one of West Ham's bogey-sides. Hurst wrong-footed Bloor to convert John Sissons' cross, but when Harry Burrows got on the end of Eastham's pass, this ageing Stoke side began to pose most of the questions. Substitute Bernard missed a sitter.											
27	H	SHEFFIELD WED		9	W	3-0	0-0	Dear 65, Hurst 75p, Sissons 84	Standen	Bovington	Charles*	Peters	Bickles	Moore	Brabrook	Sealey	Dear	Hurst	Sissons	Dawkins
	21/1		29,220	*13*	28				*Springett*	*Branfoot*	*Megson*	*Mobley*	*Ellis*	*Young*	*Pugh*	*McCalliog*	*Quinn*	*Ford*	*Eustace*	
								Ref: C Nicholls	Greenwood plays five strikers, but the breakthrough was a long time coming. Brabrook then headed back across goal to Dear. Young gave away the penalty when fouling Sissons. At the time West Ham were down to 10, Trevor Dawkins having come on as sub without permission.											
28	A	SOUTHAMPTON		11	L	2-6	0-4	Hurst 59, Burkett 76 *[Chivers 31, 75]*	Standen	Bovington	Burkett	Peters	Brown	Moore	Brabrook	Boyce	Byrne	Hurst	Sissons	
	4/2		*30,123*	*17*	28			*Hollywood 3, Davies 18, Paine 26p, 57p,*	*MacLaren*	*Webb*	*Hollywood*	*Wimshurst*	*Knapp*	*Walker*	*Paine*	*Chivers*	*Davies*	*Melia*	*Sydenham*	
								Ref: K Wynn	The Dell's biggest crowd for 18 years enjoys more misery being heaped upon Hammers. Davies fouled Brown before scoring No 2. Davies took an early knock from Moore, who was booed thereafter. Paine's penalties came after two fouls on him, first by Moore, then by Bovington.											
29	H	SUNDERLAND		11	D	2-2	1-1	Byrne 17, Hurst 89	Standen	Burnett	Burkett	Dawkins	**Andrew**	Bovington	Redknapp	Boyce	Byrne	Hurst	Peters	
	11/2		27,965	*15*	29			*Mulhall 16, Martin 73*	*Montgomery*	*Irwin*	*Harvey*	*Todd*	*Kinnell*	*Baxter*	*Kerr*	*O'Hare*	*Martin*	*Herd*	*Mulhall*	
								Ref: R Windle	Greenwood starts to rebuild. Johnny Byrne is expected to sign for Stoke, and signs off with a goal. Peters and Hurst were anonymous. Hurst missed from the spot after Byrne was tripped, but redeemed himself in the closing seconds when heading in Byrne's cross from a tight angle.											
30	A	EVERTON		13	L	0-4	0-3	*[Husband 46]*	Standen	Burnett	Bovington	Dawkins	Andrew	Boyce	Redknapp	Bennett	Brabrook	Hurst	Sissons	
	25/2		*42,504*	*7*	29			*Temple 10, Young 14, Morrissey 37,*	*West*	*Wright*	*Wilson*	*Hurst*	*Labone*	*Harvey*	*Young*	*Ball*	*Temple**	*Husband*	*Morrissey*	*Brown*
								Ref: K Burns	Everton's Alan Ball masterminded this feast of attacking football. Temple netted from Husband's pull-back. Young chipped Standen for the second. Morrissey added a third when running from the halfway line. The nearest Hammers came was when Labone headed onto his own bar.											
31	A	NOTT'M FOREST		14	L	0-1	0-0		Standen	Burkett	**Kitchener**	Peters	**Heffer**	Moore	Brabrook	Boyce	Bennett*	Hurst	Sissons	Redknapp
	18/3		*31,426*	*3*	29			*Baker 79*	*Grummitt*	*Hindley*	*Winfield*	*Hennessey*	*McKinlay*	*Newton*	*Lyons*	*Barnwell*	*Baker*	*Wignall*	*Storey-Moore*	
								Ref: R Prichard	The highest scorers in Division 1 take on the meanest defenders, and the latter win. Mind you, it took a freakish goal from Joe Baker – the ball looping over Standen after bouncing off Moore – to separate the sides. Greenwood bloodied two more youngsters in this transitional team.											

No	Venue / Date	Opponent / Att	Pos	Res / Pts	F-A	H-T	Scorers, Times, Referees	1	2	3	4	5	6	7	8	9	10	11	subs used
32	H	ASTON VILLA	14	W	2-1	1-1	Boyce 37, Peters 48	Standen	Burkett	Kitchener	Peters	Heffer	Moore	Redknapp	Boyce	Hurst	Sissons	Brabrook	
	24/3	28,716	*18*	31			*Anderson 13*	*Withers*	*Wright*	*Aitken*	*Tindall*	*Sleeu'nhoek*	*Pountney*	*Anderson*	*Chatterley*	*Stobart*	*Broadbent*	*MacLeod*	
							Ref: D Counsell	Bobby Moore played a part in all three goals. First, his mistimed clearance bounced kindly for Willie Anderson to put Villa ahead. Then his free-kick paved the way for Boyce's header. Yet another Moore free-kick was finished off by Peters for the winner. Villa are going down.											
33	H	BURNLEY	11	W	3-2	1-1	Peters 13, 64, Sissons 68	Standen	Charles	Kitchener	Bovington	Heffer	Moore	Redknapp	Boyce	Peters	Hurst	Sissons	
	25/3	24,428	*12*	33			*Morgan 11, O'Neil 59*	*Thomson*	*Smith*	*Latcham*	*O'Neil*	*Miller*	*Merrington*	*Morgan*	*Todd*	*Blant*	*Harris*	*Coates*	
							Ref: N Burtenshaw	Hurst failed to score but made all three goals for his team-mates. He also laid out Fred Smith, who was foolish enough to get in the way of a belter. Sissons claimed the winner after a blunder by Dave Merrington, who had cleared straight to Sissons' feet. Hammers go above Burnley.											
34	A	ASTON VILLA	10	W	2-0	1-0	Hurst 4, 62	Standen	Charles	Kitchener	Bovington	Heffer	Moore	Brabrook	Boyce	Peters	Hurst	Sissons*	Redknapp
	28/3	*22,033*	*19*	35				*Withers*	*Wright*	*Aitken*	*Tindall*	*Sleeu'nhoek*	*Pountney*	*Anderson*	*Chatterley*	*Stobart*	*Broadbent*	*MacLeod*	
							Ref: D Laing	An unexceptional match, except for Geoff Hurst, who takes his season's tally to 41. West Ham's Easter double over Villa is something from which Villa never recover. They appeared to know their fate as early as the fourth minute when Hurst nipped in to convert Brabrook's pass.											
35	A	MANCHESTER U	11	L	0-3	0-1		Standen	Charles	Kitchener	Bovington	Heffer	Moore	Redknapp	Boyce	Peters	Hurst	Brabrook	
	1/4	***61,380***	*1*	35			*Charlton 3, Best 86, Law 89*	*Stepney*	*Dunne*	*Noble*	*Crerand*	*Foulkes*	*Stiles*	*Best*	*Law*	*Sadler*	*Charlton*	*Aston*	
							Ref: W Handley	The magic threesome score the goals that keep Man U two points ahead of Forest. In a one-sided affair, West Ham trailed through Hurst's wayward pass till the closing minutes. Charles fouled Best but Law hit the post from the spot. Best's volley and Law's hook seal an easy win.											
36	H	SHEFFIELD UTD		L	0-2	0-0		Mackleworth	Charles	Kitchener	Bovington	Heffer	Moore	Redknapp	Boyce	Peters	Hurst	Sissons	
	4/4	22,006		35			*Jones 56, Munks 73*	*Hodgkinson*	*Badger*	*Shaw*	*Munks*	*Matthewson*	*Wagstaff*	*Woodward*	*Mallender*	*Jones*	*Barlow*	*Cliff*	
							Ref: R Johnson	Upton Park at the end resembled a morgue. Norman Giller described the Hammers as 'tigers suddenly transformed into tortoises.' The Blades were little better, but were sparked into life by Mick Jones' bullet from 15 yards. Munks then netted a rebound after Woodward had hit the bar.											
37	H	LEEDS	14	L	0-1	0-1		Standen	Charles	Kitchener	Peters	Moore	Bovington	Brabrook	Boyce	Bennett	Hurst	Sissons	
	22/4	25,429	*4*	35			*Lorimer 34*	*Sprake*	*Reaney*	*Cooper*	*Bremner*	*Madeley*	*Hunter*	*Lorimer*	*Belfitt*	*Greenhoff*	*Gray*	*Johanneson*	**Bates*
							Ref: H Davies	West Ham return from playing Real Madrid in the Houston Astrodome. Leeds are distracted by their looming FA Cup semi-final, but win with ease. Lorimer's angled 30-yarder squeezed inside the far post. Near the end Eddie Gray started mickey-taking West Ham's feeble efforts.											
38	A	NEWCASTLE	14	L	0-1	0-1		Standen	Charles	Burkett	Peters	Heffer	Moore	Redknapp	Boyce	Hurst	Sissons	Brabrook	
	26/4	*38,870*	*19*	35			*Burkett 14 (og)*	*Marshall*	*Craig*	*Clark*	*Elliott*	*McNamee*	*Iley*	*Bennett*	*Noble*	*Davies*	*Hilley*	*Robson*	
							Ref: K Dagnall	Newcastle haul themselves out of the relegation places, courtesy of Burkett's own-goal. Attempting to intercept from Pop Robson, Burkett steered the ball into his own net. And Burkett was only playing because Bill Kitchener had flu. Wyn Davies later headed against an upright.											
39	A	WEST BROM		L	1-3	0-2	Bennett 89	Standen	Charles	Burkett	Peters	Heffer	Moore	Redknapp	Bennett	**Hartley**	Hurst	Boyce	
	28/4	*23,219*		35			*Brown 24p, 32p, Astle 79*	*Osborne*	*Fairfax*	*Williams*	*Talbut*	*Colquhoun*	*Brown*	*Foggo*	*Astle*	*Kaye*	*Hope*	*Clark*	
							Ref: R Darlington	Debutant Trevor Hartley is blameless as the Hammers crash to their fifth straight defeat. Albion were helped on their way by two controversial penalties, for pushes by Heffer and Charles on Astle and Clark respectively. Charles' foul on Clark also led to a free-kick, headed in by Astle.											
40	H	MANCHESTER U	17	L	**1-6**	0-4	Charles 46 *[Best 25, Law 63p, 79]*	Mackleworth	Burkett	Charles	Peters	Heffer	Moore	Redknapp	Bennett	Boyce	Hurst	Sissons	
	6/5	**38,424**	*1*	35			*Charlton 2, Crerand 7, Foulkes 10,*	*Stepney*	*Brennan*	*Dunne*	*Crerand*	*Foulkes*	*Stiles*	*Best*	*Law*	*Sadler*	*Charlton*	*Aston*	
							Ref: R Spittle	Upton Park's biggest gate since the war sees Man U clinch the championship. Burkett made a hash of a clearance and Charlton netted. It was soon 0-4. Charles conceded a penalty for No 5, pushing Law after he had been slapped round the face. Crowd trouble erupted at the end.											
41	H	TOTTENHAM	17	L	0-2	0-0		Standen	Burnett	Charles	Bovington	Bickles	Moore	Peters	Boyce	Hurst	Sealey	**Eadie**	
	9/5	35,750	*3*	35			*Greaves 70, Gilzean 89*	*Jennings*	*Kinnear*	*Knowles*	*Mullery*	*England*	*Mackay*	*Robertson*	*Greaves*	*Gilzean*	*Venables*	*Saul*	
							Ref: J Taylor	Spurs' G-men – Greaves and Gilzean – clinched a place in Europe with two smart goals. They extend Spurs unbeaten run to 22 matches, and also inflict a seventh straight loss on the Hammers. Cyril Knowles pushed Hurst over the barrier into the crowd. Spurs have an FA Cup final.											
42	H	MANCHESTER C	16	D	1-1	1-0	Peters 42	Standen	Charles	Kitchener	Peters	Bickles	Moore	Sealey	Boyce	Hartley	Hurst	Eadie	
	13/5	**17,186**	*15*	36			*Bell 75*	*Dowd*	*Book*	*Pardoe*	*Connor*	*Heslop*	*Oakes*	*Summerbee*	*Bell*	*Crossan*	*Young*	*Coleman*	
	Home	Away					Ref: T Dawes	Doug Eadie crossed low and hard for Martin Peters to net. But West Ham fell to pieces trying to protect their lead and Colin Bell rounded Kitchener to equalise. West Ham earn their first point since 28 March. Standen plays his last game. Ken Brown shortly receives a testimonial.											
Average	29,265	33,302																	

League Cup					F-A	H-T	Scorers, Times, and Referees	1	2	3	4	5	6	7	8	9	10	11	12 sub used
2	H	TOTTENHAM	17	W	1-0	1-0	Hurst 8	Standen	Burnett	Charles	Peters	Brown	Moore	Brabrook	Boyce	Bennett	Hurst	Sissons	
	14/9	34,000	*4*					*Jennings*	*Kinnear*	*Knowles*	*Mullery*	*Beal*	*Clayton*	*Robertson*	*Greaves*	*Gilzean !*	*Venables*	*Saul*	
							Ref: H New	Alan Gilzean is sent off after 65 minutes for verbally abusing a linesman. That did not help Spurs' cause, already trailing to Hurst's seventh goal of the season – thumping home Moore's cross after Beal had failed to clear. Fisticuffs enlivened the North Bank during the interval.											
3	A	ARSENAL	12	W	3-1	1-1	Peters 26, Hurst 52, 55	Standen	Burnett	Charles	Peters	Brown	Moore	Brabrook	Boyce	Byrne	Hurst	Sissons	
	5/10	*33,647*	*14*				*Jenkins 29*	*Furnell*	*Simpson*	*Storey*	*Woodward*	*Ure*	*Boot*	*Coakley*	*Jenkins*	*Walley*	*Sammels*	*Armstrong*	
							Ref: G Roper	West Ham extend their unbeaten run to nine games, but owe a debt to Hurst for a bullet header and a rasping left-foot drive which put the game beyond Arsenal's reach. Earlier Peters had run 25 yards before heading the first goal. Jenkins levelled with an overhead that deceived Standen.											
4	H	LEEDS	14	W	7-0	4-0	Sissons 2, 28, 34, Hurst 41, 60, 73,	Standen	Bovington	Charles	Peters	Brown	Moore	Brabrook	Boyce	Byrne	Hurst	Sissons	
	7/11	27,474	*9*				[Peters 70]	*Harvey*	*Reaney*	*Bell*	*Bremner*	*Charlton*	*Hunter*	*Madeley*	*Belfitt*	*Greenhoff*	*Giles*	*O'Grady*	
							Ref: E Jennings	Six against Fulham on Saturday. Seven v Leeds on Monday. Leeds had won away just once all season. Sissons' hat-trick all came with his left foot. Hurst's hat-trick was of the ballistic sort, but it was only afterwards that it was confirmed that his first goal would not go down to Byrne.											
QF	A	BLACKPOOL	10	W	3-1	2-0	Hurst 2, 25, Byrne 52	Standen	Burnett	Charles	Bovington	Brown	Moore	Boyce	Hurst	Byrne	Peters	Sissons	
	7/12	*15,831*	*22*				*Charnley 59*	*Waiters*	*Armfield*	*Hughes*	*Fisher*	*James*	*McPhee*	*Skirton*	*Robson*	*Charnley*	*Moir*	*Lea*	
							Ref: K Stokes	Hurst's 25th and 26th goals of this prolific season put this tie beyond poor Blackpool. His first is a belter from 18 yards, his second a close-range knock in from Sissons' cross. Blackpool had little luck – Hughes hit the bar from 30 yards – forcing Hammers into desperate defence.											
SF	A	WEST BROM	11	L	0-4	0-4		Standen	Burnett	Burkett	Bovington	Brown	Moore	Brabrook	Peters	Byrne	Hurst	Sissons	
1	18/1	*29,796*	*20*				*Astle 1, 23, 45, Collard 14*	*Sheppard*	*Cram*	*Williams*	*Collard*	*Jones*	*Fraser*	*Brown*	*Astle*	*Kaye*	*Hope*	*Clark*	
							Ref: J Cattlin	Ken Brown has a stinker, and knows he is partially to blame for the first three goals. Astle headed in after 50 seconds. By half-time it is clear that West Ham won't be contesting an all-London final with QPR and that Moore won't be lifting his fourth trophy at Wembley in four years.											
SF	H	WEST BROM	11	D	2-2	2-1	Byrne 13, Hurst 35	Standen	Bovington	Burkett	Peters	Brown	Moore	Brabrook	Boyce	Byrne	Hurst	Sissons	
2	8/2	35,790	*20*				*Hope 22, Clark 63*	*Sheppard*	*Cram*	*Williams*	*Collard*	*Jones*	*Fraser*	*Foggo*	*Brown*	*Kaye*	*Hope*	*Clark*	
							Ref: T Dawes (Hammers lose 2-6 on aggregate)	Jimmy Hagan's Albion have to withstand an electric atmosphere inside Upton Park. West Ham set out to retrieve their huge deficit with pride and passion. Hurst was marked by two or three defenders, but escaped to score from Brabrook's cross. Then Clark broke clear down the left.											

FA Cup																			
3	H	SWINDON	9	D	3-3	2-1	Hurst 20, 30, 76	Standen	Bovington	Burkett	Peters	Bickles	Moore	Brabrook	Sealey	Dear	Hurst	Sissons	
	28/1	37,400	*3:8*				*Rogers 26, 71, Brown 59*	*Hicks*	*Thomas*	*Trollope*	*Morgan*	*Nurse*	*Harland*	*Brown*	*Penman*	*Skeen*	*Smart*	*Rogers*	
							Ref: J Osborne	West Ham's biggest gate for seven years looks forward to a contest between Hurst and Swindon's rising superstar Don Rogers. Rogers scores two and makes one for the Division 3 outfit. In the middle of the second half Swindon are on top, but then Peters chips onto Hurst's head.											
3R	A	SWINDON	9	L	1-3	0-1	Sissons 78	Standen	Bovington	Burkett	Peters	Bickles	Moore	Dear	Boyce	Byrne	Hurst	Sissons	
	31/1	*25,789*	*3:8*				*Penman 18, Rogers 84, Skeen 88*	*Hicks*	*Thomas*	*Trollope*	*Morgan*	*Nurse*	*Harland*	*Brown*	*Penman*	*Skeen*	*Smart*	*Rogers*	
							Ref: J Osborne	'This is the blackest month we have known,' admitted Greenwood afterwards. Moore backed off to permit Willie Penman's rocket. Sissons hit the equaliser from a corner taken by the recalled Byrne. Rogers set the stadium alight when diving between Bovington and Standen to score.											

		Home					Away					
	P	W	D	L	F	A	W	D	L	F	A	Pts
1 Manchester U	42	17	4	0	51	13	7	8	6	33	32	60
2 Nott'm Forest	42	16	4	1	41	13	7	6	8	23	28	56
3 Tottenham	42	15	3	3	44	21	9	5	7	27	27	56
4 Leeds	42	15	4	2	41	17	7	7	7	21	25	55
5 Liverpool	42	12	7	2	36	17	7	6	8	28	30	51
6 Everton	42	11	4	6	39	22	8	6	7	26	24	48
7 Arsenal	42	11	6	4	32	20	5	8	8	26	27	46
8 Leicester	42	12	4	5	47	28	6	4	11	31	43	44
9 Chelsea	42	7	9	5	33	29	8	5	8	34	33	44
10 Sheffield Utd	42	11	5	5	34	22	5	5	11	18	37	42
11 Sheffield Wed	42	9	7	5	39	19	5	6	10	17	28	41
12 Stoke	42	11	5	5	40	21	6	2	13	23	37	41
13 West Brom	42	11	1	9	40	28	5	6	10	37	45	39
14 Burnley	42	11	4	6	43	28	4	5	12	23	48	39
15 Manchester C	42	8	9	4	27	25	4	6	11	16	27	39
16 WEST HAM	42	8	6	7	40	31	6	2	13	40	53	36
17 Sunderland	42	12	3	6	39	26	2	5	14	19	46	36
18 Fulham	42	8	7	6	49	34	3	5	13	22	49	34
19 Southampton	42	10	3	8	49	41	4	3	14	25	51	34
20 Newcastle	42	9	5	7	24	27	3	4	14	15	54	33
21 Aston Villa	42	7	5	9	30	33	4	2	15	24	52	29
22 Blackpool	42	1	5	15	18	36	5	4	12	23	40	21
	924	232	110	120	836	551	120	110	232	551	836	924

Odds & ends

Double wins: (3) Sheffield Wed, Blackpool, Aston Villa.
Double losses: (5) Leicester, Everton, Sheff Utd, Leeds, Manchester U.

Won from behind: (4) Sunderland (a), Fulham (h), Villa (h), Burnley (h).
Lost from in front: (1) Leeds (a).

High spots: Reaching semi-final of League Cup.
Beating Leeds 7-0 in League Cup.
Beating Fulham 6-1 in the league.
Scoring 32 goals in just nine league games in November and December.
Only champions Manchester U scored more than Hammers' 80 goals.

Low spots: Losing to Third Division Swindon in FA Cup.
Losing seven league games in a row in April and May.
Conceding six goals at Southampton and at home to Manchester U.
Conceding more league goals than everyone except Southampton and Aston Villa.

Hammer of the Year: Geoff Hurst.
Ever-presents: (0).
Hat-tricks: (4) Geoff Hurst (3), John Sissons (1).
Leading scorer: (41) Geoff Hurst.

	Appearances						Goals			
	Lge	*Sub*	LC	*Sub*	FAC	*Sub*	Lge	LC	FAC	Tot
Andrew, George	**2**									
Bennett, Peter	**7**	*1*	1				**1**			**1**
Bickles, Dave	**8**				2					
Bovington, Eddie	**28**		4		2		**1**			**1**
Boyce, Ronnie	**37**		5		2		**4**			**4**
Brabrook, Peter	**32**		5				**5**			**5**
Brown, Ken	**18**		6							
Burkett, Jackie	**11**	*1*	2		2		**1**			**1**
Burnett, Dennis	**24**	*2*	4							
Byrne, Johnny	**25**		5		2		**11**	2		**13**
Charles, John	**31**		4				**1**			**1**
Dawkins, Trevor	**2**	*1*								
Dear, Brian	**4**	*1*			2		**3**			**3**
Eadie, Doug	**2**									
Hartley, Trevor	**2**									
Heffer, Paul	**9**									
Howe, Bobby		*1*								
Hurst, Geoff	**41**		6		2		**29**	9	3	**41**
Kitchener, Bill	**8**									
Mackleworth, Colin	**3**									
Moore, Bobby	**40**		6		2		**2**			**2**
Peters, Martin	**41**		6		2		**14**	2		**16**
Redknapp, Harry	**10**	*2*					**1**			**1**
Sealey, Alan	**4**									
Sissons, John	**34**	*1*	6		2		**7**	3	1	**11**
Standen, Jim	**39**		6		2					
26 players used	**462**	***10***	**66**		**22**		**80**	**16**	**4**	**100**

No	Date	Att	Pos	Pt	F-A	H-T	Scorers, Times, and Referees	1	2	3	4	5	6	7	8	9	10	11	12 sub used
1	H SHEFFIELD WED			L	2-3	0-1	Hurst 58, Peters 60	**Ferguson**	**Bonds**	Charles	Bovington	**Cushley**	Moore	Redknapp	Peters	Hurst	Boyce	Sissons	
	19/8	29,603		–			*Fantham 16, Ritchie 70, McCalliog 88*	*Springett*	*Smith*	*Megson*	*Mobley*	*Ellis*	*Young*	*Fantham*	*McCalliog*	*Ritchie*	*Usher*	*Quinn**	*Eustace*
							Ref: G Roper	Greenwood has splashed out £65,000 on Ferguson and £55,000 on Bonds. Together with other new boy, John Cushley, the defence has been remodelled. West Ham were 2-1 up when the ball came off Cushley's knee to Ritchie. Ferguson then let McCalliog's dolly shot over his head.											
2	H BURNLEY			W	4-2	0-1	Peters 53, Hurst 54, 63, Redknapp 79	Ferguson	Bonds	Charles	Peters	Cushley	Moore	Redknapp	Dear	Hurst	Boyce	Sissons	
	21/8	30,420		2			*Irvine 25, Casper 58*	*Thomson*	*Angus*	*Latcham*	*O'Neil*	*Merrington*	*Todd*	*Morgan*	*Bellamy*	*Irvine*	*Harris*	*Casper*	
							Ref: R Spittle	Great entertainment for the fans, dreadful blunders by both defences. Irvine headed Burnley ahead when Ferguson missed a cross. Peters' 35-yard rocket put West Ham level, before Hurst converted crosses by Redknapp and Sissons. Managerless Coventry are after Ron Greenwood.											
3	A TOTTENHAM		19	L	**1-5**	0-2	Sissons 80 *[Saul 77]*	Ferguson	Bonds	Charles	Peters	Cushley	Moore	Redknapp	Boyce	Hurst	Dear	Sissons	
	26/8	*55,831*	*4*	2			*Greaves 36, 76p, Jon es 39, Mullery 68*	*Jennings*	*Kinnear*	*Knowles*	*Mullery*	*England*	*Mackay**	*Robertson*	*Greaves*	*Saul*	*Venables*	*Jones*	*Beal*
							Ref: K Dagnall	Greenwood adopts back to the wall away tactics, with Peters as an auxiliary full-back. But West Ham are blown away from the moment Greaves escapes his marker, John Charles. When Jones headed the second, school-kids invaded the pitch. Bonds felled Greaves for the penalty.											
4	A BURNLEY			D	3-3		Moore 10, Peters 60, Hurst 77	Ferguson	Bonds	Charles	Peters	Cushley	Moore	Redknapp	**Brooking**	Hurst	Boyce	Sissons	
	29/8	*16,620*		3			*Lochead 45, Bellamy 46, Harris 70p*	*Thomson*	*Latcham*	*Buxton*	*O'Neil*	*Angus*	*Bellamy*	*Morgan*	*Lochhead*	*Irvine*	*Harris*	*Casper*	
							Ref: N Callender	Bobby Moore was at the heart of everything, scoring a sweet goal at one end and twice kicking off the line at the other. Volleys by Lochhead and Bellamy, seconds before and seconds after the interval, changed the complexion of the game. Redknapp fouled Latcham for the penalty.											
5	H MANCHESTER U		20	L	1-3	0-0	Peters 78	Ferguson	Bonds*	Charles	Peters	Cushley	Moore	Redknapp	Dear	Hurst	Boyce	Sissons	Brooking
	2/9	**36,562**	*9*	3			*Kidd 53, Sadler 54, Ryan 80*	*Stepney*	*Dunne*	*Burns*	*Crerand*	*Foulkes*	*Stiles*	*Ryan*	*Sadler*	*Charlton*	*Kidd*	*Best*	
							Ref: E Jennings	West Ham had the better of the first half against the defending champions, but Hurst and Dear missed good chances. When Bobby Charlton hooked the ball over Cushley's head to Kidd, the die was cast. Peters headed in Redknapp's corner. 18-year old sub Brooking caught the eye.											
6	A EVERTON			L	0-2	0-1		Ferguson	Charles	Kitchener	Peters	Cushley	Moore	Redknapp	Brooking	Hurst	Boyce	Sissons	
	5/9	*46,762*		3			*Kendall 35, Young 52*	*West*	*Wright*	*Brown*	*Kendall*	*Labone*	*Harvey*	*Young*	*Ball*	*Royle*	*Hurst*	*Temple*	
							Ref: R Harper	Only Everton's profligacy in front of goal saved Hammers from a hammering. £60,000 signing Howard Kendall scored with a fine header, then hit the post twice. Young dispossessed Peters and shot from 30 yards. Ferguson appeared to have saved it, but appearances can be deceptive.											
7	A SUNDERLAND		16	W	5-1	0-1	Peters 60, Hurst 61, 75, Redknapp 63,	Standen	Charles	Kitchener	Peters	Cushley	Moore	Redknapp	Brooking	Hurst	Boyce	Brabrook	
	9/9	*39,772*	*7*	5			*Moore 12 (og)* [Moore 76]	*Montgomery*	*Parke*	*Ashurst*	*Todd*	*Kinnell*	*Baxter*	*Herd*	*Suggett*	*Martin*	*Heslop*	*Mulhall*	
							Ref: G McCabe	When Moore turned Martin's cross past Ferguson, it seemed Sunderland's unbeaten home record was safe. None could have predicted the second-half turnaround. Peters' scorcher was the first of three goals in three minutes. Both Redknapp and Moore scored with 30-yard bullets.											
8	H WOLVES		20	L	1-2	1-1	Hurst 36	Standen	Charles	Kitchener	Peters	Cushley	Moore	Redknapp	Boyce	Brooking	Hurst	Sissons	
	16/9	30,780	*14*	5			*Dougan 35, 88*	*Parkes*	*Taylor*	*Thomson*	*Bailey*	*Woodfield*	*Holsgrove*	*Wharton*	*Knowles*	*Dougan*	*Evans*	*Wagstaffe*	
							Ref: R Johnson	Derek Dougan spent the match ankle-tapping defenders, in between scoring the goals that brought Wolves only their second win at Upton Park in 12 seasons. The first goal came when Standen missed a cross from 17-year-old Alun Evans; the winner when Dougan sidestepped Cushley.											
9	A FULHAM		16	W	3-0	2-0	Hurst 7, Moore 39, Sissons 89	Ferguson	Bovington	Charles	Peters	Cushley	Moore	Redknapp	Boyce	Brabrook	Hurst	Sissons	
	23/9	*29,234*	*18*	7				*McClelland*	*Cohen**	*Dempsey*	*Ryan*	*Callaghan*	*Conway*	*Brown*	*Moss*	*Clarke*	*Haynes*	*Barrett*	*Earle*
							Ref: R Weedon	Fulham are struggling once again. Only Haynes looks to have any ideas and Craven Cottage starts emptying long before the end. Ferguson did not help his confidence by letting Alan Clarke outjump him twice near the end, but headers by Hurst and Moore had long sealed the result.											
10	H LEEDS		15	D	0-0	0-0		Ferguson	Bonds	Charles	Bovington	Cushley	Moore	Redknapp	Boyce	Hurst	Peters	Brabrook	
	30/9	29,740	*9*	8				*Sprake*	*Reaney*	*Madeley*	*Bremner*	*Charlton*	*Hunter*	*Greenhoff*	*Lorimer*	*Jones*	*Gray*	*Cooper*	
							Ref: R Kirkpatrick	England boss Alf Ramsey watches a match policed exuberantly by referee Roger Kirkpatrick, whose high-stepping Tiller Girl antics have the crowd in stitches. Leeds were in almost total control by the end, but somehow could not force the goal their abundant possession merited.											

No	Date	Venue	Opponent	Att	Pos	Pts	Res	F-A	H-T	Scorers, Times, and Referees	1	2	3	4	5	6	7	8	9	10	11	12 sub used
11		H	STOKE		17		L	3-4	3-0	Hurst 24, 40, Peters 35	Ferguson	Bonds	Charles	Peters	Cushley	Moore	Redknapp	Bovington	Brabrook	Hurst	Sissons	
	7/10			24,471	*8*	8				*Burrows 65, 72, Dobing 67, 72*	*Banks*	*Skeels*	*Bentley*	*Palmer*	*Bloor**	*Allen*	*Bridgwood*	*Eastham*	*Dobing*	*Vernon*	*Burrows*	*Bernard*
										Ref: C Nicholls	A catastrophic collapse. Upton Park echoed to the chants of 'easy, easy' in the first half, as Hurst's side-foot and header and Peters' hook made it 3-0. But Stoke plundered four goals in seven minutes, with Hammers' defence standing like statues pointing accusing fingers at each other.											
12		A	LIVERPOOL		19		L	1-3	0-2	Peters 75	Ferguson	Bonds	Charles	Peters	Cushley	Moore	Redknapp	Boyce	Brabrook	Hurst	Sissons	
	14/10			*46,951*	*1*	8				*St John 14, 37, Smith 68*	*Lawrence*	*Lawler*	*Byrne*	*Smith*	*Yeats*	*Hughes*	*Callaghan*	*Hunt*	*Hateley*	*St John*	*Thompson*	
										Ref: I Thacker	West Ham set out with a safety-first approach, which was rendered useless once Ian St John was left unmarked to poach an easy goal. Worse was to come when Tommy Smith robbed Sissons and sent a 40-yard cross over Ferguson's head. Hammers only came to life when 0-3 down.											
13		H	SOUTHAMPTON		19		L	0-1	0-1		Ferguson	Bonds	Charles	Peters	Cushley	Moore	Redknapp	Bovington	Brabrook	Hurst	Sissons	
	23/10			32,550	*10*	8				*Paine 11*	*Martin*	*Jones*	*Hollywood*	*Fisher*	*Webb*	*Walker*	*Paine*	*Chivers*	*Davies*	*Melia*	*Gabriel*	
										Ref: K Walker	Both sides set their sights on mutual destruction in this Monday night match. West Ham were no angels, kicking Ron Davies over the wall into the crowd. The goal came when Ferguson pushed Gabriel's shot out to Paine, who scored from a tight angle. Saints conceded corners a-plenty.											
14		A	CHELSEA		18		W	3-1	1-1	Dear 9, Hurst 53, Peters 69	Ferguson	Bonds	Charles	Peters	Cushley	Moore	Burkett	Boyce	Brabrook	Hurst	Dear	
	28/10			*40,303*	*19*	10				*Osgood 17*	*Bonetti*	*Butler*	*McCreadie*	*Hollins*	*Hinton*	*Harris*	*Fascione*	*Baldwin*	*Osgood*	*Boyle*	*Cook*	
										Ref: J Finney	Greenwood rings the changes and switches to 4-3-3, pushing Bobby Moore into midfield. Dave Sexton's Chelsea are sunk by the power of Hurst, who made two goals and headed the other from Moore's cross. Peter Osgood's fantastic solo goal brought Stamford Bridge to its feet.											
15		A	NEWCASTLE		19		L	0-1	0-0		Ferguson	Bonds	Burkett	Charles	Cushley	Peters	Brabrook	Brooking	Hurst	Boyce	Sissons	
	11/11			*32,850*	*9*	10				*Davies 69*	*Marshall*	*Burton*	*Clarke*	*Elliott*	*McNamee*	*Moncur*	*Scott*	*Bennett*	*Davies*	*Iley*	*Robson*	
										Ref: F Nicholson	Newcastle extend their unbeaten run to 16 games thanks to Wyn Davies' towering header. Brooking conceded a needless free-kick. Iley took it, Ferguson didn't get to it and Wyn Davies did. Brabrook missed two easy chances in the first half. Newcastle have dropped just one home point.											
16		H	MANCHESTER C		20		L	2-3	1-2	Peters 29, Hurst 78	Ferguson	**Lampard**	Burkett	Peters	Cushley	Moore	Redknapp	Boyce	Brabrook	Hurst	Sissons	
	18/11			25,425	*3*	10				*Lee 24, 60, Summerbee 28*	*Mulhearn*	*Book*	*Pardoe*	*Doyle*	*Heslop*	*Oakes*	*Lee*	*Bell*	*Summerbee*	*Young*	*Coleman*	
										Ref: W Gow	This defeat leaves West Ham with the worst home record in all four divisions. Not the sort of match in which to give 19-year-old Frank Lampard his debut. Francis Lee and Tony Coleman gave him a baptism of fire. Star of the show was undoubtedly Lee, with two super goals.											
17		A	ARSENAL		20		D	0-0	0-0		Ferguson	Bonds	Burkett	Peters	Cushley	Moore	Redknapp	Brabrook	Hurst	Boyce	Sissons	
	25/11			*42,029*	*8*	11					*Furnell*	*Storey*	*McNab*	*McLintock*	*Neill*	*Simpson*	*Radford*	*Johnston*	*Graham*	*Sammels*	*Armstrong*	
										Ref: N Burtenshaw	Hurst played in midfield to disguise a painful foot injury and also to reinforce a packed defence. Arsenal spent the entire match battering the Hammers goal and late on Ferguson saved from McLintock from point-blank range. Arsenal, unbeaten at home, fail to score for the first time.											
18		H	SHEFFIELD UTD		20		W	3-0	2-0	Sissons 5, 62, Brabrook 33	Standen	Bonds	Burkett	Peters	Heffer	Moore	Redknapp	Boyce	Brabrook	Hurst	Sissons	
	2/12			22,510	*22*	13					*Hodgkinson*	*Badger*	*Shaw*	*Munks*	*Mallender*	*Barlow**	*Woodward*	*Carlin*	*Hill*	*Addison*	*Reece*	*Wagstaff*
										Ref: D Corbett	Sissons scored both his goals with his right foot, a rarity. Detroit-bound Jim Standen steps in for the flu-stricken Ferguson. The Blades go bottom as a result of this defeat, which was hard on them. Colin Addison twice hit the woodwork. West Ham's first home win since August.											
19		A	COVENTRY		20		D	1-1	1-1	Hurst 30	Ferguson	Charles	Burkett	Peters	Bonds	Moore	Redknapp	Boyce	Brabrook	Hurst	Sissons	
	8/12			*28,393*	*22*	14				*Baker 8*	*Glazier*	*Kearns*	*Bruck*	*Coop*	*Setters*	*Clements*	*Hannigan*	*Gibson*	*Baker*	*Machin*	*Rees*	
										Ref: J Osborne	Jimmy Hill's promoted Coventry have won only twice all season. Both managers, Greenwood and Cantwell, wanted this Friday night match postponed on account of the thick snow. Baker headed in Gibson's corner. Sissons hit the bar before Hurst chested down Peters' free-kick.											
20		H	WEST BROM				L	2-3	1-0	Hurst 7p, Brabrook 85	Ferguson	Charles	Burkett	Peters	Bonds	Moore	Redknapp	Boyce	Brabrook	Hurst*	Sissons	Bennett
	11/12			**18,340**		14				*Kryzwicki 50, Astle 78, Hope 87p*	*Osborne*	*Colquhoun*	*Williams*	*Brown*	*Talbut*	*Fraser*	*Kryzwicki*	*Kaye*	*Astle*	*Hope*	*Clark*	
										Ref: H New	West Ham's seventh home defeat was watched by their smallest crowd. They ended up making their own entertainment, booing or cheering, whoever was in possession. Brown shoved Sissons for Hurst's penalty. Albion's spot-kick came when Peter Bennett impeded Kryzwicki.											
21		A	SHEFFIELD WED		19		L	1-4	1-3	Dear 24	Ferguson	Charles	Burkett	Bonds	Cushley	Bovington	Dear	Boyce	Brooking	Hurst	Sissons	
	16/12			*24,003*	*5*	14				*Ritchie 22, 43, Fantham 32, Whitham 59*	*Springett*	*Smith*	*Megson*	*Mobley*	*Ellis*	*Young*	*Whitham*	*Fantham*	*Ritchie*	*McCalliog*	*Branfoot*	
										Ref: P Baldwin	Wednesday forced Hammers to change kit, lending them body-hugging white shirts that squeezed the life out of the players. The Owls are now unbeaten at home in 19 games. West Ham's only consolation was to score the best goal of the match – Brian Dear's swerving left-footer.											

No	Date	Att	Pos	Pt	F-A	H-T	Scorers, Times, and Referees	1	2	3	4	5	6	7	8	9	10	11	12 sub used
22	H TOTTENHAM		19	W	2-1	1-1	Bonds 26, Dear 75	Ferguson	Bonds	Lampard	Peters	Cushley	Moore	Dear	Boyce	Brooking	Hurst	Sissons	
	23/12	32,116	*10*	16			*Robertson 39*	*Jennings*	*Kinnear*	*Knowles*	*Mullery*	*Beal*	*Mackay*	*Robertson*	*Greaves**	*Saul*	*Bond*	*Jones*	*Venables*
							Ref: P Walters	West Ham avenge August's 1-5 thrashing in a hot-tempered affair. Jennings' helped Bonds' 25-yarder into the net. Ferguson and Cushley collided with each other going for Mackay's free-kick, and Robertson equalised. Dear's was a messy winner. Greaves went off with a cut eye.											
23	H LEICESTER		17	W	4-2	2-2	Dear 32, 61, 74, Brooking 40	Ferguson	Bonds	Lampard	Peters	Cushley	Moore	Dear	Boyce	Brooking	Hurst	Sissons	
	26/12	26,520	*18*	18			*Large 8, Sinclair 12*	*Shilton*	*Rodrigues*	*Bell*	*Roberts*	*Sjoberg*	*Nish*	*Tewley*	*Large*	*Stringfellow*	*Gibson*	*Sinclair*	
							Ref: R Pritchard	For half an hour West Ham looked a defensive shambles. Large's header and Sinclair's chip gave Leicester a two-goal lead, but when Dear rounded Shilton it sparked an epic fight-back. Hurst squared for Brooking to equalise with his first ever league goal. Dear back-heeled No 3.											
24	A LEICESTER		14	W	4-2	1-2	Brooking 8, Dear 55, 87, Sissons 64	Ferguson	Bonds	Lampard	Peters	Cushley	Moore	Dear	Boyce	Brooking	Hurst	Sissons	
	30/12	*24,589*	*18*	20			*Svarc 21, Large 42*	*Shilton*	*Rodrigues*	*Bell*	*Roberts*	*Sjoberg*	*Nish*	*Tewley*	*Large*	*Svarc*	*Gibson*	*Glover*	
							Ref: R Harper	A repeat score, once again after West Ham had trailed. Youth internationals Lampard and Brooking are behind the 4-3-3 revival of Hammers' fortunes, plus the scoring feats of overweight Dear. Sissons scores direct from a corner. West Ham's first win at Filbert Street since 1948.											
25	A MANCHESTER U		15	L	1-3	1-1	Brooking 22	Ferguson	Bonds	Lampard	Peters	Cushley	Moore	Dear	Boyce	Brooking	Hurst	Brabrook	
	6/1	***58,598***	*1*	20			*Charlton 11, Best 50, Aston 75*	*Stepney*	*Dunne*	*Burns*	*Crerand*	*Sadler*	*Fitzpatrick*	*Best*	*Kidd*	*Charlton*	*Law*	*Aston*	
							Ref: K Howley	Bobby Charlton celebrates his 400th league game for Man U with a 20-yarder. Dear's cross set up Trevor Brooking's equaliser. George Best somehow got in a scoring header despite being surrounded by defenders. The defending champions are now unbeaten at home in 36 games.											
26	A WOLVES		18	W	2-1	0-0	Dear 47, Hurst 52	Ferguson	Bonds	Lampard	Peters	Cushley	Moore	Dear	Boyce	Brooking	Hurst	Sissons	
	20/1	*32,273*	*17*	22			*Dougan 88*	*Williams*	*Taylor*	*Wilson*	*Bailey*	*Woodfield*	*Holsgrove*	*Kenning*	*Knowles*	*Dougan*	*Munro*	*Farrington*	
							Ref: G McCabe	Wolves crash to their sixth successive defeat. Two quick-fire headers early in the second half reduce the Molineux crowd to numbed silence. Hurst's was his first goal in two months. The result was signed and sealed long before Derek Dougan turned in a low centre as a consolation.											
27	H FULHAM		16	W	**7-2**	3-1	Dear 30, Brooking 42, 43, Moore 49,	Ferguson	Bonds	Lampard	Peters	Cushley	Moore	Dear	Boyce	Brooking	Hurst	Sissons	
	3/2	31,248	*22*	24			*Earle 18, Clarke 69* [Hurst 54, 78,]	*Macedo*	*Drake*	*Dempsey*	*Brown*	*Ryan*	*Conway*	*Haynes*	*Earle*	*Gilroy*	*Clarke*	*Barrett*	
							Ref: D Lyden [Peters 63]	Fulham had the cheek to score first – Haynes setting up Steve Earle. There seemed little chance of West Ham matching last season's 6-1 win. When Peters made it 6-1 this time there was still nearly half an hour to play. Fulham's new boss, Bobby Robson, knows his team are doomed.											
28	A LEEDS		16	L	1-2	1-1	Dear 43	Ferguson	Bonds	Lampard	Peters	Cushley	Moore	Dear	Bennett	Brooking	Hurst	Sissons	
	10/2	*41,814*	*2*	24			*Lorimer 4, 49*	*Sprake*	*Reaney*	*Cooper*	*Bremner*	*Madeley*	*Hunter*	*Greenhoff*	*Lorimer*	*Belfitt*	*Giles*	*Gray*	
							Ref: W Handley	Moore's early slip not only presents a goal for Peter Lorimer, it also sets up a refrain of 'Hunter for England' from the crowd. When Lorimer restored the lead from a fortunate rebound, Leeds exhibited all that was worst about Revie's team. Time-wasting at the corner flag by Giles.											
29	A STOKE		16	L	0-2	0-0		Ferguson	Bonds	Lampard	Peters	Cushley	Moore	Dear	Bennett	Brooking	Hurst	Sissons	
	26/2	***16,092***	*15*	24			*Dobing 50, Mahoney 51*	*Banks*	*Elder*	*Bentley*	*Moore*	*Bloor*	*Stevenson*	*Conroy*	*Eastham*	*Dobing*	*Mahoney*	*Burrows*	
							Ref: R Pritchard	Stoke enjoy swift revenge for their FA Cup loss. When Terry Conroy reached up and grabbed the ball inside the box the ref gave a free-kick outside it. Two quick goals sealed West Ham's fate. First, Cushley's miscued pass fell to Eastham, who fed Dobing. Mahoney volleyed No 2.											
30	A SOUTHAMPTON		19	D	0-0	0-0		Ferguson	Bonds	Lampard	Peters	**Stephenson**	Moore	Dear	Boyce	Brooking	Hurst	Sissons	
	16/3	*27,734*	*15*	25				*Martin*	*Kirkup*	*Jones*	*Walker*	*McGrath*	*Gabriel*	*Channon*	*Saul*	*Davies*	*Paine*	*Sydenham*	
							Ref: L Callaghan	On a bone hard pitch, Hurst and Dear missed so many chances that Saints fans jeered and applauded them. One of Hurst's misses was so bad – skying over – that no one could believe it. Max Marquis wrote : 'Southampton were so bad they couldn't have won with an Act of Parliament.'											
31	H CHELSEA		19	L	0-1	0-1		Ferguson	Bonds	Lampard	Peters	Stephenson	Moore	Dear	Boyce	Brooking	Hurst	Sissons	
	23/3	36,301	*9*	25			*Osgood 4*	*Bonetti*	*Harris*	*McCreadie*	*Boyle*	*Hinton*	*Hollins*	*Cooke*	*Tambling*	*Osgood*	*Birchenall*	*Houseman*	
							Ref: J Finney	Even though they are struggling, only two teams have scored more goals than West Ham. You would not have guessed it, from the way Ron Harris snuffed out Hurst. Hinton also kept Dear in his pocket. Alf Ramsey admired Osgood's sweet turn and shot. Ferguson dived over the top.											

No	V	Opponent	Att	Pos	Pts	Res	F-A	H-T	Scorers, Times, and Referees	1	2	3	4	5	6	7	8	9	10	11	12
32	H	ARSENAL		19		D	1-1	1-1	Brooking 13	Ferguson	Bonds	Lampard	Peters	Stephenson	Moore	Redknapp	Boyce	Brooking	Dear	Sissons	
	29/3		33,942	*11*	26				*Armstrong 3*	*Wilson*	*McNab*	*Storey*	*McLintock*	*Neill*	*Simpson*	*Radford*	*Gould*	*Graham*	*Court*	*Armstrong*	
									Ref: H Davey	Arsenal's ferocious tackling threatened a shortage of stretchers. Not to be intimidated, West Ham gave as good as they got in the second half. The Gunners' goal was a joke, Armstrong's cross squeezing past Ferguson, who was deceived by Graham's dummy. Lampard set up Brooking.											
33	H	NEWCASTLE		17		W	5-0	1-0	Brooking 25, 64, 75, Sissons 58, 89	Ferguson	Bonds	Lampard	Peters	Stephenson	Moore	Redknapp	Boyce	Brooking	Dear	Sissons	
	6/4		27,780	*7*	28					*Marshall*	*Burton*	*Clark*	*Iley*	*McNamee*	*Moncur*	*Sinclair*	*Scott*	*Davies*	*Robson B*	*Robson T*	
									Ref: T Dawes	On a sun-drenched pitch, high-flying Newcastle are put to the sword. The result is even more surprising as Hammers were without the injured Hurst. Marshall 'lost' Redknapp's free-kick and Brooking pounced. Sissons' header made it 2-0. Brooking's volley completed his hat-trick.											
34	H	NOTT'M FOREST		15		W	3-0	1-0	Sissons 4, Dear 46, 55	Ferguson	Bonds	Lampard	Peters	Stephenson	Moore	Redknapp	Boyce	Brooking	Dear	Sissons	
	12/4		36,589	*10*	30					*Williamson*	*Hindley*	*Winfield*	*Baxter**	*McKinlay*	*Newton*	*Lyons*	*Barnwell*	*Baker*	*Storey-Moore*	*Hall*	*Hilley*
									Ref: K Dagnall	A Good Friday thriller. Hurst was fit enough to be named substitute, which meant the strikers played out of their skins to stop him coming on. John Sissons played in the middle and volleyed in Brooking's cross. The third goal came when Williamson's goal-kick went straight to Dear.											
35	A	MANCHESTER C		15		L	0-3	0-1		Ferguson	Bonds	Lampard	Peters	Stephenson	Moore	Redknapp	Boyce	Brooking*	Dear	Hurst	Charles
	13/4		*38,754*	*3*	30				*Young 12, 58, Doyle 82*	*Mulhearn*	*Book*	*Pardoe*	*Kennedy*	*Heslop*	*Oakes*	*Lee*	*Doyle*	*Summerbee*	*Young*	*Coleman*	
									Ref: W Handley	Joe Mercer's City are third now, but will finish champions. Hurst only got his place back because John Sissons was conveniently injured. Tony Coleman's cross was turned in by Young, whose second goal was set up by a pass from Francis Lee, who was lying on his back at the time.											
36	A	NOTT'M FOREST				D	1-1	0-1	Peters 51	Ferguson	Bonds	Lampard	Peters	Stephenson	Moore	Redknapp	Boyce	Hurst	Dear	Sissons	
	16/4		*22,198*		31				*Baker 32*	*Williamson*	*Brindley*	*Winfield*	*Hindley*	*McKinlay*	*Newton*	*Lyons*	*Baxter*	*Baker*	*Storey-Moore*	*Hilley*	
									Ref: R Spittle	Baker's goal came totally against the run of play, when Lyons' cross somehow bypassed the whole West Ham defence. Peters levelled in a goal-mouth scramble following a corner. Williamson had a great game in goal for Forest. The recuperating Hurst managed to hit the crossbar.											
37	H	LIVERPOOL		15		W	1-0	1-0	Peters 40	Ferguson	Bonds	Lampard	Peters	Stephenson	Moore	Redknapp	Boyce	Dear	Hurst	Sissons	
	20/4		33,060	*4*	33					*Lawrence*	*Lawler*	*Hughes*	*Smith*	*Yeats*	*Wall*	*Callaghan*	*Hunt*	*Hateley**	*St John*	*Thompson*	*Livermore*
									Ref: P Bye	Alf Ramsey watches Moore and Peters at their best. Hurst's lack of fitness saw him play in midfield, but he still forced Tommy Lawrence to pull off the save of the match. Peters ran in on the blind side to head in Redknapp's cross. This defeat puts the nail in Liverpool's title hopes.											
38	H	SUNDERLAND		14		D	1-1	0-1	Dear 72	Ferguson	Bonds	Lampard	Brooking	Stephenson	Moore	Redknapp	Boyce	Dear	Hurst	Sissons	
	24/4		29,153	*17*	34				*Mulhall 10*	*Montgomery*	*Harvey*	*Ashurst*	*Hurley*	*Kinnell*	*Todd*	*Harris*	*Herd*	*Brand*	*Suggett*	*Mulhall*	
									Ref: I Jones	Ferguson stretched for Herd's cross, missed it, and Mulhall netted from three yards. White-shirted Sunderland then stood back and watched West Ham demonstrate their ability to miss chances by the dozen. Brian Dear glanced home the equaliser from Bobby Moore's corner-kick.											
39	A	SHEFFIELD UTD		11		W	2-1	1-0	Hurst 9, 74	Ferguson	Bonds	Lampard*	Peters	Stephenson	Moore	Redknapp	Boyce	Brooking	Hurst	Sissons	Dear
	27/4		*19,530*	*20*	36				*Reece 67*	*Hodgkinson*	*Badger*	*Shaw*	*Munks*	*Wagstaff*	*Barlow*	*Woodward*	*Carlin*	*Currie*	*Fenoughty*	*Reece*	
									Ref: E Jennings	Four minutes from time Frank Lampard emerges from a collision with Willie Carlin with a broken right leg. The crack could be heard all around the ground. The good news is that Hurst is back to form, volleying his first goal, hooking the second over Alan Hodgkinson's head.											
40	A	WEST BROM		12		L	1-3	1-2	Peters 3	Ferguson	Bonds	Charles	Peters	Cushley	Moore	Dear	Boyce	Brooking	Hurst	Sissons	
	1/5		*25,009*	*7*	36				*Astle 21, 29, 53*	*Osborne*	*Clark*	*Fairfax*	*Lovett*	*Talbut*	*Kaye*	*Rees*	*Collard*	*Astle*	*Hope*	*Hartford*	
									Ref: K Dagnall	The uncapped Jeff Astle scores his second hat-trick in three days. WBA's supporters don't like the fact that Hurst, who had a poor game, is the incumbent England No 9. Martin Peters' early header only served to light the touch-paper under Astle, whose first two goals were headers.											
41	H	COVENTRY		12		D	0-0	0-0		Ferguson	Bonds	Howe	Peters	Stephenson	Moore	Redknapp	Boyce	Dear	Hurst	Sissons	
	4/5		30,180	*19*	37					*Glazier*	*Bruck*	*Cattlin*	*Hill*	*Setters*	*Clements*	*Hannigan*	*Machin*	*Martin*	*Tudor*	*Carr*	
									Ref: W Gow	It's nip and tuck for Coventry down at the bottom. They man the barricades, determined only to keep West Ham out, and this point gained will ultimately keep them up. They might have won had they not wasted two early headers. At the death Ernie Machin hit the bar from 30 yards.											
42	H	EVERTON		12		D	1-1	0-1	Peters 63	Ferguson	Bonds	Howe	Peters	Stephenson	Moore	Redknapp	Boyce	Brooking	Dear	Sissons	
	11/5	Home	28,880 Away	*5*	38				*Husband 23*	*Barnett*	*Wright*	*Brown*	*Kendall*	*Kenyon*	*Harvey*	*Humphries*	*Husband*	*Young*	*Hurst*	*Morrissey*	
	Average	29,818	33,778						Ref: M Fussey	Everton, headed for the FA Cup final, leave out West, Ball, Royle, Labone, and Wilson. But West Ham showed few signs of superiority and Bonds has a stinker. Peters' volley, which went in off a defender, averted defeat. Had Hammers won they would have finished in the top half.											

League Cup			F-A	H-T	Scorers, Times, and Referees	1	2	3	4	5	6	7	8	9	10	11	12 sub used
2 A WALSALL	16	W	5-1	3-0	Brabrook 2, Peters 22, 83, Hurst 44p,	Standen	Charles	Kichener	Peters	Cushley	Moore	Redknapp	Boyce	Brabrook	Hurst	Sissons	
13/9 17,752	*3:7*				*Jackson 73p* [Evans 86 (og)]	*Ball*	*Gregg*	*Evans*	*Simpson*	*Bennett*	*Atthey*	*Middleton**	*Baker*	*Murray*	*McMorran*	*Taylor*	*Jackson*
					Ref: R Egan	Third Division Walsall had 12 shots to West Ham's four in the first half, but Hammers led 3-0. Both sides scored a penalty. Boyce fouled Baker for Walsall's; Evans tripped Peters from behind for West Ham's. The luckless Evans also put through his own goal. It wasn't his night.											
3 H BOLTON	17	W	4-1	3-1	Hurst 11, 14, 38p, 65	Ferguson	Bonds	Charles	Peters	Cushley	Moore	Redknapp	Boyce	Brabrook	Hurst	Sissons	
11/10 20,510	*2:12*				*Byrom 6*	*Hopkinson*	*Hatton*	*Farrimond*	*Ritson*	*Hulme*	*Greaves*	*Rimmer*	*Bromley*	*Byrom*	*Hill*	*Taylor*	
					Ref: G Roper	Hurst takes his tally in this competition over the past three years to 25. He was unmarked for his first two headers, extraordinarily generous of Bolton, who led after Gordon Taylor's shot came back off the bar. Handball on the line gave Hurst his hat-trick, admired by Alf Ramsey.											
4 A HUDDERSFIELD	18	L	0-2	0-1		Ferguson	Bonds	Charles	Peters	Cushley	Moore	Burkett	Boyce*	Brabrook	Hurst	Dear	Redknapp
1/11 17,729	*2:17*				*Worthington 2, Cattlin 70*	*Oldfield*	*Parkin*	*Cattlin*	*Nicholson*	*Ellam*	*Meagan*	*Hellawell*	*Dobson*	*Worthington*	*McGill*	*Hill*	
					Ref: Lyden	Lowly Second Division side Huddersfield expel Hammers from the League Cup. 19-year-old Frank Worthington couldn't believe his luck when Ferguson missed Cattlin's early cross. Ferguson was also at fault with Chris Cattlin's 25-yarder which many keepers would have saved.											

FA Cup																	
3 A BURNLEY	16	W	3-1	1-1	Dear 23, Peters 50, 55	Ferguson	Bonds	Lampard	Peters	Cushley	Moore	Dear	Boyce	Brooking	Hurst	Sissons	
27/1 *23,452*	*12*				*Casper 15*	*Thomson*	*Ternent*	*Latcham*	*O'Neil*	*Waldron*	*Merrington*	*Morgan*	*Lochhead*	*Casper*	*Bellamy**	*Coates*	*Irvine*
					Ref: K Howley	Burnley might have been more than one goal ahead by the time West Ham got going. Ferguson made save after save from shoot-on-sight full-back Latcham. The referee pulled a muscle in the opening seconds. Yet Latcham helped Peters' free-kick on its way to put West Ham in front.											
4 A STOKE	16	W	3-0	1-0	Sissons 2, 77, Hurst 86	Ferguson	Bonds	Lampard	Peters	Cushley	Moore	Dear	Bennett	Brooking	Hurst	Sissons	
17/2 *36,704*	*15*					*Banks*	*Skeels*	*Bloor*	*Allen*	*Elder*	*Mahoney**	*Dobing*	*Stevenson*	*Palmer*	*Vernon*	*Burrows*	*Eastham*
					Ref: J Carr	Alf Ramsey must have been impressed with Bonds, who rampaged down the right flank throughout the match. Sissons scored his first goal at the second attempt, after Banks had parried. Hurst was then brought down but drove the penalty against the bar. He atoned with a 30-yarder.											
5 H SHEFFIELD UTD	18	L	1-2	1-1	Dear 43	Ferguson	Bonds	Lampard	Peters	Cushley	Moore	Dear	Bennett	Brooking	Hurst	Sissons	
9/3 38,440	*19*				*Cliff 33, 84*	*Hodgkinson*	*Badger*	*Shaw*	*Munks*	*Mallender*	*Barlow*	*Cliff*	*Carlin*	*Hill*	*Wagstaff T*	*Reece*	
					Ref: L Hamer	Blades boss John Harris admits: 'We love playing West Ham'. The Hammers were so dire that Greenwood left his seat in the directors' box to come down to the dug-out. Moore found himself playing centre-forward. To no avail. Cliff scored No 1 with a long-range looping header.											

		Home					Away					
	P	W	D	L	F	A	W	D	L	F	A	Pts
1 Manchester C	42	17	2	2	52	16	9	4	8	34	27	58
2 Manchester U	42	15	2	4	49	21	9	6	6	40	34	56
3 Liverpool	42	17	2	2	51	17	5	9	7	20	23	55
4 Leeds	42	17	3	1	49	14	5	6	10	22	27	53
5 Everton	42	18	1	2	43	13	5	5	11	24	27	52
6 Chelsea	42	11	7	3	34	25	7	5	9	28	43	48
7 Tottenham	42	11	7	3	44	20	8	2	11	26	39	47
8 West Brom	42	12	4	5	45	25	5	8	8	30	37	46
9 Arsenal	42	12	6	3	37	23	5	4	12	23	33	44
10 Newcastle	42	12	7	2	38	20	1	8	12	16	47	41
11 Nott'm Forest	42	11	6	4	34	22	3	5	13	18	42	39
12 WEST HAM	42	8	5	8	43	30	6	5	10	30	39	38
13 Leicester	42	7	7	7	37	34	6	5	10	27	35	38
14 Burnley	42	12	7	2	38	16	2	3	16	26	55	38
15 Sunderland	42	8	7	6	28	28	5	4	12	23	33	37
16 Southampton	42	9	8	4	37	31	4	3	14	29	52	37
17 Wolves	42	10	4	7	45	36	4	4	13	21	39	36
18 Stoke	42	10	3	8	30	29	4	4	13	20	44	35
19 Sheffield Wed	42	6	10	5	32	24	5	2	14	19	39	34
20 Coventry	42	8	5	8	32	32	1	10	10	19	39	33
21 Sheffield Utd	42	7	4	10	25	31	4	6	11	24	39	32
22 Fulham	42	6	4	11	27	41	4	3	14	29	57	27
	924	244	111	107	850	548	107	111	244	548	850	924

Odds & ends

Double wins: (3) Fulham, Sheffield Utd, Leicester.
Double losses: (5) Sheff Wed, Man U, Man C, Stoke, WBA.

Won from behind: (7) Burnley (h), Sunderland (a), Leicester (h&a), Fulham (h), Bolton LC (h), Burnley FAC (a).
Lost from in front: (4) Sheff W (h), Stoke (h), WBA (h&a).

High spots: Five league wins out of six, December to February.
Beating Fulham 7-2.

Low spots: West Ham lost four times to the two Manchester clubs.
Following the 7-2 win over Fulham by failing to win any of their next five games
Losing in the FA Cup to Second Division Huddersfield.

West Ham did the double over Sheff Utd but lost to them in the FA Cup

Hammer of the Year: Bobby Moore.
Ever-presents: (0).
Hat-tricks: (3) Brian Dear, Trevor Brooking, Geoff Hurst..
Leading scorer: (25) Geoff Hurst.

	Appearances						Goals			
	Lge	*Sub*	LC	*Sub*	FAC	*Sub*	Lge	LC	FAC	Tot
Bennett, Peter	**2**	*1*			2					
Bonds, Billy	**37**		2		3		**1**			**1**
Bovington, Eddie	**6**									
Boyce, Ronnie	**38**		3		1					
Brabrook, Peter	**14**		3				**2**	1		**3**
Brooking, Trevor	**24**	*1*			3		**9**			**9**
Burkett, Jackie	**8**		1							
Charles, John	**19**	*1*	3							
Cushley, John	**27**		3		3					
Dear, Brian	**25**	*1*	1		3		**14**		2	**16**
Ferguson, Bobby	**39**		2		3					
Heffer, Paul	**1**									
Howe, Bobby	**2**									
Hurst, Geoff	**38**		3		3		**19**	5	1	**25**
Kitchener, Bill	**3**		1							
Lampard, Frank	**19**				3					
Moore, Bobby	**40**		3		3		**4**			**4**
Peters, Martin	**40**		3		3		**14**	2	2	**18**
Redknapp, Harry	**28**		2	*1*			**2**			**2**
Sissons, John	**37**		2		3		**8**		2	**10**
Standen, Jim	**3**		1							
Stephenson, Alan	**12**									
(own-goals)								*1*		**1**
22 players used	**462**	***4***	**33**	***1***	**33**		**73**	**9**	**7**	**89**

Tommy Taylor tussles with ex-Hammer Martin Peters and Martin Chivers in 1972-73

Keith Robson and QPR's Dave Clement take the plunge in season 1974-75

No	Date		Att	Pos	Pt	F-A	H-T	Scorers, Times, and Referees	1	2	3	4	5	6	7	8	9	10	11	12 sub used
1	A	NEWCASTLE			D	1-1	0-0	Dear 90	Ferguson	Bonds	Charles*	Peters	Stephenson	Moore	Redknapp	Boyce	Dear	Hurst	Brooking	Sissons
	10/8		*36,830*		1			*Robson 50*	*McFaul*	*Craig*	*Clark*	*Elliott*	*McNamee*	*Burton*	*Robson B*	*Bennett**	*Davies*	*Ross*	*Sinclair*	*Robson T*
								Ref: R Harper	There is great expectation attending the Hammers this season, but they have only won at Newcastle once in 36 attempts. Dave Elliott turned the ball back for Pop Robson to score. In injury-time Peters miscued Redknapp's low cross against a post and Brian Dear pounced on the rebound.											
2	A	STOKE			W	2-0	0-0	Peters 59, Sissons 86	Ferguson	Bonds	Charles	Peters	Stephenson	Moore	Redknapp	Boyce	Dear	Hurst	Sissons	
	14/8		*22,131*		3				*Banks*	*Skeels*	*Elder*	*Allen*	*Bloor*	*Stevenson*	*Conroy*	*Dobing*	*Herd*	*Eastham*	*Burrows*	
								Ref: L Callaghan	Two of Division 1's lightweights collide, and Stoke prove to be featherweights. Peters strolled through their defence to collect Sissons' shrewd pass. Sissons skated away on his own to seal the win, though David Herd narrowly missed two late chances. Bonds and Dobing were booked.											
3	H	NOTT'M FOREST		2	W	1-0	1-0	Hurst 13	Ferguson	Bonds	Charles	Peters	Stephenson	Moore	Redknapp	Boyce	Dear	Hurst	Sissons	
	17/8		31,114	*16*	5				*Williamson*	*Hindley*	*Winfield*	*Hennessey*	*McKinlay*	*Newton*	*Lyons*	*Richardson*	*Baker*	*Baxter*	*Moore*	
								Ref: T Lockett	West Ham opened with a roar, finished with a whimper. Johnny Carey's Forest could have been swept away by half-time, but lost to a messy goal. Peters' shot flew off Newton's leg onto the bar and rebounded to Hurst. Another Hurst shot hit the keeper in the face and k.o.'d him.											
4	H	EVERTON			L	**1-4**	0-1	Peters 51 *[Harvey 88]*	Ferguson	Bonds	Charles	Peters	Stephenson	Moore	Redknapp	Boyce	Dear*	Hurst	Sissons	Brooking
	19/8		34,895		5			*Husband 14, Royle 63, Ball 70,*	*West*	*Wright*	*Brown*	*Kendall*	*Labone*	*Harvey*	*Husband*	*Ball*	*Royle*	*Hurst*	*Morrissey*	
								Ref: I Jones	The Hammers would have gone top had they won. They looked good going forward but dreadful in defence. Every high cross spelled danger. Ferguson flapped at Morrissey's cross for the first goal. Peters' reply was erased by Royle's free header. The best goal was Colin Harvey's.											
5	A	COVENTRY		5	W	2-1	1-1	Peters 3, Brooking 58	Ferguson	Bonds	Charles	Peters	Stephenson	Moore	Redknapp	Boyce	Brooking	Hurst	Sissons	
	24/8		*33,716*	*22*	7			*Setters 32*	*Glazier*	*Bruck*	*Cattlin*	*Machin*	*Setters*	*Hill*	*Hannigan*	*Tudor*	*Baker*	*Gibson*	*Clements*	
								Ref: A Jones	Ex-Hammer Noel Cantwell's Coventry have still to earn their first point, but would have deserved one here. Peters' header from Redknapp's cross put West Ham in front. Maurice Setters then hit Hannigan's corner inside a post, but Boyce's through ball set up Brooking's winner.											
6	H	BURNLEY		1	W	5-0	4-0	Peters 18, Hurst 21, 31, Brooking 40, 58	Ferguson	Bonds	Charles	Peters	Stephenson	Moore	Redknapp	Boyce	Brooking	Hurst	Sissons*	**Cross**
	26/8		28,430	*12*	9				*Thomson*	*Smith*	*Latcham*	*O'Neil*	*Waldron*	*Bellamy*	*Coates*	*Lochhead*	*Casper*	*Kindon*	*Thomas*	
								Ref: E Wallace	West Ham go top amid a flurry of goals, controversy, and a slice of luck. This came at the end of the first half when the ref, having been hit on the head by the ball, was replaced by a linesman plucked from the crowd, who ignored Brooking being yards offside to permit the fourth goal.											
7	H	WEST BROM		3	W	4-0	1-0	Peters 19, 68, 80, Redknapp 77	Ferguson	Bonds	Charles	Peters	Stephenson	Moore	Redknapp	Boyce	Brooking	Hurst	Sissons	
	31/8		29,908	*14*	11				*Sheppard*	*Clarke*	*Williams*	*Lovett*	*Talbut*	*Kaye*	*Rees*	*Brown*	*Astle*	*Hope*	*Clark*	
								Ref: C Thomas	Martin Peters' hat-trick against the FA Cup-holders takes his tally to seven. Geoff Hurst also caught the eye, looking far more menacing than his England rival Jeff Astle. Hurst made the third goal, crossing for Redknapp, then rounded off the scoring by heading in Redknapp's centre.											
8	A	MANCHESTER U		3	D	1-1	0-0	Hurst 67	Ferguson	Bonds	Charles	Peters	Stephenson	Moore	Redknapp	Boyce	Brooking	Hurst	Sissons	
	7/9		***63,274***	*9*	12			*Law 59*	*Stepney*	*Dunne*	*Burns*	*Fitzpatrick*	*Foulkes*	*Stiles*	*Morgan*	*Sadler*	*Charlton*	*Law*	*Best*	
								Ref: E Jennings	West Ham laboured under a transparent inferiority complex for more than an hour. George Best chipped a gem of a pass to the far post where Law headed in, but Redknapp loaded the gun for the impressive Hurst's equaliser. Charlton, Law and Best were not at their best. Fortunately.											
9	H	TOTTENHAM		4	D	2-2	0-0	Peters 59, Hurst 61	Ferguson	Bonds	Charles	Peters	Stephenson	Moore	Redknapp	Boyce	Brooking	Hurst	Sissons	
	14/9		35,802	*12*	13			*Gilzean 62, Greaves 88*	*Jennings*	*Kinnear*	*Knowles*	*Mullery*	*England*	*Beal*	*Robertson*	*Greaves*	*Chivers*	*Venables*	*Gilzean*	
								Ref: M Fussey	Driving rain, quagmire pitch, insufferable Hammers arrogance as they stroll about playing out time before Mike England sends Greaves away to steal a point. Peters' volley and Hurst's cheeky lob had put West Ham firmly in charge, but Gilzean hit back within seconds with a header.											
10	A	CHELSEA		5	D	1-1	0-1	Peters 81	Ferguson	Bonds	Howe	Peters	Stephenson	Moore	Redknapp	Boyce	Brooking	Hurst	Sissons	
	21/9		*58,062*	*4*	14			*Tambling 2*	*Bonetti*	*Harris*	*McCreadie*	*Hollins*	*Webb*	*Boyle*	*Baldwin*	*Cooke*	*Osgood*	*Birchenall*	*Tambling*	
								Ref: N Burtenshaw	West Ham's pulling power lures an extra 10,000 to Chelsea's previous highest gate. Chelsea looked dangerous in breakaways, but otherwise stubbornly defended Tambling's early goal. Peters' header hits the bar and comes down over the line. Bonetti claws it out but the goal is given.											

No	Date	Opponent / Att	Pos	Res / Pts	F-A	H-T	Scorers, Times, Referees	1	2	3	4	5	6	7	8	9	10	11	subs used
11	H	SHEFFIELD WED	4	D	1-1	1-1		Ferguson	Bonds	Charles	Peters	Stephenson	Moore	Redknapp	Boyce	Brooking	Hurst	Sissons	
	28/9	31,182	*7*	15			*Witham 29*	*Springett*	*Young*	*Megson*	*Ellis*	*Mobley*	*Eustace*	*Witham*	*McCalliog*	*Warboys*	*Ford*	*Fantham*	
							Ref: D Counsell	The Owls did the double over West Ham last season and are becoming one of their bogey sides. The Hammers' run of draws continues even though they put Springett's goal under siege. Hurst's early header was cancelled by Witham, with Hammers' defenders appealing for offside.											
12	H	SOUTHAMPTON	6	D	0-0	0-0		Ferguson	Bonds	Charles	Peters	Stephenson	Moore	Redknapp	Boyce	Brooking	Hurst	Sissons	
	5/10	29,558	*14*	16				*Gurr*	*Kirkup*	*Hollywood**	*Kemp*	*McGrath*	*Gabriel*	*Payne*	*Channon*	*Davies*	*Fisher*	*Walker*	*Saul*
							Ref: V Batty	Saints have an unsavoury reputation for thuggery and are happy to pack eight players in defence. Denis Hollywood fouled everything that moved before limping off after 25 minutes. On the hour Saints broke away and Ron Davies hit the post. West Ham never came that close.											
13	A	BURNLEY		L	1-3	0-2	Brooking 60	Ferguson	Bonds	Charles	Peters	Stephenson	Moore	Redknapp	Boyce	Brooking*	Hurst	Sissons	Lindsay
	8/10	***13,869***		16			*Murray 8, Kindon 27, Dobson 59*	*Thomson*	*Smith*	*Latcham*	*Todd*	*Waldron*	*Blant*	*Thomas*	*Murray*	*Casper*	*Dobson*	*Kindon*	
							Ref: D Corbett	Injury-hit Burnley field their youngest ever side, including a debut for former rugby wing three-quarter Steve Kindon. Burnley's kids inflict a first away defeat on full-strength Hammers. John Murray's header was his first league goal. Kindon's burst of speed earned him a goal too.											
14	A	LEEDS	6	L	0-2	0-1		Ferguson	Bonds	Charles	Peters	Stephenson	Moore	Redknapp !	Boyce	Brooking	Hurst	Sissons	
	12/10	*40,786*	*1*	16			*Lorimer 13, Giles 62p*	*Sprake*	*Reaney*	*Cooper*	*Bremner*	*Charlton*	*Hunter*	*O'Grady*	*Giles*	*Jones*	*Madeley*	*Lorimer*	
							Ref: T Pallister	After 30 minutes Harry Redknapp lashes out at Bremner's shins in retaliation and becomes only the second Hammer to be sent off under Ron Greenwood's reign. Ferguson was still lining up the wall when the first goal flashed past him. Bremner's swallow dive earned Leeds a penalty.											
15	H	SUNDERLAND	6	W	**8-0**	4-0	Hurst 18, 34, 44, 48, 61, 71, [Moore 26, Brooking 62]	Ferguson	Bonds	Charles	Peters	Stephenson	Moore	Redknapp	Boyce	Brooking	Hurst	Sissons	
	19/10	**24,718**	*13*	18				*Montgomery*	*Irwin*	*Palmer*	*Hurley*	*Harvey*	*Porterfield*	*Herd*	*Harris*	*Brand*	*Suggett*	*Hughes*	
							Ref: K Burns	The season's lowest crowd witness Hammers' biggest win and Geoff Hurst's record-breaking feat of scoring a hat-trick in each half. The post-match atmosphere was soured by Hurst's frank admission that he had punched in his first goal with a left hook. Sunderland were not amused.											
16	A	ARSENAL	6	D	0-0	0-0		Ferguson	Bonds	Charles	Peters	Stephenson	Moore	Redknapp	Boyce	Brooking	Hurst	Sissons*	**Hartley**
	26/10	*59,533*	*4*	19				*Wilson*	*Storey*	*McNab*	*McLintock*	*Neill*	*Ure*	*Robertson*	*Radford*	*Graham*	*Simpson*	*Armstrong*	
							Ref: K Howley	This is the fourth successive draw between the sides, though had it been a boxing match Arsenal would have won on points. Arsenal won on corners 11-4. Long diagonal balls into the Hammers' box caused Ferguson no end of trouble. Twice his defenders had to clear off the line.											
17	H	QP RANGERS	6	W	4-3	3-1	Moore 30, Peters 39, Hurst 42, [Redknapp 69]	Ferguson	Bonds	Charles	Peters	Stephenson	Moore	Redknapp	Boyce	Brooking	Hurst	Hartley	
	2/11	36,008	*22*	21			*Bridges 19, Leach 56, 66*	*Springett*	*Watson*	*Harris*	*Keen*	*Hunt*	*Hazell*	*Bridges*	*Leach*	*Allen*	*Wilks*	*Morgan*	
							Ref: Finney	This was the right match to televise, since the other Division 1 matches produced only nine goals between them. QPR fought back gamely from 1-3 down but were sunk by Redknapp's volley, the best goal of the match. QPR veteran Les Allen was a constant thorn in Hammers' defence.											
18	A	WOLVES	7	L	0-2	0-2		Ferguson	Bonds	Charles	Peters	Stephenson	Moore	Redknapp	Boyce	Brooking	Hurst	Hartley	
	9/11	*29,704*	*15*	21			*Farrington 4, Bailey 14*	*Parkes*	*Parkin*	*Thomson*	*Bailey*	*Woodfield*	*Holsgrove*	*Farrington*	*Knowles*	*Dougan*	*Wilson*	*Wagstaffe*	
							Ref: F Nicholson	Hammers' England trio are exhausted after their midweek game in Romania, and none of their team-mates seem able to assume the baton of responsibility. John Farrington netted after Derek Dougan's shot rebounded off Ferguson, and Wolves' skipper Mike Bailey volleyed a second.											
19	H	LEICESTER	6	W	4-0	2-0	Woollett 20 (og), Dear 43, 89, Peters 64	Ferguson	Bonds	Charles	Cushley	Stephenson	Moore	Peters	Boyce	Dear	Hurst	Sissons	
	16/11	26,328	*20*	23				*Shilton*	*Potts*	*Woollett*	*Cross*	*Manley*	*Nish*	*Glover*	*Clarke*	*Lochhead**	*Fern*	*Hutchins*	*Sjoberg*
							Ref: T Dawes	Brian Dear celebrates his eighth anniversary as a West Ham pro by scoring twice on his recall. Dear has the Indian sign on 20-year-old Peter Shilton, having scored seven times against him in three matches. Woollett's own-goal from Geoff Hurst's cross opened the flood-gates.											
20	A	IPSWICH	5	D	2-2	2-0	Hurst 35, 43p	Ferguson	Bonds	Charles	Cushley	Stephenson	Moore	Peters	Boyce	Dear	Hurst	Sissons*	**Miller**
	23/11	*28,964*	*17*	24			*Morris 60, Viljoen 78*	*Hancock*	*Mills*	*Houghton*	*Morris*	*Baxter*	*Jefferson*	*Hegan*	*Viljoen*	*Crawford*	*O'Rourke*	*Brogan*	
							Ref: J Hunting5	Two days earlier Ipswich manager Bill McGarry resigned. West Ham looked razor sharp for an hour, but once Bobby Ferguson was beaten by Peter Morris's absurdly optimistic effort from 35 yards, they lost their nerve. Jefferson had fouled Hurst for the penalty, which looked harsh.											
21	H	MANCHESTER C	5	W	2-1	2-0	Hurst 3, Peters 15	Ferguson	Bonds	Charles	Cushley	Stephenson	Moore	Redknapp	Boyce	Dear	Hurst	Peters	
	30/11	33,082	*16*	26			*Lee 78p*	*Dowd*	*Pardoe*	*Mann*	*Doyle*	*Book*	*Oakes*	*Lee*	*Bell*	*Summerbee*	*Young*	*Connor*	
							Ref: W Gow	Another Jekyll and Hyde performance, so good early on, so bad once the pitch cut up badly. Peters and Hurst each crossed for the other to head a goal. Bonds fell on the ball and handled it. He was so incensed by the penalty decision that he belted the ball into the crowd and was booked.											

No	Date	Att	Pos	Pt	F-A	H-T	Scorers, Times, and Referees	1	2	3	4	5	6	7	8	9	10	11	12 sub used
22	A LIVERPOOL		5	L	0-2	0-1		Ferguson	Bonds	Charles	Cushley	Stephenson	Moore	Redknapp	Boyce	Dear	Hurst	Peters	
	7/12	*48,632*	*1*	26			*Hughes 45, Thompson 47*	*Lawrence*	*Lawler*	*Strong*	*Smith*	*Yeats*	*Hughes*	*Callaghan*	*Hunt*	*Evans*	*St John*	*Thompson*	
							Ref: W Handley	West Ham are the last London side to have won at Anfield, five years ago, and wasted early chances to have taken the lead this time. Seconds before half-time Emlyn Hughes drives through a forest of legs for his first goal of the season. West Ham are now 10 points adrift from the top.											
23	H LEEDS		5	D	1-1	0-1	Peters 88	Ferguson	Bonds	Charles	Cushley	Stephenson	Moore	Redknapp	Boyce	Dear	Hurst	Peters	
	14/12	**24,718**	*2*	27			*Gray 19*	*Sprake*	*Reaney*	*Madeley*	*Bremner*	*Charlton*	*Hunter*	*O'Grady*	*Lorimer*	*Jones*	*Giles*	*Gray*	
							Ref: P Walters	The pitch is icy and Leeds are at their cynical worst. When Cushley lost his footing, Eddie Gray took advantage to score. Hurst then chipped a free-kick over Sprake's head and Peters outjumped Charlton. Had not Brian Dear missed from a couple of yards, West Ham might have won.											
24	A SUNDERLAND		6	L	1-2	1-2	Hurst 27	Ferguson	Bonds	Charles	Cushley	Stephenson	Moore	Redknapp	Boyce	Hurst	**Lindsay**	Peters	
	21/12	*23,094*	*13*	27			*Palmer 6, Harris 13*	*Montgomery*	*Irwin*	*Harvey*	*Hurley*	*Todd*	*Palmer*	*Kerr*	*Harris*	*Hughes*	*Suggett*	*Mulhall**	*Porterfield*
							Ref: A Robinson	Jimmy Lindsay makes his debut as Sunderland take quick revenge for their 0-8 drubbing. Ferguson was partly at fault for both goals, first when Palmer scored at the second attempt from a free-kick, then when Hurley headed on to Harris. Montgomery blundered for West Ham's goal.											
25	A SOUTHAMPTON		6	D	2-2	1-0	Hurst 45p, 55	Ferguson	Bonds	Charles	Cushley	Stephenson	Moore	Redknapp	Boyce	Hurst	Lindsay	Peters	
	26/12	*27,465*	*11*	28			*Davies 49, 84*	*Gurr*	*Kirkup*	*Hollywood*	*Gabriel*	*McGrath*	*Kemp*	*Paine*	*Channon*	*Davies*	*Walker*	*Saul*	
							Ref: J Taylor	Yet again Hammers fail to cling on to a lead. In this case twice. On the stroke of half-time ex-Hammer Joe Kirkup felled Redknapp in the box. Walker's deep cross over Stephenson's head brought Ron Davies' 100th Saints goal. Paine's cross was bulleted in by Davies for the second.											
26	A QP RANGERS		6	D	1-1	1-1	Dear 36	Ferguson	Bonds	Charles*	Peters	Stephenson	Cushley	Redknapp	Lindsay	Brooking	Hurst	Dear	Boyce
	11/1	*28,645*	*22*	29			*Clarke 33*	*Spratley*	*Watson*	*Clement*	*Sibley*	*Hunt*	*Keetch*	*Morgan I*	*Leach*	*Clarke*	*Marsh*	*Morgan R*	
							Ref: H New	QPR are in deep relegation trouble, yet few Hammers fans want them to go down. The last 11 meetings have yielded 42 goals. Rodney Marsh returned to the QPR side and chipped audaciously onto the bar. Clarke turned in Roger Morgan's low cross and Dear headed in at the far post.											
27	A LEICESTER		6	D	1-1	0-0	Dear 57	Ferguson	Bonds	Charles	Peters	Stephenson	Moore	Redknapp	Lindsay	Brooking	Hurst	Dear	
	1/2	*31,002*	*19*	30			*Clarke 89*	*Shilton*	*Rodrigues*	*Nish*	*Roberts*	*Woollet*	*Cross*	*Fern*	*Gibson*	*Lochhead*	*Clarke*	*Glover*	
							Ref: F Cowen	West Ham have not won away in the league since August, though they were seconds away from doing so here. When Dear scored off a post it was his eighth goal in four matches against Leicester. But Allan Clarke eluded Moore for the only time to convert Lochhead's knock-down.											
28	H LIVERPOOL		7	D	1-1	1-0	Sissons 31	Ferguson	Bonds	Charles*	Peters	Stephenson	Moore	Redknapp	Lindsay	Brooking	Hurst	Sissons	Boyce
	22/2	36,498	*2*	31			*Hunt 51*	*Lawrence*	*Lawler*	*Strong*	*Smith*	*Yeats*	*Hughes*	*Callaghan*	*Hurst*	*Evans*	*St John*	*Thompson*	
							Ref: D Smith	Liverpool's heavyweight keeper Tommy Lawrence is much maligned. But he enjoys a distinguished match, keeping out everything West Ham throw at him apart from Sissons' goal, from Hurst's cross, and even getting his hand to that. Roger Hunt levelled from Callaghan's cross.											
29	H NEWCASTLE		5	W	3-1	2-0	Brooking 2, Peters 14, Hurst 72	Ferguson	Bonds	Howe	Peters	Stephenson	Moore	Redknapp	Boyce	Brooking	Hurst	Sissons	
	1/3	26,336	*15*	33			*Davies 70*	*McFaul*	*Craggs*	*Clark*	*Gibb*	*Burton*	*Moncur*	*Scott*	*Horsfield*	*Davies*	*Robson*	*Hindson*	
							Ref: M Fussey	West Ham must pick themselves up after the Cup debacle at Mansfield. Brooking turned Moncur to ease the nerves, and Peters' half-volley from Redknapp's cross had the crowd roaring. When Ron Davies floated over a 45-yard cross it sailed over Ferguson's head for a farcical goal.											
30	A NOTT'M FOREST		6	W	1-0	0-0	Hurst 71	Ferguson	Bonds	Howe	Peters	Stephenson	Moore	Redknapp	Boyce	Brooking	Hurst	Sissons	
	8/3	*24,303*	*19*	35				*Marshall*	*Hindley*	*Winfield*	*Hennessey*	*McKinlay*	*Newton*	*Lyons*	*Barnwell*	*Baker*	*Chapman*	*Rees*	
							Ref: P Baldwin	This is the weakest Forest side of recent years and they get off lightly. Three times West Ham hit the woodwork, though their winner had a touch of luck. Boyce's chip sent Hurst away, but he mis-hit his shot which bobbled in at the far post. West Ham's first double of the season.											
31	H COVENTRY		6	W	5-2	2-0	Sissons 2, Peters 12, Hurst 59p, 81p	Ferguson	Bonds	Howe	Peters	Stephenson	Moore	Redknapp	Boyce	Brooking	Hurst	Sissons	
	14/3	29,053	*21*	37			*Machin 47, Hunt 73* [Bonds 86]	*Glazier*	*Coop*	*Cattlin*	*Machin*	*Curtis*	*Blockley*	*Hannigan*	*Hunt*	*Martin*	*Carr*	*Clements*	
							Ref: R Johnson	Coventry played their part in this Friday night thriller and were not finally despatched till the final minutes. They got off to a bad start, Sissons' shot turned in by Curtis, and Peters' header going through Glazier's hands. Machin felled Sissons for one penalty, Coop handled for the other.											

No / Date	Venue	Opponent / Att			Score	HT	Scorers / Ref	1	2	3	4	5	6	7	8	9	10	11	Sub
32	H	IPSWICH	6	L	1-3	1-1	Hurst 29	Ferguson	Bonds	Howe	Peters	Stephenson	Moore	Redknapp	Boyce	Brooking	Hurst	Sissons	
21/3		32,574	*11*	37			*Woods 11, Wigg 47, O'Rourke 50* Ref: E Jennings	*Best*	*Mills*	*Houghton*	*Morris*	*McNeill*	*Jefferson*	*Hegan*	*Viljoen*	*Wigg*	*O'Rourke*	*Woods*	
								West Ham forced five corners in the first six minutes but were hit by three classic counter-attacks. Wigg nodded down for Woods to volley in before Hurst levelled with a glancing header. Wigg then brushed off Stephenson's challenge to restore the lead. Viljoen crossed for O'Rourke.											
33	H	WOLVES	6	W	3-1	1-0	Peters 32, 63, Brooking 55	Ferguson	Charles	Howe	Peters	Stephenson	Moore	Bonds	Boyce	Brooking	Hurst	Sissons	
24/3		25,221	*12*	39			*Wilson 80* Ref: C Nicholls	*Parkes*	*Taylor*	*Parkin*	*Bailey*	*Holsgrove*	*McAlle*	*Wilson*	*Knowles*	*Dougan*	*Seal*	*Farrington*	
								Wolves arrive at Upton Park with an unenviable reputation for uncompromising play. They concede 24 free-kicks, two of which produce goals. Peters headed the first from Moore's chipped free-kick. Keeper Parkes blundered for the second goal, spilling Brooking's volley over the line.											
34	H	MANCHESTER U	6	D	0-0	0-0		Ferguson	Charles	Howe	Peters	Stephenson	Moore	Bonds	Boyce	Brooking	Hurst	Sissons	
29/3		**41,546**	*11*	40			Ref: I Jones	*Stepney*	*Fitzpatrick*	*Dunne*	*Crerand*	*James*	*Stiles*	*Ryan*	*Kidd*	*Aston*	*Law*	*Best*	
								This was an all-action goalless draw under the eyes of England boss Alf Ramsey. Young Stephen James handled the experienced Hurst as well as anyone. A game of few fouls but plenty of injuries. Dunne fractured his jaw when colliding with Stephenson, and Crerand broke his nose.											
35	A	EVERTON	6	L	0-1	0-0		Ferguson	Howe	Charles	Peters	Stephenson	Moore	Redknapp	Bonds*	Boyce	Hurst	Sissons	Brooking
1/4		*37,212*	*4*	40			*Husband 51* Ref: G Kew	*West*	*Wright*	*Brown*	*Jackson*	*Labone*	*Harvey*	*Husband*	*Ball*	*Royle*	*Hurst*	*Morrissey*	
								Everton achieve their sixth double of the season. Both sides went into the match chasing a place in next season's Fairs Cup, but West Ham's chances have gone. West Ham played their usual 4-3-3 'away' formation, but it merely extended their winless run at Goodison to seven years.											
36	A	SHEFFIELD WED	6	D	1-1	1-1	Hurst 31	Ferguson	Bonds	Charles	Peters	Stephenson	Moore	Redknapp	Boyce	Brooking	Hurst	Sissons	
5/4		*24,268*	*14*	41			*Warboys 25* Ref: W Handley	*Springett*	*Smith*	*Megson*	*Eustace*	*Mobley*	*Young*	*Irvine*	*McCalliog*	*Ritchie*	*Warboys*	*Fantham*	
								The Owls favour the big welly, the ball living in the sky. For all that, they deserved to win this match. Moore handled unseen by the ref, and both Warboys and Eustace hit Ferguson's crossbar. Owls' forwards hadn't scored for 11 games. A local bus-strike kept down the attendance.											
37	H	STOKE	6	D	0-0	0-0		Ferguson	Howe	Charles	Peters	Stephenson	Moore	Redknapp	Bonds	Brooking	Hurst	Sissons	
8/4		26,577	*17*	42			Ref: T Reynolds	*Banks*	*Marsh*	*Pejic*	*Lacey*	*Smith*	*Stevenson*	*Eastham*	*Dobing*	*Herd*	*Vernon*	*Burrows*	
								Stoke have now not won in 19 away games. They created little themselves. Not that Gordon Banks was overstretched. He spent the 90 minutes watching West Ham's forwards shoot high, wide and handsome. Everyone lost count of the number of times Denis Smith fouled Geoff Hurst.											
38	H	CHELSEA	6	D	0-0	0-0		Ferguson	Bonds	Charles	Howe	Stephenson	Moore	Bennett	Boyce	Hurst	Peters	Sissons	
12/4		32,332	*5*	43			Ref: R Spittle	*Bonetti*	*Webb*	*McCreadie*	*Hollins*	*Dempsey*	*Osgood*	*Boyle**	*Birchenall*	*Hutchinson*	*Harris*	*Houseman*	*Tambling*
								A Fairs Cup place may still be open to the winners, but neither side can raise a sweat. Bobby Moore's 28th birthday brings West Ham's third successive home 0-0 draw. Chelsea erected an eight-man defence and Hurst wasted the best chance of the match, firing over from four yards.											
39	A	WEST BROM	6	L	1-3	0-0	Peters 80	Ferguson	Bonds	Charles	Howe	Stephenson	Moore	Redknapp	Boyce	Brooking	Hurst	Peters	
14/4		*20,092*	*13*	43			*Astle 65, 70, Brown 81* Ref: V James	*Osborne*	*Fraser*	*Williams*	*Brown*	*Talbut*	*Kaye*	*Martin*	*Lovett*	*Astle*	*Hope*	*Clark*	
								Ferguson gives away another bizarre goal, directing a goal-kick straight to Jeff Astle who put it away with Ferugson's arms raised in surrender. When Astle shortly headed in Hope's cross, the Hawthorns gave vent to a chorus of 'Geoff Hurst out, Astle in!' Alf Ramsey was in the stand.											
40	A	TOTTENHAM	7	L	0-1	0-0		**Grotier**	Bonds	Charles*	Howe	Stephenson	Moore	Redknapp	Boyce	Hurst	Peters	Sissons	Brooking
19/4		*50,970*	*8*	43			*Greaves 47* Ref: K Walker	*Jennings*	*Beal*	*Knowles*	*Mullery*	*England*	*Pratt*	*Johnson*	*Greaves*	*Gilzean*	*Pearce*	*Morgan*	
								Alan Gilzean's flick bounces off Bobby Moore's chest and Greaves pokes the ball through debutant Grotier's legs. Grotier let another shot rebound off his legs to Greaves, who frivolously shot over. This result means Spurs become the first London club to beat Hammers this season.											
41	H	ARSENAL	7	L	1-2	1-2	Sissons 15	Grotier	Bonds	Howe	Cushley	Stephenson	Moore	**Holland**	Brooking	Hurst	Peters	Sissons	
21/4		34,941	*3*	43			*Graham 30, Sammels 43* Ref: R Castle	*Wilson*	*Storey*	*McNab*	*McLintock*	*Simpson**	*Graham*	*Robertson*	*Sammels*	*Court*	*Radford*	*Armstrong*	*Gould*
								A frighteningly physical match which showed that West Ham, in the mood, need no lessons in thuggery. Sissons beat the stranded Wilson from 25 yards. Grotier got a hand to Graham's equaliser. Sammels chested down the ball to fire the winner. With the goal open, Brooking hit a post.											
42	A	MANCHESTER C	8	D	1-1	0-0	Peters 52	**Death**	Bonds	Lampard	Peters	Stephenson	Moore	Redknapp	Boyce	Brooking	Hurst	Sissons	
30/4		*31,846*	*13*	44			*Pardoe 66* Ref: J Finney	*Dowd*	*Book*	*Pardoe*	*Doyle*	*Booth*	*Oakes*	*Summerbee*	*Bell*	*Lee*	*Young*	*Coleman*	
Home / Average 30,991		Away / 34,971						West Ham applaud Man C onto the pitch with their FA Cup. Lampard plays his first game since breaking his leg last season. Stephenson kept ruffling Death's hair, presumably to give him encouragement. West Ham haven't won in nine games. A win would have lifted them to sixth.											

League Cup					F-A	H-T	Scorers, Times, and Referees	1	2	3	4	5	6	7	8	9	10	11	12 sub used
2	H	BOLTON	3	W	7-2	4-1	Hurst 4p, 28, 32, Peters 7, Sissons 69,	Ferguson	Bonds	Charles	Peters	Stephenson	Moore	Redknapp	Boyce	Brooking	Hurst	Sissons	
	4/9	24,937 *2:17*					*Wharton 40p, Taylor 78,* [Brooking 79]	*Hopkinson*	*Ritson*	*Farrimond*	*Williams*	*Hulme*	*Hatton*	*Wharton*	*Hill*	*Greaves*	*Bromley*	*Taylor*	
							Ref: R Spittle [Redknapp 89]	Hurst scored all four against Bolton in the League Cup last season. Now he adds three more. Bolton's caretaker boss Nat Lofthouse describes the Hammers as 'magnificent'. Hatton handled for Hurst's early penalty; Stephenson fouled Roy Greaves for Wharton's twice-taken spot-kick.											
3	H	COVENTRY	5	D	0-0	0-0		Ferguson	Bonds	Charles	Peters	Stephenson	Moore	Redknapp	Boyce	Brooking	Hurst	Sissons	
	25/9	27,594 *19*						*Glazier*	*Coop*	*Cattlin*	*Curtis*	*Setters*	*Hill*	*Hannigan*	*Machin*	*Hunt*	*Carr*	*Clements*	
							Ref: R Johnson	Coventry lined up with a defensive 4-2-4 in their quest for a draw. Bill Glazier was man of the match, if only for his save from Redknapp's half-volley. Bobby Moore lent his skills to the Hammers front line in the second half, but he too was thwarted by Glazier – three times.											
3R	A	COVENTRY	4	L	2-3	1-2	Hurst 45, Peters 86	Ferguson	Howe	Charles	Peters	Cushley	Moore	Redknapp	Boyce	Brooking	Hurst	Dear	
	1/10	*25,988 17*					*Hunt 43, Tudor 44, Clements 53*	*Glazier*	*Coop*	*Bruck*	*Machin*	*Curtis*	*Hill*	*Hunt*	*Carr*	*Tudor*	*Gibson**	*Clements*	*Hannigan*
							Ref: I Jones	A riotous end to the first half. Ernie Hunt shoves Charles in the back and scores in the confusion. Seconds later Tudor raced through to score an 'offside' goal. Hurst's instant volley set up a keen second half. Tudor hit a post and Clements turned the ball in. Coventry now meet Swindon.											

FA Cup																			
3	H	BRISTOL CITY	6	W	3-2	1-1	Peters 14, 65, Hurst 53	Ferguson	Bonds	Charles	Cushley	Stephenson	Moore	Redknapp	Boyce	Hurst	Lindsay	Peters	
	4/1	32,526 *2:20*					*Galley 10, Skirton 89*	*Gibson*	*Jacobs*	*Briggs*	*Wimshurst*	*Connor*	*Parr*	*Skirton*	*Garland*	*Galley*	*Kellard*	*Sharpe*	
							Ref: E Jennings	When Moore trotted out he belted a ball into the face of a trombonist in the band. City are 20th in Division 2, so put up more of a fight than they had a right to. Martin Peters equalised Galley's goal with a fierce downward header in a crowded box that went through a defender's legs.											
4	A	HUDDERSFIELD	6	W	2-0	0-0	Peters 51, Hurst 62	Ferguson	Heffer	Bonds	Peters	Stephenson	Moore	Redknapp	Lindsay	Brooking	Hurst	Boyce	
	25/1	*30,992 2:6*						*Poole*	*Smith*	*Hutt*	*Nicholson*	*Ellam*	*Cherry*	*Dobson*	*Lawson*	*Aimson*	*McGill*	*Hill*	
							Ref: D Corbett	The Hammers lost on this ground last year in the League Cup and Division 2 Huddersfield gave West Ham a first-half pounding. A sweet counter-attack climaxed with Hurst crossing low to Peters. Harry Redknapp then flighted West Ham's first corner of the match to Hurst.											
5	A	MANSFIELD	7	L	0-3	0-2		Ferguson	Bonds	Howe	Peters	Stephenson	Moore	Redknapp	Lindsay*	Brooking	Hurst	Sissons	Boyce
	26/2	*21,117 3:15*					*Roberts 23, Keeley 38, Sharkey 51*	*Hollins*	*Pate*	*Hopkinson*	*Quigley*	*Boam*	*Waller*	*Keeley*	*Sharkey*	*Ledger*	*Roberts*	*Goodfellow*	
							Ref: W Gow	Division 3 Mansfield enjoy the greatest night in their history. And yet West Ham could not have asked for better chances to come their way. But Redknapp and Hurst missed them, and Dudley Roberts netted neatly from Goodfellow's cross. Ray Keeley thumped in a volley for No 2.											

		Home					Away					
	P	W	D	L	F	A	W	D	L	F	A	Pts
1 Leeds	42	18	3	0	41	9	9	10	2	25	17	67
2 Liverpool	42	16	4	1	36	10	9	7	5	27	14	61
3 Everton	42	14	5	2	43	10	7	10	4	34	26	57
4 Arsenal	42	12	6	3	31	12	10	6	5	25	15	56
5 Chelsea	42	11	7	3	40	24	9	3	9	33	29	50
6 Tottenham	42	10	8	3	39	22	4	9	8	22	29	45
7 Southampton	42	13	5	3	41	21	3	8	10	16	27	45
8 WEST HAM	42	10	8	3	47	22	3	10	8	19	28	44
9 Newcastle	42	12	7	2	40	20	3	7	11	21	35	44
10 West Brom	42	11	7	3	43	26	5	4	12	21	41	43
11 Manchester U	42	13	5	3	38	18	2	7	12	19	35	42
12 Ipswich	42	10	4	7	32	26	5	7	9	27	34	41
13 Manchester C	42	13	6	2	49	20	2	4	15	15	35	40
14 Burnley	42	11	6	4	36	25	4	3	14	19	57	39
15 Sheffield Wed	42	7	9	5	27	26	3	7	11	14	28	36
16 Wolves	42	7	10	4	26	22	3	5	13	15	36	35
17 Sunderland	42	10	6	5	28	18	1	6	14	15	49	34
18 Nott'm Forest	42	6	6	9	17	22	4	7	10	28	35	33
19 Stoke	42	9	7	5	24	24	0	8	13	16	39	33
20 Coventry	42	8	6	7	32	22	2	5	14	14	42	31
21 Leicester	42	8	8	5	27	24	1	4	16	12	44	30
22 QP Rangers	42	4	7	10	20	33	0	3	18	19	62	18
	924	233	140	89	757	456	89	140	233	456	757	924

Odds & ends

Double wins: (2) Nott'm Forest, Coventry.
Double losses: (1) Everton.

Won from behind: (2) QPR (h), Bristol C FAC (h).
Lost from in front: (1) Arsenal (h).

High spots: A record league win, 8-0 over Sunderland.
Briefly going top of the league at the end of August.

Low spots: Losing to Third Division Mansfield in FA Cup.
Failing to win any of the last nine league games, dropping to 8th.

West Ham drew 5 games in a row, and later drew 4 games in a row.

Hammer of the Year: Geoff Hurst.
Ever-presents: (2) Martin Peters, Geoff Hurst.
Hat-tricks: (3) Geoff Hurst (2), Martin Peters (1).
Leading scorer: (31) Geoff Hurst.

	Appearances						Goals			
	Lge	*Sub*	LC	*Sub*	FAC	*Sub*	Lge	LC	FAC	Tot
Bennett, Peter	**1**									
Bonds, Billy	**42**		2		3		**1**			**1**
Boyce, Ronnie	**37**	*2*	3		2	*1*				
Brooking, Trevor	**29**	*3*	3		2		**7**	1		**8**
Charles, John	**35**		3		1					
Cross, Roger		*1*								
Cushley, John	**9**		1		1					
Dear, Brian	**11**		1				**5**			**5**
Death, Steve	**1**									
Ferguson, Bobby	**39**		3		3					
Grotier, Peter	**2**									
Hartley, Trevor	**2**	*1*								
Heffer, Paul					1					
Holland, Pat	**1**									
Howe, Bobby	**13**		1		1					
Hurst, Geoff	**42**		3		3		**25**	4	2	**31**
Lampard, Frank	**1**									
Lindsay, Jimmy	**5**	*1*			3					
Miller, Keith		*1*								
Moore, Bobby	**41**		3		3		**2**			**2**
Peters, Martin	**42**		3		3		**19**	2	3	**24**
Redknapp, Harry	**36**		3		3		**2**	1		**3**
Sissons, John	**31**	*1*	2		1		**4**	1		**5**
Stephenson, John	**42**		2		3					
(own-goals)							**1**			**1**
24 players used	**462**	***10***	**33**		**33**	***1***	**66**	**9**	**5**	**80**

No	Date	Att	Pos	Pt	F-A	H-T	Scorers, Times, and Referees	1	2	3	4	5	6	7	8	9	10	11	12 sub used
1	H NEWCASTLE			W	1-0	0-0	Hurst 67	Ferguson	Bonds	Charles	Peters	Stephenson	Moore	Redknapp	Boyce	Bennett	Hurst	Sissons	
	9/8	33,323		2				*McFaul*	*Craig**	*Clark*	*Gibb*	*Burton*	*Moncur*	*Sinclair*	*Robson*	*Davies*	*Arentoft,*	*Foggon*	*Duffy*
							Ref: L Callaghan	Newcastle have just won the Fairs Cup. Geoff Hurst conceded five free-kicks, the most of any player on the field, as he refused to bee reduced to a Geordie punch-bag. It was his 301st league game, played in high humidity, settled in West Ham's favour from Harry Redknapp's corner.											
2	H CHELSEA			W	2-0	0-0	Peters 65, Hurst 85	Ferguson	Bonds	Charles	Peters	Moore	Boyce	Redknapp	Lindsay	Bennett	Hurst	Sissons	
	11/8	39,003		4				*Bonetti*	*Harris*	*McCreadie*	*Hollins*	*Dempsey*	*Osgood*	*Cooke*	*Hinton*	*Hutchinson**	*Houseman*	*Tambling*	*Baldwin*
							Ref: J Finney	More crowd trouble, this time under a herringbone sky. On the pitch, Martin Peters snatches the ball off Peter Osgood for the first goal, then plays a one-two with Hurst to crash through the Chelsea defence like a tank for the second. Chelsea have now lost two games and six goals.											
3	A STOKE		11	L	1-2	1-1	Lindsay 29	Ferguson	Bonds	Charles	Peters	Moore	Boyce	Redknapp	Lindsay	Bennett	Hurst	Sissons	
	16/8	*23,361*	*8*	4			*Ritchie 37, Dobing 88*	*Banks*	*Marsh*	*Elder*	*Skeels*	*Smith*	*Allen*	*Conroy**	*Dobing*	*Ritchie*	*Greenhoff*	*Burrows*	*Eastham*
							Ref: I Jones	John Ritchie's power in the air gives Moore a testing time. Ritchie scored when the ball rebounded off Ferguson to his feet, then set up the winner with a cross that Dobing headed in. At the other end, Denis Smith had the measure of Geoff Hurst, leaving the Hammers lightweight.											
4	A CHELSEA		7	D	0-0	0-0		Ferguson	Bonds	Lampard	Peters	Moore	Boyce	Cross	Lindsay	Bennett	Hurst	Sissons	
	20/8	*43,347*	*15*	5				*Bonetti*	*McCreadie*	*Houston*	*Hollins*	*Dempsey*	*Hinton*	*Osgood*	*Tambling**	*Hutchinson*	*Houseman*	*Cooke*	*Birchenall*
							Ref: K Walker	Stamford Bridge's new floodlights are not yet securely mounted, and the beams dance giddily across the pitch. Chelsea ended the game with 11 walking wounded. Hinton had a strapped thigh, Hutchinson and Dempsey facial injuries. West Ham did nothing more than pump high crosses.											
5	H WEST BROM		10	L	1-3	1-2	Peters 44	Ferguson	Bonds	Charles	Peters	Stephenson	Moore	Lindsay	Boyce	Bennett	Hurst	Sissons	
	23/8	32,867	*12*	5			*Suggett 21, Brown 37, Krzywicki 83*	*Cumbes*	*Fraser*	*Williams*	*Brown*	*Talbut*	*Merrick*	*Hegan*	*Suggett*	*Krzywicki*	*Hughes*	*Hartford*	
							Ref: P Walters	This deplorable performance provoked a slow-handclap from the crowd. West Ham had opened brightly but got steadily worse. Alan Ashman's Albion went in front through Suggett's hook, from Kryzwicki's corner, then extended their lead when Brown raced through to beat Ferguson.											
6	H ARSENAL		10	D	1-1	1-0	Cross 10	Ferguson	Bonds	Lampard*	Peters	Stephenson	Moore	**Best**	Boyce	Brooking	Hurst	Cross	Howe
	25/8	39,590	*8*	6			*Lampard 52 (og)*	*Wilson*	*Storey*	*McNab*	*McLintock*	*Neill*	*Simpson*	*Robertson*	*George*	*Court*	*Graham*	*Radford*	
							Ref: G Hill	Bermudan Clyde Best makes his debut. Roger Cross headed in Bonds' free-kick, only for Lampard to turn George's cross into his own net. West Ham twice hit the bar, Arsenal once. At the start of the second half Arsenal's Court and Graham both emerged wearing No 9 shirts.											
7	A NOTT'M FOREST		13	L	0-1	0-0		Ferguson	Bonds	Lampard	Peters	Stephenson	Moore	Best	Boyce	Brooking	Hurst	Cross*	Miller
	30/8	*29,097*	*11*	6			*Hilley 75*	*Hill*	*Hindley*	*Winfield*	*Chapman*	*Hennessey*	*Newton*	*Rees*	*Lyons*	*Hilley*	*Barnwell*	*Moore*	
							Ref: W Gow	The City Ground's main stand was destroyed by fire last year. West Ham sacrificed flair in order to try to secure a 0-0 draw against Matt Gillies' Forest, but Hilley netted from Storey-Moore's centre. The home crowd sang 'Saved by the bell' as they trooped away at the end.											
8	H TOTTENHAM		17	L	0-1	0-0		Ferguson	Bonds	Lampard	Howe	Stephenson	Moore	Best*	Peters	Brooking	Hurst	Sissons	Boyce
	6/9	40,561	*4*	6			*Pearce 75*	*Jennings*	*Beal*	*Knowles*	*Mullery**	*England*	*Collins*	*Pearce*	*Greaves*	*Gilzean*	*Pratt*	*Morgan*	*Want*
							Ref: D Smith	Few observers could genuinely say Spurs were the better side, but West Ham's defence stood staring at a linesman as Pearce sprinted through to score. Though the flag went up, the referee ignored it. Clyde Best limped off after 33 minutes and Spurs Alan Mullery was carried off.											
9	A EVERTON		20	L	0-2	0-0		Ferguson	Bonds	Lampard	Peters	Stephenson	Moore	Howe	Boyce	Brooking	Hurst	Cross	
	13/9	*49,052*	*3*	6			*Ball 73, Husband 77*	*West*	*Wright*	*Brown*	*Kendall*	*Labone*	*Harvey*	*Husband*	*Ball*	*Royle*	*Hurst*	*Morrissey*	
							Ref: W Gow	With Brian Labone having the upper hand over Hurst, this game was largely one-way traffic. West saved superbly from Roger Cross's header, but Hammers were defending in numbers when Ball snapped up Kendall's miscued shot. Husband scored when Ferguson parried from Wright.											
10	H SHEFFIELD WED		15	W	3-0	1-0	Redknapp 7, Branfoot 62 (og), Hurst 67	Ferguson	Bonds	Lampard	Boyce	Stephenson	Moore	Redknapp	Brooking	Hurst	Cross	Peters	
	20/9	23,487	*20*	8				*Wicks*	*Smith*	*Megson*	*young*	*Ellis*	*Craig*	*Branfoot*	*Pugh*	*Prendergast*	*Ford*	*Fantham**	*Prophett*
							Ref: T Dawes	West Ham's incessant barrage of attacks would have deflated better teams than Wednesday, who played in a strange strip of orange shirts and blue shorts. Redknapp scored off a post, then Branfoot inadvertently steered Hurst's cross past his own keeper. Hurst's header rounded it off.											

No	Venue / Date	Opponent / Att	Pos	Res / Pts	FT	HT	Scorers, Times, and Referees	1	2	3	4	5	6	7	8	9	10	11	12 sub used
11	A	MANCHESTER U	17	L	2-5	1-2	Hurst 25, 77 *[Kidd 85]*	Ferguson	Bonds	Lampard	Howe	Stephenson	Moore	Redknapp	Lindsay	Best	Hurst	Peters	
	27/9	***58,579***	*8*	8			*Burns 5, Best 12, 83, Charlton 66,*	*Stepney*	*Fitzpatrick*	*Dunne*	*Burns*	*Ure*	*Sadler*	*Morgan*	*Kidd*	*Charlton*	*Aston*	*Best*	
							Ref: R Tinkler	Greenwood: 'With one or two reservations, that's the best we have played all season.' Only in the closing minutes did the score look one-sided. Clyde Best constantly beat Ian Ure. Pick of the goals was Best's solo run and cross onto Hurst's head. Peters has gone on the transfer list.											
12	H	BURNLEY	15	W	3-1	2-0	Best 12, 15, Brooking 64	Ferguson	Bonds	Lampard	Howe	Stephenson	Moore	Redknapp	Lindsay	Brooking	Hurst*	Best	Sissons
	4/10	26,445	*20*	10			*Kindon 80*	*Mellor*	*Angus*	*Latcham*	*O'Neil*	*Merrington*	*Todd*	*Thomas*	*Coates*	*Casper*	*Dobson*	*Kindon*	
							Ref: D Corbett	This is the first time since the 1966 World Cup final that both Hurst and Peters have been missing together. Mind you, West Ham were leading 2-0 when Hurst went off after 74 minutes with back trouble, having set up both Best goals. Brooking took unsettled Peters' role in midfield.											
13	H	STOKE	15	D	3-3	3-0	Best 3, Brooking 11, Sissons 20	Ferguson	Bonds	Lampard*	Howe	Stephenson	Boyce	Redknapp	Lindsay	Brooking	Sissons	Best	Cross
	6/10	26,860	*5*	11			*Smith 67, 87, Burrows 83*	*Banks*	*Marsh*	*Pejic*	*Skeels*	*Smith*	*Bloor*	*Conroy**	*Dobing*	*Ritchie*	*Eastham*	*Burrows*	*Herd*
							Ref: R Spittle	All three World Cup stars are missing as West Ham stage an astonishing collapse. 3-0 up after 20 minutes, they are still 3-0 up after 66. Then Smith heads in Eastham's corner. At 3-3 Burrows hit the bar. What is more, the limping, thigh-strained Gordon Banks couldn't take goal-kicks.											
14	A	COVENTRY	15	D	2-2	1-1	Brooking 30, Sissons 46	Ferguson	Bonds	Lampard	Howe	Stephenson	Moore	Redknapp	Lindsay	Brooking	Sissons	Best	
	11/10	*34,277*	*6*	12			*Joicey 31, Clements 54*	*Glazier*	*Coop*	*Bruck*	*Setters**	*Curtis*	*Blockley*	*Hunt*	*Joicey*	*Martin*	*Carr*	*Clements*	*Mortimer*
							Ref: H New	Although twice in front, West Ham are left still searching for their first away win. At one point, Best stood nonchalantly by the ball at the corner-flag, like Mohammed Ali, daring opponents to come and get it. Coventry's Brian Joicey, on his debut, had a goal ruled out for offside.											
15	A	WOLVES	16	L	0-1	0-0		Ferguson	Bonds	Lampard	Howe*	Stephenson	Moore	Redknapp	Lindsay	Brooking	Sissons	Best	Hurst
	18/10	*28,762*	*4*	12			*McCalliog 81*	*Parkes*	*Taylor*	*Parkin*	*Wilson*	*Holsgrove*	*Munro*	*McCalliog*	*O'Grady*	*Dougan*	*Curran*	*Wagstaffe*	
							Ref: G Kew	Jim McCalliog's goal was late but not undeserved for Wolves, for whom Hugh Curran twice had 'goals' disallowed. A 15th-minute injury to Bobby Howe allowed Hurst to return to the side in the unfamiliar role of substitute. Best and Redknapp's pairing up front was unproductive.											
16	H	SUNDERLAND	16	D	1-1	1-0	Peters 19	Ferguson	Bonds	Lampard	Howe	Stephenson	Moore	Redknapp	Peters	Brooking	Hurst	Best	
	25/10	29,171	*22*	13			*Hughes 47*	*Montgomery*	*Irwin*	*Ashurst*	*Todd*	*Heslop*	*McGiven*	*Park*	*Hughes*	*Baker*	*Kerr*	*Tueart*	
							Ref: M Fussey	Transfer-seeking Martin Peters returns to the side, controls Moore's lob and slides the ball past Jim Montgomery. Geoff Hurst misses three sitters, one of them from five yards when he balloons over. Moore is regularly caught in possession and is at fault for Sunderland's equaliser.											
17	A	SOUTHAMPTON	16	D	1-1	1-0	Brooking 32	Ferguson	Bonds	Lampard	Howe	Stephenson	Moore	Best	Peters	Brooking	Hurst	Sissons	
	1/11	*26,894*	*20*	14			*Channon 82*	*Martin*	*Kirkup*	*Hollywood*	*Kemp*	*McGrath*	*Gabriel**	*Paine*	*Channon*	*Davies*	*Walker*	*Sydenham*	*Byrne*
							Ref: C Thomas	Lampard retaliates at Terry Paine, and his third booking of the season means he will face an FA disciplinary enquiry. West Ham faded after a bright start and increasingly relied on Alan Stephenson to keep out energetic Saints. Twice in the closing minutes Saints might have clinched it.											
18	H	CRYS PALACE	14	W	2-1	2-0	Best 10, Hurst 26	Ferguson	Bonds	Lampard	Howe	Stephenson	Moore	Redknapp	Peters	Brooking	Hurst	Best	
	8/11	31,515	*18*	16			*Bonds 83 (og)*	*Jackson*	*Loughlan*	*Blyth*	*Payne*	*McCormick*	*Hynd*	*Kember*	*Taylor*	*Hoy*	*Queen*	*Dawkins*	
							Ref: K Walker	On the balance of play, Bert Head's Palace should have lost by five or six goals. Instead, West Ham are almost made to pay for their strolling arrogance. Hurst, Peters and Best might each have claimed a hat-trick. Despite having just one forward, Palace are pressing strongly at the end.											
19	A	LIVERPOOL	14	L	0-2	0-1		Ferguson	Bonds	Lampard	Howe	Stephenson	Moore	Redknapp	Boyce	Brooking	Hurst	Best	
	15/11	*39,668*	*3*	16			*Lawler 28, Graham 89*	*Lawrence*	*Lawler*	*Strong*	*Smith*	*Yeats*	*Hughes*	*Callaghan*	*Peplow**	*Graham*	*St. John*	*Thompson*	*Hunt*
							Ref: B Lyden	When Peters flew back to attend to his sick baby, 18-year-old Bobby Sutton was named as sub. His mother works in the canteen at Upton Park. Sutton left his boots behind and in any case was considered too risky to play, so Billy Bonds, injured at the start had to play on despite his pain.											
20	H	DERBY	14	W	3-0	1-0	Hurst 20, 70, Peters 57	Ferguson	Bonds	Lampard	Howe	Stephenson	Moore	Redknapp	Peters	Brooking	Hurst	Best	
	22/11	32,485	*6*	18				Green	Webster	Robson*	Durban	McFarland	Mackay	McGovern	Carlin	O'Hare	Hector	Hinton	Stewart
							Ref: E Jennings	Derby made the mistake of allowing West Ham to play football. Only stalwart Dave Mackay looked in the mood to resist, as Redknapp and Brooking took control. Full-backs Bonds and Lampard enjoyed the luxury of pushing up to join the attack. On this form, West Ham look great.											
21	A	IPSWICH	15	L	0-1	0-0		Ferguson	Bonds	Lampard	Howe	Stephenson	Moore	Redknapp	Peters	Brooking	Hurst	Best	
	29/11	*17,456*	*18*	18			*Mills 64*	*Best*	*Carroll*	*Mills*	*Morris*	*Baxter*	*McNeil*	*Woods*	*Collard*	*Hill*	*Viljoen*	*Lambert*	
							Ref: E Wallace	It was so cold that several Hammers sported gloves. Having squandered chance after chance, West Ham are beaten by a sucker punch out of the blue. Mick Mills' well-directed shot caught Ferguson flat-footed. Clyde Best seldom got involved and Peters was twice just off target.											

No Date	Att	Pos	Pt	F-A	H-T	Scorers, Times, and Referees	1	2	3	4	5	6	7	8	9	10	11	12 sub used
22 H MANCHESTER C		16	L	0-4	0-1		Ferguson	Bonds	Lampard	Howe	Stephenson	Moore	Redknapp	Peters	Brooking	Hurst	Best	
6/12	27,491	4	18			Lee 10, Bowyer 63, 75, Doyle 87	Corrigan	Book	Pardoe	Doyle	Booth	Oakes	Summerbee	Bell	Lee	Young*	Bowyer	Connor
						Ref: M Kerkhof	Alf Ramsey watches as all three of his England Hammers have stinkers. West Ham are run off their feet by Francis Lee and Colin Bell. Poor Bobby Ferguson was at fault to some extent with all four City goals. Whenever Hammers attacked, City packed their goalmouth to good effect.											
23 H EVERTON		17	L	0-1	0-1		Ferguson	Bonds	Lampard	Howe	Stephenson*	Moore	Sissons	Peters	Boyce	Hurst	Best	Brooking
13/12	26,689	1	18			Whittle 29	West	Wright*	Brown	Kendall	Labone	Jackson	Whittle	Ball	Royle	Hurst	Morrissey	D'arcy
						Ref: A Oliver	Harry Catterick's Everton top the league but West Ham were hard done by. They had 21 direct shots at goal, twice hit the inside of a post, and had two penalty claims turned down. Bobby Moore's blunder let in Alan Whittle. Royle whacked Stephenson so hard that he was hospitalised.											
24 A LEEDS		17	L	**1-4**	0-2	Hurst 82	Ferguson	Bonds	Lampard	Howe	Peters	Boyce	Redknapp	Bennett	Brooking	Hurst	Sissons	
17/12	30,659	1	18			Lorimer 29, 39, Clarke 50, Giles 73	Sprake	Reaney	Cooper	Bremner	Charlton	Hunter*	Lorimer	Clarke	Jones	Giles	Madeley	Yorath
						Ref: A Jones	Leeds go top, and look far superior to Everton, who they overtake. Moore is missing with a knee injury. Peter Lorimer scored the first goal from Giles' low cross and the second when Terry Cooper's cross was deflected to him. As well as the goals, Leeds hit the wood three times.											
25 A TOTTENHAM		15	W	2-0	2-0	Hurst 12, Peters 14	Ferguson	Bonds	Lampard	Howe	Moore	Boyce	Redknapp	Peters	Brooking	Hurst	Sissons	
20/12	23,375	14	20				Jennings	Kinnear	Knowles	Mullery	Beal	Evans	Johnson	Greaves	Pearce	Perryman	Morgan	
						Ref: L Callaghan	West Ham's first away win in nine months is so clear-cut that Spurs fans stream away long before the end. Moore's frailty in the air was often exposed. Spurs' last chance came with a penalty which Jimmy Greaves side-footed wide. Greaves was often caught in possession by Howe.											
26 A WEST BROM		16	L	1-3	1-1	Peters 33	Ferguson	Bonds	Lampard	Howe	Moore	Boyce	Redknapp	Hurst	Bennett	Sissons	Peters	
26/12	32,867	15	20			Suggett 19, 50, Astle 80	Osborne	Fraser	Wilson	Brown	Potter	Kaye	Martin	Suggett	Astle	Hartford	Hope*	Hughes
						Ref: J Finney	Two mistakes by Bobby Ferguson cost West Ham two goals and the match. He drops Asa Hartford's corner for the first goal, and mis-punches a ball he should have held for the third. In the second half Jeff Astle twice brushed off Bobby Moore's presence to head against the crossbar.											
27 H NOTT'M FOREST		16	D	1-1	1-0	Bonds 28	Ferguson	Bonds	Lampard	Howe	Moore	Boyce	Redknapp	Peters	Hurst	Brooking*	Best	Bennett
27/12	31,829	13	21			Moore 80	Hill	Hindley	Winfield	Chapman	O'Kane	Newton	Rees	Lyons*	Hilley	Richardson	Moore	McCaffrey
						Ref: R Johnson	Bobby Moore's 387th appearance is a post-war West Ham record. His team should have sealed the points in the first half, but Geoff Hurst's incredible misses and Redknapp's terrible crosses keep Forest alive. Ian Storey-Moore led the fightback which nearly resulted in a Forest win.											
28 A SHEFFIELD WED		16	W	3-2	1-0	Peters 26, 46, Hurst 61p	Ferguson	Bonds	Howe	Peters	Stephenson	Moore	Holland	Lindsay	Hurst	**Eustace**	Best	
10/1	28,135	22	23			Craig 51, Prophett 73	Springett	Wilcockson	Megson	Pugh	Prophett	Craig	Sinclair	Whitham*	Downes	Smith	Coleman	Warboys
						Ref: D Smith	Peter Eustace has signed from Sheffield Wednesday for £90,000 but has an inconspicuous debut. Owls' Peter Springett is to blame for two goals, though not for Hurst's ballistic penalty. Yet again a match that Hammers should have won comfortably has them hanging on desperately.											
29 H MANCHESTER U		16	D	0-0	0-0		Ferguson	Bonds	Howe	Peters	Stephenson	Moore	Holland	Lindsay	Hurst	Eustace	Best	
17/1	**41,643**	8	24				Rimmer	Edwards	Burns	Crerand	Ure	Sadler	Morgan	Sartori	Charlton	Kidd	Aston	
						Ref: W Gow	Man U are without the suspended George Best, so only one Best takes the field. This was an eventful goalless draw, with chances at either end. Peters' header is hooked off the line, while two solo runs by Brian Kidd end up with wayward shots. 19-year-old Pat Holland performs well.											
30 A BURNLEY		16	L	2-3	0-2	Eustace 50, Lindsay 84	Ferguson	Bonds	Howe	Peters	Stephenson	Moore	Holland*	Lindsay	Hurst	Eustace	Best	Heffer
31/1	**14,454**	17	24			Thomas 24, Kindon 43, Coates 73	Mellor	Angus	Thomson	Merrington	Dobson	O'Neil	Thomas	Coates	Casper	Wilson	Kindon	
						Ref: J Taylor	With West Ham knocked out of the FA Cup by Middlesbrough at the first hurdle, Ron Greenwood remodels his side. Though Eustace plays his best game yet, two first-first blunders by Ferguson prove fatal. This result leaves the Hammers just seven points clear of the relegation places.											
31 H COVENTRY		17	L	1-2	1-1	Hurst 10p	Grotier	Bonds	Howe	Peters	Stephenson	Moore	Brooking	Lindsay	Eustace	Hurst	Best	
11/2	22,723	4	24			Martin 23, 52	Glazier	Coop	Cattlin	Hunt	Barry	Clements*	Hannigan	Carr	Martin	O'Rourke	Mortimer	Hill
						Ref: G Hartley	West Ham have drawn 1-1 with Slovan Bratislava in a friendly. Hurst's penalty is his 154th league goal, a post-war Hammers record. But Noel Cantwell's side go fourth with two goals from Martin – the second a strong header. Upton Park echoes to the sound of slow hand-clapping.											

No	Venue/Date	Opponent/Att	Pos	Res	F-A	H-T	Scorers, Times, and Referees	1	2	3	4	5	6	7	8	9	10	11	12
32	A	SUNDERLAND	17	W	1-0	1-0	Hurst 43	Grotier	Bonds	Howe	Peters	Stephenson	Moore	Redknapp	Lindsay	Hurst	Eustace	Sissons	
	21/2	*16,900*	*22*	26				*Montgomery*	*Irwin*	*Ashurts*	*Todd*	*Heslop*	*McGiven*	*Tueart*	*Park*	*Baker**	*Harris*	*Hughes*	*Kerr*
							Ref: K Burns	Clyde Best has been dropped, but recalled wingers Redknapp and Sissons achieved little. Sunderland look dire, good bets for relegation. Jimmy Lindsay missed two good chances and a hat-trick was there for the taking for Peters. Moore was superb and Eustace purposeful and aggressive.											
33	H	SOUTHAMPTON	17	D	0-0	0-0		Grotier	Bonds	Howe	Peters	Stephenson	Moore	Redknapp	Lindsay	Hurst	Eustace	Sissons	
	28/2	27,088	*18*	27				*Martin*	*Kirkup*	*Byrne*	*Fisher*	*McGrath*	*Gabriel*	*Paine*	*Channon*	*Davies*	*Walker*	*Jenkins*	
							Ref: G Lyden	Banners are waved proclaiming 'Greenwood Out!' Feguson and Boyce have already been axed, but on the evidence of this match more heads need to roll. West Ham failed to create a single opening. Saints' half-fit Ron Davies hit the bar and Channon forced a great save from Grotier.											
34	A	NEWCASTLE	17	L	1-4	1-2	Eustace 28 *[Foggon 81]*	Grotier	Bonds	Howe	Peters	Stephenson	Moore	Redknapp	Lindsay	Hurst	Eustace	Sissons	
	2/3	*27,500*	*10*	27			*Davies 8, Robson 40, Dyson 74,*	*McFaul*	*Craig*	*Craggs*	*Gibb*	*McNamee*	*Moncur*	*Robson*	*Smith*	*Davies*	*Foggon*	*Dyson*	
							Ref: W Castle	West Ham are outfought and out-thought by the Fairs Cup holders. Under the eyes of Alf Ramsey, Wyn Davies out-jumps Stephenson for the first goal, but Eustace's volley squares it. Robson stabbed a low drive inside a post before Robson and Smith combined for Dyson's clincher.											
35	A	DERBY	17	L	0-3	0-0		Grotier	Bonds	Lampard	Cushley	Stephenson	Moore	Best	Peters	Hurst	Eustace	Howe	
	7/3	*35,615*	*4*	27			*Durban 58, Hinton 78p, O'Hare 84*	*Green*	*Webster*	*Robson*	*Hennessey*	*McFarland*	*Mackay*	*Durban*	*Carlin*	*O'Hare*	*Hector*	*Hinton*	
							Ref: V Batty	This result was harsh on West Ham. Martin Peters had a goal disallowed and Clyde Best sliced a chance wide from 10 yards. Derby's second goal, a penalty, was dubious, but the Hammers are so short on confidence that they fell away in the final stages. Seven goals lost in two games.											
36	H	IPSWICH	17	D	0-0	0-0		Grotier	Bonds	Lampard	Cushley	Stephenson	Moore	Best*	Peters	Hurst	Eustace	Howe	Boyce
	14/3	**20,934**	*20*	28				*Best*	*Carroll*	*Harper*	*Morris*	*Baxter*	*Jefferson*	*Woods*	*Collard*	*Whymark*	*Mills*	*Lambert*	
							Ref: R Kirkpatrick	An inept performance against an Ipswich side who look even worse. Keeper David Best hurt an arm in the opening stages but was not put under serious pressure. Best miskicked in front of an open goal. Near the end Lambert chipped onto the bar and Whymark hit the side-netting.											
37	A	MANCHESTER C	17	W	**5-1**	3-1	Greaves 10, 37, Hurst 45, 88, Boyce 83	Grotier	Bonds	Lampard	Boyce	Stephenson	Moore	Holland	Eustace*	Hurst	**Greaves**	Howe	**Llewellyn**
	21/3	*28,353*	*11*	30			*Lee 13*	*Corrigan*	*Book*	*Mann*	*Doyle*	*Booth*	*Oakes*	*Towers*	*Lee*	*Bowyer*	*Young*	*Pardoe*	
							Ref: P Baldwin	Peters has signed for Spurs and Jimmy Greaves for West Ham for £200,000. City were without Bell and Summerbee but had few excuses by the end. Greaves supplied two ice-cool finishes and Ronnie Boyce thumped a huge shot past Corrigan from somewhere near the centre-circle.											
38	A	CRYS PALACE	17	D	0-0	0-0		Grotier	Bonds	Lampard	Boyce*	Stephenson	Moore	Holland	Bennett	Hurst	Greaves	Howe	Llewellyn
	24/3	*34,801*	*21*	31				*Jackson J*	*Sewell*	*Hoadley*	*Payne*	*McCormick*	*Blyth*	*Scott*	*Kember*	*Hoy*	*Queen*	*Taylor*	
							Ref: R Nicholson	Palace fight ruthlesssly for every ball in an effort to stave off relegation. They are Greaves' bogey team, for he played them four times while with Spurs without scoring. Boyce went off after colliding with Kember. Palace came nearest to a goal when Payne clipped the top of the bar.											
39	H	LIVERPOOL	17	W	1-0	1-0	Holland 14	Grotier	Bonds	Lampard	Bennett	Stephenson	Moore	Holland	Eustace	Hurst	Greaves	Howe	
	28/3	38,239	*5*	33				*Clemence*	*Lawler*	*Evans R*	*Smith*	*Lloyd*	*Hughes*	*Thompson*	*Livermore*	*Evans A*	*Callaghan*	*Graham*	
							Ref: R Tinkler	Greaves' home debut pulls in a huge crowd for this otherwise meaningless end-of-season fixture. For their part, Liverpool field a team of kids. Greaves did little, other than hit the roof of the stand with a volley. Holland's goal was so classy that Greaves stood open-mouthed to applaud.											
40	H	WOLVES	17	W	3-0	1-0	Greaves 2, Bonds 57, Howe 84	Grotier	Bonds	Lampard	Bennett	Stephenson	Moore	Holland	Eustace	Hurst	Greaves	Howe	
	31/3	26,386	*11*	35				*Parkes*	*Taylor*	*Parkin*	*Wilson*	*Holsgrove*	*Shaw*	*Bailey*	*McCalliog*	*Dougan*	*Curran*	*Wagstaffe*	
							Ref: R Reynolds	Wolves' boss Bill McGarry described his team's defence as the worst in the world after this defeat. Greaves headed in Lampard's cross with Parkes rooted to his line. Parkes failed to cut out a corner for No 2. Curran and Wilson hit the bar and Dougan's diving header was disallowed.											
41	H	LEEDS	16	D	2-2	2-1	Best 33, Bonds 36	Grotier	Bonds	Charles	Eustace	Moore	Miller	Redknapp	Lindsay	Best	Greaves	Sissons	
	2/4	26,140	*2*	36			*Clarke 22, 78*	*Sprake*	*Reaney*	*Davey*	*Yorath*	*Madeley*	*Gray*	*Lorimer*	*Clarke*	*Belfitt**	*Bates*	*Giles*	*Hibbitt*
							Ref: J Finney	Leeds' England full-back Paul Reaney broke his leg in the 48th minute after a collision with Keith Miller, playing his first full game. The crack could be heard all around the ground. West Ham fielded a pack of reserves in protest against Don Revie's broad hint that he might do the same.											
42	A	ARSENAL	16	L	1-2	1-2	Greaves 4	Grotier	Bonds	Lampard	Bennett	Stephenson	Moore	Holland	Eustace	Hurst	Greaves	Sissons	
	4/4	*36,218*	*9*	36			*Kelly 29, Radford 44*	*Wilson*	*Storey*	*McNab*	*Kelly*	*McLintock*	*Simpson*	*Marinello*	*Sammels*	*Radford*	*George*	*Graham*	
	Home	Away					Ref: R Capey	Greaves is a mini-god at the moment. His goals have put paid to fears of relegation and this is West Ham's first defeat since he came. 36 points is West Ham's lowest since returning to Division 1, 10 years earlier. Kelly's soft goal let Arsenal back into a game that West Ham began well.											
Average	30,689	31,399																	

League Cup							F-A	H-T	Scorers, Times, and Referees	1	2	3	4	5	6	7	8	9	10	11	12 sub used
2	H	HALIFAX		13		W	4-2	2-0	Lampard 15, Best 34, Hurst 71, 88	Ferguson	Bonds	Lampard	Peters	Stephenson	Moore	Redknapp	Lindsay	Brooking	Hurst	Best	
	3/9		20,717	*3:18*					*Lawther 50, Wallace 89*	*Smith*	*Burgin*	*Pickering*	*Lennard*	*McCarthy*	*Robertson*	*Shawcross*	*Hill*	*Ryden**	*Lawther*	*Flower*	*Wallace*
									Ref: J Osborne	The eye-catching duel in this untidy cup-tie was between Hurst and his rugged marker, Dave Lennard. Hurst got so angry by his mistreatment that he took the law into his own hands and got booked. He also scored the goal of the match, a perfect run and header from Redknapp's cross.											
3	A	NOTT'M FOREST		15		L	0-1	0-1		Ferguson	Bonds	Lampard	Boyce	Stephenson	Moore	Redknapp	Brooking	Hurst	Cross	Peters	
	23/9		*20,939*	*12*					*Lyons 30*	*Hill*	*Hindley*	*Winfield*	*Chapman*	*Hennessey*	*Newton*	*Rees*	*Lyons*	*Hilley*	*Barnwell*	*Moore*	
									Ref: N Burtenshaw	This is the first season that all 92 league clubs have entered the League Cup. West Ham are beaten by Hilley's through ball to Lyons which flummoxed Bonds. Ian Storey-Moore also hit the bar with a bender free-kick. West Ham had the edge after going behind but couldn't get back.											

FA Cup										1	2	3	4	5	6	7	8	9	10	11	12 sub used
3	A	MIDDLESBROUGH		16		L	1-2	0-1	Stephenson 86	Ferguson	Bonds	Lampard	Howe	Stephenson	Moore	Boyce	Peters	Best*	Hurst	Sissons	Redknapp
	3/1		*31,295*	*2:4*					*McIlmoyle 29, Downing 83*	*Whigham*	*Smith A*	*Jones*	*Smith G*	*Gates*	*Spraggon*	*Laidlaw*	*Maddren*	*McIlmoyle*	*Hickton*	*Downing*	
									Ref: T Pughe	Three hairline offside decisions went against West Ham, who were up against a team happy to use spoiling tactics. Moore and Bonds were booked in the second half and at the end sarcastically applauded the officials off the pitch. For this West Ham will be reported to the FA.											

	P	W	D	L	F	A	W	D	L	F	A	Pts
		Home					Away					
1 Everton	42	17	3	1	46	19	12	5	4	26	15	66
2 Leeds	42	15	4	2	50	19	6	11	4	34	30	57
3 Chelsea	42	13	7	1	36	18	8	6	7	34	32	55
4 Derby	42	15	3	3	45	14	7	6	8	19	23	53
5 Liverpool	42	10	7	4	34	20	10	4	7	31	22	51
6 Coventry	42	9	6	6	35	28	10	5	6	23	20	49
7 Newcastle	42	14	2	5	42	16	3	11	7	15	19	47
8 Manchester U	42	8	9	4	37	27	6	8	7	29	34	45
9 Stoke	42	10	7	4	31	23	5	8	8	25	29	45
10 Manchester C	42	8	6	7	25	22	8	5	8	30	26	43
11 Tottenham	42	11	2	8	27	21	6	7	8	27	34	43
12 Arsenal	42	7	10	4	29	23	5	8	8	22	26	42
13 Wolves	42	8	8	5	30	23	4	8	9	25	34	40
14 Burnley	42	7	7	7	33	29	5	8	8	23	32	39
15 Nott'm Forest	42	8	9	4	28	28	2	9	10	22	43	38
16 West Brom	42	10	6	5	39	25	4	3	14	19	41	37
17 WEST HAM	42	8	8	5	28	21	4	4	13	23	39	36
18 Ipswich	42	9	5	7	23	20	1	6	14	17	43	31
19 Southampton	42	3	12	6	24	27	3	5	13	22	40	29
20 Crys Palace	42	5	6	10	20	36	1	9	11	14	32	27
21 Sunderland	42	4	11	6	17	24	2	3	16	13	44	26
22 Sheffield Wed	42	6	5	10	23	27	2	4	15	17	44	25
	924	205	143	114	702	510	114	143	205	510	702	924

Odds & ends

Double wins: (1) Sheffield Wed.
Double losses: (2) WBA, Everton.

Won from behind: (0).
Lost from in front: (3) Stoke (a), Coventry (h), Arsenal (a).

High spots: Winning first two league games.
Seven league games with only one defeat from early October.
Winning 5-1 at Manchester City.

Low spots: Losing to Second Division Middlesbrough in League Cup.
Losing four league games on the trot in November and December.

Hammer of the Year: Bobby Moore.
Ever-presents: (1) Billy Bonds.
Hat-tricks: (0).
Leading scorer: (18) Geoff Hurst.

	Appearances						Goals			
	Lge	*Sub*	LC	*Sub*	FAC	*Sub*	Lge	LC	FAC	Tot
Bennett, Peter	**11**	*1*								
Best, Clyde	**24**		1		1		**5**	1		**6**
Bonds, Billy	**42**		2		1		**3**			**3**
Boyce, Ronnie	**18**	*2*	1		1		**1**			**1**
Brooking, Trevor	**20**	*1*	2				**4**			**4**
Charles, John	**5**									
Cross, Roger	**5**	*1*	1				**1**			**1**
Cushley, John	**2**									
Eustace, Peter	**14**						**2**			**2**
Ferguson, Bobby	**30**		2		1					
Greaves, Jimmy	**6**						**4**			**4**
Grotier, Peter	**12**									
Heffer, Paul		*1*								
Holland, Pat	**8**						**1**			**1**
Howe, Bobby	**32**	*1*			1		**1**			**1**
Hurst, Geoff	**38**	*1*	2		1		**16**	2		**18**
Lampard, Frank	**30**		2		1			1		**1**
Lindsay, Jimmy	**17**		1				**2**			**2**
Llewellyn, David		*2*								
Miller, Keith	**1**	*1*								
Moore, Bobby	**40**		2		1					
Peters, Martin	**31**		2		1		**7**			**7**
Redknapp, Harry	**23**		2			*1*	**1**			**1**
Sissons, John	**19**	*1*			1		**2**			**2**
Stephenson, John	**34**		2		1				1	**1**
(own-goals)							**1**			**1**
25 players used	**462**	***12***	**22**		**11**	***1***	**51**	**4**	**1**	**56**

Alan Taylor scores the first goal against Fulham in the 1975 FA Cup final

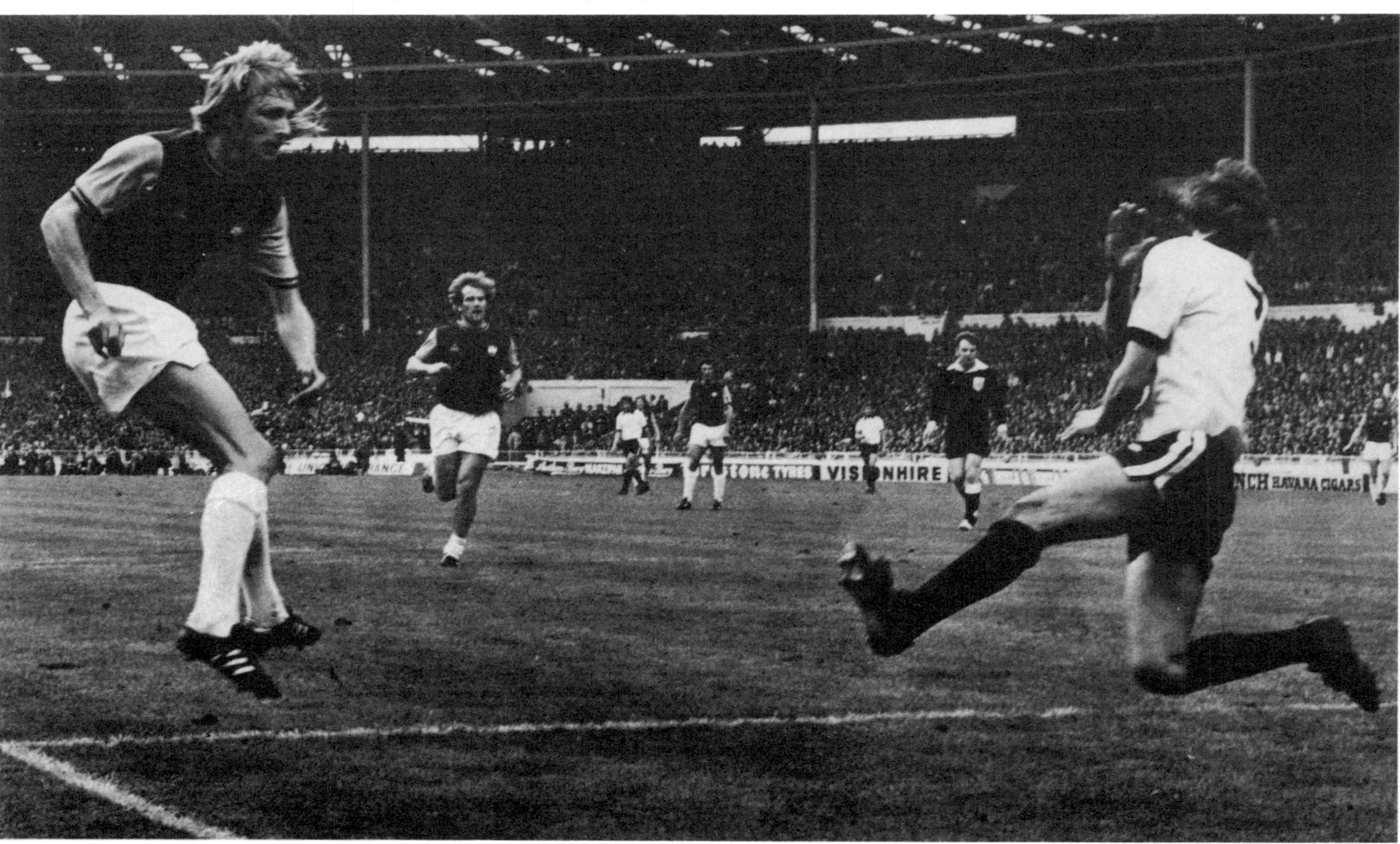

John McDowell tries on some fancy headgear after the 1975 FA Cup final

LEAGUE DIVISION 1 — Manager: Ron Greenwood — SEASON 1970-71

No	Date		Att	Pos	Pt	F-A	H-T	Scorers, Times, and Referees	1	2	3	4	5	6	7	8	9	10	11	12 sub used
1	A	TOTTENHAM			D	2-2	1-2	Greaves 32, Bennett 59	Grotier	Bonds	Lampard	Bennett	Stephenson	Moore	Best	Brooking	Hurst	Greaves	Howe	
	15/8		***53,640***		1			*Gilzean 31, 39*	*Jennings*	*Evans*	*Knowles*	*Mullery*	*England*	*Bond*	*Gilzean*	*Perryman*	*Chivers*	*Peters*	*Pearce*	
								Ref: R Matthewson	Four of England's World Cup team from Mexico are on show. There is much national head-shaking at England's elimination, but this vibrant match raises spirits. All the goals were special, notably Gilzean's diving header. This is a worthy game for Sunday afternoon's The Big Match.											
2	H	ARSENAL			D	0-0	0-0		Grotier	Bonds	Lampard	Bennett	Stephenson	Moore	Best	Brooking	Hurst	Greaves	Howe	
	17/8		39,004		2				*Wilson*	*Storey*	*McNab*	*Kelly*	*McLintock*	*Roberts*	*Armstrong*	*Kennedy*	*Radford*	*Marinello*	*Graham*	
								Ref: J Finney	'Nought plus nought equals nought' wrote *The Times* scathingly about this 'paupers' ration of football'. The only action was on the terraces, which saw some argy-bargy. Two 'goals' were handled in what would later be called 'Maradona style'. Greaves was hacked mercilessly.											
3	H	CHELSEA			D	2-2	2-0	Howe 11, Hurst 21	Grotier	Bonds	Lampard	Bennett	Stephenson	Moore	Best	Brooking	Hurst	Greaves	Howe	
	22/8		39,240		3			*Weller 60, 74*	*Bonetti*	*Mulligan*	*Harris*	*Hollins*	*Dempsey*	*Hinton*	*Weller*	*Hudson*	*Osgood*	*Hutchinson*	*Houseman*	
								Ref: F Nicholson	Greaves did not score but he was a constant threat to Chelsea in this thriller. The other star was another ex-Spur, Keith Weller, who netted from two half-chances which made his £100,000 fee seem cheap. Bobby Moore was not at his best, nor was young Grotier, particularly at crosses.											
4	A	LEEDS		15	L	0-3	0-1		Grotier	Bonds	Lampard	Bennett	Stephenson	Moore	Best	Brooking	Hurst	Greaves	Howe	
	26/8		*42,677*	*1*	3			*Giles 43p, Jones 55, Belfitt 89*	*Sprake*	*Madeley*	*Cooper*	*Bates*	*Charlton*	*Hunter*	*Lorimer*	*Clarke*	*Jones*	*Giles**	*Gray*	*Belfitt*
								Ref: J Taylor	West Ham could have been hit for six, their only chance coming when Brooking burst through but shot against Sprake's legs. Lorimer danced round Lampard, who inexplicably handled. In addition to the goals Gray and Lorimer hit the woodwork. Elland Road gave a standing ovation.											
5	A	MANCHESTER U		15	D	1-1	1-1	Hurst 2	Grotier	Bonds	Lampard	Bennett	Stephenson	Moore	Best	Brooking	Hurst	Greaves	Howe	
	29/8		*50,643*	*17*	4			*Fitzpatrick 28*	*Rimmer*	*Edwards*	*Dunne*	*Fitzpatrick*	*Ure*	*Sadler*	*Morgan*	*Law*	*Charlton*	*Stiles*	*Best*	
								Ref: E Wallace	Man U still can't win at home. With Bonds policing George Best as well as anybody could, Old Trafford was uncharacteristically subdued. Sadly for West Ham, Greaves was equally nondescript. Old Trafford has never seen the best of him, though his shrewd pass did set up Hurst.											
6	H	SOUTHAMPTON		18	D	1-1	0-1	Hurst 65p	Grotier	Bonds	Lampard	Bennett*	Stephenson	Moore	Best	Brooking	Hurst	Greaves	Howe	Eustace
	31/8		26,213	*9*	5			*Jenkins 8*	*Martin*	*Kirkup*	*Hollywood*	*Fisher*	*McGrath*	*Walker*	*Paine*	*Channon*	*Davies*	*O'Neill*	*Jenkins*	
								Ref: R Kirkpatrick	This feeble affair was not worth the admission money, other than to see Jenkins' solo goal for Saints. He beat five defenders and sent a soft shot under Grotier. West Ham had given him a 'free': it is his first ever goal for Saints. David Walker 'fouled' Greaves for a laughable penalty.											
7	H	EVERTON		18	L	1-2	0-2	Moore 67	Grotier	Bonds	Lampard	Eustace	Stephenson	Moore	Best*	Brooking	Hurst	Greaves	Howe	Redknapp
	5/9		29.171	*17*	5			*Royle 30, Husband 39*	*West*	*Wright*	*Newton K*	*Kendall*	*Kenyon*	*Harvey*	*Husband*	*Ball*	*Royle*	*Hurst*	*Morrissey**	*Brown*
								Ref: K Howley	The defending champions have yet to win a match, until now. Joe Royle's unchallenged header was followed by Jimmy Husband shooting in off Stephenson. Moore scored from long range and Bonds hit a post. Peter Eustace was cheered at the start but jeered long before the end.											
8	A	WEST BROM		19	L	1-2	1-1	Howe 7	Grotier	Bonds	Lampard	Bennett	Stephenson	Moore	Brooking	Eustace	Best	Greaves	Howe	
	12/9		*24,913*	*15*	5			*Suggett 6, 84*	*Cumbes*	*Hughes*	*Merrick*	*Brown*	*Talbut*	*Kaye*	*McVitie*	*Suggett*	*Astle*	*Hope*	*Cantello*	
								Ref: G Jones	Jimmy Greaves is still searching for the 350th goal of his career. He might have taken a lesson from Colin Suggett, whose late winner was out of the Greaves' handbook. The referee ignored a linesman's raised flag, enabling Bobby Howe to quickly equalise Suggett's shot on the turn.											
9	H	NEWCASTLE		20	L	0-2	0-1		Grotier	Bonds	Lampard	Bennett	Stephenson	Moore	Redknapp*	Eustace	Hurst	Greaves	Best	Brooking
	19/9		25,841	*10*	5			*Robson 21, 55*	*McFaul*	*Craig*	*Clark*	*Gibb*	*Burton*	*Moncur*	*Robson*	*Dyson*	*Davies*	*Arentoft*	*Young*	
								Ref: R Darlington	Redknapp looks to be the only Hammer on form, and his substitution produces howls of boos from the crowd. The player to catch the eye is Newcastle's all-action Pop Robson, who volleyed the first goal and headed the second. West Ham now fly off to USA to play Pele's Santos.											
10	A	HUDDERSFIELD		20	D	1-1	0-1	Hurst 62p	Grotier	Bonds	Lampard	Boyce	Stephenson	Moore	Best	Brooking	Hurst	Eustace	Howe	
	26/9		*20,887*	*18*	6			*Smith 3*	*Poole*	*Jones*	*Hutt*	*Nicholson*	*Ellam*	*Clarke*	*Smith*	*Kryzwicki*	*Worthington*	*McGill*	*Dobson*	
								Ref: W Castle	West Ham drew 2-2 with Santos and return to UK to stage another draw. Bonds' miscued clearance let in Smith to volley past Grotier. Hurst levelled from the spot after he had been fouled by McGill, then Hammers fell back in defence. Greaves missed the game with back trouble.											

No	Venue	Opponent	Att	Pos	Res	Score	H-T	Scorers, Times, and Referees	1	2	3	4	5	6	7	8	9	10	11	12
11	H	BURNLEY		18	W	3-1	2-0	Hurst 27, 38, 80	Grotier	Bonds	Lampard	Boyce*	Eustace	Moore	**Ayris**	Brooking	Hurst	Best	Howe	Heffer
		3/10	23,295	*22*	8			*Coates 82*	*Waiters*	*Angus*	*Merrington*	*Docherty*	*Waldron*	*Probert**	*Thomas*	*Coates*	*Casper*	*Wilson*	*West*	*Nulty*
								Ref: R Tinkler	Both teams are seeking their first win, and Jimmy Adamson's abject Burnley must wait awhile longer. Cockney-kid Johnny Ayris enjoys a confident debut, supplying the corner from which Hurst scored his first goal. His hat-trick came with a shot that flew in off Colin Waldron.											
12	A	STOKE		19	L	1-2	1-1	Greaves 22	Grotier	Bonds	Lampard	Lindsay	Stephenson	Moore	Boyce*	Best	Hurst	Brooking	Greaves	Eustace
		10/10	23,035	*9*	8			*Greenhoff 33, Dobing 89*	*Banks*	*Marsh*	*Pejic*	*Bernard*	*Smith D*	*Bloor*	*Conroy*	*Greenhoff*	*Ritchie*	*Dobing*	*Burrows*	
								Ref: J Thacker	Vintage acrobatics from Greaves, whose overhead kick flies in off a post to leave Banks dumbstruck. Peter Dobing squared to Greenhoff for the equaliser, then collected Conroy's pass for the winner. Stephenson needs a cartilage operation, so a new centre-half must be found quickly.											
13	H	TOTTENHAM		20	D	2-2	1-2	Eustace 21, Hurst 51	Grotier	Bonds	Lampard	Eustace	**Taylor**	Moore	Ayris	Lindsay	Hurst	Greaves	Dear	
		17/10	**42,322**	*4*	9			*Mullery 6, England 40*	*Jennings*	*Kinnear*	*Knowles*	*Mullery*	*England*	*Beal*	*Gilzean*	*Perryman*	*Chivers*	*Peters*	*Pearce*	
								Ref: B Homewood	Tommy Taylor, signed from Orient for £78,000, has a daunting debut against England's Martin Chivers. Moore stands tall as West Ham look to be falling apart before half-time, but driven on by Eustace – who had publicly disparaged the club a few hours earlier – they finish strongly.											
14	A	CRYS PALACE		20	D	1-1	1-0	Howe 5	Grotier	Bonds	Lampard	Eustace	Taylor	Moore	Howe	Lindsay	Hurst	Greaves	Dear	
		24/10	*41,486*	*4*	10			*Taylor 75*	*Jackson*	*Sewell*	*Wall*	*Payne*	*McCormick*	*Blyth*	*Taylor*	*Kember*	*Queen**	*Birchenall*	*Tambling*	*Hoadley*
								Ref: R Johnson	Palace's record against London clubs is dreadful, but this season is better than usual for Bert Head's annual strugglers, who point to two strong penalty claims waived away. West Ham might have been three goals up by half-time and only looked shaky after Palace had drawn level.											
15	H	BLACKPOOL		16	W	2-1	1-1	Greaves 27, Eutstace 76	Grotier	**McDowell**	Lampard	Eustace*	Taylor	Moore	Ayris	Lindsay	Hurst	Greaves	Dear	Heffer
		31/10	26,239	*21*	12			*Green 26*	*Thomson*	*Armfield*	*Mowbray*	*Craven*	*James*	*Alcock*	*Suddick*	*Green*	*Burns*	*Bentley*	*Hutchison*	
								Ref: J Yates	This was a ridiculously hard-earned win over the team that will finish bottom of the division. Even Bobby Moore had a stinker, as Blackpool found themselves with unexpected space in midfield. Mind you, West Ham wasted chances galore. Johnny Ayris laid on both Hammers' goals											
16	A	IPSWICH		17	L	1-2	1-0	Hurst 25	Grotier	McDowell	Lampard	Heffer*	Taylor	Eustace	Redknapp	Lindsay	Hurst	Best	Howe	Holland
		7/11	*22,990*	*15*	12			*Hill 52, Mills 54*	*Sivell*	*Hammond*	*Mills*	*Morris*	*Baxter*	*McNeill**	*Robertson*	*Viljoen*	*Clarke*	*Woods*	*Hill*	*Lambert*
								Ref: W Gow	Max Marquis wrote 'this scrappy game, full of unforced errors, refereed with lamentable lack of authority.' Eustace played in Moore's shirt. Injury-hit Hammers went in front through acting skipper Hurst's 25-yarder. Hill drove in Morris's cross and Mills' winner flew in off Taylor.											
17	H	WOLVES		18	D	3-3	1-1	Best 34, 75, Moore 52	Grotier	McDowell	Lampard	Eustace	Taylor	Moore	Ayris	Lindsay	Best	Hurst	Howe	
		14/11	23,978	5	13			*McCalliog 6, 83, Gould 88*	*Parkes*	*Shaw*	*Parkin**	*Bailey*	*Munro*	*McAlle*	*McCalliog*	*Hibbitt*	*Gould*	*Curran*	*Wagstaffe*	*Richards*
								Ref: Lewis	3-1 up with seven minutes to go, and West Ham blow it. Tommy Taylor was partially at fault with both late goals. Injuries to Greaves and Dear allowed Best to grab the limelight. Moore, who blasted a goal with his injured right foot, now looks forward to his testimonial against Celtic.											
18	A	MANCHESTER C		19	L	0-2	0-1		Ferguson	McDowell	Lampard	Eustace	Taylor	Moore	Holland	Lindsay*	Greaves	Hurst	Best	Howe
		21/11	*28,485*	5	13			*Lee 9, 84*	*Corrigan*	*Book*	*Pardoe*	*Doyle*	*Heslop*	*Oakes*	*Summerbee*	*Bell*	*Lee*	*Mann*	*Towers*	
								Ref: D Corbett	Bobby Ferguson returns after an eight-month lay-off and plays superbly. Not even his heroics can stunt the skills of Colin Bell and Francis Lee, but one save from Alan Oakes' thunderbolt drew applause from Maine Road. It was the same old story for West Ham. Skill yes, effort no.											
19	H	COVENTRY		19	L	1-2	0-2	Best 57	Ferguson	McDowell	Lampard	Eustace	Taylor	Moore	Holland	Howe	Best	Hurst	Greaves	
		28/11	**22,800**	*10*	13			*Clements 36, O'Rourke 38*	*Glazier*	*Coop*	*Smith*	*Mortimer*	*Blockley*	*Parker*	*Hill*	*Carr*	*Martin*	*O'Rourke*	*Clements*	
								Ref: L Callaghan	The first half was so bad the players were treated to bouts of slow-handclapping, and at the end Greenwood locked his players indoors for an ear-wagging. Bobby Moore had ducked under a corner, which was headed in by Dave Clements. Ferguson then failed to come out for a cross.											
20	A	DERBY		19	W	**4-2**	2-2	Greaves 16, Brooking 19, Best 71, 88	Ferguson	Bonds	Lampard	Eustace	Taylor	Moore	Lindsay	Brooking	Best	Hurst	Greaves	
		5/12	*30,806*	*16*	15			*Wignall 9, Durban 28*	*Green*	*Webster*	*Robson*	*Durban*	*Hennessey*	*Mackay*	*McGovern*	*Wignall*	*O'Hare*	*Hector*	*Gemmill*	
								Ref: G Hartley	Two main talking points from this match. First, Greaves marking his 500th league match with a typical goal. Second, Ferguson's 81st-minute penalty save after Eustace had blocked Gemmill's run. Ferguson clearly moved early to save from Dave Mackay, denying Derby a 3-3 draw.											
21	H	LIVERPOOL		19	L	1-2	1-2	Greaves 41	Ferguson	Bonds	Lampard	Eustace	Taylor	Moore	Lindsay*	Brooking	Best	Hurst	Greaves	Ayris
		12/12	27,459	*5*	15			*Witham 25, Boersma 43*	*Clemence*	*Lawler*	*Boersma**	*Smith*	*Lloyd*	*Hughes*	*Hall*	*McLaughlin*	*Heighway*	*Witham*	*Thompson*	*Ross*
								Ref: D Nippard	Even without towering John Toshack, Liverpool still possess sufficient aerial threat to beat West Ham with two headers. Jack Witham's is his first goal for Liverpool. He, like Boersma, was grateful to Ferguson staying rooted to his line. Greaves scored a gem, but missed two sitters.											

No	Date		Att	Pos	Pt	F-A	H-T	Scorers, Times, and Referees	1	2	3	4	5	6	7	8	9	10	11	12 sub used
22	A	CHELSEA		19	L	1-2	1-2	Lampard 40	Ferguson	Bonds	Lampard*	Eustace	Taylor	Moore	Ayris	Brooking	Dear	Lindsay	Greaves	Best
	19/12		*42,075*	*3*	15			*Osgood 19, 21*	*Bonetti*	*Boyle*	*Harris*	*Hollins*	*Hinton*	*Webb*	*Weller**	*Cooke*	*Osgood*	*Baldwin*	*Houseman*	*Hudson*
								Ref: D Pugh	West Ham's defence was regularly opened up by Chelsea's powerful surges. Peter Osgood's first was splendidly opportunist, though his second bobbled in off Ferguson. Lampard volleyed in from 15 yards. Only when Best came on at half-time did West Ham threaten Chelsea.											
23	A	ARSENAL		19	L	0-2	0-1		Ferguson	McDowell	Lampard	Bonds	Taylor	Howe	Redknapp	Lindsay	Best*	Brooking	Eustace	Llewellyn
	9/1		*49,007*	*2*	15			*Graham 40, Kennedy 80*	*Wilson*	*Rice*	*Nelson*	*Storey*	*McLintock*	*Simpson*	*Armstrong*	*Sammels*	*Radford*	*Kennedy*	*Graham*	
								Ref: A Taylor	Moore, Greaves, Best and Dear have been dropped for nightclubbing before a cup-tie. Bonds is acting skipper. Pat Rice crosses for Graham's stooping header. Ferguson's blunder gave Ray Kennedy a simple goal. The ref later signalled a 'goal' after Sammels' shot hit the side-netting.											
24	H	LEEDS		20	L	2-3	0-1	Eustace 78, Brooking 81	Grotier	McDowell	Lampard	Bonds	Taylor	Howe	Redknapp	Lindsay	Hurst	Brooking	Eustace	
	16/1		34,396	*1*	15			*Giles 32, Hunter 65, Belfitt 84*	*Sprake*	*Reaney*	*Cooper*	*Bates*	*Charlton*	*Hunter*	*Lorimer*	*Clarke*	*Jones**	*Giles*	*Madeley*	*Belfitt*
								Ref: V Batty	Hurst is acting captain. Leeds looked to be winning effortlessly when West Ham hauled themselves back with two headers in three minutes. Leeds immediately reasserted themselves. Jack Charlton said: 'Apart from the last 10 minutes this was the worst West Ham side I have seen.'											
25	H	DERBY		20	L	**1-4**	0-3	Eustace 48	Grotier	McDowell	Lampard	Bonds	Taylor	Howe*	Redknapp	Lindsay	Hurst	Brooking	Eustace	Moore
	6/2		26,606	*15*	15			*Hector 7, 19, Hinton 29, 68*	*Boulton*	*Webster*	*Robson*	*Durban*	*McFarland*	*Mackay*	*McGovern*	*Gemmill*	*O'Hare*	*Hector*	*Hinton*	
								Ref: J Finney	A game of two halves, as they say. Derby ran rampant in the first. For the second, the floodlights and Moore came on. West Ham fought their way back into contention. Grotier's feeble goal-kick cost the Hammers the first goal, then he failed to cut out Hinton's corner for the second.											
26	A	COVENTRY		20	W	1-0	1-0	Greaves 25	Ferguson	McDowell	Lampard	Bonds	Taylor	Moore	Redknapp	Boyce	Hurst	Greaves*	Eustace	Lindsay
	9/2		*25,083*	*12*	17				*Glazier*	*Coop*	*Smith*	*Mortimer*	*Blockley*	*Parker*	*Hunt*	*Carr*	*Martin*	*Joicey*	*Alderson*	
								Ref: G Kew	Moore, reappointed as captain, has seldom played better than now, on his recall from club suspension. Greaves, another of the Blackpool 'bad boys' caps his return with a crucial goal, after Glazier had repulsed Hurst's shot. When Coventry did threaten, they found Ferguson inspired.											
27	A	LIVERPOOL		20	L	0-1	0-0		Ferguson	McDowell	Lampard	Bonds	Taylor	Moore	Redknapp	Boyce	Hurst	Eustace	Greaves	
	16/2		*38,082*	*5*	17			*Toshack 58*	*Clemence*	*Lawler*	*Yeats*	*Smith*	*Lloyd*	*Hughes*	*Boersma*	*McLaughlin*	*Heighway*	*Toshack*	*Hall*	
								Ref: L Callaghan	John Toshack's flying header settled the points. It is the big Welshman's 7th goal in 15 games since his £110,000 signing. But West Ham could have few complaints. Twice Moore appeared to handle without the referee giving a penalty, and Taylor came within inches of an own-goal.											
28	H	MANCHESTER C		20	D	0-0	0-0		Ferguson	McDowell	Lampard	Bonds	Taylor	Moore	Redknapp	Boyce	Hurst	Eustace	Greaves	
	20/2		30,168	*7*	18				*Corrigan*	*Book*	*Towers*	*Doyle*	*Booth*	*Oakes*	*Jeffries*	*Young*	*Lee*	*Hill*	*Bowyer*	
								Ref: E Wallace	City have just lost in the FA Cup to Arsenal. Ron 'Ticker' Boyce is still only 28 and his return to the team is well merited. His superb pass into the path of Peter Eustace almost brought a winner. If West Ham escape the drop it will only be because Blackpool and Burnley are so far adrift.											
29	H	NOTT'M FOREST		20	W	2-0	1-0	Hurst 16, Robson 56	Ferguson	McDowell	Lampard	Bonds	Taylor	Moore	Redknapp	**Robson**	Hurst	Eustace*	Greaves	Lindsay
	24/2		35,601	*19*	20				*Barron*	*Hindley*	*Winfield*	*Chapman*	*O'Kane*	*Jackson*	*Lyons*	*Fraser*	*Martin*	*Cormack*	*Moore*	
								Ref: D Nippard	'Pop' Robson, a £120,000 buy from Newcastle, is an instant hit. His work-rate lifts the spirits of team-mates. His goal, following Redknapp's chip to the near post, was rapturously received. Geoff Hurst's far-post header from Moore's free-kick was his first goal since 7 November.											
30	A	BLACKPOOL		19	D	1-1	0-1	Hurst 73p	Ferguson	McDowell	Lampard	Bonds	Taylor	Moore	Redknapp	Boyce	Hurst	Eustace*	Robson	Greaves
	27/2		***15,639***	*22*	21			*Kemp 1*	*Ramsbottom*	*Armfield*	*Suddaby*	*Kemp*	*James*	*Hatton*	*Burns*	*Mowbray*	*Craven*	*Coleman**	*Hutchison*	*Johnston*
								Ref: G Hill	Blackpool had won only twice at home in 14 games, plus the 4-0 FA Cup debacle. Fred Kemp capitalised on Ferguson's weak punch out after just 26 seconds. Craven and Burns should have extended the lead before Suddaby panicked and handled Moore's cross. Hurst hit the penalty.											
31	H	CRYS PALACE		19	D	0-0	0-0		Ferguson	McDowell	Lampard	Bonds	Taylor	Moore	Redknapp	Boyce	Hurst	Robson	Greaves	
	6/3		26,157	*11*	22				*Jackson*	*Sewell*	*McCormick*	*Payne*	*Hoadley*	*Blyth*	*Wharton*	*Tambling*	*Queen*	*Birchenall*	*Taylor*	
								Ref: H Williams	Billy Bonds has been a revelation since his switch to midfield, in partnership with Boyce. John Jackson's saves earned Palace a point, none better than that from Robson at the death. Motiveless Palace had no thrust, and seemed to be daydreaming of their coming holiday to Jersey.											

No Date	H/A	Opponent Att	Pos	Res Pts	F-A	H-T	Scorers, Times, Referees	1	2	3	4	5	6	7	8	9	10	11	12
32	A	WOLVES	20	L	0-2	0-0		Ferguson	McDowell	Lampard	Bonds	Taylor	Moore	Redknapp*	Robson	Hurst	Boyce	Eustace	Greaves
13/3		*25,066*	*4*	22			*Gould 56, 80*	*Parkes*	*Shaw*	*Parkin*	*Bailey*	*Munro*	*McAlle*	*McCalliog*	*Hibbitt*	*Gould*	*Dougan**	*Wagstaffe*	*Walker*
							Ref: P Partridge	A horror-show for Hurst, who has one of those games when nothing goes in. At 0-0 Greaves set up a goal on a plate, but Hurst tries to pass to Robson and the chance is gone. Greaves turns pale in disgust. Gould dived to head a daisy cutter for No 1, then Moore messes up a back-pass.											
33	H	IPSWICH	20	D	2-2	1-0	Greaves 14, 74	Ferguson	McDowell	Lampard	Bonds	Taylor	Moore	Ayris	Boyce	Hurst	Robson*	Greaves	Best
20/3		25,957	*17*	23			*Bell 59, Robertson 67*	*Sivell*	*Hammond*	*Mills*	*Morris*	*Bell*	*Jefferson*	*Robertson*	*Woods*	*Clarke*	*Collard*	*Hill*	
							Ref: R Mathewson	The spotlight is on Jimmy Greaves, partly for two once-typical, smash-and-grab goals, partly because of mounting rumours that he is set to retire. West Ham looked to Pop Robson for drive and inspiration until he went off injured. Lampard and Boyce both hit the Ipswich woodwork.											
34	A	EVERTON	20	W	1-0	1-0	Kendall 34 (og)	Ferguson	McDowell	Lampard	Bonds	Taylor	Moore	Redknapp	Boyce	Hurst	Robson	Greaves	
30/3		*28,794*	*12*	25				*Rankin*	*Wright*	*Newton H*	*Kendall*	*Kenyon*	*Harvey*	*Whittle*	*Ball*	*Royle*	*Hurst*	*Morrissey*	
							Ref: V James	Everton are down in the dumps after losing an FA Cup semi-final. Redknapp returns from injury and drives in a low cross that Howard Kendall diverts into his own goal. Thereafter West Ham man the barricades to keep Everton out and register their first win at Goodison for 11 years.											
35	H	MANCHESTER U	20	W	2-1	2-0	Hurst 4, Robson 10	Ferguson	McDowell	Lampard	Bonds	Taylor	Moore	Redknapp	Boyce	Hurst	Robson	Greaves	
3/4		38,507	*10*	27			*Best 56*	*Stepney*	*Fitzpatrick*	*Dunne*	*Crerand*	*Edwards*	*Sadler**	*Morgan*	*Law*	*Charlton*	*Best*	*Aston*	*Burns*
							Ref: D Lyden	After 10 minutes West Ham led by two and it might have been four. The first half showing is a revelation, as Hurst's fierce shot and Robson's deft placement has Upton Park roaring its approval. Aston's cross deflected off the referee into the path of Best. Then Law headed onto the bar.											
36	H	WEST BROM	19	W	2-1	0-1	Robson 67, Greaves 86	Ferguson	McDowell	Lampard	Bonds	Taylor	Moore	Redknapp	Boyce*	Hurst	Robson	Greaves	Brooking
9/4		34,981	*16*	29			*Astle 30*	*Osborne*	*Hughes*	*Merrick*	*Cantello*	*Wile*	*Kaye*	*McVitie**	*Brown*	*Astle*	*Hope*	*Hartford*	*Suggett*
							Ref: T Reynolds	This win stretches West Ham's lead over 21st-placed Burnley to eight points, and survival seems assured. Albion have not won away for 16 months, but were a mite unlucky here. Astle missed three easy chances and Greaves hit the winner after the ball bounced kindly off a defender.											
37	A	NOTT'M FOREST	20	L	0-1	0-1		Ferguson	McDowell	Lampard*	Bonds	Taylor	Moore	Redknapp	Lindsay	Hurst	Robson	Greaves	Stephenson
10/4		*23,032*	*17*	29			*Moore 45*	*Barron*	*Hindley*	*Winfield*	*Chapman*	*O'Kane*	*Fraser*	*Jackson*	*Richardson**	*Martin*	*Cormack*	*Moore*	*Rees*
							Ref: J Finney	Burnley's win over Blackpool cuts West Ham's safety margin at the bottom to six points. Hammers were sunk on half-time when Ian Storey-Moore outpaced the defence and side-stepped Ferguson. Pat Gibson wrote: 'It must have been the most overwhelming 1-0 win of the season.'											
38	A	BURNLEY	20	L	0-1	0-0		Ferguson	McDowell	Howe	Bonds	Taylor	Moore	Redknapp	Eustace	Hurst	Robson	Best	
13/4		*15,822*	*21*	29			*Nulty 65*	*Waiters*	*Angus*	*Latcham*	*Docherty*	*Dobson*	*Nulty*	*Casper*	*Coates*	*Fletcher*	*Bellamy*	*Collins*	
							Ref: D Smith	The safety gap is now down to four, and Burnley have a game in hand too. When Ralph Coates crossed, three Burnley players were queuing up to head it in. West Ham came unashamedly for a point. They must hope that Burnley's run in – four away games out of five – proves too much.											
39	H	STOKE	20	W	1-0	0-0	Hurst 56	Ferguson	McDowell	Lampard	Stephenson	Taylor	Moore	Redknapp	Bonds	Hurst	Robson	Greaves	
17/4		26,269	*15*	31				*Banks*	*Skeels*	*Pejic*	*Bernard*	*Smith D*	*Bloor*	*Jump**	*Greenhoff*	*Ritchie*	*Mahoney*	*Haslegrave*	*Lees*
							Ref: E Merchant	Despite the need for points, West Ham failed to display any urgency. Only Billy Bonds and Robson were above criticism. Bonds has just been named Hammer of the Year. Robson initiated the move that was finished off by Hurst. If Arsenal beat Burnley tomorrow, West Ham are safe.											
40	A	NEWCASTLE	20	D	1-1	1-1	Hurst 43	Ferguson	McDowell	Lampard	Stephenson	Taylor	Moore	Redknapp	Bonds	Hurst	Robson	Howe	
24/4		*22,720*	*11*	32			*Tudor 38*	*McFaul*	*Craggs*	*Clark*	*Gibb*	*McNamee*	*Moncur*	*Foggan*	*Tudor*	*Dyson*	*Smith*	*Young*	
							Ref: F Nicholson	Robson returns to St James' and is booed throughout. John Tudor's half-hit shot deceived Ferguson, who was going the wrong way. Harry Redknapp's centre was then pushed home by Hurst. Because of the high wind, the referee took off his toupee rather than have it blown away.											
41	A	SOUTHAMPTON	17	W	2-1	1-0	Taylor 17, Hurst 65	Ferguson	McDowell	Lampard	Stephenson	Taylor	Moore	Llewellyn	Bonds	Hurst	Robson	Howe	
27/4		*19,395*	*7*	34			*Davies 73*	*Martin*	*Kirkup*	*Hollywood*	*Fisher*	*McGrath*	*Gabriel*	*Paine*	*Channon*	*Davies*	*O'Neill*	*Jenkins*	
							Ref: Walker	This is Hammers' first win over Southampton in 10 Division 1 matches, and it wrecks the Saints hopes of playing in Europe next season. The home team attacked throughout. Mick Channon volleyed against the bar before Tommy Taylor ambled up unchallenged to score from 30 yards.											
42	H	HUDDERSFIELD	20	L	0-1	0-0		Ferguson	McDowell	Lampard	Stephenson	Taylor	Moore	Redknapp	Bonds	Hurst	Robson	Greaves	
1/5		24,983	*15*	34			*Lawson J 49*	*Lawson D*	*Clarke*	*Jones*	*Nicholson*	*Ellam*	*Cherry*	*Barry*	*Mahoney*	*Worthington*	*McGill*	*Lawson J*	
Home		Away					Ref: N Burtenshaw	Greaves' piledriver was kicked off the line and Robson hit the underside of the bar. It was that sort of day for West Ham, who wasted countless other chances, and lost when Mike Barry's shot was deflected in off Jimmy Lawson's hip. Lawson knew nothing about the goal he had scored.											
Average 29,961		30,680																	

LEAGUE DIVISION 1 (CUP-TIES) Manager: Ron Greenwood SEASON 1970-71

League Cup

Rd	Venue	Opponent / Date	Att	Pos	Res	F-A	H-T	Scorers, Times, and Referees	1	2	3	4	5	6	7	8	9	10	11	12 sub used
2	H	HULL		18	W	1-0	0-0	Eustace 85	Grotier	Bonds !	Lampard	Eustace	Stephenson	Moore	Best	Redknapp	Hurst	Greaves	Howe	
		9/9	19,116	*2:5*					*McKechnie*	*Beardsley*	*de Vries*	*Wilkinson*	*Neill*	*Simpkin*	*Lord*	*Houghton**	*Chilton*	*Wagstaff*	*Jarvis*	*Greenwood*
								Ref: N Burtenshaw												

Three minutes from time Billy Bonds is sent off for spitting at Hull's Chris Simpkin. Bonds already has a three-match suspension hanging over him from last season. The referee needed a police escort from the pitch at the end. Terry Neill's Hull were beaten by Peter Eustace's left-footer.

Rd	Venue	Opponent / Date	Att	Pos	Res	F-A	H-T	Scorers, Times, and Referees	1	2	3	4	5	6	7	8	9	10	11	12 sub used
3	A	COVENTRY		18	L	1-3	0-1	Hurst 85	Grotier	Bonds	Lampard	Lindsay	Stephenson	Moore	Ayris	Best	Hurst	Brooking	Eustace	
		6/10	*19,362*	*14*				*Martin 41p, O'Rourke 71, Carr 90*	*Glazier*	*Coop*	*Bruck*	*Clements*	*Blockley*	*Strong*	*Hunt*	*Carr*	*Martin*	*O'Rourke*	*Alderson*	
								Ref: A Jones												

On Saturday Coventry beat champions Everton, courtesy of Ernie Hunt's famous free-kick, and now easily boot West Ham out of the League Cup. Eustace fisted over Alderson's header. Penalty! O'Rourke scored off the bar from 20 yards. Hurst's late bullet breathed life into the game.

FA Cup

Rd	Venue	Opponent / Date	Att	Pos	Res	F-A	H-T	Scorers, Times, and Referees	1	2	3	4	5	6	7	8	9	10	11	12 sub used
3	A	BLACKPOOL		19	L	0-4	0-2		Ferguson	Bonds	Lampard	Eustace	Taylor	Moore	Ayris*	Lindsay	Best	Greaves	Howe	Dear
		2/1	*21,814*	*21*				*Green 30, 38, Craven 47, Mowbray 80*	*Taylor*	*Armfield*	*Mowbray*	*Kemp*	*James*	*Hatton*	*Burns*	*Green*	*Craven*	*Coleman*	*Hutchison*	
								Ref: E Wallace												

Blackpool's new boss, Bob Stokoe, enjoys this win. Pool have won only two other cup games in the past 10 years. Tony Green capped a mazy run with the first goal and beat Moore with ease for the second. This match has repercussions for Moore and others for off-field 'activities'.

	P	W	D	L	F	A	W	D	L	F	A	Pts
		Home					Away					
1 Arsenal	42	18	3	0	41	6	11	4	6	30	23	65
2 Leeds	42	16	2	3	40	12	11	8	2	32	18	64
3 Tottenham	42	11	5	5	33	19	8	9	4	21	14	52
4 Wolves	42	13	3	5	33	22	9	5	7	31	32	52
5 Liverpool	42	11	10	0	30	10	6	7	8	12	14	51
6 Chelsea	42	12	6	3	34	21	6	9	6	18	21	51
7 Southampton	42	12	5	4	35	15	5	7	9	21	29	46
8 Manchester U	42	9	6	6	29	24	7	5	9	36	42	43
9 Derby	42	9	5	7	32	26	7	5	9	24	28	42
10 Coventry	42	12	4	5	24	12	4	6	11	13	26	42
11 Manchester C	42	7	9	5	30	22	5	8	8	17	20	41
12 Newcastle	42	9	9	3	27	16	5	4	12	17	30	41
13 Stoke	42	10	7	4	28	11	2	6	13	16	37	37
14 Everton	42	10	7	4	32	16	2	6	13	22	44	37
15 Huddersfield	42	7	8	6	19	16	4	6	11	21	33	36
16 Nott'm Forest	42	9	4	8	29	26	5	4	12	13	35	36
17 West Brom	42	9	8	4	34	25	1	7	13	24	50	35
18 Crys Palace	42	9	5	7	24	24	3	6	12	15	33	35
19 Ipswich	42	9	4	8	28	22	3	6	12	14	26	34
20 WEST HAM	42	6	8	7	28	30	4	6	11	19	30	34
21 Burnley	42	4	8	9	20	31	3	5	13	9	32	27
22 Blackpool	42	3	9	9	22	31	1	6	14	12	35	23
	924	215	135	112	652	437	112	135	215	437	652	924

Odds & ends

Double wins: (0).
Double losses: (2) Leeds, Liverpool.

Won from behind: (3) Blackpool (h), Derby (a), WBA (h).
Lost from in front: (2) Stoke (a), Ipswich (a).

High spots: Three successive league wins in March and April.
Avoiding relegation, but only because Burnley and Blackpool were even worse.

Low spots: Failing to win any of the first 10 league fixtures, dropping to 20th.
Losing five league games on the trot, December to February.
The nature of the capitulation at Blackpool in the FA Cup.

Only two of West Ham's league matches featured four goals by either side. Both were against Derby.

Hammer of the Year: Billy Bonds.
Ever-presents: (0).
Hat-tricks: (1) Geoff Hurst.
Leading scorer: (15) Geoff Hurst.

	Appearances						Goals			
	Lge	*Sub*	LC	*Sub*	FAC	*Sub*	**Lge**	LC	FAC	**Tot**
Ayris, Johnny	**6**	*1*	1		1					
Bennett, Peter	**8**						**1**			**1**
Best, Clyde	**20**	*2*	2		1		**5**			**5**
Bonds, Billy	**37**		2		1					
Boyce, Ronnie	**13**									
Brooking, Trevor	**17**	*2*	1				**2**			**2**
Dear, Brian	**4**					*1*				
Eustace, Peter	**25**	*2*	2		1		**4**	1		**5**
Ferguson, Bobby	**23**				1					
Greaves, Jimmy	**30**	*2*	1		1		**9**			**9**
Grotier, Peter	**19**		2							
Heffer, Paul	**1**	*2*								
Holland, Pat	**2**	*1*								
Howe, Bobby	**20**	*1*	1		1		**3**			**3**
Hurst, Geoff	**39**		2				**14**	1		**15**
Lampard, Frank	**41**		2		1		**1**			**1**
Lindsay, Jimmy	**14**	*2*	1		1					
Llewellyn, David	**1**	*1*								
McDowell, John	**25**									
Moore, Bobby	**38**	*1*	2		1		**2**			**2**
Redknapp, Harry	**20**	*1*	1							
Robson, Bryan	**14**						**3**			**3**
Stephenson, Alan	**15**	*1*	2							
Taylor, Tommy	**30**				1		**1**			**1**
(own-goals)							**2**			**2**
24 players used	**462**	***19***	**22**		**11**	***1***	**47**	**2**		**49**

No	Date	Att	Pos	Pt	F-A	H-T	Scorers, Times, and Referees	1	2	3	4	5	6	7	8	9	10	11	12 sub used
1	H WEST BROM			L	0-1	0-1		Ferguson	McDowell	Lampard	Bonds	Stephenson	Moore	Ayris	Best	Hurst	Taylor	Robson	
	14/8	27,420		–			*Brown 38*	*Cumbes*	*Hughes*	*Wilson*	*Cantello*	*Wile*	*Kaye*	*Hope*	*Suggett*	*Astle*	*Brown*	*Merrick*	
							Ref: T Dawes	Jimmy Greaves has quit. Don Howe's new-look Albion present more threat than West Ham, for whom Pop Robson looks forlorn and wasted wide on the wing. The goal stemmed from a long ball to Tony Brown, with the Hammers' defence spreadeagled. Jim Cumbes did well in goal.											
2	A DERBY			L	0-2	0-2		Ferguson	McDowell	Lampard	Bonds	Stephenson	Moore	Ayris*	Best	Hurst	Taylor	Robson	Howe
	18/8	*30,583*		–			*O'Hare 2, Wignall 8*	*Boulton*	*Webster*	*Robson*	*McGovern*	*Hennessey*	*Todd*	*Gemmill*	*Wignall*	*O'Hare*	*Hector*	*Hinton*	
							Ref: J Hunting	A new FA directive states: 'Referees must issue cautions for dissent.' In which case Moore and several team-mates should have been booked for protesting against a caution for Taylor. In fact, Moore *et al* escaped punishment. Moore had a bad night: his back-header put Derby in front.											
3	A NOTT'M FOREST		22	L	0-1	0-1		Ferguson	McDowell	Lampard	Bonds	Taylor	Moore	Ayris	Robson	Best	Brooking	Howe	
	21/8	*17,185*	*17*	–			*Moore 42p*	*Barron*	*Hindley*	*Chapman*	*O'Kane*	*Winfield*	*Rees*	*Fraser*	*Cormack*	*Moore*	*Martin*	*McKenzie*	
							Ref: W Johnson	Forest pick up their first points, leaving Hammers pointless and goalless. The decisive moment came when Lampard shoved Martin to concede the penalty. West Ham protested vigorously, but no one had their name taken. Martin admitted that Lampard had stumbled. Hurst was dropped!											
4	H IPSWICH		22	D	0-0	0-0		Ferguson	McDowell	Lampard	Bonds	Taylor	Moore	Ayris*	Best	Hurst	Brooking	Robson	Howe
	23/8	25,714	*5*	1				*Best*	*Carroll*	*Harper*	*Morris*	*Bell*	*Jefferson*	*Robertson*	*Mills*	*Clarke*	*Hamilton*	*Miller*	
							Ref: D Pugh	Four games and still no goals. Hurst played the first half on the wing. Only Clyde Best looked capable of besting David Best in the Town goal, though all of his good shots were fired from outside the area. Morris volleyed against a post and Bryan Hamilton missed a sitter at the death.											
5	H EVERTON		21	W	1-0	0-0	Best 54	Ferguson	McDowell	Lampard	Bonds	Taylor	Moore	Ayris	Best	Hurst	Brooking	Robson	
	28/8	26,878	*19*	3				*West*	*Scott*	*Newton*	*Kendall*	*Lyons*	*Harvey**	*Husband*	*Ball*	*Johnson*	*Hurst*	*Morrissey*	*Kenyon*
							Ref: H New	Greenwood bravely sticks with the same team that drew with Ipswich. Guts and endeavour won this game. Clyde Best outjumped keeper West from Bobby Moore's free-kick. Thereafter West Ham funnelled back in numbers, giving way to panic from time to time. Best also hit the bar.											
6	H COVENTRY			W	**4-0**	2-0	Best 17, 51, Hurst 35, Robson 52	Ferguson	McDowell	Lampard	Bonds	Taylor	Moore	Ayris	Best	Hurst	Brooking	Robson	
	30/8	28,176		5				*Glazier*	*Smith*	*Cattlin*	*Mortimer*	*Blackley*	*Barry*	*Young*	*Carr*	*O'Rourke*	*Hurst*	*McGuire*	
							Ref: M Kerkhof	Noel Cantwell's Coventry come unstuck in a fixture that, the previous season, saw Greenwood lambast his players behind closed doors. Once Best had burst through a plodding defence the outcome was clear. Brooking lit the fuses and Geoff Hurst's confidence returned after his goal.											
7	A NEWCASTLE		12	D	2-2	2-1	Hurst 14, Robson 32	Ferguson	McDowell	Lampard	Bonds	Taylor	Moore	Ayris	Best	Hurst	Brooking	Robson	
	4/9	*31,910*	*18*	6			*Tudor 12, Cassidy 66*	*McFaul*	*Craig*	*Clark*	*Gibb*	*Burton*	*Moncur**	*Hindson*	*Tudor*	*Macdonald*	*Guthrie*	*Hibbitt*	*Cassidy*
							Ref: C Fallon	Newcastle lost 1-5 at Leeds in midweek and are so inferior to West Ham that the home team are brutally barracked by their supporters. Robson returns to the ground he left in February and makes one goal and scores one. The man bought to replace him, Malcolm Macdonald, did little.											
8	H CHELSEA		9	W	2-1	0-0	Best 60, 80	Ferguson	McDowell	Lampard	Bonds	Taylor	Moore	Ayris*	Best	Hurst	Brooking	Robson	Howe
	11/9	36,866	*15*	8			*Hollins 74*	*Phillips*	*Mulligan*	*Harris*	*Hollins*	*Dempsey*	*Webb*	*Boyle*	*Garland*	*Osgood*	*Hudson*	*Houseman*	
							Ref: P Walters	Six unbeaten games is West Ham's best run for three years. The much-publicised clampdown by refs on foul play and tackles from behind has played its part. Best is dubbed the new Pele, with his feints and shimmies, and might have had five goals. Ferguson fumbled Hollins' effort.											
9	A MANCHESTER U		12	L	2-4	1-2	Best C 25, Brooking 57	Ferguson	McDowell	Lampard	Bonds	Taylor	Moore	Redknapp	Best	Hurst	Brooking	Robson	
	18/9	*53,334*	*2*	8			*Best G 21, 41, 79, Charlton 62*	*Stepney*	*O'Neil*	*Dunne*	*Gowling*	*James*	*Sadler*	*Morgan*	*Kidd*	*Charlton*	*Law*	*Best*	
							Ref: R Kirkpatrick	West Ham looked good in the first half; Frank O'Farrell's Man U in the second, as Hammers changed tactics and tried to raid down the middle rather than down the flanks. Clyde Best was overshadowed by the limping George Best. Moore dived to head off the line from Law at the end.											
10	H STOKE		10	W	2-1	1-0	Best 26, Moore 79	Ferguson	McDowell	Lampard	Bonds	Taylor	Moore	**Durrell**	Best	Hurst	Brooking	Robson	
	25/9	29,193	*12*	10			*Ritchie 59*	*Banks*	*Marsh*	*Pejic*	*Bernard*	*Smith*	*Bloor*	*Conroy**	*Greenhoff*	*Ritchie*	*Dobing*	*Jump*	*Stevenson*
							Ref: C Thomas	A lenient ref allowed Stoke to go unpunished for crippling tackles. West Ham were so much on top that John Ritchie's equaliser threatened to make a mockery of the game. As is was, West Ham needed a freak winner – Moore's shot looping off Denis Smith's foot and over Banks.											

No	H/A	Opponent / Att	Pos	Res / Pts	F-A	H-T	Scorers, Times, Referees	1	2	3	4	5	6	7	8	9	10	11	12 sub used
11	A	LEEDS	10	D	0-0	0-0		Ferguson	McDowell	Lampard	Bonds	Taylor	Moore	Redknapp	Best	Hurst	Brooking	Robson	
2/10		*30,942*	*5*	11				*Sprake*	*Reaney*	*Cooper*	*Yorath*	*Charlton*	*Hunter*	*Lorimer*	*Mann**	*Belfitt*	*Giles*	*Madeley*	*Galvin*
							Ref: G Jones	Injury-hit Leeds lack their usual thrust, enabling West Ham a more comfortable draw than they might have hoped for. Had Best's late header gone in instead of bouncing off the bar, it would have ended Leeds' unbeaten home record. Moore escaped a caution for deliberate handball.											
12	H	LEICESTER	12	D	1-1	0-0	Hurst 85	Ferguson	McDowell	Lampard	Bonds	Taylor	Moore	Redknapp	Best	Hurst	Brooking	Robson	
9/10		31,060	*20*	12			*Cross 87*	*Shilton*	*Whitworth*	*Nish*	*Cross*	*Sjoberg*	*Manley*	*Glover*	*Weller*	*Fern*	*Sammels*	*Birchenall*	
							Ref: R Gow	City's Cross presented a goal on a plate for Hurst, only to redeem himself seconds later by moving upfield for an equally scrappy equaliser. A boring, tactical game was enlivened only by Shilton, who pulled off a 'Banks-Pele' save from Pop Robson and also kept out Brooking's volley.											
13	A	WEST BROM	11	D	0-0	0-0		Ferguson	McDowell	Lampard	Bonds	Taylor	Moore	Redknapp	Best	Hurst	Brooking	Robson	
16/10		*20,740*	*16*	13				*Osborne*	*Hughes*	*Wilson*	*Cantello*	*Wile*	*Robertson*	*McLean*	*Brown*	*Astle*	*Gould*	*Hartford*	
							Ref: C Howell	Albion narrowly avoided a fifth successive home defeat, but have still scored only three goals since the end of August. In the latter stages Best, Bonds and Hurst all had chances to secure West Ham's first away win but were thwarted by the excellent Osborne, newly restored in goal.											
14	H	WOLVES	9	W	1-0	1-0	Best 10	Ferguson	McDowell	Lampard	Bonds	Taylor	Moore	Durrell	Best	Hurst	Brooking*	Robson	Howe
23/10		33,883	*11*	15				*Parkes*	*Shaw*	*Parkin*	*Bailey*	*Taylor*	*McAlle*	*Hegan**	*McCalliog*	*Richards*	*Dougan*	*Hibbitt*	*Wilson*
							Ref: K Sweet	Newboy Joe Durrell supplies the pass which Best converts from a tight angle. He also provided the crosses from which Robson and Hurst should have added further goals. Reprieved, Wolves pressed strongly at the close, when Ferguson repulsed Kenny Hibbitt's thunderbolt.											
15	A	CRYS PALACE	9	W	3-0	2-0	Coker 7, Bonds 14, Best 65	Grotier	McDowell	Lampard	Bonds	Taylor	Moore	Redknapp	Best	**Coker**	Brooking	Robson	
30/10		*41,540*	*21*	17				*Jackson*	*Payne*	*Wall*	*Goodman*	*McCormick*	*Blyth*	*Tambling*	*Craven*	*Hughes**	*Kellard*	*Taylor*	*Wallace*
							Ref: K Walker	Ade Coker is the latest youth product to burst through. It takes him just seven minutes to fire West Ham into the lead. Robson won the ball so easily to set up the second goal that Palace boss Bert Head was fuming. October has been a wonderful month for West Ham in league and cup.											
16	H	SHEFFIELD UTD	10	L	1-2	0-1	Robson 48	Ferguson	McDowell*	Lampard	Bonds	Taylor	Moore	Redknapp	Best	Hurst	Brooking	Robson	Ayris
6/11		36,595	*5*	17			*Rees 42, 75*	*Hope*	*Badger*	*Hemsley*	*Flynn*	*Colquhoun*	*Hockey*	*Woodward*	*Salmons*	*Reece*	*Currie*	*Scullion*	
							Ref: R Crabb	Blades overturn the form book to win comfortably in this League Cup rehearsal. Redknapp could not get going and Johnny Ayris was not brought on till the 83rd minute. Two headers by Rees won the game and but for erratic shooting by Scullion the margin could have been wider.											
17	A	HUDDERSFIELD	10	L	0-1	0-0		Ferguson	McDowell	Lampard	Bonds	Taylor	Moore	Redknapp	Best	Coker	Brooking	Robson	
13/11		***14,177***	*18*	17			*Smith D 77*	*Lawson D*	*Clarke*	*Hutt*	*Jones*	*Ellam*	*Cherry*	*Smith D*	*Smith S*	*Worthington*	*Lawson J*		
							Ref: F Nicholson	Wrote Frank Green: 'Having reached the dizzy heights of 10th West Ham relapsed into bad habits, including back-passing to Ferguson at a pace allowing opposing forwards a sporting chance of intervention.' Chapman dispossessed Bonds to set up the goal. Town's first win in nine.											
18	H	MANCHESTER C	13	L	0-2	0-1		Ferguson	Bonds	Lampard	Eustace	Taylor	Moore	Redknapp	Best	Coker*	Brooking	Robson	Durrell
20/11		33,694	*3*	17			*Lee 37p, Davies 60*	*Corrigan*	*Book*	*Donachie*	*Doyle*	*Booth*	*Oates*	*Summerbee*	*Bell*	*Davies*	*Lee*	*Mellor*	
							Ref: W Castle	Tommy Taylor's bitter feud with Wyn Davies, broadcast in detail on TV, cost West Ham a penalty. Davies himself scored City's second, bursting through from the halfway line. Bonds later pushed forward to replace the luckless Eustace, but it was too late. League form is sagging.											
19	A	LIVERPOOL	10	L	0-1	0-0		Ferguson	McDowell	Lampard	Bonds	Taylor	Moore	Redknapp	Best	Hurst	Brooking	Robson	
27/11		*43,399*	*6*	17			*Hughes 69*	*Clemence*	*Lawler*	*Lindsay*	*Smith*	*Ross*	*Hughes*	*Graham*	*Boersma*	*Heighway*	*Whitham*	*Callaghan*	
							Ref: N Burtenshaw	West Ham drew 4-4 with a European XI in Hurst's testimonial. James Mossop now writes: 'Emlyn Hughes cut through the West Ham defence as though its members were obstacles on a training exercise, used Jack Whitham for a quick wall-pass, and rammed in a fierce right-footer.'											
20	H	ARSENAL	13	D	0-0	0-0		Ferguson	McDowell	Lampard	Bonds	Taylor	Moore	Redknapp	Best	Hurst	Brooking	Robson	
4/12		35,155	*8*	18				*Wilson*	*Rice*	*McNab*	*Storey*	*McLintock*	*Simpson*	*Armstrong*	*Kelly*	*Radford*	*Kennedy*	*Graham*	
							Ref: C Nicholls	It is now five years and 11 matches since West Ham defeated Arsenal. They might have ended that sequence had Wilson not saved brilliantly from Robson. Wilson was voted man of the match by most Sunday papers. When Kelly's shot hit Taylor amidships, he appealed for a penalty.											
21	A	SOUTHAMPTON	12	D	3-3	3-2	Bonds 12, Best 21, Brooking 27	Ferguson	McDowell	Lampard	Bonds	Taylor	Moore	Redknapp	Best	Hurst	Brooking*	Robson	Llewellyn
11/12		*20,506*	*18*	19			*Gabriel 28p, Channon 35, Paine 77*	*Martin*	*Kirkup*	*Fry*	*Walker**	*Gabriel*	*Byrne*	*Paine*	*Channon*	*Davies*	*Stokes*	*Jenkins*	*O'Brien*
							Ref: R Tinkler	Hammers fans can hardly believe their eyes as a three-goal lead is casually tossed away. The decisive moment comes seconds after Brooking made it 3-0. Taylor fouled Jenkins and Gabriel clawed a goal back from the spot. Channon rounded Moore to set up Terry Paine's equaliser.											

No	Date	Att	Pos	Pt	F-A	H-T	Scorers, Times, and Referees	1	2	3	4	5	6	7	8	9	10	11	12 sub used
22	H NEWCASTLE		13	L	0-1	0-1		Ferguson	McDowell	Lampard	Bonds	Taylor	Moore	Ayris	Best	Hurst	Brooking	Robson	
	18/12	21,991	*16*	19			*Busby 5*	*McFaul*	*Clark*	*Guthrie*	*Nattrass*	*Burton*	*Howard*	*Barr'clough**	*Busby*	*Macdonald*	*Reid*	*Hibbitt*	*Gibb*
							Ref: T Reynolds	West Ham's league form is in tatters, and they soon trail to Viv Busby's header from a corner. Newcastle always seemed to win the 50-50 balls. Best hit a post and then faded, and McFaul pulled off two good stops from Robson. At least Taylor handled Malcolm Macdonald well.											
23	A TOTTENHAM		12	W	1-0	0-0	Best 47	Ferguson	McDowell	Lampard	Bonds	Taylor	Moore	Redknapp	Best	Hurst	Brooking	Robson	
	27/12	**53,888**	*7*	21				*Jennings*	*Evans*	*Knowles*	*Coates*	*England*	*Beal*	*Pratt*	*Perryman*	*Chivers*	*Peters*	*Gilzean*	
							Ref: R Challis	The rub of the green went West Ham's way when Mike England burst clear to miss early on, and when Neighbour shot against a defender's hand with no penalty given. Best nipped between Evans and England to head in Hurst's cross. The teams could meet in the League Cup final.											
24	H MANCHESTER U		11	W	3-0	1-0	Robson 40, Best 56, Hurst 82p	Ferguson	McDowell	Lampard	Bonds	Taylor	Moore	Redknapp	Best	Hurst	Brooking	Robson	
	1/1	**41,892**	*1*	23				*Stepney*	*Dunne*	*Burns*	*Gowling*	*Edwards*	*Sadler*	*Morgan*	*Kidd*	*Charlton*	*Law*	*Best*	
							Ref: J Taylor	A joyous match with no malicious fouls and neither trainer called upon. Robson, Brooking and Bonds dominated midfield. Man U had lost just twice in 23 matches and were unlucky when Law and Best hit the woodwork. Taylor took fright when his back-pass fell to Law, who missed.											
25	A EVERTON		14	L	1-2	1-2	Hurst 26p	Ferguson	McDowell	Lampard	Bonds	Taylor	Moore	Redknapp	Best	Hurst	Brooking	Robson	
	8/1	*38,482*	*12*	23			*Johnson 8, Harvey 14*	*West*	*Scott*	*McLaughlin*	*Kendall*	*Kenyon*	*Darracott*	*Johnson*	*Harvey*	*Royle*	*Lyons*	*Whittle*	
							Ref: D Turner	Everton chairman George Watts says: 'West Ham are the best side I have seen for years.' David Johnson whipped the ball off Moore's toe for the first goal, and Everton's second bobbled in after hitting both posts. Peter Scott punched away Geoff Hurst's header to concede the penalty.											
26	H DERBY		12	D	3-3	1-1	Lampard 42, Robson 49, Brooking 80	Ferguson	McDowell	Lampard	Bonds	Taylor	Moore	Redknapp	Best	Hurst	Brooking	Robson	
	22/1	31,045	*4*	24			*Hinton 4, Durban 65, Hector 87*	*Boulton*	*Webster*	*Robson*	*Durban*	*McFarland*	*Todd*	*McGovern*	*Gemmill*	*O'Hare*	*Hector*	*Hinton*	
							Ref: J Thacker	Taylor's error presents a quick goal to Marvin Hinton. Lampard levelled through a crowded box. Hurst and Best then set up Robson, but Alan Durban stabbed home Hinton's cross. Brooking went past three defenders for 3-1. Derby equalised a third time from yet another Hinton cross.											
27	A IPSWICH		13	L	0-1	0-0		Grotier	McDowell	Lampard	Bonds	Taylor	Moore	Redknapp	Best	Hurst	Brooking	Robson	
	29/1	*22,766*	*14*	24			*Morris 89*	*Best*	*Mills*	*Hunter*	*Jefferson*	*Harper*	*Morris*	*Viljoen*	*Miller*	*Robertson*	*Belfitt*	*Hill*	
							Ref: H Williams	A last-minute goal by Peter Morris – his first of the season in his 150th first-team game – gave Bobby Robson's Ipswich an ill-deserved win. Mick Hill ducked out of the way and the ball clipped Moore on its way past Grotier. This follows the League Cup disaster with Stoke City.											
28	A WOLVES		15	L	0-1	0-0		Ferguson	McDowell	Lampard*	Bonds	Taylor	Moore	Ayris	Best	Hurst	Brooking	Robson	Stephenson
	12/2	*26,852*	*6*	24			*Richards 62*	*Parkes*	*Shaw*	*Parkin*	*Taylor*	*Munro*	*McAlle*	*McCalliog*	*Hibbitt*	*Richards*	*Dougan*	*Wagstaffe*	
							Ref: G Hartley	West Ham face a tricky cup replay with Hereford. They have lost their scoring touch and Molineux, where Wolves have yet to lose this season, is hardly the place to find it. Yet Best blazes a great chance at Parkes and West Ham pay the price when Dougan heads down for Richards.											
29	H CRYS PALACE		13	D	1-1	0-0	Best 70	Ferguson	McDowell*	Lampard	Bonds	Taylor	Moore	Durrell	Best	Hurst	Brooking	Robson	Heffer
	19/2	28,209	*20*	25			*Payne 89*	*Jackson*	*Payne*	*Goodwin*	*Kellard*	*McCormick*	*Blyth*	*Craven*	*Queen*	*Wallace*	*Taylor*	*Tambling*	
							Ref: D Corbett	Both sides wasted chances to win, especially Palace, who looked frustrated when Tambling headed over the bar. Durrell hit a post for West Ham. Payne's late equaliser means West Ham remain just five points ahead of Palace. With just one goal in three games, Hammers lack punch.											
30	A SHEFFIELD UTD		14	L	**0-3**	0-1		Ferguson	McDowell	Lampard	Bonds	Taylor	Moore	Eustace	Best	Llewellyn*	Brooking	Robson	**Lock**
	29/2	*24,034*	*10*	25			*Dearden 12, 48, 74*	*Hope*	*Badger*	*Hemsley*	*MacKenzie*	*Colquhoun*	*Salmons*	*Woodward*	*Scullion*	*Dearden*	*Currie*	*Ford*	
							Ref: D Laing	Sheffield have not won in seven games and had lost 0-5 to West Ham earlier. Blades' boss John Harris is looking for new strikers, and Billy Dearden, whose place is under threat, responds with three goals – a header sandwiched between two drives. West Ham look in a state of shock.											
31	H HUDDERSFIELD		12	W	3-0	1-0	Best 37, 64, Robson 82	Ferguson	McDowell	Lampard	Bonds	Taylor	Moore	Redknapp	Best	Hurst	Brooking	Robson	
	4/3	18,521	*21*	27				*Lawson D*	*Clarke*	*Hutt*	*Smith S*	*Ellam*	*Cherry*	*Smith D*	*Dolan*	*Worthington*	*Lawson J*	*Chapman*	
							Ref: C Thomas	Huddersfield have just knocked West Ham out of the cup, though on this showing how they did so is a major mystery. Clyde Best tormented Ellam from first to last, heading in from Redknapp for the first goal, then sprinting past Ellam for the second. A flowing move preceded No 3.											

No	Venue	Opponent / Att	Pos	Res / Pts	F-A	H-T	Scorers, Times, and Referees	1	2	3	4	5	6	7	8	9	10	11	12 sub used
32	A	LEICESTER	14	L	0-2	0-0		Ferguson	McDowell	Lampard	Bonds	Taylor	Moore	Redknapp	Best	Hurst	Brooking	Robson	
11/3		*23,345*	*15*	27			*Nish 69, 82*	*Wallington*	*Whitworth*	*Cross*	*Sjoberg*	*Nish*	*Fern*	*Sammels*	*Weller*	*Glover*	*Farrington**	*Birchenall*	*Manley*
							Ref: H Hackney	Windswept Filbert St saw a lesson in artistry by West Ham and a lesson in finishing by full-back David Nish, who was switched to attack after half-time. He scores with a header and a lob. Mark Wallington makes his debut in place of the injured Shilton. Best hit the bar from five yards.											
33	H	NOTT'M FOREST	12	W	4-2	3-0	Robson 2, 30, Hurst 8, Brooking 89	Ferguson	McDowell	Lampard	Bonds	Taylor	Moore	Holland	Best	Hurst	Brooking	Robson	
18/3		20,960	*22*	29			*McKenzie 75, 90*	*Barron*	*Hindley*	*Gemmell*	*Chapman*	*Cottam*	*Fraser*	*Lyons*	*O'Neill*	*Buckley*	*Richardson*	*McKenzie*	
							Ref: D Smith	Three goals up at the break, West Ham went to sleep in the second half. McKenzie's late goal made no difference to Forest's prospects, but even though neither trainer was called upon, the ref allowed plenty of injury-time. This produced two more goals that distort the scoreline.											
34	A	COVENTRY	12	D	1-1	1-1	Best 35	Ferguson	McDowell	**Charles C**	Bonds	Taylor	Moore	Holland	Best	Hurst	Brooking	Robson	
21/3		*18,640*	*18*	30			*Smith 14*	*Glazier*	*Smith*	*Cattlin*	*Machin*	*Blockley*	*Barry*	*McGuire*	*Carr*	*Chilton*	*Graham*	*Hunt*	
							Ref: R Lea	Debutant Clive Charles created the goal that brought Hammers' equaliser, sending over the cross that Holland headed down to Best. Full-back Wilf Smith had fired Sky Blues into the lead. Coventry chief Jimmy Hill had appealed before the start for more vocal backing for the team.											
35	A	CHELSEA	12	L	1-3	0-1	Best 90	Ferguson	McDowell	Lampard	Bonds	Taylor	Moore	Holland	Best	Hurst	Brooking	Robson	
25/3		*45,137*	*10*	30			*Osgood 39, Mulligan 65, Hollins 84*	*Bonetti*	*Mulligan*	*Boyle*	*Hollins*	*Dempsey*	*Harris*	*Kember*	*Webb*	*Osgood*	*Hudson*	*Cooke*	
							Ref: R Matthewson	A meaningless match illuminated only by occasional flashes from Osgood, Hudson or Cooke. Osgood bagged his 30th goal of the season, Paddy Mulligan's 25-yarder somehow eluded a mass of bodies, and West Ham defenders stood by idly as five passes preceded Hollins' goal.											
36	H	LEEDS	12	D	2-2	2-0	Bonds 4, Hurst 35	Grotier	McDowell	Lampard	Bonds	Taylor	Moore	Redknapp	Best	Hurst	Brooking	Robson	
31/3		41,003	*2*	31			*Gray 62, 74*	*Sprake*	*Reaney*	*Cooper*	*Bremner*	*Charlton*	*Hunter*	*Lorimer*	*Clarke*	*Jordan**	*Gray*	*Madeley*	*Bates*
							Ref: H New	A huge crowd comes to see the 'new' Leeds, TV entertainers, but Upton Park was treated to the 'old' Leeds – hard and professional. Robson appeared to handle before crossing for Hammers' second goal. Gray 'bent' Leeds' first goal. Grotier's weak punch preceded Leeds' equaliser.											
37	H	TOTTENHAM	11	W	2-0	1-0	Brooking 40, Coker 89	Grotier	McDowell	Charles	Bonds	Taylor	Moore	Ayris*	Best	Coker	Brooking	Robson	Lock
1/4		30,763	*5*	33				*Jennings*	*Evans*	*Knowles*	*Pratt*	*Collins*	*Naylor*	*Gilzean*	*Perryman*	*Chivers*	*Peters*	*Pearce*	
							Ref: D Nippard	Brooking has been voted Hammer of the Year and he celebrates by scoring one of the goals of the season. He bemused Peter Collins before curling in a 20-yard lob. That strike was against the run of play. Gilzean fell over the ball and Chivers missed a sitter before Lock set up Coker.											
38	A	STOKE	12	D	0-0	0-0		Grotier	McDowell	Lampard	Bonds	Taylor	Moore	Redknapp	Best	Hurst	Brooking	Robson	
4/4		*24,688*	*14*	34				*Banks*	*Marsh*	*Elder*	*Bernard*	*Bloor*	*Skeels*	*Conroy*	*Greenhoff*	*Ritchie*	*Dobing*	*Eastham*	
							Ref: E Wallace	On a rain-soaked pitch Banks once again defies the Hammers in this, the sixth meeting of the sides this season. Hammers missed three chances in the first three minutes, Best missing twice and Hurst once. At the other end Eastham had one effort headed off the line, another hit the post.											
39	A	MANCHESTER C	14	L	1-3	0-1	Hurst 82	Grotier	McDowell	Lampard	Bonds	Taylor	Moore	Redknapp	Best	Hurst	Brooking	Robson	
8/4		*38,491*	*4*	34			*Marsh 11, 68, Bell 49,*	*Healey*	*Book*	*Donachie*	*Towers*	*Booth*	*Oakes*	*Lee*	*Bell*	*Davies*	*Marsh*	*Summerbee*	
							Ref: J Hunting	Rodney Marsh has yet to convince City fans that Malcolm Allison was wise to buy him. Two goals against lifeless Hammers, his first goals for City, helps his cause. Had Redknapp done better than to rattle Healey's crossbar in the sixth minute the outcome might have been different.											
40	H	LIVERPOOL	14	L	0-2	0-1		Ferguson	McDowell	Lampard	Bonds	Taylor	Moore	Redknapp	Best	Hurst	Brooking	Robson	
15/4		32,660	*3*	34			*Toshack 9, Heighway 46*	*Clemence*	*Lawler*	*Lindsay*	*Smith*	*Lloyd*	*Hughes*	*Keegan*	*Hall*	*Heighway*	*Toshack*	*Callaghan*	
							Ref: K Wynn	John McDowell's lamentable attempt to clear Lawler's effort presented an early goal for Toshack. Straight after the turnaround, the previously impeccable Moore was dispossessed by Steve Heighway for the second. Later, the unmarked Clyde Best saw his effort cleared off the line.											
41	A	ARSENAL	15	L	1-2	1-1	Brooking 37	Ferguson	McDowell	Charles	Bonds	Taylor	Lock	Durrell	Best	Coker	Brooking	Robson	
22/4		*42,251*	*6*	34			*Ball 13, 46*	*Barnett*	*Rice*	*McNab*	*Storey*	*McLintock**	*Simpson*	*Armstrong*	*Ball*	*Radford*	*Kennedy*	*Graham*	*Batson*
							Ref: V James	Bertie Mee's Arsenal have their minds on their impending FA Cup final. Despite this, and stand-in keeper Geoff Barnett's tendency to panic, they were still too good for West Ham. Best moment of the game came when Durrell beat two men and crossed for Brooking's classic header.											
42	H	SOUTHAMPTON	14	W	1-0	0-0	Robson 60	Ferguson	Lampard	Charles	Bonds	Stephenson	Taylor	Durrell	Best	Holland	Brooking*	Robson	Boyce
1/5		**18,479**	*19*	36				*Martin*	*McCarthy*	*Hollywood*	*Steele*	*Bennett*	*Talkes*	*Paine*	*Channon*	*Davies*	*O'Brien**	*O'Neill*	*Gabriel*
Average	Home 30,007	Away 31,556					Ref: T Spencer	Ron Davies and Mick Channon look knackered from their efforts to stave off relegation for the Saints. Hammers were defied by Eric Martin in goal. He was beaten once, when Robson turned in Lampard's low cross. Bonds and Durrell hit the bar; Steele and Gabriel cleared off the line.											

League Cup	F-A	H-T	Scorers, Times, and Referees	1	2	3	4	5	6	7	8	9	10	11	12 sub used
2 H CARDIFF 12 D	1-1	1-0	Bonds 32	Ferguson	McDowell	Lampard	Bonds	Taylor	Moore	Ayris	Best	Hurst	Brooking	Robson	
8/9 24,432 *2:19*			*Foggon 63*	*Eadie*	*Jones**	*Bell*	*Sutton*	*Murray*	*Phillips*	*Gibson*	*Clark*	*Woodruff*	*Warboys*	*Foggon*	*Parsons*
			Ref: J Taylor	Pop Robson is being played in midfield rather than up front, which is why he wanted to leave Newcastle. Greenwood placed Brooking on the transfer list last season, but he will have to take him off if he continues playing like this. Five minutes from time Clark hit Ferguson's crossbar.											
2R A CARDIFF 12 W	2-1	0-1	Hurst 83, 84	Ferguson	McDowell	Lampard	Bonds	Taylor	Moore	Redknapp	Best	Hurst	Brooking	Robson	
22/9 *30,100 2:19*			*Clark 15*	*Eadie*	*Jones*	*Bell*	*Sutton*	*Murray*	*Phillips*	*Gibson*	*Clark*	*Woodruff*	*Warboys*	*Hoy*	
			Ref: J Taylor	When Warboys headed down to Clark it looked grim for the Hammers. Hurst collected Redknapp's pass to smash a late equaliser, and within seconds Hurst nipped through a stunned defence for the winner. The prize for the winners is a plum home draw against either Derby or Leeds.											
3 H LEEDS 10 D	0-0	0-0		Ferguson	McDowell	Lampard	Bonds	Taylor	Moore	Redknapp	Best	Hurst	Brooking	Robson	
6/10 35,890 *5*				*Sprake*	*Davie*	*Cooper*	*Bremner*	*Charlton*	*Hunter*	*Lorimer*	*Yorath*	*Belfitt*	*Giles*	*Madeley*	
			Ref: R Matthewson	Even without four internationals, Leeds soaked up West Ham pressure. The ref disallowed two West Ham 'goals', Terry Cooper twice cleared off the line, and Hurst hit the bar. After the match a beer can was thrown at the ref and a brick tossed through the Leeds dressing room window.											
3R A LEEDS 11 W	1-0	0-0	Best 98	Ferguson	McDowell	Lampard	Bonds	Taylor	Moore	Redknapp	Best	Hurst	Brooking	Robson	
20/10 *26,504 7*	*aet*			*Harvey*	*Reaney*	*Cooper*	*Bremner*	*Charlton*	*Hunter*	*Lorimer*	*Clarke*	*Jones**	*Giles*	*Madeley*	*Gray*
			Ref: R Matthewson	Leeds have now failed to score against West Ham in three quick matches. The home team were undone by a gem of a goal, Redknapp's cross being turned in by a towering Best header. Moore began the move, played brilliantly, and shrugged off the wolf-whistles of the home crowd.											
4 H LIVERPOOL 9 W	2-1	1-1	Hurst 42, Robson 84	Ferguson	McDowell	Lampard	Bonds	Taylor	Moore	Redknapp	Best	Hurst*	Brooking	Robson	Howe
27/10 40,878 *7*			*Graham 30*	*Clemence*	*Lawler*	*Ross*	*Smith*	*Lloyd*	*Hughes*	*Graham*	*Evans*	*Heighway*	*Toshack*	*Callaghan*	
			Ref: D Turner	Geoff Hurst cancelled out Bobby Graham's goal, having been set up by Clyde Best. Hurst, however, had aggravated a thigh injury and failed to reappear after the interval. Redknapp crossed for Robson's winner at the far post. 'I'm forever blowing bubbles' echoed round Upton Park.											
QF H SHEFFIELD UTD 10 W	5-0	3-0	Robson 5, 33, 87, Best 40, 76	Ferguson	McDowell	Lampard	Bonds	Taylor	Moore	Redknapp	Best	Hurst*	Brooking	Robson	Howe
17/11 36,834 *4*				*Hope*	*Badger*	*Goulding*	*Flynn*	*Colquhoun*	*Hockey*	*Woodward*	*Salmons*	*Reece*	*Currie*	*Scullion*	
			Ref: D Smith	11 days earlier the Blades beat West Ham in the league. This is their first defeat in eight games against London opponents. Robson scored the classic hat-trick, one goal with his head, another with his right foot and one with his left. London has three semi-finalists – Chelsea and Spurs.											
SF A STOKE 13 W	2-1	1-1	Hurst 28p, Best 62	Ferguson	McDowell	Lampard	Bonds	Taylor	Moore	Redknapp	Best	Hurst	Brooking	Robson	
1 8/12 *36,400 11*			*Dobing 14*	*Banks*	*Marsh*	*Pejic*	*Bernard*	*Bloor*	*Jump*	*Conroy*	*Greenhoff*	*Ritchie*	*Dobing*	*Eastham*	
			Ref: A Morrissey	West Ham failed to withstand Stoke's ferocious early onslaught, but inspired by Bonds they come from behind. They are odds on to reach the final. A four-man move preceded Best's volley in off the bar. Moore's professional foul on Greenhoff earned the second booking of his career.											
SF H STOKE 12 L	0-1	0-0		Ferguson	McDowell	Lampard	Bonds	Taylor	Moore	Redknapp	Best	Hurst	Brooking	Robson	
2 15/12 38,771 *11*	*aet*		*Ritchie 73*	*Banks*	*Marsh*	*Pejic*	*Bernard*	*Bloor*	*Skeels*	*Conroy*	*Greenhoff*	*Ritchie*	*Dobing*	*Eastham**	*Mahoney*
			Ref: K Walker (Hammers draw 2-2 on aggregate)	Only once before has a team which lost the first leg of a League Cup semi-final reached the final. The error by Taylor and McDowell that set up Ritchie would have counted for nothing had not Banks pulled off a super save from Hurst's penalty, after Banks had taken Redknapp's legs.											
SF N STOKE 11 D	0-0	0-0		Ferguson	McDowell	Lampard	Bonds	Taylor	Moore	Redknapp	Best	Hurst	Brooking	Robson	
R 5/1 *49,247 12*	*aet*			*Banks*	*Marsh*	*Pejic*	*Bernard*	*Smith*	*Bloor*	*Conroy*	*Dobing*	*Ritchie*	*Greenhoff**	*Eastham*	*Skeels*
(At Hillsborough)			Ref: R Matthewson	Stoke have won nothing in their 108-year history, and had Gordon Banks not saved twice from Best they would still be waiting. Yet Stoke had much of the play, with Conroy and Eastham orchestrating their attacks. Stoke fans gave Moore the bird for an undignified tackle on Greenhoff.											
SF N STOKE 12 L	2-3	1-1	Bonds 39, Brooking 46	Ferguson	McDowell	Lampard	Bonds	Taylor	Moore	Redknapp*	Best	Hurst	Brooking	Robson	Eustace
2R 26/1 *49,247 11*			*Bernard 33, Dobing 50, Conroy 55*	*Banks*	*Marsh*	*Pejic*	*Bernard*	*Smith*	*Bloor*	*Conroy*	*Greenhoff*	*Ritchie*	*Dobing*	*Eastham*	
(At Old Trafford)			Ref: P Partridge	Conroy's nasty foul on Ferguson takes the concussed keeper temporarily from the field. Moore saves Bernard's penalty, but not the follow up. Marvellous goals for Bonds and Brooking give West Ham the edge, but Stoke not only scored twice themselves, but missed other chances too.											

FA Cup

Rd	Venue	Opponent	Pos	Res	Score	HT	Scorers, Times, and Referees											
3	H	LUTON	12	W	2-1	2-0	Hurst 2, Best 25	Ferguson	McDowell	Lampard	Bonds	Taylor	Moore*	Redknapp	Best	Hurst	Brooking	Robson	Eustace
15/1		32,099	*2:13*				*Givens 53*	*Read*	*Ryan*	*Slough*	*Keen*	*Nicholl*	*Moore*	*Anderson*	*Court*	*Halom*	*Givens*	*Hindson*	
							Ref: K Burns	A gripping cup-tie. Brooking set up Hurst in 91 seconds. At 2-0 everything seems settled, but Don Givens' header transformed the match. On 68 minutes Read saved Hurst's penalty. On 78 minutes Gordon Hindson misses one at the other end. Nicholl then shot against Ferguson's legs.											
4	A	HEREFORD	13	D	0-0	0-0		Ferguson	McDowell	Lampard	Bonds	Taylor	Moore	Redknapp	Best	Hurst	Brooking	Robson	
9/2		*15,000*	*SL*					*Potter*	*Gough*	*Mallender*	*Jones*	*McLaughlin*	*Addison*	*George*	*Tyler*	*Meadows*	*Owen*	*Radford*	
							Ref: R Tinkler	Greenwood sighs with relief as his team avoid the greatest humiliation in their history. The Southern Leaguers, who had beaten Newcastle in Round 3 and launched the career of commentator John Motson, pressed relentlessly. Tyler's shot, deflected by Moore, was cleared by Taylor.											
4R	H	HEREFORD	15	W	3-1	1-0	Hurst 43, 52, 74	Ferguson	McDowell	Lampard	Bonds	Taylor	Moore	Redknapp	Best	Hurst	Brooking	Robson	
14/2		42,271	*SL*				*Meadows 84*	*Potter*	*Gough*	*Mallender**	*Jones*	*McLaughlin*	*Addison*	*George*	*Tyler*	*Meadows*	*Owens*	*Radford*	*Tucker*
							Ref: R Tinkler	Hereford played their part but never seriously threatened once Best's direct run had carved out Hurst's first goal. But for appalling casualness in front of goal, the score might have been embarrassing. Reg Pratt pledges his support for Hereford's application to join the Football League.											
5	A	HUDDERSFIELD	13	L	2-4	1-1	Robson 45, Best 83 *[Worth'ton 70]*	Ferguson	McDowell	Lampard	Bonds	Taylor	Moore	Redknapp	Best	Hurst*	Brooking	Robson	Heffer
26/2		*27,080*	*21*				*Lawson J 23, Dolan 51, Smith D 68,*	*Lawson D*	*Clarke*	*Hutt*	*Smith S*	*Ellam*	*Cherry*	*Smith D*	*Dolan*	*Worthington*	*Lawson J*	*Chapman*	
							Ref: N Burtenshaw	The pain of this defeat showed in Ron Greenwood's face. Memories of the capitulation at Blackpool a year earlier came flooding back. West Ham couldn't cope with big Frank Worthington. Five of his blockbuster shots from outside the box almost carried Ferguson into the net.											

		Home					Away					
	P	W	D	L	F	A	W	D	L	F	A	Pts
1 Derby	42	16	4	1	43	10	8	6	7	26	23	58
2 Leeds	42	17	4	0	54	10	7	5	9	19	21	57
3 Liverpool	42	17	3	1	48	16	7	6	8	16	14	57
4 Manchester C	42	16	3	2	48	15	7	8	6	29	30	57
5 Arsenal	42	15	2	4	36	13	7	6	8	22	27	52
6 Tottenham	42	16	3	2	45	13	3	10	8	18	29	51
7 Chelsea	42	12	7	2	41	20	6	5	10	17	29	48
8 Manchester U	42	13	2	6	39	26	6	8	7	30	35	48
9 Wolves	42	10	7	4	35	23	8	4	9	30	34	47
10 Sheffield Utd	42	10	8	3	39	26	7	4	10	22	34	46
11 Newcastle	42	10	6	5	30	18	5	5	11	19	34	41
12 Leicester	42	9	6	6	18	11	4	7	10	23	35	39
13 Ipswich	42	7	8	6	19	19	4	8	9	20	34	38
14 WEST HAM	42	10	6	5	31	19	2	6	13	16	32	36
15 Everton	42	8	9	4	28	17	1	9	11	9	31	36
16 West Brom	42	6	7	8	22	23	6	4	11	20	31	35
17 Stoke	42	6	10	5	26	25	4	5	12	13	31	35
18 Coventry	42	7	10	4	27	23	2	5	14	17	44	33
19 Southampton	42	8	5	8	31	28	4	2	15	21	52	31
20 Crys Palace	42	4	8	9	26	31	4	5	12	13	34	29
21 Nott'm Forest	42	6	4	11	25	29	2	5	14	22	52	25
22 Huddersfield	42	4	7	10	12	22	2	6	13	15	37	25
	924	227	129	106	723	437	106	129	227	437	723	924

Odds & ends

Double wins (1) Spurs.
Doubles losses: (3) Sheffield Utd, Manchester C, Liverpool.

Won from behind: (2) Cardiff LC (a), Liverpool LC (h).
Lost from in front: (1) Stoke LC (n).

High spots: 12 league games with just one defeat from 23 August.
This lifted the Hammers to 9th.
Knocking both Leeds and Liverpool out of the League Cup.

Low spots: Losing the first three league games.
Losing all four league fixtures in November.
Losing to Stoke in dubious circumstances in League Cup semi-final.

Hammer of the Year: Trevor Brooking.
Ever-presents: (4) Bonds, Taylor, Best, and Robson.
Hat-tricks: (2) Geoff Hurst (1), Bryan Robson (1).
Leading scorer: (23) Clyde Best.

	Appearances						Goals			
	Lge	*Sub*	LC	*Sub*	FAC	*Sub*	Lge	LC	FAC	Tot
Ayris, Johnny	**11**	*1*	1							
Best, Clyde	**42**		10		4		**17**	4	2	**23**
Bonds, Billy	**42**		10		4		**3**	2		**5**
Boyce, Ronnie		*1*								
Brooking, Trevor	**40**		10		4		**6**	1		**7**
Charles, Clive	**4**									
Coker, Ade	**5**						**2**			**2**
Durrell, Joe	**5**	*1*								
Eustace, Peter	**2**			*1*		*1*				
Ferguson, Bobby	**36**		10		4					
Grotier, Peter	**6**									
Heffer, Paul		*1*				*1*				
Holland, Pat	**4**									
Howe, Bobby	**1**	*4*		*2*						
Hurst, Geoff	**34**		10		4		**8**	4	4	**16**
Lampard, Frank	**39**		10		4		**1**			**1**
Llewellyn, Dave	**1**	*1*								
Lock, Kevin	**1**	*2*								
McDowell. John	**40**		10		4					
Moore, Bobby	**40**		10		4		**1**			**1**
Redknapp, Harry	**22**		9		4					
Robson, Bryan	**42**		10		4		**9**	4	1	**14**
Stephenson, John	**3**	*1*								
Taylor, Tommy	**42**		10		4					
24 players used	**462**	*12*	**110**	*3*	**44**	*2*	**47**	**15**	**7**	**69**

John Lyall and Ron Greenwood hold the 1975 FA Cup

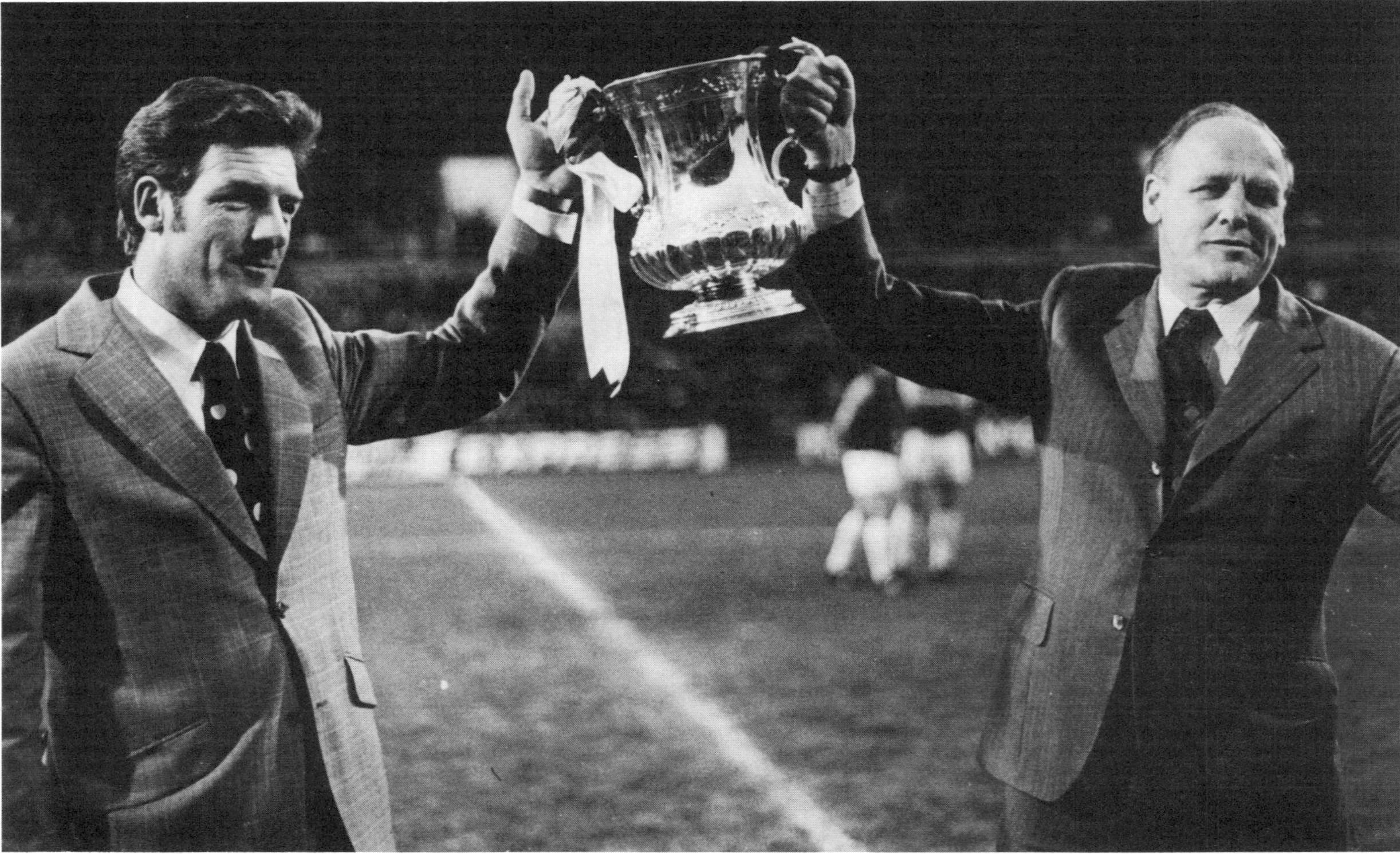

The FA Cup winning team returns to joyous scenes in east London

LEAGUE DIVISION 1 — Manager: Ron Greenwood — SEASON 1972-73

No	Date	Att	Pos	Pt	F-A	H-T	Scorers, Times, and Referees	1	2	3	4	5	6	7	8	9	10	11	12 sub used
1	A WEST BROM			D	0-0	0-0		Ferguson	McDowell	Lampard	Bonds	Taylor	Moore	**Tyler**	Best	Coker	Brooking	Robson	
	12/8	*21,509*		1				*Smith*	*Nisbet*	*Wilson*	*Cantello*	*Wile*	*Robertson*	*Brown T*	*Brown A*	*Gould*	*Suggett*	*Hartford*	
							Ref: H Hackney	Geoff Hurst has signed for Stoke and West Ham have bought 27-year-old Dudley Tyler from Hereford for £25,000. Tyler, Robson and Brooking all missed chances that might have earned West Ham two points instead of one. There is talk of signing Bill Garner from Southend.											
2	H COVENTRY			W	1-0	0-0	Best 53	Ferguson	McDowell	Lampard	Bonds	Taylor	Moore	Tyler	Best	Coker	Brooking	Robson	
	14/8	27,498		3				*Glazier*	*Coop*	*Cattlin*	*Machin*	*Blockley*	*Barry*	*Mortimer*	*Graham*	*Hunt*	*Carr*	*Smith*	
							Ref: J Gow	Coventry erected a 4-4-2 midfield barrage designed to stifle the game and earn them a point. Best hit the bar early on, but the life was being squeezed out of the game when Best headed in. Glazier scooped the ball out but the linesman confirmed a goal. Coventry players were angry.											
3	H LEICESTER		5	W	5-2	2-2	Moore 17, Coker 38, Robson 53, 78,	Ferguson	McDowell	Lampard	Bonds	Taylor	Moore	Tyler	Best	Coker	Brooking	Robson	
	19/8	25,414	*20*	5			*Stringfellow 3, Glover 32* [Tyler 70]	*Shilton*	*Whitworth*	*Nish*	*Woollett*	*Sjoberg*	*Cross*	*Farrington*	*Sammels*	*Weller*	*Stringfellow*	*Glover*	
							Ref: S Kayley	Dudley Tyler's ability to drift into menacing positions was the source of two Hammers goals. He also netted his first for the club. Leicester manager Jimmy Bloomfield admitted afterwards: 'They destroyed us'. Transfer talk is increasing: Hurst's intended replacement is Bill Garner.											
4	A WOLVES		5	L	**0-3**	0-0		Ferguson	McDowell	Lampard	Bonds	Taylor	Moore	Tyler	Best	Coker	Brooking	Robson	
	22/8	*21,958*	*8*	5			*McCalliog 74, Richards 88, Dougan 90*	*Parkes*	*Shaw*	*McAlle*	*Sunderland*	*Munro*	*Owen*	*McCalliog*	*Hibbitt*	*Richards*	*Dougan*	*Daley*	
							Ref: E Jolly	Derek Dougan's last-minute header made him the first Irishman to score 200 goals in the Football League. Injury-strapped Wolves had to play their youth-team coach, Brian Owen. McCalliog's cheeky chip broke the deadlock, and as West Ham piled forward they left gaps at the back.											
5	A LIVERPOOL		12	L	2-3	2-1	Robson 38, 43 *[Hughes 64]*	Ferguson	McDowell	Lampard	Bonds	Taylor	Moore	Tyler	Best	Holland	Brooking	Robson	
	26/8	*50,491*	*1*	5			*Toshack 42, Ferguson 60 (og),*	*Clemence*	*Lawler*	*Lindsay*	*Smith*	*Lloyd*	*Hughes*	*Keegan*	*Hall*	*Heighway*	*Toshack*	*Callaghan*	
							Ref: J Yates	The flash-point comes with Liverpool's second equaliser. Challenged by Keegan, Ferguson drops the ball over his head. Moore earns a four-point caution for dissent. Not many visitors score two at Anfield, and Robson is convinced he was denied a penalty when felled by Lawler.											
6	A ARSENAL		12	L	0-1	0-1		Grotier	McDowell	Lampard	Bonds	Taylor	Moore	Tyler	Best	Holland	Brooking	Robson*	Lock
	29/8	*43,802*	*2*	5			*Ball 1p*	*Barnett*	*Rice*	*McNab*	*Storey*	*McLintock*	*Simpson*	*Armstrong**	*Ball*	*Radford*	*Kennedy*	*Graham*	*George*
							Ref: J Hunting	Both teams went in search of goals, though the one that mattered came very early. Pat Rice fell at the feet of two defenders and Alan Ball took the penalty. Geoff Barnett made fine saves from Clyde Best and Tommy Taylor. Bobby Moore looks classy, pushed forward into midfield.											
7	H MANCHESTER U		12	D	2-2	1-1	Robson 31, 78	Grotier	McDowell	Lampard	Bonds	Taylor	Moore	Tyler	Best	Holland	Brooking	Robson	
	2/9	31,939	*21*	6			*Best 10, Moore 77*	*Stepney*	*O'Neil*	*Dunne*	*Buchan*	*James*	*Sadler*	*Morgan*	*Law**	*Charlton*	*Best*	*Moore*	*McIlroy*
							Ref: G Hill	Man U have yet to win. Clyde Best struggled under the burden of being Hurst's replacement. A revitalised George Best fended off Robson for No 1. Robson took Brooking's pass to level. Ian Storey-Moore's first goal of the season was cancelled out by Robson, from McDowell's cross.											
8	A CHELSEA		11	W	3-1	2-1	Taylor 4, Moore 23, Bonds 82	Grotier	McDowell	Lampard	Bonds	Taylor	Moore	Tyler	Best	Holland	Brooking	Robson	
	9/9	*34,392*	*7*	8			*Garland 15*	*Bonetti*	*Mulligan*	*McCreadie*	*Hollins*	*Webb*	*Harris*	*Garland*	*Kember*	*Osgood*	*Hudson**	*Houseman*	*Garner*
							Ref: K Walker	Chelsea poached Bill Garner from under the noses of West Ham following a League Cup-tie at Roots Hall, when Garner impressed. Injury to Hudson brought Garner off the bench after just nine minutes. Moore sidefooted a free-kick to Taylor, then restored the lead with a corker.											
9	H NORWICH		9	W	4-0	3-0	Brooking 29, Robson 37, 78p,	Grotier	McDowell	Lampard	Bonds	Taylor	Moore	Tyler	Best	Holland	Brooking	Robson	
	16/9	27,780	*12*	10			[Taylor 41]	*Keelan*	*Payne*	*Butler*	*Anderson*	*Forbes*	*Briggs*	*Livermore*	*Bone*	*Cross*	*Paddon*	*O'Donnell*	
							Ref: A Jones	Moore's incisive passing in midfield is the inspiration for all West Ham's attacking moves. He crosses to Brooking for the first goal, then floats a cross onto Robson's head from 35 yards. Brooking was fouled in the box for the penalty. Will Ramsey play Moore in England's midfield?											
10	A TOTTENHAM		12	L	0-1	0-0		Grotier	McDowell*	Lampard	Bonds	Taylor	Moore	Tyler	Brooking	Holland	Best	Robson	Charles
	23/9	***51,700***	*2*	10			*Lampard 88 (og)*	*Jennings*	*Evans*	*Knowles*	*Pratt*	*England*	*Beal*	*Gilzean*	*Perryman*	*Chivers*	*Peters**	*Pearce*	*Coates*
							Ref: V James	Just before Spurs' late winner Pop Robson hit Jennings' crossbar. Instead of 1-0 it was shortly 0-1. Mike England's header was going wide until Lampard attempted an awkward clearance and directed the ball into goal off his posterior. A kick on the thigh took Peters off at half-time.											

No / Date	H/A	Opponent / Att	Pos	Res / Pts	FT	HT	Scorers, Times, Referees	1	2	3	4	5	6	7	8	9	10	11	12 sub used
11	H	BIRMINGHAM	11	W	2-0	1-0	Bonds 3, Best 68	Grotier	Charles	Lampard	Bonds	Taylor	Moore	Tyler	Best	Holland	Brooking	Robson	
30/9		26,482	*16*	12				*Latchford D*	*Martin*	*Pendrey*	*Campbell**	*Hynd*	*Page*	*Burns*	*Francis*	*Latchford R*	*Hope*	*Taylor*	*Harland*
							Ref: Nicholls	Clyde Best has lost so much confidence that he is delighted with his 12-yard effort that seals victory. Bonds had put West Ham in front with a shot from 18 yards. The ref gave City a penalty when Taylor 'fouled' Gordon Taylor (later of the PFA). Grotier saved Campbell's spot kick.											
12	A	IPSWICH	10	D	1-1	0-0	Best 65	Grotier	Lampard	Charles	Bonds	Taylor	Moore	Tyler	Best	Holland	Brooking	Robson	
7/10		*22,377*	*9*	13			*Hamilton 83*	*Best*	*Mills*	*Harper*	*Collard*	*Hunter*	*Beattie*	*Hamilton*	*Viljoen*	*Belfitt*	*Whymark*	*Lambert*	
							Ref: K Wynn	A pleasant autumn afternoon saw West Ham go in front with a picture goal. Brooking crossed to the far post where Clyde Best headed the ball past David Best. Had they hung on, Hammers would have notched their first win at Ipswich in almost a decade. Hamilton headed the equaliser.											
13	H	SHEFFIELD UTD	7	W	3-1	3-0	Brooking 16, Robson 33, 39	Grotier	McDowell	Lampard	Bonds	Taylor	Moore	Tyler	Best	Holland	Brooking	Robson	
14/10		25,379	*9*	15			*Taylor 50 (og)*	*McAlister*	*Goulding*	*Hemsley**	*Flynn*	*Colquhoun*	*Hockey*	*Woodward*	*Badger*	*Warboys*	*Currie*	*Holmes*	*Mackenzie*
							Ref: D Turner	Alf Ramsey takes in this match. Pop Robson is scoring so frequently that he is rumoured to be Ramsey's target. Robson himself, having at last been pushed from midfield to attack, reckons West Ham need a ball winner, especially away from home, where Robson has scored only twice.											
14	A	MANCHESTER C	10	L	3-4	2-4	Best 16, Ayris 44, Moore 68	Grotier	McDowell	Lampard	Bonds	Taylor	Moore	Ayris	Best	Holland	Brooking	Robson	
21/10		*30,890*	*17*	15			*Towers 4, Marsh 24, 34, Summerbee 35*	*Healey*	*Book*	*Donachie*	*Doyle*	*Booth*	*Jeffries*	*Summerbee*	*Bell*	*Marsh*	*Lee*	*Towers*	
							Ref: K Burns	Moore scored with a header, a rarity. It brought the score back to 3-4 and gave West Ham a fighting chance of drawing. Ayris had also scored a peach of a goal, skipping past Doyle and Donachie. Maine Road in recent years has seen 3-5, 1-6, 1-4, 1-5, and now this latest goal-bonanza.											
15	H	CRYS PALACE	8	W	**4-0**	2-0	Brooking 5, 21, McDowell 61, [Robson 65]	Ferguson	Lampard	Charles	McDowell	Taylor	Moore	Ayris	Best	Holland	Brooking	Robson	
28/10		28,894	*22*	17				*Hammond*	*Payne*	*Taylor*	*Phillip*	*McCormick*	*Blyth*	*Pinkney*	*Cooke*	*Craven*	*Hinshelwood*	*Tambling*	
							Ref: E Wallace	Immediately after the match, which leaves Palace still bottom, Palace boss Bert Head signs Don Rogers from Swindon. Palace could have done with him against West Ham. Bobby Moore set up both Brooking goals with astute passes. John McDowell's was his first ever league goal.											
16	H	WOLVES	6	D	2-2	0-0	Robson 55, Brooking 88	Ferguson	McDowell	Lampard	Lock	Taylor	Moore	Tyler*	Best	Holland	Brooking	Robson	Ayris
4/11		29,524	*11*	18			*Kindon 64, 75*	*Parkes*	*Shaw*	*McAlle*	*Bailey*	*Munro*	*Jefferson*	*McCalliog*	*Hibbitt*	*Richards*	*Kindon*	*Wagstaffe*	
							Ref: K Styles	This perky game had Wolves' skipper Mike Bailey saying what a pleasure it was to play West Ham. He might have added what a pleasure it was to meet such a generous defence, since Kindon twice took advantage of dithering. Brooking's late header prevented a Wolves' double.											
17	A	COVENTRY	9	L	1-3	0-1	McDowell 64	Ferguson	McDowell	Lampard	Bonds	Taylor	Moore	Tyler	Best	Holland	Brooking	Robson	
11/11		*27,189*	*13*	18			*Hutchison 25, Stein 58, Alderson 84*	*Glazier*	*Coop*	*Cattlin*	*Smith*	*Barry*	*Parker*	*Mortimer*	*Alderson*	*Stein*	*Carr**	*Hutchison*	*McGuire*
							Ref: I Williams	Coventry general manager Joe Mercer is full of praise for Moore, who played both in defence and midfield. Coventry extend their unbeaten run to six, helped by expensive signings Colin Stein and Tommy Hutchison. West Ham appealed in vain that Coventry's opener was offside.											
18	H	DERBY	11	L	1-2	0-2	Robson 56	Ferguson	Charles	Lampard	Bonds	Taylor	Moore	Tyler	Ayris*	Holland	Brooking	Robson	Best
18/11		28,154	*15*	18			*Hector 1, 15*	*Boulton*	*Webster*	*Nish*	*Hennessey*	*McFarland*	*Todd*	*McGovern*	*Gemmill*	*O'Hare*	*Hector*	*Hinton*	
							Ref: N Burtenshaw	Coker, Best and Ayris all look disenchanted, and Dudley Tyler is much less effective than when he arrived. Derby spring on West Ham their first home defeat of the season, which looked on the cards from the moment Clive Charles presented the ball to Kevin Hector in 53 seconds.											
19	A	EVERTON	8	W	2-1	1-1	Brooking 44, Best 65	Ferguson	McDowell	Lampard*	Bonds	Taylor	Moore	Tyler	Best	Holland	Brooking	Robson	Lock
25/11		*27,558*	*14*	20			*Wright B 32*	*Lawson*	*Scott*	*Newton*	*Kendall*	*Kenyon*	*Hurst*	*Wright B*	*Darracott*	*Belfitt*	*Harvey*	*Connolly*	
							Ref: J Taylor	Bobby Moore marks his 500th league game by threading a reverse pass for Brooking's equaliser. Goodison's smallest crowd of the season had welcomed Bernie Wright's earlier header. Clyde Best's 60-yard run climaxed with a dummy round the keeper. A goal of the month contender.											
20	H	NEWCASTLE	7	D	1-1	0-0	Brooking 80	Ferguson	McDowell	Lock	Bonds	Taylor	Moore	Ayris	Best	Holland	Brooking	Robson	
2/12		23,785	*8*	21			*Craig 81*	*McFaul*	*Craig*	*Clark*	*Nattrass*	*Howard*	*Moncur*	*Barrowclough*	*Smith*	*Macdonald*	*Tudor*	*Hibbitt*	
							Ref: N Paget	It took David Craig just 16 seconds to equalise Brooking's goal, which was his sixth in eight games. Alf Ramsey is watching, but has still to be convinced that Brooking is ready. Robson wasn't sharp either, missing a good chance. With Leeds losing, Hammers could have closed the gap.											
21	A	LEEDS	9	L	0-1	0-1		Ferguson	McDowell	Charles	Bonds	Taylor	Moore	Ayris*	Best	Holland	Brooking	Robson	Boyce
9/12		*30,270*	*3*	21			*Jones 31*	*Harvey*	*Reaney*	*Cherry*	*Bremner*	*Madeley*	*Hunter*	*Lorimer*	*Clarke*	*Jones*	*Bates*	*Yorath*	
							Ref: A Morrissey	Leeds played all their football before half-time, and West Ham did enough afterwards to feel hard done by at not earning a point. Jones headed the only goal from Lorimer's pin-point centre. Lorimer also hit a post. Best missed a sitter from six yards and Ayris's crosses spelled danger.											

No	Date	Att	Pos	Pt	F-A	H-T	Scorers, Times, and Referees	1	2	3	4	5	6	7	8	9	10	11	12 sub used
22	H STOKE		7	W	3-2	2-1	Robson 32, 36, Best 76	Ferguson	McDowell	Lampard	Bonds	Taylor	Moore	Ayris	Best	Holland	Brooking	Robson	
	16/12	**23,269**	*18*	23			*Hurst 9, Ritchie 89*	*Farmer*	*Lees*	*Elder*	*Mahoney*	*Smith*	*Skeels*	*Conroy*	*Greenhoff*	*Ritchie*	*Hurst*	*Eastham**	*Robertson*
							Ref: R Toseland	Johnny Ayris gets the man-of-the-match vote after this thriller. And this after Geoff Hurst heads in for Stoke within nine minutes of his return to the Boleyn. He cost Stoke £80,000 and this is his 11th goal for them. Robson's two take him to 15. Best of the goals was Best's scorcher.											
23	A SOUTHAMPTON		8	D	0-0	0-0		Ferguson	McDowell*	Lampard	Bonds	Taylor	Moore	Ayris	Best	Holland	Brooking	Robson	Lock
	23/12	*19,429*	*12*	24				*Martin*	*McCarthy*	*Burns*	*Fisher*	*Bennett*	*Steele*	*Paine*	*Channon*	*Gilchrist*	*O'Neil*	*Stokes*	
							Ref: M Sinclair	Niggling overcame skills in this disappointing match. Mick Channon was blatantly 'obstructed' in the box without winning a penalty. The best move of the match was a 50-yard run between Brooking and Robson that split the Saints' defence open, but Brooking's shot was well saved.											
24	H TOTTENHAM		9	D	2-2	0-0	Robson 78, 82p	Ferguson	McDowell	Lampard	Bonds	Taylor	Moore	Lock	Best	Holland	Brooking	Robson	
	26/12	37,397	*7*	25			*Pearce 54, Peters 60*	*Jennings*	*Evans*	*Knowles*	*Pratt*	*Dillon*	*Naylor*	*Coates*	*Perryman*	*Chivers*	*Peters*	*Pearce*	
							Ref: T Reynolds	What a turnaround. After fumbling for 75 minutes West Ham turned into football furies to rescue a point from this Boxing Day morning clash. Ferguson flapped at two crosses to gift Spurs two goals. Robson hit back with a diving header and a penalty, after Terry Naylor had handled.											
25	A LEICESTER		10	L	1-2	1-1	Brooking 4	Ferguson	McDowell	Lampard	Bonds	Taylor	Moore	Ayris	Best	Holland	Brooking*	Robson	Boyce
	30/12	***19,341***	*17*	25			*Farrington 1, Worthington 71*	*Shilton*	*Whitworth*	*Rofe*	*Woollett*	*Manley*	*Tomlin*	*Farrington*	*Birchenall*	*Weller*	*Worthington*	*Glover*	
							Ref: C Howell	It took Leicester 29 seconds for Farrington to put away Tomlin's cross. Brooking equalised with a shot that went in off Manley, but when Brooking limped off after half an hour West Ham lost their rhythm. Farrington headed the ball on for Frank Worthington to nudge the winner.											
26	H LIVERPOOL		12	L	0-1	0-0		Ferguson	McDowell	Lampard	Lock*	Taylor	Moore	Ayris	Best	Holland	Tyler	Robson	Charles
	6/1	34,480	*1*	25			*Keegan 74*	*Clemence*	*Lawler*	*Thompson*	*Smith*	*Lloyd*	*Hughes*	*Keegan*	*Cormack*	*Heighway*	*Boersma*	*Callaghan*	
							Ref: R Tinkler	Shankly's Liverpool are 2-1 on for the title, and against a Hammers team minus both Bonds and Brooking in midfield were not stretched. Once Lock had gone off with a torn hamstring on 38 minutes Liverpool took complete control. Heighway's strong run and cross set up the goal.											
27	A MANCHESTER U		8	D	2-2	2-1	Robson 15, Best 28	Ferguson	McDowell	Charles	Bonds	Taylor	Moore	Tyler	Best	Holland	Ayris	Robson	
	20/1	*50,878*	*22*	26			*Charlton 31p, Macari 80*	*Stepney*	*Young*	*Forsyth*	*Law**	*Holton*	*Buchan*	*Morgan*	*MacDougall*	*Charlton*	*Macari*	*Graham*	*Davies*
							Ref: P Baldwin	Man U, with eight Scots in their team, stay bottom even though Tommy Docherty has spent over £1 million to buy success. Clyde Best set up Robson before scoring the second himself. Taylor handled Morgan's cross for the penalty. Macari's neat equaliser has Old Trafford on its feet.											
28	H CHELSEA		7	W	3-1	1-1	Taylor 13, Robson 68, 81	Ferguson	McDowell	Lampard	Bonds	Taylor	Moore	Tyler	Best	Holland	Brooking	Robson	
	27/1	33,336	*13*	28			*Garner 21*	*Phillips*	*Locke*	*Harris*	*Hollins*	*Dempsey*	*Webb*	*Baldwin*	*Kember*	*Osgood*	*Hudson*	*Garner*	
							Ref: R Matthewson	Trevor Brooking returns after injury and is involved in all three Hammers goals. Pop Robson takes his personal tally to 20, and this is the eighth time this season he has bagged two in a match. Chelsea's goal came when Steve Kember's shot was blocked and fell to Bill Garner.											
29	A NORWICH		7	W	1-0	1-0	Robson 32	Ferguson	McDowell	Lampard	Bonds	Taylor	Moore	Ayris	Best	**Lutton**	Brooking	Robson	
	10/2	*32,597*	*17*	30				*Keelan*	*Payne*	*Butler*	*Stringer*	*Anderson*	*Briggs*	*Livermore*	*Bone**	*Cross*	*Paddon*	*Howard*	*O'Donnell*
							Ref: W Castle	Ron Saunders' Norwich have now gone 11 games without a win, and face Spurs in the League Cup final. Stylish Brooking, industrious Bonds, deadly Robson. The three players combined for Robson's 21st goal of the season – Brooking's corner, Bonds' nod-down, Robson's strike.											
30	H WEST BROM		7	W	2-1	1-0	Bonds 16, Robson 90	Ferguson	McDowell	Lampard	Bonds	Taylor	Moore	Ayris	Best	Holland	Brooking	Robson	
	17/2	26,071	*22*	32			*Brown T 70*	*Latchford*	*Nisbet*	*Wilson*	*Cantello*	*Wile*	*Merrick*	*Woolgar*	*Brown T*	*Robertson*	*Hartford*	*Johnston**	*Glover*
							Ref: M Kherkof	Albion's time-wasting tactics irk the referee to such an extent that he allows seven minutes injury-time. It is well that he did, for the extension permitted Robson to pop in the winner. McDowell's ill-judged back-pass had presented bottom-placed Albion with an ill-deserved equaliser.											
31	A STOKE		7	L	0-2	0-2		Ferguson	McDowell	Lampard	Bonds	Taylor	Moore	Ayris*	Best	Holland	Brooking	Robson	Lock
	24/2	*21,855*	*17*	32			*Greenhoff 3, Robertson 16*	*Farmer*	*Marsh*	*Pejic*	*Mahoney*	*Smith*	*Bloor*	*Robertson*	*Greenhoff*	*Hurst*	*Eastham*	*Conroy*	
							Ref: R Raby	Ted MacDougall has signed from Man U for £170,000, but too late to play. He moans about his 150 days at Old Trafford. Greenhoff's volley from Eastham's free-kick, followed by Robertson's long-range daisy-cutter, leave Hammers with too much to do. Who steps down for Mac?											

No	Venue	Opponent / Date	Att	Pos	Res	Pts	F-A	H-T	Scorers, Times, and Referees	1	2	3	4	5	6	7	8	9	10	11	12
32	H	IPSWICH		8	L		0-1	0-0		Ferguson	McDowell	Lampard	Bonds	Taylor	Moore	Tyler	Best	Holland	Brooking	Robson	
		2/3	37,004	*4*		32			*Johnson 55*	*Sivell*	*Mills*	*Harper*	*Morris*	*Hunter*	*Beattie*	*Hamilton*	*Viljoen*	*Johnson*	*Whymark*	*Lambert*	
									Ref: H New	This Friday evening fixture was interrupted by a bottle thrown on the pitch. A huge crowd had turned up expecting to see Ted MacDougall's debut, but his forms have not cleared. Ipswich's new buy, Johnson, not only scored but also hit the bar. The North Bank sang 'We want Mac'.											
33	A	SHEFFIELD UTD		9	D		0-0	0-0		Ferguson	McDowell	Lampard	Bonds	Taylor	Moore	Best	Lock	**MacDougall**	Brooking	Robson	
		10/3	*24,024*	*17*		33				*McAlister*	*Badger*	*Hemsley*	*Flynn*	*Colquhoun*	*Eddy*	*Woodward*	*Salmons*	*Dearden*	*Currie*	*Bone*	
									Ref: R Capey	Who will be dropped for Supermac? Will it be Holland or will it be Best? It is Holland. The draw condemns the Blades to a sixth game without a win, and is largely due to Ferguson's two saves from Woodward's twice-taken penalty. Lampard had brought down Woodward in the box.											
34	H	MANCHESTER C		7	W		2-1	0-0	MacDougall 60, Robson 67	Ferguson	McDowell	Lampard*	Bonds	Taylor	Moore	Best	Lock	MacDougall	Brooking	Robson	Holland
		17/3	29,370	*13*		35			*Doyle 85*	*Corrigan*	*Book*	*Donachie*	*Doyle*	*Booth*	*Jeffries**	*Summerbee*	*Bell*	*Whelan*	*Lee*	*Oakes*	*Carrodus*
									Ref: R Crabb	An atmosphere fit for an end-of-season game. Ted MacDougall twists round Tony Book for his first goal for West Ham and his first for anyone since Christmas. A fine run by Holland was then finished off by Robson. Frank Carrodus crossed for Mike Doyle to pull one back for City.											
35	A	CRYS PALACE		7	W		3-1	1-0	Robson 45, Brooking 55, MacDougall 85	Ferguson	McDowell	Holland	Bonds	Taylor	Moore	Best	Lock	MacDougall	Brooking	Robson	
		24/3	*36,915*	*20*		37			*Possee 80*	*Jackson*	*Roffey*	*Taylor*	*Phillip*	*Bell*	*Blyth*	*Possee*	*Hinshelwood*	*Whittle*	*Cooke*	*Rogers*	
									Ref: D Turner	Palace's battle against relegation lends this match an unwelcome violent undercurrent, which culminates with Bobby Bell laying out Ted MacDougall. Jackson failed to hold Best's shot and Robson pounced. Supermac then took Moore's pass and wrong-footed Palace's defence.											
36	H	EVERTON		7	W		2-0	0-0	Robson 67, Lock 89	Ferguson	McDowell	Lampard	Bonds*	Taylor	Moore	Lock	Best	MacDougall	Brooking	Robson	Holland
		31/3	25,531	*17*		39				*Lawson*	*Wright T*	*Styles*	*Kendall*	*Kenyon*	*Hurst*	*Harper*	*Darracott*	*Lyons**	*Buckley*	*Connolly*	*Belfitt*
									Ref: I Jones	The Israeli national team spy on West Ham, whom they shortly play in a testimonial. They fear Brooking, whose run set up Robson's 25th goal of the season. Just before the end Kevin Lock scored his first ever league goal. Bonds and Harper were lucky not to be sent off for fighting.											
37	A	NEWCASTLE		5	W		2-1	1-1	MacDougall 18, 48	Ferguson	McDowell	Lampard	Bonds	Taylor	Moore	Best	Lock	MacDougall	Brooking	Robson	
		7/4	*24,030*	*6*		41			*Tudor 9*	*Burleigh*	*Craig*	*Clark*	*Nattrass*	*Howard*	*Moncur*	*Barrowclough*	*Smith*	*Macdonald*	*Tudor*	*Hibbitt*	
									Ref: K Styles	A gale-force wind ruined the match as a spectacle, but could not prevent Mac bagging two super headed goals, both laid on by Brooking. John Tudor's earlier goal came with Hammers defenders standing still appealing for offside. Later, Ferguson and Taylor squared up to each other.											
38	H	LEEDS		5	D		1-1	0-0	Holland 90	Ferguson	McDowell	Lampard	Bonds	Lock	Moore	Best*	Holland	MacDougall	Brooking	Robson	Lutton
		14/4	**38,804**	*3*		42			*Clarke 83*	*Harvey*	*Reaney*	*Cherry*	*Bremner*	*Yorath*	*Hunter*	*Lorimer*	*Clarke*	*Jones*	*Giles*	*Bates**	*Jordan*
									Ref: N Burtenshaw	When McDowell collides with Ferguson play is held up for 10 minutes and rumours sweep the stadium that the keeper has broken his neck or his back. Ferguson is surrounded by doctors and trainers. He went off suffering from concussion. Allan Clarke then headed past stand-in Best.											
39	H	SOUTHAMPTON		5	W		4-3	2-2	Robson 14, 18, 66, Brooking 84	Grotier	McDowell*	Lampard	Bonds	Lock	Moore	Best	Holland	MacDougall	Brooking	Robson	Lutton
		20/4	33,039	*10*		44			*Gilchrist 28, 42, Channon 89*	*Martin*	*Kirkup*	*Steele**	*Fisher*	*Bennett*	*Walker*	*Paine*	*Channon*	*Gilchrist*	*O'Neil*	*Talkes*	*Beaney*
									Ref: P Walters	Robson had already scored twice in a game eight times. Now at last he gets a hat-trick. His total now stands at 28, compared with 15 for Saints' Channon, who might have had a hat-trick himself in this cracker. Robson might have had five, narrowly missing with two diving headers.											
40	A	DERBY		5	D		1-1	0-0	Lutton 75	Grotier	Charles	Lampard	Bonds	Lock	Moore	Best	Lutton	MacDougall	Brooking	Robson	
		21/4	*28,727*	*9*		45			*Gemmill 87p*	*Moseley*	*Nish*	*Daniel*	*Parry**	*McFarland*	*Todd*	*McGovern*	*Gemmill*	*O''Hare*	*Hector*	*Powell*	*Durban*
									Ref: E Wallace	Greenwood, normally the calmest of managers, storms out of the Baseball Ground following a penalty decision against Moore, for bringing down Hector. Needless to say, Brian Clough said it *was* a penalty. With five regulars injured, Greenwood had to play Pop Robson in defence.											
41	A	BIRMINGHAM		5	D		0-0	0-0		Ferguson	McDowell	Lampard	Bonds	Lock	Moore	Best	Lutton	MacDougall	Brooking	Robson	
		23/4	*36,942*	*11*		46				*Latchford D*	*Martin*	*Pendrey*	*Page*	*Hynd*	*Roberts*	*Campbell*	*Francis*	*Latchford R*	*Burns*	*Taylor*	
									Ref: P Partridge	With City seeking their sixth straight win, and West Ham unbeaten in eight, this match always looked a likely draw. Dreadful weather did not keep the crowd down, though goal chances were at a premium. West Ham penetrated City's penalty box just three times in the whole match.											
42	H	ARSENAL		6	L		1-2	0-2	Rice 73 (og)	Ferguson	McDowell	Lampard	Bonds	Lock	Moore	Best*	Lutton	MacDougall	Brooking	Robson	Ayris
		28/4	37,366	*2*		46			*Kennedy 30, Radford 43*	*Wilson*	*Rice*	*McNab*	*Storey*	*Kelly*	*Simpson*	*Armstrong*	*Ball*	*Radford*	*Kennedy*	*George*	
		Home	Away						Ref: B Homewood	Pop Robson needs one goal to equal Geoff Hurst's post-war Hammers record of 29. He fails to get it, as West Ham slump to their first defeat in 10 games. Robson will later be locked in transfer negotiations. If they fail, Spurs are favourites to sign him as a replacement for Alan Gilzean.											
Average		30,025	31,280																		

League Cup

Rd		Opponent	Pos	Res	F-A	H-T	Scorers, Times, and Referees	1	2	3	4	5	6	7	8	9	10	11	12 sub used
2	H	BRISTOL CITY	12	W	2-1	1-0	McDowell 45, Best 77	Groiter	McDowell	Lampard	Bonds	Taylor	Moore	Tyler	Best	Holland	Brooking	Robson	
6/9		17,688 *2:5*					*Galley 89*	*Cashley*	*Wilson*	*Drysdale*	*Sweeney*	*Rodgers**	*Merrick*	*Tainton*	*Spiring*	*Galley*	*Gow*	*Ritchie*	*Broomfield*
							Ref: N Paget												

A forgettable match, other than for two spectacular West Ham goals. Tyler set up the first, for John McDowell to record his first senior goal, and Clyde Best fired in the second from the edge of the area. City's dull second-half pressure was finally rewarded with a late consolation.

Rd		Opponent	Pos	Res	F-A	H-T	Scorers, Times, and Referees	1	2	3	4	5	6	7	8	9	10	11	12 sub used
3	A	STOCKPORT	11	L	1-2	1-2	Best 27	Groiter	McDowell	Lampard	Bonds	Taylor	Moore	Tyler	Best	Holland	Brooking	Robson	
4/10		*13,410 4:11*					*Russell 18, Spratt 42p*	*Ogley*	*Ingle*	*Charter*	*Spratt*	*Hart*	*Ashworth*	*Garbett*	*Ryden*	*Griffiths*	*Russell*	*Davidson*	
							Ref: P Partridge												

Never before have West Ham lost to a Division 4 team in a competitive fixture, so this is as dark a day as they come. The critical moment came just before half-time when McDowell felled John Ryden, leaving Tom Spratt to convert the penalty. Near the end Best was thwarted by Ogley.

FA Cup

Rd		Opponent	Pos	Res	F-A	H-T	Scorers, Times, and Referees	1	2	3	4	5	6	7	8	9	10	11	12 sub used
3	A	PORT VALE	12	W	1-0	0-0	Holland 62	Ferguson	McDowell	Lampard*	Bonds	Taylor	Moore	Tyler	Best	Holland	Brooking	Robson	Charles
13/1		*20,619 3:6*						*Boswell*	*Brodie*	*Lacey*	*Sum'rscales*	*Cross*	*Mountford*	*Williams*	*Goodwin*	*Morgan*	*Tartt*	*McLaren**	*Gough*
							Ref: A Jones												

Vale boss Gordon Lee said: 'To say we deserved a draw is an understatement.' His team had 75% of the play. Mountford's 'goal', early on, was ruled out for pushing and Clive Charles appeared to handle a net-bound shot. Moore's free-kick was headed down by Best to Pat Holland.

Rd		Opponent	Pos	Res	F-A	H-T	Scorers, Times, and Referees	1	2	3	4	5	6	7	8	9	10	11	12 sub used
4	A	HULL	7	L	0-1	0-1		Ferguson	McDowell	Lampard	Bonds	Taylor	Moore	Tyler*	Best	Holland	Brooking	Robson	Lock
3/2		*32,290 2:13*					*Houghton 29*	*McKechnie*	*Banks*	*Beardsley*	*Kaye*	*Neill*	*Knighton*	*McGill*	*Houghton*	*Pearson*	*Holme*	*Greenwood*	
							Ref: N Burtenshaw												

West Ham crash to another cup disaster, this time on foggy Humberside. Moore makes the error that lets in Ken Houghton – a bad back-pass that puts Ferguson in trouble. A minute earlier, Clyde Best had hit the post. Hull player-boss Terry Hull now faces an away trip to Coventry.

	Home						Away						
	P	W	D	L	F	A	W	D	L	F	A	Pts
1 Liverpool	42	17	3	1	45	19	8	7	6	27	23	60
2 Arsenal	42	14	5	2	31	14	9	6	6	26	29	57
3 Leeds	42	15	4	2	45	13	6	7	8	26	32	53
4 Ipswich	42	10	7	4	34	20	7	7	7	21	25	48
5 Wolves	42	13	3	5	43	23	5	8	8	23	31	47
6 WEST HAM	42	12	5	4	45	25	5	7	9	22	28	46
7 Derby	42	15	3	3	43	18	4	5	12	13	36	46
8 Tottenham	42	10	5	6	33	23	6	8	7	25	25	45
9 Newcastle	42	12	6	3	35	19	4	7	10	25	32	45
10 Birmingham	42	11	7	3	39	22	4	5	12	14	32	42
11 Manchester C	42	12	4	5	36	20	3	7	11	21	40	41
12 Chelsea	42	9	6	6	30	22	4	8	9	19	29	40
13 Southampton	42	8	11	2	26	17	3	7	11	21	35	40
14 Sheffield Utd	42	11	4	6	28	18	4	6	11	23	41	40
15 Stoke	42	11	8	2	38	17	3	2	16	23	39	38
16 Leicester	42	7	9	5	23	18	3	8	10	17	28	37
17 Everton	42	9	5	7	27	21	4	6	11	14	28	37
18 Manchester U	42	9	7	5	24	19	3	6	12	20	41	37
19 Coventry	42	9	5	7	27	24	4	4	13	13	31	35
20 Norwich	42	7	9	5	22	19	4	1	16	14	44	32
21 Crys Palace	42	7	7	7	25	21	2	5	14	16	37	30
22 West Brom	42	8	7	6	25	24	1	3	17	13	38	28
	924	236	130	96	724	436	96	130	236	436	724	924

Odds & ends

Double wins: (4) Chelsea, Norwich, Palace, Everton.
Double losses: (2) Liverpool, Arsenal.

Won from behind: (4) Leicester (h), Everton (a), Stoke (h), Newcastle (a).
Lost from in front: (1) Liverpool (a).

High spots: Nine unbeaten league games from 10 March.
Bryan Robson's remarkable scoring exploits.

Low spots: Three successive league defeats in August.
Losing to Second Division Hull in the League Cup and, worst of all, to Fourth Division Stockport in FA Cup.

Hammer of the Year: Bryan Robson.
Ever-presents: (2) Bobby Moore and Bryan Robson.
Hat-tricks: (1) Bryan Robson.
Leading scorer: (28) Bryan Robson.

	Appearances						Goals			
	Lge	*Sub*	LC	*Sub*	FAC	*Sub*	Lge	LC	FAC	Tot
Ayris, Johnny	**13**	*2*					**1**			**1**
Best, Clyde	**41**	*1*	2		2		**7**	2		**9**
Bonds, Billy	**39**		2		2		**3**			**3**
Boyce, Ronnie		*2*								
Brooking, Trevor	**40**		2		2		**11**			**11**
Charles, John	**7**	*2*				*1*				
Coker, Ade	**4**						**1**			**1**
Ferguson, Bobby	**31**				2					
Grotier, Peter	**11**		2							
Holland, Pat	**30**	*2*	2		2		**1**		1	**2**
Lampard, Frank	**38**		2		2					
Lock, Kevin	**14**	*4*				*1*	**1**			**1**
Lutton, Bertie	**4**	*2*					**1**			**1**
McDowell, John	**38**		2		2		**2**	1		**3**
MacDougall, Ted	**10**						**4**			**4**
Moore, Bobby	**42**		2		2		**3**			**3**
Robson, Bryan	**42**		2		2		**28**			**28**
Taylor, Tommy	**37**		2		2		**3**			**3**
Tyler, Dudley	**21**		2		2		**1**			**1**
19 players used	**462**	***15***	**22**	***0***	**22**	***2***	**67**	**3**	**1**	**71**

No	Date	Opponent	Att	Pos	Pt	F-A	H-T	Scorers, Times, and Referees	1	2	3	4	5	6	7	8	9	10	11	12 sub used
1	H	NEWCASTLE			L	1-2	1-0	Robson 37	Ferguson	Lampard	Charles	Bonds	Taylor	Moore	Best*	Lutton	MacDougall	Brooking	Robson	Holland
	25/8		28,169		–			*Macdonald 56, 80*	*McFaul*	*Craig*	*Clark*	*Gibb*	*Nattrass*	*Moncur*	*Barrowclough*	*Smith*	*Macdonald*	*Tudor*	*Hibbitt*	
								Ref: G Hill	Bobby Moore is still playing in midfield. Brooking's cross should have been put away by Best and MacDougall before it reached Pop Robson. Malcolm Macdonald headed in Terry Hibbitt's cross and claimed the winner with a shot that slipped through Bobby Ferguson's fingers.											
2	H	IPSWICH			D	3-3	2-1	Bonds 5 Brooking 7, Best 80	**Day**	Lampard	Lock	Bonds	Taylor	Moore	Best	Holland	MacDougall	Brooking	Robson	
	27/8		23,335		1			*Whymark 13, Johnson 64, 72*	*Best*	*Mills*	*Harper*	*Morris*	*Keeley*	*Beattie*	*Hamilton*	*Viljoen*	*Johnson*	*Whymark*	*Lambert*	
								Ref: D Biddle	Topsy-turvy Hammers. Ferguson asked to be left out for personal reasons. A Trevor Brooking 'special' made it 2-0 after just seven minutes, but when Mervyn Day punched the air at Harper's free-kick West Ham fell apart. Best rescued a point when Glen Keeley missed a cross.											
3	A	NORWICH		14	D	2-2	1-1	Best 12, Robson 71	Ferguson	Lampard	Lock	Bonds	Taylor	Moore	Best	Holland	MacDougall	Brooking	Robson	
	1/9		*25,706*	*16*	2			*Mellor 35, Paddon 80p*	*Keelan*	*Prophett*	*Black*	*Stringer*	*Rollings*	*Briggs*	*Anderson*	*Suggett*	*Cross*	*Paddon*	*Mellor*	
								Ref: J Hunting	Twice West Ham take the lead against Ron Saunders' Norwich. There was nothing fluky about the first goal, Best heading home off the post. But the second, from Brooking's corner, went in off Robson's ear. Lampard then fluffs a clearance and Billy Bonds has to bring down Paddon.											
4	A	QP RANGERS			D	0-0	0-0		Ferguson	Lampard	Lock	Bonds	Taylor	Moore	Best	Holland	Ayris	Brooking	Robson	
	4/9		*28,360*		3				*Parkes*	*Clement*	*Watson*	*Venables*	*Mancini*	*Hazell*	*Thomas*	*Francis*	*Leach*	*Bowles*	*Givens*	
								Ref: R Challis	Rangers totally dominated this draw, and West Ham's offside trap was not welcomed by the crowd, who slow-handclapped in frustration. Man-of-the-match Dave Thomas hit a post, had three goals disallowed, and Frank Lampard unwittingly blocked Stan Bowles' header on the line.											
5	H	TOTTENHAM		17	L	0-1	0-0		Ferguson	McDowell	Lampard	Bonds	Taylor	Moore	Best	Lock	MacDougall*	Brooking	Robson	Holland
	8/9		30,888	*15*	3			*Chivers 66*	*Jennings*	*Evans*	*Knowles*	*Coates*	*Dillon*	*Beal*	*Gilzean**	*Perryman*	*Chivers*	*Peters*	*Neighbour*	*Kinnear*
								Ref: D Smith	The attendance is 7,000 down on the corresponding fixture last season. The crowd don't like what they see and hundreds leave the ground long before the end. Lock and Best, in particular, rile the fans. Though Ferguson made several fine saves, he was beaten by Chivers' half-hit shot.											
6	H	QP RANGERS		17	L	2-3	0-2	Robson 47, Bonds 67p	Ferguson	McDowell	Lampard	Bonds	Taylor	Moore	Tyler	Lock	Lutton	Brooking	Robson	
	10/9		26,042	*10*	3			*Givens 5, 15, Abbott 52*	*Parkes*	*Clement*	*Watson*	*Venables*	*Mancini*	*Hazell*	*Abbott*	*Francis*	*Leach*	*Bowles*	*Givens*	
								Ref: D Turner	Greenwood has now used 17 players in six games. Taylor's error gave Don Givens his first goal and McDowell his second. 19-year-old Ron Abbott headed in Venables' free-kick to make it 1-3. Brooking's corner was handled by Dave Clement for the penalty. QPR deserved to win.											
7	A	MANCHESTER U		21	L	1-3	0-1	Bonds 79p	Ferguson	McDowell	Lampard	Bonds	Taylor	Lock	Tyler*	Holland	MacDougall	Brooking	Robson	Lutton
	15/9		***44,757***	*14*	3			*Kidd 7, 62, Moore I 83*	*Stepney*	*Buchan M*	*Young*	*Martin*	*Holton**	*James*	*Morgan*	*Kidd*	*Anderson*	*Graham*	*Moore*	*Buchan G*
								Ref: H Williams	The talk is of Bobby Moore demanding a transfer. Because of this, he is dropped. Brian Kidd's two goals – both thumping, long-range efforts, look to have settled the outcome. Martin Buchan topples Brooking for the penalty, but Ian Storey-Moore's half-hit shot clinches the points.											
8	H	LEICESTER		21	D	1-1	1-0	Robson 36	Ferguson	McDowell	Lampard	Bonds	Taylor	Moore	Tyler	Lock	MacDougall*	Brooking	Robson	Coker
	22/9		23,567	*5*	4			*Worthington 87*	*Shilton*	*Whitworth*	*Rofe*	*Farrington*	*Munro*	*Cross*	*Weller*	*Sammels*	*Worthington*	*Birchenall*	*Glover*	
								Ref: P Partridge	Lock failed to clear, leaving Frank Worthington to run through to level the scores for Jimmy Bloomfield's Leicester and leave West Ham still looking for their first win. They only once got the better of the outstanding Shilton, when he miscued a goal-kick to Tyler, who fed Robson.											
9	A	STOKE		21	L	0-2	0-1		Ferguson	McDowell	Lampard	Bonds	Taylor	Moore	Tyler	Lock	MacDougall	Brooking	Robson	
	29/9		***16,395***	*17*	4			*Goodwin 40, Hurst 65*	*Farmer*	*Marsh*	*Pejic*	*Dodd*	*Smith*	*Bloor**	*Haslegrave*	*Greenhoff*	*Hurst*	*Goodwin*	*Eastham*	*Ritchie*
								Ref: W Johnson	Stoke's first win of the season dumps West Ham deeper into trouble. Stoke owe their win to an 18-year-old debutant, who nodded Greenhoff's flick over Ferguson, and to ex-Hammer Hurst, who headed in Ritchie's knock-on. MacDougall has a stinker, but Moore and Bonds play well.											
10	H	BURNLEY		21	L	0-1	0-0		Day	**Coleman**	Lampard	Bonds	McDowell	Moore	Lutton*	Holland	MacDougall !	Brooking	Robson	Lock
	6/10		23,604	*2*	4			*Waldron 64*	*Stevenson*	*Noble*	*Newton*	*Dobson*	*Waldron*	*Thomson*	*Nulty*	*Hankin*	*Fletcher*	*Collins*	*James*	
								Ref: R Crabb	Ferguson has been dropped for saying: 'There are too many gutless, spineless men in the team.' Day steps in and saves well from Dobson late in the game. Colin Waldron plays a one-two with Nulty to score. Seven minutes later MacDougall is ordered off for head-butting Doug Collins.											

No	Venue / Opponent / Date	Att	Pos	Res	F-A	H-T	Scorers, Times, Referees	1	2	3	4	5	6	7	8	9	10	11	12
11	A EVERTON		22	L	0-1	0-1		Day	Coleman	Lampard	Bonds	Taylor	Moore	Ayris	Best	MacDougall	Brooking	Robson	
	13/10	*34,708*	*5*	4			*Harper 32*	*Lawson*	*Darracott*	*McLaughlin*	*Clements*	*Kenyon*	*Hurst*	*Bernard*	*Buckley*	*Lyons**	*Harper*	*Connolly*	*Irving*
							Ref: P Reeves	Hary Catterick's Everton are going well. McDougall hit a post from one of Brooking's early openings. Coleman's bad back-pass leaves Harper in the clear for the only goal. Day saved a lot, and dropped a lot, too. Clyde Best missed a simple chance to equalise in the closing minutes.											
12	A COVENTRY		21	W	1-0	0-0	McDowell 68	Day	Coleman	Lampard	Bonds	Taylor	Moore	Tyler	McDowell	Best	Brooking	Robson*	Lock
	20/10	*21,097*	*6*	6				*Glazier*	*Coop*	*Holmes*	*Mortimer*	*Craven**	*Dugdale*	*Smith*	*Alderson*	*Stein*	*Green*	*Hutchison*	*Cartwright*
							Ref: I Jones	Greenwood abandons the safety-first policy that had brought few rewards on opposing grounds and it pays off against a strong Coventry team. McDowell, an England-Under-23 full-back, was switched to midfield but took time off from shadowing Hutchison to volley the winning goal.											
13	H DERBY		21	D	0-0	0-0		Day	Coleman	Lampard	Bonds	Taylor	Moore	Tyler	McDowell	Best	Brooking	Lock	
	27/10	31,237	*4*	7				*Boulton*	*Webster*	*Nish*	*Newton*	*McFarland*	*Todd*	*McGovern*	*Gemmill*	*Davies*	*Hector*	*Hinton*	
							Ref: A Morrissey	Without both Robson and MacDougall, West Ham's attack was bound to struggle. Greenwood juggled his resources and played McDowell in midfield while pushing Brooking – under protest – into attack. Neither man played well. Now West Ham must focus on the Liverpool replay.											
14	A LEEDS		21	L	**1-4**	0-2	MacDougall 83	Day	Coleman	Lampard	Bonds	Taylor	Moore	Tyler	McDowell	Best	Brooking	MacDougall	
	3/11	*36,869*	*1*	7			*Bates 19, Jones 21, 51, Clarke 58*	*Harvey*	*Reaney*	*Cherry*	*Bremner*	*McQueen*	*Hunter*	*Lorimer*	*Clarke*	*Jones*	*Bates*	*Madeley*	
							Ref: J Williams	Leeds have dropped just three points all season and extend their lead at the top to six points. Madeley's cross comes back off the bar for Bates to net the first, and Jones collects a return pass from Lorimer to add a second. MacDougall's header from Bonds' cross was too little, too late.											
15	H SHEFFIELD UTD		21	D	2-2	0-2	Bonds 50, Brooking 51	Ferguson	Coleman	Lampard	Bonds	Taylor	Moore	Tyler	McDowell	Robson	Brooking	MacDougall	
	10/11	21,243	*12*	8			*Woodward 14, 45*	*Connaughton*	*Goulding*	*Ogden*	*Flynn*	*Colquhoun*	*Speight*	*Woodward*	*Salmons*	*Dearden*	*Currie*	*Bone*	
							Ref: A Jones	Greenwood misses his first home match for years, spying on another player. He misses a famous recovery. Teased by Currie in the first half, Hammers trail through two deflections – off Taylor and Moore. Bonds' back-header goes in off a post, whereupon Brooking hits the equaliser.											
16	A WOLVES		21	D	0-0	0-0		Day	Coleman	Lampard	Bonds	Taylor	Moore	Best	McDowell	MacDougall	Brooking	Robson	
	17/11	*19,587*	*19*	9				*Parkes*	*Palmer*	*Parkin*	*Bailey*	*Munro*	*McAlle*	*Powell*	*Hibbitt*	*Kindon**	*Dougan*	*Wagstaffe*	*McCalliog*
							Ref: H Davy	Robson hates playing in midfield; Brooking hates playing in attack, and Greenwood can't keep upsetting his players like this, especially as Best wants to move on. Greenwood is said to be about to buy two players, Graham Paddon from Norwich and Dennis Tueart from Sunderland.											
17	H ARSENAL		21	L	1-3	1-1	Bonds 37	Day	Coleman	Lampard	Bonds	Taylor	Moore	**Gould**	McDowell	MacDougall	Brooking	Robson	
	24/11	28,287	*11*	9			*George 29, Ball 55, 87*	*Wilson*	*Rice*	*McNab*	*Storey*	*Simpson*	*Kelly*	*Ball*	*George*	*Hornsby*	*Kennedy*	*Armstrong*	
							Ref: R Capey	Bobby Gould makes his debut in a match where Upton Park resounds to chants of: 'Greenwood out'. Charlie George received a short free-kick and curled the ball into the top corner. Bonds scrambles a goal off his knee, but Ball restores Arsenal's lead with a 'dolly' shot from 20 yards.											
18	A LIVERPOOL		21	L	0-1	0-1		Day	Coleman	Lampard	Bonds	**McGiven**	Moore	Gould	McDowell	MacDougall	Brooking	Holland	
	1/12	*34,857*	*2*	9			*Cormack 14*	*Clemence*	*Smith*	*Lindsay*	*Thompson*	*Lloyd*	*Hughes*	*Keegan*	*Cormack*	*Heighway*	*Waddle*	*Callaghan*	
							Ref: E Wallace	This was not the tight match the score suggests. Liverpool were always in control after Tommy Smith's cross picked out Cormack, who took the ball round Day. The game was also one to remember for Bobby Moore, playing in midfield, who was booked for back-chatting the ref.											
19	H MANCHESTER C		20	W	2-1	1-1	Brooking 43, Doyle 60 (og)	Day	McDowell	Lampard	Bonds	Taylor	Moore	Ayris	**Paddon**	Gould	Brooking*	Best	Coleman
	8/12	20,790	*16*	11			*Lee 18*	*MacRae*	*Pardoe*	*Donachie*	*Doyle*	*Booth*	*Towers*	*Summerbee*	*Bell*	*Lee*	*Leman*	*Marsh*	
							Ref: R Toseland	Graham Paddon in, MacDougall out. A first home win of the season, secured against Ron Saunders' City with the aid of an own-goal by Mike Doyle, who headed in Paddon's cross. Francis Lee's earlier header had been answered when Brooking shot through the legs of Keith MacRae.											
20	A BIRMINGHAM		22	L	1-3	1-1	Gould 4	Day	McDowell	Lampard	Bonds	Taylor	Moore	Ayris	Paddon	Gould	Coleman	Best	
	15/12	*23,787*	*20*	11			*Burns 44, 63, Hatton 76*	*Latchford D*	*Martin*	*Gallagher*	*Pendrey*	*Hynd*	*Roberts*	*Burns*	*Francis*	*Latchford R*	*Hatton*	*Hendrie*	
							Ref: E Jolly	Freddie Goodwin's City overtake West Ham, who slump to the bottom despite Gould's first goal for the club. It was a fine goal, too, a superb volley from Bonds' cross. Trevor Francis and Kenny Burns turned the match around, Burns 'chesting' his first goal and driving in his second.											
21	H STOKE		22	L	0-2	0-0		Day	McDowell	Lampard	Holland	Taylor	McGiven	Ayris*	Paddon	Gould	Coleman	Best	**Wooler**
	22/12	**16,513**	*18*	11			*Robertson 49, Greenhoff 84*	*McDonald*	*Dodd*	*Pejic*	*Skeels*	*Smith*	*Bloor*	*Robertson*	*Greenhoff*	*Hurst*	*Mahoney*	*Haslegrave*	
							Ref: W Castle	Stoke's first away win is achieved against a team minus the unfit Moore, Brooking, Robson, and the suspended Bonds. Mick McGiven is on loan from Sunderland. Hurst's shot is blocked but runs to Jimmy Robertson. Stoke settle it when Mahoney and Haslegrave set up Greenhoff.											

No	Date		Att	Pos	Pt	F-A	H-T	Scorers, Times, and Referees	1	2	3	4	5	6	7	8	9	10	11	12 sub used
22	A	CHELSEA		21	W	4-2	0-2	Lampard 48, Gould 57, Best 63, 84	Day	Coleman	Lampard	McDowell	Taylor	Moore	McGiven	Paddon	Gould	Brooking	Best	
	26/12		*26,982*	*15*	13			*Britton 10, Hudson 42*	*Bonetti*	*Locke*	*Harris*	*Hollins*	*Webb*	*Kember*	*Britton*	*Baldwin*	*Osgood*	*Hudson*	*Houseman*	
								Ref: R Tinkler	One of the great Hammers fight-backs. Keeper Peter Bonetti was badly positioned when Lampard pulled the first goal back. The turning point came when Peter Osgood volleyed against the bar. Day's huge goal-kick bounced perfectly for Gould. Best won the game with two headers.											
23	A	TOTTENHAM		21	L	0-2	0-0		Day	McDowell	Lampard	Bonds	Taylor	Moore	McGiven	Paddon	Gould	Coleman*	Best	Holland
	29/12		*33,172*	*15*	13			*Pratt 77, Chivers 87*	*Jennings*	*Evans*	*Naylor*	*Pratt*	*England*	*Beal*	*Gilzean*	*Perryman*	*Chivers*	*Peters*	*Coates**	*McGrath*
								Ref: K Styles	West Ham look to be holding out, by hook or by crook. Ralph Coates had hit the post and on 68 minutes McGiven floors Gilzean in the box. Day saves Chivers' penalty after Clyde Best pointed which way to go. But McGrath engineers Pratt's close-range goal and Chivers heads No 2.											
24	H	NORWICH		21	W	4-2	0-2	Gould 23, Paddon 44, 59, Brooking 63	Day	McDowell	Lampard	Bonds	Taylor	Moore	McGiven	Paddon	Gould	Brooking*	Best	Coleman
	1/1		32,259	*22*	15			*McDougall 50, 89*	*Keelan*	*Howard*	*Govier*	*Stringer*	*Rollings*	*Prophett**	*Grapes*	*MacDougall*	*Suggett*	*Briggs*	*Sissons*	*Silvester*
								Ref: K Burns	Paddon and MacDougall each score twice against their former club. Norwich's new manager, John Bond, sees his side stuck to the bottom. Brooking limps off after 70 minutes with a groin strain, but his super goal – bending the ball round Keelan – had assured his team of the win.											
25	H	MANCHESTER U		19	W	2-1	0-0	Bonds 49, Holland 83	Day	Coleman	Lampard	Bonds	Taylor	Wooler	McGiven	Paddon	Lutton	Holland	Best	
	12/1		34,147	*21*	17			*McIlroy 66*	*Stepney*	*Forsyth*	*Houston*	*Greenhoff*	*Holton*	*Buchan M*	*Morgan*	*Macari*	*Kidd**	*Young*	*Graham*	*McIlroy*
								Ref: R Perkin	Just before kick-off the suspended George Best is told he can leave Old Trafford. Clyde Best heads on for Bonds to hit the first goal. A slack pass by Wooler let in McIlroy, after which Man U had two efforts cleared off the line. Holland won the game with a harmless-looking header.											
26	A	NEWCASTLE		19	D	1-1	0-1	Holland 51	Day	Coleman	Lampard	Bonds	Taylor	Brooking	McGiven	Paddon	Gould*	Holland	Best	Lutton
	19/1		*27,216*	*9*	18			*Macdonald 15*	*McFaul*	*Craig*	*Kennedy*	*McDermott*	*Howard*	*Clark*	*Barrowclough*	*Smith*	*Macdonald*	*Tudor*	*Cassidy*	
								Ref: G Hill	Malcolm Macdonald flings himself full length to head Kennedy's cross past Day. With the wind behind them after half-time, West Ham level within six minutes. Holland beat McFaul to Brooking's cross and the ball cannoned in off the keeper. John Tudor blasted a sitter over the bar.											
27	H	BIRMINGHAM		19	D	0-0	0-0		Day	Coleman	Lampard	Bonds	Taylor	McGiven	Holland	Paddon	McDowell	Brooking	Best	
	2/2		27,948	*20*	19				*Sprake*	*Martin*	*Clarke*	*Pendrey*	*Gallagher*	*Hynd*	*Campbell*	*Burns*	*Latchford R*	*Hatton*	*Calderwood*	
								Ref: C Thomas	The critical moment arrives after 52 minutes when Gary Sprake – Britain's most expensive goalkeeper – fells Pat Holland, but Billy Bonds' spot-kick goes wide. Pop Robson has been out for nine weeks now, and without him West Ham still seem far too lightweight up front.											
28	A	IPSWICH		19	W	3-1	2-0	Mills 32 (og), McDowell 37, Best 71	Day	Coleman	Lampard	Bonds	Taylor	McGiven	Holland	Paddon	McDowell	Brooking	Best	
	5/2		*25,747*	*7*	21			*Hamilton 69*	*Sivell*	*Burley*	*Mills*	*Morris*	*Hunter*	*Beattie*	*Hamilton*	*Viljoen**	*Johnson*	*Whymark*	*Lambert*	*Gates*
								Ref: P Reeves	Last Saturday Ipswich beat Southampton 7-0. Hammers borrow Ipswich's all-white strip. In a rain-drenched game Brooking's shot goes in off Mills and a post. McDowell's 30-yarder made it 2-0. Hamilton put in Whymark's header, and Best pounced after Holland's shot was parried.											
29	A	LEICESTER		19	W	1-0	0-0	Best 58	Day	Coleman	Lampard	Bonds	Taylor	McGiven	Holland	Paddon	McDowell	Brooking	Best	
	9/2		*27,032*	*7*	23				*Shilton*	*Whitworth*	*Rofe*	*Earle*	*Munro*	*Cross*	*Weller*	*Sammels*	*Worthington*	*Birchenall*	*Glover*	
								Ref: L Hayes	Two moments won this match for West Ham. The first was when Clyde Best bulleted home a stunning shot. The second came when Day saved Frank Worthington's 75th-minute penalty. The referee had only given the kick on the advice of a linesman, who saw Bonds manhandle Rofe.											
30	H	EVERTON		19	W	4-3	2-2	Paddon 33, Best 41, 49, Bonds 84	Day	Coleman	Lampard	Bonds	Taylor	McGiven	Holland	Paddon	McDowell	Brooking	Best	
	16/2		29,347	*6*	25			*Telfer 5, 20, Harvey 73*	*Lawson*	*Darracott*	*McLaughlin*	*Hurst*	*Kenyon*	*Bernard*	*Harvey*	*Buckley*	*Latchford*	*Jones*	*Telfer*	
								Ref: V James	Clyde Best answers his critics by dominating this thriller. He scored twice, headed down for Graham Paddon's opener, and at one point juggled the ball on his knee and chest and defied any Everton player to take it away. Billy Bonds clinched the victory by heading in Paddon's corner.											
31	A	BURNLEY		19	D	1-1	0-1	Paddon 55	Day	Coleman	Lampard	Bonds	Taylor	McGiven	Holland	Paddon	McDowell	Brooking	Best	
	23/2		*18,216*	*6*	26			*Nulty 33*	*Stevenson*	*Noble*	*Newton*	*Dobson*	*Waldron*	*Thomson*	*Nulty*	*Hankin*	*Fletcher*	*Collins*	*James*	
								Ref: D Smith	A high-class match that might easily have finished 4-4. Jimmy Adamson's Burnley went in front through Nulty's deft header from Thompson's cross. Paddon equalised from outside the box when Holland shielded the ball before laying it into his path. Nulty hit the underside of the bar.											

No	Date	Venue	Opponent	Att	Pos	Pts	Res	F-A	H-T	Scorers, Times, Referees	1	2	3	4	5	6	7	8	9	10	11	12 sub used
32		H	CHELSEA		16		W	3-0	2-0	Bonds 5, 37, 57	Day	Coleman	Lampard	Bonds	Taylor	McGiven	Holland	Paddon	McDowell	Brooking	Best	
	2/3			34,043	*19*	28					*Phillips*	*Locke*	*Harris*	*Hollins*	*Droy*	*Webb*	*Britton*	*Garland*	*Kember*	*Garner*	*Cooke*	
										Ref: G Kew	Billy Bonds' first ever hat-trick comprised a header from Paddon's cross, a rebound when Phillips blocked Best's header, and another rebound when Phillips parried Paddon's screamer. Dave Sexton's Chelsea were beaten in midfield, where Bonds, Paddon and McDowell took control.											
33		A	DERBY		16		D	1-1	0-0	Bonds 73	Day	Coleman	Lampard	Bonds	Taylor	McGiven	Holland	Paddon	McDowell	Brooking	Best	
	9/3			*24,684*	*3*	29				*Rioch 63p*	*Boulton*	*Webster*	*Nish*	*Rioch*	*McFarland*	*Todd*	*Powell*	*Newton*	*Davies**	*Hector*	*Bourne*	*Hinton*
										Ref: R Matthewson	Derby boss Dave Mackay is none too impressed by West Ham's packed defence, but it has brought 16 points from 10 unbeaten games, and probably earned survival. West Ham did not like the penalty decision, given for McDowell's foul on Hector. Bonds' header went in off a post.											
34		H	COVENTRY		18		L	2-3	1-2	Bonds 26p, 75	Day	Coleman	Lampard	Bonds	Taylor	McGiven	Holland	Paddon	Robson	Brooking	Best	
	16/3			26,502	*9*	29				*Cross 2, Alderson 38, Carr 86*	*Glazier*	*Smith*	*Holmes*	*Mortimer*	*Craven*	*Dugdale*	*McGuire*	*Alderson*	*Cross*	*Carr*	*Hutchison*	
										Ref: H New	Day drops Alderson's shot to Cross. Taylor's error gives Coventry their second goal. West Ham level when Wilf Smith's weak header is driven back by Bonds. Willie Carr ran the length of the pitch and tricked Lampard for the late winner. Bonds wasted a hat-trick when heading wide.											
35		A	SHEFFIELD UTD		19		L	0-1	0-0		Day	Coleman	Lampard	Bonds	Taylor	McGiven	Holland	Paddon	Robson	Brooking	Best	
	23/3			*19,467*	*9*	29				*Field 82*	*Brown*	*Badger*	*Hemsley*	*Eddy*	*Colquhoun*	*Salmons*	*Woodward*	*Garbett*	*Nicholl*	*Currie*	*Field*	
										Ref: J Hunting	Booby Moore signed for Fulham before the Coventry game. New skipper Billy Bonds is just eight minutes from leading the team to a precious point when Blades' Tony Field, a new £60,000 signing from Blackburn, headed in a free-kick at the far post. The relegation panic now returns.											
36		H	LEEDS		18		W	3-1	0-1	Best 50, Robson 62, Brooking 84	Day	Coleman	Lampard	Bonds	Taylor	McGiven	McDowell	Paddon	Robson	Brooking	Best	
	30/3			**38,416**	*1*	31				*Clarke 32*	*Harvey*	*Reaney*	*Cherry*	*Bremner*	*McQueen*	*Hunter*	*Giles*	*Clarke*	*Jordan**	*Yorath*	*Madeley*	*Jones*
										Ref: J Yates	This shock win threatens to throw open the championship. Best outpaced McQueen to equalise Allan Clarke's opener. Robson's header was his first goal since September. Paddon's corner was knocked on to Brooking. Liverpool close the gap on Leeds but have still to visit Upton Park.											
37		A	ARSENAL		18		D	0-0	0-0		Day	Coleman	Lampard	Bonds	Taylor	McGiven	McDowell	Paddon	Robson	Brooking	Best	
	6/4			*37,868*	*15*	32					*Wilson*	*Rice*	*Nelson*	*Storey*	*Blockley*	*Kelly*	*Armstrong*	*Ball*	*Radford*	*Kennedy*	*George*	
										Ref: H Hackney	Like West Ham, Arsenal are having a terrible season. Pop Robson wasted Hammers' best chance when failing to convert a cross to the near post. But Arsenal nearly stole both points in the last minute when Charlie George's 25-yard effort bounced off the bar into the North Bank.											
38		H	SOUTHAMPTON		17		W	**4-1**	1-1	Robson 26, 53, Best 49, 82	Day	Coleman	Lampard	Bonds	Taylor	McGiven	McDowell	Paddon	Robson	Brooking	Best	
	12/4			34,163	*19*	34				*Channon 24p*	*Martin*	*McCarthy*	*Mills*	*Fisher**	*Bennett*	*Steele*	*Paine*	*Channon*	*Osgood*	*O'Neil*	*Stokes*	*Gilchrist*
										Ref: W Gow	Saints splashed out £285,000 on Peter Osgood from Chelsea, but he has yet to score in five games for his new club. He was, however, brought down by McGiven for Channon's penalty. Within two minutes Robson headed in Bonds' cross with Saints defenders appealing for offside.											
39		H	WOLVES		17		D	0-0	0-0		Day	Coleman	Lampard	Bonds	Taylor	McGiven	McDowell	Paddon	Robson	Brooking	Best	
	13/4			29,488	*11*	35					*Parkes*	*Palmer*	*Parkin*	*Bailey*	*Munro*	*McAlle*	*Powell**	*Hibbitt*	*Sunderland*	*Kindon*	*Daley*	*Dougan*
										Ref: R Crabb	Struggling Man U beat Newcastle to close the gap with West Ham to six points. Bonds rolled his socks down but not even his all-action game could conjure a goal. Wolves came nearest when Parkin rattled the bar with a 30-yard free-kick. The second half was much ado about nothing.											
40		A	SOUTHAMPTON		17		D	1-1	1-0	Best 44	Day	Coleman	Lampard	Bonds	Taylor	McGiven*	McDowell	Paddon	Robson	Brooking	Best	Gould
	15/4			*26,515*	*19*	36				*Stokes 53*	*Turner*	*McCarthy*	*Peach*	*Fisher*	*Earls*	*Steele*	*Paine*	*Channon*	*Osgood*	*Gilchrist*	*Stokes*	
										Ref: H Davey	McMenemy's Saints need to win more than West Ham, and could be pitched into Division 2 if Man U continue their revival. On 15 December Saints lay 5th, since when they have totally collapsed. Best headed in Paddon's corner. Stokes received a short free-kick to fire the equaliser.											
41		A	MANCHESTER C		18		L	1-2	0-2	Gould 52	Day	Coleman	Lampard	Bonds	Taylor	Holland	McDowell	Paddon	Gould	Brooking	Best	
	20/4			*29,700*	*13*	36				*Booth 3, Bell 17*	*Corrigan*	*Barrett*	*Donachie*	*Doyle*	*Booth*	*Oakes*	*Summerbee*	*Bell*	*Lee*	*Law*	*Tueart*	
										Ref: J Taylor	Two looping headers from Booth and Bell seemed to have put City in command, but the recalled Gould netted from a tight angle to open up the match. West Ham thought they had levelled when Gould 'scored' after Corrigan had dropped the ball but the ref gave a foul against the keeper.											
42		H	LIVERPOOL		18		D	2-2	1-0	Lampard 32, Brooking 67	Day	Coleman	Lampard	Bonds	Taylor	McDowell	Holland	Paddon	Gould	Brooking	Best	
	27/4			36,160	*2*	37				*Toshack 58, Keegan 89*	*Clemence*	*Smith*	*Lindsay*	*Thompson*	*Cormack*	*Hughes*	*Keegan*	*Hall*	*Heighway*	*Toshack*	*Callaghan*	
		Home		Away						Ref: T Reynolds	The great escape is complete. There is much talk of how West Ham discovered their form only after they had sold Bobby Moore to Fulham. Bill Shankly agrees that Mervyn Day has been the find of the season, and he proves the point by saving Alec Lindsay's 39th-minute penalty.											
Average		28,388		27,749																		

League Cup					F-A	H-T	Scorers, Times, and Referees	1	2	3	4	5	6	7	8	9	10	11	12 sub used
2	H	LIVERPOOL	21	D	2-2	1-1	McDougall 39, Robson 84	Day	McDowell	Lampard	Coleman	Taylor	Lock*	Ayris	Best	MacDougall	Brooking	Robson	Holland
8/10		25,840	*5*				*Cormack 35, Heighway 55*	*Clemence*	*Lawler*	*Lindsay*	*Smith*	*Lloyd*	*Hughes*	*Keegan*	*Cormack*	*Heighway*	*Hall*	*Callaghan*	
							Ref: J Taylor	Ferguson has been placed on the transfer list. He is no longer the most expensive keeper in Britain, having been overtaken by Lawson and Sprake. West Ham twice come from behind, first when MacDougall heads his first goal of the season, then when heading a pass to Robson.											
2R	A	LIVERPOOL	21	L	0-1	0-1		Day	Coleman	Lampard	Bonds	Taylor	Moore	Tyler	McDowell	Best	Brooking	Lock*	Holland
29/10		*26,002*	*6*				*Toshack 22*	*Clemence*	*Lawler*	*Lindsay*	*Smith*	*Lloyd*	*Hughes*	*Keegan*	*Cormack*	*Heighway*	*Toshack*	*Callaghan*	
							Ref: J Taylor	A patchy football match is settled by a fine goal. Keegan whips over a low centre and John Toshack dives headlong to nod the ball past Day at the far post. West Ham, as so often on their travels, were too preoccupied with defensive duties to produce much sustained power and skill.											
FA Cup																			
3	H	HEREFORD	21	D	1-1	0-1	Holland 88	Day	McDowell	Lampard	Bonds	Taylor	Moore*	McGiven	Paddon	Gould	Coker	Best	Holland
5/1		23,087	*3:12*				*Redrobe 21*	*Hughes*	*Radford*	*Naylor*	*McLaughlin*	*Jones*	*Tavener*	*Redrobe**	*Tyler*	*Hinch*	*Evans*	*Rudge*	*Owen*
							Ref: R Challis	Bobby Moore limps off after 30 minutes, never to play for West Ham again. He had earlier been dispossessed by Redrobe for Hereford's goal. Hinch then hit a post. When McDowell went off after 67 minutes Hammers were down to 10 men, but Holland's solo goal kept them alive.											
3R	A	HEREFORD	21	L	1-2	1-1	Best 35	Day	Coleman	Lampard	Bonds	Taylor	Wooler	McGiven	Paddon	Lutton	Holland	Best	
8/1		*17,423*	*3:12*				*Naylor 37p, Jones 74*	*Hughes*	*Radford*	*Naylor*	*McLaughlin*	*Jones*	*Taverner*	*Redrobe**	*Tyler*	*Hinch*	*Rudge*	*Evans*	*Owen*
							Ref: E Wallace	West Ham must regret voting for Hereford's admission to the Football League. Tyler is back with Hereford. Best headed in Lampard's cross for the perfect start, but when Evans was upended Naylor levelled. Alan Jones then lashed in Evans' cross. Hereford now play Bristol City.											

		Home					Away					
	P	W	D	L	F	A	W	D	L	F	A	Pts
1 Leeds	42	12	8	1	38	18	12	6	3	28	13	62
2 Liverpool	42	18	2	1	34	11	4	11	6	18	20	57
3 Derby	42	13	7	1	40	16	4	7	10	12	26	48
4 Ipswich	42	10	7	4	38	21	8	4	9	29	37	47
5 Stoke	42	13	6	2	39	15	2	10	9	15	27	46
6 Burnley	42	10	9	2	29	16	6	5	10	27	37	46
7 Everton	42	12	7	2	29	14	4	5	12	21	34	44
8 QP Rangers	42	8	10	3	30	17	5	7	9	26	35	43
9 Leicester	42	10	7	4	35	17	3	9	9	16	24	42
10 Arsenal	42	9	7	5	23	16	5	7	9	26	35	42
11 Tottenham	42	9	4	8	26	27	5	10	6	19	23	42
12 Wolves	42	11	6	4	30	18	2	9	10	19	31	41
13 Sheffield Utd	42	7	7	7	25	22	7	5	9	19	27	40
14 Manchester C	42	10	7	4	25	17	4	5	12	14	29	40
15 Newcastle	42	9	6	6	28	21	4	6	11	21	27	38
16 Coventry	42	10	5	6	25	18	4	5	12	18	36	38
17 Chelsea	42	9	4	8	36	29	3	9	9	20	31	37
18 WEST HAM	42	7	7	7	36	32	4	8	9	19	28	37
19 Birmingham	42	10	7	4	30	21	2	6	13	22	43	37
20 Southampton	42	8	10	3	30	20	3	4	14	17	48	36
21 Manchester U	42	7	7	7	23	20	3	5	13	15	28	32
22 Norwich	42	6	9	6	25	27	1	6	14	12	35	29
	924	218	149	95	674	433	95	149	218	433	674	924

Odds & ends

Double wins: (1) Chelsea.
Double losses: (2) Spurs, Stoke.

Won from behind: (5) Man C (h), Chelsea (a), Everton (h), Leeds (h), Southampton (h).
Lost from in front: (3) Newcastle (h), Birmingham (a), Hereford FAC (a).

High spots: 10 unbeaten games, January to March, climbing to 16th.
Beating champions Leeds.

Low spots: Losing to Third Division Hereford in FA Cup.
Failing to win any of the first 11 league games, dropping to last place.

West Ham's average home attendance was higher than the average for the First Division as a whole.

Hammer of the Year: Billy Bonds.
Ever-presents: (1) Frank Lampard.
Hat-tricks: (1) Billy Bonds.
Leading scorer: (13) Clyde Best and Billy Bonds.

	Appearances						Goals			
	Lge	*Sub*	LC	*Sub*	FAC	*Sub*	Lge	LC	FAC	Tot
Ayris, Johnny	**5**		1							
Best, Clyde	**34**		2		2		**12**		1	**13**
Bonds, Billy	**40**		1		2		**13**			**13**
Brooking, Trevor	**38**		2				**6**			**6**
Charles, Clive	**1**									
Coker, Ade		*1*			1					
Coleman, Keith	**31**	*2*	2		1					
Day, Mervyn	**33**		2		2					
Ferguson, Bobby	**9**									
Gould, Bobby	**11**	*1*			1		**4**			**4**
Holland, Pat	**20**	*3*		*2*	1	*1*	**2**		1	**3**
Lampard, Frank	**42**		2		2		**2**			**2**
Lock, Kevin	**9**	*2*	2							
Lutton, Bertie	**4**	*2*			1					
MacDougall, Ted	**14**		1				**1**	1		**2**
McDowell, John	**33**		2		1		**2**			**2**
McGiven, Mike	**21**				2					
Moore, Bobby	**22**		1		1					
Paddon, Graham	**24**				2		**4**			**4**
Robson, Bryan	**22**		1				**7**	1		**8**
Taylor, Tommy	**40**		2		2					
Tyler, Dudley	**8**		1							
Wooler, Alan	**1**	*1*			1					
(own-goals)							**2**			**2**
23 players used	**462**	***12***	**22**	***2***	**22**	***1***	**55**	**2**	**2**	**59**

Billy Jennings heads West Ham's second goal against Den Haag on 3 March 1976

Pre-season training in the summer of 1979

No	Date		Att	Pos	Pt	F-A	H-T	Scorers, Times, and Referees	1	2	3	4	5	6	7	8	9	10	11	12 sub used
1	A	MANCHESTER C			L	**0-4**	0-1		Day	Coleman*	Lampard	Bonds	Taylor T	McDowell	Holland	Paddon	Gould	Brooking	Best	Lock
	17/8		*30,240*		–			*Tueart 10, Marsh 47, 62, Doyle 77*	*MacRae*	*Barrett*	*Donachie*	*Doyle*	*Clarke*	*Oakes*	*Henson*	*Bell*	*Marsh*	*Hartford*	*Tueart*	
								Ref: J Taylor	John Lyall has taken over team affairs from Ron Greenwood, who is off scouting. City parade several new signings, among them Asa Hartford, who did much to undermine the hapless Hammers. A combination of the woodwork and Mervyn Day's excellence prevented a worse defeat.											
2	H	LUTON			W	2-0	2-0	Lampard 4, Bonds 16	Day	McDowell	Lampard	Bonds	Taylor T	Lock	Holland	Paddon	Ayris	Brooking	Best	
	19/8		23,182		2				*Horn*	*John Ryan*	*Thomson*	*Anderson*	*Litt*	*Garner**	*Aston*	*Husband*	*Butlin*	*West*	*Hindson*	*Shanks*
								Ref: R Kirkpatrick	Luton return to Division 1 after 14 years. They lost their opener 1-2 to Liverpool, and look a poor team now. Greenwood is away watching Alf Wood of Millwall. Lampard scored early with a low volley and Bonds added a second with a header after Horn had punched the ball out.											
3	H	EVERTON		16	L	2-3	0-2	Bonds 71p, McDowell 73	Day	Coleman	Lampard	Bonds	Taylor T	Lock	Holland	Paddon	Gould	McDowell	Best	
	24/8		22,486	*5*	2			*Royle 39p, Latchford 45, Harvey 80*	*Lawson*	*Darracott*	*Seargeant*	*Clements*	*Lyons*	*Hurst*	*Buckley*	*Harvey*	*Royle*	*Latchford*	*Connolly**	*Pearson*
								Ref: K Burns	Again it is West Ham's defenders who get the goals. Buckley was pulled down by McDowell for Everton's penalty; West Ham's was given for handball. The ball came off the bar for Latchford's goal. McDowell dodged Everton's offside trap. Harvey won the game with a rising drive.											
4	A	LUTON			D	0-0	0-0		Day	Coleman	Lampard	Bonds	Taylor T	Lock	Holland	Paddon	Gould	McDowell	Best	
	28/8		*16,931*		3				*Barber*	*Shanks*	*Thomson*	*Anderson*	*Faulkner*	*John Ryan*	*Hindson*	*Husband*	*Butlin*	*West*	*Aston**	*Alston*
								Ref: C Thomas	West Ham's goal-shy forwards also failed to score in three Texaco Cup games. Clyde Best lacked support. His one shot was pushed aside by Barber. Luton are still looking for their first win and did most of the attacking. Elsewhere, Bill Nicholson has resigned at Tottenham.											
5	A	NEWCASTLE		18	L	0-2	0-2		Day	Coleman	Lampard	Bonds	Taylor T	Lock	Holland	Paddon	Gould*	McDowell	Best	Ayris
	31/8		*30,780*	*11*	3			*Tudor 5, Macdonald 24*	*McFaul*	*Craig D*	*Clark*	*McDermott*	*Keeley*	*Howard*	*Burns*	*Nattrass*	*Macdonald*	*Tudor*	*Hibbitt*	
								Ref: H Hackney	Goal-shy Hammers miss Trevor Brooking's midfield guile. Newcastle win so comfortably that after the final whistle they heap salt on the wounds by saying the team they want to play in Round 3 of the FA Cup is West Ham! Little do they know that Hammers are destined to win it.											
6	H	SHEFFIELD UTD		21	L	1-2	1-0	Jennings 18	Day	McDowell	Lampard	Bonds	Taylor T	Lock	Ayris	Paddon	**Jennings**	Holland	Best	
	7/9		**20,977**	*6*	3			*Woodward 76, Dearden 85*	*Brown*	*Badger*	*Hemsley*	*Eddy*	*Colquhoun*	*Franks*	*Woodward*	*Speight*	*Dearden*	*Currie*	*Field*	
								Ref: I Jones	5ft 9in Billy Jennings has signed from Watford for £115,000. He turned in Lampard's long ball and saw another effort superbly saved by Jim Brown. Holland's sloppy square pass let in Alan Woodward. Soon afterwards Dearden scored at the second attempt for Ken Furphy's Blades.											
7	A	TOTTENHAM		22	L	1-2	0-0	Lampard 79	Day	McDowell	Lampard	Bonds	Taylor T	Lock	Holland	Paddon	Jennings	Brooking	Best	
	14/9		*27,959*	*18*	3			*England 56, Chivers 74*	*Jennings*	*Evans*	*Knowles*	*Pratt*	*England*	*Beal*	*Neighbour*	*Perryman*	*Chivers*	*Peters*	*Coates*	
								Ref: R Tinkler	Bill Nicholson resigned two weeks ago. Greenwood watches the Hammers for the first time this season. England outjumped Bonds and Chivers outjumped Taylor for Spurs' goals. Lampard replied with a diving header. Spurs' win hauls them above West Ham, who are now bottom.											
8	H	LEICESTER		19	W	**6-2**	3-1	Jennings 24, 50, Bonds 35, Gould 40, 56,	Day	McDowell	Lampard	Bonds	Taylor T	Lock	Jennings*	Paddon	Gould	Brooking	**Robson**	Holland
	21/9		21,377	*13*	5			*Worthington 10p, 89* [Robson 68]	*Wallington*	*Whitworth*	*Rofe*	*Sammels*	*Munro*	*Woollett*	*Weller*	*Earle*	*Worthington*	*Birchenall**	*Glover*	*Cross*
								Ref: R Crabb	Keith Robson signs for £60,000 from Newcastle and scores. John Lyall switches to 4-3-3 to accommodate him. Worthington 'dives' to win a penalty. Jennings' looping header makes it 1-1.Bonds' right-footer and Gould's diving header make it 3-1. Brooking is man of the match.											
9	H	BIRMINGHAM		13	W	3-0	1-0	Paddon 44, Jennings 64, Robson 80	Day	McDowell	Lampard	Bonds	Taylor T	Lock	Jennings	Paddon	Gould	Brooking	Robson	
	25/9		29,495	*21*	7				*Latchford*	*Martin*	*Styles*	*Kendall*	*Gallagher*	*Page**	*Campbell*	*Francis*	*Burns*	*Hatton*	*Taylor*	*Hynd*
								Ref: A Lees	Hammers hit the woodwork three times in the opening 20 minutes, but the score was harsh on Freddie Goodwin's City, who had a goal chalked off and live-wire Trevor Francis also hit the bar. Graham Paddon's 30-yarder was followed by Billy Jenning's header from McDowell's cross.											
10	A	BURNLEY		12	W	5-3	1-1	Robson 18, 55, Brooking 65, Jennings 71,	Day	McDowell	Lampard	Bonds	Taylor T	Lock	Jennings	Paddon	Gould	Brooking	Robson	
	28/9		*17,613*	*13*	9			*Fletcher 3, 86, Noble 57* [Bonds 83]	*Stevenson*	*Newton*	*Brennan*	*Ingham*	*Waldron*	*Rodaway*	*Noble*	*Flynn*	*Fletcher*	*Collins*	*James*	
								Ref: G Hill	It is hard to know which is the more remarkable, the thrill-a-minute football match or Trevor Brooking's first ever booking, for a challenge on Leighton James. Jimmy Adamson's Burnley had won at Anfield in midweek but their keeper has one of those matches he would wish to forget.											

No	Venue	Opponent / Date	Att	Pos	Pts	F-A	H-T	Scorers, Times, and Referees	1	2	3	4	5	6	7	8	9	10	11	12
11	H	DERBY		12	D	2-2	1-1	Robson 8, Bonds 59	Day	McDowell*	Lampard	Bonds	Taylor T	Lock	Jennings	Paddon	Gould	Brooking	Robson	Holland
		5/10	32,900	*9*	10			*Lee 29, Hector 80*	*Boulton*	*Webster*	*Nish*	*Rioch*	*Daniel*	*Todd*	*Newton*	*Gemmill*	*Davies*	*Hector*	*Lee*	
								Ref: P Walters	Brooking is scintillating, despite playing in attack against his wishes. Keith Robson appears to handle before scoring the first goal. After Lee levelled, Lampard crossed for Robson to head on to Bonds. Though Hector equalised, it does not stop talk of Hammers challenging at the top.											
12	A	COVENTRY		12	D	1-1	0-0	Gould 77	Day	Coleman	Lampard	Bonds	Taylor T	Lock	Jennings	Paddon	Gould	Brooking	Robson	
		12/10	*22,519*	*13*	11			*Hutchison 71*	*Ramsbottom*	*Oakey*	*Catlin*	*Mortimer*	*Lloyd*	*Hindley*	*Holmes*	*Alderson*	*Stein*	*Cross*	*Hutchison*	
								Ref: L Hayes	The City match programme devoted three pages to the return of Bobby Gould: the home crowd booed him lethargically and former team-mates playfully kicked him. Gould responded by cracking in a superb volley. That equalised Day's mishap, letting a corner float through his hands.											
13	A	EVERTON		12	D	1-1	1-0	Gould 40	Day	Coleman	Lampard	Bonds	Taylor T	Lock	Jennings	Paddon	Gould	Brooking	Robson	
		15/10	*31,855*	*3*	12			*Lyons 59*	*Davies*	*Bernard*	*Seargeant*	*Lyons*	*Kenyon*	*Clements*	*Buckley*	*Dobson*	*Pearson*	*Royle*	*Connolly*	
								Ref: D Wallace	Never has 19-year-old Day performed better than this, and all under the appreciative eye of England boss Don Revie. Hammers were swamped in midfield, yet took the lead when Gould slid in to connect with Robson's back-header. Lyons ran from half-way to level from a sharp angle.											
14	H	IPSWICH		10	W	1-0	1-0	Jennings 34	Day	Coleman	Lampard	Bonds	Taylor T	Lock	Jennings	Paddon	Gould	Brooking	Robson	
		19/10	33,543	*3*	14				*Sivell*	*Mills*	*Harper*	*Talbot*	*Hunter*	*Beattie*	*Hamilton*	*Collard*	*Johnson*	*Woods*	*Lambert**	*Gates*
								Ref: R Perkin	West Ham extend their unbeaten league record to seven with an uncompromisingly physical performance. Billy Jennings won the game with a super goal, taking a short cross from Robson and slipping past three defenders. The goal had supporters comparing it with Greaves - at his best.											
15	A	ARSENAL		11	L	0-3	0-2		Day	McDowell*	Lampard	Bonds	Taylor T	Lock	Jennings	Paddon	Gould	Brooking	Robson	Coleman
		26/10	*41,004*	*21*	14			*Radford 14, Brady 42, Kidd 50*	*Rimmer*	*Rice**	*McNab*	*Kelly*	*Mancini*	*Simpson*	*Storey*	*Ball*	*Radford*	*Brady*	*Kidd*	*Armstrong*
								Ref: T Reynolds	England boss Don Revie runs his eye over Brooking, but West Ham's midfield is swamped by Arsenal's 4-4-2 formation. Arsenal had so much freedom that Eddie Kelly started taking the mickey. The turning point came when McNab cleared off the line from Gould just after half-time.											
16	H	MIDDLESBROUGH		10	W	3-0	1-0	Robson 29, Boam 84 (og), Paddon 87	Day	Coleman	Lampard	Bonds	Taylor T	Lock	Jennings	Paddon	Gould	Brooking	Robson	
		2/11	28,915	*6*	16				*Platt*	*Craggs*	*Spraggon*	*Souness*	*Boam*	*Maddren*	*Murdoch*	*Mills**	*Hickton*	*Foggon*	*Armstrong*	*Willey*
								Ref: R Mathewson	Kevin Lock plays a stormer alongside Tommy Taylor, locking the door against Hickton and Mills. Gould's cross was unwittingly turned in by Robson. Brooking made the game safe with a goal that went in off Stuart Boam. Paddon's free-kick then flew in from the edge of the box.											
17	A	CARLISLE		9	W	1-0	0-0	Lampard 48	Day	Coleman	Lampard	Bonds	Taylor T	Lock	Jennings	Paddon	Gould	Brooking	Robson	
		9/11	***14,141***	*17*	18				*Clarke T*	*Carr*	*Gorman*	*O'Neill*	*Green*	*Parker*	*Martin*	*Train*	*Clarke F*	*McIlmoyle*	*Balderstone*	
								Ref: K Styles	Lampard's goal leaves West Ham just four points behind the leaders, and even Lyall is foolish enough to start talking about the championship. The bookies are unimpressed, quoting the Hammers at 20-1 for the title. The looming match at Anfield will sort the men from the boys.											
18	H	WOLVES		7	W	5-2	2-0	Bonds 37p, Brook 44, Lamp' 62, Jen' 78,	Day	Coleman	Lampard	Bonds	Taylor T	Lock	Jennings	Paddon	Gould	Brooking	Robson	
		16/11	31,708	*13*	20			*Richards 70, Kindon 88* [Gould 85]	*Parkes*	*Palmer*	*Parkin*	*Bailey*	*Jefferson*	*McAlle*	*Hibbitt*	*Powell*	*Richards*	*Kindon*	*Farley*	
								Ref: H Davey	'Brooking for England; West Ham for champions' sing the crowd. Wolves had not lost in London on their previous 11 visits, over 27 months. A penalty conceded by Ken Hibbitt – who handled Brooking's cross – lit the touch-paper. Brooking played a part in all but one of the goals.											
19	A	LIVERPOOL		6	D	1-1	1-1	Robson 11	Day	Coleman	Lampard	Bonds	Taylor T	Lock	Jennings	Paddon	Gould	Brooking	Robson	
		23/11	***46,346***	*2*	21			*Smith 12*	*Clemence*	*Smith*	*Lindsay*	*McDermott*	*Lawler*	*Hughes*	*Keegan*	*Cormack*	*Boersma**	*Kennedy*	*Callaghan*	*Heighway*
								Ref: R Capey	West Ham looked full of ideas early on, but were hanging on desperately by the close, when Mervyn Day saved well from Lindsay's point-blank effort. Afterwards Day was hospitalised with tummy pains. X-rays showed his stomach contained gravel. He was told to drink water.											
20	A	QP RANGERS		6	W	2-0	1-0	Jennings 31, Paddon 70	Day	Coleman	Lampard	Bonds*	Taylor T	Lock	Jennings	Paddon	Gould	Brooking	Robson	Holland
		30/11	*28,356*	*17*	23				*Parkes*	*Clement*	*Gillard*	*McLintock*	*Webb*	*Hazell*	*Thomas*	*Francis*	*Rogers*	*Bowles*	*Givens*	
								Ref: M Sinclair	David Webb's error let in Billy Jennings to head the first goal. Man-of-the-match Graham Paddon deserved to score the second, decisive goal, a left-footer from the edge of the box. The chance was set up by Brooking. Kevin Lock padlocked danger-man Stan Bowles out of the game.											
21	H	LEEDS		5	W	2-1	1-0	Gould 29, Jennings 69	Day	Coleman	Lampard	Bonds	Taylor T	Lock	Jennings*	Paddon	Gould	McDowell	Robson	**Taylor A**
		7/12	39,562	*12*	25			*McKenzie 90*	*Harvey*	*Reaney*	*Cherry*	*Bremner*	*McQueen*	*Madeley*	*McKenzie*	*Clarke*	*Jordan*	*Lorimer*	*Yorath*	
								Ref: W Gow	The gates were locked 30 minutes before kick-off. Paddon's corner-kicks brought two goals. The first was headed on by Robson to Gould. The second was headed in by Jennings. Leeds feigned injury and back-chatted the ref throughout, then blamed West Ham for being too physical.											

No Date		Att	Pos	Pt	F-A	H-T	Scorers, Times, and Referees	1	2	3	4	5	6	7	8	9	10	11	12 sub used
22 H	MANCHESTER C		6	D	0-0	0-0		Day	Coleman	Lampard	Bonds	Taylor T	Lock	Jennings*	Paddon	Gould	Brooking	Robson	McDowell
14/12		33,908	*4*	26				*MacRae*	*Hammond*	*Donachie*	*Henson*	*Doyle**	*Oakes*	*Horswill*	*Bell*	*Marsh*	*Hartford*	*Tueart*	*Daniels*
							Ref: J Hunting	City skipper Rodney Marsh admits to having agreed during a team-talk to stop rampant West Ham by employing negative tactics. City tried to interrupt Hammers' rhythm with constant time-wasting. Gould missed the best chance, but Day pulled off a super save to prevent a travesty.											
23 A	CHELSEA		5	D	1-1	0-0	Gould 85	Day	Coleman	Lampard	Bonds*	Taylor T	Lock	McDowell	Paddon	Gould	Brooking	Robson	Best
21/12		*34,969*	*19*	27			*Hutchinson 65*	*Phillips*	*Locke*	*Harris*	*Hollins*	*Droy*	*Hay*	*Kember**	*Wilkins R*	*Garland*	*Hutchinson*	*Cooke*	*Dempsey*
							Ref: R Perkins	Day turned Lock's miscued clearance onto the bar, with Hutchinson waiting for the rebound. Gould, previously marked tight by Droy, chested down and fired the equaliser past Phillips. After 35 matches Best returned to first-team football, but was booked immediately and looked stale.											
24 H	TOTTENHAM		5	D	1-1	1-1	Robson 26	Day	Coleman	Lampard	McDowell	Taylor T	Lock	Jennings*	Paddon	Gould	Brooking	Robson	Taylor A
26/12		37,682	*18*	28			*Peters 18*	*Jennings*	*Kinnear*	*Knowles*	*Pratt*	*England*	*Naylor*	*Coates*	*Perryman*	*Chivers*	*Peters*	*Duncan*	
							Ref: G Kew	Spurs have lost their last two games. Martin Peters chipped Day from the edge of the box, then Keith Robson headed in Brooking's near-post corner. Robson's fourth booking will bring him an automatic ban. Had West Ham won they would have gone top of the league for four hours.											
25 A	STOKE		6	L	1-2	0-0	Holland 52	Day	Coleman	Lampard	Holland	Taylor T	Lock	Taylor A*	Paddon	Gould	McDowell	Best	Ayris
28/12		*33,498*	*5*	28			*Salmons 69p, Hurst 79*	*Shilton*	*Marsh*	*Pejic*	*Mahoney*	*Smith*	*Dodd*	*Conroy*	*Greenhoff*	*Hurst*	*Hudson*	*Salmons*	
							Ref: D Richardson	Stoke had lost at home just once, so this was a tough fixture, especially without Brooking, Bonds, Jennings, and Robson. Alan Taylor went off with a twisted knee. Defeat was made worse because Stoke's first goal was a disputed penalty and their second was headed in by Geoff Hurst.											
26 A	LEEDS		9	L	1-2	1-1	Robson 10	Day	Coleman	Lampard	Bonds	McDowell	Lock	Holland	Paddon	Best	Brooking	Robson	
11/1		*40,099*	*10*	28			*Clarke 37, McKenzie 59*	*Harvey*	*Reaney*	*Gray F*	*Bremner*	*McQueen*	*Madeley*	*McKenzie*	*Clarke*	*Lorimer*	*Giles*	*Gray E*	
							Ref: J Rice	When Keith Robson headed in Bonds' cross it seemed that the Elland Road jinx might be lifted. Hammers had not won here in Division 1 since 1930. Lock's bad back-pass let in Clarke, and Jimmy Armfield's Leeds were on top when McKenzie fired in after Clarke's shot was blocked.											
27 H	QP RANGERS		10	D	2-2	2-1	Jennings15, Bonds 44p	Day	Coleman*	Lampard	Bonds	Taylor T	Lock	Jennings	Paddon	McDowell	Brooking	Robson	Best
18/1		28,772	*12*	29			*Masson 32, Bowles 73p*	*Parkes*	*Clement*	*Gillard*	*Masson*	*McLintock*	*Webb*	*Thomas*	*Francis*	*Beck*	*Bowles*	*Givens*	
							Ref: P Willis	Jennings side-foots Paddon's cross. Bowles slips a quick free-kick to Masson. Robson signs off before he starts a suspension with a cracking run that earns a penalty. Bowles levelled from another penalty, both of which – against Webb and Lampard – were shown by TV to be correct.											
28 H	CARLISLE		6	W	2-0	2-0	Jennings 18, Holland 38	Day	McDowell	Lampard	Bonds	Taylor T	Lock	Jennings	Paddon	Robson	Brooking*	Holland	Best
1/2		26,805	*20*	31				*Ross*	*Spearritt*	*Gorman*	*O'Neill*	*Green*	*Parker*	*Martin**	*Train*	*Owen*	*Laidlaw*	*Clarke*	*Barry*
							Ref: R Crabb	Carlisle pressed hard but seldom threatened, not helped by striker Bobby Owen playing deep in midfield. Jennings missed his first shot but scored with his second, with Carlisle defenders standing like statues. Holland snapped up a bad back-pass by Les O'Neill for the second goal.											
29 A	MIDDLESBROUGH		7	D	0-0	0-0		Day	McDowell	Lampard	Bonds*	Taylor T	Lock	Jennings	Paddon	Best	Brooking	Holland	Coleman
8/2		*29,179*	*8*	32				*Platt*	*Craggs*	*Spraggon*	*Murdoch*	*Boam*	*Maddren*	*Brine*	*Mills*	*Hickton*	*Willey*	*Armstrong**	*Taylor*
							Ref: J Williams	Boro boss Jack Charlton is full of praise for West Ham's football. Boro didn't play any, but still felt they should have won when Day appeared to impede David Mills in the box. Best Hammers' chance fell to Clyde Best, who shimmied through three tackles, then lost control of the ball.											
30 H	LIVERPOOL		6	D	0-0	0-0		Day	McDowell	Lampard	Bonds	Taylor T	Lock	Jennings	Paddon	Robson	Brooking	Holland	
19/2		**40,256**	*5*	33				*Clemence*	*Neal*	*Smith*	*Thompson*	*McDermott**	*Hughes*	*Keegan*	*Hall*	*Heighway*	*Kennedy*	*Callaghan*	*Waddle*
							Ref: T Reynolds	Tommy Smith is recalled by Liverpool to curtail Robson, and within 36 seconds has kicked him into orbit. The rusty Smith also presents West Ham with their best chance, fluffing a back-pass that Jennings volleyed against a post, with Pat Holland hooking the rebound over the bar.											
31 A	WOLVES		9	L	1-3	0-2	Gould 82	Day	Coleman*	Lampard	McDowell	Taylor T	Lock	Jennings	Paddon	Robson	Brooking	Holland	Gould
22/2		*24,791*	*14*	33			*Kindon 17, Richards 41, 64*	*Pierce*	*Palmer*	*Parkin*	*Bailey*	*Munro*	*Jefferson*	*Hibbitt*	*Daley*	*Richards*	*Kindon*	*Wagstaffe*	
							Ref: H Hackney	Lyall has no one to do the job of the absent Bonds. West Ham had lost at Molineux, without scoring, for the previous six years, so the result is no surprise, though Gould's goal is. No wonder McGarry's team like playing West Ham, who afterwards retreat to Bournemouth for a break.											

32	H	NEWCASTLE		13	L	0-1	0-1		Day	McDowell	Lampard	Robson	Taylor T	Lock	Jennings	Paddon	Gould	Brooking	Holland*	Taylor A
	28/2		32,753	*11*	33			*Macdonald 26*	*McFaul*	*Craig D*	*Barker*	*Smith*	*Keeley*	*Nattrass*	*Barrowclough*	*Nulty*	*Macdonald*	*Tudor*	*Craig T*	
								Ref: D Biddle	It's now just one win in 11 games as West Ham's slide continues. Malcolm Macdonald ran 40 yards to beat Hammers' offside-trap for his 16th league goal of the season. Both sides wasted chances. Keith Robson headed against a post and Billy Jennings shot wide from six yards.											
33	H	BURNLEY		12	W	2-1	0-1	Robson 66, Taylor A 76	Day	McDowell	Lampard	Bonds*	Taylor T	Lock	Jennings	Paddon	Taylor A	Brooking	Robson	Gould
	15/3		28,830	*2*	35			*Collins 42*	*Stevenson*	*Ingham*	*Newton*	*Noble*	*Waldron*	*Thomson*	*Flynn**	*Hankin*	*Fletcher*	*Collins*	*James*	*Rodaway*
								Ref: T Spencer	Bonds is carried off in the first minute with a knee injury. Doug Collins chipped Day, but Keith Robson's cross sailed over Alan Stevenson for the equaliser. Afterwards Bobby Gould claimed he got the faintest of touches and jokingly tried to claim the goal. Lyall awarded it to Robson.											
34	A	BIRMINGHAM			D	1-1	1-0	Taylor A 29	Day	Coleman	Lampard	McDowell	Taylor T	Lock	Gould	Paddon	Taylor A	Brooking	Robson	
	18/3		*34,000*		36			*Bryant 67*	*Latchford*	*Calderwood*	*Bryant*	*Kendall**	*Gallagher*	*Roberts*	*Morton*	*Francis*	*Hendrie*	*Hatton*	*Taylor*	*Want*
								Ref: P Partridge	Brooking set up Alan Taylor's fourth goal in three games, but Francis, back after five months out through injury, manufactures City's equaliser through Bryant's first senior goal. After the match Robson suffers from internal bleeding, which together with a leg injury has him on crutches.											
35	A	SHEFFIELD UTD		12	L	2-3	2-1	Gould 7, Jennings 28	Day	Coleman	Lampard	McDowell	Taylor T	Lock	Jennings	Paddon	Taylor A	Brooking	Gould	
	22/3		*25,527*	*8*	36			*Currie 8, 78, Woodward 58*	*Brown*	*Badger*	*Bradford*	*Eddy*	*Colquhoun*	*Flynn*	*Woodward*	*Speight*	*Cammack*	*Currie*	*Field*	
								Ref: J Taylor	It is one defeat in 11 for the Blades, who are now only five points behind leaders Everton. The game got off to a furious start, Gould driving in from McDowell's lay-off. Seconds later Cammack hit the post and Currie tapped in the rebound. Man-of-the-match Currie mis-hit the winner.											
36	H	STOKE		12	D	2-2	1-1	Brooking 39, Jennings 69	Day	Coleman	Lampard*	McDowell	Taylor T	Lock	Jennings	Paddon	Taylor A	Brooking	Gould	Ayris
	28/3		29,811	*5*	37			*Conroy 40, 49*	*Shilton*	*Bloor*	*Bowers*	*Mahoney*	*Dodd*	*Skeels*	*Conroy*	*Greenhoff*	*Hurst**	*Hudson*	*Salmons*	*Moores*
								Ref: H Davey	Had Tony Waddington's Stoke won they would have been just one point off the top. Carrot-top Conroy scored twice and was at the heart of everything. Brooking had impudently taken the ball around Shilton to put West Ham one up. Jennings side-stepped two defenders to level.											
37	H	CHELSEA		12	L	0-1	0-1		Day	Coleman	McDowell	**Curbishley**	Taylor T	Lock	Jennings*	Paddon	Taylor A	Brooking	Gould	Ayris
	29/3		31,025	*18*	37			*Droy 22*	*Phillips*	*Locke*	*Harris*	*Hollins*	*Droy*	*Hinton*	*Kember*	*Hay*	*Langley*	*Houseman*	*Cooke*	
								Ref: A Morrissey	Chelsea are fighting desperately against the drop, and with West Ham's minds on the FA Cup this is the perfect time to play them. Semi-fit giant Mick Droy glanced a header for the only goal. Young Alan Curbishley took the eye on his debut, drafted in for the injured Billy Bonds.											
38	A	LEICESTER		12	L	0-3	0-1		Day	Coleman	McDowell	Holland	Taylor T	Lock	Best	Wooler	Taylor A	Brooking	Gould	
	1/4		*30,408*	*18*	37			*Worthington 13p, Garland 86, 87*	*Wallington*	*Whitworth*	*Rpfe*	*Lee*	*Blockley*	*Cross*	*Weller*	*Sammels*	*Worthington**	*Birchenall*	*Garland*	*Glover*
								Ref: K McNally	All the bottom clubs are beating West Ham of late. With an FA Cup semi-final looming, Lyall does not relish a punishing Easter schedule, and rests Jennings and Paddon. Pat Holland's foul on Frank Worthington allowed Jimmy Bloomfield's City to go in front. Garland sealed the win.											
39	A	DERBY		13	L	0-1	0-0		Day	McDowell	Lampard	Bonds	Taylor T	Lock	Jennings	Paddon	Taylor A*	Brooking	Gould	Holland
	12/4		*31,336*	*1*	37			*Rioch 67*	*Boulton*	*Thomas*	*Nish*	*Rioch*	*McFarland*	*Todd*	*Newton*	*Gemmill*	*Davies*	*Hector*	*Lee*	*Hinton*
								Ref: M Lowe	Bruce Rioch's 20th goal of the season keeps Derby two points out in front with two matches to play. It came when Hinton's corner was only half-cleared, and Rioch slammed the ball in. Sub Hinton had only been on two minutes. Derby boss Dave Mackay: 'I died a death out there'.											
40	H	COVENTRY		14	L	1-2	1-2	Holland 44	Day	Coleman	Lampard	Holland	McDowell	Lock	Jennings	Paddon*	Taylor A	Brooking	Gould	Curbishley
	19/4		27,431	*12*	37			*Green 4, Mortimer 45*	*Ramsbottom*	*Oakey*	*Cattlin !*	*Craven*	*Lloyd*	*Dugdale*	*Mortimer*	*Holmes*	*Ferguson*	*Green*	*Hutchison*	
								Ref: R Tinkler	West Ham extend their dismal league run to seven games without a win. Players feared injury against Gordon Milne's Coventry, for whom Chris Cattlin was sent off after just nine minutes. City were leading at the time through Alan Green's effort, when Day and Lampard dithered.											
41	A	IPSWICH		16	L	1-4	1-1	Holland 36	Day	Coleman	Lampard	Holland	McDowell	Lock	Jennings	Best	Taylor A	Brooking	Gould	
	26/4		*31,592*	*3*	37			*Talbot 27, Whymark 61, Beattie 87, [Hunter 89]*	*Sivell*	*Burley*	*Mills*	*Talbot*	*Hunter*	*Beattie*	*Hamilton*	*Viljoen*	*Woods*	*Whymark*	*Lambert*	
								Ref: D Turner	In the 86th minute Talbot sends Brooking flying in the box but the referee waves play on. Ipswich immediately broke downfield for Kevin Beattie to make it 1-3. Ipswich's first goal had come when the ref penalised Day for time-wasting and awarded a free-kick on the 18-yard line.											
42	H	ARSENAL		13	W	1-0	1-0	Paddon 3	Day	McDowell	Lampard	Bonds	Taylor T	Lock	Jennings*	Paddon	Taylor A	Brooking	Holland	Gould
	28/4		30,195	*16*	39				*Barnett*	*Storey*	*Nelson*	*Kelly*	*Mancini*	*Matthews*	*Ball*	*Brady*	*Hornsby*	*Kidd*	*Rostron*	
	Home		Away					Ref: R Matthewson	West Ham's first league win in nine attempts, and only their third in five months. Kelly's mistake gave Paddon the chance of a left-footer over Barnett's shoulder. Taylor missed two good chances, one of which hit the bar. No one can take it easy for fear of being dropped for Wembley.											
Average	30,077		29,673																	

League Cup					F-A	H-T	Scorers, Times, and Referees	1	2	3	4	5	6	7	8	9	10	11	12 sub used
2	A	TRANMERE	21	D	0-0	0-0		Day	McDowell	Lampard	Bonds	Taylor T	Lock	Ayris	Paddon	Holland	Brooking	Best	
11/9		*8,638*	*3:21*					*Johnson*	*Matthias*	*Flood*	*Moore*	*Philpotts*	*Veitch*	*Coppell*	*Palios*	*Young*	*Tynan*	*Crossley*	
							Ref: A Grey	Hammers' first ever visit to Prenton Park. New signing Billy Jennings is cup-tied. Tranmere knocked out Arsenal last year and had the chances to win this one too. They had Mervyn Day to blame for not taking them. Tranmere 'scored' after 16 minutes, but Ronnie Moore was offside.											
2R	H	TRANMERE	7	W	6-0	2-0	Bonds 23p, 87, Gould 44, 56, 89p,	Day	McDowell	Lampard	Bonds	Taylor T	Lock	Ayris	Paddon	Gould	Brooking	Robson	
18/9		15,854	*3:14*				[Ayris 59]	*Johnson*	*Matthias*	*Flood*	*Moore*	*Philpotts*	*Veitch*	*Coppell*	*Palios**	*Mitchell*	*Tynan*	*Crossley*	*Webb*
							Ref: A Grey	Gould was almost set to join Portsmouth, but takes the place of Jennings to record his first hat-trick in three seasons. That he did so was down to skipper Bonds, who had two goals himself when West Ham were given a last-minute penalty. Bonds selflessly handed the ball to Gould.											
3	A	FULHAM	6	L	1-2	1-0	Brooking 34	Day	Coleman	Lampard	Bonds	Taylor T	Lock	Ayris*	Paddon	Gould	Brooking	Robson	Holland
8/10		*29,611*	*2:8*				*Mullery 47, Slough 59*	*Mellor*	*Cutbush*	*Strong*	*Mullery*	*Lacy*	*Moore*	*Conway*	*Slough*	*Busby*	*Lloyd*	*Barrett*	
							Ref: H New	Bobby Moore is made Fulham's captain for the day. A floodlight failure interrupted the game at 1-1 for 30 minutes. The ref then asked Day if three pylons were bright enough to continue. Day said yes, and minutes later was beaten by a messy goal by Slough, deflected in by Paddon.											

FA Cup																			
3	A	SOUTHAMPTON	6	W	2-1	2-0	Lampard 25, Gould 40	Day	Coleman	Lampard	Bonds	McDowell	Lock	Jennings	Paddon	Gould*	Brooking	Robson	Holland
4/1		*24,615*	*2:16*				*Channon 67p*	*Martin*	*Mills*	*Steele*	*Holmes*	*Bennett*	*Blyth*	*Stokes**	*Channon*	*Osgood*	*Crabbe*	*O'Brien*	*Peach*
							Ref: G Hill	Eric Martin fumbles Lampard's free-kick into the net. Southampton never recover. Gould doubles the lead with a header, having received the injury for which he will be substituted. Lampard pushed Bobby Stokes for the penalty. The bookies now make West Ham 9-1 for the Cup.											
4	H	SWINDON	10	D	1-1	0-0	Jennings 75	Day	McDowell	Lampard	Bonds	Taylor T	Lock	Jennings	Paddon	Best	Brooking	Holland	
25/1		35,679	*3:4*				*Eastoe 83*	*Barron*	*Dixon*	*Trollope*	*Jenkins*	*Burrows*	*Prophett*	*Moss*	*McLaughlin*	*Eastoe*	*Butler*	*Anderson*	
							Ref: C Thomas	The last time these teams met in the FA Cup was in 1964. West Ham won 3-1 and went on to win it. Manager Danny Williams was angry that Tommy Taylor's shirt-tugging went unpunished seconds before Jennings fired through Jim Barron's legs. Moss crossed for Eastoe's equaliser.											
4R	A	SWINDON	10	W	2-1	0-1	Brooking 59, Holland 86	Day	McDowell	Lampard	Bonds	Taylor T	Lock	Jennings	Paddon	Best	Brooking	Holland	
28/1		*27,749*	*3:4*				*Anderson 29*	*Barron*	*Dixon*	*Trollope*	*Jenkins*	*Burrows*	*Prophett*	*Moss*	*McLaughlin*	*Eastoe*	*Butler*	*Anderson*	
							Ref: C Thomas	A thrilling cup-tie. Trevor Anderson heads in Moss's cross. Hammers level when, from a disputed free-kick, Billy Jennings heads down to Brooking. The winner is a messy business. McDowell hits a post, Jennings returns the ball in, and Holland volleys through a ruck of players.											
5	H	QP RANGERS	7	W	2-1	1-1	Holland 34, Robson 46	Day	McDowell	Lampard	Bonds	Taylor T	Lock	Jennings	Paddon	Robson	Brooking	Holland	
15/2		39,193	*12*				*Clement 27*	*Parkes*	*Clement*	*Gillard*	*Masson*	*McLintock*	*Webb*	*Thomas*	*Leach*	*Beck*	*Bowles**	*Givens*	*Rogers*
							Ref: G Kew	Robson's weak back-pass was cut out by Dave Clement, who beat Lampard and Lock before scoring. Pat Holland, playing these days wide on the right, created and executed the equaliser. The brilliant Brooking laid the ball back to Jennings, who crossed for Keith Robson's winner.											
QF	A	ARSENAL	13	W	2-0	1-0	Taylor A 15, 46	Day	McDowell	Lampard	Bonds	Taylor T	Lock	Jennings	Paddon	Taylor A	Brooking	Robson	
8/3		*56,742*	*18*					*Rimmer*	*Rice*	*McNab*	*Storey*	*Mancini*	*Ssimpson*	*Matthews*	*Ball*	*Radford**	*Kidd*	*Brady*	*Armstrong*
							Ref: K Burns	Alan Taylor is brought in for his first full game, the idea being to discomfort the pedestrian Terry Mancini. The new boy prods in Paddon's chip, then scores the best goal of his life with a fierce right-footer. Just before the break Day rugby-tackled John Radford and got away with it.											
SF	N	IPSWICH	12	D	0-0	0-0		Day	McDowell	Lampard	Bonds	Taylor T	Lock	Jennings	Paddon	Taylor A	Brooking	Gould*	Holland
5/4		*58,000*	*3*					*Sivell*	*Burley*	*Mills*	*Talbot*	*Hunter**	*Beattie*	*Hamilton*	*Viljoen*	*Woods*	*Whymark*	*Lambert*	*Osborne*
		(At Villa Park)					Ref: C Thomas	Lucky Hammers. Ipswich lose both centre-halves – Beattie and Hunter – and switch centre-forward Trevor Whymark to central defence, where he plays a blinder. Ipswich dominated the game from first to last. In injury-time Billy Jennings cleared off the line with Mervyn Day beaten.											

SF	N	IPSWICH	12	W	2-1	1-1	Taylor A 29, 82	Day	McDowell	Lampard	Bonds	Taylor T	Lock	Jennings*	Paddon	Taylor A	Brooking	Gould	Holland
R	9/4	*45,344*	*3*				*Jennings 44 (og)*	*Sivell*	*Burley*	*Mills*	*Talbot*	*Wark*	*Beattie*	*Hamilton*	*Viljoen*	*Woods*	*Whymark*	*Lambert*	
		(At Chelsea)					Ref: C Thomas	Yet again West Ham are outplayed by Bobby Robson's Ipswich, who have two 'goals' disallowed. Alan Taylor's far-post header put West Ham ahead, until Jennings sliced Lambert's corner past Day. Alan Taylor fired Paddon's free-kick in off a post from 25 yards for the winner.											
F	N	FULHAM	13	W	2-0	0-0	Taylor A 61, 64	Day	McDowell	Lampard	Bonds	Taylor T	Lock	Jennings	Paddon	Taylor A	Brooking	Holland	
	3/5	*100,000*	*2:9*					*Mellor*	*Cutbush*	*Lacy*	*Moore*	*Fraser*	*Mullery*	*Conway*	*Slough*	*Mitchell*	*Busby*	*Barrett*	
		(At Wembley)					Ref: P Partridge	Alec Stock's Fulham knocked West Ham out of the League Cup in October. They might have won this one too, but for Day's two sharp saves from John Mitchell. Fulham had the edge until Peter 'Teflon' Mellor failed to gather two shots, which spilled into the path of Alan Taylor.											

		Home					Away					
	P	W	D	L	F	A	W	D	L	F	A	Pts
1 Derby	42	14	4	3	41	18	7	7	7	26	31	53
2 Liverpool	42	14	5	2	44	17	6	6	9	16	22	51
3 Ipswich	42	17	2	2	47	14	6	3	12	19	30	51
4 Everton	42	10	9	2	33	19	6	9	6	23	23	50
5 Stoke	42	12	7	2	40	18	5	8	8	24	30	49
6 Sheffield Utd	42	12	7	2	35	20	6	6	9	23	31	49
7 Middlesbro	42	11	7	3	33	14	7	5	9	21	26	48
8 Manchester C	42	16	3	2	40	15	2	7	12	14	39	46
9 Leeds	42	10	8	3	34	20	6	5	10	23	29	45
10 Burnley	42	11	6	4	40	29	6	5	10	28	38	45
11 QP Rangers	42	10	4	7	25	17	6	6	9	29	37	42
12 Wolves	42	12	5	4	43	21	2	6	13	14	33	39
13 WEST HAM	42	10	6	5	38	22	3	7	11	20	37	39
14 Coventry	42	8	9	4	31	27	4	6	11	20	35	39
15 Newcastle	42	12	4	5	39	23	3	5	13	20	49	39
16 Arsenal	42	10	6	5	31	16	3	5	13	16	33	37
17 Birmingham	42	10	4	7	34	28	4	5	12	19	33	37
18 Leicester	42	8	7	6	25	17	4	5	12	21	43	36
19 Tottenham	42	8	4	9	29	27	5	4	12	23	36	34
20 Luton	42	8	6	7	27	26	3	5	13	20	39	33
21 Chelsea	42	4	9	8	22	31	5	6	10	20	41	33
22 Carlisle	42	8	2	11	22	21	4	3	14	21	38	29
	924	235	124	103	753	460	103	124	235	460	753	924

Odds & ends

Double wins: (2) Burnley, Carlisle.
Double losses: (2) Newcastle, Sheff U.

Won from behind: (5) Leicester (h), Burnley (h&a), Swindon FAC (a), QPR FAC (h).
Lost from in front: (5) Sheff U (h&a), Stoke (a), Leeds (a), Fulham LC (a).

High spots: Winning the FA Cup.
Only one defeat in 17 league games, September to December, up to 5th.

Low spots: Losing to Second Division Fulham in League Cup.
Terrible start, bottom of the league after seven games.
Terrible finish to league season, winning just once in 13 games from February to April.

Hammer of the Year: Billy Bonds.
Ever-presents: (1) Mervyn Day.
Hat-tricks: (1) Bobby Gould.
Leading scorer: (14) Billy Jennings.

	Appearances						Goals			
	Lge	*Sub*	LC	*Sub*	FAC	*Sub*	Lge	LC	FAC	Tot
Ayris, Johnny	**2**	*4*	3					1		**1**
Best, Clyde	**12**	*3*	1		2					
Bonds, Billy	**31**		3		8		**7**	2		**9**
Brooking, Trevor	**36**		3		8		**3**	1	1	**5**
Coleman, Keith	**27**	*2*	1		1					
Curbishley, Alan	**1**	*1*								
Day, Mervyn	**42**		3		8					
Gould, Bobby	**31**	*3*	2		3		**9**	3	1	**13**
Holland, Pat	**18**	*4*	1	*1*	4	*3*	**4**		2	**6**
Jennings, Billy	**32**				8		**13**		1	**14**
Lampard, Frank	**40**		3		8		**4**		1	**5**
Lock, Kevin	**41**	*1*	3		8					
McDowell, John	**33**	*1*	2		8		**1**			**1**
Paddon, Graham	**40**		3		8		**4**			**4**
Robson, Keith	**25**		2		3		**10**		1	**11**
Taylor, Alan	**11**	*3*			4		**2**		6	**8**
Taylor, Tommy	**39**		3		7					
Wooler, Alan	**1**									
(own-goals)							**1**			**1**
18 players used	**462**	***22***	**33**	***1***	**88**	***3***	**58**	**7**	**13**	**78**

No	Date		Att	Pos	Pt	F-A	H-T	Scorers, Times, and Referees	1	2	3	4	5	6	7	8	9	10	11	12 sub used
1	A	STOKE			W	2-1	2-0	Gould 26, Taylor A 44	Day	McDowell	Lampard	Holland	Taylor T	Lock	Taylor A	Paddon	Gould	Brooking	Robson	
	16/8		*23,744*		2			*Moores 88*	*Shilton*	*Dodd*	*Pejic*	*Mahoney*	*Smith*	*Bloor*	*Skeels**	*Moores*	*Conroy*	*Hudson*	*Salmons*	*Haslegrave*
								Ref: L Hayes	Both teams play open, attacking soccer. Billy Bonds misses the game, owing to a groin operation. Pat Holland played a part in both Hammers goals, the second of which seemed to be turned into his own net by Denis Smith. Alan Taylor claimed he got a touch and Smith did not argue.											
2	A	LIVERPOOL			D	2-2	1-1	Taylor A 35, 63	Day	McDowell	Lampard	Holland	Taylor T	Lock	Taylor A	Paddon	Gould*	Brooking	Robson	Jennings
	19/8		*40,564*		3			*Callaghan 25, Toshack 81*	*Clemence*	*Neal*	*Jones*	*Thompson*	*Cormack*	*Hughes*	*Keegan*	*McDermott*	*Heighway*	*Toshack*	*Callaghan*	
								Ref: H Hackney	Liverpool lost at QPR on Saturday, and seldom do they lose their first two of the season. Yet West Ham were nine minutes from their first win at Anfield in 12 years when Peter Cormack set up Toshack's equaliser. Brooking's inch-perfect pass had paved the way for Hammers' second.											
3	H	BURNLEY		6	W	3-2	0-1	Taylor A 60, 77, Paddon 80	Day	McDowell	Lampard	Holland	Taylor T	Lock	Taylor A	Paddon	Jennings*	Brooking	Robson	Ayris
	23/8		28,048	*15*	5			*James 22, Noble 67*	*Stevenson*	*Docherty*	*Newton*	*Noble*	*Waldron*	*Thomson*	*Flynn*	*Hankin*	*Summerbee*	*Collins**	*James*	*Morgan*
								Ref: K Baker	Burnley boss Jimmy Adamson wanted to buy Alan Taylor when he was at Rochdale, and now pays the price for losing him. James' low shot slipped from Day's grasp for the first goal. Noble and Taylor both headed goals from corners. Paddon side-stepped two players for the winner.											
4	H	TOTTENHAM		1	W	1-0	1-0	Robson 45	Day	McDowell	Lampard	Holland	Taylor T	Lock	Taylor A	Paddon	Jennings	Brooking	Robson	
	25/8		36,567	*11*	7				*Jennings*	*Naylor*	*Knowles*	*Pratt*	*Osgood*	*McAllister*	*Conn*	*Perryman*	*Chivers*	*Jones*	*Duncan**	*McNab*
								Ref: W Gow	Lyall is so impressed with this emphatic win – which takes West Ham top of the table – that he gives his players a day off as a reward. Paddon, Brooking and Holland ruled the midfield. Robson headed in when Pat Jennings came too far out for Holland's cross and exposed an open goal.											
5	A	QP RANGERS		2	D	1-1	0-1	Jennings 82	Day	McDowell	Lampard	Holland	Taylor T	Lock	Taylor A	Paddon	Jennings	Brooking	Robson	
	30/8		*28,408*	*3*	8			*Givens 30*	*Parkes*	*Clement*	*Gillard*	*Leach*	*Abbott*	*Tagg*	*Thomas*	*Francis**	*Masson*	*Bowles*	*Givens*	*Hollins*
								Ref: P Partridge	QPR's opening salvo is rewarded when Day mishandles a Masson free-kick, which falls to Don Givens. Billy Jennings rescues a point late on with a sharp shot from a tight angle. West Ham drop down to second, and in midweek will lose 0-1 to Fiorentina in the Anglo-Italian Cup.											
6	H	MANCHESTER C		2	W	1-0	0-0	Lampard 77	Day	McDowell	Lampard	Holland	Taylor T	Lock	Taylor A*	Paddon	Jennings	Brooking	Robson	Bonds
	6/9		29,752	*13*	10				*Corrigan*	*Clements*	*Donachie*	*Doyle*	*Watson*	*Oakes*	*Hartford*	*Bell*	*Leman*	*Marsh*	*Tueart*	
								Ref: D Nippard	Bonds makes his first appearance of the season. Frank Lampard plays a one-two with Paddon before striking a first-timer that was the least West Ham deserved against fancied City. Alan Taylor limped off with a swollen ankle. Only Man U keep the Hammers off the top of the table.											
7	A	LEICESTER		2	D	3-3	0-3	Bonds 60, Lampard 66, Holland 89	Day	McDowell	Lampard	Bonds	Taylor T	Lock	Holland	Paddon	Jennings	Brooking	Robson	
	13/9		*21,413*	*17*	11			*Worthington 8, Sammels 9, 19*	*Wallington*	*Whitworth*	*Rofe*	*Kember*	*Sims*	*Woollett*	*Weller*	*Alderson*	*Worthington*	*Sammels*	*Lee*	
								Ref: A Morrissey	Three down at half-time, West Ham stage a stirring fight-back. Frank Worthington's header was his first goal since April. In the second half Sammels and Weller are denied the space they relish. In the final seconds Brooking crosses and Pat Holland heads the equaliser at close range.											
8	H	SHEFFIELD UTD		2	W	2-0	0-0	Taylor T 71, Best 87	Day	McDowell	Lampard	Bonds	Taylor T	Lock	Taylor A*	Paddon	Jennings	Brooking	Holland	Best
	20/9		28,744	*22*	13				*Brown*	*Flynn*	*Calvert*	*Eddy*	*Colquhoun*	*Bradford*	*Woodward*	*Speight*	*Guthrie*	*Currie**	*Field*	*Irving*
								Ref: R Crabb	Ken Furphy's rock-bottom Blades carry little threat, other than from striker Chris Guthrie, who beat Tommy Taylor in the air 18 times out of 21. Yet it is Guthrie's wayward pass that leads to his marker firing the first goal. Clyde Best, on as sub, scores in his first game of the season.											
9	A	WOLVES		2	W	1-0	0-0	Paddon 62	Day	McDowell	Lampard	Bonds	Taylor T	Lock	Taylor A	Paddon	Best	Brooking	Holland	
	27/9		*18,455*	*21*	15				*Pierce*	*Palmer*	*McNab*	*Bailey*	*Munro*	*McAlle*	*Hibbitt*	*Carr*	*Richards*	*Kindon**	*Daley*	*Sunderland*
								Ref: E Garner	Graham Paddon reckons his 40-yard rocket is the best goal of his career. Wolves have taken only five points from six home games and scored just four goals, which is relegation form. Leaders QPR and West Ham, who have a game in hand, are the only unbeaten teams in the division.											
10	H	EVERTON		3	L	0-1	0-0		Day	McDowell	Lampard	Bonds	Taylor T	Lock	Robson	Paddon	Best*	Brooking	Holland	Taylor A
	4/10		31,005	*7*	15			*Jones G 62*	*Davies*	*Seargeant*	*Clements*	*Pearson**	*Kenyon*	*Lyons*	*Buckley*	*Dobson*	*Latchford*	*Telfer*	*Jones G*	*McNaught*
								Ref: T Reynolds	Everton came to defend, yet succeeded in inflicting a first defeat on the Hammers. It might have been averted had Lampard not blazed over a gaping goal after 27 minutes. Jones's header from Buckley's free-kick was deflected in by McDowell. Too many aimless balls from Hammers.											
11	H	NEWCASTLE		3	W	2-1	1-0	Curbishley 2, Taylor A 52	Day	McDowell	Lampard	Bonds	Taylor T	Coleman	Taylor A	Paddon	Best	Curbishley	Holland	
	11/10		30,400	*16*	17			*Howard 47*	*Mahoney*	*Nattrass*	*Kennedy*	*Nulty*	*Bird*	*Howard*	*Barrowclough*	*Burns*	*Macdonald*	*Gowling*	*Craig T*	
								Ref: P Walters	On *Match of the Day* afterwards, Jimmy Hill raves over the performance of 18-year-old Alan Curbishley, who only played because of injury to Brooking. Curbishley netted after two minutes, controlling the ball and shooting in one sweet movement. He then laid on Alan Taylor's header.											

No	Venue	Opponent / Date / Att	Pos	Res	F-A	H-T	Scorers, Times, and Referees	1	2	3	4	5	6	7	8	9	10	11	12 sub used
12	A	MIDDLESBROUGH	3	L	0-3	0-1		Day	McDowell	Lampard*	Bonds	Taylor T	Coleman	Taylor A	Paddon	Best	Brooking	Holland	Curbishley
		18/10 *25,831*	*6*	17			*Souness 42, Armstrong 58, Foggon 72*	*Platt*	*Craggs*	*Cooper*	*Souness*	*Boam*	*Maddren*	*Murdoch*	*Mills*	*Hickton*	*Foggon*	*Armstrong*	
							Ref: R Capey	Unbeaten at home, Middlesbrough look the ultimate professionals. They had two 'goals' disallowed before Graeme Souness sprinted 50 yards to convert a return pass. Only Mervyn Day prevented a complete rout. Frank Lampard had to withdraw at half-time with a thigh strain.											
13	H	MANCHESTER U	3	W	2-1	1-0	Taylor A 6, Gould 70	Day	McDowell	Lampard	Holland	Taylor T	Coleman	Taylor A	Paddon	Gould	Brooking	Robson	
		25/10 **38,528**	*2*	19			*Macari 56*	*Stepney*	*Nicholl*	*Houston*	*Jackson*	*Greenhoff*	*Buchan*	*Coppell*	*McIlroy*	*Pearson*	*Macari*	*Daly**	*McCreery*
							Ref: P Reeves	A shameful match, marred by fighting on the terraces and by fighting between Buchan and Gould. Early in the second half play was held up for 18 minutes when a gate was broken at a corner of the ground. Macari scored on the resumption. Gould then connected with Paddon's cross.											
14	A	BIRMINGHAM	2	W	**5-1**	2-1	Brooking 15, Pendrey 37 (og), Lampard 67, [Taylor A 69, 72]	Day	McDowell	Lampard	Bonds	Taylor T	Coleman	Taylor A	Paddon	Holland	Brooking	Robson	
		1/11 *28,474*	*20*	21			*Francis 5*	*Latchford*	*Martin*	*Pendrey*	*Kendall*	*Gallagher**	*Roberts*	*Campbell*	*Francis*	*Burns*	*Hatton*	*Hibbitt*	*Taylor*
							Ref: J Goggins	John Lyall plays a tactical trump-card which masterminds this crushing victory. He plays an extra man in midfield, which has the effect of giving Brooking, who is pushed into the 'hole' between midfield and attack, more room to wreak havoc. Brooking shines magnificently.											
15	H	COVENTRY	1	D	1-1	0-0	Robson 48	Day	McDowell	Lock	Bonds*	Taylor T	Coleman	Taylor A	Paddon	Holland	Brooking	Robson	Gould
		8/11 29,501	*16*	22			*Powell 67*	*King*	*Coop*	*Brogan*	*Dugdale*	*Lloyd*	*Holmes*	*Powell*	*Mortimer*	*Cross*	*Murphy*	*Hutchison*	
							Ref: K Styles	Lucky Hammers, who struggled to stay afloat once Billy Bonds had limped out of the fray. Pop Robson's blast was cancelled out by Barry Powell's 20-yard rocket. Mortimer and Cross both hit the woodwork for Coventry, although Alan Taylor did the same for West Ham.											
16	A	DERBY	5	L	1-2	1-1	Brooking 42	Day	McDowell	Lampard	Lock	Taylor T	Coleman	Taylor A	Gould*	Holland	Brooking	Robson	Ayris
		15/11 *31,172*	*1*	22			*Rioch 32, George 64*	*Boulton*	*Thomas*	*Nish*	*Rioch*	*McFarland*	*Todd*	*Newton*	*Gemmill*	*Lee*	*Hector*	*George*	
							Ref: R Rice	Though Brooking scores the best goal of the match, West Ham are dumped from the top and plummet to fifth. They are now quoted at 11-1 for the title, with Derby 2-1. Hammers top the Fair Play league, having conceded no penalties, had no players sent off and only three booked.											
17	H	MIDDLESBROUGH	4	W	2-1	1-1	Jennings 35, Holland 70	Day	McDowell	Lock	Holland	Taylor T	Coleman	Taylor A	Paddon	Jennings	Brooking	Robson	
		22/11 26,914	*9*	24			*Mills 12*	*Platt*	*Craggs*	*Spraggon*	*Murdoch*	*Boam*	*Maddren*	*Brine*	*Mills*	*Hickton**	*Cooper*	*Armstrong*	
							Ref: R Newsome	Boro boss Jack Charlton rages against the stand-in ref, taking charge of his first ever game in Division 1. West Ham had been well beaten on Wearside, so revenge is sweet. Billy Jennings' second league goal prompted Trevor Brooking to ignite West Ham's second-half onslaught.											
18	H	ARSENAL	3	W	1-0	1-0	Taylor A 22	Day	McDowell	Lampard	Coleman	Taylor T	Lock	Taylor A	Paddon	Holland	Jennings	Robson	
		29/11 31,012	*18*	26				*Rimmer*	*Rice*	*Nelson*	*Storey*	*O'Leary*	*Powling*	*Ball*	*Armstrong*	*Stapleton*	*Kidd*	*Brady*	
							Ref: G Kew	McDowell plays a stormer, and Graham Paddon marks Alan Ball out of the game. The only goal provoked a storm of controversy. TV replays showed Alan Taylor to be offside when knocking in Jennings' downward header from Lock's cross. Lyall gives his players another holiday.											
19	A	NORWICH	6	L	0-1	0-0		Day	McDowell	Lampard	Coleman	Taylor T	Lock	Taylor A	Paddon	Holland	Brooking	Robson	
		6/12 *27,020*	*16*	26			*MacDougall 78*	*Keelan*	*Jones*	*Sullivan*	*Morris*	*Forbes*	*Stringer*	*Machin*	*MacDougall*	*Boyer*	*Suggett*	*Peters*	
							Ref: H Davey	The tabloids stir up Ted MacDougall's war of words. He is alleged to have said: 'I hate West Ham even more than I hate Manchester United – and that's saying something.' He caps this fine match by heading in Peters' cross, then rugby-tackling an invading fan before officials arrived.											
20	A	BURNLEY	7	L	0-2	0-2		Day	Coleman	Lampard	Curbishley*	Taylor T	Lock	Taylor A	Paddon	Holland	Brooking	Jennings	Ayris
		13/12 ***14,907***	*19*	26			*Hankin 19, Kennerley 35*	*Peyton*	*Docherty*	*Newton*	*Ingham*	*Waldron*	*Thomson*	*Summerbee*	*Kennerley*	*Hankin*	*Flynn*	*Bradshaw*	
							Ref: J Taylor	Hammers have gone off the boil, and have lost at home to Fiorentina in the Anglo-Italian Cup. On a frozen pitch at Turf Moor they slither to another defeat. Hankin scored from under Day's nose. Now that Gould has been transferred, Lyall is looking at Southampton's Mick Channon.											
21	H	STOKE	6	W	3-1	2-1	Jennings 28, 35, 61	Day	Coleman	Lampard	McDowell	Taylor T	Lock	Taylor A	Paddon	Holland	Jennings	Robson	
		20/12 21,135	*8*	28			*Bloor 32*	*Shilton*	*Marsh*	*Pejic*	*Mahoney*	*Dodd*	*Bloor*	*Robertson*	*Greenhoff*	*Moores**	*Hudson*	*Salmons*	*Haslegrave*
							Ref: D Nippard	Billy Jennings has got himself fit, at last, and celebrates with a famous hat-trick. He headed into the top corner for the first goal, blasted in Robson's knock-down from a tight angle for No 2, and headed in Coleman's cross for his third. These are Hammers' first goals in three games.											
22	A	ASTON VILLA	6	L	1-4	1-2	Jennings 40	Day	Coleman	Lampard	McDowell	Taylor T	Lock	Taylor A	Paddon	Holland	Jennings	Robson	
		26/12 *51,300*	*12*	28			*Deehan 6, 19, Gray 55, Hamilton 88*	*Burridge*	*Gidman*	*Robson*	*Ross*	*Nicholl*	*Mortimer*	*Graydon*	*Deehan*	*Gray*	*Hamilton*	*Carrodus*	
							Ref: A Jones	Ron Saunders' team leave the field to a standing ovation. Villa have scored 16 goals in their last five home games. Dennis Mortimer makes his debut and sets up John Deehan's first goal. This, and Deehan's second – a volley from Graydon's free-kick – might have been saved by Day.											
23	H	IPSWICH	6	L	1-2	0-0	Taylor T 75p	Day	Coleman*	McDowell	Holland	Taylor T	Lock	Taylor A	Paddon	Brooking	Jennings	Robson !	Curbishley
		27/12 *32,741*	*11*	28			*Lambert 50, Peddelty 84*	*Cooper*	*Burley*	*Beattie*	*Talbot*	*Hunter*	*Peddelty*	*Woods*	*Mills*	*Austin*	*Whymark*	*Lambert*	
							Ref: T Spencer	Keith Robson was booked and sent off in the 67th minute after throwing a punch at George Burley. That completed a disastrous Christmas schedule for the Hammers, who enjoyed an iffy penalty when Paddon appeared to dive. Bobby Robson's Ipswich have lost one game in 13.											

No		Date	Att	Pos	Pt		F-A	H-T	Scorers, Times, and Referees	1	2	3	4	5	6	7	8	9	10	11	12 sub used
24	H	LEICESTER		6		D	1-1	0-0	Taylor A 65	Day	McDowell	Lampard	Holland	Taylor T	Lock	Taylor A	Best	Brooking	Jennings	Curbishley	
		10/1	24,615	*15*	29				*Lee 78*	*Wallington*	*Whitworth*	*Rofe*	*Kember*	*Blockley*	*Woollett*	*Weller*	*Alderson*	*Garland**	*Lee*	*Worthington*	*Sammels*
									Ref: A Lees	Paddon has strained a hamstring and young Alan Curbishley shines until he tires. Alan Taylor 'kneed' in Brooking's curled pass. But Tommy Taylor then stubbed his toe and messed up a back-pass. City boss Jimmy Bloomfield's verdict: 'The wind spoiled it and the pitch was bumpy.'											
25	A	MANCHESTER C		8		L	0-3	0-2		Day	McDowell	Lampard	Holland	Taylor T	Lock	Taylor A*	Paddon	Jennings	Brooking	Curbishley	Best
		17/1	*32,147*	*6*	29				*Royle 11, 58p, Oakes 25*	*Corrigan*	*Barrett*	*Donachie*	*Doyle*	*Clements*	*Oakes*	*Power*	*Keegan*	*Royle*	*Hartford*	*Barnes*	
									Ref: G Courtney	Day's 100th league game is not one to remember fondly. Joe Royle was left unmarked for his first goal, and scored City's third from the spot after Lock had upended Barnes. In between, veteran Alan Oakes seized on Royle's pass to burst through. City have lost Rodney Marsh to USA.											
26	H	QP RANGERS		6		W	1-0	1-0	Taylor A 42	Day	McDowell	Lampard	Holland	Taylor T	Coleman	Taylor A	Paddon	Brooking	Jennings	**Orhan**	
		24/1	26,677	*5*	31					*Parkes*	*Clement*	*Gillard*	*Hollins*	*McLintock**	*Webb*	*Thomas*	*Beck*	*Masson*	*Leach*	*Givens*	*Nutt*
									Ref: A Morrissey	A fast and furious London derby, illuminated by Hammers' Turkish Cypriot debutant, but won by Alan Taylor's 15th goal of the season. QPR were without Bowles (transfer listed), Gerry Francis (injured), and – after half-time – by the concussed McLintock, who sat wrapped in a coat.											
27	H	LIVERPOOL		6		L	0-4	0-0		Day	McDowell	Lampard	Holland	Taylor T	Coleman	Taylor A	Paddon	Jennings*	Brooking	Orhan	Robson
		31/1	26,741	*2*	31				*Toshack 63, 75, 86, Keegan 88*	*Clemence*	*Smith*	*Neal*	*Thompson*	*Kennedy*	*Hughes*	*Keegan*	*Case*	*Heighway*	*Toshack*	*Callaghan*	
									Ref: J Hunting	Liverpool had just lost to Derby in the FA Cup. Ray Clemence said he was glad he wore track-suit bottoms on an icy pitch, otherwise he would have got frostbite. Bob Paisley added: 'I wish we could come here more often.' Toshack completed his hat-trick heading in Heighway's cross.											
28	A	TOTTENHAM		6		D	1-1	0-0	Brooking 77	Day	Coleman	Lampard	Holland	Taylor T	McGiven	Taylor A	Paddon	Jennings	Brooking	Robson	
		7/2	*32,832*	*15*	32				*Duncan 65*	*Jennings*	*Naylor*	*McAllister*	*Pratt*	*Young*	*Osgood*	*Coates*	*Perryman*	*Duncan*	*Jones*	*Neighbour**	*Chivers*
									Ref: R Toseland	Keith Robson returns but after 20 minutes could easily have been sent off for an over-the-top tackle on Keith Osgood that will dominate the sports headlines. John Duncan headed in a cross from man-of-the-match Coates before Lampard's overlap down the left set up the equaliser.											
29	A	COVENTRY		6		L	0-2	0-1		Day	McDowell	Lampard	Holland	Taylor T	McGiven	Taylor A	Paddon	Jennings	Brooking	Robson	
		14/2	*16,173*	*14*	32				*Powell 44, Coop 54*	*Blyth*	*Oakey*	*Cattlin*	*Craven*	*Dugdale*	*Coop*	*Cartwright*	*Powell*	*Cross*	*Murphy*	*Hutchison*	
									Ref: N Ashley	Mervyn Day is showing signs of strain. He helps Mick Coop's sliced cross into his own net for Coventry's second goal. Day was blameless with the first, Barry Powell shooting on the run from 25 yards. West Ham had no answer to the jinking skills of left-winger Tommy Hutchison.											
30	H	DERBY		9		L	1-2	0-0	Brooking 84	Day	Coleman	Lampard	Holland	Taylor T	McGiven	McDowell	Paddon	Orhan*	Brooking	Robson	Jennings
		21/2	24,941	*4*	32				*George 60, Rioch 82*	*Moseley*	*Thomas*	*Nish*	*Rioch*	*McFarland*	*Todd*	*Powell*	*Gemmill*	*Hector*	*George*	*James*	
									Ref: T Reynolds	Derby boss Dave Mackay fanned the flames afterwards when saying he was more worried by Southend United in the FA Cup last week than by West Ham, whose build-up was slow and ponderous. Spies for Den Haag in the Cup-Winners' Cup are equally unimpressed with West Ham.											
31	H	LEEDS				D	1-1	0-0	Taylor A 66	Day	McDowell	Lampard	Holland*	Taylor T	McGiven	Taylor A	Paddon	Curbishley	Brooking	Robson	Jennings
		23/2	28,025		33				*McKenzie 76*	*Harvey*	*Reaney*	*Gray F*	*Bates*	*Madeley*	*Hunter*	*McKenzie*	*Cherry*	*Jordan*	*Yorath*	*Gray E*	
									Ref: R Crabb	Keith Robson missed a sitter at the death that would have given West Ham a deserved win. Under the eyes of the watching England boss Don Revie, Alan Taylor converts Paddon's corner, headed on by Lampard. Joe Jordan's over-the-top lunge at Tommy Taylor inflames the crowd.											
32	A	MANCHESTER U		9		L	0-4	0-0	*[Pearson 86]*	Day	McDowell	Lock	Bonds	Taylor T	McGiven	Taylor A*	Paddon	Curbishley	Brooking	Robson	Jennings
		28/2	***57,240***	*3*	33				*Forsyth 49, Macari 56, McCreery 76,*	*Stepney*	*Forsyth*	*Houston*	*Daly*	*Greenhoff*	*Buchan*	*Coppell*	*McIlroy**	*Pearson*	*Macari*	*Hill*	*McCreery*
									Ref: K Baker	Lyall's five-man defence keeps Tommy Docherty's Man U at bay for the first half. Forsyth then fired a hard shot through a crowded goalmouth and Daly did likewise, the ball glancing off Macari's head as it flew past Day. Coppell and Hill sent over a string of crosses to test Day and Co.											
33	H	BIRMINGHAM		12		L	1-2	0-1	Curbishley 76	Day	Coleman	Lampard	Bonds	Taylor T	Wooler	Taylor A	Paddon	Curbishley	Orhan*	Robson	**Pike**
		6/3	19,868	*19*	33				*Withe 35, Emmanuel 48*	*Latchford*	*Martin*	*Styles*	*Kendall*	*Gallagher*	*Burns*	*Emmanuel*	*Francis*	*Withe*	*Page*	*Hibbitt**	*Calderwood*
									Ref: A Gray	Lyall is in bed with flu, leaving Greenwood to marshal the only 13 fit players available. Terry Hibbitt's free-kick is nodded in by Peter Withe, and Emmanuel converts Trevor Francis' cross. Curbishley's goal went in off Martin. Defeat sends West Ham into the bottom half of the table.											
34	A	LEEDS		12		D	1-1	0-0	Jennings 54	Day	Coleman	Lampard	Bonds	Taylor T	Taylor A	Ayris*	Paddon	Jennings	Curbishley	Robson	Pike
		9/3	28,453	*5*	34				*Jordan 68*	*Harvey*	*Reaney**	*Gray F*	*Bates*	*Madeley*	*Hunter*	*McKenzie*	*Clarke*	*Jordan*	*Yorath*	*Cherry*	*Gray E*
									Ref: P Willis	This match had been scheduled for the autumn. Hammers have now won once in 15 games, and taken only six points since Christmas. Without Brooking, Lock and McDowell they seldom looked like subduing Jimmy Armfield's Leeds. Bonds and Clarke were booked for wrestling.											

35 A NEWCASTLE 11 L 1-2 1-1 Jennings 16
13/3 32,842 *14* 34 *Macdonald 20, Craig T 67p*
Ref: K Ridden

Day	Coleman	Lampard*	Bonds	Taylor T	Taylor A	Ayris	Paddon	Jennings	Curbishley	Robson	McDowell
Jones	*Blackhall*	*Kennedy*	*Barrowclough*	*Bird*	*Howard*	*Burns*	*Cassidy*	*Macdonald*	*Gowling*	*Craig T*	

Bonds plays his best game since returning form injury. Tommy Taylor is upset about conceding the penalty that cost West Ham the points. He admits that he handled the ball but insists that his arm had been knocked against it and that he should have won a free-kick. Now for Den Haag.

36 A ARSENAL 12 L **1-6** 1-4 Jennings 23
20/3 *34,011* *13* 34 *Ball 2, 29p, Armstrong 30, Kidd 44, 55, 85*
Ref: K McNally

Day	Coleman*	Lampard	Bonds	Taylor T	Lock	Taylor A	Curbishley	Jennings	Brooking	Robson	McGiven
Rimmer	*Rice**	*Nelson*	*Ross*	*Mancini*	*Powling*	*Armstrong*	*Ball*	*Radford*	*Kidd*	*Brady*	*Stapleton*

Having triumphed over Den Haag, this is a painful let-down. Brian Kidd completed one hat-trick but might have had two. Alan Ball might even have had a hat-trick himself, scoring one penalty and missing another – both were for trips on Kidd. West Ham might have conceded 10.

37 H NORWICH 12 L 0-1 0-0
27/3 20,628 *15* 34 *MacDougall 16*
Ref: R Matthewson

Day	Coleman	Lampard	Bonds	Taylor T	Lock	Paddon	Curbishley	Jennings	McDowell	Robson	
Keelan	*Jones*	*Sullivan*	*McGuire*	*Forbes*	*Powell*	*Miller*	*MacDougall*	*Boyer*	*Suggett*	*Peters*	

Martin Peters, now playing out his days for Norwich, says afterwards: 'They never bothered us'. West Ham showed little fight in a fixture that should have been a full-scale dress rehearsal for Eintracht. Norwich keeper Kevin Keelan never had to make a save. Relegation may yet loom.

38 H WOLVES 13 D 0-0
3/4 **16,769** *20* 35
Ref: D Nippard

Day	Coleman	Lampard	McDowell	Taylor T	Lock*	Holland	Paddon	Jennings	Brooking	Robson	Ayris
Parkes	*Sunderland*	*Palmer*	*Parkin*	*Bailey*	*McAlle*	*Daley*	*Carr*	*Kindon*	*Kelly*	*Gould**	*Hibbitt*

Wolves are fighting to stay up. They won't make it, but they extend West Ham's winless league sequence to two and half months, in which they have taken just four points from 12 games. Wolves' Bobby Gould was kept quiet, and West Ham frittered away what chances they had.

39 A SHEFFIELD UTD 16 L 2-3 1-0 Jennings 16, 60
10/4 *18,797* *22* 35 *Woodward 57, Guthrie 61, Stainrod 63*
Ref: D Civil

Day	Coleman	Lampard	Bonds	Taylor T	McDowell	Holland	Paddon	Jennings	Brooking	Robson*	Ayris
Brown	*Franks*	*Garner*	*Speight*	*Colquhoun*	*Kenworthy*	*Woodward*	*Bradford*	*Guthrie*	*Currie*	*Stainrod*	

Blades are so far behind that they are already doomed. West Ham manage more than one goal for the first time in 1976, and lead twice, but still lose. Guthrie's header made it 2-2. 17-year-old Simon Stainrod marked his home debut by scoring off a post. Jennings' goals count for nothing.

40 H ASTON VILLA 17 D 2-2 1-2 Robson 14, Brooking 89
17/4 21,642 *18* 36 *Deehan 4, Hunt 10*
Ref: T Bune

Ferguson	Coleman	Lampard	Lock*	Taylor T	McDowell	Holland	Paddon	Jennings	Brooking	Robson	Ayris
Findlay	*Gidman*	*Robson*	*Phillips*	*Nicholl*	*Mortimer*	*Deehan*	*McDonald*	*Gray*	*Hunt*	*Carrodus*	

Villa are seconds away from their first away win of the season when Brooking lets fly and the ball bounces like a leg-break past Findlay. Two quick Villa headers had silenced Upton Park. Had it not been for Robson's riposte, a header from Brooking's corner, it may have stayed silent.

41 A IPSWICH 18 L 0-4 0-2
19/4 28,217 *6* 36 *Bertschin 24, Talbot 45, Whymark 70,* *[Peddelty 89]*
Ref: K Styles

Day	Bonds	McDowell	Curbishley	Taylor T	McGiven	Ayris	Paddon	Orhan*	Brooking	Robson	Pike
Cooper	*Burley*	*Mills*	*Sharkey*	*Hunter*	*Peddelty*	*Talbot*	*Osborne*	*Bertschin*	*Whymark*	*Lambert*	

West Ham lost 1-4 at Portman Road last season, and 0-4 this, so it is becoming a bogey ground. The Hammers were chasing a lost cause from the moment 19-year-old Keith Bertschin swerved the opening goal from 20 yards. He had also scored on his debut at Highbury on Saturday.

42 A EVERTON 18 L 0-2 0-2
24/4 *26,101* *11* 36 *Bernard 5p, Pearson 23*
Home Away
Average 27,345 29,433
Ref: A Robinson

Day	Coleman	Lampard	Bonds	Taylor T	McDowell	Holland	Paddon	Jennings	Brooking	Robson*	Taylor A
Lawson	*Bernard*	*Jones D*	*Lyons*	*McNaught*	*King*	*Buckley*	*Dobson*	*Latchford*	*Connolly*	*Pearson*	

Hammers conclude the league season without a win in their last 16 games. They were not helped by a disputed penalty when Tommy Taylor tugged Latchford's shirt. Day fumbled a cross which led to Pearson's goal. Skipper Bonds apologises to fans afterwards on behalf of the team.

Charity Shield

9/8 DERBY L 0-2 0-2
59,000 *Hector 20, McFarland 43*
(at Wembley)
Ref: G Kew

Day	McDowell	Lampard	Holland	Taylor T	Lock	Taylor A	Paddon	Jennings*	Brooking	Gould^	Robson/Coleman
Boulton	*Thomas*	*Nish*	*Rioch*	*McFarland*	*Todd*	*Newton*	*Gemmill*	*Lee*	*Hector*	*George*	

Last year was the first Charity Shield to be staged at Wembley, and it was sullied by the dismissal of Liverpool's Keegan and Leeds' Bremner. No such problems this time. Hector won the game with a 20-yard goal followed by a back-heel to McFarland. How West Ham missed Bonds.

League Cup

2 H BRISTOL CITY 2 D 0-0 0-0
9/9 19,837 *2:5*
Ref: A Robinson

Day	McDowell	Lampard	Bonds	Taylor T	Lock	Holland*	Paddon	Jennings	Brooking	Robson	Ayris
Cashley	*Sweeney*	*Drysdale*	*Gow*	*Collier*	*Merrick*	*Tainton*	*Ritchie*	*Mann !*	*Cheesley*	*Brolly**	*Gillies*

Just after the hour City striker Jimmy Mann was fouled by Jennings, retaliated and was ordered off. Barely was he off the pitch than Merrick handled in the box. Paul Cheesley had played at Norwich with Graham Paddon and pointed to keeper Cashley which way to go. He was right.

2R A BRISTOL CITY 2 W 3-1 0-1 Brooking 75, Best 80, Taylor A 82
24/9 *19,643* *2:4* *Cheesley 20*
Ref: A Robinson

Day	McDowell	Lampard	Bonds	Taylor T	Lock	Taylor A	Paddon	Best	Brooking	Holland	
Cashley	*Sweeney*	*Drysdale*	*Gow*	*Collier*	*Merrick*	*Tainton*	*Ritchie*	*Mann*	*Cheesley*	*Brolly**	*Gillies*

Lyall decides to play Clyde Best – back from America – as an all-muscle striker in the manner of Hurst. The tactic works, though Day – whose boob let in Cheesley – has to save a twice-taken penalty after McDowell fouled Ritchie. Sweeney missed, but Tommy Taylor had encroached.

League Cup			F-A	H-T	Scorers, Times, and Referees	1	2	3	4	5	6	7	8	9	10	11	12 sub used
3 H DARLINGTON	3	W	3-0	0-0	Paddon 52, Robson 72, Bonds 74p	Day	McDowell	Lampard	Bonds	Taylor T	Lock*	Robson	Paddon	Best	Taylor A	Holland	Jennings
8/10	19,844 *4:17*					*Ogley*	*Nattrass*	*Cochrane*	*Cattrell*	*Noble*	*Blant*	*Holbrook**	*Sinclair*	*Webb*	*Crosson*	*Young*	*Rowles*
					Ref: R Kirkpatrick	Darlington, struggling in the soccer basement, make West Ham sweat for this victory. Webb had a 48th-minute 'goal' disallowed, and Eric Young appeared to equalise with a header that was dubiously annulled. Young later handled in his own area for Bonds to round off the scoring.											
4 A TOTTENHAM	1	D	0-0	0-0		Day	McDowell	Lock	Bonds	Taylor T	Coleman	Taylor A	Paddon	Holland	Brooking	Robson	
12/11	*49,125 14*					*Jennings*	*Naylor*	*McAllister*	*Pratt*	*Young*	*Osgood*	*Coates*	*Perryman*	*Duncan**	*Jones*	*Neighbour*	*Conn*
					Ref: M Sinclair	Brooking is again played as a deep-lying centre-forward, though this time without conspicuous success. When he went forward he was marked by Keith Osgood, when he fell back he was picked up by Perryman. Early on Pat Jennings saved when his feet were behind the goal-line.											
4R H TOTTENHAM	4	L	0-2	0-0		Day	McDowell	Lampard	Bonds	Taylor T	Lock	Taylor A	Paddon	Holland	Brooking*	Robson	Jennings
24/11	38,443 *16*		*aet*		*Duncan 101, Young 109*	*Jennings*	*Naylor*	*McAllister*	*Pratt*	*Young*	*Osgood*	*Coates*	*Perryman*	*Duncan*	*Jones*	*Neighbour*	
					Ref: M Sinclair	Fourth Division Doncaster Rovers are the plum awaiting the winners. Terry Neill's Spurs are the lucky ones, but they were distinctly second best until Trevor Brooking went off with a ricked back. Bonds returned after injury but was embarrassingly run off his feet by Ralph Coates.											

FA Cup																	
1 H LIVERPOOL	6	L	0-2	0-1		Day	Coleman	Lampard	Holland	McGiven	Lock	Taylor A	Paddon	Brooking	Jennings	Curbishley	
3/1	32,363 *1*				*Keegan 36, Toshack 83*	*Clemence*	*Smith*	*Neal*	*Thompson*	*Kennedy*	*Hughes*	*Keegan*	*Case*	*Heighway*	*Toshack*	*Callaghan*	
					Ref: P Partridge	West Ham are dethroned at the first hurdle. With Bonds, McDowell and Tommy Taylor injured, and Keith Robson suspended, Hammers had their work cut out. Keegan ran the show on his own, scoring the first with Toshack's assistance, then returning the favour for the second goal.											

European Cup-Winners' Cup																	
1:1 A LAHDEN REIPAS	2	D	2-2	1-1	Brooking 29, Bonds 76	Day	McDowell	Lampard	Bonds	Taylor T	Lock	Holland	Paddon	Taylor A	Brooking	Robson*	Jennings
17/9 (Finland)	*4,587*				*Lindholm 4, Tupasela 55*	*Holli*	*Kosonen*	*Kautonen M*	*Riutto*	*Repo*	*Toivanen*	*Kautonen T*	*Tupasela*	*Jantunen*	*Hamaleinen*	*Lindholm*	
					Ref: U Eriksson	This match was played at Helsinki's Olympic Stadium. The Finns played in red and black stripes that made them look like bees. They scored first when the ball bounced off Day's chest. Brooking's free-kick sailed past everybody and Bonds' goal followed a one-two with Holland.											
1:2 H LAHDEN REIPAS	2	W	3-0	0-0	Robson 60, Holland 77, Jennings 89	Day	McDowell	Lampard	Bonds	Taylor T	Lock	Taylor A*	Paddon	Robson	Brooking	Holland	Jennings
1/10	24,131					*Holli*	*Kosonen*	*Kautonen M*	*Riutto*	*Repo*	*Toivanen**	*Kautonen T*	*Tupasela*	*Jantunen*	*Hamaleinen*	*Lindholm*	*Nordman*
					Ref: A Briguglio (Malta) (Hammers win 5-2 on aggregate)	Clyde Best has returned from USA but is ineligible. The Finns defied predictions and came out to attack, knowing that if they did not score they would go out on the away-goals rule. The tie was effectively settled when Bonds crossed and Robson's shot flew in off post and keeper.											
2:1 A ARARAT EREVAN	3	D	1-1	0-0	Taylor A 56	Day	McDowell	Lampard	Bonds	Taylor T	Coleman	Taylor A	Paddon	Gould	Holland	Robson	
22/10 (USSR)	*66,662*				*Petrosian S 66*	*Abramian*	*Gevorkian*	*Sarkissian*	*Martirosian*	*Mesropian*	*Andreassian*	*Azarian**	*Oganesian*	*Markarov*	*Petrosian S*	*Petrosian N^*	*Bondarenko*
					Ref: H Weyland (W Germany) (Ararat's 2nd sub Pogosian)	Mervyn Day stands holding the ball wondering where to kick it, when Petrosian heads it out of his hands and into the net. Day stands aghast, waiting for a foul that is never given. That farcical goal wiped out Alan Taylor's effort, and raised questions about the West German referee.											
2:2 H ARARAT EREVAN	2	W	3-1	2-0	Paddon 16, Robson 27, Taylor A 59	Day	McDowell	Lampard	Bonds	Taylor T	Coleman	Taylor A	Paddon	Holland	Brooking	Robson	
5/11	30,399				*Petrosian N 46*	*Abramian*	*Martirosian*	*Sarkissian*	*Gevorkian*	*Mesropian*	*Andreassian*	*Azarian*	*Oganesian*	*Markarov**	*Petrosian S*	*Petros'n N^*	*Ishtoyan/Bond'*
					Ref: R Helies (France) (Hammers win 4-2 on aggregate)	The experiment of playing Brooking further forward continues, though on this occasion he plays no part in any of the goals. Paddon's spinning left-footer was followed by Robson heading in Alan Taylor's cross, and Taylor himself rounded things off with a disputed offside goal.											
QF 1 A DEN HAAG	9	L	2-4	0-4	Jennings 50, 58	Day	McGiven*	Lampard	Bonds	Taylor T	Lock	Taylor A	Paddon	Jennings	Curbishley	Robson	Coleman
3/3 (Holland)	*26,000*				*Mansveld 13, 15p, 38p, Schoenmaker 42*	*Thie*	*Mansvelt*	*de Caluwe*	*van Vliet*	*Korevaar*	*Kila*	*Perazic*	*Schoenmaker*	*Ouwenhand*	*van Leeuwen*	*Swanenburg*	
					Ref: R Glockner (E Germany)	Flu keeps Lyall in bed, so Ron Greenwood takes charge. Herr Glockner refereed the 1970 World Cup final between Brazil and Italy. He tells Lock to pull his socks up and awards two disputed penalties when Lock and McGiven handle. Two Paddon crosses yield two Jennings goals.											
QF 2 H DEN HAAG	11	W	3-1	3-0	Taylor A 28, Lampard 33, Bonds 38	Day	Coleman	Lampard	Bonds	Taylor T*	Lock	Taylor A	Paddon^	Jennings	Brooking	Robson	McGiv/Curbishley
17/3	29,829				*Schoenmaker 59*	*Thie*	*Mansvelt*	*Ouwehand*	*van Vliet*	*Korevaar*	*Kila**	*Perazic*	*Schoenmaker*	*Bres*	*van Leeuwen*	*Albertsen^*	*Jol/Swanenburg*
					Ref: K Palotai (Hungary) (Hammers win on away goals)	An emotional night, though a frustrating one, with West Ham caught offside 18 times. Thie drops Brooking's shot to make it 3-4 overall. Brooking then curls a pass onto Lampard's boot, before Tommy Taylor goes down in the box. Shoenmaker's goal made Hammers sweat it out.											

SF	A	EINTRACHT		12	L	1-2	1-1	Paddon 9	Day	Coleman	Lampard	Bonds	Taylor T	McDowell	Holland	Paddon	Jennings	Brooking	Robson	
1	31/3	(W Germ)	*45,000*					*Neuberger 28, Kraus 47*	*Kunter*	*Reichel*	*Neuberger*	*Simons*	*Beverungen*	*Kraus**	*Korbel*	*Holzenbein*	*Wenzel*	*Grabowski*	*Nickel*	*Weidle*
								Ref: V Rudnev	Eintracht's 35-year-old reserve keeper, Kunter, is a part-time dentist. Paddon's early 30-yarder keeps up West Ham's record of scoring in every away leg. Though they take a 2-1 lead in the Wald Stadium, Eintracht know they need a bigger advantage. They become ragged and frustrated.											
SF	H	EINTRACHT		16	W	3-1	0-0	Brooking 49, 78, Robson 67	Day	Coleman	Lampard	Bonds	Taylor T	McDowell	Holland	Paddon	Jennings	Brooking	Robson	
2	14/4		39,202					*Beverungen 87*	*Kunter*	*Reicehl*	*Neuberger*	*Lorenz*	*Beverungen*	*Weidle*	*Korbel*	*Holzenebin*	*Wanzel*	*Grabowski*	*Nickel*	
								Ref: W Hungerbuhler (Switz) (Hammers win 4-3 on aggregate)	Eintracht were the only team in Europe to have won every tie, home and away. They might have maintained that record but for Mervyn Day's fine early saves from Wanzel and Nickel. Brooking's delicate header put the Hammers ahead on away goals. Robson then curled a 30-yarder.											
F	N	ANDERLECHT		18	L	2-4	1-1	Holland 29, Robson 69	Day	Coleman	Lampard*	Bonds	Taylor T	McDowell	Holland	Paddon	Jennings	Brooking	Robson	Taylor A
	5/5	(Belgium)	*58,000*					*Rensenbrink 42, 73p, Van d Elst 48, 85*	*Ruiter*	*Lomme*	*Broos*	*Van Binst*	*Thissen*	*Dockx*	*Coeck**	*Van der Elst*	*Ressel*	*Haan*	*Rensenbrink*	*Vercauteren*
		(Heysel Stadium)						Ref: R Wurtz (France)	Bonds heads down for Holland's opener. Lampard blames his crazy back-pass that made it 1-1 on the long grass. Van der Elst makes it 1-2 and will later sign for West Ham. Robson levels with a header off a post. Pat Holland concedes the penalty. Rensenbrink was man of the match.											

		Home					Away					
	P	W	D	L	F	A	W	D	L	F	A	Pts
1 Liverpool	42	14	5	2	41	21	9	9	3	25	10	60
2 QP Rangers	42	17	4	0	42	13	7	7	7	25	20	59
3 Manchester U	42	16	4	1	40	13	7	6	8	28	29	56
4 Derby	42	15	3	3	45	30	6	8	7	30	28	53
5 Leeds	42	13	3	5	37	19	8	6	7	28	27	51
6 Ipswich	42	11	6	4	36	23	5	8	8	18	25	46
7 Leicester	42	9	9	3	29	24	4	10	7	19	27	45
8 Manchester C	42	14	5	2	46	18	2	6	13	18	28	43
9 Tottenham	42	6	10	5	33	32	8	5	8	30	31	43
10 Norwich	42	10	5	6	33	26	6	5	10	25	32	42
11 Everton	42	10	7	4	37	24	5	5	11	23	42	42
12 Stoke	42	8	5	8	25	24	7	6	8	23	26	41
13 Middlesbro	42	9	7	5	23	11	6	3	12	23	34	40
14 Coventry	42	6	9	6	22	22	7	5	9	25	35	40
15 Newcastle	42	11	4	6	51	26	4	5	12	20	36	39
16 Aston Villa	42	11	8	2	32	17	0	9	12	19	42	39
17 Arsenal	42	11	4	6	33	19	2	6	13	14	34	36
18 WEST HAM	42	10	5	6	26	23	3	5	13	22	48	36
19 Birmingham	42	11	5	5	36	26	2	2	17	21	49	33
20 Wolves	42	7	6	8	27	25	3	4	14	24	43	30
21 Burnley	42	6	6	9	23	26	3	4	14	20	40	28
22 Sheffield Utd	42	4	7	10	19	32	2	3	16	14	50	22
	924	229	127	106	736	494	106	127	229	494	736	924

Odds & ends

Double wins: (1) Stoke.
Double losses: (4) Everton, Derby, Norwich, Ipswich.

Won from behind: (5) Burnley (h), Birmingham (a), Middlesbrough (h), Bristol C LC (a), Den Haag CWC.
Lost from in front (3) Newcastle (a), Sheff Utd (a), Anderlecht CWC,

High spots: Unbeaten in first nine league games, up to 2nd.
Reaching final of European Cup-Winners' Cup.

Low spots: Terrible end to league season, failing to win any of last 16 games, and only one in 1976.
Relinquishing hold on FA Cup at the first attempt, to Liverpool.
Leading in Cup-Winners' Cup final, and then coming back to equalise, but still losing.

Hammer of the Year: Trevor Brooking.
Ever-presents: (0).
Hat-tricks: (1) Billy Jennings.
Leading scorer: (17) Alan Taylor.

	Appearances								Goals				
	Lge	*Sub*	LC	*Sub*	FAC	*Sub*	Eur	*Sub*	Lge	LC	FAC	Eur	Tot
Ayris, Johnny	**3**	*6*		*1*									
Best, Clyde	**5**	*2*	2						**1**	1			**2**
Bonds, Billy	**17**	*1*	5				9		**1**	1		2	**4**
Brooking, Trevor	**34**		4		1		7		**5**	1		3	**9**
Coleman, Keith	**26**		1		1		6	*1*					
Curbishley, Alan	**12**	*2*			1		1	*1*	**1**				**1**
Day, Mervyn	**41**		5		1		9						
Ferguson, Bobby	**1**												
Gould, Bobby	**4**	*1*					1		**2**				**2**
Holland, Pat	**35**		5		1		7		**2**			2	**4**
Jennings, Billy	**26**	*4*	1	*2*	1		5	*2*	**11**			3	**14**
Lampard, Frank	**37**		4		1		9		**3**			1	**4**
Lock, Kevin	**26**		5		1		4						
McDowell, John	**36**	*1*	5				7						
McGiven, Mike	**6**	*1*			1		1	*1*					
Orhan, Yilmaz	**5**												
Paddon, Graham	**39**		5		1		9		**2**	1		2	**5**
Pike, Geoff		*3*											
Robson, Bryan '	**33**	*1*	4				9		**3**	1		4	**8**
Taylor, Alan	**33**	*2*	4		1		6	*1*	**13**	1		3	**17**
Taylor, Tommy	**42**		5				9		**2**				**2**
Wooler, Alan	**1**												
(own-goals)									**2**				**2**
22 players used	**462**	***24***	**55**	***3***	**11**		**99**	***6***	**48**	**6**		**20**	**74**

No	Date	Att	Pos	Pt	F-A	H-T	Scorers, Times, and Referees	1	2	3	4	5	6	7	8	9	10	11	12 sub used
1	A ASTON VILLA			L	0-4	0-0		Day	Coleman	Lampard	Taylor T	**Green**	Bonds	Taylor A	Paddon	Holland	Brooking	Curbishley	
	21/8	*39,012*		–			*Gray 49, 75, Graydon 54, 60p*	*Burridge*	*Gidman*	*Smith*	*Phillips*	*Nicholl*	*Mortimer*	*Graydon*	*Little*	*Gray*	*Robson*	*Carrodus*	
							Ref: C Thomas	Bill Green has signed from Carlisle for £100,000, allowing Tommy Taylor to play up front as experimental striker. Green gives away a penalty with a foul on Andy Gray, but Graydon, set for his hat-trick, fired over the bar. Bonds brought down Carrodus for Villa's second penalty.											
2	H QP RANGERS			W	1-0	0-0	Paddon 76	Day	Coleman	Lampard	Holland	Green	Bonds	Taylor T	Paddon	Taylor A	Brooking	Curbishley	
	23/8	31,668		2				*Parkes*	*Clement*	*Gillard*	*Hollins*	*McLintock*	*Leach*	*Thomas*	*Leach*	*Masson*	*Bowles*	*Givens*	
							Ref: A Glasson	Like West Ham, Dave Sexton's QPR lost their opening match 0-4. Day is the busier keeper and in the space of seconds Bowles and Givens break clear but miss. Paddon's 30-yarder dipped under the bar to give Hammers their first home win in seven months. That was versus QPR.											
3	H LEICESTER		17	D	0-0	0-0		Day	Coleman	McGiven	Holland	Green	Bonds	Taylor T	Paddon	Taylor A	Brooking	Jennings	
	28/8	24,960	*14*	3				*Wallington*	*Whitworth*	*Rofe*	*Kember**	*Blockley*	*Woollett*	*Weller*	*Alderson*	*Worthington*	*Lee*	*Garland*	*Birchenall*
							Ref: A Grey	Leicester manager Jimmy Bloomfield admitted: 'We were lucky'. His side is full of expensive new signings, but survived only because the woodwork three times came to their assistance. Both matches with Leicester last season were drawn, and both have drawn all matches so far.											
4	A STOKE		20	L	1-2	0-1	Taylor A 70	Day	Coleman	Lampard	McGiven	Green	Bonds	Taylor T*	Paddon	Taylor A	Brooking	Holland	Jennings
	4/9	*19,131*	*6*	3			*Crooks 32, Conroy 51*	*Shilton*	*Marsh*	*Pejic*	*Mahoney*	*Dodd*	*Bloor*	*Salmons*	*Greenhoff*	*Conroy*	*Hudson*	*Crooks*	
							Ref: W Gow	Stoke are going well and on this evidence deserve to be doing so. 18-year-old Garth Crooks nets his first ever Division 1 goal, and man-of-the-match Terry Conroy fired a screamer. Alan Taylor deflected Brooking's shot past Shilton, and Tommy Taylor hit a post against the run of play.											
5	H ARSENAL		21	L	0-2	0-1		Day	Coleman*	Lampard	Bonds	Green	McGiven	Taylor T	Paddon	Taylor A	Brooking	Holland	Orhan
	11/9	31,965	*6*	3			*Stapleton 28, Ross 46*	*Rimmer*	*Rice*	*Nelson*	*Ross*	*O'Leary**	*Howard*	*Ball*	*Armstrong*	*Stapleton*	*Cropley*	*Brady*	*Storey*
							Ref: A Robinson	Terry Neill's Arsenal are without £300,000 signing Malcolm Macdonald. Alan Taylor hit a post with one effort and the bar seconds later. Stapleton's header and Trevor Ross's volley earned Arsenal the points. Billy Bonds and Mick McGiven kept feuding between themselves.											
6	A BRISTOL CITY		20	D	1-1	0-1	Taylor A 69	Day	Coleman	Lampard*	Bonds	Green	Taylor T	Jennings	Paddon	Taylor A	Brooking	Holland	McGiven
	18/9	*28,932*	*5*	4			*Fear 10*	*Cashley*	*Sweeney*	*Drysdale*	*Gow*	*Collier*	*Merrick*	*Tainton*	*Fear*	*Mann*	*Gillies*	*Whitehead*	
							Ref: L Burden	A minute before half-time Pat Holland collides with Jimmy Mann and breaks a shin-bone. With Lampard already off with a strained hip, West Ham must play the second half with 10 men. Strangely, they played better, and deserved their equaliser when Brooking crossed to Alan Taylor.											
7	H SUNDERLAND		20	D	1-1	0-0	Jennings 52	Day	Coleman	Lock	Bonds	Green	Taylor T	Jennings	Paddon	Taylor A	Brooking	McGiven	
	25/9	24,319	*22*	5			*Bolton 70*	*Montgomery*	*Ashurst*	*Bolton*	*Towers*	*Clarke*	*Holton*	*Train*	*Hughes**	*Greenwood*	*Robson*	*Foggon*	*Rowell*
							Ref: K Baker	Bob Stokoe's Sunderland are searching for their first win. Such is the tension within West Ham's ranks that when Billy Jennings heads in Trevor Brooking's cross he does not celebrate but V-signs the crowd who had baited him. Full-back Bolton levelled from Towers' pass.											
8	A MANCHESTER C		21	L	2-4	0-1	Taylor A 63, Doyle 84 (og)	Day	Coleman	Lock	Bonds	Green	Taylor T	Jennings	Paddon	Taylor A	Brooking	McGiven*	Ayris
	2/10	*37,795*	*2*	5			*Owen 44, Tueart 50, 89, Hartford 79*	*Corrigan*	*Clements*	*Donachie*	*Doyle*	*Watson*	*Owen*	*Barnes*	*Kidd*	*Royle*	*Hartford*	*Tueart*	
							Ref: J Taylor	Gary Owen's cheeky lob over the stranded Day ignites a second-half goal blitz. When Corrigan punched out Paddon's cross and Doyle headed unwittingly into his own net, West Ham sensed a reprieve. Mick McGiven was carried off. Lyall hopes to sign Plymouth striker Paul Mariner.											
9	H LEEDS			L	1-3	1-1	Jennings 22	Day	Coleman	Lock	Bonds	Green	Taylor T	Jennings	Paddon	Taylor A	Brooking	Ayris	
	6/10	21,909		5			*Gray E 5, Lorimer 77, Harris 83*	*Harvey*	*Reaney*	*Hampton*	*Madeley*	*McQueen*	*Hunter*	*Cherry*	*Lorimer*	*Jordan*	*Gray F*	*Gray E**	*Harris*
							Ref: R Challis	The crowd is small, morale is low, and Jimmy Armfield's strugglers put the shackles on Brooking by man-marking him with Trevor Cherry. Day is to blame for Eddie Gray's opener. Although Jennings levels with a deflection, by the close Leeds look like scoring with every attack.											
10	H IPSWICH		21	L	0-2	0-1		Day	Coleman	Lock	Bonds	Green	Taylor T	Jennings	Paddon	Taylor A*	Brooking	Robson B	Ayris
	16/10	24,534	*7*	5			*Woods 10, 87*	*Cooper*	*Burley*	*Mills*	*Talbot*	*Hunter*	*Beattie*	*Osborne*	*Wark*	*Bertschin**	*Whymark*	*Woods*	*Lambert*
							Ref: T Bent	Even though Pop Robson has come back from Sunderland, this is a pathetic showing. Ipswich's Kevin Beattie says: 'They'll be in the Second Division next season.' Man-of-the-match Clive Woods got off the mark following Bertschin's dummy. Ipswich should have scored five or six.											

11 A	EVERTON		21	L	2-3	0-1	McNaught 76 (og), Bonds 87	Day	Bonds	Lampard	Curbishley	Green*	Taylor T	Orhan	Paddon	Robson B	Brooking	Robson K	Lock
23/10		*23,163*	*4*	5			*Lyons 13, King 54, Latchford 65*	*Davies*	*Darracott*	*Jones*	*Lyons*	*McNaught*	*Hamilton*	*King*	*Dobson**	*Latchford*	*Goodlass*	*Telfer*	*Pearson*
							Ref: R Perkin	When Bob Latchford climaxes a 30-yard run with a 30-yard shot to put Everton three up, West Ham look doomed. But Ken McNaught's own-goal, finishing off a shot from the Cypriot Yilmaz Orhan, breathes life into the Hammers. Bonds' shot went through keeper Dai Davies' hands.											
12 A	WEST BROM		22	L	0-3	0-1		Day	Bonds	Lampard	Curbishley	Lock	Taylor T	**Devonshire**	Paddon	Robson B	Brooking	Robson K*	Orhan
30/10		*19,856*	*10*	5			*Martin 43, Brown A 76, 86*	*Osborne*	*Mulligan*	*Cantello*	*Brown T*	*Wile*	*Robertson*	*Martin*	*Treacy*	*Edwards**	*Giles*	*Brown A*	*Trewick*
							Ref: G Flint	Six successive defeats, five points from 12 games. That is West Ham's worst run since 1958. Once Johnny Giles' Albion went in front, West Ham failed to create any chances. Day was at fault with both Ally Brown goals, dropping Martin's cross and failing to hold Trewick's shot.											
13 H	TOTTENHAM		21	W	**5-3**	2-1	Robson 21, Bonds 30, Jen' 69, Brook 54,	Day	Bonds	Lampard	Curbishley	Lock	Taylor T	Devonshire	Pike	Jennings	Brooking	Robson B	
6/11		28,997	*19*	7			*Duncan 41, Hoddle 78, Osgood 83p*	*Daines*	*Naylor*	*McAllister*	*Hoddle*	*Young*	*Osgood*	*Pratt*	*Perryman*	*Duncan*	*Conn*	*Taylor**	*Coates*
							Ref: D Lloyd [Goal 5. Curbishley 72]	John Lyall plays four in midfield, most of them kids, and none a natural ball-winner. Spurs have now shipped 24 goals in six away games. Lyall has also signed Anton Otulakowski for £60,000 from Barnsley. He is ineligible, serving a week's notice as a gas board draughtsman.											
14 A	NORWICH		21	L	0-1	0-1		Day	Bonds	Lampard	Curbishley	Lock*	Taylor T	Devonshire	Pike	Jennings	Brooking	Robson B	Coleman
10/11		*24,762*	*18*	7			*Peters 17*	*Keelan*	*Ryan*	*Sullivan*	*Steele**	*Jones*	*Powell*	*Neighbour*	*Osgood*	*Boyer*	*Suggett*	*Peters*	*Machin*
							Ref: C Maskell	Peter Osgood makes his Norwich debut on loan. Suggett's corner, headed in by Martin Peters, settles a match that West Ham let slip away. They saw enough of the ball, but lacked a cutting edge. Graham Paddon re-signs for Norwich after the game. 'It's great to be back,' he says.											
15 H	NEWCASTLE		22	L	1-2	1-1	Robson B 36	Day	Bonds	Lampard	Curbishley	Lock	Taylor T*	Devonshire	Pike	Jennings	Brooking	Robson B	Robson K
20/11		21,324	*5*	7			*Nulty 35, Burns 53*	*Mahoney*	*Nattrass*	*Kennedy*	*Cassidy*	*McCaffery*	*Nulty*	*Barrowclough*	*Cannell*	*Burns*	*Gowling*	*Craig T*	
							Ref: H Robinson	Brooking's 300th game for the Hammers is not a happy one. Tommy Craig's free-kick was deflected in by Magpies' skipper Geoff Nulty. Pop Robson's instant equaliser counted for nothing when Mervyn Day hesitated about coming out, leaving Mickey Burns to nip in for the winner.											
16 A	MANCHESTER U		22	W	2-0	2-0	Brooking 19, Jennings 30	Day	Lock	Lampard	**Otulakowski**	Taylor T	Bonds	Devonshire	Pike	Jennings	Brooking	Robson B	
27/11		*55,366*	*15*	9				*Stepney*	*Forsyth*	*Albiston*	*Daly*	*Greenhoff B*	*Houston*	*Coppell*	*McIlroy*	*Pearson*	*Greenhoff J*	*Hill*	
							Ref: P Reeves	The first away win for a year, against a Man U side who have won just once at home in seven games. 20-year-old, 5ft 6in Anton Otulakowski enjoys a fine debut. Jennings knocked on for Brooking to dash between two defenders for the first. West Ham stay bottom on goal-difference.											
17 H	MIDDLESBROUGH		22	L	0-1	0-1		Day	Lock	Lampard	Otulakowski	Taylor T	Bonds	Devonshire	Pike	Jennings*	Brooking	Robson B	Curbishley
4/12		20,184	*10*	9			*Boersma 8*	*Platt*	*Craggs*	*Cooper*	*Souness*	*Boam*	*Maddren*	*McAndrew*	*Mills*	*Brine*	*Boersma**	*Armstrong*	*Hickton*
							Ref: C Thomas	Jack Charlton's joyless Boro snatch their first away win of the season with only their third away goal. Charlton is gracious enough to admit the win is undeserved. He did not, however, apologise for his team's stifling, negative tactics as they sought to protect Phil Boersma's early goal.											
18 H	LIVERPOOL		21	W	2-0	0-0	Brooking 59, Jennings 86	Day	Lock	Lampard	Green	Taylor T	Bonds	Robson K	**Radford**	Jennings	Brooking	Robson B	
18/12		24,175	*2*	11				*Clemence*	*Neal*	*Jones*	*Thompson*	*Kennedy*	*Hughes*	*Keegan*	*McDermott*	*Heighway*	*Toshack**	*Callaghan*	*Case*
							Ref: K Baker	Lyall leaves out most of his youngsters against the defending champions. John Radford, an £80,000 signing from Arsenal, makes his debut. The magnificent Brooking beats the offside trap and side-steps Emlyn Hughes for the first goal. Radford headed down to Jennings for No 2.											
19 A	BIRMINGHAM		21	D	0-0	0-0		Day	Lock	Lampard	Green	Taylor T	Bonds	Robson K	Radford	Jennings	Brooking	Robson B	
27/12		*39,978*	*8*	12				*Latchford*	*Rathbone*	*Styles*	*Kendall*	*Gallagher*	*Page*	*Jones*	*Francis*	*Burns*	*Hibbitt*	*Connolly*	
							Ref: A Porter	West Ham had the chances in the first half, but Radford and Pop Robson missed them. The defence had to earn their corn after the turnaround, and Mervyn Day enjoyed one of his most defiant displays. Billy Bonds took the eye with the way he controlled the boy-wonder Trevor Francis.											
20 A	TOTTENHAM		21	L	1-2	1-0	Brooking 2	Day	Lock	Lampard	Green	Taylor T	Bonds	Robson K	Radford*	Jennings	Brooking	Robson B	Otulakowski
1/1		*44,972*	*18*	12			*Osgood 54p, Duncan 61*	*Jennings*	*Naylor*	*Gorman*	*Hoddle*	*Pratt*	*Osgood*	*Conn*	*Perryman*	*Duncan*	*Coates*	*Taylor*	
							Ref: K Burns	Pouring rain, freak goals, bags of controversy. The freak goal was Brooking's, his free-kick aquaplaning through the puddles. The controversy attended Bonds' tackle on Alfie Conn. The linesman's yellow flag signalled a penalty. Then Perryman felled Brooking but this time no penalty.											
21 H	WEST BROM		21	D	0-0	0-0		Day	Lock	Lampard	Green	Taylor T	Bonds	Robson K	Devonshire	Jennings	Brooking	Robson B	
3/1		25,236	*9*	13				*Osborne*	*Mulligan*	*Robson*	*Brown T*	*Wile*	*Robertson*	*Martin*	*Treacy*	*Cross*	*Trewick*	*Johnston*	
							Ref: L Shapter	Many referees would have postponed this match rather than let it go ahead on a treacherous pitch that made football impossible. Albion stopper John Wile had a comfortable time without the hamstrung John Radford to mark. The best chance fell to Jennings but was acrobatically saved.											

No Date	Att	Pos	Pt	F-A	H-T	Scorers, Times, and Referees	1	2	3	4	5	6	7	8	9	10	11	12 sub used
22 H ASTON VILLA		21	L	0-1	0-1		Day	Lock	Lampard	Green	Taylor T	Bonds	Curbishley	Pike*	Jennings	Brooking	Robson B	Devonshire
22/1	27,577	*4*	13			*Gray 3*	*Burridge*	*Gidman*	*Robson*	*Phillips*	*Nicholl*	*Mortimer*	*Deehan*	*Little*	*Gray*	*Cropley**	*Carrodus*	*Smith*
						Ref: A Grey	Tommy Taylor is so fed up with being told to play in midfield that he gives Lyall an ultimatum: 'Let me play in defence or I quit.' John Deehan fed Andy Gray for his 23rd goal of the season. Ron Saunders' Villa become the 10th side to keep out West Ham's so-called attack.											
23 A LEICESTER		21	L	0-2	0-1		Day	Bonds	Lampard	Otulakowski	Green	Lock	Taylor A	Radford	Devonshire	Brooking	Robson B	
5/2	16,201	*9*	13			*Worthington 20, Weller 71*	*Wallington*	*Whitworth*	*Rofe*	*Kember*	*Blockley*	*Sims*	*Weller*	*Sammels*	*Worthington*	*Alderson**	*Earle*	*Birchenall*
						Ref: W Gow	This was better than it appears. West Ham held their own against a team beaten at home just twice, but lost to two stupid mistakes. Dennis Rofe's centre was deflected by Bonds to Frank Worthington. When Pop Robson lost possession, Keith Weller made the game safe for City.											
24 H STOKE		21	W	1-0	1-0	Robson B 8	Day	Bonds	Lampard	Otulakowski	Green	Lock	Taylor A	Radford	Devonshire	Brooking	Robson B*	Robson K
12/2	**20,160**	*16*	15				*Shilton*	*Dodd*	*Bowers*	*Mahoney*	*Smith*	*Bloor*	*Crooks*	*Suddick**	*Goodwin*	*Conroy*	*Salmons*	*Marsh*
						Ref: A Robinson	Pop Robson's near-post glancing header was oh-so-nearly saved by Shilton. Bonds missed with a 65th-minute penalty and poor Mervyn Day looked increasingly edgy. He saved from Dave Goodwin with his knees and looked as though the final whistle could not come quickly enough.											
25 A ARSENAL		20	W	3-2	2-1	Taylor A 23, 75, Jennings 34	Day	Bonds	Lampard	Otulakowski	Green	Lock	Taylor A	Radford	Devonshire	Brooking	Jennings	
19/2	*38,221*	*9*	17			*Brady 13, Stapleton 62*	*Rimmer*	*Rice*	*Nelson*	*Ross*	*Powling*	*Simpson*	*Hudson*	*Brady*	*Macdonald*	*Stapleton*	*Armstrong*	
						Ref: R Challis	This televised match was finally turned West Ham's way when Alan Taylor launched himself at Lampard's low cross and the ball flew into the net. How much Taylor knew of it was debatable. Young Devonshire played a blinder for the Hammers and Lock twice cleared off the line.											
26 H BRISTOL CITY		18	W	2-0	1-0	Bonds 26p, Jennings 67	Day	Bonds	Lampard	Otulakowski	Green	Lock	Taylor A	Radford	Devonshire	Brooking	Jennings	
26/2	29,713	*20*	19				*Shaw*	*Gillies*	*Merrick*	*Sweeney*	*Collier*	*Hunter*	*Gow*	*Fear*	*Garland**	*Cormack*	*Whitehead*	*Tainton*
						Ref: A Turvey	The return of Alan Taylor to the side seems to have injected life into a lifeless team. Gerry Gow toppled him for the penalty. Geoff Merrick then deflected Billy Jennings' effort past Shaw. Jennings claimed the goal. Alan Dick's City spent the afternoon running around in circles.											
27 A SUNDERLAND		20	L	**0-6**	0-3	[Lee 85]	Day	Bonds	Lampard	Otulakowski	Green	Lock	Robson K	Radford	Devonshire	Brooking	Jennings	
5/3	*35,357*	*18*	19			*Holden 3, 30, Rowell 9, 65, Kerr 53,*	*Siddall*	*Docherty*	*Bolton*	*Arnott*	*Waldron*	*Ashurst*	*Kerr*	*Elliott**	*Holden*	*Lee*	*Rowell*	*Brown*
						Ref: A Jones	West Ham had won their last three. Sunderland had won their last four and had climbed off the bottom by winning 6-1 in their last home game, against WBA. This is Roker's best result for 14 years and ITV's *The Big Match* cameras are there to record it. Rowell set up Holden's opener.											
28 H MANCHESTER C		18	W	1-0	1-0	Robson B 20	Day	Bonds	Lampard	Otulakowski	Green*	Lock	Pike	Robson B	Devonshire	Brooking	Jennings	Curbishley
12/3	24,974	*3*	21				*Corrigan*	*Clements*	*Donachie*	*Doyle**	*Watson*	*Conway*	*Barnes*	*Kidd*	*Royle*	*Hartford*	*Tueart*	*Owen*
						Ref: E Read	Disaster for Bill Green as he collides with Joe Royle, cracks a fibula in his right leg and fractures his temple bone too. Just before half-time Bonds misses his second penalty in three weeks. This left the Hammers hanging on to Pop Robson's flick from Trevor Brooking's cross.											
29 A IPSWICH		22	L	1-4	0-0	Robson B 86p	Day	Bonds	Lampard	Otulakowski	Taylor T	Lock	Pike	Robson B	Devonshire	Brooking	Jennings	
22/3	*27,315*	*1*	21			*Taylor 56 (og), Mariner 68, 72, 82*	*Cooper*	*Burley*	*Mills*	*Talbot*	*Hunter*	*Roberts*	*Osborne*	*Wark*	*Mariner*	*Whymark**	*Woods*	*Bertschin*
						Ref: B Martin	This fixture was brought forward four days in view of England's World Cup clash with Luxembourg. Tommy Taylor returns after six weeks' absence and heads an own-goal. Talbot felled Devonshire for the penalty. The result sends Ipswich top above Liverpool and West Ham bottom.											
30 H EVERTON		22	D	2-2	1-1	Robson B 29p, 83	Day	Bonds	Lampard	Otulakowski	Taylor T	Lock	Radford	Robson B	Devonshire	Brooking	Jennings	
2/4	22,518	*14*	22			*Goodlass 10, Pearson 58*	*Lawson*	*Jones*	*Pejic*	*Lyons*	*McNaught*	*Darracott*	*Hamilton*	*Dobson*	*Latchford*	*Telfer**	*Goodlass*	*Pearson*
						Ref: L Burden	Gordon Lee's Everton extend their unbeaten run to 11. They took the lead twice, despite having come to defend. Mervyn Day, off his line, is catastrophically lobbed by Ronnie Goodlass from near the halfway line. Many supporters identify that goal as the beginning of the end for Day.											
31 A QP RANGERS		22	D	1-1	0-0	Robson B 62	Day	Bonds	Lampard	Pike	Taylor T	Lock	Radford	Robson B	Devonshire*	Brooking	Jennings	Otulakowski
4/4	*24,930*	*16*	23			*Eastoe 57*	*Parkes*	*Shanks*	*Gillard*	*Hollins*	*McLintock*	*Abbott*	*Eastoe*	*Leach*	*Masson*	*Webb*	*Givens*	
						Ref: C Biddle	QPR remain three points above West Ham as a result of this draw. Givens headed on to Peter Eastoe, but the lead was cancelled out by Pop Robson, thanks to Brooking's slide-rule pass. It is Robson's fifth goal in four games. Lyall had told him to do less work, and stop chasing back.											

No	Date	Opponent / Att	Pos	Res / Pts	F-A	H-T	Scorers, Times, and Referees	1	2	3	4	5	6	7	8	9	10	11	12 sub used
32	H	BIRMINGHAM	22	D	2-2	1-2	Jennings 7, Pike 56	Day	Bonds	Coleman	Pike	Taylor T	Lock	Radford	Robson B	Devonshire*	Brooking	Jennings	Taylor A
	8/4	28,167	*12*	24			*Gallagher 22, Francis 23*	*Montgomery*	*Calderwood*	*Pendrey*	*Kendall*	*Gallagher*	*Want*	*Emmanuel*	*Francis*	*Burns*	*Hibbitt*	*Connolly*	
							Ref: R Crabb	The turning point comes in the 48th minute. Pop Robson has taken over responsibility for penalties from Bonds. He is now up against Jim Montgomery, who he knows from their time at Sunderland. Monty guesses right and saves. Day is lobbed by Francis and V-signs the crowd.											
33	A	COVENTRY	21	D	1-1	0-0	Robson B 87	Day	Bonds	Lampard	Pike	Taylor T	McGiven	Taylor A	Robson B	Devonshire	Brooking	Jennings	
	9/4	***15,816***	*19*	25			*Ferguson 76*	*Blyth*	*Roberts*	*McDonald**	*Gooding*	*Yorath*	*Coop*	*Beck*	*Powell*	*Wallace*	*Ferguson*	*Hutchison*	*Green*
							Ref: T Reynolds	Coventry lose their keeper with a knee injury after an hour. Bobby McDonald volunteers to go in goal. Ferguson heads Yorath's free-kick over Day to put City in front. McDonald was all set to celebrate his stint in goal when Robson headed the equaliser from Devonshire's centre.											
34	H	NORWICH	20	W	1-0	0-0	Pike 74	Day	Bonds	Lampard	Pike	Taylor T	McGiven	Radford	Robson B	Devonshire	Brooking	Taylor A	
	11/4	27,084	*13*	27				*Keelan*	*Ryan*	*Sullivan*	*Machin*	*Jones*	*Powell*	*Neighbour*	*Reeves*	*Boyer*	*Steele*	*Peters*	
							Ref: P Reeves	Day looks a bag of nerves and his confidence is not helped by sections of the crowd who are happy to jeer his every touch. At least he has learned his lesson and offers no more V-signs. Geoff Pike's winner was a 25-yarder, capitalising on a half-clearance from Lampard's cross.											
35	A	NEWCASTLE	21	L	0-3	0-1		Day	Bonds	Lampard	Pike	Taylor T	McGiven	Radford	Robson B	Devonshire	Brooking	Taylor A*	Jennings
	16/4	*30,967*	*4*	27			*Gowling 45, Cannell 67, Nulty 78*	*Mahoney*	*Nattrass*	*Kennedy*	*Cassidy**	*McCaffrey*	*Nulty*	*Barrowclough*	*Cannell*	*Burns*	*Gowling*	*Craig T*	*Blackhall*
							Ref: A Morrissey	Pop Robson says: 'We are great at playing but hopeless at scoring.' Newcastle, unbeaten at home, are given a first-half lesson by Brooking and Devonshire and are booed off at half-time. In the second half Gowling nodded in from Nulty, then Day fumbled Burns' cross to Paul Cannell.											
36	A	DERBY	21	D	1-1	0-0	Pike 86p	Day	Bonds*	Lampard	Pike	Taylor T	McGiven	Radford	Robson B	Devonshire	Brooking	Taylor A	Jennings
	20/4	*21,380*	*17*	28			*Daly59p*	*Boulton*	*Langan*	*Webster*	*Daly*	*McFarland*	*Todd*	*Powell*	*Gemmill*	*Hales*	*Hector*	*James*	
							Ref: R Toseland	Twice Mick McGiven clatters Derek Hales in the box, but only once is a penalty awarded. Two minutes after Daly converts it, Billy Bonds hobbles off. But late in the game Kevin Hector inadvertently handled. Geoff Pike was the only Hammer brave enough to volunteer to take it.											
37	A	LEEDS	21	D	1-1	0-0	Robson B 73	Day	Coleman	Lampard	Pike	Taylor T	McGiven	Radford	Robson B	Devonshire	Brooking	Taylor A	
	26/4	*16,891*	*10*	29			*Jordan 53*	*Stewart*	*Stevenson*	*Hampton*	*Cherry*	*McQueen*	*Madeley*	*Harris*	*McNiven*	*Jordan*	*Currie*	*Gray E*	
							Ref: K Butcher	England manager Don Revie always seems to turn up to watch Leeds play West Ham. Leeds are rebuilding. Tony Currie's corner is volleyed in by Joe Jordan. Brooking then squeezed past three defenders before laying the ball off to Devonshire, who provided Pop Robson's equaliser.											
38	A	MIDDLESBROUGH	19	D	1-1	1-0	Robson B 12	Day	Bonds	Lampard	Pike	Taylor T	McGiven	Jennings	Robson B	Devonshire	Brooking	Taylor A	
	29/4	*16,500*	*11*	30			*Mills 73*	*Platt*	*Craggs*	*Cooper*	*Souness*	*Ramage*	*Maddren*	*McAndrew*	*Mills*	*Wood*	*Brine**	*Armstrong*	*Boersma*
							Ref: K McNally	West Ham squeeze out of the bottom three with this point. When Alan Taylor's shot was blocked it ran to Robson to poke the ball in. Hammers were desperate to hang on to both points, but when Alan Taylor under-hit a back-pass Mills drew Day from his goal to score from a tight angle.											
39	H	COVENTRY	18	W	2-0	1-0	Robson B 20, Pike 51p	Day	Bonds	Lampard	Pike	Taylor T	McGiven	Radford	Robson B	Devonshire	Brooking	Taylor A	
	4/5	25,461	*16*	32				*Sealey*	*Cartwright*	*McDonald*	*Yorath*	*Holton*	*Coop*	*Beck*	*Wallace*	*Ferguson*	*Powell*	*Hutchison*	
							Ref: R Lewis	In the mud and rain, Brooking lights up a fighting performance by the Hammers, feeding Robson, who wriggled round Coop for the first goal. Terry Yorath conceded the second by handling. He angrily claimed the ball had hit him. Sunderland, Spurs and Bristol C are the bottom three.											
40	H	DERBY	19	D	2-2	1-1	Pike 2, Jennings 84	Day	Bonds	Lampard	Pike	Taylor T	McGiven*	Radford	Robson B	Devonshire	Brooking	Taylor A	Jennings
	7/5	**32,079**	*15*	33			*James 44, McGiven 76 (og)*	*Boulton*	*Langan*	*Webster*	*Daly*	*McFarland*	*Todd*	*Powell*	*Gemmill*	*Hector*	*George*	*James*	
							Ref: H Robinson	It takes Pike 98 seconds to bag the first goal. Most unpopular man at Upton Park is Derby's Leighton James, who keeps tumbling whenever a defender gets near. He fired in a free-kick when felled by Taylor and later prompted McGiven's own-goal. The referee needed a police escort.											
41	A	LIVERPOOL	19	D	0-0	0-0		Day	Bonds	Lampard	Pike	Taylor T	McGiven	Jennings	Robson B	Devonshire	Brooking	Taylor A	
	14/5	***55,675***	*1*	34				*Clemence*	*Neal*	*Jones*	*Smith*	*Kennedy*	*Hughes*	*Keegan*	*Case*	*Heighway*	*Johnson**	*McDermott*	*Fairclough*
							Ref: C Seel	West Ham conclude their season by facing both FA Cup finalists, who are bound to be distracted. The magnificent Steve Heighway steals the show and forces a fine save from Day. West Ham have lost once in 14 games, and with Spurs already down have survival in their own hands.											
42	H	MANCHESTER U	19	W	4-2	1-1	Lampard 29, Pike 53, Robson 60, 74	Day	Bonds	Lampard	Pike	Taylor T	McGiven	Radford	Robson B	Devonshire	Brooking	Taylor A	
	16/5	29,311	*6*	36			*Hill 1, Pearson 67*	*Roche*	*Nicholl*	*Albiston*	*McIlroy*	*Greenhoff B*	*Buchan*	*Coppell*	*Greenhoff J**	*Pearson*	*Macari*	*Hill*	*McCreery*
Average	Home 26,015	Away 30,106					Ref: C Thomas	A terrace ban on Man U fans means more space for Hammers supporters. Even though the FA Cup final is just five days away, Tommy Docherty's side show great commitment. They take the lead in 25 seconds. Lampard levels off a post from 30 yards and West Ham turn it on.											

League Cup

League Cup					F-A	H-T	Scorers, Times, and Referees	1	2	3	4	5	6	7	8	9	10	11	12 sub used
2	H	BARNSLEY	17	W	3-0	2-0	Holland 21, 60, Paddon 45	Day	Coleman	McGiven	Holland	Green	Bonds	Taylor T	Paddon	Taylor A	Brooking	Jennings	
1/9		17,889	*4:7*					*Springett*	*Murphy*	*Gorry*	*Otulakowski*	*Burke*	*Pickering*	*Felton*	*Peachey*	*Joicey*	*Brown*	*Millar**	*Price*
							Ref: R Lewis	Barnsley boss Jim Iley admits: 'West Ham have taught us a lot.' He may not have been so generous had Kenny Brown not scooped over Day's crossbar at 0-0. Tommy Taylor is still playing as striker. He is so desperate to score he claimed one of Holland's, though he was yards away.											
3	A	CHARLTON	20	W	1-0	0-0	Taylor A 82	Day	Coleman	McGiven	Bonds	Green	Taylor T	Jennings	Paddon	Taylor A	Brooking	Lock	
21/9		*32,898*	*2:15*					*Wood*	*Berry*	*Warman*	*Hunt*	*Giles*	*Curtis*	*Powell*	*Hales*	*Flanagan*	*Bowman*	*Peacock*	
							Ref: J Homewood	Charlton's biggest crowd for 14 years are not too impressed by the Hammers, who adopt negative tactics and pass back to Day whenever danger threatens. Nor is manager Andy Nelson impressed with the referee. Alan Taylor won the match after Paddon's shot was blocked.											
4	H	QP RANGERS	21	L	0-2	0-1		Day	Bonds	Lampard	Curbishley	Lock	Taylor T	Orhan	Paddon	Devonshire	Brooking	Robson K	
27/10		24,565	*13*				*Bowles 38, Clement 87*	*Parkes*	*Clement*	*Gillard*	*Hollins*	*McLintock*	*Webb*	*Thomas**	*Kelly*	*Masson*	*Bowles*	*Givens*	*Leach*
							Ref: R Capey	Alan Devonshire plays his first match after being signed by scout Eddie Baily from Southall for £5,000. Nasty fouls committed by Lampard, Lock and Keith Robson do little for West Ham's nice-guy image. Dave Thomas was carried off after eight minutes, following Lampard's foul.											

FA Cup

FA Cup					F-A	H-T	Scorers, Times, and Referees	1	2	3	4	5	6	7	8	9	10	11	12 sub used
3	H	BOLTON	21	W	2-1	1-0	Jennings 29, Pike 89	Day	Lock	Lampard	Green	Taylor T	Bonds	Curbishley	Pike	Jennings	Brooking	Robson B	
8/1		24,147	*2:2*				*Waldron 90*	*McDonagh*	*Nicholson*	*Dunne*	*Greaves*	*Jones**	*Walsh*	*Morgan*	*Whatmore*	*Taylor*	*Reid*	*Smith*	*Waldron*
							Ref: A Hamil	As Ian Greaves' side like to build from the back, Lyall gets his forwards to pressure their defence. When McDonagh scooped out Pike's shot after 50 minutes the ball had crossed the line, though the linesman disagreed. Jennings had already outjumped Jones to put West Ham in front.											
4	A	ASTON VILLA	21	L	0-3	0-0		Day	Lock	Lampard	Green	Taylor T	Bonds	Taylor A	Radford	Jennings	Brooking	Robson B	
29/1		*46,954*	*4*				*Deehan 58, 66, Mortimer 78*	*Burridge*	*Gidman*	*Robson*	*Phillips*	*Nicholl*	*Mortimer*	*Deehan*	*Little*	*Gray*	*Cowans*	*Carrodus*	
							Ref: P Partridge	West Ham lost to Villa last week in the league. Alan Taylor returns after three months out. Tommy Taylor plays in midfield in the first half but switched with Bonds after the turnaround. Villa's John Deehan made the breakthrough when Day, at a corner, lost his footing on the icy pitch.											

		Home					Away					
	P	W	D	L	F	A	W	D	L	F	A	Pts
1 Liverpool	42	18	3	0	47	11	5	8	8	15	22	57
2 Manchester C	42	15	5	1	38	13	6	9	6	22	21	56
3 Ipswich	42	15	4	2	41	11	7	4	10	25	28	52
4 Aston Villa	42	17	3	1	55	17	5	4	12	21	33	51
5 Newcastle	42	14	6	1	40	15	4	7	10	24	34	49
6 Manchester U	42	12	6	3	41	22	6	5	10	30	40	47
7 West Brom	42	10	6	5	38	22	6	7	8	24	34	45
8 Arsenal	42	11	6	4	37	20	5	5	11	27	39	43
9 Everton	42	9	7	5	35	24	5	7	9	27	40	42
10 Leeds	42	8	8	5	28	26	7	4	10	20	25	42
11 Leicester	42	8	9	4	30	28	4	9	8	17	32	42
12 Middlesbro	42	11	6	4	25	14	3	7	11	15	31	41
13 Birmingham	42	10	6	5	38	25	3	6	12	25	36	38
14 QP Rangers	42	10	7	4	31	21	3	5	13	16	31	38
15 Derby	42	9	9	3	36	18	0	10	11	14	37	37
16 Norwich	42	12	4	5	30	23	2	5	14	17	41	37
17 WEST HAM	42	9	6	6	28	23	2	8	11	18	42	36
18 Bristol City	42	8	7	6	25	19	3	6	12	13	29	35
19 Coventry	42	7	9	5	34	26	3	6	12	14	33	35
20 Sunderland	42	9	5	7	29	16	2	7	12	17	38	34
21 Stoke	42	9	8	4	21	16	1	6	14	7	35	34
22 Tottenham	42	9	7	5	26	20	3	2	16	22	52	33
	924	240	137	85	753	430	85	137	240	430	753	924

Odds & ends

Double wins: (1) Manchester U.
Double losses: (3) Villa, Ipswich, Newcastle.

Won from behind: (1) Arsenal (a).
Lost from in front: (1) Spurs (a).

High spots: Avoiding relegation, after it looked so likely.
Losing only one of the last 13 league games.

Low spots: Five consecutive league defeats in October, down to 22nd.
Being crushed 0-6 at Sunderland.
An anticlimactic season after reaching the Cup-Winners' Cup final the previous year.

Hammer of the Year: Trevor Brooking.
Ever-presents: (2) Mervyn Day and Trevor Brooking.
Hat-tricks: (0).
Leading scorer: (14) Bryan Robson.

	Appearances						**Goals**			
	Lge	*Sub*	LC	*Sub*	FAC	*Sub*	**Lge**	LC	FAC	**Tot**
Ayris, Johnny	**1**	*2*								
Bonds, Billy	**41**		3		2		**3**			**3**
Brooking, Trevor	**42**		3		2		**4**			**4**
Coleman, Keith	**12**	*1*	2							
Curbishley, Alan	**8**	*2*	1		1		**1**			**1**
Day, Mervyn	**42**		3		2					
Devonshire, Alan	**27**	*1*	1							
Green, Bill	**22**		2		2					
Holland, Pat	**6**		1					2		**2**
Jennings, Billy	**27**	*4*	2		2		**8**		1	**9**
Lampard, Frank	**36**		1		2		**1**			**1**
Lock, Kevin	**25**	*1*	2		2					
McGiven, Mike	**15**	*1*	2							
Orhan, Yilmaz	**1**	*2*	1							
Otulakowski, Anton	**10**	*2*								
Paddon, Graham	**12**		3				**1**	1		**2**
Pike, Geoff	**20**				1		**6**		1	**7**
Radford, John	**18**				1					
Robson, Bryan	**30**				2		**14**			**14**
Robson, Keith	**7**	*2*	1							
Taylor, Alan	**24**	*1*	2		1		**5**	1		**6**
Taylor, Tommy	**36**		3		2					
(own-goals)							**3**			**3**
22 players used	**462**	***19***	**33**		**22**		**46**	**4**	**2**	**52**

Jim Callaghan is introduced to West Ham before the 1980 FA Cup final

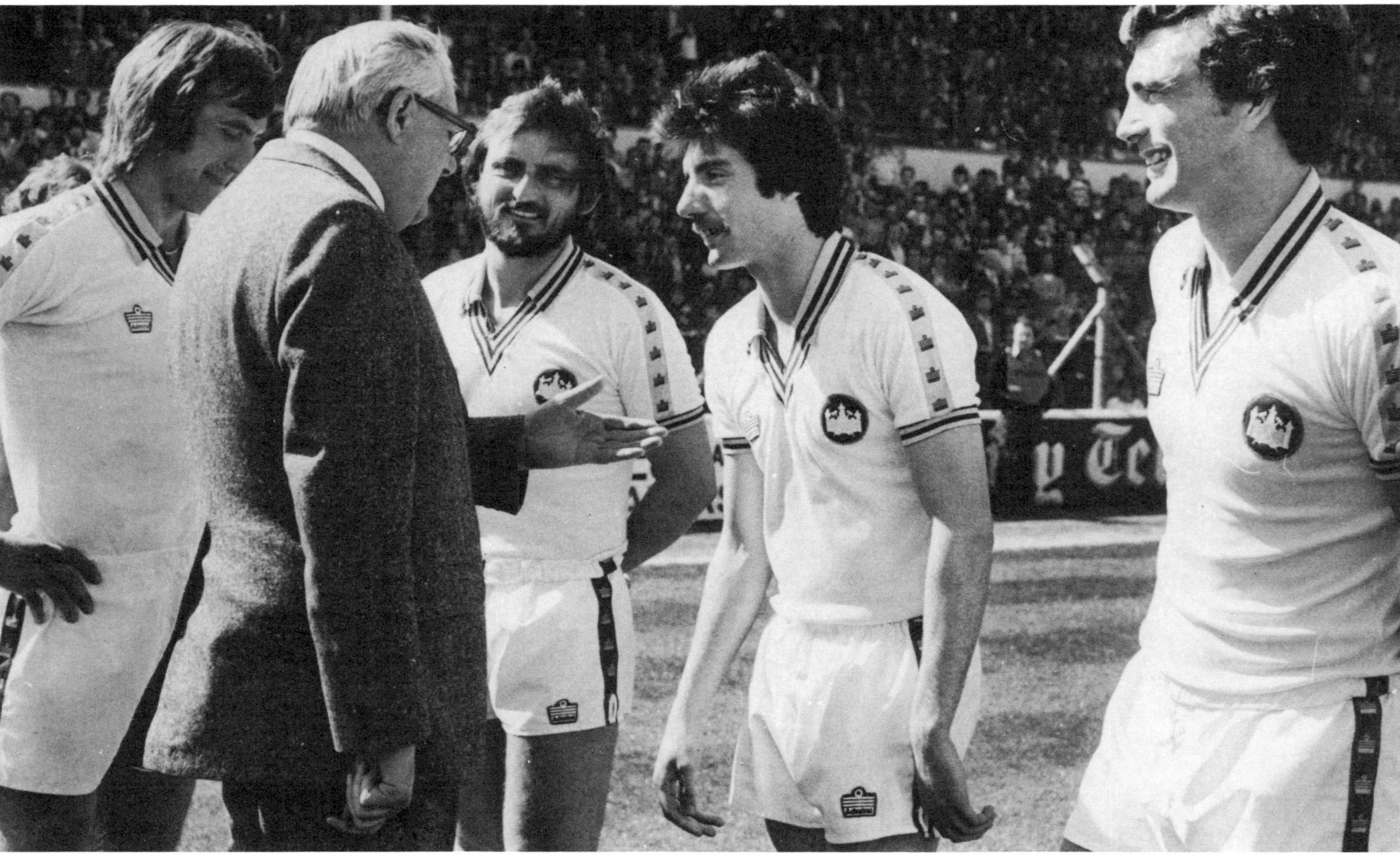

Happy Hammers parade the 1980 FA Cup around Wembley

No	Date	Att	Pos	Pt	F-A	H-T	Scorers, Times, and Referees	1	2	3	4	5	6	7	8	9	10	11	12 sub used
1	H NORWICH			L	1-3	0-1	Robson 71p	Day	Lampard	**Brush**	Pike	Taylor T	Lock	Taylor A	Robson	Radford	Brooking	Devonshire	
	20/8	28,178		–			*Ryan 32, Jones 59, 73*	*Keelan*	*Ryan*	*Sullivan*	*Evans*	*Jones*	*Powell*	*Neighbour*	*Busby*	*Reeves*	*Suggett*	*Gibbins*	
							Ref: K Baker	Ron Greenwood is now manager of England. Keith Robson has signed for Cardiff for £30,000. This awful season-opener did not see its first foul for 15 minutes and so lethargic were the players that the crowd was drifting away before the end. Jones felled Alan Taylor for the penalty.											
2	A LEICESTER			L	0-1	0-0		Day	Brush	Lampard	Pike	Taylor T	Lock	Taylor A	Robson	Radford	Curbishley	Devonshire*	Otulakowski
	24/8	*18,310*		–			*Kember 71*	*Wallington*	*Whitworth*	*Rofe*	*Kember*	*Sims**	*Woollett*	*Alderson*	*Sammels*	*Worthington*	*Kelly*	*Weller*	*Blockley*
							Ref: D Lloyd	Frank Worthington headed down, Day slipped in the mud, and the ball ricocheted off his body and Kember's arm into the net. This cruel goal condemns Hammers to defeat. Brooking was out with a groin strain. Alan Taylor, Pop Robson and Radford missed chances to save the game.											
3	H MANCHESTER C		21	L	0-1	0-0		Day	Lampard	Brush	Pike	Taylor T	Lock	Taylor A*	Robson	Radford	Curbishley	Devonshire	Otulakowski
	27/8	25,278	*4*	–			*Royle 50*	*Corrigan*	*Clements*	*Donachie*	*Doyle*	*Watson*	*Booth*	*Kidd*	*Channon*	*Royle*	*Hartford*	*Tueart*	
							Ref: A Glasson	John Radford is wondering where his first goal is coming from. He joined the Hammers at Christmas but can't find the net. The club face a worrying fine after a 'fan' rushed onto the pitch to grapple with City's Willie Donachie, who was in the process of being booked by the referee.											
4	A NEWCASTLE		18	W	3-2	1-2	Jennings 37, Taylor A 49, Robson 80	Day	Lampard	Brush	Holland	Taylor T	Lock	Taylor A	Robson	Jennings	Curbishley	Devonshire	
	3/9	*26,983*	*20*	2			*Burns 8, Cassidy 23*	*Mahoney*	*Blackhall*	*Kennedy*	*Cassidy*	*McCaffrey*	*Bird*	*McLean*	*Mitchell**	*Burns*	*Oates*	*Craig T*	*Nattrass*
							Ref: W Johnson	Newcastle have also made a dreadful start to the season, allowing a two-goal lead to slip through their fingers. Robson's hopeful cross was headed in by Jennings. Three home defenders then failed to clear Holland's cross, which fell to Alan Taylor. Robson headed a simple winner.											
5	H QP RANGERS		17	D	2-2	1-2	Holland 11, Lock 78	Day	Lampard	Brush	Holland	Taylor T	Lock	Pike	Robson	Jennings*	Curbishley	Devonshire	Otulakowski
	10/9	26,922	*14*	3			*Eastoe 7, Lock 13 (og)*	*Parkes*	*Clement*	*Shanks*	*Hollins*	*Needham*	*Webb*	*Eastoe*	*Francis*	*Masson*	*Bowles*	*Givens**	*Williams*
							Ref: A Robinson	Billy Jennings ruptures an Achilles' tendon; his season is over. Pat Holland is enjoying a rich vein of form, and scores when Tommy Taylor flicks on Lampard's cross to him. Kevin Lock, trying to clear, belted the ball past Day, but made amends with a screamer that rescued a point.											
6	A BRISTOL CITY		20	L	2-3	1-2	Robson 5, Pike 86	Day	Lampard	Brush	Holland	Taylor T	Lock	Taylor A	Robson	Curbishley	Brooking	Devonshire*	Pike
	17/9	*21,180*	*17*	3			*Mabbutt 6, Ritchie 23, 64*	*Shaw*	*Gillies*	*Sweeney*	*Gow*	*Collier*	*Hunter*	*Tainton*	*Ritchie*	*Mabbutt*	*Cormack*	*Whitehead*	
							Ref: L Burden	City bag their first win of the season, recovering from Robson's 30-yard thunderbolt to equalise within seconds. Clive Whitehead laid on both City's first two goals. Day might have saved the second. Though Hammers' problems lie in defence, Lyall wants Swansea striker Alan Curtis.											
7	H EVERTON		17	D	1-1	1-0	Dobson 35 (og)	Day	Lampard	Brush	Holland	Taylor T	McGiven	Taylor A	Robson	Curbishley	Brooking	Devonshire	
	24/9	25,296	*6*	4			*McKenzie 52*	*Wood*	*Darracott*	*Pejic*	*Lyons*	*Higgins*	*Rioch*	*King*	*Dobson*	*Latchford*	*McKenzie*	*Thomas**	*Jones*
							Ref: D Nippard	Pop Robson's header flies into the net off Everton's Martin Dobson. The Toffees equalise when Tommy Taylor is caught dithering in his penalty box and is dispossessed by Duncan McKenzie. London Weekend TV pictures confirm that Robson's disallowed header wasn't offside.											
8	A ARSENAL		20	L	0-3	0-1		Day	Lampard	Brush	Holland	Taylor T	McGiven	Taylor A	Robson	Curbishley*	Brooking	Devonshire	Pike
	1/10	*41,245*	*9*	4			*Stapleton 31, Rice 38, Brady 79p*	*Jennings*	*Rice*	*Nelson*	*Price*	*O'Leary*	*Simpson*	*Brady*	*Ross*	*Macdonald*	*Stapleton*	*Rix*	
							Ref: B Homewood	Hammers' worst display so far. When Jennings saved Devonshire's shot with his feet it amounted to West Ham's one and only serious effort. Stapleton battled past McGiven to score with power; Rice ran from halfway to head in from six yards; and Day toppled Macdonald in the box.											
9	H MIDDLESBROUGH		20	L	0-2	0-0		Day	Lampard	Brush	Holland	Taylor T	McGiven	Taylor A	Robson	**Hales***	Brooking	Pike	Devonshire
	3/10	26,508	*14*	4			*Mills 70, 81*	*Platt*	*Craggs*	*Cooper*	*Souness*	*Boam*	*Ramage*	*Mahoney*	*Mills*	*Ashcroft*	*McAndrew*	*Armstrong*	
							Ref: A Turvey	Derek Hales, formerly of Charlton, has signed from Derby for £110,000. Two minutes into his debut he collides with Alan Ramage and injures his knee. He is subbed early in the second half. The team will now stay in the Grosvenor Hotel prior to turning out for Brooking's testimonial.											
10	H NOTT'M FOREST		20	D	0-0	0-0		Day	Lampard	Brush	Curbishley	Taylor T	McGiven	Devonshire	Robson	Radford	Brooking	Pike	
	8/10	26,126	*1*	5				*Shilton*	*Anderson*	*Barrett*	*McGovern*	*Lloyd*	*Burns*	*O'Neill*	*Bowyer**	*Withe*	*Woodcock*	*Robertson*	*Gemmill*
							Ref: C Maskell	Brian Clough's Forest sit top of the league. He praises the Hammers' fighting spirit, though raises an eyebrow at Frank Lampard launching 20-yard tackles at John Robertson. Lampard had been given the runaround last time he faced the Scot and was determined to keep face this time.											

No	Venue	Opponent	Att	Pos	Res	F-A	H-T	Scorers, Times, and Referees	1	2	3	4	5	6	7	8	9	10	11	12 sub used
11	A	WOLVES		20	D	2-2	2-1	Pike 28, Robson 38	Day	Lampard	Brush	Bonds	Taylor T	Pike	Devonshire	Robson	Radford	Brooking	Hales	
15/10			*19,366*	*13*	6			*Richards 43, Hibbitt 84*	*Bradshaw*	*Palmer*	*Daly*	*Patching*	*Brazier*	*Parkin*	*Hibbitt*	*Carr*	*Richards*	*Bell*	*Sunderland*	
								Ref: B Stevens	Billy Bonds returns after his long injury and adds welcome steel to the Hammers. He also lends an arm, for it is that part of his anatomy that turns Geoff Pike's shot into the net for the first goal. Bonds deflected Kenny Hibbitt's equaliser. John Richards scored his 100th league goal.											
12	H	ASTON VILLA		20	D	2-2	1-1	Taylor T 22, Hales 75	Day	Lampard	Brush	Bonds	Taylor T	Pike	Devonshire	Robson	Radford	Brooking	Hales	
22/10			26,599	*9*	7			*McNaught 27, Gray 78*	*Rimmer*	*Gidman*	*Smith*	*Phillips*	*McNaught*	*Mortimer*	*Deehan**	*Little*	*Gray*	*Cropley*	*Carrodus*	*Cowans*
								Ref: A Gunn	Ron Saunders' Villa have only lost once away. West Ham were winning 2-1 when Day took his eye off the ball to concede a soft equaliser. Back in 1973 Greenwood had said: 'Mervyn will be our first-team goalkeeper for the next 10 years.' It is a heavy burden for the young keeper.											
13	A	IPSWICH		19	W	2-0	1-0	Hales 25, 82	Day	Lampard	Brush	Bonds	Taylor T	Pike	Devonshire	Robson	Radford	Brooking	Hales	
29/10			*27,308*	*10*	9				*Cooper*	*Mills*	*Tibbott*	*Talbot*	*Hunter*	*Osman*	*Osborne**	*Gates*	*Mariner*	*Whymark*	*Woods*	*Geddis*
								Ref: M Sinclair	Ipswich had dropped just one home point, to Liverpool, so this win is a headline-grabber. Radford headed down for Hales to fire past Paul Cooper. Radford made Hales' second goal too, this time a lob. Hales said later that he had never before played alongside a big target man.											
14	A	COVENTRY		19	L	0-1	0-1		Day	Lampard	Brush	Bonds	Taylor T	Pike	Devonshire	Robson	Radford	Brooking	Hales	
5/11			*23,276*	*4*	9			*Wallace 43*	*Blyth*	*Oakey*	*McDonald*	*Yorath*	*Beck*	*Coop*	*Nardiello*	*Wallace*	*Ferguson**	*Powell*	*Hutchison*	*Graydon*
								Ref: E Hughes	Bonds has been named in the England squad. A minute's silence for the death of City chairman Sir Jack Scamp. Gordon Milne's City have lost at home only once, playing just three at the back. Coop shot wide from the spot when Lampard handled. Ian Wallace back-headed the goal.											
15	H	WEST BROM		20	D	3-3	1-2	Robson 20p, Devonshire 48,	Day	Lampard	Brush	Bonds	Taylor T	Pike	Devonshire	Robson	Curbishley	Brooking	Hales	
12/11			23,601	*3*	10			*Wile 37, 39, Cunningham 75*	*Godden*	*Mulligan*	*Statham*	*Brown T*	*Wile*	*Robertson*	*Cantello*	*Cunningham*	*Cross*	*Robson*	*Johnston*	
								Ref: E Read	Brooking has had a testimonial against an England XI. Both Devonshire's goals v WBA took deflections, and the penalty given when the ball was driven against Wile's hand seemed harsh. Wile made amends with two headers. Little Laurie Cunningham also found space to head a goal.											
16	A	DERBY		20	L	1-2	0-1	Bonds 52	Day	Lampard	Brush	Bonds	Taylor T	Pike	Devonshire	Robson	Radford	Brooking	Hales	
19/11			*23,273*	*17*	10			*Nish 11, Rioch 51*	*Middleton*	*Langan*	*Nish*	*Rioch*	*McFarland*	*Todd*	*Curran*	*Hughes*	*Masson*	*George*	*Ryan*	
								Ref: K Walmsley	Derby welcome back Charlie George, who had fractured his cheekbone in a car crash. They need him, having won only one of seven home games. Man-of-the-match Brooking produced a wonderful pass for Bonds to score, but it was not enough to prevent Derby's second home win.											
17	H	LEEDS		20	L	0-1	0-0		Day	Lampard	Brush	Bonds	Taylor T	Pike	Devonshire	Robson	Radford*	Brooking	Hales	Curbishley
26/11			26,883	*9*	10			*Hankin 53*	*Harvey*	*Cherry*	*Gray F*	*Currie*	*Parkinson*	*Madeley*	*Harris*	*Hankin*	*Jordan*	*Flynn*	*Graham*	
								Ref: W Gow	10 minutes into the game John Radford collides accidentally with Tony Currie and breaks his jaw in two places. The Hammers are beaten by Ray Hankin's fierce header from Frank Gray's cross. Despite their late fight-back they now have the worst home record in the Football League.											
18	A	LIVERPOOL		20	L	0-2	0-1		Day	Lampard	Brush	Bonds	Taylor T*	Pike	Devonshire	Robson	Curbishley	Brooking	Hales	Holland
3/12			*39,659*	*4*	10			*Dalglish 37, Fairclough 81*	*Clemence*	*Neal*	*Smith*	*Thompson*	*Kennedy*	*Hughes*	*Dalglish*	*McDermott*	*Heighway*	*Fairclough*	*Callaghan*	
								Ref: A Morrissey	Pat Holland returns after a two-month injury. 20 minutes from time Tommy Taylor dislocates his knee. West Ham had created plenty of chances in the first half but Ray Clemence was equal to them. Lyall wanted to buy Roger Davies from Bruges, but he has signed for Leicester.											
19	H	MANCHESTER U		20	W	2-1	1-1	Hales 6, Brooking 81	Day	Lampard*	Brush	Bonds	Taylor T	Pike	Devonshire	Robson	Curbishley	Brooking	Hales	McDowell
10/12			20,759	*13*	12			*McGrath 19*	*Roche*	*Nicholl*	*Albiston*	*Coppell*	*Greenhoff B*	*Houston*	*McGrath*	*Greenhoff J*	*Pearson*	*Grimes*	*Hill*	
								Ref: A Grey	At last a home win, though Day's fragility in the air almost put paid to it. The continuing ban on Man U's away supporters has the curious effect of making this the lowest gate since February. Ron Greenwood has officially been appointed England manager, so leaves West Ham Utd.											
20	A	WEST BROM		21	L	0-1	0-0		Day	McDowell	Brush	Bonds	Taylor T	Pike	Devonshire	Robson	**Cross**	Brooking	Hales	
17/12			*18,868*	*4*	12			*Brown A 76*	*Godden*	*Mulligan*	*Statham*	*Brown T*	*Wile*	*Robertson*	*Martin*	*Regis*	*Brown A*	*Robson*	*Johnston*	
								Ref: A Hughes	David Cross cost £200,000 from WBA, whom he faces in his first match. Albion were unbeaten at home, so this was a creditable display. The game was lost to a disputed goal. A linesman flagged Tony Brown offside. The ref consulted the linesman but allowed namesake Ally's goal.											
21	H	BIRMINGHAM		19	W	1-0	0-0	Curbishley 87	Day	McDowell	Lampard	Bonds	Taylor T	Pike	Devonshire	Robson	Cross	Brooking	Curbishley	
26/12			25,572	*18*	14				*Montgomery*	*Calderwood*	*Pendrey*	*Towers*	*Howard*	*Want*	*Page*	*Francis*	*Bertschin*	*Hibbitt*	*Emmanuel*	
								Ref: R Lewis	A stomach bug lays low Derek Hales. His place goes to Alan Curbishley, who nets the precious winner. It is 'Whizz's' second league goal of his career, struck from 25 yards, and it needed a slight deflection to get the better of Montgomery. Brooking had hit a post after 10 minutes.											

LEAGUE DIVISION 1 — Manager: John Lyall — SEASON 1977-78

No	Date		Att	Pos	Pt	F-A	H-T	Scorers, Times, and Referees	1	2	3	4	5	6	7	8	9	10	11	12 sub used
22	A	CHELSEA		19	L	1-2	0-1	Robson 71	Day	McDowell	Lampard	Bonds	Taylor T	Pike	Devonshire	Robson	Cross	Brooking	Curbishley	
	27/12		*44,093*	*14*	14			*Langley 34, Garner 77*	*Bonetti*	*Harris*	*Wilkins G*	*Britton*	*Droy*	*Wicks*	*Garner*	*Lewington**	*Langley*	*Swain*	*Walker*	*Finnieston*
								Ref: T Bune	Poor Day makes two more howlers, which are made all the more glaring in the light of Bonetti's brilliance at the other end. Day flapped at Clive Walker's cross for Chelsea's first, then played silly-beggers with Bonds on the six-yard line, allowing Garner to nip in for the winner.											
23	H	LEICESTER		19	W	3-2	2-0	McDowell 4, Hales 31, Cross 65	Ferguson	McDowell	Lampard	Bonds	Taylor T	Curbishley	Devonshire	Robson	Cross	Brooking	Hales	
	31/12		25,455	*22*	16			*Kember 73, Sims 75*	*Wallington*	*Williams**	*Rofe*	*Kember*	*Sims*	*Webb*	*Sammels*	*Davies*	*Hughes*	*Kelly*	*Armstrong*	*Earle*
								Ref: C Maskell	Mervyn Day has at last been dropped and veteran Bobby Ferguson gets a chance to show what he can do. The result? Ferguson permits Steve Kember's 40-yard cross to float over his head. Hammers had been coasting 3-0, but by the final whistle they are hanging on desperately.											
24	A	NORWICH		19	D	2-2	1-0	Devonshire 7, Hales 85	Ferguson	Brush	Lampard	Bonds	Taylor T	Curbishley	Devonshire	Robson	Cross	Brooking	Hales	
	2/1		*29,480*	*8*	17			*Ryan 66p, Peters 78*	*Keelan*	*Bond*	*Sullivan*	*Ryan*	*Jones*	*Powell*	*Neighbour*	*Suggett*	*Gibbins*	*Reeves*	*Peters*	
								Ref: K Baker	Norwich are unbeaten at home but have to turn to Hammers old-boy Martin Peters to rescue them. Bonds shoved him in the back to give away a penalty, a decision which so incensed Robson that he was booked. West Ham secured their point when Hales back-headed Brooking's cross.											
25	A	MANCHESTER C		19	L	2-3	1-2	Brooking 41, Cross 88	Ferguson	McDowell	Lampard	Bonds	Taylor T	Curbishley	Devonshire	Robson	Cross	Brooking	Hales	
	14/1		*43,627*	*5*	17			*Kidd 20, Booth 30, Barnes 57*	*Corrigan*	*Clements**	*Donachie*	*Booth*	*Watson*	*Owen*	*Barnes*	*Bell*	*Kidd*	*Hartford*	*Tueart*	*Channon*
								Ref: P Partridge	The result may appear close but it condemns West Ham to their eighth successive defeat at Maine Road. Trevor Brooking deserved better, making one goal, scoring another. But the damage had already been done. Kidd's header and Booth's shot were executed without interference.											
26	H	NEWCASTLE		19	W	1-0	1-0	Hales 10	Ferguson	McDowell	Lampard	Bonds	Taylor T	Curbishley	Devonshire*	Pike	Cross	Taylor A	Hales	Holland
	21/1		25,461	*21*	19				*Mahoney*	*Nattrass*	*Barker*	*Cassidy**	*Bird*	*Kennedy*	*Burns*	*Hudson*	*McGhee*	*Larnach*	*Barrowclough*	*Gowling*
								Ref: M Taylor	Both sides desperately need to win this four-pointer. The match had too much at stake to make it pretty. When Newcastle failed to withdraw 10 yards at a free-kick, Bonds bulldozed his way into it to make space. McDowell took aim and the ball flew off a defender and the post to Hales.											
27	H	BRISTOL CITY		19	L	1-2	1-1	Robson 13	Day	McDowell	Lampard	Bonds	Taylor T	Green	Devonshire	Robson	Cross	Brooking	Hales*	Taylor A
	11/2		19,934	*14*	19			*Mann 45, Royle 62*	*Shaw*	*Sweeney*	*Merrick*	*Gow*	*Rodgers*	*Hunter*	*Mann*	*Ritchie*	*Royle*	*Cormack*	*Whitehead*	
								Ref: C Thomas	West Ham paid the price for scoring first then falling back to protect their advantage. Derek Hales is suffering from flu and is pulled off to give Alan Taylor a chance to stretch the City defence. He is the only player on Lyall's books able to pose as a winger. The Hammers have no width.											
28	A	EVERTON		19	L	1-2	1-1	Hales 35	Ferguson	Bonds*	Lampard	Pike	Taylor T	Green	Devonshire	Robson	Cross	Brooking	Hales	McDowell
	18/2		*33,862*	*2*	19			*McKenzie 24, Thomas 60*	*Wood*	*Jones*	*Pejic*	*Lyons*	*Higgins*	*Ross*	*King*	*Dobson*	*Latchford**	*McKenzie*	*Thomas*	*Telfer*
								Ref: T Farley	Dave Thomas always seems to turn it on against West Ham. Once Billy Bonds limped off in the second half with a calf strain Hammers had no one capable of dealing with him or cutting out his crosses. Thomas' winner is his first goal for Everton. Ross missed a penalty for the Toffees.											
29	H	ARSENAL		19	D	2-2	0-2	Taylor A 48, Cross 89	Ferguson	McDowell*	Lampard	Curbishley	Taylor T	Green	Devonshire	Robson	Cross	Brooking	Taylor A	Pike
	25/2		31,675	*5*	20			*Macdonald 25, 28*	*Jennings*	*Rice*	*Nelson*	*Price*	*O'Leary*	*Young*	*Brady*	*Sunderland*	*Macdonald*	*Stapleton*	*Rix**	*Walford*
								Ref: R Crabb	Malcolm Macdonald's second goal sparks trouble in the crowd. Hammers' defence had seen the linesman's raised flag and foolishly not played to the whistle. Full-back Pat Rice also appeared to push Cross before crossing for Macdonald's first goal, a header that went in off a post.											
30	A	NOTT'M FOREST		19	L	0-2	0-0		Ferguson	McDowell	Lampard	Curbishley	Taylor T	Green*	Devonshire	Robson	Cross	Brooking	Hales	Holland
	4/3		*33,924*	*1*	20			*Needham 79, Robertson 81p*	*Shilton*	*Bowyer*	*Clark*	*O'Hare*	*Needham*	*Burns*	*O'Neill*	*Gemmill*	*Withe*	*Woodcock*	*Robertson*	
								Ref: K Hackett	Brian Clough admits that had Derek Hales not committed the miss of the century in the 69th minute, his table toppers would have been sunk. Reprieved, they steal the points through Needham's header and a twice-taken penalty after Trevor Brooking had handled O'Hare's cross.											
31	H	WOLVES		20	L	1-2	0-0	Hales 71	Ferguson	McDowell*	Lampard	Curbishley	Taylor T	Bonds	Devonshire	Holland	Cross	Brooking	Hales !	Otulakowski
	11/3		23,525	*17*	20			*Rafferty 50, Carr 60*	*Parkes*	*Palmer*	*Parkin !*	*Daley*	*Hazell*	*McAlle*	*Brazier*	*Carr*	*Richards*	*Rafferty*	*Patching**	*Daly*
								Ref: A Turvey	10 minutes from time Derek Parkin grabs Hales' shirt, Hales swings a punch, and both are sent off. McDowell and Cross both hit the bar in the first half, and Hammers pay the price when Bill Rafferty netted. He had signed from Carlisle and was thought to be on Lyall's wanted list.											

No	H/A	Opponent	Pos	Res	F-A	H-T	Scorers, Times, and Referees	1	2	3	4	5	6	7	8	9	10	11	12 sub used
32	A	QP RANGERS	20	L	0-1	0-1		Ferguson	McDowell	Lampard	Bonds	Taylor T	Curbishley	Devonshire	Holland	Cross	Brooking	Pike	
14/3		*20,394*	*19*	20			*Cunningham 37*	*Parkes*	*Clement*	*Gillard*	*Hollins*	*Howe*	*Cunningham*	*Shanks*	*Busby*	*James**	*Bowles*	*Givens*	*McGee*
							Ref: C Maskell	Six weeks previously QPR had thrashed West Ham 6-1 in the Cup. This time the Hammers were unlucky. They were frustrated by Phil Parkes' save from Devonshire's chip. Tommy Cunningham headed in Leighton James' corner. QPR boss Frank Sibley: 'We played rubbish and won.'											
33	A	ASTON VILLA	20	L	**1-4**	1-2	Brooking 26 *[Mortimer 77]*	Ferguson	McDowell	Lampard	Curbishley	Taylor T	Bonds	Devonshire*	Holland	Cross	Brooking	Hales	**Martin**
18/3		*28,275*	*10*	20			*Gregory 18, 80, Deehan 34,*	*Rimmer*	*Gidman*	*Smith*	*Phillips*	*McNaught*	*Mortimer*	*Gregory*	*Little*	*Deehan*	*Cowans*	*Carrodus*	
							Ref: D Nippard	It is clutching at straws to suggest this result was worse than West Ham deserved. Frank Lampard hit the bar, Trevor Brooking scored a classic goal, but their fate was sealed when Mortimer headed in Carrodus's corner. West Ham, Newcastle and Leicester are now adrift at the bottom.											
34	H	IPSWICH	20	W	**3-0**	0-0	Cross 51, 44, 59	Ferguson	Bonds	Lampard	Curbishley	Taylor T	Green	Pike	Holland	Cross	Brooking	Hales	
24/3		23,867	*17*	22				*Cooper*	*Mills*	*Tibbott*	*Talbot*	*Hunter*	*Beattie*	*Osborne**	*Wark*	*Mariner*	*Turner*	*Woods*	*Lambert*
							Ref: H Robinson	'Our worst performance of the season,' complains Ipswich boss Bobby Robson, after emerging from a stormy session with his players. West Ham completed their second double of the season with a tabloid writer's dream headline: 'Hot Cross Fun.' Two headers and an angled shot.											
35	H	CHELSEA	19	W	3-1	0-1	Brooking 79, Green 88, Holland 89	Ferguson	Bonds	Lampard	Curbishley	Taylor T	Green	Pike	Holland	Cross	Brooking	Robson	
25/3		24,987	*17*	24			*Garner 10*	*Phillips*	*Locke*	*Harris*	*Britton*	*Hay*	*Wicks*	*Finnieston*	*Swain*	*Garner**	*Lewington*	*Walker*	*Langley*
							Ref: J Bent	On 55 minutes Phillips is kicked in the face by Tommy Taylor and is replaced in goal by Langley, leaving Chelsea with 10 men. The incident sparks crowd trouble. Of the game's 36 fouls, 22 were committed by West Ham. Brooking scored from a corner. Bill Green headed the winner.											
36	A	BIRMINGHAM	19	L	0-3	0-2		Ferguson	Bonds	Lampard	Curbishley	Taylor T	Green*	Pike	Holland	Cross	Brooking	Robson	Hales
28/3		*23,554*	*13*	24			*Francis 31, 43p, Bertschin 89*	*Montgomery*	*Calderwood*	*Pendrey*	*Towers*	*Gallagher*	*Howard*	*Page*	*Francis*	*Bertschin*	*Hibbitt*	*Fox*	
							Ref: S Bates	For half an hour Hammers looked the more positive. But Trevor Francis knocked the ball in after Hibbitt had hit the bar and from that moment West Ham were not at the races. Bobby Ferguson brought down Bertschin for the penalty. Hales has been missing rather than scoring recently.											
37	H	COVENTRY	19	W	2-1	1-0	Taylor T 20, Holland 60	Ferguson	Bonds	Lampard	Curbishley	Taylor T	Green	Pike*	Holland	Hales	Brooking	Robson	Martin
1/4		**19,260**	*6*	26			*McDonald 62*	*Blyth*	*Roberts*	*McDonald*	*Yorath*	*Holton*	*Osgood*	*Beck*	*Wallace*	*Thompson**	*Powell*	*Hutchison*	*Coop*
							Ref: R Challis	On this evidence, West Ham want First Division survival more than Coventry want a place in the UEFA Cup. 28-year-old Brooking does not relish life in Division 2 and he plays a stormer, supplying the corner for Tommy Taylor's header and the pass from which Holland netted No 2.											
38	A	LEEDS	18	W	2-1	1-1	Martin 44, Hales 53	Ferguson	Bonds	Brush	Martin	Taylor T	Green	Curbishley	Holland	Hales	Brooking	Robson	
8/4		*22,953*	*7*	28			*Graham 25*	*Harvey*	*Reaney*	*Gray F*	*Flynn*	*Hart*	*Madeley*	*Lorimer*	*Gray E*	*Currie*	*Harris*	*Graham*	
							Ref: K Walmsley	It was 48 years ago that West Ham last won here in Division 1. Alvin Martin, in his first full game, marks Currie out of the match and heads a fine goal. Hales beats the offside trap for the winner. Peter Lorimer misses a 77th-minute penalty, awarded after Currie had run into Robson.											
39	H	DERBY	17	W	**3-0**	2-0	Robson 3, 71, Cross 23	Ferguson	Lampard	Brush	Martin	Taylor T	Green	Curbishley*	Holland	Cross	Brooking	Robson	Otulakowski
15/4		25,424	*14*	30				*Middleton*	*Langan*	*Buckley*	*Rioch*	*McFarland*	*Todd*	*Powell**	*Daly*	*Masson*	*George*	*Nish*	*Bartlett*
							Ref: T Reynolds	The Indian Summer to West Ham's season has brought five wins out of six and probable survival. Robson played despite a severely bruised instep and is rewarded with his first goals in two months. Cross also scored on his return from suspension. Pat Holland was man of the match.											
40	A	MANCHESTER U	19	L	0-3	0-0		Ferguson	Bonds	Lampard	Martin*	Taylor T	Green	Curbishley	Holland	Cross	Brooking	Robson	Brush
22/4		***54,089***	*10*	30			*Grimes 68p, McIlroy 75, Pearson 77*	*Stepney*	*Albiston*	*Houston*	*McIlroy*	*McQueen*	*Buchan*	*Coppell*	*Jordan*	*Pearson*	*Grimes*	*Greenhoff B*	
							Ref: T Mills	Alvin Martin's honeymoon is over. Two second-half blunders result in two penalties for Man U. First he handles under pressure from Jordan. Although Ferguson saves Pearson's spot-kick, he then drags Pearson down. But when Martin topples Jordan in the box, the ref looks away.											
41	A	MIDDLESBROUGH		W	2-1	1-1	Cross 42, 80	Ferguson	Bonds	Lampard	Martin	Taylor T	Green	Curbishley	Holland	Cross	Brooking	Robson	
25/4		***13,247***		32			*Johnston 17*	*Brown*	*Craggs*	*Bailey**	*Johnston*	*Boam*	*Ramage*	*Mills*	*Cummins*	*Ashcroft*	*McAndrew*	*Armstrong*	*Hickton*
							Ref: D Richardson	17-year-old Australian Craig Johnston gives Boro a dream start, but Frank Lampard's chip presents David Cross with an easy equaliser. The winner came from a goalmouth scramble. Keeper David Brown failed to gather a corner cleanly and Cross poked the ball over the goal-line.											
42	H	LIVERPOOL	20	L	0-2	0-1		Ferguson	Bonds	Lampard	Martin	Taylor T*	Green	Curbishley	Holland	Cross	Brooking	Robson	
29/4		**37,448**	*3*	32			*McDermott 39, Fairclough 67*	*Clemence*	*Neal*	*Hansen*	*Thompson*	*Kennedy*	*Hughes*	*Dalglish*	*Case*	*Fairclough*	*McDermott*	*Souness*	
Home		Away					Ref: D Reeves	Even if West Ham win they are not safe, since other strugglers have games to play. Hammers wasted early half-chances, and once Case had set up McDermott's goal Liverpool dominated. Wolves must lose their last two games to go down instead, but on 2 May Wolves beat Aston Villa.											
Average 25,655		28,903																	

League Cup					F-A	H-T	Scorers, Times, and Referees	1	2	3	4	5	6	7	8	9	10	11	12 sub used
2	A	NOTT'M FOREST	21	L	0-5	0-2	*[Woodcock 63, Withe 80]*	Day	Lampard	Brush*	Pike	Green	Lock	Taylor A	Robson	Radford	Curbishley	Devonshire	Otulakowski
30/8		*18,224*	*1*				*O'Neill 10, Bowyer 26, 87,*	*Middleton*	*Anderson*	*Clark*	*McGovern*	*Lloyd*	*Burns*	*O'Neill*	*Bowyer*	*Withe*	*Woodcock*	*Robertson*	
							Ref: D Turner	Clough's Forest inflict West Ham's worst ever defeat in the League Cup. John Robertson handed out the kind of punishment that Lampard will have nightmares over. An early booking was the least of Lampard's worries. Robson and Alan Taylor had missed early chances for Hammers.											

FA Cup																			
3	H	WATFORD	19	W	1-0	0-0	Robson 80	Ferguson	McDowell	Lampard	Bonds	Taylor T	Curbishley*	Devonshire	Robson	Cross	Brooking	Hales	Pike
7/1		36,745	*4:1*					*Rankin*	*Geidmintis*	*Pritchett*	*Booth*	*Bolton*	*Garner*	*Downes**	*Blissett*	*Jenkins*	*Joslyn*	*Mayes*	*Pollard*
							Ref: J Hunting	BBC planned to show this game on Saturday night, then decided against. Viewers missed a thriller. Elton John's money and Graham Taylor's know-how are building a fine team. Blissett missed early chances. West Ham only won after they started pumping high balls over the defence.											
4	H	QP RANGERS	19	D	1-1	1-0	Bonds 43	Ferguson	McDowell	Lampard	Bonds	Taylor T	Curbishley	Devonshire	Robson	Cross	Brooking	Hales	
28/1		35,566	*20*				*Howe 75*	*Parkes*	*Clement*	*Gillard*	*Hollins*	*Howe*	*Abbott*	*Shanks*	*Busby*	*James*	*Bowles*	*Givens*	
							Ref: P Reeves	Torrential rain threatens to postpone the match and in Stan Bowles' opinion it should have. The turning point was Phil Parkes' splendid save from Lampard's thunderbolt, when West Ham were already leading 1-0. QPR capitalised when Ernie Howe headed in John Hollins' free-kick.											
4R	A	QP RANGERS	19	L	1-6	1-1	Robson 4 *[Bowles 70p, James 83]*	Ferguson	McDowell	Lampard	Bonds	Taylor T	Curbishley	Devonshire*	Robson	Cross	Holland	Hales	Taylor A
31/1		*24,057*	*20*				*Givens 38, Hollins 50, Busby 54, 62,*	*Parkes*	*Clement*	*Gillard*	*Hollins*	*Howe*	*Abbott*	*Shanks*	*Busby*	*James*	*Bowles*	*Givens*	
							Ref: P Reeves	Three pitch inspections are necessary. Without Brooking, nursing his ankle, and with Tommy Taylor having a stinker, Hammers are pulverised. Four QPR goals came from set-pieces. Givens equalised Robson's opener from Hollins' free-kick. Tommy Taylor handled for Bowles' penalty.											

		Home					Away					
	P	W	D	L	F	A	W	D	L	F	A	Pts
1 Nott'm Forest	42	15	6	0	37	8	10	8	3	32	16	64
2 Liverpool	42	15	4	2	37	11	9	5	7	28	23	57
3 Everton	42	14	4	3	47	22	8	7	6	29	23	55
4 Manchester C	42	14	4	3	46	21	6	8	7	28	30	52
5 Arsenal	42	14	5	2	38	12	7	5	9	22	25	52
6 West Brom	42	13	5	3	35	18	5	9	7	27	35	50
7 Coventry	42	13	5	3	48	23	5	7	9	27	39	48
8 Aston Villa	42	11	4	6	33	18	7	6	8	24	24	46
9 Leeds	42	12	4	5	39	21	6	6	9	24	32	46
10 Manchester U	42	9	6	6	32	23	7	4	10	35	40	42
11 Birmingham	42	8	5	8	32	30	8	4	9	23	30	41
12 Derby	42	10	7	4	37	24	4	6	11	17	35	41
13 Norwich	42	10	8	3	28	20	1	10	10	24	46	40
14 Middlesbro	42	8	8	5	25	19	4	7	10	17	35	39
15 Wolves	42	7	8	6	30	27	5	4	12	21	37	36
16 Chelsea	42	7	11	3	28	20	4	3	14	18	49	36
17 Bristol City	42	9	6	6	37	26	2	7	12	12	27	35
18 Ipswich	42	10	5	6	32	24	1	8	12	15	37	35
19 QP Rangers	42	8	8	5	27	26	1	7	13	20	38	33
20 WEST HAM	42	8	6	7	31	28	4	2	15	21	41	32
21 Newcastle	42	4	6	11	26	37	2	4	15	16	41	22
22 Leicester	42	4	7	10	16	32	1	5	15	10	38	22
	924	223	132	107	741	490	107	132	223	490	741	924

Odds & ends

Double wins: (2) Newcastle, Ipswich.
Double losses: (3), Manchester C, Bristol C, Liverpool.

Won from behind: (4) Newcastle (a), Chelsea (h), Leeds (a), Midd'bro (a).
Lost from in front: (3) Bristol C (h&a), QPR FAC (a).

High spots: Five league wins out of six in March and April to stand a fair chance of avoiding relegation.

Low spots: Relegation.
Having to wait three days after the last match, v Liverpool, to have that fate confirmed.
Failing to beat any of the top six sides in the league.
Taking just one point from seven games in February and March.
Suffering their heaviest ever defeats in League Cup and FA Cup in the same season (by Forest and QPR respectively).

Hammer of the Year: Trevor Brooking.
Ever-presents: (0).
Hat-tricks: (1) David Cross.
Leading scorer: (11) Bryan Robson.

	Appearances						Goals			
	Lge	*Sub*	LC	*Sub*	FAC	*Sub*	**Lge**	LC	FAC	**Tot**
Bonds, Billy	**29**				3		**1**		1	**2**
Brooking, Trevor	**37**				2		**4**			**4**
Brush, Paul	**23**	*1*	1							
Cross, David	**21**				3		**9**			**9**
Curbishley, Alan	**31**	*1*	1		3		**1**			**1**
Day, Mervyn	**23**		1							
Devonshire, Alan	**32**	*2*	1		3		**3**			**3**
Ferguson, Bobby	**19**				3					
Green, Bill	**13**		1				**1**			**1**
Hales, Derek	**23**	*1*			3		**10**			**10**
Holland, Pat	**18**	*3*			1		**3**			**3**
Jennings, Billy	**2**						**1**			**1**
Lampard, Frank	**40**		1		3					
Lock, Kevin	**6**		1				**1**			**1**
Martin, Alvin	**5**	*2*					**1**			**1**
McDowell, John	**12**	*2*			3		**1**			**1**
McGiven, Mick	**4**									
Otulakowski, Anton		*5*								
Pike, Geoff	**25**	*3*	1			*1*	**2**			**2**
Radford, John	**10**		1							
Robson, Bryan	**37**		1		3		**9**		2	**11**
Taylor, Alan	**10**	*1*	1			*1*	**2**			**2**
Taylor, Tommy	**42**				3		**2**			**2**
(own-goals)							**1**			**1**
23 players used.	**462**	*21*	**11**		**33**	*2*	**52**		**3**	**55**

Liverpool's Terry McDermott handles in the 1981 League Cup final

Ray Stewart fires a penalty past Liverpool's Ray Clemence in the 1981 League Cup final

No	Date		Att	Pos	Pt	F-A	H-T	Scorers, Times, and Referees	1	2	3	4	5	6	7	8	9	10	11	12 sub used
1	H	NOTTS CO			W	5-2	4-0	Cross 9, 20, 59, Blockley 11 (og),	Ferguson	Lampard	Brush	Holland	Taylor T	Bonds	Curbishley	Devonshire	Cross	Brooking	Robson	
	19/8		25,387		2			*McCulloch 61, 68* [Devonshire 16]	*McManus*	*Richards*	*O'Brien*	*Benjamin*	*Blockley*	*Stubbs*	*Carter*	*McCulloch*	*Hooks**	*Mann*	*Vinter*	*McVay*
								Ref: H Robinson	This astonishing match sees West Ham 4-0 up after 20 minutes. Frank Lampard made the first three goals with crosses or free-kicks, the most enjoyable of which saw Jeff Blockley bullet an own-goal. But when Ferguson started spilling crosses an unthinkable fightback looked possible.											
2	A	NEWCASTLE			W	3-0	1-0	Devonshire 6, Cross 60, Robson 71	Ferguson	Lampard	Brush	Holland	Taylor T	Bonds	Curbishley	Devonshire	Cross	Brooking*	Robson	Taylor A
	23/8		*27,233*		4				*Mahoney*	*Kelly*	*Barker*	*Cassidy*	*Bird*	*Blackley*	*Walker*	*Suggett*	*Pearson*	*Hibbitt*	*Connolly*	
								Ref: M Peck	Newcastle field six new players since they were relegated, but they are powerless to prevent Brooking's neat pass to Devonshire, who cuts inside two defenders to score. Brooking limped off after 28 minutes, and West Ham were grateful for their second goal, set up by Devonshire.											
3	A	CRYS PALACE		2	D	1-1	1-1	Taylor A 42	Ferguson	Lampard	Brush	Holland	Taylor T	Bonds	Curbishley	Devonshire	Cross	Taylor A	Robson	
	26/8		*32,611*	*6*	5			*Gilbert 45*	*Burridge*	*Hinshelwood*	*Sansom*	*Chatterton*	*Cannon*	*Gilbert*	*Nicholas*	*Murphy*	*Swindlehurst*	*Elwiss*	*Hilaire*	
								Ref: Ref: T Reynolds	This match is best remembered for Billy Gilbert's freak equaliser for Palace on the stroke of half-time. Hit from 35 yards, the ball dipped and swerved and completely bemused Ferguson. His captain, Bonds, exonerates him from blame. Stoke overtake West Ham to go top of the table.											
4	H	FULHAM		4	L	0-1	0-1		Ferguson	Lampard	Brush	Holland	Taylor T	Bonds	Curbishley	Pike	Cross	Taylor A*	Robson	McDowell
	2/9		25,778	*18*	5			*Margerrison 16*	*Peyton*	*Strong*	*Lock*	*Money*	*Banton*	*Gale*	*Bullivant*	*Davies*	*Mahoney*	*Margerrison*	*Evanson*	
								Ref: C Maskell	Minus Brooking and Devonshire, West Ham laboured. Fulham made ex-Hammer Kevin Lock skipper for the day. Evanson's long ball enabled John Margerrison to lob Ferguson, after which Fulham defended in depth. Bonds was pushed into midfield as West Ham grew desperate.											
5	A	BURNLEY		7	L	2-3	2-1	Cross 33, 35	Ferguson	Lampard	Brush	Holland	Taylor T	Bonds	Curbishley	Devonshire	Cross	Martin	Robson	
	9/9		*12,303*	*4*	5			*Brennan 37, Fletcher 50, Thomson 82*	*Stevenson*	*Scott*	*Brennan*	*Noble*	*Thomson*	*Rodaway*	*Cochrane*	*Hall*	*Fletcher*	*Kindon*	*Smith*	
								Ref: A Challinor	Lyall cannot explain how his team can look so good in the first half and so bad in the second. Both Robson and Martin hit the wood. Fletcher levelled with a blind-side goal that might have been averted, and Thomson hit the winner when Bonds and Ferguson left the ball to each other.											
6	H	BRISTOL ROV		4	W	2-0	0-0	Robson 59, Brooking 76	Ferguson	Lampard	Brush	Holland	Taylor T	Bonds	Curbishley	Devonshire	Cross !	Brooking	Robson	
	16/9		22,189	*11*	7				*Thomas*	*Pulis*	*Bater*	*Day*	*Taylor*	*Prince*	*Dennehy**	*Williams*	*Staniforth*	*Randall*	*Barry*	*Hendrie*
								Ref: R Toseland	Ironically, it was the 52nd-minute dismissal of David Cross that changed the course of the game. Cross had been fouling all afternoon, and his expulsion for lunging at Graham Day was inevitable. From that moment West Ham stopped tossing up high balls. Robson netted with a header.											
7	H	SHEFFIELD UTD		3	W	2-0	0-0	Robson 75p, 84 p	Ferguson	Lampard*	Brush	Holland	Taylor T	Bonds	Curbishley	Devonshire	Jennings	Brooking	Robson	Pike
	23/9		24,361	*18*	9				*Conroy*	*Cutbush*	*Calvert*	*Kenworthy*	*Matthews*	*Keeley*	*Guy**	*Speight*	*Franks*	*Sabella*	*Hamson*	*Anderson*
								Ref: A Robinson	Two penalties seal the Blades' fate. The first was a result of Chris Calvert fisting out Lampard's effort; the second was given when Brooking's cross smacked against Tony Kenworthy at close range. Blades' boss Harry Haslam set out to defend, which negated Alex Sabella's skills.											
8	A	SUNDERLAND		6	L	1-2	0-1	Cross 59	Ferguson	McDowell	Brush	Holland	Taylor T	Bonds	Curbishley	Devonshire	Cross	Brooking	Robson	
	30/9		*23,676*	*5*	9			*Rowell 27p, 71*	*Siddall*	*Coady*	*Rostron*	*Docherty*	*Clarke*	*Elliott*	*Chisholm*	*Lee*	*Entwhistle*	*Brown*	*Rowell*	
								Ref: C Seel	A mysterious penalty set West Ham on the road to defeat. Brush was alleged to have hauled back Rowell, a decision which led to bookings for Robson and Tommy Taylor. Rowell netted himself, then scored a second with a mis-hit shot that trundled wide of the wrong-footed Ferguson.											
9	H	MILLWALL		4	W	3-0	1-0	Robson 35, 71, 75p	Ferguson	Lampard	Brush	Holland	Taylor T	Bonds	Curbishley	Devonshire	Cross	Brooking	Robson	
	7/10		22,000	*22*	11				*Cuff*	*Hamilton B**	*Gregory*	*Tagg*	*Kitchener*	*Gale*	*Donaldson*	*Seasman*	*Mitchell*	*Pearson*	*Walker*	*Cross*
								Ref: C White	Basement club Millwall have scored just one away goal, so this result goes to form. Devonshire revelled in the space afford by the Lions' obsession with tight-marking Brooking. Leaflets distributed before the game warned of crowd trouble; a police helicopter hovered overhead.											
10	A	OLDHAM		3	D	2-2	1-0	Robson 6, 47	Ferguson	Lampard	Brush	Holland	Taylor T	Bonds	Curbishley*	Devonshire	Cross	Brooking	Robson	McDowell
	14/10		*10,143*	18	12			*Taylor 69, 74*	*McDonnell*	*Wood*	*Blair*	*Bell*	*Hicks**	*Hurst*	*Valentine*	*Taylor*	*Young*	*Chapman*	*Gardner*	
								Ref: B Newsome	West Ham took their foot off the throttle after half-time. Brooking could have sealed the win but missed an inviting chance when Hammers were 2-0 ahead. But his miss fired up Oldham, who equalised through two goals from Steve Taylor, following a free-kick and a corner.											

No	Venue	Opponent	Att	Pos	Pts	Res	F-A	H-T	Scorers, Times, Referees	1	2	3	4	5	6	7	8	9	10	11	12
11	H	STOKE		5		D	1-1	0-0	Brooking 85	Ferguson	McDowell	Brush	Holland	Taylor T	Bonds	Curbishley	Devonshire	Cross	Brooking	Robson	
21/10			27,859	2	13				*Richardson 89*	*Jones*	*Marsh*	*Scott*	*Kendall*	*Smith*	*Doyle*	*Dodd*	*Irvine*	*O'Callaghan*	*Crooks*	*Richardson*	
									Ref: T Bune	Alan Durban's Stoke look a capable team, though when Cross heads down for Brooking to slide a late goal it looked curtains. City are grateful to McDowell's even later error, hooking a clearance against Sammy Irvine to put Stoke in possession. O'Callaghan headed on to Richardson.											
12	A	BRIGHTON		4		W	2-1	2-1	Robson 27, 43	Day	McDowell	Brush	Holland	Taylor T	Bonds	Curbishley	Devonshire	Cross	Brooking	Robson	
28/10			*32,634*	*12*	15				*Sayer 39*	*Moseley*	*Tiler*	*Williams*	*Horton*	*Rollings**	*Lawrenson*	*Ryan*	*Ward*	*Maybank*	*Clark*	*O'Sullivan*	*Sayer*
									Ref: R Lewis	33-year-old Pop Robson has turned down an offer to return north as player-manager of Darlington. Paul Brush laid on both goals with left-wing crosses. Tommy Taylor sports a cut eye following a clash with Maybank. His defiance was typical of Hammers' battling back four.											
13	H	PRESTON		2		W	3-1	1-1	Lampard 19, Devonshire 64, Cross 89	Day	Lampard	Brush	Holland	Taylor T	Bonds	Curbishley	Devonshire	Cross	Brooking	Robson	
4/11			23,579	*21*	17				*Thomson 37*	*Tunks*	*McMahon*	*Cameron*	*Doyle*	*Baxter*	*O'Riordan*	*Coleman*	*Haslegrave*	*Robinson*	*Thomson*	*Bruce*	
									Ref: L Burden	Lyall is away scouting, dampening speculation that he is about to sell Brooking to Coventry. Bonds' continuing vendetta with Alex Bruce costs West Ham a goal. Bonds was out of position when Thomson fired in from 30 yards. In injury-time Taylor handled, but Thomson shot wide.											
14	A	NOTTS CO		4		L	0-1	0-0		Day	Lampard	Brush	Holland	Taylor T	Bonds	Curbishley	Devonshire	Cross	Brooking	Robson	
11/11			*11,002*	*11*	17				*O'Brien 81p*	*McManus*	*Richards*	*O'Brien*	*Benjamin*	*Stubbs*	*Mann*	*McCulloch*	*Masson*	*Hooks*	*Hunt*	*Vinter*	
									Ref: N Ashley	Notts Co are unbelievably negative, playing five men in defence even when at home. Had West Ham come to defend, there wouldn't have been a contest at all. County cannot believe their luck as Robson misses several chances and Brush topples Paul Hooks to concede a late penalty.											
15	H	CRYS PALACE		3		D	1-1	1-0	Bonds 31	Day	Lampard	Brush	Holland*	Taylor T	Bonds	Curbishley	Devonshire	Cross	Brooking	Robson	Taylor A
18/11			31,245	*1*	18				*Elwiss 75*	*Burridge*	*Fenwick*	*Sansom*	*Kember*	*Cannon*	*Gilbert*	*Nicholas*	*Murphy*	*Swindlehurst*	*Walsh*	*Hilaire**	*Elwiss*
									Ref: R Kirkpatrick	Leaders Palace have only lost once away. They trail to Bonds' goal for a long time until Murphy shoots. Day half-saves, but the ball comes off his arm to Elwiss. Day hangs his head. Five minutes from time Alan Taylor comes on in an attempt to inject width. But it is far too late.											
16	A	FULHAM		3		D	0-0	0-0		Day	Lampard	Brush	Holland	Taylor T	Bonds	Curbishley	Devonshire	Cross	Taylor A	Robson	
21/11			*26,556*	*4*	19					*Peyton*	*Evans*	*Strong*	*Lock*	*Money*	*Gale*	*Margerrison*	*Evanson*	*Guthrie*	*Beck*	*Greenaway*	
									Ref: M Baker	West Ham won on points, so to speak, with central defenders Bonds and Taylor giving Fulham barely a sniff at goal. But Bonds' booking – his fifth – for a foul on John Evanson will earn him a three-match ban. Trevor Brooking missed the game, having twisted an ankle in training.											
17	A	LEICESTER		3		W	2-1	1-0	Cross 20, 83	Day	Lampard	Brush	Holland	Taylor T	Bonds	McDowell	Devonshire	Cross	Taylor A	Robson	
25/11			*16,149*	*17*	21				*Christie 56*	*Wallington*	*Whitworth*	*Rofe*	*May*	*Williams*	*Kelly*	*Weller*	*Ridley*	*Christie*	*Henderson**	*Hughes*	*Goodwin*
									Ref: A Morrissey	Lyall admitted afterwards that Jock Wallace's Leicester had been hard done by. City pounded forward after Cross had swept in Alan Taylor's cross, though it took another Day fumble – dropping Weller's free-kick – to let in Christie. Cross's spectacular winner came out of the blue.											
18	H	CAMBRIDGE		3		W	5-0	1-0	Taylor A 3, Robson 69, 88, Bonds 86, [Curbishley 87]	Day	Lampard	Brush	Holland	Taylor T	Bonds	Curbishley	Devonshire	Cross	Taylor A	Robson	
2/12			21,379	*15*	23					*Webster*	*Corbin**	*Smith L*	*Stringer*	*Fallon*	*Leach*	*Christie*	*Spriggs*	*Garner*	*Finney*	*Biley*	*Murray*
									Ref: L Shapter	Bonds staged a 90-minute commercial for his coming testimonial against Spurs with this all-action display. He heads in Holland's corner and bows out for a three-match ban. Alan Taylor's diving header divided the teams for over an hour, during which Alan Biley wasted a free header.											
19	A	WREXHAM		3		L	3-4	1-2	Cross 26, Lampard 84, Robson 89	Day	Lampard	Brush	Holland	Taylor T	Martin	Curbishley	Devonshire	Cross	Taylor A	Robson	
9/12			*15,787*	*6*	23				*Lyons 1, 21p, 49 p, Hill 53*	*Davies*	*Jones J*	*Dwyer*	*Davis*	*Roberts J*	*Cegielski*	*Shinton*	*Sutton*	*McNeil**	*Lyons*	*Hill*	*Evans*
									Ref: K Hackett	A 34-second goal and two penalties. That sums up West Ham's misery at the Racecourse Ground. John Lyons was responsible for all three – netting the quick-fire opener from Bobby Shinton's pass, then netting twice from the spot after Devonshire fouled Shinton and Martin handled.											
20	H	CHARLTON		3		W	2-0	1-0	Robson 37, Cross 63	Day	Lampard	Brush	Holland*	Taylor T	McDowell	Curbishley	Devonshire	Cross	Taylor A	Robson	Pike
16/12			23,833	*11*	25					*Wood*	*Shaw*	*Campbell*	*Gritt*	*Shipperley*	*Berry*	*Brisley*	*Robinson**	*Flanagan*	*Madden*	*Peacock*	*Powell*
									Ref: M Sinclair	Pop Robson nets his 200th league goal – a sweet half-volley from 20 yards. It is his 17th goal of the season. Stand-in skipper Frank Lampard supplied the pass for David Cross to dive waist-high among the flying boots and nod the ball into the net via the keeper's body and the post.											
21	H	ORIENT		4		L	0-2	0-1		Day	Lampard	Brush	Pike	Taylor T	McDowell	Curbishley*	Devonshire	Cross	Taylor A	Robson	Jennings
26/12			29,220	*10*	25				*Mayo 17, Chiedozie 85*	*Jackson*	*Fisher*	*Roffey*	*Grealish*	*Gray N*	*Went*	*Kitchen*	*Moores*	*Mayo*	*Chiedozie*	*Coates**	*Banjo*
									Ref: C Downey	Upton Park's second highest gate of the season saw this Boxing Day upset. Without Bonds and Brooking, West Ham lacked bite and flair. Orient went ahead when Moores nodded the ball over and Joe Mayo tapped it in. Chiedozie's goal was special, running from the halfway line.											

LEAGUE DIVISION 2 — Manager: John Lyall — SEASON 1978-79

No	Date	Att	Pos	Pt	F-A	H-T	Scorers, Times, and Referees	1	2	3	4	5	6	7	8	9	10	11	12 sub used
22	H BLACKBURN		4	W	4-0	1-0	Robson 33, Taylor A 60, Cross 64,	Day	Lampard	Brush	Bonds	Martin	McDowell	Taylor A	Devonshire	Cross	Brooking	Robson	
	30/12	21,269	*21*	27			[Curtis 67 (og)]	*Butcher*	*Hird*	*Curtis*	*Metcalfe*	*Keeley*	*Round*	*Fowler*	*Radford*	*Craig**	*Garner*	*Birchenall*	*Morris*
							Ref: P Reeves	Brooking returns to spark three goals. Though they are next to bottom, over the years no team has won at the Boleyn in the league as frequently as Rovers, though they seldom looked likely to add to their 13 wins on this freezing afternoon. Curtis rubbed it in with his headed own-goal.											
23	A BRISTOL ROV		4	W	1-0	1-0	Robson 34	Day	McDowell	Brush	Curbishley	Martin	Bonds	Taylor A	Devonshire	Cross	Brooking	Robson	
	20/1	12,418	*13*	29				*Thomas*	*Day*	*Bater*	*Harding*	*Taylor*	*Aitken*	*Emmanuel*	*Williams**	*White*	*Staniforth*	*Hendrie*	*Dennehy*
							Ref: T Reyolds	Rovers' second home defeat of the season is mostly down to Trevor Brooking, who treats the pitch as if it were his own. Off the pitch, the air is thick with transfer talk. Chelsea's centre-half Steve Wicks is said to be headed for Upton Park. If he comes, is that the end for Tommy Taylor?											
24	H SUNDERLAND		4	D	3-3	1-2	Cross 22, 58, Robson 50	Day	McDowell	Brush	Curbishley	Taylor T	Bonds	Holland	Devonshire	Cross	Brooking	Robson*	Jennings
	10/2	24,998	*5*	30			*Lee 3, Rostron 35, 63*	*Siddall*	*Henderson*	*Gilbert*	*Arnott*	*Clarke*	*Elliott*	*Chisholm*	*Rostron*	*Entwhistle*	*Lee*	*Rowell*	
							Ref: R Hamil	A match of gladiatorial cruelty. Mervyn Day, Young Footballer of the Year in 1975, makes a hash of Sunderland's second goal and is jeered off the pitch. All this overshadowed Robson's volley, his 20th goal of the season, and Lee's bad back-pass that let in Cross for Hammers' third.											
25	H OLDHAM		4	W	3-0	1-0	Holland 21, Martin 59, Robson 83	**Parkes**	McDowell	Brush	Curbishley	Martin	Bonds	Holland	Devonshire	Cross	Brooking	Robson	
	24/2	26,052	*19*	32				*McDonnell*	*Wood*	*Blair*	*Bell*	*Hicks**	*Hurst*	*Keegan*	*Halom*	*Young*	*Chapman*	*Gardner*	*Heaton*
							Ref: R Challis	Day is finished. Phil Parkes has signed from QPR for a world record £565,000. He is an instant hit with the Upton park crowd, saving Alan Young's header with aplomb. There is thankfully no animosity between Day and his successor, who both shake hands warmly before kick-off.											
26	A LUTON		3	W	4-1	1-0	Cross 6, 88, Devonshire 60, Robson 89	Parkes	McDowell	Brush	Curbishley	Martin	Bonds	Holland	Devonshire	Cross	Brooking	Robson	
	26/2	*14,205*	*10*	34			*Turner 75*	*Findlay*	*Stephens*	*Aizlewood*	*West*	*Turner C*	*Price*	*Silkman*	*Carr*	*Taylor*	*Hatton*	*Hill*	
							Ref: D Civil	West Ham's early goal, deflected in off the bar, sparked a sustained spell of Luton pressure. Hatton headed against Phil Parkes' crossbar. A second Hammers goal was followed soon after by Turner's header. Two late clinchers take West Ham above Crystal Palace on goal-difference.											
27	A STOKE		4	L	0-2	0-1		Parkes	McDowell	Brush	Curbishley	Martin	Bonds	Holland	Devonshire	Cross	Brooking	Robson	
	3/3	*24,912*	*1*	34			*Doyle 9, Randall 85*	*Jones*	*Dodd*	*Scott*	*Kendall*	*Smith*	*Doyle*	*Randall*	*Irvine*	*O'Callaghan*	*Crooks*	*Richardson*	
							Ref: J Bray	On the way to the stadium the windscreen of the team coach shattered, showering glass over all those seated near the front, and especially Phil Parkes. He is lucky to escape serious lacerations. In pouring rain Mike Doyle heads Stoke in front, after which Hammers look impotent.											
28	H BRIGHTON		5	D	0-0	0-0		Parkes	Lampard	Brush	Curbishley	Martin	Bonds	Holland	Devonshire	Cross	McDowell	Robson	
	10/3	35,802	*1*	35				*Steele*	*Cattlin*	*Williams*	*Horton*	*Rollings*	*Lawrenson*	*Ryan*	*Ward**	*Maybank*	*Clark*	*O'Sullivan*	*Poskett*
							Ref: D Hutchinson	Alan Mullery's Brighton set up an eight-man defensive barricade to face a Hammers team depleted by the late withdrawal of flu-stricken Trevor Brooking. Paul Clark had been designated to mark him. Now he had other duties to perform, including being booked for time-wasting.											
29	A PRESTON		5	D	0-0	0-0		Parkes	Lampard	Brush	McDowell	Martin	Bonds	Holland	Devonshire	Cross	Brooking	Robson	
	17/3	*15,376*	*12*	36				*Tunks*	*Taylor*	*Cameron*	*Doyle**	*Baxter*	*O'Riordan*	*Coleman*	*Haslegrave*	*Elliott*	*Potts*	*Bruce*	*Wilson*
							Ref: M Peck	This match was billed as the 'High Noon' shoot-out between Division 2's top scorers, Alex Bruce and Pop Robson. In the event it was a dreary match with hardly a shot fired in anger at either end. Preston boss Nobby Stiles was diplomatic enough to say that West Ham were going up.											
30	H NEWCASTLE		5	W	5-0	4-0	Devonshire 20, Robson 22, Lampard 34,	Parkes	Lampard	Brush	McDowell	Martin	Bonds	Holland	Devonshire	Cross	Brooking*	Robson	Pike
	24/3	24,650	*16*	38			[McDowell 37, 50]	*Hardwick*	*Brownlie*	*Mitchell*	*Martin*	*Bird*	*Nattrass*	*Shoulder*	*Walker**	*Withe*	*Hibbitt*	*Connolly*	*Wharton*
							Ref: D Biddle	Just before half-time Brooking limps off with a twisted ankle. But by then the damage had been done. Oddly, only one of the four goals already scored was manufactured by Brooking. McDowell scored his first 'double' for the Hammers. This game was shown on ITV's *The Big Match*.											
31	H LEICESTER		5	D	1-1	0-0	Robson 58	Parkes	Lampard	Brush	McDowell*	Martin	Bonds	Holland	Devonshire	Cross	Pike	Robson B	Curbishley
	31/3	23,992	*12*	39			*Henderson 51*	*Wallington*	*Goodwin*	*Rofe*	*Williams*	*May*	*O'Neill*	*Peake*	*Kelly*	*Henderson*	*Buchanan**	*Smith*	*Ridley*
							Ref: L Shapter	Jock Wallace's young Leicester team go in front when Henderson eludes Bonds and heads past Parkes. Robson levelled, heading in a cross from Devonshire. Near the end a post denied Devonshire the winner. After the game Anton Otulakowski was transferred to Southend United.											

No	Date	Venue	Opponent	Att	Pos	Pts	Res	F-A	H-T	Scorers, Times, and Referees	1	2	3	4	5	6	7	8	9	10	11	12 sub used
32		A	SHEFFIELD UTD		5		L	0-3	0-1		Parkes	Lampard	Brush	McDowell	Martin	Bonds	Holland	Devonshire	Cross	Pike	Robson	
	2/4			*17,720*	*18*	39				*Finnieston 42, Anderson 46, 59*	*Conroy*	*Speight*	*Tibbott*	*Kenworthy*	*MacPhail*	*Matthews*	*Anderson*	*Rioch*	*Finnieston*	*Sabella*	*Hamson*	
										Ref: J Hough	Those who say West Ham are a one-man team find support in this limp showing. Brooking's ankle keeps him out, and no one else provides any spark. Blades' Argentine, Alex Sabella, rules imperiously over the pitch. Steve Finnieston headed in at the near post from Matthews' corner.											
33		A	CAMBRIDGE		5		D	0-0	0-0		Parkes	Lampard*	Brush	Bonds	Martin	Taylor T	Holland	Devonshire	Cross	McDowell	Robson	Pike
	7/4			*11,406*	*12*	40					*Webster*	*Graham*	*Smith L*	*Stringer*	*Fallon*	*Murray*	*Christie**	*Spriggs*	*Buckley*	*Finney*	*Biley*	*Garner*
										Ref: A Jenkins	Cambridge are the division's draw specialists. This is their 10th at home. The home side welcome their biggest ever league crowd, but the game does not deserve them. Hammers came nearest when Robson's header came back off the bar and bounced to the feet of keeper Webster.											
34		H	LUTON		5		W	1-0	0-0	Carr 65 (og)	Parkes	McDowell	Brush	Bonds	Martin	Taylor T	Holland	Devonshire	**Morgan**	Pike	Robson	
	9/4			25,498	*6*	42					*Findlay*	*Stephens*	*Aizlewood*	*Donaghy*	*P-Masters*	*Carr*	*Hill*	*West*	*Stein*	*Hatton*	*Moss**	*Taylor*
										Ref: D Reeves	Cross's twisted ankle permits a debut for Nicky Morgan, who was told he was playing one hour before kick-off. The points were won when Pike's low cross was turned in by David Carr. Luton boss David Pleat was angry that McDowell's 'foul' on David Moss wasn't a penalty.											
35		A	ORIENT		5		W	2-0	1-0	Holland 5, Pike 89	Parkes	McDowell	Brush	Bonds	Martin	Taylor T	Holland	Devonshire	Cross	Pike	Robson	
	14/4			*17,517*	*9*	44					*Jackson*	*Hughton*	*Roffey*	*Grealish*	*Gray N*	*Went*	*Chiedozie*	*Moores*	*Mayo**	*Whittle*	*Coates*	*Clarke*
										Ref: R Lewis	Pike's spectacular goal was missed by those who left early. He sprinted 25 yards to fire an explosive shot from a similar range past Jackson. Holland would have been forgiven a sigh, for he had scored a slick goal himself, from a tight angle. Now the headlines would belong to Pike.											
36		H	CARDIFF		5		D	1-1	1-0	Holland 6	Parkes	McDowell	Brush	Bonds	Martin	Taylor T	Holland	Devonshire	Cross	Pike	Robson	
	16/4			29,058	*19*	45				*Bishop 79*	*Healey*	*Jones*	*Sullivan*	*Campbell*	*Roberts*	*Dwyer*	*Bishop*	*Evans*	*Moore*	*Stevens*	*Buchanan*	
										Ref: A Glasson	Both teams are fighting desperate battles, albeit at either end of the division. Holland's brave header might have clinched the points, but Ray Bishop's volley – one of the best goals seen at the Boleyn all season – means both clubs are likely to stay in the Second Division next season.											
37		A	CHARLTON		5		D	0-0	0-0		Parkes	McDowell	Brush	Bonds	Martin	Taylor T	Holland	Devonshire	Cross	Pike	Jennings*	Lampard
	21/4			*22,816*	*17*	46					*Johns*	*Shaw*	*Campbell*	*Tydeman*	*Berry*	*Madden*	*Powell*	*Robinson*	*Gritt*	*Peacock*	*Churchouse**	*Brisley*
										Ref: M Sinclair	Charlton's biggest gate of the season. Robson is out with a groin strain. Billy Jennings is recalled but pulls a hamstring after just 13 minutes. Devonshire's 'goal' was disallowed because Jennings was lying injured in an offside position. Parkes keeps his eighth clean sheet in 13 games.											
38		H	BURNLEY		5		W	3-1	2-1	Bonds 6, Pike 10, Robson 53	Parkes	McDowell	Brush	Bonds	Martin	Taylor T	Holland	Devonshire	Cross	Pike	Robson	
	24/4			24,139	*7*	48				*Noble 1*	*Stevenson*	*Scott*	*Brennan*	*Noble*	*Thomson*	*Rodaway*	*Jakub**	*Ingham*	*Robinson*	*Morley*	*James*	*Hall*
										Ref: C Thomas	Referee Clive Thomas says later that it is a pleasure to officiate at games like this. Noble headed in Morley's cross in the first minute. Cross's low centre was missed by Robson but not by Bonds. Pike's shot goes in off Cross's back. Pike wants Cross to claim it but is not permitted to.											
39		H	WREXHAM		5		D	1-1	1-0	Bonds 28	Parkes	McDowell	Brush	Bonds	Martin	Taylor T	Holland	Devonshire	Cross	Pike*	Robson	**Lansdowne**
	28/4			28,865	*17*	49				*Shinton 88*	*Davies !*	*Cegielski*	*Dwyer*	*Jones J*	*Roberts J*	*Giles*	*Shinton*	*Sutton*	*McNeil*	*Lyons**	*Fox*	*Buxton*
										Ref: K Baker	Drama as Bonds gives West Ham the lead. A West Ham player clearly handled moments before, and was gracious (or foolish) enough to admit it later. Dai Davies man-handled the referee and was sent off. 10-man Wrexham felt justice was done when Shinton headed a late equaliser.											
40		A	BLACKBURN		5		L	0-1	0-0		Parkes	Lampard	Brush	Bonds	Martin	Taylor T	Holland	Devonshire	Cross	McDowell*	Robson	Taylor A
	5/5			*7,585*	*21*	49				*McKenzie 49*	*Butcher*	*Rathbone*	*Bailey*	*Garner*	*Round*	*Fazackerley*	*Brotherston*	*Fowler*	*Craig*	*McKenzie*	*Aston*	
										Ref: K Redfern	Much-travelled Duncan McKenzie blazes a shot from 30 yards to finally scupper Hammers' promotion hopes. To make matters worse, Rovers are next to bottom and will finish bottom. Alan Devonshire is voted Hammer of the Year, yet he had wasted the best chance of the match.											
41		A	CARDIFF		5		D	0-0	0-0		Parkes	Lampard	Brush	Bonds	Martin	Taylor T	Holland	Devonshire	Cross	McDowell*	Morgan	**Brignull**
	11/5			*13,140*	*9*	50					*Healey*	*Jones*	*Sullivan*	*Campbell*	*Roberts*	*Dwyer*	*Grapes*	*Evans*	*Moore*	*Stevens*	*Buchanan*	
										Ref: T Spencer	Cardiff's unbeaten run is extended to 10 games. Afterwards, Pat Holland, in the bath, unknowingly poured industrial cleaning fluid down his throat. The club doctor made him drink milk and salt water to try to rinse him out, but Holland had to be rushed to hospital with a police escort.											
42		A	MILLWALL				L	1-2	1-0	Robson 12	Parkes	Lampard	Brush	Bonds	Martin	Taylor T	Holland	Devonshire	Cross	Brooking	Robson	
	14/5			*11,917*		50				*Mehmet 66, Chatterton 81*	*Cuff*	*Donaldson*	*Gregory**	*Chambers*	*Kitchener*	*Coleman*	*Towner*	*Seasman*	*Tagg*	*Walker*	*Chatterton*	*Mehmet*
	Home			Away						Ref: White	Millwall have two games to play after this, so relegation is not yet confirmed. West Ham, on the other hand, have nothing to play for. Brooking returns for his first match in six weeks. Pop Robson's goal is his 24th in the league and his last for West Ham. He shortly signs for Sunderland.											
Average	25,779			17,946																		

LEAGUE DIVISION 2 (CUP-TIES)

Manager: John Lyall

SEASON 1978-79

League Cup				F-A	H-T	Scorers, Times, and Referees	1	2	3	4	5	6	7	8	9	10	11	12 sub used
2 H SWINDON	2	L		1-2	0-0	Robson 80	Ferguson	Lampard	Brush	Holland	Taylor T	Bonds	Curbishley	Devonshire	Cross	Taylor A*	Robson B	Pike
30/8	19,672	*3:8*				*Miller 58, Guthrie 61*	*Ogden*	*McLaughlin*	*Ford*	*McHale*	*Aizlewood*	*Stroud*	*Miller*	*Carter*	*Guthrie**	*Bates*	*Williams*	*Kamara*
						Ref: M Taylor	West Ham have only themselves to blame for losing to Bobby Smith's 3rd Division side. Alan Taylor's miss was so bad he was pulled off immediately. In the 73rd minute Andy Ford handled Geoff Pike's effort on the goal-line, but David Cross squandered the ensuing penalty.											

FA Cup				F-A	H-T	Scorers, Times, and Referees	1	2	3	4	5	6	7	8	9	10	11	12 sub used
3 A NEWPORT	4	L		1-2	1-1	Robson 21	Day	Lampard	Brush	Bonds	Martin	McDowell	Taylor A	Devonshire	Cross	Brooking	Robson B	
9/1	*14,124*	*4:8*				*Goddard 14, Woods 81*	*Plumley*	*Walden*	*Byrne*	*Thompson*	*Davies*	*Bruton*	*Oakes*	*Lowndes*	*Goddard*	*Woods*	*Vaughan*	
						Ref: J Worrall	When Robson equalised – a fantastic effort from 30 yards – the money should have been on West Ham. Howard Goddard's glancing header had put Newport in front, and they regained the lead when Day failed to cut out Goddard's cross, leaving Eddie Woods to head a simple goal											

		Home					Away					
	P	W	D	L	F	A	W	D	L	F	A	Pts
1 Crys Palace	42	12	7	2	30	11	7	12	2	21	13	57
2 Brighton	42	16	3	2	44	11	7	7	7	28	28	56
3 Stoke	42	11	7	3	35	15	9	9	3	23	16	56
4 Sunderland	42	13	3	5	39	19	9	8	4	31	25	55
5 WEST HAM	42	12	7	2	46	15	6	7	8	24	24	50
6 Notts Co	42	8	10	3	23	15	6	6	9	25	45	44
7 Preston	42	7	11	3	36	23	5	7	9	23	34	42
8 Newcastle	42	13	3	5	35	24	4	5	12	16	31	42
9 Cardiff	42	12	5	4	34	23	4	5	12	22	47	42
10 Fulham	42	10	7	4	35	19	3	8	10	15	28	41
11 Orient	42	11	5	5	32	18	4	5	12	19	33	40
12 Cambridge	42	7	10	4	22	15	5	6	10	22	37	40
13 Burnley	42	11	6	4	31	22	3	6	12	20	40	40
14 Oldham	42	10	7	4	36	23	3	6	12	16	38	39
15 Wrexham	42	10	6	5	31	16	2	8	11	14	26	38
16 Bristol Rov	42	10	6	5	34	23	4	4	13	14	37	38
17 Leicester	42	7	8	6	28	23	3	9	9	15	29	37
18 Luton	42	11	5	5	46	24	2	5	14	14	33	36
19 Charlton	42	6	8	7	28	28	5	5	11	32	41	35
20 Sheffield Utd	42	9	6	6	34	24	2	6	13	18	45	34
21 Millwall	42	7	4	10	22	29	4	6	11	20	32	32
22 Blackburn	42	5	8	8	24	29	5	2	14	17	43	30
	924	218	142	102	725	449	102	142	218	449	725	924

Odds & ends

Double wins: (3) Newcastle, Bristol R, Luton.
Double losses: (0).

Won from behind: (1) Burnley (h).
Lost from in front: (2) Burnley (a), Millwall (a).

High spots: Winning first two league matches.
Four wins and a draw from five matches from 30 December.

Low spots: Slowly slipping out of the promotion race, and failing to win any of the last four games.
Losing to Third Division Swindon in League Cup and, which was worse, to Fourth Division Newport in FA Cup.

Hammer of the Year: Alan Devonshire.
Ever-presents: (1) Paul Brush.
Hat-tricks: (2) David Cross (1), Bryan Robson (1).
Leading scorer: (26) Bryan Robson.

	Appearances						Goals			
	Lge	*Sub*	LC	*Sub*	FAC	*Sub*	**Lge**	LC	FAC	**Tot**
Bonds, Billy	**39**		1		1		**4**			**4**
Brignull, Phil	**0**	*1*								
Brooking, Trevor	**21**				1		**2**			**2**
Brush, Paul	**42**		1		1					
Cross, David	**40**		1		1		**18**			**18**
Curbishley, Alan	**26**	*1*	1				**1**			**1**
Day, Mervyn	**13**				1					
Devonshire, Alan	**41**		1		1		**5**			**5**
Ferguson, Bobby	**11**		1							
Holland, Pat	**39**		1				**3**			**3**
Jennings, Billy	**2**	*2*								
Lampard, Frank	**28**	*1*	1		1		**3**			**3**
Lansdowne, Billy	**0**	*1*								
Martin, Alvin	**22**				1		**1**			**1**
McDowell, John	**26**	*2*			1		**2**			**2**
Morgan, Nicky	**2**									
Parkes, Phil	**18**									
Pike, Geoff	**10**	*4*		*1*			**1**			**1**
Robson, Bryan	**40**		1		1		**24**	1	1	**26**
Taylor, Alan	**10**	*3*	1		1		**3**			**3**
Taylor, Tommy	**32**		1							
(own-goals)	**0**						**3**			**3**
21 players used	**462**	***15***	**11**	***1***	**11**		**70**	**1**	**1**	**72**

LEAGUE DIVISION 2 — Manager: John Lyall — SEASON 1979-80

No	Date		Att	Pos	Pt	F-A	H-T	Scorers, Times, and Referees	1	2	3	4	5	6	7	8	9	10	11	12 sub used
1	A	WREXHAM			L	0-1	0-0		Parkes	Lampard	Brush	Pike	Martin	Bonds	Holland	Devonshire	Cross	Brooking	**Pearson**	
	18/8		*13,036*		–			*Vinter 60*	*Niedzwiecki*	*Jones J*	*Dwyer*	*Davis*	*Roberts J**	*Giles*	*Sutton*	*Vinter*	*McNeil*	*Whittle*	*Cartwright*	*Fox*
								Ref: D Clarke	Pop Robson has gone for £400,000; Stuart Pearson, with 15 England caps, arrives from Man U for £220,000. Hammers lost at the Racecourse Ground 3-4 last season, so it is becoming an unhappy venue. Parkes and Bonds get in a tizzy over a throw-out and Mick Vinter nips in to score.											
2	H	CHELSEA			L	0-1	0-1		Parkes	Lampard	Brush	Bonds	Martin	Holland	Pike	Pearson*	Cross	Brooking	Devonshire	**Banton**
	20/8		31,627		–			*Johnson 6*	*Borota*	*Locke*	*Stride*	*Nutton*	*Droy*	*Harris*	*Britton*	*Bannon*	*Langley*	*Johnson*	*Fillery*	
								Ref: A Robinson	Martin boobed with his clearance to give Danny Blanchflower's Chelsea an early goal. West Ham forced 21 corners but could not equalise. On the hour keeper Borota high-tackled Pearson in the crutch. Pearson had to go off and West Ham were given an indirect free-kick, not a penalty.											
3	H	OLDHAM		15	W	1-0	0-0	Holland 59	Parkes	Lampard	Brush	Bonds	Martin	Holland	Pike	Morgan	Cross	Brooking	Devonshire	
	25/8		18,319	*22*	2				*Platt*	*Wood*	*Blair*	*Keegan*	*Hicks*	*Hurst*	*Atkinson*	*Halom*	*Steel*	*Stainrod*	*Heaton*	
								Ref: T Spencer	Two opening defeats mean Upton Park sees its lowest home crowd for almost six years. Oldham had also lost both openers, now they have lost their first three, thanks to Holland's goal. Upon scoring, the barracked player rushes over to the crowd and cups his ear to hear the applause.											
4	A	WATFORD		21	L	0-2	0-1		Parkes	Lampard	Brush	Bonds	Martin	Holland	Pike	Pearson*	Cross	Brooking	Devonshire	Lansdowne
	1/9		*23,329*	*12*	2			*Blissett 36, 60*	*Rankin*	*How*	*Harrison*	*Booth*	*Sims*	*Bolton !*	*Joslyn**	*Blissett*	*Jenkins*	*Train*	*Downes*	*Mercer*
								Ref: G Napthine	Luther Blissett wasted two early chances for Watford, but rather than encourage the Hammers they were merely a taster of what was to come. Blissett headed in unchallenged from How's cross. Stuart Pearson was kicked black and blue, and Ian Bolton was sent off for kicking Pike.											
5	A	PRESTON		19	D	1-1	0-0	Cross 61	Parkes	Lampard	Brush	Bonds	**Stewart**	Holland	Pike	Banton	Cross	Brooking	Morgan	
	8/9		*10,460*	*6*	3			*Coleman 44*	*Tunks*	*Taylor*	*Cameron*	*Doyle*	*Baxter*	*O'Riordan*	*Coleman*	*Haslegrave*	*Elliott*	*Potts*	*Thomson*	
								Ref: P Willis	19-year-old Ray Stewart has signed from Dundee United for £400,000, and helps West Ham to their first away point of the season. Coleman scored at the second attempt through a packed penalty area. Hammers' equaliser was bizarre – Pike's wayward shot was volleyed in by Cross.											
6	H	SUNDERLAND		17	W	2-0	0-0	Cross 57, Pearson 73	Parkes	Lampard	Brush	Bonds	Martin	Stewart	**Neighbour**	Pearson	Cross	Brooking	Devonshire	
	15/9		24,021	*9*	5				*Siddall*	*Whitworth*	*Bolton*	*Clarke*	*Elliott**	*Buckley*	*Ashurst*	*Rostron*	*Brown*	*Robson*	*Arnott*	*Chisholm*
								Ref: A Glasson	A vibrant match. Spectators at Upton Park cast their eyes on two new Hammers, Jimmy Neighbour from Norwich and Ray Stewart. Sunderland boss Ken Knighton watches his new signing Pop Robson blotted out of the game by Billy Bonds. Stuart Pearson bags his 100th league goal.											
7	A	QP RANGERS		19	L	0-3	0-1		Parkes	Lampard	Brush	Bonds	Martin	Stewart	Neighbour	Pike*	Cross	Brooking	Devonshire	Holland
	22/9		*24,692*	*4*	5			*Allen 10, 46, Goddard 59*	*Woods*	*Shanks*	*Gillard*	*McCreery*	*Hazell*	*Roeder*	*Bowles*	*Currie*	*Allen*	*Goddard*	*Burke*	
								Ref: M Taylor	QPR's teenage scorers will both end up playing for West Ham, sooner or later. Clive Allen steered in Bowles' quickly taken free-kick and then headed in Bowles' cross. Paul Goddard was sent clear by Bowles for No 3. All in all, a triumph for QPR's new manager, Tommy Docherty.											
8	H	BURNLEY		16	W	2-1	0-1	Stewart 66p, Lansdowne 69	Parkes	Stewart	Brush	Bonds	Martin	**Allen**	Neighbour	Lansdowne	Cross	Brooking	Devonshire	
	29/9		18,327	*21*	7			*Scott 42*	*Stevenson*	*Scott*	*Jakub*	*Hall*	*Thomson*	*Rodaway*	*Young**	*Dobson*	*Fletcher*	*Kindon*	*James*	*Brennan*
								Ref: D Hutchinson	Teenager Paul Allen makes his league debut. Poor Burnley have not won a league fixture since Easter. Brooking and Cross both hit the bar early on, but Burnley take the lead. Keeper Alan Stevenson then flattens Brooking and Ray Stewart demonstrates his ferocious penalty-taking.											
9	H	NEWCASTLE		16	D	1-1	1-1	Cross 7	Parkes	Stewart	Brush	Bonds	Martin	Allen	Neighbour*	Lansdowne	Cross	Brooking	Devonshire	Holland
	6/10		23,206	*1*	8			*Withe 37*	*Hardwick*	*Brownlie*	*Davies*	*Martin*	*Barton*	*Boam*	*Shoulder*	*Walker*	*Withe*	*Hibbitt*	*Cartwright*	
								Ref: C Thomas	This fixture last season ended 5-0, so Newcastle have stiffened up. Cross opened the scoring by stooping to head in Neighbour's free-kick. When Parkes then claimed a cross with his leg raised, the ref penalised him with an indirect free-kick, taken by Martin and converted by Withe.											
10	A	LEICESTER		14	W	2-1	1-1	Martin 29, Cross 51	Parkes	Stewart	Lampard	Bonds	Martin	Holland	Allen	Lansdowne	Cross	Brooking	Neighbour	
	13/10		*22,472*	*6*	10			*Williams 1*	*Wallington*	*Williams*	*Rofe*	*Peake*	*May*	*Welsh*	*Byrne**	*Henderson*	*Young*	*Wilson*	*Smith*	*Lineker*
								Ref: J Worrall	Although falling behind in 15 seconds to a shot deflected in off Lampard, West Ham recover to record their first away win in 11 games. Lyall's tactics of playing two wide men, Neighbour and Holland, to squeeze Newcastle's marauding full-backs paid off. Both goals were low shots.											
11	H	LUTON		16	L	1-2	0-2	Allen 64	Parkes	Stewart	Lampard	Bonds	Martin	Holland	Allen	Lansdowne	Cross	Pike	Neighbour	
	20/10		25,049	*1*	10			*Stein 16, Saxby 36*	*Findlay*	*Stephens*	*Donaghy*	*Grealish*	*Saxby*	*Price*	*Hill*	*West*	*Stein*	*Ingram*	*Moss*	
								Ref: W Bombroff	Luton top the league. Both their goals came from set pieces, and Lyall rages against his players at half-time and full-time. Cross did not track Paul Price for Luton's first, and Saxby outjumped Martin for the second. The defeat overshadowed Paul Allen's first league goal for Hammers.											

No	Venue	Opponent / Date	Att	Pos	Res / Pts	F-A	H-T	Scorers, Times, Referees	1	2	3	4	5	6	7	8	9	10	11	12 sub used
12	A	NOTTS CO		14	W	1-0	0-0	Holland 55	Parkes	Stewart	Lampard	Bonds	Martin	Holland	Allen	Pike	Cross	Brooking	Neighbour	
		27/10	*12,256*	*5*	12				*Avramovic*	*Richards*	*O'Brien*	*Hunt*	*Stubbs*	*Blockley*	*McCulloch*	*Masson*	*Hooks*	*Benjamin*	*Mair**	*Christie*
								Ref: N Midgley	West Ham's poor run of results is making them much more defensive in outlook these days. Out of necessity, some might say. This was a backs-to-the-wall win, County's first home defeat of the season, secured when Holland dived among the flying boots to head Martin's flick-on.											
13	H	WREXHAM		14	W	1-0	0-0	Pike 51	Parkes	Stewart	Lampard	Bonds	Martin	Holland	Allen	Pike	Cross	Devonshire*	Neighbour	Lansdowne
		3/11	20,595	*6*	14				*Davies*	*Hill*	*Dwyer*	*Davis*	*Jones J*	*Giles*	*Fox*	*Cartwright*	*Edwards*	*McNeil*	*Buxton**	*Roberts I*
								Ref: H Robinson	Lyall's more cautious outlook results in just one player up front – Cross. But the tactics work. Holland gets in a shot, Dai Davies blocks, but Pike follows up. High-flying Wrexham looked strangely subdued, and Alvin Martin dealt comfortably with free-scoring striker Dixie McNeil.											
14	A	FULHAM		11	W	2-1	0-0	Stewart 66p, Cross 72	Ferguson	Stewart	Lampard	Bonds	Martin	Holland	Allen	Pike	Cross	Devonshire	Neighbour	
		10/11	*16,476*	*21*	16			*Davies 83*	*Digweed*	*Peters**	*Strong*	*Bullivant*	*Money*	*Gale*	*Marinello*	*Beck*	*Guthrie*	*Lock*	*Davies*	
								Ref: T Bune	The deaths in quick succession of Phil Parkes' father and father-in-law mean that he is given compassionate leave. When John Beck up-ends Pike, it gives Stewart the chance to put away his third penalty. Cross doubles the lead with a looping far-post header from Lampard's cross.											
15	A	CHELSEA		11	L	1-2	1-1	Holland 25	Ferguson	Stewart	Lampard	Bonds	Martin	Holland	Allen*	Devonshire	Cross	Brooking	Neighbour	Lansdowne
		14/11	*30,859*	*5*	16			*Frost 29, Fillery 76*	*Borota*	*Locke*	*Sparrow*	*Bumstead*	*Droy*	*Chivers*	*Britton*	*Fillery*	*Frost*	*Walker*	*Harris*	
								Ref: R Challis	Chelsea are managed by Geoff Hurst. First blood to the Hammers, when Brooking and Stewart set up a chance for Holland. But Martin then headed out to Frost, who drove into the net through a forest of legs. Clive Walker made the winner, turning Stewart inside out before crossing.											
16	H	SWANSEA		8	W	2-0	0-0	Brooking 56, Cross 75	Parkes	Stewart	**Smith**	Bonds	Martin	Holland	Allen	Devonshire	Cross	Brooking	Lansdowne	
		17/11	21,210	*9*	18				*Letheran*	*Evans*	*Rushbury*	*Charles*	*Phillips*	*Stevenson*	*Craig*	*Attley*	*James R*	*Mahoney**	*Callaghan*	*Waddle*
								Ref: J Martin	Lampard's torn hamstring rules him out. Mark Smith is his late replacement. Brooking oozed class throughout, and had Billy Lansdowne's finishing been of equal quality Swansea would have taken a hiding. Brooking made Cross's goal and scored himself. Martin also hit the bar.											
17	H	CARDIFF		7	W	3-0	2-0	Cross 27, Stewart 44p, 85p	Parkes	Stewart	Lampard	Bonds	Martin	Holland	Allen	Pearson	Cross	Brooking	Devonshire	
		24/11	20,242	*13*	20				*Davies J*	*Jones**	*Sullivan*	*Campbell*	*Pontin*	*Thomas*	*Bishop*	*Dwyer*	*Moore*	*Ronson*	*Lewis*	*Stevens*
								Ref: D Reeves	Both penalties were conceded by Rod Thomas, first when tripping Devonshire, then by fisting away Pearson's header. Both penalties were blasted in by Stewart. The FA have introduced random drugs tests. Phil Parkes is chosen but is unable to give a urine sample. He is excused.											
18	A	CHARLTON		7	L	0-1	0-1		Parkes	Stewart	Lampard	Bonds	Martin	Holland*	Allen	Pearson	Cross	Brooking	Devonshire	Neighbour
		1/12	*19,021*	*18*	20			*Gritt 14*	*Wood*	*Hazell*	*Shaw*	*Tydeman*	*Berry*	*Madden*	*Powell*	*Jacobson*	*Hales*	*Walker*	*Gritt*	
								Ref: T Spencer	Players' minds are distracted by the looming cup-tie with Forest, and Lyall loses his rag. Mike Bailey's Charlton won the points through Steve Gritt's far-post header from Powell's cross. That Charlton registered their first clean-sheet so far indicates the flimsiness of West Ham's attack.											
19	H	BRISTOL ROV		7	W	2-1	1-1	Cross 29, 52	Parkes	Stewart	Lampard	Bonds	Martin	Allen	Neighbour	Pearson	Cross	Brooking	Devonshire	
		8/12	17,763	*21*	22			*Barrowclough 2*	*Thomas*	*Bater*	*Williams*	*Mabbutt*	*Taylor*	*Aitken*	*Barrowclough*	*Emmanuel*	*Brown**	*Penny*	*Pulis*	*Jones V*
								Ref: C White	David Cross celebrates his 29th birthday with two goals, taking his total for the season to 14. Rovers' manager Bobby Campbell is not inclined to celebrate, having seen Tony Pulis set Barrowclough clear in the second minute. But Rovers were unable to stem Cross's aerial menace.											
20	A	SHREWSBURY		9	L	0-3	0-0		Parkes	Stewart	Lampard	Bonds	Martin	Pike	Allen	Pearson	Cross	Brooking	Neighbour	
		15/12	*8,513*	*19*	22			*Maguire 59, Chapman 85, Atkins 87*	*Mulhearn*	*King*	*Larkin*	*Lindsay*	*Griffin*	*Keay*	*Tong*	*Atkins*	*Chapman*	*Dungworth*	*Maguire*	
								Ref: L Robinson	For the second time in four days, West Ham fold under late pressure. Parkes comes out, Atkins heads down, and Maguire blasts the ball into the empty net. Pearson might have scored in the opening minutes against Graham Turner's strugglers, but Keay cleared his shot off the line.											
21	H	CAMBRIDGE			W	3-1	0-1	Stewart 47, Pearson 61, Neighbour 70	Parkes	Stewart	Lampard	Bonds	Martin	Devonshire	Allen	Pearson	Cross*	Brooking	Neighbour	Pike
		21/12	11,721		24			*Biley 36*	*Webster*	*Stringer*	*Christie**	*Calderwood*	*Fallon*	*O'Neill*	*Biley*	*Spriggs*	*Reilly*	*Gibbins*	*Murray*	*Turner*
								Ref: C Thomas	A Friday match on a frozen pitch produces a worrying knee injury to Cross, who collides with the keeper after 35 minutes and is stretchered off. Half-time was enlivened briefly by a middle-aged, poorly-endowed streaker. A second-half blizzard almost brought an abandonment.											
22	A	ORIENT			W	4-0	3-0	Pearson 11, 40, Devonshire 24, Pike 54	Parkes	Stewart	Lampard	Bonds	Martin	Devonshire	Allen	Pearson	Pike	Brooking	Neighbour	
		1/1	*23,885*		26				*Day*	*Fisher*	*Smith**	*Taylor*	*Gray N*	*Moores*	*Chiedozie**	*Hughton*	*Mayo*	*Jennings*	*Coates*	*Godfrey*
								Ref: C Downey	A skating rink pitch sees the Hammers scamper about in space-age boots with tiny pimples on the sole. Lyall switched his full-backs so Stewart could mark tricky John Chiedozie. Former West Ham keeper Mervyn Day now plays for Jimmy Bloomfield's Orient and lets in four goals.											
23	H	WATFORD		7	D	1-1	0-0	Bonds 84	Parkes	Stewart	Lampard	Bonds	Martin	Devonshire	Allen	Pearson	Pike	Brooking	Neighbour	
		12/1	*23,553*	*16*	27			*Rostron 48*	*Steele*	*Henderson*	*Harrison*	*Patching*	*Sims*	*Bolton*	*Booth*	*Blissett**	*Ward*	*Train*	*Rostron*	*Poskett*
								Ref: C Maskell	Watford boss Graham Taylor decides to pack the midfield, which forces West Ham to resort to the long ball. These tactics don't impress young Paul Allen, who has lost his way lately. Not the best of games for TV. Not the best advertisement either, when a linesman is hit by something.											

No	Date		Att	Pos	Pt	F-A	H-T	Scorers, Times, and Referees	1	2	3	4	5	6	7	8	9	10	11	12 sub used
24	H	PRESTON		6	W	2-0	0-0	Stewart 55p, Allen 77	Parkes	Lampard	Brush	Bonds*	Martin	Devonshire	Allen	Pearson	Pike	Stewart	Neighbour	Banton
	19/1		17,603	*10*	29				*Tunks*	*Taylor*	*McAteer*	*Doyle*	*Anderson*	*O'Riordan*	*Bell*	*Haslegrave*	*Elliott*	*McGee**	*Bruce*	*Coleman*
								Ref: R Toseland	Preston boss Nobby Stiles can have few complaints as Don O'Riorden barges into Geoff Pike. Stewart's penalty went in off keeper Tunks' fingers and almost removed them. Tunks then dropped Martin's cross to Allen. Bonds gets kicked in the head by Martin and has seven stitches.											
25	H	QP RANGERS		7	W	2-1	1-1	Pearson 39, Hazell 71 (og)	Parkes	Lampard	Brush	Stewart	Martin	Devonshire	Allen	Pearson	Cross	Brooking	Pike	
	9/2		26,037	*9*	31			*Goddard 35*	*Woods*	*Shanks*	*Gillard*	*McCreery*	*Wicks*	*Hazell*	*Goddard*	*Roeder*	*Allen*	*Currie*	*Burke**	*Waddock*
								Ref: B Hill	Clive Allen's shot goes in off Paul Goddard's head to put Rangers in front. Bob Hazell returns from suspension to accomplish an extraordinary own-goal from David Cross's centre. This is Stuart Pearson's best game so far for the Hammers. He hits the crossbar in addition to his goal.											
26	A	BURNLEY		5	W	1-0	1-0	Devonshire 19	Parkes	Lampard	Brush	Stewart	Martin	Devonshire	Allen	Neighbour	Cross	Brooking	Pike	
	19/2		*10,610*	*20*	33				*Stevenson*	*Arins*	*Brennan*	*Burke**	*Overson V*	*Dixon*	*James*	*Dobson*	*Hamilton*	*Young*	*Smith*	*Cavener*
								Ref: G Owen	Alan Devonshire has been under the weather with a bug for some weeks, but shakes it off to dominate the game. The only goal, a delightful scissors movement with Brooking, finished off from 20 yards, is enough to take West Ham to within three points of leaders Luton Town.											
27	H	LEICESTER		6	W	3-1	0-1	Pike 69, Cross 75, Holland 79	Parkes	Lampard	Brush	Stewart	Martin	Devonshire	Allen	Holland	Cross	Brooking	Pike	
	23/2		27,762	*1*	35			*Young 11*	*Wallington*	*Williams*	*Scott*	*Kelly*	*May*	*O'Neill !*	*Goodwin*	*Henderson*	*Young*	*Peake*	*Smith*	
								Ref: B Steven	Leicester top the table but are beaten by a candidate for goal of the season. England boss Ron Greenwood watches as Pike lobs Wallington. O'Neill is sent off for pulling Devonshire's shirt. This is the 14th match of the season in which West Ham recover from being a goal down.											
28	A	LUTON		5	D	1-1	0-1	Stewart 70	Parkes	Lampard	Brush	Stewart	Martin	Devonshire	Allen	Holland*	Cross	Brooking	Pike	Pearson
	1/3		*20,040*	*3*	36			*Hill 3*	*Findlay*	*Stephens*	*Donaghy*	*Grealish*	*Price*	*Price*	*Hill*	*West*	*Stein**	*Hatton*	*Moss*	*White*
								Ref: S Bates	The pre-match entertainment comprised scantily-clad girls, suspended from ropes, wriggling free from straitjackets. The on-field entertainment gave us Hill's volley. Then Stephens dragged down Brooking. Stewart missed his first penalty. Findlay saved, but Stewart got to the loose ball.											
29	H	NOTTS CO		7	L	1-2	0-0	Pike 90	Parkes	Lampard*	Brush	Stewart	Martin	Devonshire	Allen	Pearson	Cross	Brooking	Pike	Holland
	11/3		24,844	*15*	36			*Christie 65, Stubbs 69*	*Avramovic*	*Richards*	*O'Brien*	*Benjamin*	*Stubbs*	*Kilcline*	*McCulloch*	*Masson*	*Christie*	*Hunt*	*Mair*	
								Ref: D Letts	After the Cup win over Villa, this was an anti-climax, West Ham's first defeat in 14 games. Jimmy Sirrel's County employ an offside trap and win the points through Trevor Christie's header, from Richards' cross, and another header from Stubbs, from Don Masson's free-kick.											
30	A	NEWCASTLE		8	D	0-0	0-0		Parkes	Lampard	Brush	Stewart	Martin	Devonshire	Allen	Pearson	Cross	Brooking	Pike*	Holland
	15/3		*25,431*	*7*	37				*Hardwick*	*Brownlie*	*Davies*	*Walker*	*Bird*	*Boam*	*Shoulder*	*Cartwright*	*Rafferty*	*Hibbitt*	*Shinton*	
								Ref: R Bridges	Newcastle boast just one home defeat in 16 games, so this is a point gained rather than a point lost. Paul Allen has found his form again, while Lampard finds the referee's notebook again. He faces a suspension. West Ham are five points behind leaders Chelsea with three games in hand.											
31	H	FULHAM		8	L	2-3	2-2	Devonshire 6, Stewart 16p	Parkes	Lampard	Brush*	Stewart	Martin	Devonshire	Allen	Pearson	Cross	Brooking	Holland	Pike
	22/3		30,030	*21*	37			*Maybank 12, Banton 34, 40*	*Peyton*	*Money*	*Strong*	*Lock*	*Banton*	*Gale*	*Gayle*	*Beck*	*Davies*	*Maybank*	*Lewington*	
								Ref: A Seville	This was the match where dreams of promotion died. Fulham's Geoff Banton scored his first ever league goals, both identical, and both from corners, both the result of Parkes' dislike of having a defender on the far post. Beck flattened Brooking to allow Stewart a twice-taken penalty.											
32	A	SWANSEA		8	L	1-2	0-0	Devonshire 50	Parkes	Stewart	Brush	Bonds	Martin	Devonshire	Allen*	Pearson	Pike	Brooking	Holland	Cross
	29/3		*13,275*	*16*	37			*Craig 56p, 75*	*Stewart*	*Robinson*	*Evans*	*Charles**	*Phillips*	*Stevenson*	*Craig*	*Attley*	*Waddle*	*Giles*	*Mahoney*	*Baker*
								Ref: V Callow	A few weeks earlier bookies had stopped taking bets on West Ham's promotion. Now they are giving odds of 12-1 against their taking the title. Lyall's 4-4-2 formation ensures this match offers little excitement. Martin impeded Waddle for the penalty; Parkes left his line for the winner.											
33	A	CAMBRIDGE		8	L	0-2	0-2		Parkes	Lampard	Brush	Bonds	Martin	Devonshire	Stewart	Pearson	Cross	Brooking	Holland	
	1/4		*8,863*	*15*	37			*Finney 20, 35*	*Webster*	*Donaldson*	*Murray*	*Smith*	*Fallon*	*Gibbins*	*Streete*	*Spriggs*	*Reilly*	*Finney*	*Christie*	
								Ref: M Scott	On the balance of play this result was laughable. Lyall sends out an attacking formation, but a muddy pitch and Malcolm Webster's heroics combine to frustrate the Hammers, who have taken just one point from five games. Tom Finney netted with a header; then from a rebound.											
34	H	ORIENT		9	W	2-0	0-0	Gray 68 (og), Brooking 73	Parkes	Lampard*	Brush	Bonds	Martin	Devonshire	Stewart	Pearson	Cross	Brooking	Holland	Pike
	5/4		22,066	*8*	39				*Day*	*Fisher*	*Roffey*	*Taylor*	*Gray N*	*Hughton*	*Chiedozie*	*Jennings*	*Moores*	*Margerrison*	*Coates*	
								Ref: P Reeves	Nigel Gray's own-goal – turning in Alan Devonshire's cross – means Orient have gifted West Ham an own-goal in all three meetings this season, and Gray has donated two of them – the other being in the FA Cup. This match was Frank Lampard's 500th West Ham appearance.											

No / Date	Venue	Opponent / Att	Pos	Res / Pts	F-A	H-T	Scorers, Times, Referees	1	2	3	4	5	6	7	8	9	10	11	12
35	A	BIRMINGHAM	8	D	0-0	0-0		Parkes	Stewart	Brush	Bonds	Martin	Devonshire	Allen	Pearson	Cross	Brooking	Holland	
7/4		*28,377*	*1*	40				*Wealands*	*Broadhurst*	*Dennis*	*Curbishley*	*Gallagher**	*Towers*	*Todd*	*Ainscow*	*Bertschin*	*Gemmill*	*Dillon*	*Lynex*
							Ref: D Shaw	Jim Smith's Birmingham tackle like demons, and this point will ultimately earn them promotion. Mind you, West Ham hardly deserved their draw. Wealands was untroubled by West Ham's attack. City won 14 corner-kicks. When Parkes dropped Bertschin's header, Holland cleared.											
36	A	CARDIFF	8	W	1-0	1-0	Stewart 29	Parkes	Lampard	Brush	Stewart	Bonds	Devonshire	Allen	Pearson	Cross	Brooking	Pike	
19/4		*12,076*	*13*	42				*Grotier*	*Grapes*	*Lewis*	*Campbell*	*Pontin*	*Thomas*	*Ronson*	*Bishop**	*Stevens*	*Buchanan*	*Harris*	*Sullivan*
							Ref: D Lloyd	Former Hammer Peter Grotier was told he was playing just an hour before kick-off. It is his mistake that keeps West Ham's promotion hopes theoretically alive. He misjudges Brooking's inswinging corner and palms the ball to Cross – who squares to Stewart. It's his ninth league goal.											
37	H	BIRMINGHAM	8	L	1-2	0-1	Martin 53	Parkes	Lampard	Brush	Bonds !	Martin	Devonshire	Allen*	Pearson	Cross	Brooking	Stewart	Pike
22/4		37,167	*1*	42			*Ainscow 37, Bertschin 71*	*Wealands*	*Broadhurst*	*Dennis*	*Curbishley*	*Gallagher*	*Todd !*	*Ainscow*	*Lynex*	*Bertschin*	*Gemmill*	*Dillon*	
							Ref: A Gunn	When Billy Bonds and Colin Todd exchanged kicks on the ground, expulsion was inevitable. It took some effort to keep them apart on their way to the tunnel. Martin's fierce header was followed by Bertschin's easy header, which won the game and hoisted City from fourth to first.											
38	H	SHREWSBURY	9	L	1-3	0-2	Brooking 79	Parkes	Lampard	Brush	Stewart	Martin	Neighbour	Allen	Pearson	Cross*	Brooking	Pike	Morgan
26/4		19,765	*14*	42			*Maguire 17, Keay 40p, Biggins 84*	*Wardle*	*King*	*Leonard*	*Turner*	*Griffin*	*Keay*	*Tong*	*Atkins*	*Biggins*	*Dungworth*	*Maguire*	
							Ref: L Shapter	Even though they are Wembley bound, the Hammers get the bird from their demanding supporters after this shoddy display. Brooking's was an untypical goal, a rasping cross-shot. It briefly brought the game to life, following Maguire's shot and a penalty for Lampard's foul on Maguire.											
39	A	OLDHAM		D	0-0	0-0		Parkes	Lampard	Brush	Bonds	Martin	Allen	Neighbour	Pike*	Cross	Brooking	Stewart	Morgan
29/4		*8,214*		43				*McDonnell*	*Hoolickin*	*Holt*	*Kowenicki*	*Clements*	*Blair*	*Keegan*	*Heaton*	*Steel**	*Stainrod*	*Atkinson*	*Wood*
							Ref: J Haugh	Both teams went through the motions. West Ham bored the crowd by constantly passing back to Parkes. Lyall's players are terrified of picking up injuries before the Cup Final and when Brooking goes off with a dislocated finger one feared the worst. Happily he was soon back in action.											
40	A	BRISTOL ROV	7	W	2-0	0-0	Devonshire 61, Cross 78	Parkes	Lampard	Stewart	Bonds	Martin	Devonshire	Allen	Morgan	Cross	Pike	Neighbour	
3/5		*9,824*	*19*	45				*Thomas*	*Bater*	*Cooper*	*Hughes**	*Mabbutt*	*Griffiths*	*Barrowclough*	*Pulis*	*Penny*	*Bates*	*Barrett*	*Williams*
							Ref: J Lovatt	After 40 seconds Ashley Griffiths' studs shatters Paul Allen's shin pad, but mercifully spares his shin. Allen will be okay for Wembley. Devonshire blasts a great goal from 25 yards and Cross adds another with his head. Rovers were already sure of staying up, so weren't fired up.											
41	H	CHARLTON	7	W	4-1	4-0	Pike 1, Morgan 12, Cross 22, Stewart 45p	Parkes	Stewart	Brush	Bonds	Martin	Banton	Neighbour	Pike	Cross*	Brooking	Morgan	Lampard
5/5		19,314	*22*	47			*Hales 85*	*Johns*	*Hazell !*	*Walker*	*Tydeman*	*Berry*	*Shaw*	*Churchouse*	*Walsh*	*Hales*	*Ostergaard**	*Robinson*	*Smith*
							Ref: E Read	Charlton are so far adrift they have long since given up the ghost. They have not registered an away win for 18 months and were not likely to end that run now. Pike headed the first goal after 20 seconds, and proved such a thorn that on the hour Hazell was sent off for fouling him.											
42	A	SUNDERLAND	7	L	0-2	0-1		Parkes	Stewart	Brush	Bonds	Martin	Devonshire	Neighbour	Pearson*	Cross	Brooking	Pike	Holland
12/5		*47,000*	*2*	47			*Arnott 29, Cummins 67*	*Turner*	*Whitworth*	*Hinnigan*	*Chisholm*	*Hindmarch*	*Elliott*	*Arnott*	*Buckley*	*Hawley*	*Robson*	*Cummins*	
	Home	Away					Ref: J Worrall	Two days after winning the FA Cup Hammers head for Sunderland, who will be promoted at the expense of Chelsea if they win. Hence the electric atmosphere. West Ham lost Pearson and Stewart to injury and finished with 10 men. Cummins' 30-yard clincher ignited a huge party.											
Average	22,868	18,510																	

League Cup

No / Date	Venue	Opponent / Att	Pos	Res / Rnd	F-A	H-T	Scorers, Times, Referees	1	2	3	4	5	6	7	8	9	10	11	12
2:1	H	BARNSLEY	15	W	3-1	2-0	Brooking 17, Pearson 32, Cross 77	Parkes	Lampard	Brush	Bonds	Martin	Holland	Pike	Pearson	Cross	Brooking	Devonshire	
28/8		12,320	*3:21*				*Glavin 54*	*Pierce*	*Flavell*	*Collins*	*Glavin*	*Dugdale*	*McCarthy*	*Little*	*Riley*	*Pugh*	*Millar*	*Bell*	
							Ref: L Burden	The lowest crowd for 20 years welcomes Allan Clarke's Barnsley to Upton Park. League Cup-ties are now played over two-legs. Lampard's deflected shot was turned in by Pearson, his first Hammers' goal. Sections of the crowd have taken to baiting Geoff Pike, the latest boo-boy.											
2:2	A	BARNSLEY	21	W	2-0	1-0	Cross 19, 76	Parkes	Lampard	Brush	Bonds	Stewart	Holland	Pike	Banton	Cross	Brooking	Morgan	
4/9		*15,898*	*3:23*					*Pierce*	*Flavell**	*Collins*	*Glavin*	*Dugdale*	*McCarthy*	*Little*	*Riley*	*Pugh*	*Banks*	*Bell*	*Millar*
							Ref: K Walmsley (Hammers win 5-1 on aggregate)	When Martin fails a late fitness test, Ray Stewart is pressed into midfield. He became one of four Hammers to be booked, as Barnsley raised the temperature. Though the scoreline does not show it, Phil Parkes had much to do. David Cross's second goal looked to many to be offside.											
3	H	SOUTHEND	19	D	1-1	1-1	Cross 43	Parkes	Stewart	Brush	Bonds	Martin	Holland	Allen	Lansdowne	Cross	Brooking	Devonshire	
25/9		19,658	*3:11*				*Pountney 11*	*Cawston*	*Dudley*	*Moody*	*Cusack*	*Yates*	*Stead*	*Otulakowski*	*Pountney*	*Morris*	*Tuohy*	*Gray*	
							Ref: R Lewis	Southend beat Division 1 Bolton in the 1st Round and set off at a furious pace. Colin Morris's pass was thumped in by Ron Pountney. Phil Dudley missed a sitter and Cross's strong header from Stewart's cross came out of the blue. After the break Southend lived on their nerves.											

League Cup			F-A	H-T	Scorers, Times, and Referees	1	2	3	4	5	6	7	8	9	10	11	12 sub used
3R A SOUTHEND	16	D	0-0	0-0		Parkes	Stewart	Brush	Bonds	Martin	Holland	Allen	Lansdowne	Cross	Brooking	Devonshire	
1/10	*22,497 3:15*		*aet*			*Cawston*	*Dudley*	*Moody*	*Cusack*	*Yates**	*Stead*	*Otulakowski*	*Pountney*	*Morris*	*Tuohy*	*Gray*	*Walker*
					Ref: J Sewell	Despite the lack of goals this replay had its share of thrills. West Ham resorted to brawn rather than brain and Paul Allan and Ray Stewart were booked. Hammers created and wasted most of the chances, the best of which fell to Cross. Blues' boss Dave Smith then lost the toss for venue.											
3 H SOUTHEND	16	W	5-1	2-1	Lansdowne 25, 36, 46, Holland 60,	Parkes	Stewart	Smith	Bonds	Martin	Holland	Allen	Lansdowne	Cross	Brooking	Pike	
RR 8/10	19,718 *3:17*				*Gray 23* [Stewart 79p]	*Cawston*	*Dudley*	*Moody*	*Cusack*	*Walker*	*Stead*	*Otulakowski**	*Morris*	*Pountney*	*Hadley*	*Gray*	*Hull*
					Ref: M Baker	Yet again Southend score first at Upton Park, but this time their lead is erased in seconds by the first instalment of Billy Lansdowne's hat-trick. It is his first hat-trick and came shortly after his father was sacked as Hammers' reserve-team coach. Dudley fouled Paul Allen for the penalty.											
4 A SUNDERLAND	14	D	1-1	0-1	Pike 68	Parkes	Stewart	Lampard	Bonds	Martin	Holland	Allen	Pike	Cross	Brooking*	Devonshire	Lansdowne
31/10	*30,302 11*				*Brown 11*	*Siddall*	*Whitworth*	*Gilbert*	*Clarke*	*Hindmarch*	*Elliott*	*Arnott*	*Lee*	*Brown*	*Robson*	*Rowell*	
					Ref: G Nolan	Alan Brown sprinted through for a fine goal, but not as fine as Geoff Pike's dipping 30-yarder. Trevor Brooking failed to reappear after half-time, and Sunderland's spirits visibly lifted. Pop Robson, playing for Ken Knighton's Sunderland, reckoned that West Ham look a good team.											
4R H SUNDERLAND	14	W	2-1	1-1	Martin 9, Cross 49	Ferguson	Stewart	Lampard	Bonds	Martin	Holland	Allen	Pike	Cross	Devonshire	Lansdowne	
5/11	24,454 *10*				*Brown 6*	*Siddall*	*Whitworth*	*Bolton*	*Clarke*	*Elliott*	*Hindmarch*	*Arnott*	*Gilbert*	*Brown*	*Rowell*	*Dunn*	
					Ref: S Bates	The winners will play European champions Forest, so this is a rare old ding-dong. A bereavement means Phil Parkes is left out. Alan Brown scores another scorcher, but it is soon cancelled out by Martin's header. The winner came from a deflection after Devonshire had hit the post.											
QF H NOTT'M FOREST	7	D	0-0	0-0		Parkes	Stewart	Lampard	Bonds	Martin	Holland	Allen	Pearson	Cross	Brooking	Devonshire	
4/12	35,856 *1:5*					*Shilton*	*Anderson*	*Gray*	*Bowyer*	*Lloyd*	*Burns*	*O'Neill*	*O'Hare*	*Birtles*	*Francis*	*Robertson*	
					Ref: A Grey	A sardine-packed Upton Park welcomes Clough's European champions, who are unbeaten in 21 games but spend the 90 minutes desperately trying to survive. Gary Birtles and Trevor Francis hardly had a kick until the 82nd minute, when Phil Parkes saved superbly at Francis's feet.											
QF A NOTT'M FOREST	7	L	0-3	0-0		Parkes	Stewart	Lampard	Bonds	Martin	Pike	Allen	Pearson	Cross	Brooking	Devonshire	
R 12/12	*25,462 1:7*		*aet*		*O'Hare 99, Birtles 101, O'Neill 108*	*Shilton*	*Anderson*	*Gray*	*Bowyer*	*Lloyd*	*Burns*	*O'Neill*	*O'Hare*	*Birtles*	*Francis*	*Robertson*	
					Ref: N Ashley	Phil Parkes was the main reason this cup-tie stayed goalless throughout normal time. How cruel, then, that it should be his mistake that decides the outcome, when dropping Birtles' cross at John O'Hare's feet. Early in the game Stewart's free-kick had slithered out of Shilton's hands.											

FA Cup																	
3 A WEST BROM	9	D	1-1	1-0	Pearson 33	Parkes	Stewart	Lampard	Bonds	Martin	Devonshire	Allen	Pearson	Pike	Brooking	Neighbour	
5/1	*20,572 1:16*				*Regis 90*	*Godden*	*Batson*	*Statham*	*Trewick*	*Wile*	*Robertson*	*Deehan*	*Brown A*	*Regis*	*Owen*	*Barnes*	
					Ref: J Hunting	Ron Atkinson's Albion are left stunned by Phil Parkes' goalkeeping display, which is admired by his family up in the stand. Best of his many saves was when pushing Statham's effort against a post. Pearson's header was cancelled out by Regis's effort, which may have been handled.											
3R H WEST BROM	9	W	2-1	0-0	Pike 53, Brooking 83	Parkes	Stewart	Lampard	Brush	Martin	Devonshire	Allen	Pearson	Pike	Brooking	Neighbour	
8/1	30,689 *1:16*				*Brown T 86*	*Godden*	*Batson*	*Statham*	*Trewick*	*Wile*	*Robertson*	*Deehan*	*Brown A*	*Regis*	*Owen**	*Barnes*	*Brown T*
					Ref: J Hunting	Geoff Pike is drafted in as makeshift striker and plays a blinder, side-footing the first goal. John Deehan contrived an improbable miss for WBA in the first half and paid the price. Albion's goal came from a Parkes mistake. He flapped at Barnes's cross and Tony Brown capitalised.											
4 A ORIENT	6	W	3-2	2-1	Gray 28 (og), Stewart 34p, 81	Parkes	Brush	Lampard	Bonds	Martin	Devonshire	Allen	Pearson	Pike	Stewart	Neighbour	
26/1	*21,521 13*				*Taylor 11p, Chiedozie 61*	*Rafter*	*Fisher*	*Roffey*	*Taylor*	*Gray*	*Moores*	*Chiedozie*	*Hughton*	*Jennings*	*Margerrison*	*Coates*	
					Ref: S Bates	O's Day is injured. Ex-Hammer Tommy Taylor is now Orient's skipper. Bonds handled for the O's early penalty. Nigel Gray headed an own-goal for West Ham before they won a penalty of their own when Moores handled. Stewart saw Taylor point one way, so he aimed the other.											
5 H SWANSEA	6	W	2-0	0-0	Allen 85, Cross 86	Parkes	Lampard	Brush	Stewart	Martin	Devonshire	Neighbour	Pearson*	Cross	Brooking	Pike	Allen
16/2	30,497 *13*					*Letheran*	*Robinson*	*Rushbury*	*Phillips*	*Stevenson*	*Giles*	*Craig*	*James*	*Charles*	*Toshack*	*Callaghan*	
					Ref: K Baker	John Toshack's Swansea felt robbed by this result. They had two 'goals' disallowed for offside. Hammers avoided an uncomfortable replay when Swansea's keeper dropped Cross's volley. West Ham reach the quarter-finals of both domestic cups in the same season for the first time.											

QF	H	ASTON VILLA	5	W	1-0	0-0	Stewart 89p
	8/3	36,393 *1:6*					Ref: D Richardson

Parkes, Lampard, Brush, Stewart, Martin, Devonshire, Allen, Pearson, Cross, Brooking, Pike
Rimmer, Linton, Gibson, Ormsby, McNaught, Mortimer, Bremner, Little, Donovan, Cowans, Bullivant

Drama in the dying seconds. Villa's Ken McNaught goes up with Alvin Martin with his arm in the air. It makes contact with the ball and a penalty ensues. Villa boss Ron Saunders dismissed it as 'a complete freak'. McNaught's arm had been driven against the ball by Martin's back.

SF	N	EVERTON	8	D	1-1	0-1	Pearson 70
	12/4	47,685 *1:18*					*Kidd 42p*
		(at Villa Park)					Ref: C Seel

Parkes, Stewart, Brush, Bonds, Martin, Devonshire, Allen, Pearson*, Cross, Brooking, Holland, Pike
Hodge, Gidman, Bailey, Wright, Lyons, Eastoe, Megson, King, Kidd !, Hartford, Ross, Latchford*

A highly-charged match sees Devonshire concede a penalty with a challenge on Andy King that seemed fair. Brian Kidd was sent off following a fracas with Stewart. Ross escaped expulsion when scything Brooking. Pearson forced a replay when side-footing home Brooking's cross.

SF	N	EVERTON	8	W	2-1	0-0	Devonshire 94, Lampard 118
R	16/4	40,720 *1:18*			*aet*		*Latchford 113*
		(at Elland Road)					Ref: C Seel

Parkes, Lampard, Brush, Stewart, Bonds, Devonshire, Allen, Pearson, Cross, Brooking, Pike
Hodge, Gidman, Bailey, Wright, Lyons, Ratcliffe, King, Eastoe, Latchford, Hartford, Ross, Varadi*

Bonds plays out of his skin to take the tie into extra-time, having had a header ruled out for pushing. Latchford's diving header made it 1-1. With two minutes left Lampard, who only played because Martin had tonsillitis, launched himself at Cross's flick-on to earn a Wembley date.

F	N	ARSENAL	7	W	1-0	1-0	Brooking 13
	10/5	100,000 *1:4*					
		(at Wembley)					Ref: G Courtney

Parkes, Stewart, Lampard, Bonds, Martin, Devonshire, Allen, Pearson, Cross, Brooking, Pike
Jennings, Rice, Devine, Talbot, O'Leary, Young, Brady, Sunderland, Stapleton, Price, Rix, Nelson*

Arsenal are holders of the Cup, and needed four matches to get past Liverpool in their semi-final. This is their third successive final, but they are beaten by Brooking's header. Young should have been sent off for tripping Allen. Four days later Arsenal lose the Cup-Winners' Cup final.

		Home					Away					
	P	W	D	L	F	A	W	D	L	F	A	Pts
1 Leicester	42	12	5	4	32	19	9	8	4	26	19	55
2 Sunderland	42	16	5	0	47	13	5	7	9	22	29	54
3 Birmingham	42	14	5	2	37	16	7	6	8	21	22	53
4 Chelsea	42	14	3	4	34	16	9	4	8	32	36	53
5 QP Rangers	42	10	9	2	46	25	8	4	9	29	28	49
6 Luton	42	9	10	2	36	17	7	7	7	30	28	49
7 WEST HAM	42	13	2	6	37	21	7	5	9	17	22	47
8 Cambridge	42	11	6	4	40	23	3	10	8	21	30	44
9 Newcastle	42	13	6	2	35	19	2	8	11	18	30	44
10 Preston	42	8	10	3	30	23	4	9	8	26	29	43
11 Oldham	42	12	5	4	30	21	4	6	11	19	32	43
12 Swansea	42	13	1	7	31	20	4	8	9	17	33	43
13 Shrewsbury	42	12	3	6	41	23	6	2	13	19	30	41
14 Orient	42	7	9	5	29	31	5	8	8	19	23	41
15 Cardiff	42	11	4	6	21	16	5	4	12	20	32	40
16 Wrexham	42	13	2	6	26	15	3	4	14	14	34	38
17 Notts Co	42	4	11	6	24	22	7	4	10	27	30	37
18 Watford	42	9	6	6	27	18	3	7	11	12	28	37
19 Bristol Rov	42	9	8	4	33	23	2	5	14	17	41	35
20 Fulham	42	6	4	11	19	28	5	3	13	23	46	29
21 Burnley	42	5	9	7	19	23	1	6	14	20	50	27
22 Charlton	42	6	6	9	25	31	0	4	17	14	47	22
	924	227	129	106	699	463	106	129	227	463	699	924

Odds & ends

Double wins: (5) Burnley, Leicester, Cardiff, Bristol R, Orient.
Double losses: (2) Chelsea, Shrewsbury.

Won from behind: (9) Burnley (h), Leicester (h&a), Bristol R (h), Cambridge (h), QPR (h), Southend LC (h), Sunderland LC (h), Orient FAC (a).
Lost from in front: (3) Chelsea (a), Fulham (h), Swansea (a).

High spots: Winning FA Cup.
Dropping just one point in seven league games from 21 December.

Low spots: Bad league run from March, just two points from six games, to spoil chances of promotion.

West Ham played a total of 17 cup-ties, six of them replays.
The gate at Sunderland in the league was 10,000 than the next biggest away gate.

Hammer of the Year: Alvin Martin.
Ever-presents: (0).
Hat-tricks: (1) Billy Lansdowne.
Leading scorer: (18) David Cross.

	Appearances						Goals			
	Lge	*Sub*	LC	*Sub*	FAC	*Sub*	Lge	LC	FAC	Tot
Allen, Paul	**31**		7		7	*1*	**2**		1	**3**
Banton, Dale	**2**	*2*	1							
Bonds, Billy	**34**		9		5		**1**			**1**
Brooking, Trevor	**37**		8		7		**3**	1	2	**6**
Brush, Paul	**27**		4		6					
Cross, David	**38**	*1*	9		5		**12**	5	1	**18**
Devonshire, Alan	**34**		7		8		**5**		1	**6**
Ferguson, Bobby	**2**		1							
Holland, Pat	**21**	*5*	8		1		**4**	1		**5**
Lampard, Frank	**35**	*1*	6		7				1	**1**
Lansdowne, Billy	**5**	*3*	4	*1*			**1**	3		**4**
Martin, Alvin	**40**		8		7		**2**	1		**3**
Morgan, Nicky	**4**	*2*	1				**1**			**1**
Neighbour, Jimmy	**22**	*1*			4		**1**			**1**
Parkes, Phil	**40**		8		8					
Pearson, Stuart	**24**	*1*	3		8		**5**	1	2	**8**
Pike, Geoff	**27**	*4*	6		7	*1*	**5**	1	1	**7**
Smith, Mark	**1**		1							
Stewart, Ray	**38**		8		8		**10**	1	3	**14**
(own-goals)	**0**						**2**		1	**3**
19 players used	**462**	*20*	99	*1*	88	*2*	**54**	14	13	**81**

LEAGUE DIVISION 2 — Manager: John Lyall — SEASON 1980-81

No	Date		Att	Pos	Pt	F-A	H-T	Scorers, Times, and Referees	1	2	3	4	5	6	7	8	9	10	11	12 sub used
1	H	LUTON			L	1-2	0-0	Stewart 56p	Parkes	Stewart	Brush	Bonds	Martin	Devonshire	Holland	**Goddard***	Cross	Brooking	Pike	Lampard
	16/8		27,933		–			*Moss 64p, 88p*	*Findlay*	*Stephen*	*Donaghy*	*Grealish*	*Saxby*	*Price*	*Hill*	*Stein*	*White**	*Antic*	*Moss*	*West*
								Ref: R Reeves	Paul Goddard signs from QPR for a record £800,000, but is clattered by numerous tackles from behind and goes off with a bruised Achilles tendon. None of the game's three penalties was disputed. Grealish grassed Holland; Martin upended David Moss; and Bonds fouled Stein.											
2	A	BRISTOL CITY			D	1-1	1-1	Cross 19	Parkes	Stewart	Brush	Bonds	Martin	Devonshire	Holland	Goddard	Cross	Brooking	Pike	
	19/8		*13,554*		1			*Ritchie 15*	*Cashley*	*Sweeney*	*Baddeley*	*Tainton*	*Rodgers**	*Merrick*	*Fitzpatrick*	*Mabbutt*	*Ritchie*	*Mann*	*Whitehead*	*Garland*
								Ref: D Lloyd	Goddard thought he had scored his first Hammers goal until he saw the linesman's raised flag. Ritchie capitalised when Bonds couldn't repel Fitzpatrick's cross. Cross headed the equaliser from Brooking's centre. David Rodgers was carried off as a result of colliding with the scorer.											
3	A	PRESTON		17	D	0-0	0-0		Parkes	Lampard	Brush	Stewart	Martin	Devonshire	Holland	Goddard	Cross	Brooking	Pike	
	23/8		*9,063*	*14*	2				*Tunks*	*Cameron*	*McAteer*	*Burns*	*Baxter*	*Blackley**	*Bell*	*Coleman*	*Elliott*	*Potts*	*McGee*	*Doyle*
								Ref: M Warner	Preston continue their run of early-season draws. There was little to enthuse about from this fixture, which was littered with mistakes from both teams. Lampard returned to the side, with Ray Stewart switched to central defence. At least, two away draws compensate for the home defeat.											
4	H	NOTTS CO		7	W	4-0	1-0	Cross 17, Goddard 53, 75, Stewart 67p	Parkes	Stewart	Lampard	Bonds	Martin	Devonshire	Holland	Goddard	Cross	Brooking	Pike	
	30/8		*21,769*	*6*	4				*Avramovic*	*Benjamin*	*O'Brien*	*Kelly*	*Kilcline*	*Richards*	*McCulloch*	*Masson*	*Christie**	*Hunt*	*Hooks*	*Mair*
								Ref: D Hedges	Jimmy Sirrel's County like to mix it. Four of his players were booked, including McCulloch for hurling the ball into the crowd. Cross towered above Kilcline for the first goal, and later won a penalty when fouled by Pedro Richards. Goddard was denied the first hat-trick of his career.											
5	A	CHELSEA		4	W	1-0	0-0	Wilkins 88 (og)	Parkes	Stewart	Lampard	Bonds	Martin	Devonshire	Holland	Goddard	Cross	Brooking	Pike	
	6/9		***32,669***	*20*	6				*Borota*	*Wilkins*	*Rofe*	*Bumstead**	*Nutton*	*Pates*	*Britton*	*Fillery*	*Lee*	*Walker*	*Viljoen*	*Chivers*
								Ref: P Reeves	Lyall and scout Eddie Baily are away spying on Castilla in Spain. They miss the sight of Geoff Hurst's Chelsea losing in the dying minutes as a result of a bizarre own-goal by Graham Wilkins. He managed to hook the ball out, but it had already crossed the line. Pike had a good game.											
6	H	SHREWSBURY		3	W	3-0	1-0	King 7 (og), Goddard 65, Cross 67	Parkes	Stewart	Lampard	Bonds	Martin	Devonshire	Neighbour*	Goddard	Cross	Brooking	Pike	Morgan
	13/9		22,339	*20*	8				*Wardle*	*King*	*Leonard*	*Lindsay*	*Griffin*	*Keay*	*Tong*	*Atkins*	*Dungworth*	*Edwards*	*Petts*	
								Ref: C Maskell	Shrewsbury beat West Ham twice last season, but John King's own-goal from Brooking's cross ruled out any repetition. David Cross spent the 90 minutes shooting on sight, and was eventually rewarded with his 50th goal for West Ham. Neighbour's comeback lasted just 25 minutes.											
7	H	WATFORD		2	W	3-2	0-1	Cross 53, Barnes 67, Brooking 89	Parkes	Stewart	Lampard	Bonds	Martin	Devonshire	**Barnes**	Goddard	Cross	Brooking	Pike	
	20/9		24,288	*15*	10			*Poskett 25, Jackett 55*	*Steele*	*Henderson*	*Jackett*	*Blissett*	*Sims*	*Bolton*	*Callaghan**	*Poskett*	*Jenkins*	*Train*	*Rostron*	*Harrison*
								Ref: A Robinson	The mayhem of Madrid haunts West Ham and Bonds, who, according to the tabloids, labelled certain trouble-makers 'scum'. He was booed onto the pitch, where a wreath was laid for a dead fan. Brooking's late header from Lampard's cross takes Hammers second behind Blackburn.											
8	A	CAMBRIDGE		2	W	2-1	1-1	Goddard 10, Cross 71	Parkes	Stewart	Lampard	Bonds	Martin	Devonshire	Holland	Goddard	Cross	Brooking	Pike	
	27/9		*8,591*	*20*	12			*Finney 31*	*Webster*	*Donaldson*	*Buckley**	*Smith*	*Fallon*	*Gibbins*	*Evans*	*Spriggs*	*Reilly*	*Finney*	*Christie*	*O'Neill*
								Ref: P Richardson	A fourth successive league defeat for John Docherty's Cambridge brings a fifth straight win for West Ham. Goddard's low drive was answered by Tom Finney's close-range header. West Ham were in territorial control through the second half and were rewarded by Cross's firm header.											
9	A	NEWCASTLE		3	D	0-0	0-0		Parkes	Stewart	Lampard	Bonds	Martin	Devonshire	Holland	Goddard*	Cross	Neighbour	Pike	Brush
	4/10		*24,848*	*10*	13				*Carr*	*Kelly*	*Davies*	*Walker*	*Boam*	*Mitchell*	*Shoulder*	*Hibbitt*	*Shinton*	*Rafferty*	*Koenen*	
								Ref: G Nolan	Newcastle stay unbeaten at home; West Ham stay unbeaten away. The dropped point means the Hammers drop to third behind Notts County. John Lyall has been named Bell's Whisky Manager of the Month for September. A recurrent knee injury forces Paul Goddard's substitution.											
10	H	CARDIFF		2	W	1-0	0-0	Neighbour 54	Parkes	Stewart	Lampard	Bonds	Martin	Devonshire	Holland	Morgan	Cross	Neighbour	Pike	
	7/10		**20,402**	*12*	15				*Grotier*	*Grapes*	*Thomas*	*Hughes*	*Pontin*	*Roberts*	*Micallef*	*Kitchen*	*Stevens*	*Ronson*	*Buchanan*	
								Ref: A Gunn	Jimmy Neighbour plays instead of the injured Brooking and bags his second ever goal for the Hammers, turning in Devonshire's cross. The goal came seconds after Peter Kitchen's effort for Cardiff had been ruled out for handball. West Ham go back above Notts Co to second place.											
11	H	BLACKBURN		1	W	2-0	1-0	Cross 40, 53	Parkes	Stewart	Lampard	Bonds	Martin	Devonshire	Holland	Goddard	Cross	Neighbour	Pike	
	11/10		32,402	*3*	17				*Butcher*	*Branagan*	*Devries*	*Coughlin*	*Keeley*	*Fazackerley*	*Brotherston**	*Stonehouse*	*Garner*	*Comstive*	*Parkes*	*Rathbone*
								Ref: G Napthine	A titanic battle between the top two. Geoff Pike covers every blade of grass and David Cross takes his season's tally to 14 goals already. The two combined for the second goal. Pike's shot was turned by the keeper out to Cross, who was denied a hat-trick by the width of a goalpost.											

No	Venue / Opponent	Pos	Res	F-A	H-T	Scorers, Times, and Referees												
12	A OLDHAM	2	D	0-0	0-0		Parkes	Stewart	Lampard	Bonds	Martin	Devonshire*	Holland	Morgan	Cross	Neighbour	Pike	Barnes
18/10	8,344	11	18				*McDonnell*	*Sinclair*	*Blair*	*Kowenicki**	*Clements*	*Hurst*	*Keegan*	*Futcher*	*Steel*	*Stainrod*	*Heaton*	*Atkinson*
						Ref: D Civil	A stodgy pitch and a blustery wind combine to reduce the entertainment value. Oldham preserve their unbeaten home record, but with a Cup-Winners tie looming Lyall is more worried about injuries. Brooking is out with a groin strain and Devonshire limps off with the same problem.											
13	H BOLTON	2	W	2-1	1-0	Walsh 39 (og), Pike 47	Parkes	Stewart	Brush	Bonds	Martin	Devonshire	Holland	Goddard	Cross	Neighbour	Pike	
25/10	25,257	12	20			*Kidd 83*	*Poole*	*Graham*	*Burke*	*Cantello*	*Jones*	*Walsh*	*Reid*	*Whatmore*	*Carter*	*Kidd*	*Gowling*	
						Ref: A Grey	West Ham force 22 corners against Stan Anderson's Bolton, which gives a better indication of the balance of play than does the score. Mike Walsh headed an own-goal before Geoff Pike doubled the lead with one of his specials, sprinting from the halfway line to score off a post.											
14	A BRISTOL ROV	2	W	1-0	1-0	Goddard 26	Parkes	Stewart	Lampard	Bonds	Martin	Devonshire*	Holland	Goddard	Cross	Neighbour	Pike	Brush
1/11	***6,328***	22	22				*Thomas*	*Gillies*	*Bater*	*McCaffrey*	*Hughes*	*Cooper*	*Barrowclough**	*Williams G*	*Mabbutt*	*Bates*	*Barrett*	*Emmanuel*
						Ref: L Robinson	Considering Rovers are propping up the table, and are still searching for their first win, this was an unconvincing result. Parkes was the busier keeper and in the second half he was kept on his toes throughout. Paul Goddard's brilliant goal was ideal preparation for the trip to Romania.											
15	H GRIMSBY	2	W	2-1	1-0	Cross 15, 55	Parkes	Brush	Lampard	Bonds	Martin	Neighbour	Holland	Goddard	Cross	Brooking	Pike	
8/11	25,468	19	24			*Stone 89*	*Batch*	*Stone*	*Crosby*	*Waters*	*Wigginton*	*Moore K*	*Brolly*	*Kilmore*	*Drinkell*	*Mitchell*	*Liddell**	*Steeples*
						Ref: L Burden	The players looked knackered after their trip to Romania, and make hard work of beating a side who had scored only six goals all season. Cross headed two typical goals, the first from Brush's cross, the second from Brooking's. Mike Brolly's free-kick raised Grimsby's total to seven.											
16	H BRISTOL CITY	1	W	**5-0**	2-0	Goddard 11, 89, Martin 16, Brooking 71, [Cross 85]	Parkes	Stewart	Lampard	Bonds	Martin	Devonshire	Holland	Goddard	Cross	Brooking	Pike	
11/11	25,210	20	26				*Cashley*	*Sweeney*	*Hay*	*Mann*	*Marshall*	*Whitehead*	*Tainton**	*Fitzpatrick*	*Whitehead*	*Ritchie*	*Pritchard*	*Smith*
						Ref: J Martin	City haven't won away all season and permit West Ham to go top for the first time. Yet what might have happened had City not squandered an easy chance at 0-0? Alvin Martin's shot was deflected in off Merrick, and Cross takes his tally to 19, the same as that for the whole of 1979-80.											
17	A LUTON	1	L	2-3	1-2	Brooking 44, 49	Parkes	Stewart	Lampard	Bonds	Martin	Devonshire	Holland	Goddard	Cross	Brooking	Pike	
15/11	*17,031*	10	26			*Stein 14, 17, Moss 85*	*Findlay*	*Stephens*	*Donaghy*	*Grealish*	*Saxby*	*Price*	*Hill*	*Stein*	*White*	*Aizlewood**	*Moss*	*West*
						Ref: C White	Luton were the last team to beat the Hammers. They now complete the double. The last time Brooking scored twice in one match was against Palace in 1972. He hasn't scored a hat-trick since Newcastle 13 years ago. Having got to 2-2 it was galling to lose; Hill nodded down to Moss.											
18	H SWANSEA	1	W	2-0	0-0	Cross 66, Goddard 83	Parkes	Stewart	Lampard	Bonds	Martin	Devonshire*	Holland	Goddard	Cross	Brooking	Pike	Neighbour
22/11	27,376	6	28				*Stewart*	*Attley*	*Hadziabdic**	*Rushbury*	*Charles*	*Stevenson*	*Craig*	*Waddle*	*James R*	*Mahoney*	*Robinson*	*Loveridge*
						Ref: D Hutchinson	John Toshack's Swansea take no prisoners. He doesn't mince words either, demanding 'Where's the justice?' Goddard was plainly offside as Cross broke the deadlock, and the linesman duly had his flag up. On the run of play Swansea got off lightly. Phillips struck his own crossbar.											
19	A DERBY	1	L	0-2	0-1		Parkes	Stewart	Lampard	Bonds	Martin	Devonshire	Holland	Goddard	Cross	Brooking	Pike	
26/11	*18,446*	9	28			*Biley 19, Clark 88*	*Jones*	*Powell S*	*Richards*	*Clark*	*McFarland*	*Ramage*	*Powell B*	*Swindlehurst*	*Biley*	*Wilson*	*Emson*	
						Ref: D Webb	Keith Burkinshaw, manager of League Cup opponents Spurs, sees West Ham fail to score for only the third time this season. They came close against Colin Addison's Derby when Goddard and Holland hit the bar, but could never get back on terms after Biley headed in Emson's cross.											
20	A WREXHAM	1	D	2-2	1-1	Devonshire 2, Goddard 51	Parkes	Stewart	Lampard	Bonds	Martin	Devonshire	Holland	Goddard	Cross	Brooking	Pike	
29/11	*8,941*	17	29			*Cartwright 35, Edwards 67*	*Davies*	*Sutton*	*Kenworthy*	*Davis*	*Cegielski*	*Carrodus*	*Fox*	*Arkwright*	*Edwards*	*McNeil*	*Cartwright*	
						Ref: C Seel	Devonshire had had a bet with Pat Holland over who would score first this season. Devonshire wins it with a sensational individual goal that saw him waltz through half the Wrexham team. But Holland does not pay up, changing the rules to who scores the most, not who scores first.											
21	H SHEFFIELD WED	1	W	2-1	2-1	Brooking 40, Holland 42	Parkes	Stewart	Lampard	Bonds	Martin	Devonshire	Holland	Goddard	Cross	Brooking	Pike	
6/12	30,746	6	31			*Mirocevic 35*	*Bolder*	*Blackhall*	*Grant*	*Smith*	*Shirtliff*	*Sterland*	*Mirocevic**	*Johnson*	*Leman*	*McCulloch*	*Curran*	*Owen*
						Ref: D Letts	Jack Charlton's Owls provide West Ham with their 10th straight home win. Bookies rate them 8-13 on for promotion. Brooking was booked for the third time in his career for a late tackle. Bolder was only booked for a professional foul and the referee needed a police escort at the end.											
22	A BLACKBURN	1	D	0-0	0-0		Parkes	Stewart	Lampard	Bonds	Martin	Devonshire	Holland	Goddard	Cross	Brooking	Pike	
13/12	*13,279*	8	32				*Butcher*	*Speight*	*Branagan*	*Kendall*	*Keeley*	*Fazackerley*	*Brotherston*	*Stonehouse*	*Lowey*	*McKenzie**	*Parkes*	*Burke*
						Ref: A Saunders	Blackburn have slumped from first to eighth though remain unbeaten at home. West Ham score goals so freely at home that it is surprising to learn they have scored only nine in 11 away games – fewer than nine other sides in the division. In fact, Hammers are away draw specialists.											
23	H DERBY	1	W	3-1	1-1	Cross 44, Goddard 74, Brooking 85	Parkes	Stewart	Lampard	Bonds	Martin	Devonshire	Holland	Goddard	Cross	Brooking	Pike	
20/12	24,071	8	34			*Swindlehurst 42p*	*Jones*	*Emery*	*Richards*	*Clark*	*Osgood*	*Ramage*	*Powell S*	*Hector*	*Biley*	*Swindlehurst*	*Emson*	
						Ref: R Challis	When Pike hauled down Kevin Hector, Colin Addison's Derby must have hoped for an upset. But moments later Lampard's miscued shot fell kindly for Cross to equalise. Brooking dominated the second half, and his solo goal has the crowd on its feet. West Ham go five points clear.											

No	Date		Att	Pos	Pt	F-A	H-T	Scorers, Times, and Referees	1	2	3	4	5	6	7	8	9	10	11	12 sub used
24	A	QP RANGERS		1	L	**0-3**	0-1		Parkes	Stewart	Lampard	Bonds	Martin	Devonshire	Holland	Goddard	Cross*	Brooking	Pike	Neighbour
	26/12		*23,811*	*12*	34			*Silkman 30, Currie 52, Stainrod 84*	*Burridge*	*Shanks*	*Gillard*	*Fenwick*	*Wicks*	*Roeder*	*Flanagan*	*King*	*Stainrod*	*Currie**	*Silkman*	*Waddock*
								Ref: B Hill	Terry Venables' hastily rebuilt Rangers cashed in on the well-travelled Barry Silkman, who scored one goal and made the others. Silkman's bad early back-pass let in Cross, who missed and hurt his ribs. Phil Parkes was responsible for the second goal, fumbling Silkman's cross.											
25	H	ORIENT		1	W	2-1	0-0	Holland 64, Allen 82	Parkes	Stewart	Lampard*	Bonds	Martin	Devonshire	Holland	Goddard	Morgan	Brooking	Pike	Allen
	27/12		34,408	*8*	36			*Chiedozie 71*	*Day*	*Fisher*	*Roffey*	*Taylor T*	*Gray*	*Parsons*	*Chiedozie*	*Moores*	*Mayo*	*Bowles*	*Taylor P*	
								Ref: E Read	A no-holds-barred local derby. Orient boss Jimmy Bloomfield later lambasts Lampard for repeatedly kicking John Chiedozie into orbit. Pat Holland headed in Devonshire's cross; Chiedozie scored a freak equaliser when Parkes fluffed Parson's cross; Allen hit a spectacular winner.											
26	A	SWANSEA		1	W	3-1	2-0	Brooking 24, Pike 34, Cross 58	Parkes	Stewart	Lampard	Bonds	Martin	Devonshire	Holland	Goddard	Cross	Brooking	Pike	
	10/1		*22,110*	*2*	38			*Curtis 54*	*Stewart*	*Attley*	*Hadziabdic*	*Mahoney*	*Stevenson*	*Phillips*	*James R*	*Curtis*	*James L**	*Charles*	*Robinson*	*Giles*
								Ref: M Scott	Hammers win the battle of the top two to go six points clear. Lyall instructed Cross and Goddard to play tight together to frustrate Swansea's sweeper, Phillips, who was pressured into conceding the Hammers' third goal. Paul Goddard's cheeky dummy had set up Brooking's opener.											
27	A	NOTTS CO		1	D	1-1	1-0	Holland 22	Parkes	Stewart	Brush	Bonds	Martin	Devonshire	Holland*	Goddard	Cross	Brooking	Pike	Allen
	17/1		*13,718*	*3*	39			*Hooks 56*	*Avramovic*	*Benjamin*	*O'Brien*	*Kelly*	*Kilcline*	*Richards*	*McCulloch*	*Masson*	*Christie*	*Hunt*	*Hooks*	
								Ref: P Partridge	Holland pays a heavy price for scoring; he collides with Avramovic and goes off with knee ligament damage. Though County have lost just once at home, this was a point lost. Cross incredibly hit the bar from two feet out, Brooking hit a post, and Allen's 'goal' was narrowly offside.											
28	H	PRESTON		1	W	**5-0**	2-0	Goddard 10, Pike 33, Lampard 76, [Devonshire 80, 87]	Parkes	Stewart	Lampard	Bonds	Martin	Devonshire	Neighbour	Goddard	Cross	Brooking	Pike	
	31/1		26,413	*20*	41				*Tunks*	*Westwell*	*McAteer*	*Bell*	*Baxter*	*O'Riorden*	*Coleman*	*Doyle*	*Elliott*	*McGee**	*Houston*	*Sayer*
								Ref: C Thomas	West Ham shrug off defeats by Wrexham and Coventry by serving up five super goals. Pick of the bunch was Lampard's, who drove back a clearance from 30 yards. Preston manager Nobby Stiles admitted: 'They never gave us a look in.' West Ham's lead widens to seven points.											
29	A	SHREWSBURY		1	W	2-0	1-0	Devonshire 33, Cross 90	Parkes	Stewart	Lampard	Bonds	Martin	Devonshire	Neighbour	Goddard*	Cross	Brooking	Pike	Barnes
	7/2		*9,201*	*20*	43				*Wardle*	*King*	*Leonard*	*MacLaren**	*Griffin*	*Keay*	*Tong*	*Atkins*	*Bates*	*Biggins*	*Cross*	*Petts*
								Ref: H King	A statistical quirk. All other 10 games in Division 2 ended in home wins. So casual did West Ham become after half-time that they would have had only themselves to blame had this been a home win. Devonshire's header was followed by Cross connecting with Brooking's free-kick.											
30	H	CHELSEA		1	W	4-0	1-0	Brooking 26, 75, Cross 61, Devonshire 89	Parkes	Stewart	Lampard	Bonds	Martin	Devonshire	Neighbour	Goddard	Cross	Brooking	Pike	
	14/2		35,164	*3*	45				*Borota*	*Locke*	*Rofe*	*Bumstead*	*Droy*	*Chivers*	*Elmes*	*Fillery*	*Lee*	*Mayes*	*Rhr'des-Brown*	
								Ref: S Bates	Thousands are locked out of this top-of-the-table clash. Brooking illuminates it with two classic goals, the first when Cross drags a defender wide to create space; the second with an exquisite chip as Borota strays off his line. West Ham are now 10 points clear of third-placed Chelsea.											
31	H	CAMBRIDGE		1	W	4-2	2-1	Devonshire 33, Stewart 36p, 65, [Goddard 58]	Parkes	Stewart	Lampard	Bonds	Martin	Devonshire	Neighbour	Goddard	Cross	Brooking	Pike	
	21/2		**36,002**	*11*	47			*Reilly 31, Spriggs 82*	*Key*	*Donaldson**	*Murray*	*Smith*	*Fallon*	*Finney*	*Streete*	*Spriggs*	*Reilly*	*Lyons*	*Gibbins*	*O'Neill*
								Ref: T Bune	The ref takes a lenient view of a second-half punch-up between Alvin Martin and George Reilly, sending neither of them off. Reilly's header had opened the scoring for John Docherty's Cambridge. Ray Stewart's penalty was awarded after Fallon had shoved David Cross in the back.											
32	A	WATFORD		1	W	2-1	0-0	Cross 56, 63	Parkes	Stewart	Lampard	Bonds	Martin	Devonshire	Neighbour	Goddard	Cross	Brooking	Pike	
	28/2		*20,786*	*14*	49			*Poskett 85*	*Sherwood*	*Rice*	*Pritchett*	*Taylor*	*Sims*	*Bolton*	*Ward*	*Blissett*	*Armstrong*	*Jackett*	*Poskett*	
								Ref: B Stevens	Watford boss Graham Taylor reckoned the only difference between the sides was Phil Parkes' goalkeeping, especially during Watford's early assaults. Martin needed five stitches in a head wound following a mid-air collision with John Ward. Cross takes his season's goal tally to 27.											
33	H	NEWCASTLE		1	W	1-0	1-0	Cross 3	Parkes	Stewart	Lampard	Bonds	Martin	Allen*	Neighbour	Goddard	Cross	Brooking	Pike	Pearson
	7/3		26,274	*14*	51				*Carr*	*Brownlie*	*Davies*	*Martin*	*Barton*	*Halliday*	*Shoulder*	*Trewick*	*Harford*	*Wharton*	*Waddle**	*Carney*
								Ref: K Baker	West Ham have eaten humble pie after losing to Tbilisi, and this bread and butter game offered little that was memorable. Newcastle had only scored eight away goals all season and carried little threat. Cross's early header takes Hammers 10 points clear of second-placed Notts County.											
34	H	OLDHAM		1	D	1-1	0-0	Goddard 81	Parkes	Stewart	Lampard	Bonds	Martin	Brush*	Pearson	Goddard	Cross	Brooking	Pike	Barnes
	21/3		24,394	*17*	52			*Wylde 49*	*Platt*	*Edwards*	*Blair*	*Keegan*	*McDonough*	*Futcher*	*Wylde*	*Heaton*	*Steel*	*Palmer*	*Atkinson*	
								Ref: J Deakin	Another limp display following European exertions. When Parkes failed to gather a corner-kick the ball fell to Wylde. Martin's dreadful back-pass almost made it 0-2 before Goddard squared things from Barnes' corner. Stewart played in midfield and looked like a fish out of water.											

No	Date	Venue	Opponent	Att	Pos	Res	Pts	F-A	H-T	Scorers, Times, and Referees	1	2	3	4	5	6	7	8	9	10	11	12 sub used
35	28/3	A	BOLTON	*13,271*	1	D	53	1-1	0-1	Brooking 61	Parkes	Stewart	Lampard	Bonds	Martin*	Devonshire	Neighbour	Goddard	Cross	Brooking	Pike	Pearson
					15					*Whatmore 20*	*Poole*	*Nicholson*	*Walsh*	*Reid*	*Jones*	*Cantello*	*Nikolic*	*Whatmore*	*Thomas*	*Hoggan*	*Gowling*	
										Ref: M Heath	Minds are not at Burnden Park but on Liverpool in the League Cup final replay. With promotion a formality, all John Lyall cares about is that his players pick up no injuries. The only doubt is Martin, who was taken off with an ankle injury. Devonshire came through without mishap.											
36	4/4	H	BRISTOL ROV	23,544	1	W	55	2-0	1-0	Pike 32, Goddard 50	Parkes	Stewart	Lampard	Bonds	Brush	Devonshire	Neighbour	Goddard	Cross	Brooking	Pike	
					22						*McAlister*	*Gillies*	*Jones*	*McCaffrey*	*Hughes*	*Emmanuel*	*Williams G**	*Williams D*	*Randall*	*Penny*	*Mabbutt*	*Cooper*
										Ref: D Hutchinson	West Ham put defeat by Liverpool out of their minds by celebrating promotion with six matches still to play. Terry Cooper's bottom-placed Rovers have won away only once and were lambs to the slaughter. Pike took Goddard's pass to fire the first goal and launch the celebrations.											
37	11/4	A	GRIMSBY	*17,924*	1	W	57	5-1	1-0	Cross 32, 47, 88, 89, Pike 80	Parkes	Stewart	Lampard	Bonds	Martin	Devonshire	Neighbour	Goddard	Cross	Brooking	Pike	
					6					*Waters 70p*	*Batch*	*Stone*	*Crombie**	*Waters*	*Wigginton*	*Moore K*	*Brolly*	*Whymark*	*Drinkell*	*Mitchell*	*Cumming*	*Ford*
										Ref: R Toseland	David Cross had been stuck on 29 goals for five games. He races up to 33 in a magical performance with the first four-goal haul of his career. Grimsby were unlikely victims, having lost only once and conceded just four home goals all season. Stewart tripped Cumming for the penalty.											
38	18/4	A	ORIENT	*14,592*	1	W	59	2-0	2-0	Neighbour 17, Pike 40	Parkes	Stewart	Lampard	Bonds	Martin	Devonshire	Neighbour	Pearson*	Cross	Brooking	Pike	Barnes
					15						*Day*	*Fisher*	*Roffey*	*Taylor T**	*Gray*	*Moores*	*Chiedozie*	*Hughton*	*Jennings*	*Bowles*	*Taylor P*	*Mayo*
										Ref: R Lewis	Lyall missed this game, going up to Scotland to try to unearth another nugget like Ray Stewart. A boring match was illuminated only by Jimmy Neighbour bursting between two defenders for the first goal, and Pike rocketing his third in three games. West Ham are still unbeaten in 1981.											
39	21/4	H	QP RANGERS	24,599	1	W	61	3-0	2-0	Goddard 8, 28, 81	Parkes	Stewart	Lampard	Bonds	Martin	Devonshire	Neighbour	Goddard	Cross	Brooking*	Pike	Barnes
					10						*Burridge*	*Neill*	*Gillard*	*Fenwick*	*Wicks**	*Roeder*	*Waddock*	*Francis*	*Flanagan*	*Currie*	*Sealy*	*Burke*
										Ref: L Shapter	Terry Venables' QPR were the last league side to beat West Ham, back on Boxing Day. QPR have blown their own promotion hopes in recent weeks. Ex-Ranger Paul Goddard bags the first hat-trick of his career. Parkes saved Gerry Francis' penalty after Bonds had fouled Roeder.											
40	2/5	H	WREXHAM	30,515	1	W	63	1-0	1-0	Stewart 43p	Parkes	Stewart	Lampard	Bonds	Martin	Devonshire	Neighbour	Goddard*	Cross	Brooking	Pike	Pearson
					16						*Davies*	*Dowman*	*Dwyer*	*Davis*	*Cegielski*	*Carrodus*	*Fox*	*Buxton**	*Vinter*	*McNeil*	*Hill*	*Edwards*
										Ref: A Grey	West Ham's target is to beat Middlesbrough's Division 2 record of 65 points. Stewart's seventh penalty of the season keeps them on track, and avenges defeat by Wrexham in the FA Cup. Wayne Cegielski conceded the penalty when fouling Cross. Lyall wants to sign Steve Coppell.											
41	6/5	A	CARDIFF	*10,558*	1	D	64	0-0	0-0		Parkes	Stewart	Lampard	Bonds	Martin	Devonshire	Neighbour	Morgan	Cross	Brooking	Pike	
					19						*Healey*	*Jones*	*Sullivan*	*Grapes**	*Pontin*	*Dwyer*	*Lewis*	*Kitchen*	*Stevens*	*Ronson*	*Micallef*	*Thomas*
										Ref: P Reeves	Nicky Morgan plays in place of the injured Goddard and does well. This draw averts relegation for Cardiff, and dooms Preston, who won 2-1 at Derby. This is West Ham's ninth away draw in the league. Now they need to win at Hillsborough to break Middlesbrough's points record.											
42	8/5	A	SHEFFIELD WED	*21,087*	1	W	66	1-0	0-0	Morgan 64	Parkes	Stewart	Lampard	Bonds	Martin*	Devonshire	Neighbour	Morgan	Cross	Brooking	Pike	Brush
					10						*Bolder*	*Blackhall*	*Grant*	*Smith*	*Shirtliff*	*Johnson*	*Mellor*	*Taylor*	*King**	*McCulloch*	*Curran*	*Pearson*
			Home	Away						Ref: N Midgley	It is ironic that victory over Jack Charlton's Owls enables West Ham to break the 65-points record established by Jack Charlton's Boro. Against all expectations this was an entertaining game, the Hammers 61st of the season. Stuart Pearson is up for sale at a knock-down price.											
Average			27,140	15,625																		

League Cup

No	Date	Venue	Opponent	Att	Pos	Res	F-A	H-T	Scorers, Times, and Referees	1	2	3	4	5	6	7	8	9	10	11	12 sub used
2:1	26/8	A	BURNLEY	*6,818*	17	W	2-0	2-0	Goddard 14, Cross 22	Parkes	Stewart	Lampard	Bonds	Martin	Devonshire	Holland	Goddard	Cross	Brooking	Pike	
					3:13					*Stevenson*	*Wood*	*Thomson*	*Rodaway*	*Laws*	*Scott*	*Dobson*	*Cassidy*	*Cavener*	*Hamilton*	*Taylor*	
									Ref: D Shaw	Goddard is happy to score his first goal – a volley – for West Ham, who might have settled this tie with five or six goals. After David Cross outjumped Jim Thomson to head in Brooking's cross for the second, West Ham took their foot off the gas, and that might prove unwise.											
2:2	2/9	H	BURNLEY	15,216	7	W	4-0	1-0	Stewart 33p, Goddard 65, Wood 77 (og), [Pike 86]	Parkes	Stewart	Lampard	Bonds	Martin	Devonshire	Holland*	Goddard	Cross	Brooking	Pike	Allen
					3:19					*Stevenson*	*Laws*	*Holt*	*Scott**	*Dobson*	*Overson*	*Cassidy*	*Young*	*Hamilton*	*Taylor*	*Cavener*	
									Ref: A Seville (Hammers win 6-0 on aggregate)	When Brian Laws brings down Devonshire, Ray Stewart misses his second penalty in 15 attempts since joining West Ham. But as with his other miss, the ball was swept into the net, this time by Goddard. Stewart had already scored one penalty in this match, when Holt handled.											
3	23/9	A	CHARLTON	*17,884*	2	W	2-1	1-1	Cross 20, 81	Parkes	Stewart	Lampard	Bonds	Martin	Devonshire	Barnes	Goddard	Cross	Brush	Pike	
					3:10				*Robinson 21*	*Wood*	*Gritt*	*Warman*	*Shaw*	*Berry*	*Tydeman*	*Powell*	*Walsh*	*Hales*	*Smith*	*Robinson*	
									Ref: M Taylor	This vibrant cup-tie saw Phil Parkes make the first goal with a phenomenally long goal-kick, which bounced neatly for Cross to lob Jeff Wood. Charlton's Phil Warman dished out some heavy treatment on Barnes, who had the last laugh when floating over the cross for Cross's winner.											
4	28/10	H	BARNSLEY	21,548	2	W	2-1	0-0	Martin 69, Cross 71	Parkes	Stewart	Lampard*	Brush	Martin	Devonshire	Holland	Goddard	Cross	Neighbour	Pike	Allen
					3:7				*Evans 63*	*New*	*Joyce*	*Chambers*	*Glavin*	*Banks*	*McCarthy*	*Evans*	*Riley*	*Aylott*	*Lester*	*Downes*	
									Ref: A Glasson	Lucky Hammers. Barnsley boss Norman Hunter complains that David Cross handled the winning goal into the net while lying on the goal-line. Lyall admitted: 'Barnsley are the best side to come here this season.' Barnsley's bus arrived just 27 minutes before kick-off because of traffic.											

League Cup			F-A	H-T	Scorers, Times, and Referees	1	2	3	4	5	6	7	8	9	10	11	subs used
QF H TOTTENHAM	1	W	1-0	0-0	Cross 81	Parkes	Stewart	Lampard	Bonds	Martin	Devonshire	Holland	Goddard	Cross	Neighbour	Pike	
2/12 36,003 *1:10*					Ref: J Hunting	*Daines*	*McAllister*	*Hughton*	*Yorath*	*Lacy*	*Perryman*	*Ardiles*	*Archibald*	*Villa*	*Hoddle*	*Crooks*	
SF A COVENTRY	1	L	2-3	2-0	Bonds 26, Thompson 35 (og)	Parkes	Stewart	Brush	Bonds	Martin	Devonshire	Allen	Goddard	Cross	Brooking	Pike	
1 27/1 *35,468 1:15*					*Thompson 71, 90, Daly 76* Ref: G Courtney	*Sealey*	*Thomas*	*Roberts*	*Blair*	*Dyson*	*Gillespie*	*Bodak*	*Daly**	*Thompson*	*Hateley*	*Hunt*	*Jacobs*
SF H COVENTRY	1	W	2-0	0-0	Goddard 60, Neighbour 89	Parkes	Stewart	Lampard	Bonds	Martin	Devonshire	Neighbour	Goddard	Cross	Brooking	Pike	
2 10/2 36,551 *1:15*					Ref: K Hackett (Hammers win 4-3 on aggregate)	*Sealey*	*Thomas*	*Roberts*	*Blair*	*Dyson*	*Gillespie*	*Bodak**	*Daly*	*Thompson*	*Hateley*	*Hunt*	*Jacobs*
F N LIVERPOOL	1	D	1-1	0-0	Stewart 120p	Parkes	Stewart	Lampard	Bonds	Martin	Devonshire	Neighbour	Goddard*	Cross	Brooking	Pike	Pearson
14/3 *100,000 1:4* (at Wembley)			*aet*		*Kennedy A 117* Ref: C Thomas	*Clemence*	*Neal*	*Kennedy A*	*Irwin*	*Kennedy R*	*Hansen*	*Dalglish*	*Lee*	*Heighway**	*McDermott*	*Souness*	*Case*
FR N LIVERPOOL	1	L	1-2	1-2	Goddard 10	Parkes	Stewart	Lampard	Bonds	Martin	Devonshire	Neighbour	Goddard	Cross	Brooking	Pike*	Pearson
1/4 *36,693 1:4* (at Villa Park)					*Dalglish 25, Hansen 29* Ref: C Thomas	*Clemence*	*Neal*	*Kennedy A*	*Thompson*	*Kennedy R*	*Hansen*	*Dalglish*	*Lee*	*Rush*	*McDermott*	*Case*	

QF: The goal was made by Brooking and scored by Cross, yet illness or injury almost ruled out both players. This was not a match for touch-play, and Ardiles, Hoddle and Brooking were largely swamped by flying boots. The win takes West Ham to a first League Cup semi in eight years.

SF 1: West Ham stage an incredible collapse after leading 2-0 at half-time to Gordon Milne's Coventry. What's more, West Ham had been handed their two goals on a plate, first when Bonds' weak header squirmed through Sealey's hands, then when Thompson's back-pass eluded Sealey.

SF 2: Billy Bonds celebrates his 600th first-team game with this famous victory. Goddard is the only Hammer on the pitch for whom this will be a first appearance to Wembley. So it is fitting that his 20-yard belter paves the way. Earlier, Phil Parkes had saved splendidly from Daly.

F: Controversy rages as the ref allows Alan Kennedy's goal, even though Sammy Lee is lying prostrate in an offside position. In the last seconds McDermott fists Martin's header against the bar, permitting Stewart to force a replay. The 90 minutes normal play had been quite forgettable.

FR: Live TV coverage dampens the attendance. When Goddard headed in Neighbour's cross, West Ham sensed glory. But McDermott's chip produced an equaliser from Dalglish, whereupon Bonds' knee diverted Hansen's header past Parkes. This was Ian Rush's second full game.

Charity Shield			F-A	H-T	Scorers, Times, and Referees	1	2	3	4	5	6	7	8	9	10	11	subs used
N LIVERPOOL		L	0-1	0-1		Parkes	Stewart	Brush	Bonds	Martin	Devonshire	Allen	Holland	Cross	Brooking	Pike*	Morgan
9/8 *90,000* (At Wembley)					*McDermott 18* Ref: J Hunting	*Clemence*	*Neal*	*Kennedy A*	*Thompson*	*Kennedy R*	*Hansen*	*Dalglish*	*Case*	*Johnson*	*McDermott*	*Souness*	

Liverpool scored when Alan Kennedy fired in a fierce cross-shot that Parkes couldn't hold. McDermott swept the ball into the net from close range. Bob Paisley's team then wasted many chances, and West Ham might have rescued themselves when Clemence saved at Morgan's feet.

FA Cup			F-A	H-T	Scorers, Times, and Referees	1	2	3	4	5	6	7	8	9	10	11	subs used
3 H WREXHAM	1	D	1-1	0-0	Stewart 60p	Parkes	Stewart	Lampard	Bonds	Martin	Devonshire	Holland	Goddard	Cross	Brooking	Pike	
3/1 30,137 *13*					*Davis 87* Ref: A Hamil	*Davies*	*Hill*	*Jones*	*Davis*	*Cegielski*	*Arkwright*	*Buxton**	*Sutton*	*Edwards*	*McNeil*	*Cartwright*	*Fox*
3R A WREXHAM	1	D	0-0	0-0		Parkes	Stewart	Lampard	Bonds	Martin	Devonshire	Holland	Goddard	Cross	Brooking	Pike	
6/1 *13,643 13*			*aet*		Ref: A Hamil	*Davies*	*Sutton*	*Kenworthy*	*Davis*	*Cegielski*	*Carrodus*	*Fox*	*Arkwright*	*Edwards*	*McNeil*	*Cartwright*	
3 A WREXHAM	1	L	0-1	0-0		Parkes	Stewart	Brush	Bonds	Martin	Devonshire	Allen*	Goddard	Cross	Brooking	Pike	Neighbour
RR 19/1 *14,615 15*			*aet*		*McNeil 104* Ref: D Owen	*Davies*	*Hill*	*Jones*	*Davis**	*Cegielski*	*Arkwright*	*Fox*	*Sutton*	*Edwards*	*McNeil*	*Cartwright*	*Vinter*

3: 'On my baby's life I never touched him,' protests Wrexham's Joey Jones, as Holland goes down in the penalty area. Ray Stewart was relieved to score, for the Upton Park crowd had been getting at him recently. Wrexham's 33-year-old skipper, Gareth Davis, thumped the equaliser.

3R: In the second half West Ham thought they had scored. Cross was given offside, although Joey Jones looked to have played him onside. The winners will be at home to Division 4 Wimbledon in Round 4. Wrexham boss Arfon Griffiths called 'heads' correctly for the choice of venue.

3 RR: So West Ham relinquish their grip on the FA Cup at the first hurdle. Their interest might have been sustained but for bad misses by Goddard in the 4th and 73rd minutes. A 330-minute cup-tie was finally settled when Cartwright's shot was blocked by Parkes but fell to Dixie McNeil.

European Cup-Winners' Cup			F-A	H-T	Scorers, Times, and Referees	1	2	3	4	5	6	7	8	9	10	11	subs used
1:1 A CASTILLA	3	L	1-3	1-0	Cross 17	Parkes	Stewart	Lampard	Bonds	Martin	Devonshire*	Morgana^	Goddard	Cross	Brooking	Pike	Brush/Barnes
17/9 (Spain) *40,000*					*Paco 64, Balin 70, Cidon 74* Ref: Delmer (France)	*Miguel*	*Juanito**	*Casimiro*	*Salguero*	*Espinosa*	*Sanch' Lorenzo*	*Balin*	*Alvarez*	*Paco*	*Bernal*	*Cidon^*	*Chendo/Blanco*

Castilla are Real Madrid's reserve side. Cross's header gives West Ham the lead in the Bernabeu Stadium, but then they sit back. Hooligans among supporters incite frightening scenes, in which one West Ham fan loses his life. Terrible back-passes by Bonds and Pike cost two goals.

Rd	Venue	Opponent	Att	Res	F-A	H-T	Scorers, Times, and Referees	1	2	3	4	5	6	7	8	9	10	11	12 sub used
1:2	H	CASTILLA		2	W 5-1	3-0	Pike 19, Cross 30, 103, 119, Goddard 40	Parkes	Stewart	Lampard	Bond	Martin	Devonshire	Holland*	Goddard^	Cross	Brooking	Pike	Brush/Morgan
1/10		behind closed doors			aet		*Bernal 56*	*Miguel*	*Chendo*	*Casimiro*	*Salguero*	*Espinosa*	*Sanch' Lorenzo*	*Balin*	*Alvarez*	*Paco**	*Bernal*	*Cidon^*	*Ramirez/Blanco*

Ref: J Keizer (Holland)
(Hammers win 6-4 on aggregate)

West Ham were originally ordered to play this match 300 kilometres from Upton Park, but the club appealed and were ordered instead to play behind closed doors, with just 70 representatives of each side allowed. The weird atmosphere was evidently to Hammers' liking in extra-time.

Rd	Venue	Opponent	Att	Res	F-A	H-T	Scorers	1	2	3	4	5	6	7	8	9	10	11	12
2:1	H	POLI TIMISOARA		2	W 4-0	3-0	Bonds 24, Goddard 25, Stewart 27p,	Parkes	Stewart	Lampard	Bonds	Martin	Devonshire	Holland	Goddard*	Cross	Neighbour	Pike	Morgan
22/10		(Romania)	27,257				[Cross 75]	*Moise*	*Nadu*	*Paltinisanu*	*Visan*	*Sunda*	*Murar*	*Anghel*	*Dembrowsji**	*Nedelcu*	*Dumitru*	*Cotec*	*Titi*

Ref: H Fahnler (Austria)

Politecnica beat Billy McNeill's Celtic in Round 1, and he obligingly passes on his dossier to Lyall. Bonds' header put West Ham on their way, and two minutes later they lead 3-0 when Visan pushed Goddard in the area. When Moise later fouled Goddard, Stewart's penalty was saved.

Rd	Venue	Opponent	Att	Res	F-A	H-T	Scorers	1	2	3	4	5	6	7	8	9	10	11	12
2:2	A	POLI TIMISOARA		2	L 0-1	0-0		Parkes	Stewart*	Lampard	Bonds	Martin	Allen	Holland	Goddard	Cross	Neighbour^	Pike	Brush/Brooking
5/11			*25,000*				*Paltinisanu 54*	*Moise*	*Sunda*	*Paltinisanu*	*Visan*	*Titi*	*Serbanoiu*	*Anghel*	*Dembrowski**	*Nedelcu*	*Dumitru*	*Cotec*	*Sunda*

Ref: R Lattanzi (Italy)
(Hammers win 4-1 on aggregate)

The Romanians think the tie is winnable, and if not they seem determined to hospitalise as many Hammers as possible. The goal was Parkes' fault, allowing a shot to bounce over his arm. The hosts played their version of Yellow Submarine over the public address system during play.

Rd	Venue	Opponent	Att	Res	F-A	H-T	Scorers	1	2	3	4	5	6	7	8	9	10	11	12
3:1	H	DYNAMO TBILISI		1	L 1-4	0-2	Cross 54	Parkes	Stewart	Lampard	Bonds	Martin	Devonshire*	Neighbour	Goddard	Cros	Brooking	Pike	Allen
4/3		(USSR)	34,957				*Chivadze 23, Gutsaev 31, Shengelia 56, 67*	*Gabelia*	*Khisanishvili*	*Chivadze*	*Khinchagashvili*	*Tavadze*	*Daraselia*	*Svanadze*	*Sulakvelidze*	*Gutsayev*	*Kipiani*	*Shengelia*	

Ref: A Garrido (Portugal)

Had this game also been played behind closed doors West Ham fans would have been denied a sight of the finest performance many of them had seen. Tbilisi were irresistible from the moment Chivadze burst through to score from 25 yards. Lyall had said they were the best team left.

Rd	Venue	Opponent	Att	Res	F-A	H-T	Scorers	1	2	3	4	5	6	7	8	9	10	11	12
3:2	A	DYNAMO TBILISI		1	W 1-0	0-0	Pearson 88	Parkes	Stewart	Lampard	Bonds	Martin	Brush	Neighbour	Goddard*	Cross	Brooking	Pike	Pearson
18/3			*80,000*					*Gabelia*	*Chivadze*	*Khisanishvili*	*Khinchagashvili*	*Tavadze*	*Chilaya**	*Svanadze*	*Sulakvelidze*	*Gutsayev*	*Kipiani*	*Shengelia*	*Mudzhir*

Ref: W Eschweiler (W Germany)
(Hammers lose 2-4 on aggregate)

The huge bleak Lenin Stadium sees West Ham salvage their dignity, though they had no hope of progress unless they could conjure up at least four goals. A lifeless match was settled by Pearson's volley, which means they become the third side to win here in Europe in the last six years.

		Home						Away					
	P	W	D	L	F	A	W	D	L	F	A	Pts
1 WEST HAM	42	19	1	1	53	12	9	9	3	26	17	66
2 Notts Co	42	10	8	3	26	15	8	9	4	23	23	53
3 Swansea	42	12	5	4	39	19	6	9	6	25	25	50
4 Blackburn	42	12	8	1	28	7	4	10	7	14	22	50
5 Luton	42	10	6	5	35	23	8	6	7	26	23	48
6 Derby	42	9	8	4	34	26	6	7	8	23	26	45
7 Grimsby	42	10	8	3	21	10	5	7	9	23	32	45
8 QP Rangers	42	11	7	3	36	12	4	6	11	20	34	43
9 Watford	42	13	5	3	34	18	3	6	12	16	27	43
10 Sheffield Wed	42	14	4	3	38	14	3	4	14	15	37	42
11 Newcastle	42	11	7	3	22	13	3	7	11	8	32	42
12 Chelsea	42	8	6	7	27	15	6	6	9	19	26	40
13 Cambridge	42	13	1	7	36	23	4	5	12	17	42	40
14 Shrewsbury	42	9	7	5	33	22	2	10	9	13	25	39
15 Oldham	42	7	9	5	19	16	5	6	10	20	32	39
16 Wrexham	42	5	8	8	22	24	7	6	8	21	21	38
17 Orient	42	9	8	4	34	20	4	4	13	18	36	38
18 Bolton	42	10	5	6	40	27	4	5	12	21	39	38
19 Cardiff	42	7	7	7	23	24	5	5	11	21	36	36
20 Preston	42	8	7	6	28	26	3	7	11	13	36	36
21 Bristol City	42	6	10	5	19	15	1	6	14	10	36	30
22 Bristol Rov	42	4	9	8	21	24	1	4	16	13	41	23
	924	217	144	101	668	405	101	144	217	405	668	924

Odds & ends

Double wins: (9) Chelsea, Shrewsbury, Watford, Cambridge, Bristol R, Grimsby, Swansea, Sheff Wed, Orient.
Double losses: (1) Luton.

Won from behind: (4) Watford (h), Sheff W (h), Derby (h), Cambridge (h).
Lost from in front: (1) Luton (h).

High spots: Running away with the Second Division championship.
Reaching the League Cup final.
Unbeaten in any competition from 19 August to 15 November, a total of 19 games.

Low spots: Losing League Cup final replay to Liverpool.
Failing to win any of the first three league fixtures.

Hammer of the Year: Phil Parkes.
Ever-presents: (2) Phil Parkes and Geoff Pike.
Hat-tricks: (2) David Cross (1), Paul Goddard (1).
Leading scorer: (27) David Cross.

	Appearances						Goals			
	Lge	*Sub*	LC	*Sub*	FAC	*Sub*	Lge	LC	FAC	Tot
Allen, Paul	1	*2*	1	*2*	1		1			1
Barnes, Bobby	1	*5*	1				1			1
Bonds, Billy	41		8		3			1		1
Brooking, Trevor	36		7		3		10			10
Brush, Paul	8	*3*	3		1					
Cross, David	41		9		3		22	5		27
Devonshire, Alan	39		9		3		6			6
Goddard, Paul	37		9		3		17	4		21
Holland, Pat	25		4		2		3			3
Lampard, Frank	38	*1*	8		2		1			1
Martin, Alvin	41		9		3		1	1		2
Morgan, Nicky	5	*1*					1			1
Neighbour, Jimmy	22	*2*	4			*1*	2	1		3
Parkes, Phil	42		9		3					
Pearson, Stuart	2	*3*		*2*						
Pike, Geoff	42		9		3		6	1		7
Stewart, Ray	41		9		3		5	2	1	8
(own-goals)							3	2		5
17 players used	462	*17*	99	*4*	33	*1*	79	17	1	97

Paul Goddard is congratulated by Geoff Pike after scoring his first Hammers goal – against Notts County in August 1980

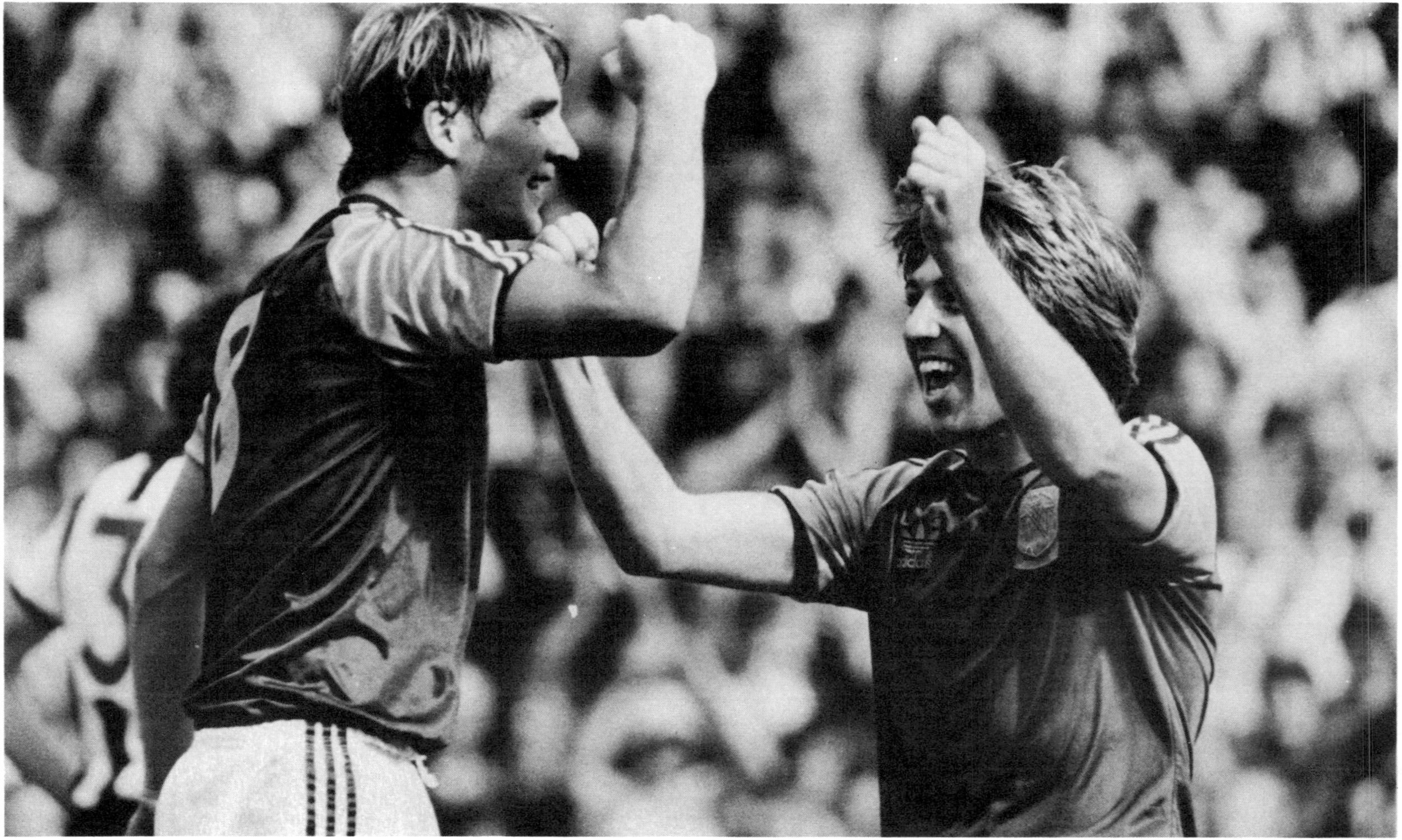

The eerie match in an empty Upton Park against Castilla in October 1980

No	Date	Att	Pos	Pt	F-A	H-T	Scorers, Times, and Referees	1	2	3	4	5	6	7	8	9	10	11	12 sub used
1	H BRIGHTON			D	1-1	0-0	Stewart 61p	Parkes	Stewart	Lampard	Bonds	Martin	Devonshire	Neighbour	Goddard	Cross	Allen	Pike	
	29/8	30,468		1			*McNab 84p*	*Moseley*	*Shanks*	*Williams*	*Grealish*	*Foster*	*Stevens*	*Case*	*Ritchie**	*Robinson*	*McNab*	*Ryan !*	*Smith*
							Ref: L Shapter	Three points for a win has been introduced. Hammers were heading for their first threesome, courtesy of Foster's push on Cross, when Devon policeman Leslie Shapter penalised Billy Bonds for shoving Michael Robinson. In injury-time Shapter sent off Ryan for a foul on Neighbour.											
2	A TOTTENHAM			W	**4-0**	1-0	Cross 10, 50, 57, 89	Parkes	Stewart	Lampard	Bonds	Martin	Devonshire	Neighbour	Goddard	Cross	Allen	Pike	
	2/9	*41,200*		4				*Clemence*	*Roberts*	*Miller*	*Price**	*Villa*	*Perryman*	*Hazard*	*Brooke*	*Galvin*	*Hoddle*	*Falco*	*Smith*
							Ref: K Baker	West Ham were determined to keep Spurs' Argentinians, Ardiles and Villa, quiet in midfield. So well did the plan succeed that David Cross was able to demonstrate superb finishing. It is not the first four-goal haul of his career. He performed the same fate versus Grimsby last season.											
3	A SUNDERLAND		1	W	2-0	1-0	Goddard 39, Cross 54	Parkes	Stewart	Lampard	Bonds	Martin	Devonshire	Neighbour	Goddard*	Cross	Allen	Pike	Pearson
	5/9	*28,347*	*14*	7				*Turner*	*Hinnigan*	*Munro*	*Buckley*	*Clarke*	*Hindmarch*	*Chisholm*	*Ritchie*	*Cooke*	*Rowell*	*Pickering**	*McCoist*
							Ref: A Challinor	Paul Goddard steals the limelight from David Cross. Devonshire laid on the chance, which Goddard stroked into the empty net. When Cross made it 2-0, shaking off his marker at the near post, it made him top scorer in Division 1. Goddard is in England's Under-21 party to Norway.											
4	H STOKE		1	W	3-2	1-1	Goddard 7, 49, Stewart 69p	Parkes	Stewart	Lampard	Bonds	Martin	Devonshire	Neighbour	Goddard	Cross	Allen	Pike	
	12/9	28,774	*7*	10			*O'Callaghan 28, Maguire 88p*	*Fox*	*Evans*	*Hampton*	*Dodd*	*O'Callaghan*	*Doyle*	*Griffiths*	*Heath*	*Chapman*	*Bracewell*	*Maguire*	
							Ref: J Martin	England have just lost 1-2 to Norway in the World Cup and the nation is in shock. West Ham triumph over Richie Barker's Stoke in a game of two penalties. Stewart scored, when Devonshire was brought down, while Stoke's arrived when Lampard handled. Cross wasted chances.											
5	A WEST BROM		1	D	0-0	0-0		Parkes	Stewart	Lampard	Bonds	Martin	Devonshire	Neighbour	Goddard	Cross	Allen	Pike	
	19/9	*19,516*	*15*	11				*Godden*	*Batson*	*Statham*	*Brown**	*Wile*	*Robertson*	*Deehan*	*Mills*	*Regis*	*Owen*	*MacKenzie*	*Cross*
							Ref: D Hedges	A rainswept match. Ronnie Allen's WBA indulge in another tough physical game. Cross clashes with Wile and plays on with his face covered in blood. Bryan Robson is out through injury, but will soon sign for Man U. Paul Allen will soon be off to Australia with the FA Youth team.											
6	H SOUTHAMPTON		1	W	4-2	2-1	Goddard 34, 38, 60, Pike 48	Parkes	Stewart	Lampard	Bonds	Martin	Devonshire	Neighbour	Goddard	Cross	Allen	Pike	
	22/9	**34,026**	*4*	14			*Armstrong 11, Waldron 66*	*Wells*	*Golac*	*Holmes*	*Agboola*	*Watson**	*Waldron*	*Keegan*	*Baker G*	*Puckett*	*Armstrong*	*Ball*	*Rogers*
							Ref: G Napthine	Goddard is violently ill before kick-off but recovers to play a blinder. His best goal is his third, beating three men before chipping Wells. The turning point is when Parkes turns Keegan's effort against a post. Lawrie McMenemy said afterwards: 'Take away the result and I enjoyed it.'											
7	H LIVERPOOL		2	D	1-1	1-0	Pike 28	Parkes	Stewart	Lampard	Bonds	Martin	Devonshire	Neighbour	Goddard	Cross	Allen	Pike	
	26/9	30,802	*12*	15			*Johnson 79*	*Grobbelaar*	*Neal*	*Kennedy A*	*Thompson*	*Kennedy R*	*Hansen*	*Dalglish*	*Lee*	*Johnson*	*McDermott*	*Souness*	
							Ref: A Robinson	Phil Parkes is struggling with a floating bone in his knee, and he gifts Johnson a simple headed equaliser when dropping Alan Kennedy's cross. The corner count – 17-2 to Liverpool – shows the balance of play. The result knocks West Ham off the top: they are replaced by Ipswich.											
8	A BIRMINGHAM		2	D	2-2	1-1	Cross 11, 61	**McAlister**	Stewart	Lampard	Bonds	Martin	Devonshire	Neighbour	Goddard	Cross	Brooking	Pike	
	3/10	*22,290*	*15*	16			*Langan 14, Dillon 89*	*Wealands*	*Langan*	*Dennis*	*Dillon*	*Broadhurst*	*Todd*	*Brocken*	*Whatmore*	*Worthington*	*Gemmill*	*Van Mierlo**	*Handysides*
							Ref: D Webb	When 2-1 up, West Ham were denied a penalty when Colin Todd held back Goddard. City boss Jim Smith admitted his player was lucky to get away with it. Trevor Brooking returns to the team but fails to prevent Dillon's late equaliser. A pitch invasion by Hammers fans spells trouble.											
9	H EVERTON		4	D	1-1	1-1	Martin 39	McAlister	Stewart	Lampard	Bonds	Martin	Devonshire	Neighbour	Goddard	Cross	Brooking	Pike	
	10/10	31,608	*14*	17			*McMahon 1*	*Arnold*	*Stevens*	*Bailey*	*Higgins*	*Lyons*	*Thomas*	*McMahon*	*Biley**	*Ferguson*	*Ross*	*McBride*	*O'Keefe*
							Ref: T Bune	John Lyall celebrates his Bell's Manager of the Month award, but within seconds watches horrified as McMahon's bobbling shot squeezes past McAlister. Martin levelled when heading in Stewart's free-kick. Lyall is reputed to be on the verge of signing Manchester Utd's Steve Coppell.											
10	A ASTON VILLA		5	L	2-3	1-3	Brooking 2, Cross 49	McAlister	Stewart	Lampard	Bonds	Martin	Devonshire	Neighbour*	Goddard	Cross	Brooking	Pike	Brush
	17/10	*32,064*	*13*	17			*Morley 25, Geddis 26, Mortimer 40*	*Rimmer*	*Williams*	*Gibson*	*Evans*	*Ormsby*	*Mortimer*	*Bremner*	*Shaw*	*Geddis**	*Cowans*	*Morley*	*Blair*
							Ref: N Glover	West Ham's first defeat is largely down to Tom McAlister, who is at fault for Morley's and Geddis's goals. Trevor Brooking scores a vintage goal and the Hammers are denied two strong second-half penalty appeals. Lyall's latest target is said to be Leeds' winger Arthur Graham.											

No	Venue	Opponent	Pos	Res	F-A	H-T	Scorers, Times, and Referees	1	2	3	4	5	6	7	8	9	10	11	subs used
11	A	NOTTS CO	6	D	1-1	0-0	Brooking 50	Parkes	Stewart	Lampard	Bonds	Martin	Devonshire	Brush	Goddard	Cross	Brooking	Pike	
24/10		*12,505*	*13*	18			*Masson 66*	*Avramovic*	*Goodwin*	*O'Brien*	*Hunt*	*Lahtinen*	*Richards*	*Chiedozie*	*Masson*	*McCulloch*	*Hooks*	*Mair*	
							Ref: Willis	Trevor Brooking's autobiography was launched on this day. He celebrated by directing a trundler that squirmed under Avramovic's body, but otherwise failed to rescue an anaemic match. Parkes returned to the side after knee surgery, but could not keep out former team-mate Masson.											
12	H	MIDDLESBROUGH	6	W	3-2	2-0	Neighbour 32, Goddard 40, Stewart 48p	Parkes	Stewart	Lampard	Bonds	Martin	Devonshire	Neighbour	Goddard	Cross	Brooking	Pike	
31/10		27,604	*20*	21			*Woof 55, Thomson 79p*	*Platt*	*Nattrass*	*Bolton*	*Angus*	*Baxter*	*McAndrew**	*Cochrane*	*Otto*	*Woof*	*Hodgson*	*Thomson*	*Shearer*
							Ref: L Burden	West Ham were coasting at 3-0 when everything collapsed. Bobby Murdoch's Boro had only scored one away goal so far, but must have thought they could retrieve a point after Jimmy Neighbour's dreadful back-pass let in Woof, and Brooking barged over Cochrane in the box.											
13	A	NOTT'M FOREST	6	D	0-0	0-0		Parkes	Stewart	Lampard	Allen*	Martin	Devonshire	Neighbour	Goddard	Cross	Brooking	Pike	Brush
7/11		*26.327*	*5*	22				*Shilton*	*Anderson*	*Gunn*	*McGovern*	*Needham*	*Aas**	*Gray*	*Wallace*	*Fashanu*	*Proctor*	*Robertson*	*Walsh*
							Ref: G Tyson	Frank Lampard was once again acting skipper. Brooking earns the sixth booking of his long career when fouling Justin Fashanu. Forest had more of the play but the best chance fell to West Ham in the final minute, when David Cross forced Peter Shilton into a scrambling save.											
14	H	COVENTRY	5	W	5-2	2-1	Brook'g 22, Neighbour 37, Martin 50, 55,	Parkes	Stewart	Lampard	Bonds	Martin	Devonshire	Neighbour	Goddard	Cross	Brooking	Pike	
21/11		26,065	*17*	25			*Hunt 6, 62* [Stewart 87p]	*Blyth*	*Thomas*	*Roberts*	*Jacobs*	*Dyson*	*Gillespie*	*Bradford*	*Daly*	*Thompson*	*Hateley*	*Hunt*	
							Ref: A Glasson	Brooking's super goal in Hungary, lodging the ball in the stanchion, is the talk of England. This thriller saw a 20-minute delay due to floodlight failure. At 4-2 West Ham were given a penalty. The crowd urged Martin to complete his hat-trick, but an angry Lyall ordered him to leave it.											
15	A	LEEDS	6	D	3-3	0-1	Brooking 55, 86, Cross 77	Parkes	Stewart	Lampard	Bonds	Martin	Devonshire	Neighbour*	Goddard	Cross	Brooking	Pike	Allen
28/11		*25,637*	*19*	26			*Graham 13, Hird 65p, Cherry 69*	*Lukic*	*Cherry*	*Gray F*	*Stevenson*	*Hart*	*Burns*	*Harris*	*Graham*	*Butterworth*	*Hamson*	*Hird*	
							Ref: P Richardson	West Ham went 1-2 behind to a disputed penalty. Stewart had already been booked for a foul on Graham when he brings him down in the box. The ref waved play on until spotting a linesman's raised flag. Cross pulled a goal back with a toe-ender, before heading down for Brooking.											
16	H	ARSENAL	7	L	1-2	0-2	Pearson 85	Parkes	Stewart	Lampard	Bonds	Martin	Devonshire	Barnes*	Pearson	Cross	Brooking	Allen	Banton
5/12		33,833	*6*	26			*Whyte 15, Hollins 45p*	*Jennings*	*Robson*	*Sansom*	*Talbot*	*O'Leary*	*Whyte*	*Hollins*	*Sunderland*	*Davis*	*Nicholas*	*Rix*	
							Ref: A Gray	The last time these teams met was in the 1980 FA Cup final. Arsenal's fifth straight win inflicts West Ham's first home league defeat in over a year. Stewart Robson made his Arsenal debut. Pearson is surprisingly recalled in place of Goddard. Stewart fouled Sansom for the penalty.											
17	A	LIVERPOOL	12	L	**0-3**	0-2		Parkes	Stewart	Lampard	Bonds	Martin	Devonshire*	Neighbour	Pearson	Cross	Brooking	Pike	Brush
5/1		28,427	*9*	26			*McDermott 22, Whelan 24, Dalglish 67*	*Grobbelaar*	*Neal*	*Lawrenson*	*Thompson*	*Whelan*	*Hansen*	*Dalglish*	*Kennedy A*	*Rush*	*McDermott*	*Souness*	
							Ref: B Newsome	West Ham did not win their first corner till the final minute. McDermott looked offside when receiving the ball to score at the second attempt. Two minutes later Dalglish set up Whelan's 20-yard scorcher. Whelan then fed Dalglish, who turned and shot in one exquisite movement.											
18	A	BRIGHTON	12	L	0-1	0-0		Parkes	Stewart	Lampard	Bonds	Martin	Devonshire*	Neighbour	Goddard	Cross	Brooking	Pike	**Van der Elst**
16/1		*22,620*	*8*	26			*Ritchie 77*	*Moseley*	*Shanks*	*Nelson*	*Grealish*	*Foster*	*Gatting*	*Ryan*	*Ritchie*	*Smith*	*McNab*	*Thomas*	
							Ref: G Napthine	These are the two draw specialists of Division 1, with 17 between them. Offside decisions marred the outcome. West Ham claimed Ritchie was offside when taking Nelson's long pass, but TV showed he had been onside. Stewart's 35-yarder was disallowed because Cross was offside.											
19	A	MANCHESTER U	12	L	0-1	0-0		Parkes	Brush	Lampard*	Bonds	Martin	**Orr**	Van der Elst	Stewart	Cross	Brooking	Pike	Goddard
27/1		***41,291***	*1*	26			*Macari 75*	*Bailey*	*Duxbury*	*Albiston*	*Wilkins*	*Moran*	*McQueen*	*Robson*	*Birtles*	*Stapleton*	*Macari*	*Coppell*	
							Ref: V Callow	Old Trafford jeers West Ham's excessive robustness, but cheer their own new signing from West Brom, Bryan Robson, who played a part in the goal. The hosts won the corner-count 21-1, and go top of the league. Trevor Brooking wasted West Ham's only chance, heading at Bailey.											
20	H	WEST BROM	12	W	3-1	1-0	Goddard 34, Cross 51, 75	Parkes	Stewart	Brush	Bonds	Martin	Orr	Van der Elst	Goddard	Cross	Brooking	Pike	
30/1		24,423	*14*	29			*King 62*	*Grew*	*Batson*	*Statham*	*King*	*Wile*	*Robertson*	*Jol*	*Whitehead**	*Regis*	*Owen*	*MacKenzie*	*Cross*
							Ref: C Maskell	This time it is WBA who take their own medicine, as Billy Bonds lunges at everything that moves. Ronnie Allen describes the Hammers as the hard men of Division 1. Bonds was also involved in both Cross's goals, the second of which might have been ruled out for a foul on the keeper.											
21	H	MANCHESTER C	12	D	1-1	0-0	Bonds 80	Parkes	Stewart	Brush*	Bonds	Martin	Orr	Van der Elst	Goddard	Cross	Brooking	Pike	Pearson
2/2		26,552	*4*	30			*Bond 73p*	*Corrigan*	*Ranson*	*McDonald*	*Ryan**	*Bond*	*Caton*	*Kinsey*	*Reeves*	*Francis*	*Hartford*	*Power*	*Hareide*
							Ref: A Gunn	Van der Elst, a £400,000 buy from New York Cosmos, has another anonymous game and the fans are getting at him. Orr brought down Trevor Francis for City's penalty. Bonds' equaliser was a comedy of errors. Orr mis-hit a free-kick and the ball went in off Van der Elst and Goddard.											

No	Date	Att	Pos	Pt	F-A	H-T	Scorers, Times, and Referees	1	2	3	4	5	6	7	8	9	10	11	12 sub used
22	A STOKE		12	L	1-2	0-1	Van der Elst 71	Parkes	Stewart	Brush	Bonds	Martin	Orr	Van der Elst	Goddard	Cross	Brooking	Pike	
	6/2	***11,987***	*16*	30			*Chapman 10, Maguire 79*	*Fox*	*Kirk*	*Hampton*	*Dodd*	*Watson*	*McAughtrie*	*Griffiths**	*O'Callaghan*	*Chapman*	*Bracewell*	*Maguire*	*Lumsden*
							Ref: J Worrall	Stoke's first home win of 1982 is earned by Maguire's left foot, after Martin failed to cut out a pass to him. West Ham were so bad in the first half that Lyall read the riot act at half-time. He was rewarded by Van der Elst's first goal for the club. But Maguire saw that justice was done.											
23	H BIRMINGHAM		12	D	2-2	0-1	Orr 46, Stewart 88p	Parkes	Lampard	Brush*	Bonds	Stewart	Orr	Van der Elst	Goddard	Cross	Brooking	Pike	Neighbour
	13/2	22,512	*19*	31			*Whatmore 35, Van Mierlo 55*	*Jones*	*Langan*	*Dennis**	*Curbishley*	*Scott*	*Broadhurst*	*Van Mierlo*	*Whatmore*	*Worthington*	*Phillips*	*Handysides*	*v d Hauwe*
							Ref: I Borrett	Martin is missing with a fractured collarbone. Worthington's rocket was parried by Parkes but fell to Whatmore for the first goal. Jim Smith's City were two minutes from their first away win in 16 months when Geoff Scott handled in the box. Ray Stewart got West Ham off the hook.											
24	A SOUTHAMPTON		14	L	1-2	1-2	Stewart 15p	Parkes	Stewart	Brush	Bonds	Orr	Van der Elst	Neighbour	Goddard	Cross	Brooking	Pike	
	20/2	*24,026*	*1*	31			*Armstrong 10, Channon 28*	*Katalinic*	*Golac*	*Holmes*	*Baker G*	*Nicholl*	*Waldron*	*Keegan*	*Channon*	*Puckett*	*Armstrong*	*Ball*	
							Ref: E Read	Saints top the table by four points from Man U. Kevin Keegan was superb, and kept winning free-kicks. Two Southampton players looked offside when Armstrong scored. Malcolm Waldron dumped Van der Elst on his backside for the penalty. Mick Channon headed the winner.											
25	A EVERTON		14	D	0-0	0-0		Parkes	Stewart	Brush	Bonds	Orr	Allen	Neighbour*	Goddard	Van der Elst	Brooking	Pike	Lampard
	27/2	*28,618*	*11*	32				*Southall*	*Borrows*	*Bailey*	*Higgins*	*Wright*	*Richardson*	*Irvine*	*Heath*	*Sharp*	*Biley*	*Ross*	
							Ref: J Key	David Cross is out with a damaged shoulder. John Motson gets into hot water when he tells Howard Kendall before a *Match of the Day* audience that this was the worst game he had seen this season. Everton came nearest to a goal when Graeme Sharp's header hit an upright.											
26	H IPSWICH		12	W	2-0	1-0	Devonshire 40, Van der Elst 64	Parkes	Stewart	Brush	Bonds	Orr	Devonshire	Allen	Goddard	Van der Elst	Brooking	Pike	
	2/3	24,846	*6*	35				*Cooper*	*Burley*	*McCall*	*Mills*	*Osman*	*Steggles**	*Wark*	*Muhren*	*D'Avray*	*Brazil*	*Gates*	*O'Callaghan*
							Ref: B Hill	Bobby Robson's Ipswich cannot afford defeats like this if they wish to sustain their title challenge. Alan Devonshire is credited with his first goal of the season, even though the ball went in off Steggles. Stewart's astute through ball sets up Van der Elst's first goal at Upton Park.											
27	H ASTON VILLA		12	D	2-2	1-1	Stewart 39p, Van der Elst 53	Parkes	Stewart	Brush	Bonds	Orr	Devonshire	Allen	Goddard	Van der Elst	Brooking	Pike	
	6/3	26,894	*14*	36			*Cowans 18, Withe 60*	*Rimmer*	*Swain*	*Willams*	*Bremner*	*McNaught*	*Mortimer*	*Blair*	*Shaw*	*Withe*	*Cowans*	*Morley*	
							Ref: J Martin	Villa have just returned from a midweek trip to the Soviet side, Tbilisi, in the European Cup. Brush's error let in Cowan for the first goal. Des Bremner upended Brooking for the penalty. Van der Elst swooped after Rimmer had saved from Goddard, but Shaw then headed on for Withe.											
28	H NOTTS CO		12	W	1-0	0-0	Stewart 47p	Parkes	Stewart	Lampard	Bonds	Orr	Devonshire	Allen	Goddard	Cross	Van der Elst	Pike	
	13/3	22,145	*14*	39				*Avramovic*	*Benjamin*	*O'Brien*	*Goodwin*	*Kilcline*	*Richards*	*Chiedozie**	*Harkouk*	*McCulloch*	*Hooks !*	*Mair*	*Christie*
							Ref: R Milford	A dreary match, settled by one of many recent penalties. Paul Hooks was the guilty man, fouling Devonshire. Injury-time witnessed a punch-up between the same two players, as a result of which Hooks was sent off. County's Jimmy Sirrel gave a hilarious speech at the press conference.											
29	A MIDDLESBROUGH		11	W	3-2	2-0	Van der Elst 15, Goddard 29, 89	Parkes	Stewart	Lampard	Bonds	Orr	Devonshire	Allen	Goddard	Van der Elst	Brooking	Pike*	Neighbour
	20/3	*12,134*	*22*	42			*McAndrew 59p, Ashcroft 74*	*Platt*	*Craggs*	*Bailey*	*Ross*	*Baxter*	*McAndrew*	*Cochrane*	*Nattrass*	*Hodgson*	*Ashcroft*	*Thomson*	
							Ref: T Hills	The bottom team provide West Ham with their first away win in 13 attempts. But it was a close thing. West Ham surrendered a two-goal lead before Brooking set up Goddard's late winner. Boro have won only three matches all season. Stewart handled from Ashcroft for the penalty.											
30	H NOTT'M FOREST		11	L	0-1	0-1		Parkes	Stewart	Lampard	Bonds	Orr	Devonshire	Van der Elst	Goddard	Cross	Brooking	Allen*	Neighbour
	27/3	24,633	*9*	42			*Wallace 30*	*Shilton*	*Anderson*	*Bowyer*	*McGovern*	*Young*	*Gunn*	*Rober*	*Wallace*	*Fashanu*	*Proctor*	*Robertson*	
							Ref: T Bune	Peter Shilton had only one save to make, from Goddard. Paul Allen was at fault for the goal, letting in Wallace, who offered a constant threat. Cross's reward for his endeavour was to get kicked in the face by Willie Young. West Ham have not scored against Forest for 750 minutes.											
31	A SWANSEA		10	W	1-0	1-0	Van der Elst 10	Parkes	Stewart	Lampard	Orr	Martin	Devonshire	Van der Elst	Goddard	Cross	Brooking	Allen	
	30/3	*20,272*	*4*	45				*Davies*	*Robinson*	*Hadziabdic**	*Irwin*	*Kennedy*	*Rajkovic*	*Curtis*	*James R*	*James L*	*Stevenson*	*Latchford*	*Stanley*
							Ref: B Stevens	The championship hopes of John Toshack's Swansea, damaged by a home defeat by Ipswich on Saturday, are extinguished by the much-maligned Van der Elst, who fires a screamer past Dai Davies. Swansea's subsequent pressure came to nothing, largely thanks to Alvin Martin.											

No	Venue	Opponents	Pos	Res	F-A	H-T	Scorers, Times, and Referees	1	2	3	4	5	6	7	8	9	10	11	12 sub used
32	A	MANCHESTER C	9	W	1-0	0-0	Goddard 80	Parkes	Stewart	Lampard	Orr	Martin	Devonshire	Van der Elst	Goddard	Cross	Brooking	Allen	
3/4		30,875	8	48				Corrigan	Ranson	McDonald	Reid	Power	Caton	Ryan	Reeves	Hareide	Hartford	Jackson	
							Ref: M Scott	West Ham's third successive away win is earned by Paul Goddard's late effort. David Cross's header fell to him and his shot went in off a post. Goddard had come close twice beforehand. Alvin Martin looked much more impressive than City's rival England hopeful, Tommy Caton.											
33	H	WOLVES	8	W	3-1	0-1	Martin 46, Goddard 50, 66	Parkes	Stewart	Lampard	Orr	Martin	Devonshire	Van der Elst	Goddard	Cross	Brooking	Allen	
6/4		20,651	20	51			Richards 13	Bradshaw	Humphrey	Palmer	Matthews	Pender	Coy	Hibbitt	Carr	Richards	Eves	Clarke	
							Ref: D Letts	The players were treated to another Lyall tirade at half-time, and this time it has the desired effect. Martin immediately headed in Devonshire's corner, and Brooking and Martin set up further goals for Paul Goddard. In the first half John Richards had looped a header over Phil Parkes.											
34	H	SWANSEA	8	D	1-1	0-1	Goddard 88	Parkes	Stewart	Lampard*	Orr	Martin	Devonshire	Van der Elst	Goddard	Cross	Brooking	Allen	Neighbour
10/4		25,566	3	52			James R 34	Davies	Marustik*	Hadziabdic	Irwin	Kennedy	Rajkovic	Curtis	James R	Staney	Stevenson	Latchford	Robinson
							Ref: A Robinson	Belgian manager Guy Thys runs his eye over Van der Elst. Thys sees Brooking and Cross squander chances galore in the first half, before Robbie James fires Swansea ahead with a spectacular 30-yarder. Paul Goddard connects with a late corner to rescue a point. It is his 14th goal.											
35	A	IPSWICH	8	L	2-3	1-2	Cross 42, 80	Parkes	Stewart	Allen	Orr	Martin	Devonshire	Van der Elst	Goddard	Cross	Brooking	Neighbour*	**Cowie**
13/4		28,767	2	52			Brazil 15, Wark 26p, Osman 51	Cooper	Burley	McCall	Mills	Osman	Butcher	Wark	Muhren	Mariner	Brazil	Gates	
							Ref: M Taylor	Portman Road's biggest crowd of the season are enticed by an exciting title chase with Liverpool. Mariner and Butcher both return after long absences. Alan Brazil went down for Ipswich's penalty. Osman's free header made it 1-3 before McCall boobs to let in Cross near the end.											
36	A	COVENTRY	8	L	0-1	0-1		Parkes	Stewart	Cowie	Orr	Martin*	Devonshire	Van der Elst	Goddard	Cross	Brooking	Allen	Laronde
17/4		13,398	15	52			Hateley 45	Sealey	Thomas	Roberts	Butterworth	Dyson	Gillespie	Whitton*	Jacobs	Hateley	Thompson	Hunt	Hormantsch'k
							Ref: L Shapter	Martin collides with Parkes, does further damage to his collarbone and is stretchered off. The team coach was returning home when it was flagged down by Martin's father, so that Alvin could climb aboard. With the World Cup finals just weeks away, Martin might not be fit.											
37	H	LEEDS	8	W	4-3	0-1	Cross 47, Brooking 52, 80, Stewart 88p	Parkes	Stewart	Laronde	Allen	Orr	Devonshire	Van der Elst	Goddard	Cross	Brooking	Pike	
24/4		24,748	21	55			Connor 20, Graham 56, Flynn 89	Lukic	Hird	Gray F	Flynn	Hart	Cherry	Gray E	Graham	Worthington	Butterworth*	Barnes	Connor
							Ref: J Bray	Allan Clarke's Leeds drop to 21st after this defeat. At 2-2 Leeds looked the likelier team, and they were pressing hard at 2-3 when Frank Gray handled in the box. Brooking's goals – one a far-post header ('Dixie' Brooking) – were his first since playing Leeds back in November.											
38	A	ARSENAL	9	L	0-2	0-2		Parkes	Stewart	Laronde	Allen	Orr	Devonshire	Van der Elst	Cowie*	Cross	Brooking	Pike	Houghton
1/5		34,977	7	55			Rix 16, Sunderland 42	Wood	Hollins	Sansom	Talbot	O'Leary	Whyte	Hawley	Sunderland	Davis	Robson	Rix	
							Ref: J Hunting	Arsenal boss Terry Neill is in despair over the dreadful crowd disturbances which disfigured this match. Smoke bombs went off in the North bank and the players were taken off during a 10-minute stoppage. Rix headed in Hawley's cross. Other than Brooking, West Ham looked poor.											
39	H	SUNDERLAND	10	D	1-1	0-1	Stewart 67p	Parkes	Stewart	Laronde	Allen	Orr	Devonshire	Van der Elst	Goddard	Cross	Brooking	Pike	
4/5		**17,130**	17	56			West40	Turner	Hinnigan	Munro	Hindmarch	Chisholm	Elliott	Buckley	West	Rowell	Pickering	Cummins	
							Ref: J Deakin	Sunderland have lost just one of their last nine. Devonshire won a penalty when wriggling into the box and fouled by Shaun Elliott, who was so incensed he refused to shake hands at the end. At half-time police broadcast a request for information regarding a death at Highbury last week.											
40	H	MANCHESTER U	10	D	1-1	0-0	Cross 48	Parkes	Stewart	Laronde	Allen	Orr	Devonshire	Cowie	Goddard	Cross	Brooking	Pike	
8/5		26,337	3	57			Moran 62	Bailey	Gidman	Albiston	Wilkins	Moran	Duxbury	Moses	Birtles*	Stapleton	Grimes	Coppell	McGarvey
							Ref: S Bates	Billy Bonds is still out with jaundice and Van der Elst misses the match with bruised toes. The crowd spilled over the wall at the South Bank, putting everyone in fear of yet more crowd disturbances. Gidman's back-pass let in Cross to bring West Ham back on terms with his 18th goal.											
41	H	TOTTENHAM	10	D	2-2	0-1	Brooking 62, Goddard 85	Parkes	Stewart	Laronde	Allen	Orr	Devonshire	Cowie*	Goddard	Cross	Brooking	Pike	Barnes
10/5		27,667	4	58			Hoddle 10p, Brooke 63	Parks	Corbett*	Miller	Price	Lacy	Perryman	Hazard	Brooke	Falco	Hoddle	Crooks	O'Reilly
							Ref: A Seville	Two Parks in goal, so to speak, as Spurs' 19-year-old Tony Parks makes his debut. Ron Greenwood comes along to watch Brooking and Hoddle, who quickly scored from the spot after Gary Brooke had been flattened. Brooking was not to be outdone, volleying home Pike's chip.											
42	A	WOLVES	9	L	1-2	1-2	Cross 13	Parkes	Stewart	Laronde	Allen	Orr	Devonshire	Cowie	Goddard	Cross*	Brooking	Pike	Barnes
15/5		13,283	21	58			Eves 3, Richards 10	Bradshaw	Humphrey	Atkinson	Eves	Gallagher	Coy	Hibbitt	Carr	Matthews	Richards	Clarke	
Home Average 26,594		Away 24,694					Ref: G Owen	Wolves had to win and WBA had to lose if Wolves were to stay up. Albion's win at Notts Co sent Wolves down. David Cross scored his 98th and last West Ham goal and is subbed at half-time. He is refusing to sign a new contract, and Man C manager John Bond is here to watch him.											

League Cup			F-A	H-T	Scorers, Times, and Referees	1	2	3	4	5	6	7	8	9	10	11	12 sub used
2:1 A DERBY	2	W	3-2	1-1	Cross 28, Brooking 48, Stewart 82p	McAlister	Stewart	Lampard	Bonds	Martin	Devonshire	Neighbour	Goddard	Cross	Brooking	Pike	
7/10	*13,764 2:17*				*Stewart 9 (og), Hector 46*	*Cherry*	*Coop*	*Buckley*	*Powell S*	*Ramage*	*Osgood**	*Skivington*	*Powell B*	*Hector*	*Swindlehurst*	*Emson*	*Clayton*
					Ref: R Bridges	Colin Addison's Derby would have been dead and buried, but for Cross and Brooking both hitting the woodwork. Ray Stewart scored at both ends, side-footing into his own net, then netting a penalty after Alan Ramage handled on the line. Kevin Hector scored his 200th Derby goal.											
2:2 H DERBY	6	W	2-0	1-0	Goddard 36, 70	Parkes	Stewart	Lampard	Bonds	Martin	Devonshire	Neighbour	Goddard	Cross	Brooking	Pike	
27/10	21,043 *2:16*					*Jones*	*Coop*	*Buckley*	*Powell S*	*Sheridan*	*Powell B*	*Hector**	*Reid*	*Clayton*	*Swindlehurst*	*Emson*	*Gibson*
					Ref: M Taylor (Hammers win 5-2 on aggregate)	Paul Goddard enjoys the nickname 'Sarge'. He was a bit fortunate with his first goal, turning in Frank Lampard's off-target effort, but his second was something special. Trevor Brooking crossed, and Sarge's volley flew in off a post. Derby's Swindlehurst gave Martin a hard time.											
3 H WEST BROM	6	D	2-2	1-2	Stewart 43p, Cross 64	Parkes	Brush	Lampard	Stewart	Martin	Devonshire	Neighbour	Goddard	Cross	Brooking	Pike	
10/11	24,168 *17*				*Regis 22, King 40*	*Grew*	*Arthur*	*Statham*	*King*	*Wile*	*Robertson*	*Jol*	*Brown*	*Regis*	*Owen*	*MacKenzie*	
					Ref: T Spencer	England manager Ron Greenwood watches this virtuoso performance by Alan Devonshire. At 0-2, Devonshire won a penalty when tripped by King. Cross then levelled after John Wile had misjudged Alvin Martin's mis-hit shot. Robust Albion might have had two players sent off.											
3R A WEST BROM	5	D	1-1	0-0	Stewart 108p	Parkes	Stewart	Lampard	Bonds	Martin	Devonshire	Neighbour	Goddard*	Cross	Brooking	Pike	Allen
24/11	*15,869 16*		*aet*		*Regis 92*	*Grew*	*Batson*	*Statham*	*King*	*Wile*	*Robertson*	*Jol*	*Brown*	*Regis*	*Owen*	*MacKenzie*	
					Ref: H King	Two minutes into extra-time Andy King's long ball enables Cyrille Regis to outpace Martin and put WBA ahead. When Wile is judged to have fouled Brooking in the box, Albion players go demented. Lyall won the post-match toss of the coin for the right of home advantage next time.											
3 H WEST BROM	6	L	0-1	0-0		Parkes	Stewart	Lampard	Bonds	Martin	Devonshire	Neighbour	Goddard	Cross*	Brooking	Pike	Allen !
RR 1/12	24,760 *17*				*Regis 80*	*Grew*	*Batson*	*Statham*	*King*	*Wile*	*Robertson*	*Jol*	*Brown !*	*Regis*	*Owen*	*MacKenzie*	
					Ref: B Martin	West Ham's first home defeat in 17 months was a tactical triumph for Ronnie Allen, who instructed Jol to stifle Trevor Brooking in midfield. When Paul Allen retaliated after Brown's foul, both were ordered off. MacKenzie put the fleet-footed Cyrille Regis away for the winner.											

FA Cup																	
3 H EVERTON	10	W	2-1	1-0	Bonds 8, Cross 57	Parkes	Stewart	Lampard	Bonds	Martin	Devonshire	Neighbour	Goddard*	Cross	Brooking	Pike	Pearson
2/1	24,431 *8*				*Eastoe 65*	*Southall*	*Stevens*	*Ratcliffe*	*Higgins*	*Lyons*	*Kendall*	*Richardson*	*Ross**	*Sharp*	*Eastoe*	*Lodge*	*O'Keefe*
					Ref: K Hackett	Everton player-manager Howard Kendall was incandescent after this defeat against a team who hadn't played for a month. All three goals were headers, but the moment that riled Kendall most was when Sharp was brought down. Ross had missed a penalty last week, and did so again.											
4 A WATFORD	12	L	0-2	0-0		Parkes	Stewart	Lampard	Bonds	Martin	Van der Elst	Neighbour*	Goddard	Cross	Brooking	Pike	Pearson
23/1	*27,004 2:3*				*Armstrong 47, Callaghan 72*	*Sherwood*	*Rice*	*Pritchett*	*Blissett*	*Terry*	*Bolton*	*Callaghan*	*Armstrong*	*Jenkins**	*Lohman*	*Barnes*	*Rostron*
					Ref: J Martin	Graham Taylor's Watford beat Man U in the previous round, and his promotion chasers do it again. The sight of Elton John leaping around the directors' box was enough to distress West Ham fans, who directed their spleen at debutant Van der Elst. What has he let himself in for?											

	Home						Away					
	P	W	D	L	F	A	W	D	L	F	A	Pts
1 Liverpool	42	14	3	4	39	14	12	6	3	41	18	87
2 Ipswich	42	17	1	3	47	25	9	4	8	28	28	83
3 Manchester U	42	12	6	3	27	9	10	6	5	32	20	78
4 Tottenham	42	12	4	5	41	26	8	7	6	26	22	71
5 Arsenal	42	13	5	3	27	15	7	6	8	21	22	71
6 Swansea	42	13	3	5	34	16	8	3	10	24	35	69
7 Southampton	42	15	2	4	49	30	4	7	10	23	37	66
8 Everton	42	11	7	3	33	21	6	6	9	23	29	64
9 WEST HAM	42	9	10	2	42	29	5	6	10	24	28	58
10 Manchester C	42	9	7	5	32	23	6	6	9	17	27	58
11 Aston Villa	42	9	6	6	28	24	6	6	9	27	29	57
12 Nott'm Forest	42	7	7	7	19	20	8	5	8	23	28	57
13 Brighton	42	8	7	6	30	24	5	6	10	13	28	52
14 Coventry	42	9	4	8	31	24	4	7	10	25	38	50
15 Notts Co	42	8	5	8	32	33	5	3	13	29	36	47
16 Birmingham	42	8	6	7	29	25	2	8	11	24	36	44
17 West Brom	42	6	6	9	24	25	5	5	11	22	32	44
18 Stoke	42	9	2	10	27	28	3	6	12	17	35	44
19 Sunderland	42	6	5	10	19	26	5	6	10	19	32	44
20 Leeds	42	6	11	4	23	20	4	1	16	16	41	42
21 Wolves	42	8	5	8	19	20	2	5	14	13	43	40
22 Middlesbro	42	5	9	7	20	24	3	6	12	14	28	39
	924	214	121	127	672	501	127	121	214	501	672	1265

Odds & ends

Double wins: (1) Middlesbrough.
Double losses: (1) Arsenal.

Won from behind: (4) South'ton, (h), Coventry (h), Wolves (h), Leeds (h).
Lost from in front: (2) Villa (a), Derby LC (a).

High spots: Not losing any of the first nine league games.
Five league wins out of six from 13 March.
David Cross's four goals against Spurs.

Low spots: Four consecutive league defeats from 5 December.
Failing to win any of the last five games.

Hammer of the Year: Alvin Martin.
Ever-presents: (1) Ray Stewart
Hat-tricks: (2) Paul Goddard (1), David Cross (1).
Leading scorer: (19) David Cross.

	Appearances						Goals			
	Lge	*Sub*	LC	*Sub*	FAC	*Sub*	Lge	LC	FAC	Tot
Allen, Paul	**27**	*1*		*2*						
Banton, Dale	**0**	*1*								
Barnes, Bobby	**1**	*2*								
Bonds, Billy	**29**		4		2		**1**		1	**2**
Brooking, Trevor	**34**		5		2		**8**	1		**9**
Brush, Paul	**10**	*3*	1							
Cowie, George	**5**	*1*								
Cross, David	**38**		5		2		**16**	2	1	**19**
Devonshire, Alan	**35**		5		1		**1**			**1**
Goddard, Paul	**38**	*1*	5		2		**15**	2		**17**
Houghton, Ray	**0**	*1*								
La Ronde, Everald	**6**	*1*								
Lampard, Frank	**27**	*1*	5		2					
McAlister, Tom	**3**		1							
Martin, Alvin	**28**		5		2		**4**			**4**
Neighbour, Jimmy	**19**	*4*	5		2		**2**			**2**
Orr, Neil	**24**						**1**			**1**
Parkes, Phil	**39**		4		2					
Pearson, Stuart	**2**	*2*				*2*	**1**			**1**
Pike, Geoff	**34**		5		2		**2**			**2**
Stewart, Ray	**42**		5		2		**10**	3		**13**
Van der Elst, François	**21**	*1*			1		**5**			**5**
22 players used	**462**	***19***	**55**	***2***	**22**	***2***	**66**	**8**	**2**	**76**

No	Date		Opponent	Att	Pos	Pt	F-A	H-T	Scorers, Times, and Referees	1	2	3	4	5	6	7	8	9	10	11	12 sub used
1		H	NOTT'M FOREST			L	1-2	1-1	Stewart 37p	Parkes	Stewart	Lampard	Bonds	Martin	Devonshire	Van der Elst	Goddard	**Clark**	Allen	Pike	
	28/8			23,796		–			*Walsh 10, Robertson 78p*	*Sutton*	*Anderson*	*Bowyer*	*Proctor**	*Young*	*Todd*	*Hodge*	*Wallace*	*Plummer*	*Walsh*	*Robertson*	*Gunn*
									Ref: A Gunn	Only Forest stopped West Ham scoring at home last season and the jinx continues. The new partnership of Goddard and Clark fails to gel and Hammers resort to screaming for penalties. It works when Allen drives the ball against Walsh. Forest got one, too, when Wallace went down.											
2		A	LUTON			W	2-0	0-0	Goddard 49, Bonds 66	Parkes	Stewart	Lampard	Bonds	Martin	Devonshire	Van der Elst	Goddard	Clark	Allen	Neighbour*	Morgan
	31/8			*13,402*		3				*Findlay*	*Stephens*	*Money*	*Horton*	*Goodyear*	*Donaghy*	*Hill*	*Stein*	*Walsh*	*Antic*	*Moss*	
									Ref: A Seville	The music of Chariots of Fire accompanies David Pleat's promoted champions on to the pitch. Billy Bonds heads on Ray Stewart's corner to Goddard. Bonds then heads in from Stewart's free-kick. Jimmy Neighbour lasts 25 minutes before torn knee ligaments takes him from the fray.											
3		A	SUNDERLAND		14	L	0-1	0-1		Parkes	Stewart	Lampard	Bonds	Martin	Devonshire	Van der Elst	Goddard	Clark	Allen	Pike	
	4/9			*19,239*	*4*	3			*Rowell 15*	*Turner*	*Venison*	*Munro*	*Atkins*	*Hindmarch*	*Elliott*	*Buckley*	*Rowell*	*McCoist*	*Pickering*	*Cummins*	
									Ref: R Chadwick	Lyall recalls Geoff Pike and gives Van der Elst a Brooking-like role in midfield. The tactics don't work and the Hammers don't get a whiff of a goal. Parkes is at fault for Sunderland's breakthrough. He tried to smother the ball at Stan Cummins' feet but it ballooned in off his shoulder.											
4		H	IPSWICH			D	1-1	0-1	Lampard 60	Parkes	Stewart	Lampard	Bonds	Martin	Devonshire	Van der Elst	Goddard	Clark	Allen	Pike	
	7/9			21,963		4			*Wark 32*	*Cooper*	*Burley*	*Mills*	*Thijssen*	*Osman*	*Butcher*	*Wark*	*McCall*	*Mariner*	*Brazil*	*Gates*	
									Ref: K Barratt	Billy Bonds' 545th league appearance breaks Bobby Moore's all-time record, and he receives a cut-glass vase beforehand. Stewart let in Wark for Ipswich's goal, then has his penalty saved when Osman fouled Van der Elst. Lampard levelled at the second go from Devonshire's corner.											
5		H	BIRMINGHAM		8	W	**5-0**	2-0	Van Elst 22, Goddard 30, Stewart 60p, [Martin 73, Clark 86]	Parkes	Stewart	Lampard	Bonds	Martin	Devonshire	Van der Elst	Goddard	Clark	Allen	Pike	
	11/9			18,754	*22*	7				*Blyth*	*Hagan*	*Dennis*	*Hawker*	*v d Hauwe**	*Phillips*	*van Mierlo*	*Dillon*	*Harford*	*Curbishley*	*Carrodus*	*Summerfield*
									Ref: M James	Ron Saunders' ragged Birmingham offer little resistance. The penalty is awarded for a foul on Clark, who later nets his first West Ham goal with a neat chip. Goddard managed one goal, a lob, but should have had a hat-trick. The game marked Lampard's 500th league appearance.											
6		A	WEST BROM		6	W	2-1	2-1	Clark 8, Van der Elst 9	Parkes	Stewart	Lampard	Bonds	Martin	Devonshire	Van der Elst	Goddard	Clark	Allen	Pike	
	18/8			*15,321*	*8*	10			*Eastoe 41*	*Grew*	*Batson*	*Whitehead*	*Zondervan*	*Bennett*	*Robertson*	*Jol*	*Brown**	*Regis*	*Owen*	*Eastoe*	*Cross*
									Ref: K Walmsley	Alvin Martin takes advantage of an injury to Liverpool's Phil Thompson to earn an England call-up for the European Championship match against Denmark. Martin keeps a tight grip on Cyrille Regis, Ally Brown and Peter Eastoe. Sandy Clark scores a fine individual goal.											
7		H	MANCHESTER C		4	W	4-1	2-0	Clark 33, 37, Goddard 47, Van Elst 71	Parkes	Stewart*	Lampard	Bonds	Martin	Devonshire	Van der Elst	Goddard	Clark	Allen	Pike	Orr
	25/9			23,883	*9*	13			*Boyer 63*	*Williams*	*Ranson*	*McDonald**	*Baker*	*Bond !*	*Caton*	*Hareide*	*Reeves*	*Boyer*	*Hartford !*	*Power*	*Tueart*
									Ref: D Letts	City end the match with nine men. Kevin Bond was sent off on 59 minutes for kicking Bonds, and Hartford's mouth got him expelled later. Ray Stewart had another penalty saved, this time by the overworked Alex Williams, only playing because England man Corrigan was injured.											
8		A	ARSENAL		4	W	3-2	2-1	Van der Elst 19, Goddard 42, Martin 62	Parkes	Stewart	Lampard	Bonds	Martin	Devonshire	Van der Elst*	Goddard	Clark	Allen	Pike	Orr
	2/10			*30,484*	*18*	16			*Talbot 22, Davis 84*	*Wood*	*Hollins*	*Sansom*	*Talbot*	*O'Leary*	*Whyte*	*Davis*	*Sunderland*	*Chapman*	*Woodcock*	*Rix*	
									Ref: T Bune	Arsenal can't stop leaking goals at home lately. Pin-point Hammers passes set up goals for Van der Elst and Goddard. Martin's goal was a looping header. West Ham had much defending to do after half-time, and Davis' headed goal from Hollins' corner provoked a furious finale.											
9		H	LIVERPOOL		2	W	3-1	1-0	Martin 36, Pike 46, Clark 79	Parkes	Stewart	Lampard	Bonds*	Martin	Devonshire	Neighbour	Goddard	Clark	Allen	Pike	Orr
	9/10			32,500	*5*	19			*Souness 75*	*Grobbelaar*	*Neal*	*Kennedy**	*Thompson*	*Whelan*	*Hansen*	*Dalglish*	*Lee*	*Lawrenson*	*Rush*	*Souness*	*Johnston*
									Ref: A Robinson	Hammers extend their winning league run to five after this exhilarating match. Neighbour and Goddard supplied the crosses for all three West Ham goals. When Liverpool pushed Lawrenson forward, they carried far greater threat. Two defeats on the trot for Liverpool, and that's rare.											
10		A	SOUTHAMPTON		2	L	0-3	0-1		Parkes	Stewart	Lampard	Bonds	Martin	Devonshire	Van der Elst	Goddard	Clark	Allen	Pike	
	16/10			*19,840*	*19*	19			*Williams 15, Ball 60, Moran 89*	*Wells*	*Rofe*	*Holmes*	*Williams*	*Nicholl*	*Wright*	*Ball*	*Moran*	*Fashanu*	*Armstrong*	*Lawrence**	*Puckett*
									Ref: J Hunting	The form book is turned upside down as West Ham's winning run comes to an end. Peter Shilton is missing from McMenemy's Saints, having hurt his shoulder when falling off a log while playing with his child. West Ham's best chance came when Van der Elst hit an upright at 0-2.											

11	A	BRIGHTON	5	L	1-3	0-1	Devonshire 89	Parkes	Stewart	Lampard !	Bonds	Martin	Devonshire	Van der Elst	Goddard	Clark	Allen	Pike	
23/10		*20,490*	*12*	19			*Smith 44, Gatting 77, Robinson 84*	*Moseley*	*Shanks*	*Pearce*	*Stille*	*Foster*	*Gatting*	*Case**	*McNab*	*Robinson*	*Ward*	*Smith*	*Ryan*
							Ref: L Burden	After 24 minutes Frank Lampard is sent off for the first time in his career, guilty of a professional foul on Michael Robinson. Brighton are still unbeaten at home, and a huge crowd at the Goldstone Ground turns out to welcome the return of Brighton's prodigal son, Mark Ward.											
12	H	MANCHESTER U	2	W	3-1	1-0	Goddard 32, Stewart 53p, Pike 70	Parkes	Stewart	Lampard	Bonds	Martin	Devonshire	Van der Elst	Goddard	Clark	Allen	Pike	
30/10		31,684	*3*	22			*Moran 90*	*Bailey*	*Duxbury*	*Albiston*	*Grimes !*	*Moran*	*Buchan*	*Robson*	*Muhren*	*Stapleton*	*Whiteside*	*Coppell*	
							Ref: D Hedges	Man U's Ashley Grimes is sent off for clipping the ref round the face after a penalty claim goes unheeded. Grimes had earlier conceded the penalty, impeding Clark. Ron Atkinson's team created 17 clear-cut chances. Coppell hit the bar, and Atkinson asks the press 'Am I dreaming?'											
13	A	STOKE	3	L	**2-5**	1-4	Stewart 43p, Pike 77 *[McIlroy 45, 76]*	Parkes	Stewart	Brush	Bonds	Martin	Devonshire	Van der Elst*	Goddard	Clark	Allen	Pike	Orr
6/11		*17,589*	*7*	22			*O'Callaghan 15, Hampton 30, Thomas 42*	*Harrison*	*Parkin D*	*Hampton*	*Bracewell*	*Watson*	*McAughtrie*	*Maguire*	*McIlroy*	*O'Callaghan**	*Thomas*	*Chamberl'n M*	*Berry*
							Ref: F Roberts	On the day Lyall receives his Bell's Manager of the Month award for October, his team are torn apart, recording their heaviest setback since Sunderland beat them 0-6 in 1967. Devonshire kept trying to beat everyone on his own, and consequently gave the ball away time after time.											
14	H	NORWICH	2	W	1-0	0-0	Clark 53	Parkes	Stewart	Lampard	Bonds	Martin	Devonshire	Van der Elst	Goddard	Clark	Allen	Pike	
13/11		22,463	*22*	25				*Woods*	*Haylock*	*Hareide*	*Van Wyk*	*Walford*	*Watson*	*Barham**	*O'Neill*	*Deehan*	*Bertschin*	*Bennett*	*Metcalf*
							Ref: B Hill	Bobby Robson watched Goddard have a poor game, but he keeps his place in the England squad to play Greece. The pattern was set after two minutes, when Goddard ran from the halfway line, rounded Chris Woods, but pushed the ball too wide. Clark hit the winner from a rebound.											
15	A	TOTTENHAM	4	L	1-2	1-0	Van der Elst 35	Parkes	Stewart	Lampard	Bonds	Martin	Neighbour	Van der Elst	Goddard	Clark	Allen	Pike	
20/11		***41,960***	*8*	25			*Archibald 55, 88*	*Clemence*	*Hughton*	*Price*	*Parks*	*Hazard*	*Perryman**	*Mabbutt*	*Archibald*	*Villa*	*Hoddle*	*Crooks*	*Brooke*
							Ref: R Lewis	Spurs' boardroom is again in upheaval. Keith Burkinshaw's team have just been knocked out of Europe. Steve Archibald misses several chances for Spurs before seizing on Neighbour's back-pass. Archibald was credited with the late winner, after the ball ricocheted off his chest.											
16	H	EVERTON	5	W	2-0	1-0	Stevens 16 (og), Bonds 85	Parkes	Stewart	Lampard	Bonds	Martin !	Devonshire*	Van der Elst	Goddard	Clark	Allen	Pike	Morgan
27/11		21,424	*15*	28				*Arnold*	*Stevens*	*Ratcliffe*	*Higgins*	*Wright*	*McMahon*	*Irvine !*	*Heath**	*Sharp*	*King*	*Sheedy*	*Johnston*
							Ref: V Callow	Two minutes from time Everton's Alan Irvine kicked the ball at the grounded Van der Elst and all hell was let loose. The outcome was red cards for Irvine and Martin, who had looked the best player on the pitch and just laid on Bonds' goal. Everton's rough play won few admirers.											
17	A	ASTON VILLA	6	L	0-1	0-0		Parkes	Stewart !	Lampard	Orr	Martin	Brush	Van der Elst	Goddard	Clark	Allen	Pike	
4/12		*24,658*	*3*	28			*Cowans 83p*	*Rimmer*	*Jones*	*Williams*	*Evans*	*McNaught*	*Mortimer**	*Bremner*	*Shaw*	*Withe*	*Cowans*	*Morley*	*Walters*
							Ref: E Read	This game exploded at the death. Peter Withe dives into Martin, who was running backwards, and wins a penalty. Stewart was then sent off for body-checking Mark Walters, having been booked moments earlier. Lyall refuses to attend the press conference, feeling his team were cheated.											
18	H	COVENTRY	7	L	0-3	0-3		Parkes	Stewart	Lampard	Orr	**Gallagher**	Devonshire*	Van der Elst	Goddard	Brush	Allen	Pike	Morgan
11/12		19,321	*8*	28			*Hateley 36, Roberts 42, Whitton 45*	*Sealey*	*Thomas*	*Roberts*	*Butterworth*	*Dyson*	*Gillespie*	*Whitton*	*Jacobs*	*Hateley*	*Melrose*	*Hunt*	
							Ref: A Grey	With half his defence injured or suspended, Lyall signs Wolves' Joe Gallagher on trial, despite his bad-boy reputation. The result is to gift Coventry their first away win of the season. Brian Roberts' goal, a 20-yard volley, was his first in a 10-year career. The third goal was farcical.											
19	A	NOTTS CO	6	W	2-1	2-0	Dickens 6, Hunt 15 (og)	Parkes	Lampard	Brush	Orr	Gallagher	**Dickens**	Van der Elst	Goddard	Clark	Allen	Pike	
18/12		***8,457***	*15*	31			*Worthington 73*	*Avramovic*	*Benjamin*	*Worthington*	*Hunt*	*Kilcline*	*Richards*	*Chiedozie*	*Fashanu*	*Christie*	*Hooks*	*Mair**	*Clarke*
							Ref: J Worrall	Another debutant, this time 18-year-old Alan Dickens, a Brooking lookalike. He enjoys a fine debut, scoring after Paul Allen's effort had been parried by the keeper. Clark's cross cannoned off David Hunt for the second goal. County debutant Justin Fashanu had a 'goal' disallowed.											
20	H	SWANSEA	4	W	3-2	0-2	Stewart 48p, Van Elst 68, Goddard 86	Parkes	Stewart	Brush	Orr	Martin	Devonshire	Van der Elst	Goddard	Clark	Allen	Pike	
27/12		23,843	*18*	34			*Latchford 26, 38*	*Davies*	*Stanley*	*Hadziabdic*	*Robinson*	*Evans*	*Rajkovic*	*James L*	*James R*	*Mahoney*	*Charles*	*Latchford*	
							Ref: I Borrett	At half-time Paul Brush is pushed up from midfield and a lost cause is transformed into an epic win. Gary Stanley toppled Devonshire for the penalty. Devonshire set up Van der Elst's goal. Goddard's late winner, a deflection off the keeper, is his first league goal for two months.											
21	A	WATFORD	5	L	1-2	0-1	Stewart 78p	Parkes	Stewart	Lampard	Gallagher	Martin	Devonshire	Van der Elst	Goddard	Clark	Allen	Pike	
29/12		*24,870*	*3*	34			*Jackett 39, Jenkins 58*	*Sherwood*	*Rice*	*Rostron*	*Taylor*	*Sims*	*Bolton*	*Callaghan*	*Blissett*	*Jenkins*	*Jackett*	*Barnes*	
							Ref: C Thomas	Graham Taylor's Watford are going well. Just before the hour, Gallagher was lucky not to be sent off for deliberate handball. But from John Barnes' free-kick Ross Jenkins headed Watford's second goal. Pat Rice brought West Ham back into contention when fouling Devonshire.											

No	Date		Att	Pos	Pt	F-A	H-T	Scorers, Times, and Referees	1	2	3	4	5	6	7	8	9	10	11	12 sub used
22	H	TOTTENHAM		5	W	3-0	1-0	Cottee 25, Stewart 70p, Pike 80	Parkes	Stewart	Gallagher	Dickens	Martin	Devonshire	Van der Elst	**Cottee**	Clark	Allen	Pike	
	1/1		**33,383**	*12*	37				*Clemence*	*Hughton*	*Mazzon*	*Price*	*Villa*	*Perryman*	*O'Reilly*	*Archibald*	*Brooke*	*Hoddle*	*Crooks*	
								Ref: M Scott	17-year-old Tony Cottee makes his senior debut and scores after Ray Clemence pushes Joe Gallagher's header against the bar. The lead was doubled when Mazzon brought down Devonshire in the area. Spurs' boss Keith Burkinshaw rages at his team, especially the invisible Hoddle.											
23	H	LUTON		5	L	2-3	1-1	Cottee 12, Clark 66	Parkes	Stewart	Gallagher	Dickens	Martin*	Devonshire	Van der Elst	Cottee	Clark	Allen	Pike	Morgan
	4/1		21,435	*17*	37			*Walsh 32, 73, 88*	*Findlay*	*Stephens*	*Thomas*	*Horton*	*Goodyear*	*Donaghy*	*Hill*	*Bunn**	*Walsh*	*Turner*	*Moss*	*Kellock*
								Ref: T Spencer	Luton have a good record at Upton Park and this win takes them out of the bottom three. England manager Bobby Robson watches as Paul Walsh hits the post inside the first minute. Ray Stewart slips to let in Walsh for Luton's very late winner, which completed his hat-trick.											
24	A	NOTT'M FOREST		6	L	0-1	0-0		Parkes	Stewart*	Lampard	Bonds	Martin	Devonshire	Van der Elst	Goddard	Clark	Allen	Pike	Gallagher
	15/1		*17,031*	*3*	37			*Wallace 74*	*Sutton*	*Swain*	*Gunn*	*Todd*	*Young*	*Bowyer*	*Proctor*	*Wallace*	*Birtles*	*Hodge*	*Robertson*	
								Ref: P Tyldesley	It is 11 years since West Ham were successful against Forest at the City Ground. Forest pressed from first to last. Clark volleyed against the bar in the first half, but Hammers would not come so close again. Wallace took Birtles' pass with his back to goal, turned and shot into the corner.											
25	H	WEST BROM		6	L	0-1	0-1		Parkes	Lampard	Gallagher	Bonds	Martin	Devonshire	Van der Elst*	Goddard	Clark	Allen	Pike	Cowie
	22/1		19,887	*13*	37			*Eastoe 10*	*Barron*	*Whitehead*	*Statham*	*Zondervan*	*Wile*	*Robertson*	*Jol*	*Bennett*	*Regis**	*Owen*	*Eastoe*	*Cross*
								Ref: M Taylor	Albion are as physical a team as they come, and Clive Whitehead seemed to foul everyone in sight. But WBA lose Cyrille Regis in the first half with a fractured cheekbone, following a collision with Gallagher. A floodlight failure delayed the start of the second half by 21 minutes.											
26	A	BIRMINGHAM		8	L	0-3	0-1		Parkes	Lampard	Gallagher	Bonds	Martin	Devonshire	Van der Elst	Goddard	Clark	Allen*	Cowie	Dickens
	5/2		*12,539*	*20*	37			*Harford 35, Ferguson 59, Gayle 90*	*Coton*	*Langan*	*Dennis*	*Stevenson*	*Blake*	*Broadhurst*	*Gayle*	*Ferguson*	*Harford*	*Curbishley*	*Dillon*	
								Ref: T Fitzharris	West Ham's sixth successive league defeat leaves veteran Billy Bonds fuming: 'We were absolute rubbish.' It would have been even worse had Kevin Dillon not missed a penalty for City – after Lampard had handled. Birmingham nonetheless win easily enough and climb off the bottom.											
27	H	SOUTHAMPTON		12	D	1-1	1-1	Lampard 44	Parkes	Stewart	Lampard	Bonds	Martin	Devonshire	Van der Elst	Goddard	Clark*	Allen	Pike	Cottee
	26/2		19,626	*10*	38			*Wallace 16*	*Shilton*	*Agboola*	*Mills*	*Williams*	*Nicholl*	*Wright*	*Holmes*	*Baird*	*Moran*	*Armstrong*	*Wallace*	
								Ref: L Robinson	The boo-boys have it in for Sandy Clark, who is barracked throughout. In the 33rd minute Parkes smothered the ball outside his area and is sent off, but a linesman was already flagging for offside. Lampard's deflected shot, through Mick Mills' legs, denies Saints a fourth straight win.											
28	H	BRIGHTON		10	W	2-1	0-0	Dickens 83, Cottee 84	Parkes	Stewart*	Lampard	Gallagher	Martin	Devonshire	Van der Elst	Morgan	Cottee	Allen	Pike	Dickens
	5/3		16,850	*21*	41			*Ryan 82*	*Moseley*	*Ramsey*	*Gatting*	*Grealish*	*Foster*	*Stevens*	*Case*	*Ritchie*	*Robinson*	*Ryan*	*Smillie*	
								Ref: J Deakin	West Ham's first win since New Year's Day looked unlikely after 82 dreadfully tedious minutes. But then the match burst into life. Alan Dickens described his 30-yard goal as the best of his life. Cottee's winner was the first goal scored by a West Ham forward since 4 January.											
29	A	LIVERPOOL		11	L	0-3	0-0		Parkes	Stewart	Lampard	Bonds	Martin	Devonshire	Van der Elst	Morgan	Goddard	Allen	Pike	
	12/3		*28,511*	*1*	41			*Pike 49 (og), Lee 55, Rush 67*	*Grobbelaar*	*Neal*	*Kennedy*	*Lawrenson*	*Whelan*	*Hansen*	*Dalglish*	*Lee*	*Rush*	*Johnston*	*Souness*	
								Ref: K Hackett	Leaders Liverpool remain 14 points clear of second-placed Watford thanks to this emphatic win. West Ham came for a draw and defended in depth. But when Pike dived to head into his own net the floodgates opened. Ian Rush scores his 100th Liverpool goal, his 26th of the season.											
30	H	STOKE		13	D	1-1	0-0	Bould 52 (og)	Parkes	Stewart	Lampard	Bonds	Martin	Devonshire	Van der Elst	Goddard	Morgan	Allen	Pike	
	19/3		**16,466**	*9*	42			*Thomas 70*	*Fox*	*Bould*	*Hampton*	*Bracewell*	*Watson*	*Berry*	*Painter*	*McIlroy*	*O'Callaghan**	*Thomas*	*Chamberl'n*	*M Griffiths*
								Ref: M Bodenham	John Lyall missed this game, taking in another fixture. With the transfer deadline looming he is anxious to make a signing. There are rumours that David Cross might be returning from Man City. Lyall missed an exquisitely scooped own-goal by Steve Bould, later bound for Arsenal.											
31	A	MANCHESTER U		13	L	1-2	0-0	Devonshire 72	Parkes	Stewart	Lampard	Bonds	Martin	Devonshire	Van der Elst	Goddard	Orr*	Allen	Pike	Dickens
	22/3		*30,227*	*3*	42			*Stapleton 46, McGarvey 63*	*Bailey*	*Gidman*	*Albiston*	*Moses*	*McGrath*	*Duxbury*	*Wilkins*	*Muhren*	*Stapleton**	*McGarvey*	*Coppell*	*Macari*
								Ref: A Challinor	Lyall has sold Clark to Glasgow Rangers and Nicky Morgan to Portsmouth, and has signed David Swindlehurst from Derby. Lyall missed the first half of this match, but had taken his seat to see Muhren's corner headed in by Stapleton. McGarvey ran on to Remi Moses' pass for No 2.											

No	Date	Venue	Opponent	Att	Pos	Pts	Result	F-A	H-T	Scorers, Times, and Referees	1	2	3	4	5	6	7	8	9	10	11	12 sub used
32		A	NORWICH		14		D	1-1	1-0	Dickens 25	Parkes	Stewart	Lampard	Bonds	Martin	Devonshire	Orr	Goddard	**Swindl'urst**	Dickens	Pike	
	26/3			*18,582*	*21*	43				*Deehan 67p*	*Woods*	*Haylock*	*Downs*	*Mendham*	*Walford*	*Watson*	*Barham*	*O'Neill*	*Deehan*	*Bertschin**	*Channon*	*Jack*
										Ref: J Bray	David Swindlehurst makes his debut, his mind troubled by his baby daughter, who has been hospitalised with pneumonia. His team-mates took his mind off her by pumping a stream of high balls at his head. West Ham might even have won, until Martin fouled Mick Channon in the area.											
33		H	WATFORD		12		W	2-1	1-1	Van der Elst 19, Swindlehurst 62	Parkes	Stewart	Lampard	Bonds	Martin	Devonshire	Van der Elst	Goddard	Swindlehurst*	Dickens	Pike	Cottee
	2/4			22,647	*3*	46				*Callaghan 6*	*Sherwood*	*Rice*	*Rostron*	*Taylor*	*Sims*	*Bolton*	*Callaghan*	*Blissett*	*Barnes*	*Lohman**	*Jobson*	*Armstrong*
										Ref: A Robinson	Devonshire played so poorly against Greece that Bobby Robson took the rare step of criticising him publicly. Whether or not by coincidence, Robson watched this match, and Devonshire was stung into playing well. Dickens made the winner, Swindlehurst's first goal for his new club.											
34		A	SWANSEA		10		W	5-1	2-1	Pike 20, 65, D'shire 45, Dickens 82, 88	Parkes	Stewart	Lampard	Bonds	Martin	Devonshire	Van der Elst	Goddard	Orr	Dickens	Pike	
	5/4			*13,303*	*19*	49				*Walsh 2*	*Sander*	*Marustik*	*Richards*	*Stevenson*	*Lewis*	*Rajkovic*	*Loveridge*	*James R*	*Walsh**	*Stanley*	*Latchford*	*Gale*
										Ref: D Civil	Six points out of six over Easter. This win is West Ham's biggest since defeating Grimsby by the same score two years earlier. Swindlehurst misses the game with hamstring trouble. Walsh's shock header was cancelled out by a slovenly half-clearance that fell neatly for Geoff Pike.											
35		H	SUNDERLAND		7		W	2-1	0-0	Dickens 60, Goddard 82	Parkes	Stewart	Lampard	Bonds	Martin	Devonshire	Van der Elst	Goddard	Swindlehurst*	Dickens	Pike	Cottee
	9/4			20,053	*16*	52				*Pickering 70*	*Turner*	*Nicholl*	*Munro*	*Elliott*	*Chisholm*	*Proctor*	*Cummins**	*Rowell*	*Worthington*	*James*	*Pickering*	*McCoist*
										Ref: H Taylor	An hour of tedium and the crowd are getting restless. Alan Dickens' sweet volley – his fourth goal in four games – lifts the tempo, but Nick Pickering replies with a spectacular volley of his own. Paul Goddard shrugs off a heavy challenge to bludgeon his first goal since Christmas.											
36		A	MANCHESTER C		9		L	0-2	0-2		Parkes	Stewart	Lampard	Bonds	Orr	Devonshire	Van der Elst	Goddard*	Allen	Dickens	Pike	Cottee
	16/4			*23,015*	*17*	52				*McDonald 13, Tueart 26p*	*Williams*	*Ranson*	*McDonald*	*Reid*	*Bond*	*Caton*	*Tueart*	*Reeves*	*Kinsey*	*Hartford*	*Power*	
										Ref: A Saunders	City boss John Bond drops leading scorer David Cross and the gamble seems to pay off. Kevin Bond's free-kick was headed in by full-back Bobby McDonald. Then Billy Bonds was ruled to have handled in the area following a City corner. Bonzo thought the decision very harsh.											
37		H	ASTON VILLA		9		W	2-0	0-0	Swindlehurst 59, Bonds 78	Parkes	Stewart	Lampard*	Bonds	Martin	Devonshire	Van der Elst	Goddard	Swindlehurst	Dickens	Pike	Orr
	23/4			21,822	*4*	55					*Spink*	*Williams*	*Gibson*	*Evans*	*McNaught*	*Walker*	*Curbishley*	*Shaw*	*Withe*	*Cowans*	*Morley*	
										Ref: C Thomas	Villa boss Tony Barton has no complaints following this clear-cut defeat. Spink failed to hold Goddard's header, allowing Swindlehurst an easy goal. Devonshire and Dickens set up Bonds' third league goal of the season. Bonds and Withe exchanged blows but escaped punishment.											
38		A	EVERTON		10		L	0-2	0-1		Parkes	Stewart	Brush	Bonds	Martin	Devonshire	Van der Elst	Goddard	Swindlehurst	Dickens	Pike	
	30/4			*16,355*	*7*	55				*Sharp 32, 82*	*Southall*	*Stevens*	*Bailey*	*Ratcliffe*	*Higgins*	*Richardson*	*Ainscow*	*Johnson*	*Sharp*	*Heath*	*Sheedy*	
										Ref: K Holbrook	England international Alvin Martin blunders to prevent Everton with their first goal. He tackles Graeme Sharp and tries to prod the ball back to Parkes, but Sharp nips in. Sharp side-foots the second goal, from Stevens' cross, as Bonds, Stewart and Parkes all stand staring at each other.											
39		A	IPSWICH				W	2-1	1-1	Goddard 10, Stewart 79p	Parkes	Stewart	Lampard	Bonds	Martin	Devonshire	Van der Elst	Goddard	Swindlehurst	Dickens	Pike	
	3/5			*18,690*		58				*D'Avray 33*	*Cooper*	*Burley*	*Barnes*	*Parkin**	*Gernon*	*Butcher*	*Wark*	*McCall*	*Mariner*	*D'Avray*	*O'Callaghan*	*Turner*
										Ref: G Napthine	This thriller was decided by a late penalty. Back in September Cooper saved a Ray Stewart penalty. This time, after Goddard had been felled by Irvin Gernon, Stewart has his revenge, scoring his 10th penalty of the season. Mich D'Avray had earlier levelled with a superb shot.											
40		H	NOTTS CO		8		W	2-0	1-0	Van der Elst 5, Goddard 70	Parkes	Stewart	Lampard	Bonds	Martin	Devonshire	Van der Elst	Goddard	Swindlehurst	Dickens	Pike	
	7/5			17,534	*16*	61					*Avramovic*	*Benjamin*	*Hunt*	*Goodwin*	*Kilcline*	*Richards*	*Chiedozie*	*Christie*	*McCulloch**	*Lahtinen*	*Worthington*	*Clarke*
										Ref: T Bune	Van der Elst's solo goal does not affect his decision to return to Belgium at the end of the season. Alan Dickens laid on the second goal for Goddard. Poor Notts Co are heartily sick of West Ham, having been beaten by them twice in the league and also knocked out of the Milk Cup.											
41		H	ARSENAL				L	1-3	0-3	Van der Elst 52	Parkes	Stewart	Lampard	Bonds	Martin	Devonshire	Van der Elst	Goddard	Swindlehurst	Brooking	Pike	
	10/5			28,930		61				*Petrovic 9, Whyte 22, McDermott 28*	*Jennings*	*Kay*	*Sansom*	*Whyte*	*O'Leary*	*Nicholas*	*Talbot*	*Davis*	*Petrovic*	*McDermott*	*Hill*	
										Ref: A Gunn	Terry Neill's Arsenal performed a first-half demolition job on West Ham. The Gunners were inspired by Vladimir Petrovic, who turned in Paul Davis' low cross, featured in the build-up to Whyte's goal, then crossed for McDermott's third. Van der Elst's consolation spun off Jennings.											
42		A	COVENTRY		8		W	4-2	1-0	Goddard 8, Cottee 54, 88, Swind'h'st 60	Parkes	Stewart	Lampard	Bonds	Orr	Devonshire	Van der Elst	Goddard	Swindlehurst	Allen	Pike	Cottee
	14/5			*10,919*	*19*	64				*Hendrie 55, Whitton 75*	*Sealey*	*Thomas*	*Roberts*	*Hormanschuk*	*Butterworth*	*Gillespie*	*Whitton*	*Singleton*	*Hateley*	*Hendrie*	*Hunt*	
		Home		Away						Ref: B Newsome	A game with no managers. John Lyall was a way scouting and Dave Sexton was sacked by Coventry just hours before kick-off. Bobby Gould takes temporary charge. Goddard shot on the run through Sealey's legs. Tony Cottee, a second-half sub, slides home Alan Devonshire's cross.											
Average		22,820		20,265																		

Milk Cup			F-A	H-T	Scorers, Times, and Referees	1	2	3	4	5	6	7	8	9	10	11	12 sub used
2:1 A STOKE	4	D	1-1	0-0	Stewart 81p	Parkes	Stewart	Lampard	Orr	Martin	Devonshire	Neighbour	Goddard	Clark	Allen	Pike	
6/10	*18,079 8*				*Thomas 70*	*Fox*	*Parkin*	*Hampton*	*Bracewell*	*Watson*	*Berry*	*Maguire*	*McIlroy*	*O'Callaghan*	*Thomas*	*Chamb'l'n M* Griffiths*	
					Ref: H King	Lampard assumes the captaincy in the absence of Bonds. An early clash between Alan Devonshire and Mark Chamberlain saw the England winger limp off the pitch. Thomas's goal went in off Phil Parkes' body. Berry's clumsy challenge on Devonshire resulted in Stewart's penalty.											
2:2 H STOKE	5	W	2-1	0-0	Goddard 80, Clark 82	Parkes	Stewart	Lampard	Bonds	Martin	Devonshire	Van der Elst	Goddard	Clark	Allen	Pike*	Neighbour
26/10	18,270 *8*				*Watson 63*	*Harrison*	*Pike*	*Hampton*	*Bracewell*	*Watson*	*McAughtrie*	*Maguire*	*McIlroy*	*O'Callaghan*	*Thomas*	*Chamberl'n M*	
					Ref: J Martin (Hammers win 3-2 on aggregate)	Bobby Robson watches as England defender Dave Watson heads Paul Maguire's cross beyond Parkes. Goddard's equaliser, after he beat three players to shoot from 20 yards, was special. Stoke were furious over Clark's winner, insisting that Devonshire's pass caught Goddard offside.											
3 A LINCOLN	3	D	1-1	1-0	Goddard 25	Parkes	Stewart	Brush	Bonds	Martin	Devonshire	Orr*	Goddard	Clark	Allen	Pike	Van der Elst
10/11	*13,899 3:1*				*Bell 82*	*Felgate*	*Carr*	*Neale*	*Cockerill*	*Peake*	*Thompson*	*Burke*	*Turner*	*Hobson*	*Bell*	*Shipley*	
					Ref: K Baker	Colin Murphy's Lincoln put West Ham under a second-half siege, forcing corner after corner on a windy night. Peake had hit a post before Bell nodded in Turner's free-kick. The Hammers had been hanging on to Goddard's earlier swerving shot, which was set up by Devonshire.											
3R H LINCOLN	5	W	2-1	1-0	Stewart 45, Clark 116	Parkes	Stewart	Lampard	Bonds	Martin	Neighbour*	Van der Elst	Goddard	Clark	Allen	Pike	Barnes
29/11	13,686 *3:1*		*aet*		*Clark 77 (og)*	*Felgate*	*Carr*	*Neale*	*Cockerill*	*Peake*	*Thompson*	*Hibberd*	*Turner*	*Hobson*	*Bell*	*Shipley*	
					Ref: A Glasson	Lyall admits his team were 'very fortunate' after this battle with the Division 3 pace-setters. Turner rugby-tackled Allen to concede a penalty, which Stewart put away only after Felgate saved. George Shipley's cross was dummied by Derek Bell and ricocheted in off Sandy Clark.											
4 A NOTTS CO	6	D	3-3	0-0	Van der Elst 66, 73, 85	Parkes	Stewart	Lampard	Orr	Martin	Devonshire	Van der Elst	Goddard	Clark*	Allen	Pike	Brush
7/12	*7,525 12*				*McCulloch 50, Christie 53p, Hunt 88*	*Avramovic*	*Benjamin*	*Worthington*	*Hunt*	*Kilcline*	*Richards*	*Chiedozie*	*Christie*	*McCulloch*	*Hooks*	*Mair*	
					Ref: G Tyson	Van der Elst celebrates being called into the Belgian national squad with his first Hammers hat-trick. Although Alvin Martin concedes yet another penalty, West Ham recovered and looked to be through – 3-2 winners – until Phil Parkes beat out Chiedozie's cross to David Hunt.											
4R H NOTTS CO	6	W	3-0	1-0	Stewart 30p, Clark 62, Allen 88	Parkes	Stewart	Brush	Orr	Martin	Devonshire	Van der Elst	Goddard	Clark	Allen	Pike	
21/12	13,140 *15*					*Avramovic*	*Benjamin*	*Worthington*	*Hunt*	*Kilcline*	*Richards*	*Chiedozie*	*Christie*	*Fashanu*	*Goodwin*	*Clarke**	*Mair*
					Ref: L Shapter	John Lyall is in bed with flu, leaving Ronnie Boyce to take charge. The Hammers have two goals disallowed before Avramovic brings downs Goddard for the penalty. Clark settled the outcome, netting the rebound after Van der Elst had hit a post. Two wins in four days over County.											
QF A LIVERPOOL	6	L	1-2	0-0	Allen 75	Parkes	Cowie	Gallagher	Bonds	Martin	Devonshire	Van der Elst	Goddard	Clark	Allen	Pike	
18/1	*23,953 1*				*Hodgson 70, Souness 86*	*Grobbelaar*	*Neal*	*Kennedy*	*Lawrenson*	*Johnston**	*Hansen*	*Dalglish*	*Lee*	*Rush*	*Hodgson*	*Souness*	*Whelan*
					Ref: M Heath	Holders Liverpool are unbeaten at Anfield in any cup-tie since 1974. Twice Goddard was through on a snow-bound pitch, but twice he spurned the chances. Time was running out when Parkes allowed Souness's shot to slither under his body. West Ham would have deserved a replay.											

FA Cup																	
3 A MANCHESTER U	5	L	0-2	0-1		Parkes	Stewart	Lampard	Bonds	Gallagher	Devonshire	Van der Elst	Cottee	Clark	Allen	Pike	
8/1	*44,143 3*				*Coppell 31, Stapleton 54*	*Bailey*	*Duxbury*	*Albiston*	*Moses*	*Moran*	*McQueen*	*Robson*	*Muhren*	*Stapleton*	*Whiteside*	*Coppell*	
					Ref: D Hutchinson	*The Times* wrote: 'West Ham made no more impact than a man reading the gas meter.' Alan Devonshire, in particular, has a shocker. Arnold Muhren's corner was headed on by Frank Stapleton to Steve Coppell. Man-of-the match Bryan Robson set up Frank Stapleton's clincher.											

	P	W	D	L	F	A	W	D	L	F	A	Pts
		Home					Away					
1 Liverpool	42	16	4	1	55	16	8	6	7	32	21	82
2 Watford	42	16	2	3	49	20	6	3	12	25	37	71
3 Manchester U	42	14	7	0	39	10	5	6	10	17	28	70
4 Tottenham	42	15	4	2	50	15	5	5	11	15	35	69
5 Nott'm Forest	42	12	5	4	34	18	8	4	9	28	32	69
6 Aston Villa	42	17	2	2	47	15	4	3	14	15	35	68
7 Everton	42	13	6	2	43	19	5	4	12	23	29	64
8 WEST HAM	42	13	3	5	41	23	7	1	13	27	39	64
9 Ipswich	42	11	3	7	39	23	4	10	7	25	27	58
10 Arsenal	42	11	6	4	36	19	5	4	12	22	37	58
11 West Brom	42	11	5	5	35	20	4	7	10	16	29	57
12 Southampton	42	11	5	5	36	22	4	7	10	18	36	57
13 Stoke	42	13	4	4	34	21	3	5	13	19	43	57
14 Norwich	42	10	6	5	30	18	4	6	11	22	40	54
15 Notts Co	42	12	4	5	37	25	3	3	15	18	46	52
16 Sunderland	42	7	10	4	30	22	5	4	12	18	39	50
17 Birmingham	42	9	7	5	29	24	3	7	11	11	31	50
18 Luton	42	7	7	7	34	33	5	6	10	31	51	49
19 Coventry	42	10	5	6	29	17	3	4	14	19	42	48
20 Manchester C	42	9	5	7	26	23	4	3	14	21	47	47
21 Swansea	42	10	4	7	32	29	0	7	14	19	40	41
22 Brighton	42	8	7	6	25	22	1	6	14	13	46	40
		255	111	96	810	454	96	111	255	454	810	1275

Odds & ends

Double wins: (2) Notts Co, Swansea.
Double losses: (1) Nott'm Forest.

Won from behind: (4) Swansea (h), Brighton (h), Watford (h), Stoke LC (h).
Lost from in front: (3) Spurs (a), Luton (h), Swansea (a).

High spots: Five successive league wins from 11 September. Up to 2nd.
Finishing the season strongly, with seven wins from the last 10 games.

Low spots: Four consecutive defeats from 4 January.
Going out of the FA Cup at the first hurdle, to Manchester U.

Hammer of the Year: Alvin Martin.
Ever-presents: (1) Phil Parkes.
Hat-tricks: (1) Van der Elst.
Leading scorer: (12) Paul Goddard and Van der Elst.

	Appearances Lge	*Sub*	LC	*Sub*	FAC	*Sub*	Goals Lge	LC	FAC	Tot
Allen, Paul	**33**		7		1			2		**2**
Barnes, Bobby	**0**			*1*						
Bonds, Billy	**34**		4		1		**3**			**3**
Brooking, Trevor	**1**									
Brush, Paul	**6**		2	*1*						
Clark, Sandy	**26**		7		1		**7**	3		**10**
Cottee, Tony	**3**	*5*			1		**5**			**5**
Cowie, George	**1**	*1*	1							
Devonshire, Alan	**39**		6		1		**3**			**3**
Dickens, Alan	**12**	*3*					**6**			**6**
Gallagher, Joe	**8**	*1*	1		1					
Goddard, Paul	**39**		7				**10**	2		**12**
Lampard, Frank	**37**		4		1		**2**			**2**
Martin, Alvin	**38**		7				**3**			**3**
Morgan, Nicky	**3**	*4*								
Neighbour, Jimmy	**3**		2	*1*						
Orr, Neil	**9**	*5*	4							
Parkes, Phil	**42**		7		1					
Pike, Geoff	**40**		7		1		**6**			**6**
Stewart, Ray	**39**		6		1		**8**	3		**11**
Swindlehurst, Dave	**9**						**3**			**3**
Van der Elst, François	**40**		5	*1*	1		**9**	3		**12**
(own-goals)	**0**						**3**			**3**
22 players used	**462**	***19***	**77**	***4***	**11**		**68**	**13**		**81**

No	Date	Opponent	Att	Pos	Pt	F-A	H-T	Scorers, Times, and Referees	1	2	3	4	5	6	7	8	9	10	11	12 sub used
1	H	BIRMINGHAM			W	**4-0**	3-0	Cottee 23, 28, Martin 36,	Parkes	Stewart	**Walford**	Bonds	Martin	Devonshire	**Whitton**	Cottee	Swindlehurst	Brooking*	Pike	Orr
	27/8		19,729		3			[Swindlehurst 52]	*Coton*	*Hagan*	*Stevenson*	*Blake*	*Wright*	*Broadhurst*	*Handysides**	*Phillips*	*Harford*	*v d Hauwe*	*Hopkins*	*Rees*
								Ref: A Robinson	18-year-old Tony Cottee is only playing because of Goddard's damaged knee-ligaments, but now he deserves his place on merit. Brooking's shot was turned in by Cottee, who netted his second when Ray Stewart's free-kick wasn't cleared. Ron Saunders' City looked weak in the air.											
2	A	EVERTON			W	1-0	0-0	Walford 69	Parkes	Stewart	Walford	Bonds	Martin	Devonshire	Whitton	Cottee	Swindlehurst	Orr	Pike	
	29/8		*20,375*		6				*Arnold*	*Harper*	*Bailey*	*Mountfield*	*Higgins*	*Richardson**	*Steven*	*Heath*	*Sharp*	*King*	*Sheedy*	*Johnson*
								Ref: P Tyldesley	Walford's fluke goal, an intended cross that floats over Jim Arnold's head, and the first goal he had ever scored with his right foot, brings West Ham their first win at Goodison since Alvin Martin was an apprentice there. Brooking, in his last season, missed the game with a thigh strain.											
3	A	TOTTENHAM		1	W	2-0	2-0	Whitton 9, Swindlehurst 39	Parkes	Stewart	Walford	Bonds	Martin	Devonshire	Whitton	Cottee	Swindlehurst	Brooking	Pike	
	3/9		*38,042*	*20*	9				*Clemence*	*Hughton*	*Thomas*	*Roberts*	*Stevens*	*Perryman*	*Mabbutt*	*Falco*	*Galvin*	*Hoddle**	*Crooks*	*Miller*
								Ref: J Hunting / D Nevin	The game lost Glenn Hoddle to injury before half-time and the referee, too, during the interval. Whitton put West Ham ahead with a volley on the turn, and Swindlehurst swept in Cottee's cross. Spurs had looked in control, though in the second half their shots were all from long range.											
4	H	LEICESTER		1	W	3-1	1-1	Walford 10, Swind'hurst 48, Cottee 49	Parkes	Stewart	Walford	Bonds	Martin	Devonshire	Whitton	Cottee	Swindlehurst	Brooking	Pike	
	6/9		22,131	*22*	12			*Lineker 8*	*Grew*	*Ramsey*	*Smith B*	*MacDonald*	*Rennie*	*Peake*	*Lynex*	*Lineker*	*Smith A*	*Jones**	*Wilson*	*English*
								Ref: L Burden	Lineker's early goal is the first Leicester have scored – and the first West Ham have conceded – this season. It was quickly cancelled out by Steve Walford's 25-yard effort. Swindlehurst headed No 2 and chipped on to Cottee for the third. West Ham's 'robust' play surprises many.											
5	H	COVENTRY		1	W	5-2	3-2	Swind'hurst 29, 35, 67, Whitton 30, 60	Parkes	Stewart	Walford	Bonds	Martin	Devonshire	Whitton	Cottee	Swindlehurst	Brooking	Pike	
	10/9		22,195	*7*	15			*Peake 10, Platnauer 15*	*Suckling*	*Hormantsch'k*	*Roberts*	*Grimes*	*Peake*	*Jacobs*	*Butterworth*	*Withey*	*Platnauer*	*Gibson*	*Adams**	*Singleton*
								Ref: A Crickmore	Bobby Gould's Coventry were unbeaten. This result is one of the great recoveries of the season. At 0-0 Stewart's penalty is saved after Grimes had handled. Before they know it the Hammers are 0-2 down, but Swindlehurst and Whitton turn the tables by half-time. Bonds is magnificent.											
6	A	WEST BROM		1	L	0-1	0-0		Parkes	Stewart	Walford	Bonds	Martin	Devonshire	Orr*	Cottee	Swindlehurst	Brooking	Pike	Goddard
	17/9		*15,161*	*14*	15			*Thompson 87*	*Barron*	*Whitehead*	*Cowdrill*	*Zondervan*	*McNaught*	*Bennett*	*Lewis*	*Thompson*	*Regis*	*Owen*	*Cross**	*Perry*
								Ref: N Wilson	Billy Bonds' 37th birthday. West Ham play for a draw and seldom pose any threat to the Albion defence. They look like surviving until Garry Thompson, the best player on view, heads in Cowdrill's cross. Cowdrill had actually been fouled by Brooking, but the ref played advantage.											
7	H	NOTTS CO		1	W	3-0	1-0	Brooking 32, Goddard 60, Stewart 89p	Parkes	Stewart	Walford	Bonds	Martin	Devonshire	Goddard	Cottee	Swindlehurst	Brooking	Pike	
	24/9		20,613	*18*	18				*McDonough*	*Benjamin*	*Worthington*	*O'Neill*	*Kilcline*	*Hunt*	*McParland*	*Christie**	*McCulloch*	*Harkouk*	*Mair*	*Chiedozie*
								Ref: M James	Paul Goddard plays in midfield and scores the all-important second goal, lifting the ball over the keeper as he rushes off his line. Brooking had earned the first-half lead when chesting down Walford's centre. Stewart's penalty was the consequence of Benjamin shoving Tony Cottee.											
8	A	STOKE		1	L	1-3	0-1	Stewart *60p* *[Thomas 85]*	Parkes	Stewart	Walford	Bonds	Martin	Devonshire	Whitton	Goddard	Swindlehurst	Brooking	Pike	
	1/10		*13,852*	*18*	18			*McAughtrie 29, Chamberlain 70,*	*Fox*	*Berry*	*Hampton*	*James*	*Dyson*	*McAughtrie*	*Painter*	*McIlroy*	*O'Callaghan*	*Thomas*	*Chamberlain*	
								Ref: B Stevens	Stoke boss Ritchie Barker describes West Ham as 'fragile'. This angers Lyall, who felt his team looked stronger once Ray Stewart had levelled from the spot, Goddard having been felled. Tiny Ian Painter outjumped Bonds to set up Stoke's second goal. Mickey Thomas then broke away.											
9	H	LIVERPOOL		2	L	1-3	0-2	Devonshire 89	Parkes	Stewart	Walford	Bonds	Martin	Devonshire	Whitton	Goddard*	Swindlehurst	Brooking	Pike	Cottee
	15/10		**32,555**	*5*	18			*Robinson 15, 27, 75*	*Grobbelaar*	*Neal*	*Kennedy*	*Lawrenson*	*Johnston !*	*Hansen*	*Dalglish*	*Lee*	*Rush**	*Robinson*	*Souness*	*Hodgson*
								Ref: L Shapter	West Ham are toppled off the top by Michael Robinson's first league goals for Joe Fagan's European champions. Poor Bonds, on his 700th appearance, was partially responsible for all three. On the hour Craig Johnston was sent off for his second yellow card, having fouled Bonds.											
10	H	NORWICH		3	D	0-0	0-0		Parkes	Stewart	Walford	Bonds	Martin	Devonshire	Whitton*	Cottee	Swindlehurst	Brooking	Pike	Dickens
	22/10		18,958	*16*	19				*Woods*	*Haylock*	*Downs*	*Mendham*	*Hareide*	*Watson*	*Donowa*	*Channon*	*Devine*	*Bertschin*	*Bennett*	
								Ref: D Brazier	Liverpool join Man U above West Ham, who slip down to third. The Hammers were poor in the first half, when they tried to play through the middle, yet improved afterwards when using the long ball. One Billy Bonds' header brings a great save from Chris Woods; another goes wide.											

No Date	Venue	Opponent Att	Pos	Res Pts	F-A	H-T	Scorers, Times, and Referees	1	2	3	4	5	6	7	8	9	10	11	12
11	A	WATFORD	4	D	0-0	0-0		Parkes	Stewart	Walford	Bonds	Martin	Devonshire	Allen	Cottee	Swindlehurst	Brooking	Orr	
28/10		*14,559*	*19*	20				*Sherwood*	*Palmer*	*Sinnott*	*Jobson*	*Sims*	*Franklin*	*Callaghan*	*Richardson*	*Barnes*	*Bolton*	*Rostron*	
							Ref: B Hill	Had West Ham won this Friday match they would have gone back to the top. It was scheduled for TV, but was scrapped at the last moment, with *Carry On Girls* broadcast instead. It was a wise choice. According to *The Times*, West Ham were 'abysmal', rarely interested in scoring.											
12	H	IPSWICH	3	W	2-1	2-1	Swindlehurst 25, 41	Parkes	Stewart	Walford	Bonds*	Martin	Devonshire	Orr	Cottee	Swindlehurst	Dickens	Pike	Lampard
5/11		20,682	*12*	23			*Osman 39*	*Cooper*	*Burley*	*McCall*	*Putney*	*Osman*	*Butcher*	*Wark*	*Gates*	*Mariner*	*Kinsella**	*O'Callaghan*	*Turner*
							Ref: T Bune	Bonds is the victim of a clash of heads that has him taken to hospital with impaired vision. Better news for David Swindlehurst, who celebrates the birth of twin sons by winning the match with twin headers. Both goals stemmed from free-kicks and both saw him outjump Russell Osman.											
13	A	WOLVES	2	W	3-0	1-0	Brooking 4, Swind'hurst 57, Cottee 89	Parkes	Stewart	Lampard	Walford	Martin	Devonshire	Orr	Cottee	Swindlehurst	Brooking	Pike	
12/11		*12,062*	*22*	26				*Bradshaw*	*Humphrey*	*Bennett**	*Blair*	*Pender*	*Dodd*	*Hibbitt*	*Clarke*	*Cartwright*	*Mardenboro'*	*Crainie*	*Rudge*
							Ref: J Deakin	Devonshire is in such irrepressible form that he seems determined to add to his seven England caps. When he is fouled in the box by Dodd, Stewart's penalty is tipped over by Bradshaw, his second miss from the spot this season. Poor Wolves have now gone 18 games without a win.											
14	A	SUNDERLAND	2	W	1-0	0-0	Swindlehurst 85	Parkes	Stewart	Lampard	Walford	Martin	Devonshire	Whitton	Cottee	Swindlehurst	Brooking	Pike	
19/11		*19,921*	*16*	29				*Turner*	*Venison*	*Pickering*	*Atkins*	*Chisholm*	*Hindmarch*	*Bracewell*	*Rowell*	*West*	*Proctor*	*James*	
							Ref: T Jones	Sunderland had lost just once in 10 games and looked set to extend that fine sequence until Swindlehurst continued his rich vein of goals with a late volley. Stewart had earlier hit the bar and Parkes had silenced the Roker Roar with a string of fine saves. Sunderland saw more of the ball.											
15	H	MANCHESTER U	2	D	1-1	0-0	Swindlehurst 58	Parkes	Stewart	Lampard	Walford	Martin	Devonshire	Whitton	Cottee	Swindlehurst	Brooking	Pike	
27/11		23,355	*3*	30			*Wilkins 56*	*Bailey*	*Moses*	*Albiston*	*Wilkins*	*Duxbury*	*McQueen*	*Robson*	*Muhren**	*Stapleton*	*Crooks*	*Graham*	*Whiteside*
							Ref: C Thomas	A live TV audience saw Bryan Robson at his magnificent best, in a match which offered skill, entertainment and controversy. Wilkins turned inside Brooking for a rare goal, immediately cancelled out by Swindlehurst's header from Pike's corner. Norman Whiteside's header hit a post.											
16	A	ASTON VILLA	2	L	0-1	0-0		Parkes	Stewart	Lampard	Walford	Martin	Devonshire	Whitton	Orr*	Swindlehurst	Brooking	Pike	Cottee
3/12		*21,297*	*7*	30			*Rideout 77*	*Spink*	*Williams*	*Gibson**	*Evans*	*Ormsby*	*Mortimer*	*Birch*	*Walters*	*Rideout*	*Walker*	*Morley*	*Deacy*
							Ref: N Glover	Two moments decided this match, both coming within seconds of one another. Brooking's shot was half-saved, the ball being whacked off the line by Williams. The ball was swept upfield and a cross from near the corner flag saw Rideout head in. Rideout later cleared off his own line.											
17	H	ARSENAL	2	W	3-1	1-0	Brooking 34, Whyte 70 (og), Pike 88	Parkes	Stewart	Lampard	Walford	Martin	Devonshire	Whitton	Orr	Swind'hurst!	Brooking	Pike	
10/12		25,118	*16*	33			*Whyte 90*	*Jennings*	*Hill**	*Sansom*	*Kay !*	*Whyte*	*Caton*	*Madden*	*Davis*	*Woodcock*	*Nicholas*	*Allinson*	*Meade*
							Ref: E Read	Kay's late lunge on Swindlehurst and the latter's retaliation brought red cards for both players. West Ham were already in front through Trevor Brooking's diving header. When Whyte stuck out a boot to deflect man-of-the-match Devonshire's cross past Jennings, Arsenal's hopes faded.											
18	A	NOTT'M FOREST	3	L	0-3	0-1		Parkes	Stewart	Lampard	Walford	Martin	Devonshire	Whitton	Orr	Swindlehurst	Brooking	Pike*	Dickens
17/12		*14,544*	*8*	33			*Hodge 27, Birtles 75, Walsh 85p*	*v Breukelen*	*Anderson*	*Swain*	*Fairclough*	*Hart**	*Bowyer*	*Wigley*	*Davenport*	*Birtles*	*Hodge*	*Walsh*	*Wallace*
							Ref: T Holbrook	Bad luck, the woodwork, and Van Breukelen's defiance combine to deny West Ham their first goal at the City Ground since 1969. Forest were flattered by the final score. Swain went past two Hammers defenders to tee up Gary Birtles for No 2 and Stewart fouled Wigley for the penalty.											
19	H	SOUTHAMPTON	5	L	0-1	0-0		Parkes	Stewart	Lampard*	Walford	Martin	Devonshire	Whitton	Orr	Cottee	Brooking	Dickens	**Donald**
26/12		22,221	*4*	33			*Wallace 64*	*Shilton*	*Mills*	*Dennis*	*Armstrong K*	*Agboola*	*Williams*	*Holmes*	*Curtis**	*Worthington*	*Armstrong D*	*Wallace*	*Puckett*
							Ref: M Bodenham	Lawrie McMenemy's Saints climb above West Ham as a result of Wallace dancing round Orr, who had been switched to left-back in place of the subbed Lampard. Father Christmas handed out presents to the crowd at half-time, but snubbed West Ham when Cottee headed onto the bar.											
20	A	LUTON	4	W	1-0	0-0	Cottee 78	Parkes	Stewart	Brush	Walford	Martin	Devonshire	Whitton	Orr	Cottee	Brooking	Barnes	
27/12		*16,343*	*5*	36				*Sealey*	*Stephens*	*Thomas*	*Horton*	*Elliott*	*Donaghy*	*Hill*	*Stein B*	*Walsh*	*Aylott**	*Daniel*	*Turner*
							Ref: K Baker	Luton saw most of the ball but succumbed to a volley by Cottee, who was only playing because Swindlehurst was suspended. The goal carried West Ham back above Luton, but the match saw more muscle than skill. Players were left black and blue, the same colour as the stormy sky.											
21	H	TOTTENHAM	3	W	4-1	1-1	Cottee 11, Martin 70, Stewart 72, [Brooking 76]	Parkes	Stewart	Brush	Walford	Martin	Devonshire	Whitton	Cottee	Swindlehurst	Brooking	Orr	
31/12		30,939	*11*	39			*Stevens 30*	*Clemence*	*O'Reilly*	*Bowen*	*Webster*	*Stevens*	*Perryman*	*Ardiles*	*Archibald*	*Falco*	*Thomas*	*Dick*	
							Ref: T Spencer	Spurs have seven first-teamers injured or suspended and their depleted side assists Devonshire and Brooking in eclipsing Ardiles in midfield. Brooking set up the first goal for Cottee and the second through Martin's header. Brooking's bobbling shot for No 4 was the least he deserved.											

No	Date		Att	Pos	Pt	F-A	H-T	Scorers, Times, and Referees	1	2	3	4	5	6	7	8	9	10	11	12 sub used
22	A	NOTTS CO		3	D	2-2	2-1	Stewart 20p, Swindlehurst 28	Parkes	Stewart	Brush	Walford	Martin	Devonshire	Whitton	Cottee	Swindlehurst	Brooking	Orr	
	2/1		***8,667***	*20*	40			*Christie 38, O'Neill 47*	*McDonough*	*Goodwin**	*Worthington*	*Richards*	*Hunt*	*Kilcline*	*O'Neill*	*Clarke*	*Christie*	*Harkouk*	*Chiedozie*	*McParland*
								Ref: G Courtney	In a gale-lashed match West Ham looked set to reclaim second spot above Man U. The ball hit Hunt's arm for the penalty. The ref waved play on until alerted by the linesman's waved flag. Swindlehurst began and ended the move for the second. Chiedozie inspired County's fight-back.											
23	A	BIRMINGHAM		3	L	0-3	0-1		Parkes	Stewart	Brush	Walford	Martin	Barnes	Whitton	Cottee	Swindlehurst	Brooking	Orr	
	14/1		10,334	*19*	40			*Harford 30, Halsall 70, Hopkins 80*	*Coton*	*Stevenson*	*v d Hauwe*	*Blake*	*Wright*	*Broadhurst*	*Gayle*	*Kuhl*	*Harford*	*Halsall*	*Hopkins*	
								Ref: D Hedges	Ron Saunders' City had lost their last six home games. This is Phil Parkes' 600th league game but he is at fault for the first goal, bungling a clearance from Gayle's cross under pressure from Harford. Gayle had the beating of Brush and set up both of Birmingham's second-half goals.											
24	H	WEST BROM		3	W	1-0	0-0	Cottee 81	Parkes	Stewart	Lampard	Walford	Orr	Brush	Barnes	Cottee	Swindlehurst	Brooking	Pike	
	21/1		17,213	*16*	43				*Barron*	*Whitehead*	*Cowdrill*	*Luke*	*McNaught*	*Robertson*	*Zondervan*	*Owen**	*Thompson*	*Regis*	*Morley*	*Jol*
								Ref: I Borrett	Alvin Martin has broken six ribs in a car crash. West Ham's desperate injury problem requires Stewart to play centre-back. Walford's through ball enabled Cottee to spring the offside trap for the only goal. A rough game saw more than 50 fouls. Sub Jol was booked within 90 seconds.											
25	H	STOKE		3	W	3-0	2-0	Barnes 6, Cottee 35, Stewart 65p	Parkes	Stewart	Lampard	Walford	Orr	Brush	Barnes	Cottee	Swindlehurst	Allen	Dickens	
	4/2		18,775	*21*	46				*Fox*	*Bould*	*Maskery*	*James*	*Dyson*	*O'Callaghan*	*Painter*	*McIlroy*	*Maguire*	*Hudson*	*Chamberlain*	
								Ref: R Milford	West Ham's young mascot sported a broken nose and the ball burst after five minutes. Fortunately, woeful Stoke were not able to put up much opposition, other than Alan Hudson in midfield. West Ham scored two simple headers before O'Callaghan fouled Tony Cottee for the penalty.											
26	A	QP RANGERS		3	D	1-1	1-1	Cottee 2	Parkes	Stewart	Lampard	Walford	Orr	Brush	Barnes	Cottee	Swindlehurst	Allen	Dickens	
	7/2		*20,102*	*5*	47			*Stainrod 15*	*Hucker*	*Neill*	*Dawes*	*Waddock*	*Wicks*	*Fenwick*	*Fillery**	*Stewart*	*Stainrod*	*Fereday*	*Gregory*	*Micklewhite*
								Ref: G Napthine	Loftus Road's notorious Omniturf pitch does not appear to discomfort West Ham, who are quickly in front as Swindlehurst's cross eludes Fenwick. Stainrod levelled when a high ball was missed by those in front of him. West Ham's nimble forwards always looked likely to score.											
27	A	COVENTRY		3	W	2-1	1-0	Bamber 18 (og), Cottee 60	Parkes	Stewart	Lampard	Walford	Orr	Brush	Barnes	Cottee	Swindlehurst	Allen	Dickens	
	11/2		*13,271*	*10*	50			*Hunt 90*	*Avramovic*	*Roberts*	*Pearce*	*Daly*	*Peake*	*Allardyce*	*Bennett*	*Hunt*	*Bamber*	*Gibson*	*Grimes*	
								Ref: L Burden	Coventry paraded two mascots beforehand, but they could not ward off defeat by the only team still chasing the league and cup double. Tony Cottee's header from Allen's corner was goalbound before deflecting off Bamber's head. But Phil Parkes was by far the busier goalkeeper.											
28	H	WATFORD		4	L	2-4	1-1	Swindlehurst 2, Barnes 60	Parkes	Stewart	Lampard	Bonds	Walford	**Hilton**	Barnes	Cottee	Swindlehurst	Allen	Dickens	
	21/2		19,241	*8*	50			*J'ston 45, Barnes 55, 75, Callaghan 79*	*Sherwood*	*Bardsley*	*Rostron*	*Sims*	*Franklin*	*Taylor*	*Jackett*	*Callaghan*	*Johnston*	*Barnes*	*Atkinson*	
								Ref: A Robinson	Watford's 20-year-old John Barnes steals the show. Playing in the middle alongside Mo Johnston, he terrorises Walford and Bonds. Barnes creates Watford's first goal, left-foots the second and heads their third. Play was held up in the second half when a glass smashed on the pitch.											
29	A	NORWICH		4	L	0-1	0-0		Parkes	Stewart	Lampard	Bonds	Walford	Hilton	Barnes	Cottee	Swindlehurst	Allen	Dickens	
	25/2		*16,294*	*7*	50			*Deehan 65*	*Woods*	*Haylock*	*Downs*	*Mendham*	*Hareide*	*Watson*	*Devine*	*Channon*	*Deehan*	*Bertschin*	*Van Wyk*	
								Ref: J Ashworth	The Hammers' third defeat in a week leaves them with nothing to play for except a UEFA Cup place. They appeared to set out with nothing other than to achieve a goalless draw. Former Norwich player Steve Walford lost out in a scramble with John Deehan for the only goal.											
30	A	IPSWICH		4	W	3-0	2-0	Hilton 4, Butcher 30 (og), Cottee 70	Parkes	Stewart	Lampard	Bonds	Walford	Hilton	Orr	Cottee	Swindlehurst	Brooking	Allen	
	3/3		*17,297*	*19*	53				*Cooper*	*Parkin*	*McCall*	*Putney*	*Osman*	*Butcher*	*Wark*	*Brennan**	*D'Avray*	*Sunderland*	*Gates*	*Dozzell*
								Ref: J Bray	The fact that Bonds and Brooking – 72 years between them – can stroll through this match shows what little fight Ipswich put up. Brooking laid on Paul Hilton's header, his first goal for the Hammers. Brooking's crafty cross then lured Terry Butcher to slice the ball into his own net.											
31	H	WOLVES		3	D	1-1	1-1	Cottee 30	Parkes	Stewart	Lampard	Bonds	Walford	Orr	Barnes*	Cottee	Swindlehurst	Brooking	Allen	Dickens
	10/3		18,111	*21*	54			*McGarvey 22*	*Burridge*	*Buckland*	*Palmer*	*Rudge*	*Pender*	*Dodd*	*Towner*	*Clarke*	*Troughton*	*McGarvey*	*Crainie*	
								Ref: E Read	This surprise result enables Wolves to climb off the bottom. Stewart's error allowed Scott McGarvey, on loan from Man U, to volley past Phil Parkes. Trevor Brooking's sweet through ball set up Cottee's equaliser on a plate. Brooking is determined to retire at the end of this season.											

No	H/A	Opponent	Att	Pos	Res	FT	HT	Scorers, Times, and Referees	1	2	3	4	5	6	7	8	9	10	11	12
32	A	LEICESTER		5	L	1-4	0-1	Stewart 89p	Parkes	Stewart	Lampard	Bonds	Walford	Orr*	Allen	Cottee	Swindlehurst	Brooking	Pike	Barnes
	17/3		*13,533*	*16*	54			*Hazell 42, Lynex 55p, 80p, Lineker 75*	*Wallington*	*Smith B*	*Wilson*	*MacDonald*	*Hazell*	*O'Neill*	*Lynex*	*Lineker*	*Smith A*	*Williams*	*Peake*	
								Ref: D Richardson	Yet more crowd trouble caused by a minority of West Ham fans. Man-of-the-match for Gordon Milne's Leicester was Steve Lynex, who was involved in all four goals. Lampard felled Lynex for the first penalty; Walford handled for the second. Pike had returned after stomach surgery.											
33	H	QP RANGERS		4	D	2-2	2-0	Pike 18, Cottee 45	Parkes	Stewart	Walford	Bonds	Martin	Orr	Allen P	Cottee	Swindlehurst	Brooking	Pike	
	31/3		21,099	*6*	55			*Allen C 76, 85*	*Hucker*	*Neill*	*Dawes*	*Waddock*	*Wicks*	*Fenwick*	*Micklewhite*	*Fillery*	*Allen C*	*Stainrod*	*Fereday**	*Burke*
								Ref: M Dimblebee	A match marred by capricious wind, slipshod passing and ill-timed tackles. Brooking's enterprise conjured two goals before the interval, but Clive Allen rescued a point for QPR single-handedly. He shrugged off Martin and Bonds to score a superb goal, then turned in Burke's corner.											
34	A	LIVERPOOL		6	L	**0-6**	0-4	*[Souness 61, 69]*	Parkes	Stewart	Walford	Bonds	Martin	Orr	Allen	Cottee	Whitton	Brooking	Pike	
	7/4		*38,359*	*1*	55			*Rush 5, 18, Dalglish 12, Whelan 29*	*Grobbelaar*	*Neal*	*Kennedy*	*Lawrenson*	*Whelan*	*Hansen*	*Dalglish*	*Lee*	*Rush*	*Wark*	*Souness*	
								Ref: D Hutchinson	How can a team lying fourth be thumped so comprehensively? Wingless Liverpool became arrogantly bored with West Ham's gutless showing and eased off. Parkes was to blame for two goals. Grobbelaar bantered with everyone. Joe Fagan sent a get-well letter to the flu-stricken Lyall.											
35	H	SUNDERLAND		6	L	0-1	0-0		Parkes	Stewart	Lampard	Bonds	Martin	Orr*	Allen	Cottee	Swindlehurst	Brooking	Pike	Barnes
	14/4		16,558	*18*	55			*Chisholm 71*	*Turner*	*Venison*	*Pickering*	*Atkins*	*Chisholm*	*Elliott*	*Bracewell*	*Robson*	*West*	*Hindmarch*	*James*	
								Ref: T Bune	A slow handclap resounds around Upton Park as Sunderland win their first away fixture in five months. Leighton James' free-kick was met by Chisholm but went in off Brooking. Biggest cheer of the night was to applaud the return of 38-year-old former Hammers idol Pop Robson.											
36	H	LUTON		6	W	3-1	2-0	Cottee 23, 81, Martin 37	Parkes	Stewart	Walford	Bonds	Martin	Barnes	Allen	Cottee	Swindlehurst	Brooking	Pike	
	17/4		**15,430**	*14*	58			*Walsh 65*	*Sealey*	*Stephens*	*Thomas*	*Horton*	*Elliott*	*Donaghy*	*Parker*	*Stein B*	*Walsh*	*Bunn**	*Moss*	*Goodyear*
								Ref: D Reeves	Luton had won just twice in 20 games, so hardly provided the most sterling opposition. Brooking chipped over the defence to Cottee for the first goal. Luton's Paul Walsh was being watched by representatives of four Italian clubs. He scored one, then missed a sitter when 1-2 down.											
37	A	SOUTHAMPTON		6	L	0-2	0-1		Parkes	Stewart	Walford	Bonds	Martin	Barnes*	Allen	Cottee	Swindlehurst	Brooking	Pike	Hilton
	21/4		*20,846*	*5*	58			*Holmes 34, Moran 77*	*Shilton*	*Mills*	*Golac*	*Curtis*	*Whitlock*	*Wright*	*Holmes*	*Moran*	*Worthington*	*Armstrong*	*D Wallace*	
								Ref: C Thomas	A sunny day, but the sun did not shine on West Ham, who seldom got within shooting range of Shilton's goal. Holmes netted the first, from Curtis's pass. The referee overruled the linesman's raised flag. Wallace hit the post before crossing for Moran, whose shot went in off Stewart.											
38	A	MANCHESTER U		7	D	0-0	0-0		Parkes	Stewart	Walford	Bonds	Martin	Hilton	Allen	Cottee	Orr	Brooking	Pike	
	28/4		***44,124***	*2*	59				*Bailey*	*Duxbury*	*Albiston*	*Wilkins*	*Moran*	*Hogg*	*McGrath**	*Moses*	*Stapleton*	*Hughes*	*Graham*	*Whiteside*
								Ref: K Hackett	West Ham line up with Cottee the sole forward and everyone else packing the defence. Cottee might have scored in the second minute, but that would have been hard on Man U, who imposed a siege around the visitors' goal. Parkes made save after save to keep the home team at bay.											
39	H	ASTON VILLA		9	L	0-1	0-1		Parkes	Stewart*	Walford	Bonds	Hilton	Orr	Allen	Cottee	Swindlehurst	Brooking	Pike	Goddard
	5/5		17,930	*8*	59			*Mortimer 19*	*Day*	*Williams*	*Deacy*	*Ormsby*	*Foster*	*Mortimer*	*Birch*	*Blair*	*Withe*	*McMahon*	*Walters**	*Walker*
								Ref: B Hill	West Ham needed to win to have any chance of pipping Arsenal and Spurs for a UEFA Cup place. But not even the return of Goddard, for his first game since October, could fashion a goal. Peter Withe's square pass from the left was thumped in by Mortimer from the edge of the box.											
40	A	ARSENAL		7	D	3-3	3-2	Whitton 4, 44, Hilton 35	Parkes	Stewart	Brush	Bonds	Walford	Hilton	Allen	Cottee	Orr	Brooking	Whitton	
	7/5		*33,347*	*6*	60			*Talbot 15, Woodcock 40, Mariner 75*	*Jennings*	*Hill*	*Sansom*	*Talbot*	*O'Leary*	*Caton*	*Robson*	*Nicholas*	*Mariner*	*Woodcock*	*Rix**	*Davis*
								Ref: R Lewis	An 11 am kick-off with five goals and a missed penalty by mid-day. It was Charlie Nicholas whose kick was saved, Orr having fouled Robson. Whitton made it 3-2 on half-time, when Allen's shot came back off the bar. Arsenal levelled yet again when Mariner stabbed in Robson's pass.											
41	H	NOTT'M FOREST		8	L	1-2	1-1	Stewart 19p	Parkes	Stewart	Brush*	Bonds	Walford	Hilton	Allen	Cottee	Orr	Brooking	Whitton	Pike
	12/5		18,468	*4*	60			*Birtles 22, Davenport 57*	*v Breukelen*	*Anderson*	*Swain*	*Fairclough*	*Hart*	*Bowyer*	*Wigley*	*Hodge*	*Birtles*	*Davenport*	*Walsh*	
								Ref: L Shapter	Brooking's six-year old son, Warren, is the secret mascot for dad's last Saturday game. Trevor had no idea. Brooking was fouled by Fairclough for the penalty – which looked like the referee's own parting gift. Birtles levelled from close range and Paul Brush's error led to the winner.											
42	H	EVERTON		9	L	0-1	0-1		Parkes	Stewart	Orr	Bonds	Walford	Donald	Allen	Cottee	Whitton	Brooking	Pike*	Swindlehurst
	14/5		25,452	*7*	60			*Richardson 14*	*Southall*	*Stevens*	*Harper*	*Ratcliffe*	*Mountfield*	*Reid*	*King*	*Richardson*	*Steven*	*Heath*	*Sharp*	
		Home	Away					Ref: M Taylor	Trevor Brooking's last match for West Ham, Warren Donald's first full 90 minutes. Everton have an appointment at Wembley in the FA Cup final, and Kevin Richardson's goal means they overtake West Ham in the league table. An angry Lyall locks his players in the dressing room.											
Average		21,247	20,111																	

CANON DIVISION 1 (CUP-TIES) Manager: John Lyall SEASON 1983-84

Milk Cup

Milk Cup					F-A	H-T	Scorers, Times, and Referees	1	2	3	4	5	6	7	8	9	10	11	12 sub used
2:1	A	BURY	1	W	2-1	1-0	Goddard 16, Orr 82	Parkes	Stewart	Walford*	Bonds	Martin	Devonshire	Whitton	Goddard	Swindlehurst	Brooking	Pike	Orr
4/10		8,050	*4:5*				*Madden 61*	*Brown*	*Gardner*	*Pashley**	*Carrodus*	*Hilton*	*Bramhall*	*Potts*	*Madden*	*Spence*	*Jakub*	*Deacy*	*Coleman*
							Ref: M Heath	Torrential rain, a small pitch, and Bury's gutsy performance erased any obvious disparity between the teams. Brooking's reverse pass to Goddard was cancelled out by Madden at the far post. Bury were pressing hard when Alvin Martin's downfield clearance left Orr in the clear.											
2:2	H	BURY	3	W	10-0	5-0	Cot' 2,34,39,63, M'tin 17, S'wart 71p,	Parkes	Stewart	Walford	Bonds*	Martin	Devonshire	Allen	Cottee	Swindlehurst	Brooking	Pike	Orr
25/10		10,896	*4:8*				[Brooking 23, 83, Devonshire 67, 81]	*Brown*	*Gardner*	*Pashley*	*Coleman*	*Hilton*	*Bramhall*	*Potts*	*Entwhistle*	*Spence*	*Jakub*	*Deacy*	
							Ref: D Letts (Hammers win 12-1 on aggregate)	The crucial moment came in the fourth minute. Bonds fouled Entwistle, but Bramhall's penalty hit a post. Bury's spirit drained away. Stewart made it 8-0 on the night with a penalty after Coleman impeded Devonshire. Ironically, the ball went in off the same post Bramhall had struck.											
3	H	BRIGHTON	3	W	1-0	0-0	Swindlehurst 81	Parkes	Stewart	Lampard	Walford	Martin	Devonshire	Orr	Cottee	Swindlehurst	Brooking	Pike	
8/11		17,082	*2:12*					*Corrigan*	*Ramsey*	*Pearce*	*Grealish*	*Young E*	*Gatting*	*O'Reagan*	*Young A**	*Ryan*	*Connor*	*Howlett*	*Smith*
							Ref: M Scott	Brighton were happy to surrender midfield and give away corner-kicks by the dozen. Centre-half Eric Young and veteran England keeper Joe Corrigan held their defence together until Swindlehurst headed in Devonshire's cross. At one point Corrigan headed clear outside his area.											
4	H	EVERTON	2	D	2-2	1-1	Mountfield 35 (og), Pike 85	Parkes	Stewart	Lampard	Walford	Martin	Devonshire	Whitton	Cottee*	Swindlehurst	Brooking	Pike	Orr
30/11		19,702	*17*				*Reid 2, Sheedy 55*	*Southall*	*Stevens*	*Ratcliffe*	*Mountfield*	*Higgins*	*Reid*	*Irvine*	*Heath*	*Sharp*	*King*	*Sheedy*	
							Ref: A Gunn	West Ham enjoy the rub of the green against Howard Kendall's goal-shy Everton. Heath sold Martin an outrageous dummy for the first goal. Hammers equalised twice, first when Brooking's shot went in off Mountfield's knee, then when Pike squeezed the ball through a crowded box.											
4R	A	EVERTON	2	L	0-2	0-0		Parkes	Stewart	Lampard	Walford	Martin	Orr	Whitton	Cottee*	Swindlehurst	Brooking	Pike	Dickens
6/12		21,609	*16*		*aet*		*King 95, Sheedy 116*	*Southall*	*Stevens*	*Ratcliffe*	*Mountfield*	*Higgins*	*Reid*	*Irvine*	*Heath*	*Sharp*	*King*	*Sheedy*	
							Ref: T Mills	Alan Devonshire misses his first game of the season. West Ham look bereft of ideas without him, and their attacks are few and lack penetration. The breakthrough in extra-time came when Irvine's corner was headed on by Derek Mountfield. The ball came off the crossbar to King.											

FA Cup

FA Cup					F-A	H-T	Scorers, Times, and Referees	1	2	3	4	5	6	7	8	9	10	11	12 sub used
3	H	WIGAN	3	W	1-0	1-0	Stewart 26p	Parkes	Stewart	Brush	Walford	Martin	Devonshire*	Whitton	Cottee	Swindlehurst	Brooking	Orr	Barnes
7/1		16,000	*3:17*					*Tunks*	*Cribley*	*Comstive*	*Butler*	*Walsh*	*Methven*	*Langley*	*Barrow*	*Lowe*	*Taylor*	*Bruce*	
							Ref: A Seville	Alan Devonshire's season is over after tearing ankle ligaments in the 15th minute. West Ham's penalty was fiercely contested. Brooking's shot struck Cribley on the hand, but it looked involuntary. Stewart drove the penalty into the centre of the goal. Keeper Tunks kept the score down.											
4	A	CRYS PALACE	3	D	1-1	0-1	Swindlehurst 80	Parkes	Stewart	Lampard	Walford	Orr	Brush*	Barnes	Cottee	Swindlehurst	Brooking	Pike	Allen
28/1		*27,590*	*2:18*				*McCulloch 29*	*Wood*	*Locke*	*Hughton*	*Stebbing*	*Cannon*	*Gilbert*	*Giles*	*Mabbutt*	*McCulloch*	*Nicholas*	*Hilaire*	
							Ref: J Hunting	A full-blooded cup-tie. Both goals were the result of goalmouth melees, with the ball finding the net at the third attempt. The ball hit the bar twice before McCulloch forced it in for Palace. Trevor Brooking's chip from the left paved the way for David Swindlehurst's late equaliser.											
4R	H	CRYS PALACE	3	W	2-0	1-0	Pike 22, Barnes 65	Parkes	Stewart	Lampard	Walford	Orr	Brush	Barnes	Cottee	Swindlehurst	Brooking	Pike*	Allen
31/1		27,127	*2:18*					*Wood*	*Locke*	*Hughton**	*Stebbing*	*Cannon*	*Gilbert*	*Giles*	*Mabbutt*	*McCulloch*	*Nicholas*	*Hilaire*	*Evans*
							Ref: J Hunting	Brooking looks head and shoulders better than anyone else, but is adamant that he will retire at the end of the season. Pike claimed West Ham's first goal, though Gilbert had turned his shot into his own net. Brush's centre was then missed by Cottee but converted by Bobby Barnes.											
5	A	BIRMINGHAM	3	L	0-3	0-2		Parkes	Stewart	Lampard	Walford	Orr	Brush*	Barnes	Cottee	Swindlehurst	Allen	Dickens	Bonds
18/2		*29,570*	*18*				*Hopkins 8, Rees 14, Wright 78p*	*Coton*	*McCarrick*	*v d Hauwe*	*Blake*	*Wright*	*Broadhurst*	*Rees*	*Kuhl*	*Harford*	*Stevenson*	*Hopkins*	
							Ref: G Courtney	Ron Saunders' City win before their biggest gate of the season. Two pitch invasions, instigated by West Ham fans after their team went 0-3 down, sparks an FA inquiry. Minus Brooking and Devonshire, West Ham lacked guile in midfield. Stewart fouled Rees to concede the penalty.											

	Home						Away					
	P	W	D	L	F	A	W	D	L	F	A	Pts
1 Liverpool	42	14	5	2	50	12	8	9	4	23	20	80
2 Southampton	42	15	4	2	44	17	7	7	7	22	21	77
3 Nott'm Forest	42	14	4	3	47	17	8	4	9	29	28	74
4 Manchester U	42	14	3	4	43	18	6	11	4	28	23	74
5 QP Rangers	42	14	4	3	37	12	8	3	10	30	25	73
6 Arsenal	42	10	5	6	41	29	8	4	9	33	31	63
7 Everton	42	9	9	3	21	12	7	5	9	23	30	62
8 Tottenham	42	11	4	6	31	24	6	6	9	33	41	61
9 WEST HAM	42	10	4	7	39	24	7	5	9	21	31	60
10 Aston Villa	42	14	3	4	34	22	3	6	12	25	39	60
11 Watford	42	9	7	5	36	31	7	2	12	32	46	57
12 Ipswich	42	11	4	6	34	23	4	4	13	21	34	53
13 Sunderland	42	8	9	4	26	18	5	4	12	16	35	52
14 Norwich	42	9	8	4	34	20	3	7	11	14	29	51
15 Leicester	42	11	5	5	40	30	2	7	12	25	38	51
16 Luton	42	7	5	9	30	33	7	4	10	23	33	51
17 West Brom	42	10	4	7	30	25	4	5	12	18	37	51
18 Stoke	42	11	4	6	30	23	2	7	12	14	40	50
19 Coventry	42	8	5	8	33	33	5	6	10	24	44	50
20 Birmingham	42	7	7	7	19	18	5	5	11	20	32	48
21 Notts Co	42	6	7	8	31	36	4	4	13	19	36	41
22 Wolves	42	4	8	9	15	28	2	3	16	12	52	29
	924	226	118	118	745	505	118	118	226	505	745	1268

Odds & ends

Double wins: (4) Spurs, Coventry, Ipswich, Luton.
Double losses (4) Liverpool, Aston Villa, Nott'm Forest, Southampton.

Won from behind: (2) Leicester (h), Coventry (h).
Lost from in front: (2) Watford (h), Nott'm Forest (h).

High spots: Winning the first five league games to top the league.
Six undefeated league games from 22 October, to stay 2nd.
Beating Bury 10-0 in the Milk Cup.

Low spots: Bad end to the season, failing to win any of the last six games.

Hammer of the Year Trevor Brooking.
Ever-presents: (2) Phil Parkes, Ray Stewart.
Hat-tricks: (2) David Swindlehurst (1), Tony Cottee (1).
Leading scorer: (19) Tony Cottee.

	Appearances						Goals			
	Lge	*Sub*	LC	*Sub*	FAC	*Sub*	Lge	LC	FAC	Tot
Allen, Paul	**19**		1		1	*2*				
Barnes, Bobby	**11**	*2*			3	*1*	**2**		1	**3**
Bonds, Billy	**27**		2			*1*				
Brooking, Trevor	**35**		5		3		**4**	3		**7**
Brush, Paul	**10**				4					
Cottee, Tony	**37**	*2*	4		4		**15**	4		**19**
Devonshire, Alan	**22**		4		1		**1**	2		**3**
Dickens, Alan	**7**	*3*		*1*	1					
Donald, Warren	**1**	*1*								
Goddard, Paul	**3**	*2*	1				**1**	1		**2**
Hilton, Paul	**7**	*1*					**2**			**2**
Lampard, Frank	**17**	*1*	3		3					
Martin, Alvin	**29**		5		1		**3**	1		**4**
Orr, Neil	**28**	*1*	2	*2*	4			1		**1**
Parkes, Phil	**42**		5		4					
Pike, Geoff	**27**	*1*	5		2		**2**	1		**3**
Stewart, Ray	**42**		5		4		**7**	1	1	**9**
Swindlehurst, Dave	**35**	*1*	5		4		**13**	1	1	**15**
Walford, Steve	**41**		5		4		**2**			**2**
Whitton, Steve	**22**		3		1		**5**			**5**
(own-goals)							**3**		1	**4**
20 players used	**462**	***15***	**55**	***3***	**44**	***4***	**60**	**15**	**4**	**79**

The Hammers celebrate promotion at Bristol Rovers in April 1981

Frank McAvennie and Paul Goddard in action at Upton Park

No		Date	Att	Pos	Pt	F-A	H-T	Scorers, Times, and Referees	1	2	3	4	5	6	7	8	9	10	11	12 sub used
1	H	IPSWICH			D	0-0	0-0		**McAlister**	Stewart	Walford	Allen	Martin	**Gale**	Whitton*	Cottee	Goddard	Dickens	Pike	Hilton
		25/8	19,032		1				*Cooper*	*Burley*	*McCall*	*Zondervan*	*Osman*	*Butcher*	*Putney*	*Brennan*	*D'Avray*	*Sunderland**	*Gates*	*O'Callaghan*
								Ref: H Taylor	A lacklustre opening to the new season. West Ham must do without the retired Brooking and the semi-retired Bonds, who declines to be named as substitute. So poorly do Lyall's youngsters – Alan Dickens, Tony Cottee, and Steve Whitton – play that all are dropped for the Anfield trip.											
2	A	LIVERPOOL			L	0-3	0-1		McAlister	Stewart	Walford	Allen	Martin	Gale	Barnes	Bonds	Goddard	Swindleh'rst*	Pike	Cottee
		27/8	*32,633*		1			*Walsh 1, Wark 75, 88*	*Grobbelaar*	*Neal*	*Kennedy*	*Lawrenson*	*Whelan*	*Hansen*	*Dalglish*	*Lee*	*Walsh*	*Wark*	*Molby*	
								Ref: G Tyson	Liverpool have won the European Cup for the fourth time, but Souness is gone and Rush injured. It takes his understudy, Paul Walsh, 14 seconds to put the skids under West Ham. Near the end Wark headed in Walsh's cross, then netted from 20 yards as defenders backed off.											
3	A	SOUTHAMPTON		12	W	3-2	2-0	Goddard 21, 44, Dickens 87	McAlister	Stewart	Walford	Allen	Martin	Gale	Barnes	Goddard*	Cottee	Dickens	Pike	Hilton
		1/9	*18,488*	*22*	4			*Armstrong 75, Jordan 88*	*Shilton*	*Mills*	*Golac**	*Williams*	*Agboola*	*Wright*	*Whitlock*	*Moran*	*Jordan*	*Armstrong*	*Wallace*	*Curtis*
								Ref: A Gunn	This was Paul Goddard's match. He had not scored in the league for almost a year and never in his career bagged two headers in one game. By the time a twisted ankle took him off he had done much to win the match. Barnes, Cottee and Goddard are the smallest attack in the league.											
4	H	COVENTRY		5	W	3-1	2-0	Stewart 24p, 65p, Cottee 32	McAlister	Stewart	Walford	Allen	Martin	Gale	Barnes*	**Campbell**	Cottee	Dickens	Pike	Bonds
		4/9	14,949	*10*	7			*Pearce 81*	*Ogrizovic*	*Stephens*	*Pearce*	*Jol*	*Kilcline*	*Peake*	*Bennett*	*Gynn*	*Latchford*	*Gibson*	*Platnauer*	
								Ref: A Robinson	A debut for former Portsmouth boss, Bobby Campbell's, son. West Ham's tiny strike force prove too nimble for plodding Coventry, for whom Hibbitt handled to concede the first penalty and Ogrizovic toppled Cottee for the second. This is Stuart Pearce's last season with Coventry.											
5	H	WATFORD		2	W	2-0	0-0	Sinnott 50 (og), Barnes 52	McAlister	Stewart	Walford	Allen	Martin	Gale	Barnes	Campbell*	Cottee	Dickens	Pike	Bonds
		8/9	20,377	*20*	10				*Sherwood*	*Bardsley*	*Sinnott*	*Terry*	*Jackett*	*Blissett*	*Callaghan*	*Johnston*	*Reilly**	*Barnes*	*Sterling*	*Porter*
								Ref: B Stevens	Seven former member of West Ham's youth team help take the team up to second, headed only by Arsenal. At 0-0 Stewart tripped Sterling, whose penalty was too close to McAlister. Paul Allen's low cross was turned into his own net by Sinnott, leaving boss Graham Taylor fuming.											
6	A	CHELSEA		6	L	0-3	0-1		McAlister	Stewart	Walford	Allen	Martin*	Gale	Barnes	Bonds	Cottee	Dickens	Pike	Goddard
		15/9	*32,411*	*12*	10			*Lee 14, Speedie 80, Nevin 84*	*Niedzwiecki*	*Lee*	*Rougvie*	*Pates*	*McLaughlin*	*Bumstead*	*Nevin*	*Spackman*	*Dixon*	*Speedie*	*Thomas*	
								Ref: T Spencer	Promoted Chelsea call upon 880 police to keep order. They make 100 arrests. Chelsea go 1-0 up from a penalty after McAlister felled Speedie. Lee's spot-kick was saved, but he volleyed in, only to have to retake it. Everything is repeated – side, save, volley – but this time it counted.											
7	H	NOTT'M FOREST		7	D	0-0	0-0		McAlister	Stewart	Walford	Allen	Bonds	Gale	Barnes	Goddard	Cottee	Dickens	Pike	
		22/9	17,434	*3*	11				*Sutton*	*Gunn*	*Swain*	*Fairclough*	*Smalley*	*Bowyer*	*Wigley*	*Metgod*	*Hodge*	*Davenport*	*Walsh*	
								Ref: J Martin	This draw knocks Forest off the top. In the first half West Ham did everything but score, stringing passes together with ease. The nearest they came was when Gale's header was pushed onto a post. After half-time Forest piled it on, and it was down to McAlister to keep the score blank.											
8	A	NEWCASTLE		8	D	1-1	0-1	Allen 55	McAlister	Stewart	Walford	Allen	Martin	Gale	Barnes	Goddard	Cottee	Bonds	Pike	
		29/9	*29,452*	*10*	12			*Beardsley 42*	*Carr*	*Brown*	*Saunders*	*Heard*	*Anderson*	*Roeder*	*McDonald*	*Wharton*	*Waddle*	*Beardsley*	*McCreery*	
								Ref: D Allison	Future England stars Chris Waddle and Peter Beardsley combine for the first goal, scored from outside the area. It was fitting that West Ham's equaliser was claimed by Paul Allen. He was the man of the match and netted his first goal for nearly two years with a blistering shot.											
9	H	LEICESTER		5	W	3-1	0-1	Stewart 68p, Bonds 75, Cottee 90	McAlister	Stewart	Walford	Allen	Martin	Gale	Barnes*	Goddard	Cottee	Bonds	Pike	Whitton
		6/10	15,306	*18*	15			*Lynex 28*	*Wallington*	*Ramsey*	*Smith R*	*MacDonald*	*Hazell*	*O'Neil*	*Lynex*	*Lineker*	*Smith A*	*Wilson*	*Peake**	*Bright*
								Ref: E Read	Lynex stuns Upton Park when capitalising on Tom McAlister's poor throw out. The Hammers rarely looked look like getting back into the game until Kevin MacDonald handled in the box. Billy Bonds' header, set up by Paul Goddard, was Bonzo's first league goal for 18 months.											
10	A	MANCHESTER U		8	L	1-5	0-2	Goddard 85 *[Moses 63, Hughes 76]*	McAlister	Stewart	Walford	Allen	Martin	Gale	Whitton	Goddard	Cottee	Bonds	Pike	
		13/10	***44,559***	*4*	15			*McQueen 26, Brazil 33, Strachan 50,*	*Bailey*	*Duxbury*	*Albiston*	*Moses*	*McQueen*	*Hogg*	*Robson*	*Strachan*	*Hughes*	*Brazil*	*Olsen*	
								Ref: T Holbrook	Ron Atkinson's United recover from a 0-3 defeat at Villa to give West Ham a thrashing. Olsen and Robson made the first goal for McQueen, playing his first game of the season. Alan Brazil's goal was a solo affair. Gale and Martin went AWOL when Strachan burst through for No 3.											

No / Date	H/A	Opponent / Att	Pos	Res / Pts	F-A	H-T	Scorers, Times, and Referees	1	2	3	4	5	6	7	8	9	10	11	12 sub used
11	A	STOKE	7	W	4-2	1-0	Berry 34 (og), Cot' 56, G'ard 72, Allen 84	McAlister	Stewart	Walford	Allen	Martin	Gale	Whitton	Goddard	Cottee	Bonds	Pike*	Orr
20/10		*9,945*	*22*	18			*Painter 80, Chamberlain 89*	*Fox*	*Bould*	*Hemming*	*Ebanks*	*Dyson*	*Berry*	*Painter*	*McIlroy**	*Heath*	*O'Callaghan*	*Chamberlain*	*Parkin*
							Ref: K Cooper	After the Old Trafford massacre, this is the perfect time to play dreadful Stoke. The score is deceptive, for former England winger Mark Chamberlain wasted two good chances at 0-0. George Berry headed an own-goal and Hemming nodded down to Cottee for Hammers' second.											
12	H	ARSENAL	5	W	3-1	2-1	Cottee 29, Goddard 36, Pike 49	McAlister	Stewart	Walford	Allen	Martin	Gale	Whitton	Goddard	Cottee	Bonds	Pike	
27/10		**33,218**	*1*	21			*Allinson 44*	*Jennings*	*Anderson*	*Sansom*	*Talbot*	*O'Leary*	*Hill*	*Robson*	*Rix*	*Allinson*	*Davis*	*Nicholas*	
							Ref: A Seville	Greenwood returns to Upton Park to promote his autobiography. Bonds and Pike are the only players remaining from his time. Bonds set up the first two goals. Goddard's was the best. Arsenal had won their last five, and afterwards Don Howe locked his players in for a roasting.											
13	A	ASTON VILLA	5	D	0-0	0-0		McAlister	Stewart	Walford	Allen	Martin	Gale*	Whitton	Goddard	Cottee	Bonds	Pike	Orr
3/11		*15,709*	*16*	22				*Day*	*Williams*	*Gibson*	*Evans*	*Ormsby*	*McMahon*	*Birch*	*Kerr*	*Withe*	*Cowans*	*Six*	
							Ref: T Jones	Both teams hit the wood. Villa in the first half, when Kerr's lob landed on top of the bar; West Ham after 87 minutes, when man-of-the-match Paul Allen rounded Mervyn Day but shot against the inside of a post. Pike blazed the rebound wide. An earlier shot had hit Ormsby in the face.											
14	H	EVERTON	6	L	0-1	0-0		McAlister	Stewart	Walford	Allen	Martin	Gale*	Whitton	Goddard	Cottee	Bonds	Pike	Dickens
10/11		24,089	*1*	22			*Heath 78*	*Southall*	*Stevens*	*v d Hauwe*	*Ratcliffe*	*Mountfield*	*Reid*	*Steven*	*Heath*	*Sharp*	*Bracewell*	*Sheedy*	
							Ref: J Ashworth	Everton have surged up the table to the top. West Ham are headed in the opposite direction, largely because their strikers have lost their touch. Having received £1,000 from sponsors Canon for being top scorers in October, West Ham have netted just once in four games in November.											
15	H	SUNDERLAND	5	W	1-0	0-0	Cottee 52	McAlister	Stewart	Walford	Allen	Martin	Gale	Whitton	Goddard	Cottee	Bonds	Pike	
17/11		15,204	*11*	25				*Turner*	*Venison*	*Pickering*	*Chisholm**	*Bennett*	*Elliott*	*Hodgson*	*Berry*	*West*	*Proctor*	*Walker*	*Gayle*
							Ref: D Letts	Having been booked just once in his career, Cottee gets another yellow card which might have been red after a contretemps with Shaun Elliott. The ref was lenient and Cottee stayed on to convert Whitlock's back-header. Dave Swindlehurst is fit again and challenging for Cottee's place.											
16	A	LUTON	5	D	2-2	1-1	Whitton 9, Martin 84	McAlister	Stewart	Walford*	Allen	Martin	Gale	Whitton	Goddard	Cottee	Bonds	Pike	Swindlehurst
24/11		*10,789*	*21*	26			*Stein 36, Nwajiobi 48*	*Findlay*	*Breacker*	*Turner*	*North*	*Droy**	*Donaghy*	*Hill*	*Stein*	*Elliott*	*Bunn*	*Nwajiobi*	*Parker*
							Ref: K Barratt	David Pleat's Luton end a run of defeats and come within six minutes of a precious win. Whitton had opened the scoring from a free-kick but Luton took command when Walford's error let in Nigerian Nwajiobi. With Swindlehurst on for Walford, Martin headed the late equaliser.											
17	H	WEST BROM	8	L	0-2	0-0		McAlister	Stewart	Walford	Allen	Martin	Gale	Whitton	Goddard	Cottee	Bonds*	Pike	Swindlehurst
1/12		15,572	*9*	26			*Hunt 49, Thompson 77*	*Godden*	*Nicholl*	*Statham*	*Hunt*	*Bennett*	*Robertson*	*Grealish*	*Thompson*	*Mackenzie*	*Cross D*	*Valentine*	
							Ref: L Burden	Bonds was on the touchline having his knee strapped – following a crushing tackle with Tony Grealish – when Hunt scored the first goal, and had been subbed by Swindlehurst when Thompson put WBA two up. In the first half both Stewart and Bonds had hit the Albion woodwork.											
18	A	NORWICH	12	L	0-1	0-1		McAlister	Stewart	Walford	Allen	Martin	Gale	Whitton	Goddard	Cottee	Dickens	Pike*	Hilton
8/12		*13,908*	*11*	26			*Farrington 29*	*Woods*	*Haylock*	*Downs*	*Bruce*	*Mendham*	*Watson*	*Channon*	*Farrington*	*Goss*	*Hartford*	*Gordon*	
							Ref: D Hedges	West Ham are plunging down the table, and their passing game seems to have gone to pieces. Tony Cottee is initially at fault for Norwich's goal. His first touch lets him down, allowing 19-year-old Mark Farrington to pounce on the loose ball and score with a scorching cross-shot.											
19	H	SHEFFIELD WED	12	D	0-0	0-0		McAlister	Allen	Walford	Dickens	Martin	Gale	Whitton	Goddard	Swindlehurst	Cottee	Pike	
15/12		14,896	*7*	27				*Hodge*	*Oliver*	*Shirtliff*	*Smith*	*Lyons*	*Worthington*	*Marwood*	*Blair*	*Varadi*	*Chapman*	*Shelton**	*Sterland*
							Ref: M James	Stewart's injury forces Paul Allen to play at right back. The Wednesday bench scream at their team to put him to the test, which he passes with flying colours. David Swindlehurst almost marked his first 90 minutes of the season with a late winner, but shot too close to Martin Hodge.											
20	H	SOUTHAMPTON	12	L	2-3	1-1	Cottee 6, 73	McAlister	Allen	Walford	Dickens*	Martin	Gale	Whitton	Goddard	Swindlehurst	Cottee	Pike	Orr
22/12		14,221	*5*	27			*McAlister 16 (og), Jordan 60, Wallace 71*	*Shilton*	*Mills*	*Dennis**	*Puckett*	*Whitlock*	*Wright*	*Holmes*	*Moran*	*Jordan*	*Armstrong*	*Wallace*	*Bond*
							Ref: I Borrett	England boss Bobby Robson runs his eye over Martin, comparing him with his main rival Mark Wright. Dickens manufactures a quick goal for Cottee, but Saints hit back thanks to a daft own-goal. Walford's back-pass is turned onto the post by McAlister, who fails to keep the ball out.											
21	A	TOTTENHAM	13	D	2-2	1-2	Cottee 43, Goddard 50	McAlister	Allen	Brush	Dickens	Martin	Gale	Orr	Hilton	Swind'hurst*	Cottee	Pike	Goddard
26/12		*37,198*	*1*	28			*Mabbutt 17, Crooks 34*	*Clemence*	*Stevens*	*Hughton**	*Roberts*	*Miller*	*Perryman*	*Chiedozie*	*Falco*	*Galvin*	*Mabbutt*	*Crooks*	*Hazard*
							Ref: J Bray	Walford and Whitton have been dropped. Peter Shreeve's Spurs are the latest team to top the division, and are so impressed by Paul Allen's performance against them that they sign him in the summer. Galvin's corners brought both Spurs' goals. Paul Goddard's equaliser was special.											

No	Date	Att	Pos	Pt	F-A	H-T	Scorers, Times, and Referees	1	2	3	4	5	6	7	8	9	10	11	12 sub used
22	A COVENTRY		12	W	2-1	0-0	Cottee 58, 87	McAlister	Allen	Brush	Dickens	Martin	Gale	Orr	Hilton*	Goddard	Cottee	Pike	Whitton
	29/12	*10,775*	*21*	31			*Stephens 62*	*Ogrizovic*	*Stephens*	*Pearce*	*Bowman*	*Kilcline*	*McGrath*	*Hibbitt*	*Gynn**	*Regis*	*Gibson*	*Barnes*	*Adams*
							Ref: N Ashley	Bobby Gould was sacked yesterday and Don Mackay takes temporary charge of the Sky Blues. Luck deserts them when Kilcline heads over an open goal and Pearce hits the bar. Stephens' effort, deflected by Orr, cancels out Cottee's first goal. But Goddard's dummy sets up his second.											
23	H QP RANGERS		12	L	1-3	1-0	Brush 4	McAlister	**Potts**	Brush	Dickens	Martin	Gale*	Allen	Hilton	Goddard	Cottee	Orr	Whitton
	1/1	20,857	*14*	31			*Byrne 54, Bannister 71, Waddock 74*	*Hucker*	*James**	*Dawes*	*Waddock*	*Chivers*	*Fenwick*	*McDonald*	*Fillery*	*Bannister*	*Byrne*	*Gregory*	*Robinson*
							Ref: M Bodenham	Three players were stretchered off. First to go was QPR keeper Hucker, who collided with Dickens as Brush nodded in – his first West Ham goal. Gary Chivers took over until Hucker returned. Debut-boy Steve Potts headed off the line before QPR levelled from a quick free-kick.											
24	H NEWCASTLE		13	D	1-1	1-0	Allen 16	McAlister	Stewart	Brush	Dickens	Martin	Walford	Allen	Barnes	Goddard	Cottee	Pike	
	2/2	17,723	*18*	32			*Waddle 64*	*Thomas*	*Brown*	*Wharton*	*Clarke*	*Roeder*	*Heard*	*McDonald*	*Megson*	*Waddle*	*Beardsley*	*McCreery*	
							Ref: J Ball	Time and again West Ham pumped up high balls to their midget strikers. John Lyall is being linked in the press with a job at managerless QPR, and he is conducting urgent negotiations with the West Ham board. Norwich manager Ken Brown is being tipped as Lyall's replacement.											
25	H ASTON VILLA		15	L	1-2	0-0	Goddard 48	McAlister	Stewart	Brush	Walford	Martin	Dickens	Allen	Barnes*	Goddard	Cottee	Pike	Swindlehurst
	23/2	14,845	*10*	32			*Walford 59 (og), Ormsby 75*	*Spink*	*Williams*	*Dorigo*	*Evans*	*Ormsby*	*Gibson*	*Birch*	*Rideout*	*Withe*	*Cowans*	*Walters*	
							Ref: J Deakin	If only Geoff Pike's second-minute effort that hit the bar had gone in. Even when Goddard did score it was not enough to secure three points, because West Ham keep surrendering leads. Mark Walters pressured Steve Walford into an own-goal, and Ormsby's 40-yarder was deflected.											
26	A ARSENAL		16	L	1-2	1-0	Cottee 28	McAlister	Stewart	Brush	Dickens	Martin	Walford	Allen	Orr	Goddard	Cottee	Pike	
	2/3	*25,818*	*6*	32			*Mariner 46, Robson 52*	*Lukic*	*Anderson*	*Sansom*	*Williams*	*O'Leary*	*Caton*	*Robson*	*Davis*	*Mariner*	*Woodcock*	*Nicholas*	
							Ref: K Baker	An 11.30 kick-off. Not a good game, but West Ham were superior except in front of goal. Cottee lobs in as Goddard and O'Leary miss a high ball. West Ham stood appealing for offside as Mariner equalised. Arsenal took the lead while Alvin Martin was being treated for a head injury.											
27	H MANCHESTER U		13	D	2-2	1-1	Stewart 25p, Duxbury 51 (og)	McAlister	Stewart	Brush	Walford	Martin	Hilton	Allen	Orr	Goddard	Cottee	Dickens*	Swindlehurst
	15/3	16,674	*3*	33			*Stapleton 31, Robson 62*	*Bailey*	*Gidman*	*Albiston*	*Duxbury*	*McGrath*	*Hogg*	*Strachan*	*Whiteside**	*Hughes*	*Stapleton*	*Olsen*	*Robson*
							Ref: A Robinson / D Keen	Man U have just won in the FA Cup. TV cameras affect the gate, with Wogan on the other channel. Hogg's arm stops Allen's shot. Penalty, after consulting a linesman. Goddard's cross was turned in by Duxbury. Man U replied with two headers. Achilles problems affect the referee.											
28	A LEICESTER		16	L	0-1	0-0		McAlister	Stewart	Brush	Walford	Martin	Gale	Allen	Orr	Goddard	Cottee	Dickens*	Swindlehurst
	23/3	*11,375*	*10*	33			*Lineker 83*	*Andrews*	*Feeley**	*Wilson*	*Smith R*	*Williams*	*O'Neil*	*Lynex*	*Lineker*	*Smith A*	*Ramsey*	*Banks*	*Bright*
							Ref: N Glover	Alan Devonshire has returned in the FA Cup, but flu denies him his first league game of the season. Alvin Martin is dispirited at being left out of Bobby Robson's England team to play the Republic of Ireland. Martin is caught out by Alan Smith's cross, which was turned in by Lineker.											
29	A NOTT'M FOREST		16	W	2-1	1-0	Cottee 20, Goddard 75	McAlister	Stewart	Walford	Allen	Martin	Gale	Orr	Cottee	Goddard*	Pike	Barnes	Swindlehurst
	30/3	*13,560*	*7*	36			*Hodge 55*	*Segers*	*McInally*	*Swain*	*Fairclough*	*Hart**	*Bowyer*	*Wigley*	*Hodge*	*Riley*	*Davenport*	*Metgod*	*Campbell*
							Ref: G Tyson	When Tony Cottee slides in to convert Bobby Barnes' cross it brings West Ham's first goal at the City Ground since Geoff Hurst scored there back in 1969. Steve Wigley makes an equaliser for Steve Hodge, but Cottee's cross is turned in by Paul Goddard to secure a precious win.											
30	A WATFORD		17	L	**0-5**	0-3	*[West 80]*	McAlister	Stewart	Orr	Walford	Martin	Gale	Allen	Barnes	Goddard	Cottee	Pike*	Swindlehurst
	2/4	*17,884*	*16*	36			*Taylor 3, Blissett 11, 16, Barnes 75,*	*Coton*	*Gibbs*	*Rostron*	*Taylor*	*Terry*	*McClelland*	*Callaghan*	*Blissett*	*West*	*Jackett*	*Barnes*	
							Ref: H King	Strangely, West Ham played well for an hour. But before and after they were ripped apart by Graham Taylor's fellow strugglers. Les Taylor's opener was mis-hit yet bobbled over McAlister's arms. John Barnes' gentle header was turned in by Luther Blissett for the second goal.											
31	H TOTTENHAM		17	D	1-1	0-1	Dickens 84	McAlister	Stewart	Orr	Walford	Martin	Gale	Allen	Barnes*	Goddard	Cottee	Dickens	Swindlehurst
	6/4	24,435	*3*	37			*Ardiles 43*	*Clemence*	*Thomas*	*Bowen*	*Roberts*	*Miller*	*Perryman*	*Ardiles*	*Falco*	*Galvin**	*Hoddle*	*Crooks*	*Chiedozie*
							Ref: R Lewis	Home defeat by Everton has scuppered Spurs' championship hopes. Roberts' miscued pass falls perfectly for Ossie Ardiles to swivel and shoot past McAlister. West Ham's second-half enterprise was rewarded when Cottee robbed the injured Roberts, Orr crossed, and Dickens swept in.											

No	Venue	Opponent	Att	Pos	Res	F-A	H-T	Scorers, Times, and Referees	1	2	3	4	5	6	7	8	9	10	11	12
32	A	QP RANGERS		17	L	2-4	1-1	Cottee 45, 84	McAlister*	Stewart	Orr	Walford	Martin	Gale	Allen	Swindlehurst	Goddard	Cottee	Dickens	Barnes
	8/4		*16,085*	*12*	37			*Byrne 1, Bannister 60, 65, Fenwick 69p*	*Hucker*	*Chivers*	*Dawes*	*Waddock*	*Wicks*	*Fenwick*	*McDonald*	*Fillery*	*Bannister*	*Byrne*	*Fereday**	*James*
								Ref: R Milford	The morning kick-off does not suit West Ham, who are behind in 38 seconds. Though Cottee turns in Walford's cross to equalise, Bannister finds space to beat the injured McAlister. Stewart takes his jersey but gives the ball to Bannister. Swindlehurst fouls McDonald for the penalty.											
33	H	CHELSEA		17	D	1-1	1-1	Cottee 23	Parkes	Stewart	Brush	Walford	Orr	Gale	Allen	Swindlehurst	Goddard	Cottee	Dickens	
	13/4		19,003	*9*	38			*Speedie 17*	*Francis*	*Jones J*	*Dublin*	*Pates*	*McLaughlin*	*Bumstead*	*Nevin*	*Spackman*	*Dixon*	*Speedie*	*Jasper*	
								Ref: N Midgley	Phil Parkes takes over from the injured McAlister. Bobby Robson watches Alvin Martin and Paul Allen. Cottee pierces the wall from a short free-kick to equalise, but the outcome hinges on Dickens' fine second-half 'goal', which was disallowed because Goddard had strayed offside.											
34	A	SUNDERLAND		17	W	1-0	1-0	Goddard 15	Parkes	Stewart	Brush	Orr	Martin	Gale	Allen	Swindlehurst	Goddard	Cottee	Dickens	
	20/4		*15,622*	*19*	41				*Turner*	*Venison*	*Pickering*	*Bennett*	*Chisholm*	*Agboola**	*Lemon*	*Wallace*	*Cummins*	*Berry*	*Walker*	*Hodgson*
								Ref: I Hendrick	A six-pointer. 'If West Ham were barely competent, Sunderland could only be described as abysmal,' said *The Times*. 'A bad match and a bad result,' lamented Sunderland boss Len Ashurst. Goddard's goal, converted at the second attempt, lifts West Ham above their relegation rivals.											
35	H	LUTON		17	D	0-0	0-0		Parkes	Stewart	Brush	Orr	Martin	Gale	Allen	Swind'hurst*	Goddard	Cottee	Dickens	Bonds
	27/4		17,303	*18*	42				*Sealey*	*Breacker*	*Thomas*	*Nicholas*	*Foster*	*Donaghy*	*Hill*	*Stein*	*Bunn**	*Nwajiobi*	*Preece*	*Parker*
								Ref: A Gunn	'A point is a point,' muses Luton's David Pleat afterwards. Though as West Ham have not won at home since November he might have felt more frustrated. Both sides marked two forwards with four defenders, stifling the life out of the game. But Les Sealey made several fine saves.											
36	A	WEST BROM		19	L	1-5	0-1	Stewart 54p *[Cross N 80]*	Parkes	Stewart	Brush	Bonds	Martin	Gale	Allen	Whitton	Goddard	Cottee	Dickens	
	4/5		***8,878***	*11*	42			*Hunt 24, Mackenzie 56, 58, Grealish 60,*	*Godden*	*Nicholl*	*Cowdrill*	*Hunt*	*Bennett*	*Robertson*	*Owen**	*Thompson*	*Mackenzie*	*Cross N*	*Valentine*	*Grealish*
								Ref: L Dilkes	Johnny Giles' Albion had been fifth at Christmas but have since collapsed. They had lost five of their last seven games, but find West Ham at their most charitable. Strange to say, when Ray Stewart levelled from the spot West Ham looked good for a point. Then the floodgates opened.											
37	H	NORWICH		19	W	1-0	0-0	Barnes 86	Parkes	Stewart	Brush	Orr	Martin	Gale	Allen	Bonds	Cottee	Goddard	Dickens*	Barnes
	6/5		16,233	*18*	45				*Woods*	*Haylock*	*Van Wyk*	*Bruce*	*Rosario*	*Watson*	*Spearing !*	*Channon**	*Deehan*	*Hartford*	*Donowa*	*Downs*
								Ref: L Shapter	Bobby Barnes, on for the injured Dickens, hooks a late goal that sees Alvin Martin sink to his knees with relief. But Barnes then fells Dave Watson in the box. Barnes admits it is a penalty but the ref says no. Spearing is sent off for dissent. The dropped point sends Norwich down.											
38	A	EVERTON		19	L	0-3	0-2		Parkes	Stewart	Brush	Orr	Martin	Gale	Allen	Bonds	Goddard	Cottee	Barnes	
	8/5		*32,657*	*1*	45			*Gray 11, Mountfield 42, 77*	*Southall*	*Stevens*	*v d Hauwe*	*Atkins*	*Mountfield*	*Reid*	*Steven*	*Sharp*	*Gray**	*Bracewell*	*Sheedy*	*Richardson*
								Ref: A Saunders	Everton are presented with the Canon championship trophy before kick-off. They extend their unbeaten run to 28 games against dismal West Ham, who get the Lyall riot act at the final whistle. Once Andy Gray had headed in Trevor Steven's corner, West Ham offered little resistance.											
39	A	SHEFFIELD WED		19	L	1-2	0-2	Cottee 77	Parkes	Stewart	Brush	Orr	Martin	Gale	Walford*	Bonds	Goddard	Cottee	Barnes	Whitton
	11/5		*24,314*	*8*	45			*Chapman 5, 32*	*Hodge*	*Sterland*	*Worthington*	*Smith*	*Lyons*	*Madden*	*Marwood*	*Blair*	*Varadi*	*Chapman*	*Shelton*	
								Ref: K Walmsley	This is the day of the Bradford City blaze that killed 56. Lyall sets out a defensive formation with Gale in midfield, but West Ham are so weak in the air that Chapman helps himself to two goals, the first from Blair's corner. Stewart had a penalty saved when Hodge floored Goddard.											
40	H	STOKE		17	W	**5-1**	3-0	Bonds 14, 89, Pike 32, Stewart 36p, [Hilton 90]	Parkes	Stewart	Brush	Gale	Martin	Pike	Orr*	Bonds	Barnes	Cottee	Goddard	Hilton
	14/5		**13,362**	*22*	48			*Painter 60p*	*Fox*	*Bould*	*Saunders*	*Dodd*	*Dyson*	*Maskrey*	*Painter*	*McIlroy*	*Hemming*	*Williams**	*Heath*	*Callaghan*
								Ref: J Martin	Awful conditions in which to face an awful team. Bonds scored two and won a penalty when fouled by Dyson. Stewart missed with his first kick but Saunders had encroached and the ref ordered a retake. When Brush fouled Saunders it brought Stoke's sixth away goal of the season.											
41	A	IPSWICH		16	W	1-0	1-0	Cottee 11	Parkes	Stewart	Brush	Walford	Martin	Hilton	Barnes	Bonds	Goddard	Cottee	Pike	
	17/5		*19,326*	*17*	51				*Cooper*	*Burley*	*Yallop*	*Zondervan*	*Osman*	*Steggles**	*Putney*	*Brennan*	*Dozzell*	*Wilson*	*Gates*	*Parkin*
								Ref: V Callow	West Ham looked safe beforehand, but Coventry will win their last three to survive yet again. Had West Ham lost at Portman Road they would have been relegated, but they win with something to spare against an injury-ravaged side. Paul Allen confirms he is leaving the Hammers.											
42	H	LIVERPOOL		16	L	0-3	0-2		Parkes	Stewart	Brush	**McPherson**	Martin	Lampard*	Barnes	**Parris**	Goddard	Walford	Pike	Gale
	20/5		22,408	*2*	51			*Walsh 27, 36, Beglin 56*	*Grobbelaar*	*Neal*	*Beglin*	*Molby**	*Nicol*	*Hansen*	*Dalglish*	*Whelan*	*Rush*	*Walsh*	*Wark*	*Lee*
	Average	Home 18,435	Away 21,158					Ref: D Axcell	An early clash of heads between Molby and Hansen sees Molby led off with a broken nose and two missing teeth. When Walsh departed after 64 minutes Liverpool played on with 10 men, but still looked streets ahead of the Hammers. Lyall gave debuts to McPherson and Parris.											

Milk Cup					F-A	H-T	Scorers, Times, and Referees	1	2	3	4	5	6	7	8	9	10	11	12 sub used
2:1	A	BRISTOL CITY	7	D	2-2	2-2	Cottee 28, Walford 37	McAlister	Stewart	Walford	Allen	Martin	Gale	Bonds	Goddard	Cottee	Dickens	Pike	
25/9		*15,894*	*3:7*				*Morgan 20, Walsh 33*	*Shaw*	*Stevens*	*Newman*	*P-Masters*	*Halliday*	*Walsh*	*Hirst*	*Crawford*	*Pritchard*	*Morgan*	*Riley*	
							Ref: V Callow	City led twice, first when Morgan broke clear to run on to Pritchard's overhead kick. Second when Walsh squeezed his shot underneath Tom McAlister's body. West Ham replied through Tony Cottee's right-foot volley and Steve Walford's 25-yarder from Paul Goddard's pass.											
2:2	H	BRISTOL CITY	5	W	6-1	1-1	Cottee 24, 70, Goddard 48, 57,	McAlister	Stewart	Walford	Allen	Martin	Gale	Whitton	Goddard	Cottee	Bonds*	Pike	Barnes
9/10		11,376	*3:9*				*Walsh 33p* [Whitton 67, Walford 79]	*Shaw*	*Stevens*	*Newman*	*Curle*	*Phil-Masters*	*Riley*	*Pritchard*	*Ritchie**	*Morgan*	*Walsh*	*Crawford*	*Smith*
							Ref: K Baker (Hammers win 8-3 on aggregate)	City boss Terry Cooper threatened to play himself, but does not. His players hold their own until half-time. They trailed to Cottee's hooked volley which went in off the bar, but levelled from the spot when Stewart fisted Walsh's header over the bar. Today Stewart would be sent off.											
3	A	MANCHESTER C	5	D	0-0	0-0		McAlister	Stewart	Walford	Allen	Martin	Gale	Whitton*	Barnes	Cottee	Bonds	Pike	Orr
31/10		*20,510*	*2:9*					*Williams*	*May*	*Power*	*Reid*	*McCarthy*	*Phillips*	*Smith**	*Baker*	*Cunningham*	*Wilson*	*Kinsey*	*Beckford*
							Ref: D Hutchinson	The critical moment came in the third minute, when Tom McAlister crashed into Baker without conceding a penalty-kick. McAlister enjoyed his let-off, knowing that fit-again Phil Parkes wants his place back, and defying Billy McNeill's City to the end. Goddard had a stomach virus.											
3R	H	MANCHESTER C	5	L	1-2	0-1	Whitton 65	McAlister	Stewart	Walford	Allen	Martin	Orr *	Whitton	Goddard	Cottee	Bonds	Pike	Dickens
6/11		17,461	*2:10*				*Cunningham 26, Kinsey 66*	*Williams*	*May*	*Power*	*Reid*	*McCarthy*	*Phillips*	*Smith*	*McNab*	*Cunningham*	*Wilson*	*Kinsey*	
							Ref: T Bune	Billy McNeill declared this to be his team's best performance since he arrived. West Ham were beaten fair and square. Whitton's 25-yarder was one of only a few efforts to trouble Alex Williams, but it was followed within seconds by Kinsey scoring off a post from Power's corner.											

FA Cup																			
3	H	PORT VALE	12	W	4-1	2-0	Dickens 31, Goddard 33, 51, 80	McAlister	Allen	Brush	Dickens	Martin	Walford	Orr	Barnes	Goddard	Cottee	Pike	
5/1		11,452	*4:15*				*Griffiths 76*	*Siddall*	*Webb*	*Bromage*	*Hunter*	*Sproson*	*Cegielski*	*Williams*	*Earle*	*Brown*	*O'Keefe*	*Griffiths P*	
							Ref: E Read	Vale boss John Rudge misses the game with flu. Paul Goddard had never previously scored in the FA Cup for QPR or West Ham, now he gets three on a treacherously icy pitch. He secured his hat-trick when Cegielski was caught dithering four minutes after Vale had come back to 3-1.											
4	H	NORWICH	13	W	2-1	0-1	Pike 60, Stewart 61p	McAlister	Stewart	Brush	Dickens	Martin	Walford	Allen	Barnes	Goddard	Cottee	Pike	
4/2		20,098	*10*				*Donowa 27*	*Woods*	*Haylock*	*Van Wyk*	*Bruce*	*Mendham*	*Watson*	*Spearing*	*Channon*	*Deehan*	*Downs*	*Corrigan*	
							Ref: R Milford	Seven home-grown Hammers carry the team into Round 5. A fast and furious match was watched by Dave Bassett, whose Wimbledon await the winners. Two goals in a minute had the crowd roaring. The penalty was controversial and was given for Van Wyk's foul on Paul Allen.											
5	A	WIMBLEDON	16	D	1-1	0-0	Cottee 72	McAlister	Stewart	Brush	Walford	Martin	Devonshire	Allen	Orr	Goddard	Cottee	Pike	
4/3		*13,500*	*2:13*				*Evans 82*	*Beasant*	*Gage*	*Winterburn*	*Galliers*	*Morris*	*Smith*	*Evans*	*Fishenden*	*Cork*	*Sanchez*	*Hodges**	*Downes*
							Ref: K Hackett	Division 2 Dons maintain their record of scoring in every home match this season when Stewart Evans heads in a long-range cross. Cottee had earlier got in the way of Stewart's shot and scored himself. Alan Devonshire returns at last, distinguished as the hairiest player on the pitch.											
5R	H	WIMBLEDON	16	W	5-1	2-1	Cottee 5, 42, 85, Dickens 56, Allen 80	McAlister	Stewart	Brush	Hilton	Martin	Devonshire	Allen	Orr	Goddard*	Cottee	Dickens	Swindlehurst
6/3		20,258	*2:13*				*Fishenden 18*	*Beasant*	*Gage*	*Winterburn*	*Galliers*	*Morris*	*Smith*	*Evans*	*Fishenden*	*Cork*	*Sanchez*	*Downes**	*Martin*
							Ref: R Lewis	Devonshire's first home game for 14 months was marked by a dreadful back-pass to Paul Fishenden. With his hair in his eyes it was a wonder Devonshire could see at all. The win could have been even more emphatic. Goddard wasted three good second-half chances and failed to score.											
QF	A	MANCHESTER U	16	L	2-4	1-2	Hogg 29 (og), Allen 85	McAlister	Stewart	Brush	Walford	Martin	Dickens	Allen	Orr	Goddard	Cottee	Pike*	Hilton
9/3		*46,769*	*3*				*Hughes 20, Whiteside 38, 75, 88p*	*Bailey*	*Gidman*	*Albiston*	*Duxbury*	*McGrath*	*Hogg*	*Strachan*	*Whiteside*	*Hughes*	*Stapleton*	*Olsen*	
							Ref: T Mills	A flu epidemic delayed Lyall's selection and almost caused a postponement. Hughes controlled, turned, and scored in one movement. West Ham's equaliser flew in off Hogg's shin but was the least they deserved. Norman Whiteside's first ever hat-trick included his first ever penalty.											

		Home						Away					
	P	W	D	L	F	A	W	D	L	F	A	Pts
1 Everton	42	16	3	2	58	17	12	3	6	30	26	90
2 Liverpool	42	12	4	5	36	19	10	7	4	32	16	77
3 Tottenham	42	11	3	7	46	31	12	5	4	32	20	77
4 Manchester U	42	13	6	2	47	13	9	4	8	30	34	76
5 Southampton	42	13	4	4	29	18	6	7	8	27	29	68
6 Chelsea	42	13	3	5	38	20	5	9	7	25	28	66
7 Arsenal	42	14	5	2	37	14	5	4	12	24	35	66
8 Sheffield Wed	42	12	7	2	39	21	5	7	9	19	24	65
9 Nott'm Forest	42	13	4	4	35	18	6	3	12	21	30	64
10 Aston Villa	42	10	7	4	34	20	5	4	12	26	40	56
11 Watford	42	10	5	6	48	30	4	8	9	33	41	55
12 West Brom	42	11	4	6	36	23	5	3	13	22	39	55
13 Luton	42	12	5	4	40	22	3	4	14	17	39	54
14 Newcastle	42	11	4	6	33	26	2	9	10	22	44	52
15 Leicester	42	10	4	7	39	25	5	2	14	26	48	51
16 WEST HAM	42	7	8	6	27	23	6	4	11	24	45	51
17 Ipswich	42	8	7	6	27	20	5	4	12	19	37	50
18 Coventry	42	11	3	7	29	22	4	2	15	18	42	50
19 QP Rangers	42	11	6	4	41	30	2	5	14	12	42	50
20 Norwich	42	9	6	6	28	24	4	4	13	18	40	49
21 Sunderland	42	7	6	8	20	26	3	4	14	20	36	40
22 Stoke	42	3	3	15	18	41	0	5	16	6	50	17
	924	237	107	118	785	503	118	107	237	503	785	1279

Odds & ends

Double wins: (3) Coventry, Stoke, Sunderland.
Double losses: (4) Liverpool, Everton, WBA, QPR.

Won from behind: (2) Leicester (h), Norwich FAC (h).
Lost from in front: (4) Southampton (h), QPR (h), Villa (h), Arsenal (a).

High spots: Three consecutive league wins in September.

Low spots: Just one league win in 13 games from 24 November.
Losing all four league matches to the two Liverpool clubs.
Being knocked out of both cups by the two Manchester clubs.

Hammer of the Year: Paul Allen.
Ever-presents: (0).
Hat-tricks: (2) Paul Goddard (1), Tony Cottee (1).
Leading scorer: (24) Tony Cottee.

	Appearances						Goals			
	Lge	*Sub*	LC	*Sub*	FAC	*Sub*	**Lge**	LC	FAC	**Tot**
Allen, Paul	**38**		4		5		**3**		2	**5**
Barnes, Bobby	**18**	*2*	1	*1*	2		**2**			**2**
Bonds, Billy	**19**	*3*	4				**3**			**3**
Brush, Paul	**18**				5		**1**			**1**
Campbell, Greg	**2**									
Cottee, Tony	**40**	*1*	4		5		**17**	3	4	**24**
Dickens, Alan	**24**	*1*	1	*1*	4		**2**		2	**4**
Devonshire, Alan					2					
Gale, Tony	**36**	*1*	3		1					
Goddard, Paul	**38**	*2*	3		5		**9**	2	3	**14**
Hilton, Paul	**5**	*4*			1	*1*	**1**			**1**
Lampard, Frank	**1**									
McAlister, Tom	**32**		4		5					
McPherson, Keith	**1**									
Martin, Alvin	**40**		4		5		**1**			**1**
Orr, Neil	**17**	*3*	1	*1*	4					
Parkes, Phil	**10**									
Parris, George	**1**									
Pike, Geoff	**30**		4		4		**2**		1	**3**
Potts, Steve	**1**									
Stewart, Ray	**37**		4		4		**6**		1	**7**
Swindlehurst, Dave	**8**	*8*				*1*				
Walford, Steve	**33**		4		3			2		**2**
Whitton, Steve	**13**	*4*	3				**1**	2		**3**
(own-goals)							**3**		1	**4**
24 players used	**462**	***29***	**44**	***3***	**55**	***2***	**51**	**9**	**14**	**74**

No	Date		Att	Pos	Pt	F-A	H-T	Scorers, Times, and Referees	1	2	3	4	5	6	7	8	9	10	11	12 sub used
1	A	BIRMINGHAM			L	0-1	0-0		Parkes	Stewart	Walford	Gale	Martin	Devonshire	**Ward**	**McAvennie**	Goddard*	Cottee	Orr	Dickens
	17/8		*11,164*		–			*Hopkins 65*	*Seaman*	*Ranson*	*Roberts*	*Wright*	*Armstrong**	*Daly*	*Bremner*	*Clarke*	*Jones*	*Geddis*	*Hopkins*	*Kuhl*
								Ref: N Glover	After Heysel and Bradford City English football is in the dock. St Andrews also witnessed awful violence on the last day of last season. Today there is nothing to note, on or off the pitch. A Test Match is going on at Edgbaston. Hopkins scores from 20 yards in this morning kick-off.											
2	H	QP RANGERS			W	3-1	2-0	McAvennie 10, 66, Dickens 24	Parkes	Stewart	Walford	Gale	Martin	Devonshire	Ward	McAvennie	Dickens	Cottee	Orr	
	20/8		15,530		3			*Byrne 54*	*Hucker*	*Chivers*	*Dawes*	*Waddock*	*McDonald*	*Fenwick*	*Byrne*	*Robinson**	*Bannister*	*Fereday*	*Gregory*	*James*
								Ref: M James	Frank McAvennie, a £340,000 buy from St Mirren, scores twice on his home debut, turning in Cottee's low cross to round off the scoring. To many the transfer fee is too high. Dickens' stooping header had made it 2-0 before Bannister crossed to the far post for Byrne to pull one back.											
3	H	LUTON		14	L	0-1	0-0		Parkes	Stewart	Walford	Gale	Martin	Devonshire	Ward	McAvennie	Dickens	Cottee*	Orr	Campbell
	24/8		14,104	*7*	3			*Harford 48p*	*Dibble*	*Johnson*	*Thomas*	*Nicholas*	*Elliott*	*Donaghy*	*Parker*	*Stein B*	*Harford*	*Nwajiobi*	*Preece*	
								Ref: T Holbrook	Having reached the FA Cup semi-finals last season, David Pleat's Luton are on the up. Ray Stewart tripped Stein for the all-important penalty, after which shots went flying in from all angles. Welsh keeper Andy Dibble made a string of fine saves as West Ham sought to equalise.											
4	A	MANCHESTER U		17	L	0-2	0-0		Parkes	Stewart	Walford	Gale	Martin	Devonshire	Ward	McAvennie	Dickens	Cottee*	Orr	Campbell
	26/8		***50,773***	*1*	3			*Hughes 55, Strachan 75*	*Bailey*	*Duxbury*	*Albiston*	*Whiteside*	*McGrath*	*Hogg*	*Robson*	*Strachan*	*Hughes*	*Stapleton*	*Olsen*	
								Ref: R Bridges	West Ham strung 10 defenders outside their box to frustrate Man U. Gordon Strachan was determined to impress watching Scotland boss, Jock Stein, and his flicked pass to Hughes opened the scoring. Gale's woeful back-pass was responsible for No 2, when Strachan rounded Parkes.											
5	H	LIVERPOOL		17	D	2-2	1-0	McAvennie 21, 71	Parkes	Stewart	Walford	Gale	Martin	Devonshire	Ward	McAvennie	Dickens	Cottee	Orr	
	31/8		19,762	*8*	4			*Johnston 52, Whelan 83*	*Grobbelaar*	*Neal*	*Kennedy*	*Lawrenson*	*Whelan*	*Hansen*	*Johnston*	*Nicol*	*Rush*	*Molby*	*Lee*	
								Ref: B Hill	The TV cameras in evidence were not for a domestic audience but to beam this vibrant match to 35 countries around the world. Frank McAvennie nipped in front of Grobbelaar for both Hammers goals. Both Liverpool equalisers were headers following intricate build-ups.											
6	A	SOUTHAMPTON		17	D	1-1	0-0	McAvennie 81	Parkes	Stewart	Walford	Gale	Martin	Devonshire	Ward	McAvennie	Dickens	Campbell*	Orr	Cottee
	3/9		*14,477*	*19*	5			*Curtis 52*	*Shilton*	*Golac*	*Dennis*	*Case*	*Wright*	*Bond*	*Townsend*	*Curtis*	*Jordan**	*Armstrong*	*Wallace*	*Lawrence*
								Ref: J Deakin	Saints, under new boss Chris Nicholl, are still seeking their first win. They are fortunate when Wallace's shot deflects off a defender to play Curtis onside. Ward's shot from outside the box was helped past Shilton by McAvennie, who had earlier been denied by the England keeper.											
7	A	SHEFFIELD WED		17	D	2-2	1-1	McAvennie 9, Cottee 88	Parkes	Stewart	Walford	Gale	Martin	Parris	Ward	McAvennie*	Dickens	Cottee	Orr	Barnes
	7/9		*19,287*	*3*	6			*Chapman 18, Thompson 58*	*Hodge*	*Morris*	*Worthington*	*Smith*	*Lyons*	*Madden*	*Marwood*	*Thompson**	*Chapman*	*Jonsson*	*Shelton*	*Stainrod*
								Ref: N Midgley	In midweek the Owls lost their first match of the season, 1-5 at home to Everton. McAvennie had to hobble off with knee trouble, leaving Tony Cottee on his own. Cottee had been rested against Southampton, feeling jaded, now he scores his first goal of the season to rescue a point.											
8	H	LEICESTER		13	W	3-0	1-0	McAvennie 31, D'shire 46, Cottee 70	Parkes	Stewart	Walford	Gale	Martin	Devonshire	Ward	McAvennie	Dickens	Cottee	Orr	
	14/9		**12,125**	*21*	9				*Andrews*	*Williams*	*Smith R*	*Ramsey**	*Osman*	*O'Neill*	*Kelly*	*Bright*	*Smith A*	*Mauchlen*	*Banks*	*Jones*
								Ref: I Borrett	A terribly small crowd is attributed to the critical state of English football. Man-of-the-match Devonshire passed a late fitness test on a bruised shin. McAvennie is now Division 1's leading scorer, having netted all but four of West Ham's goals. Yet he arrived with a dubious reputation.											
9	A	MANCHESTER C		13	D	2-2	2-1	Cottee 7, McCarthy 41 (og)	Parkes	Stewart	Walford	Gale	Martin	Devonshire	Ward	McAvennie	Dickens	Cottee	Orr	
	21/9		*22,001*	*16*	10			*Lillis 10, Melrose 49*	*Nixon*	*May*	*Wilson*	*Clements*	*McCarthy*	*Phillips*	*Lillis*	*Power*	*Melrose*	*McIlroy*	*Simpson*	
								Ref: M Robinson	Billy McNeill's City have lost their last three and failed to score. A mistake by Tony Gale, caught dwelling on the ball, presented a quick equaliser to David Lillis. West Ham twice fail to protect a lead, though afterwards McNeill rails against his own team's defensive lapses.											
10	H	NOTT'M FOREST		13	W	4-2	3-0	Cottee 6, McAv'nie 12, 20, Dickens 59	Parkes	Stewart	Walford	Gale	Martin	Devonshire	Ward	McAvennie	Dickens	Cottee	Orr	
	28/9		14,540	*16*	13			*Metgod 61, Clough 70*	*Segers**	*Walker*	*Pearce*	*Butterworth*	*Metgod*	*Bowyer*	*Mills*	*Campbell*	*Clough*	*Davenport*	*Webb*	*Walsh*
								Ref: D Axcell	Forest have a ready-made excuse for going 0-4 down. Keeper Segers was hurt colliding with Dickens during West Ham's first goal and hashed a clearance that led to the second. He was replaced in goal by Neil Webb. Johnny Metgod was behind Forest's stirring second-half fight-back.											

No	Venue / Date	Opponent / Att	Pos	Res / Pts	FT	HT	Scorers, Times, and Referees	1	2	3	4	5	6	7	8	9	10	11	12 sub used
11	A	NEWCASTLE	11	W	2-1	2-0	McAvennie 12, Cottee 25	Parkes	Stewart	Walford	Gale	Martin	Devonshire	Ward	McAvennie	Dickens	Cottee	Orr	
	5/10	26,709	7	16			Reilly 84	Thomas	Haddock	Anderson	Davies	Clarke	Roeder	McDonald	McCreery	Reilly	Beardsley	Stewart	
							Ref: D Scott	For the first time since 1968-69, when Martin Peters achieved it, a West Ham player reaches double figures in goals by the end of September. McAvennie's early strike, laid on by Mark Ward, gives him that distinction. Newcastle's first home defeat is largely due to Alvin Martin.											
12	H	ARSENAL	11	D	0-0	0-0		Parkes	Stewart	Walford	Gale	Martin	Devonshire	Ward	McAvennie	Dickens*	Cottee	Orr	Parris
	12/10	24,057	4	17				Lukic	Anderson	Sansom	Davis	O'Leary*	Caton	Whyte	Allinson	Nicholas	Woodcock	Rix	Rocastle
							Ref: A Robinson	Attention focuses on two Scots, Arsenal's Charlie Nicholas, who has been left out of Jock Stein's plans, and McAvennie, who is anxious to take his place. Nicholas even looks on the way out of Don Howe's Arsenal, whereas the wholehearted McAvennie was denied by John Lukic.											
13	H	ASTON VILLA	7	W	4-1	2-1	McAvennie 23, 79, Cottee 34, 57	Parkes	Stewart	Walford	Gale	Martin	Devonshire	Ward	McAvennie	Parris	Cottee	Orr	
	19/10	15,034	16	20			Stainrod 6	Spink	Williams*	Dorigo	Evans	Ormsby	Walker	Birch	Stainrod	Gray	Hodge	Walters	Bradley
							Ref: M Bodenham	Under the gaze of England boss Bobby Robson, Alvin Martin wages a stirring battle against Andy Gray. Pick of the goals were Cottee's 25-yard dipper to make it 3-1 and McAvennie's chip over Spink to conclude the scoring. Nine players were booked, six from naughty Villa.											
14	A	IPSWICH	7	W	1-0	1-0	Cottee 26	Parkes	Parris	Walford	Gale	Martin	Devonshire*	Ward	McAvennie	Dickens	Cottee	Orr	Potts
	26/10	16,849	21	23				Cooper	Yallop	McCall	Zondervan	Cranson	Atkins	Gleghorn*	Brennan	Wilson	Cole	Dozzell	D'Avray
							Ref: M Scott	Woeful Ipswich have now managed just eight points and seven goals from 14 league games. Tony Cottee's poached effort was his 10th of the season, but afterwards Ipswich rallied strongly. Unfortunately for them, they have no eye for goal and no cutting edge. Ipswich will go down.											
15	H	EVERTON	6	W	2-1	0-0	McAvennie 74, 81	Parkes	Stewart	Walford*	Gale	Martin	Devonshire	Ward	McAvennie	Dickens	Cottee	Orr	Parris
	2/11	23,844	7	26			Steven 60	Southall	Stevens	Harper	Ratcliffe	v d Hauwe	Heath	Steven	Lineker	Sharp	Bracewell	Sheedy	
							Ref: A Seville	McAvennie is the talk of English football, yet he managed just 18 goals last season for St Mirren. After Steven turned in Lineker's low cross McAvennie showed why he is so regarded. He takes Parris's pass and feints Southall, then takes Cottee's cross on his chest to win the game.											
16	A	OXFORD	5	W	2-1	1-1	Cottee 38, Ward 68	Parkes	Stewart	Walford	Gale	Martin	Devonshire	Ward	McAvennie	Dickens	Cottee	Orr	
	9/11	13,140	18	29			Aldridge 21	Hardwick	Langan	Slatter	Trewick	Briggs	Shotton	Houghton	Aldridge	Charles	Hebberd	R-Brown*	Brock
							Ref: J Ball	The headline is McAvennie did 'not' score. Oxford boss Maurice Evans tried to sign him when managing Reading. But this is Mark Ward's match. His 40-yard pass enabled Tony Cottee to cancel out John Aldridge's opener. Ward's 35-yard free-kick was his first Division 1 goal.											
17	H	WATFORD	4	W	2-1	1-0	McAvennie, 27 Ward 56	Parkes	Stewart	Walford	Gale	Martin	Devonshire	Ward	McAvennie	Dickens	Cottee	Orr	
	16/11	21,490	12	32			Sterling 66	Coton	Bardsley	Rostron	Talbot	Terry	Sinnott	Sterling	Allen	Barnes	Jackett	Porter*	Smillie
							Ref: H Taylor	McAvennie beats three defenders to reach Neil Orr's cross. Coton then allows Ward's free-kick to trickle through his hands and legs. At this point John Barnes took over, directing Watford's fight-back. Sterling's deflected goal was all they managed. Parkes saved well from Barnes.											
18	A	COVENTRY	4	W	1-0	0-0	McAvennie 55	Parkes	Stewart	Walford	Gale	Martin	Devonshire	Ward	McAvennie	Dickens	Cottee	Orr	
	23/11	**11,042**	15	35				Ogrizovic	Borrows	Downs	Bowman	Rodger	Peake	Adams	McGrath	Evans*	Gibson	Bennett	Turner
							Ref: J Worrall	Frank McAvennie has made his Scottish debut, scoring in the World Cup-tie with Australia. His goal against Coventry was simplicity, when Dickens' low cross looped up off a defender. Thereafter West Ham had to defend stoutly. Neil Orr had one of his best games for West Ham.											
19	H	WEST BROM	3	W	4-0	2-0	Cottee 12, Parris 31, D'shire 47, Orr 66	Parkes	Stewart	Walford	Gale	Martin	Devonshire	Ward	Parris	Dickens	Cottee	Orr	
	30/11	16,325	22	38				Bradshaw	Nicholl	Cowdrill	Hunt	Bennett	Robertson	Grealish	Whitehead*	Varadi	Thomas	Crooks	MacKenzie
							Ref: J Martin	Doomed Albion have earned just one win and seven points, yet played above themselves in the first half. With McAvennie in Australia on World Cup duty, Dickens partnered Cottee. Parris's goal was deflected in by Robertson. Devonshire ran though the Albion defence for No 3.											
20	A	QP RANGERS	3	W	1-0	0-0	McAvennie 73	Parkes	Stewart	Walford	Gale	Martin	Devonshire	Ward	McAvennie	Dickens	Cottee	Orr	
	7/12	23,836	12	41				Barron	McDonald	Dawes	Robinson	Wicks	Fenwick	Allen	Fillery	Bannister*	Byrne	Fereday	Rosenior
							Ref: J Bray	West Ham's first win at Loftus Road since 1974 was partly due to two days intense training on the plastic pitch. Bobby Robson watches as Frank McAvennie, back from Australia yesterday, converts Martin's knock-down. QPR boss Jim Smith admits West Ham have 'added steel'.											
21	H	BIRMINGHAM	3	W	2-0	2-0	McAvennie 37, Stewart 40p	Parkes	Stewart	Walford*	Gale	Martin	Devonshire	Ward	McAvennie	Dickens	Cottee	Orr	Parris
	14/12	17,481	20	44				Seaman	Ranson	Roberts	Hagan	Kuhl	Wright	Bremner	Dicks	Rees	Geddis	Platnauer	
							Ref: L Shapter	McAvennie volleys over his shoulder past David Seaman. Stewart adds a second from the spot after Alan Dickens was fouled by Jim Hagan. West Ham's ninth successive league win, and 17th unbeaten game, leaves them behind second-placed Liverpool only on goal-difference.											

No	Date		Att	Pos	Pt	F-A	H-T	Scorers, Times, and Referees	1	2	3	4	5	6	7	8	9	10	11	12 sub used
22	A	LUTON		3	D	0-0	0-0		Parkes	Stewart	Walford	Gale	Martin	Devonshire	Ward	McAvennie	Dickens	Cottee	Orr	
	21/12		*14,599*	*8*	45				*Sealey*	*Breacker*	*Thomas*	*Nicholas*	*Foster*	*Donaghy*	*Hill*	*Stein B*	*Harford*	*Daniel*	*Preece*	
								Ref: D Hedges	Luton gave away free programmes to everyone bar visiting supporters, whom they intend to ban completely from next season. Having endured a drab first half *The Times* described the second as 'like a pantomime'. Alan Devonshire was taken to hospital for treatment to a face injury.											
23	A	TOTTENHAM		3	L	0-1	0-0		Parkes	Stewart	Walford	Gale	Martin	Devonshire	Ward	McAvennie	Dickens	Cottee	Orr	
	26/12		*33,835*	*9*	45			*Perryman 85*	*Clemence*	*Thomas*	*Hughton*	*Stevens G*	*Mabbutt*	*Perryman*	*Ardiles**	*Falco*	*Allen C*	*Hoddle*	*Waddle*	*Allen P*
								Ref: C Downey	Rain and gale-force winds. West Ham are five minutes from extending their unbeaten run to 19 games when Hoddle climaxes a 12-pass move by picking out Perryman at the near post. It is his first goal of the season and he has never scored twice in a season. West Ham created nothing.											
24	A	LEICESTER		4	W	1-0	0-0	McAvennie 54	Parkes	Stewart	Walford	Gale	Martin	Devonshire	Ward	McAvennie	Dickens	Cottee	Parris	
	11/1		*11,359*	*17*	48				*Andrews*	*Feeley*	*Morgan*	*McAllister*	*Osman*	*O'Neil*	*Lynex*	*Bright**	*Smith A*	*Mauchlen*	*Banks*	
								Ref: A Robinson	Once again West Ham score first then spend the rest of the match hanging on grimly. McAvennie's looping header broke the deadlock. Parkes saved McAllister's penalty when Walford felled Lynex. Leicester missed other chances too. Martin said: 'We haven't played well for a month.'											
25	A	LIVERPOOL		5	L	1-3	0-0	Dickens 82	Parkes	Stewart !	Walford	Gale	Martin	Devonshire	Ward	McAvennie	Dickens	Cottee	Parris	
	18/1		*41,056*	*3*	48			*Molby 58p, Rush 67, Walsh 70*	*Grobbelaar*	*Nicol*	*Gillespie*	*Lawrenson*	*Whelan*	*Hansen*	*Walsh*	*Johnston*	*Rush*	*Molby*	*Wark*	
								Ref: G Tyson	The team bus pulled up at Everton by mistake. West Ham were on top, enjoying the space Mark Ward was allowed by not having a full-back to mark. Martin shoved Walsh in the box and Stewart was sent off for dissent before Molby converted. Rush then netted his 100th league goal.											
26	H	MANCHESTER U		5	W	2-1	0-1	Ward 62, Cottee 76	Parkes	Parris	Walford	Gale	Martin	Devonshire	Ward	McAvennie	Dickens	Cottee	Pike	
	2/2		22,642	*2*	51			*Robson 25*	*Bailey*	*Gidman*	*Albiston*	*Whiteside*	*McGrath*	*Moran*	*Robson**	*Olsen*	*Hughes*	*Stapleton*	*Gibson C*	*Gibson T*
								Ref: J Ball	Under the eyes of Bobby Robson, namesake Bryan lobs the first goal but limps off after 65 minutes with torn ankle ligaments. Ward's 25-yarder levels, and Whiteside's inattentive back-pass lets in Cottee for the winner. It is Man U's first defeat by any London side in 27 games.											
27	A	ARSENAL		7	L	0-1	0-0		Parkes	Stewart	Parris	Gale	Martin !	Devonshire	Ward	McAvennie	Dickens	Cottee	Pike	
	15/3		*31,240*	*5*	51			*Woodcock 76*	*Lukic*	*Anderson*	*Sansom*	*Williams*	*O'Leary*	*Keown*	*Hayes*	*Rocastle*	*Nicholas*	*Woodcock*	*Rix*	
								Ref: I Borrett	It is six weeks since West Ham's last league fixture. This disgraceful match began with Williams being booked in the first minute and ended with Martin and O'Leary exchanging blows. Others joined in. Martin was expelled, O'Leary escaped. The only goal came from a corner-kick.											
28	A	ASTON VILLA		7	L	1-2	1-1	Hunt 2 (og)	Parkes	Parris	Walford	Gale	Martin	Orr	Ward	McAvennie	Dickens	Cottee*	Pike	Goddard
	19/3		*11,579*	*20*	51			*Hodge 38, 78*	*Spink*	*Dorigo*	*Evans*	*Ormsby*	*Elliott*	*Hunt*	*Blair*	*Shaw*	*Gray*	*Hodge*	*Walters*	
								Ref: K Walmsley	Cottee played despite an ankle injury sustained at Highbury and misses three good chances. West Ham had a perfect start, Villa's new signing, Hunt, chesting the ball through Spink's legs. Pike, who had just become a father, hit a post. Steve Hodge struck twice for Villa from midfield.											
29	H	SHEFFIELD WED		7	W	1-0	1-0	McAvennie 6	Parkes	Stewart	Parris	Gale	Martin	Orr	Ward	McAvennie	Dickens	Cottee*	Pike	Goddard
	22/3		16,604	*6*	54				*Hodge*	*Sterland*	*Morris*	*Hart*	*Shirtliff*	*Worthington*	*Marwood*	*Megson*	*Thompson*	*Shutt*	*Snodin*	
								Ref: K Barratt	Revenge for the FA Cup defeat is sweet. Chris Morris miscues a back-pass into the path of Frank McAvennie, who takes the ball round Martin Hodge. West Ham squandered chances to increase the lead. The result leaves them 12 points behind leaders Everton with four games in hand.											
30	A	CHELSEA		6	W	4-0	1-0	D'shire 23, Cottee 55, 64, McAven' 68	Parkes	Stewart	Parris	Gale	Hilton	Devonshire*	Ward	McAvennie	Dickens	Cottee	Pike	Orr
	29/3		*29,955*	*4*	57				*Godden*	*Wood*	*Rougvie*	*Pates*	*McLaughlin*	*Bumstead**	*Nevin*	*Spackman*	*Lee*	*Speedie*	*McAllister*	*Hazard*
								Ref: R Lewis	The extraordinary result in this Easter fixture shows West Ham are back on the goal-trail. Chelsea, second at New Year, are chasing the title themselves, and are using their third keeper in a month. This will not be a fleeting blip for Chelsea; two days later they will lose 0-6 at QPR.											
31	H	TOTTENHAM		5	W	2-1	2-1	Cottee 17, McAvennie 43	Parkes	Stewart	Parris	Gale	Hilton	Devonshire*	Ward	McAvennie	Dickens	Cottee	Pike	Orr
	31/3		27,497	*11*	60			*Ardiles 22*	*Clemence*	*Allen P*	*Thomas*	*Roberts*	*Miller*	*Stevens G*	*Mabbutt*	*Falco*	*Galvin*	*Ardiles**	*Waddle*	*Allen C*
								Ref: B Hill	Tempers frayed on both sides, but mercifully did not mar a fiercely contested match. Dickens on the halfway line flicked on for Cottee to score. Ardiles ducked to head in a near-post corner. The winner came from Ward's corner. Cottee's shot was charged out, straight to McAvennie.											

32	A	NOTT'M FOREST	5	L	1-2	0-1	Cottee 69	Parkes	Stewart	Parris	Gale	Martin	Orr	Ward	McAvennie	Dickens	Cottee	Pike	
	2/4	*17,498*	*8*	60			*Metgod 39, Rice 88*	*Sutton*	*Fleming*	*Pearce*	*Walker*	*Metgod*	*Bowyer*	*Carr*	*Webb*	*Clough*	*Campbell*	*Rice*	
							Ref: L Dilkes	Forest's Brian Rice will remember this game for a long time. He misses an open goal at 0-0, but has the satisfaction of sinking West Ham with his late winner. Johnny Metgod earlier drove in a free-kick from 35 yards, and Stewart picked out Cottee, who wriggled clear to equalise.											
33	H	SOUTHAMPTON	4	W	1-0	1-0	Martin 26	Parkes	Stewart	Parris	Gale	Martin	Devonshire	Ward	McAvennie	Dickens	Cottee	Pike	
	8/4	22,459	*15*	63				*Shilton*	*Forrest*	*Dennis*	*Case*	*Townsend*	*Bond*	*Holmes*	*Cockerill*	*Jordan*	*Armstrong*	*Puckett**	*Whitlock*
							Ref: P Vanes	West Ham have a congested but comparatively easy run in. Saints have won away from home only once all season, and on Saturday lost an FA Cup semi-final to Spurs. Alvin Martin volleyed Gale's header past Shilton. Near the end Townsend's weak shot deceived Parkes and hit a post.											
34	H	OXFORD	5	W	3-1	0-1	Trewick 49 og, McAv 65, Stewart 81p	Parkes	Stewart	Parris	Gale	Martin	Devonshire	Ward	McAvennie	Dickens	Cottee	Pike	
	12/4	23,956	*20*	66			*Houghton 13*	*Judge*	*Langan*	*Trewick*	*Phillips*	*Briggs*	*Shotton*	*Houghton*	*Aldridge*	*Hamilton**	*Hebberd*	*Perryman*	*Charles*
							Ref: N Butler	An exhilarating match, remembered for bad things as well as good. Ward was booked for flinging the ball at a linesman, and McAvennie might have been sent off had the ref seen his retaliation on Hebberd. Stewart scored one and missed one penalty, both given for fouls by Perryman.											
35	H	CHELSEA	5	L	1-2	0-0	Cottee 51	Parkes	Stewart	Parris	Gale*	Martin	Devonshire	Ward	McAvennie	Dickens	Cottee	Pike	Orr
	15/4	29,361	*4*	66			*Spackman 55, Nevin 78*	*Godden*	*Wood*	*Millar*	*Rougvie*	*McLaughlin*	*Bumstead**	*Nevin*	*Spackman*	*Dixon*	*Hazard*	*Murphy*	*McAllister*
							Ref: M Bodenham	Chelsea gain revenge for their 4-0 mauling two weeks earlier. After Dickens had set up Cottee's opener with a diagonal pass, Neil Orr fell over the ball to present a gift to Spackman. Pat Nevin's free header won a match that was interrupted by two minutes after a brief pitch invasion.											
36	A	WATFORD	5	W	2-0	0-0	Cottee 59, McAvennie 89	Parkes	Stewart	Parris	Gale	Martin	Devonshire	Ward	McAvennie	Dickens	Cottee	Orr	
	19/4	*16,651*	*12*	69				*Coton*	*Gibbs*	*Franklin**	*Talbot*	*Terry*	*McClelland*	*Sterling*	*Bardsley*	*West*	*Jackett*	*Barnes*	*Smillie*
							Ref: J Bray	Watford manager Graham Taylor pays West Ham the ultimate compliment, saying they are a better team than Everton. The double act of Cottee and McAvennie bagged a goal apiece and might have had more. Watford carved out just one chance, which West scooped over the bar.											
37	H	NEWCASTLE	3	W	**8-1**	4-0	Martin 3, 64p, 84, Stewart 11, Orr 35, [Roeder 43 (og), G'ard 81,] [McAvennie 83]	Parkes	Stewart	Parris	Gale	Martin	Devonshire	Ward	McAvennie	Dickens*	Cottee	Orr	Goddard
	21/4	24,735	*11*	72			*Whitehurst 76*	*Thomas**	*McDonald*	*Bailey*	*McCreery*	*Anderson*	*Roeder*	*Stephenson*	*Hedworth*	*Whitehurst*	*Beadsley*	*Cunningham*	*Stewart*
							Ref: T Hamer	A game for the record books. West Ham's biggest win since October 1968 produced a hat-trick for Alvin Martin, each of whose goals was scored against a different keeper. Martin Thomas went off shell-shocked at half-time. Hedworth went in goal for a while, then Peter Beardsley.											
38	H	COVENTRY	4	W	1-0	0-0	Cottee 61	Parkes	Stewart	Parris	Gale	Martin	Devonshire	Ward	McAvennie	Dickens	Cottee	Orr	
	26/4	27,251	*18*	75				*Ogrizovic*	*Borrows*	*Downs*	*McGrath*	*Kilcline*	*Peake*	*Bennett*	*Brazil*	*Regis*	*Pickering*	*Adams*	
							Ref: I Hemley	West Ham suffer an understandable hangover after Newcastle. Coventry are desperate for points themselves and would have deserved one. They were denied it when, from Ward's throw-in, the ball reached Cottee for his 24th goal of the season. Bobby Robson watched the game.											
39	H	MANCHESTER C	3	W	1-0	1-0	Stewart 19p	Parkes	Stewart	Parris	Gale	Martin	Devonshire	Ward	McAvennie	Dickens	Cottee	Orr	
	28/4	27,153	*15*	78				*Siddall*	*Phillips*	*May*	*Reid*	*McCarthy*	*Wilson*	*Lillis*	*McIlroy*	*Davies*	*McNab*	*Simpson**	*Beckford*
							Ref: R Gifford	City have taken just three points from 11 games, yet they squander early chances against weary West Ham, who had created nothing when May tried to sell Cottee a dummy and fouled him. Stewart's penalty was his seventh in eight attempts. McCarthy and Phillips missed late chances.											
40	H	IPSWICH	2	W	2-1	0-0	Dickens 72, Stewart 86p	Parkes	Stewart	Parris	Gale	Martin	Devonshire	Ward	McAvennie	Dickens	Cottee	Orr*	Goddard
	30/4	**31,121**	*19*	81			*Wilson 63*	*Cooper*	*Atkins**	*McCall*	*Parkin*	*Cranson*	*Butcher*	*Gleghorn*	*Brennan*	*Dozzell*	*Wilson*	*Cole*	*Yallop*
							Ref: G Ashby	After three FA Cup-ties, another fiercely contested clash. The game exploded as a result of Stewart's late penalty, when Brennan and Gleghorn impeded Ward. Terry Butcher appeared to lash out at the ref after the final whistle. The point dropped will eventually send Ipswich down.											
41	A	WEST BROM	2	W	3-2	2-1	McAvennie 6, Cottee 24, Stewart 82p	Parkes	Stewart	Parris	Gale	Martin	Devonshire	Ward	McAvennie	Dickens	Cottee	Orr	
	3/5	*17,651*	*22*	84			*Madden 30, Reilly 64p*	*Naylor*	*Whitehead*	*Statham*	*Cowdrill*	*Dyson*	*Palmer*	*Dickinson*	*MacKenzie**	*Reilly*	*Madden*	*Bradley*	*Robson*
							Ref: A Robinson	WBA are sure to finish bottom but they put up sterling resistance before presenting West Ham with their sixth successive win. Stewart's third penalty in successive games earns three points after WBA had fought back from 0-2. But Liverpool's win at Chelsea has clinched the title.											
42	A	EVERTON	3	L	1-3	0-1	Cottee 89	Parkes	Stewart	Parris	Gale	Martin	Devonshire	Ward	McAvennie	Dickens*	Cottee	Orr	Goddard
	5/5	*40,073*	*2*	84			*Lineker 42, 47, Steven 72p*	*Mimms*	*Stevens*	*v d Hauwe*	*Mountford*	*Billing*	*Richardson*	*Steven*	*Lineker**	*Wilkinson*	*Heath*	*Sheedy*	*Aspinall*
	Home	Away					Ref: G Courtney	This is the battle for second place, which will be West Ham's if they draw. Sadly, they are outplayed, but win £15,000 from sponsors Canon. Cottee's 26th goal of the season is eclipsed by Lineker's 30th. At the final whistle players go to salute 6,000 supporters who had made the trip.											
Average	21,992	22,608																	

CANON DIVISION 1 (CUP-TIES) Manager: John Lyall SEASON 1985-86

Milk Cup					F-A	H-T	Scorers, Times, and Referees	1	2	3	4	5	6	7	8	9	10	11	12 sub used
2:1	H	SWANSEA	13	W	3-0	0-0	Cottee 48, McAven' 56, Stewart 90p	Parkes	Stewart	Walford	Gale	Martin	Devonshire	Ward	McAvennie	Dickens	Cottee	Orr	
24/9		9,282	*3:20*					*Rimmer*	*Lewis*	*Sullivan*	*Price*	*Stevenson*	*Marustik*	*Hutchinson*	*Randell*	*Turner*	*Harrison*	*Pascoe*	
							Ref: A Gunn	Ex-Hammer, John Bond, is in charge of struggling Swansea. Tommy Hutchison looks dangerous during the 10 minutes that Devonshire is off receiving treatment. The breakthrough came when Dickens chipped to the near post for Cottee. Stevenson fouled Alvin Martin for the penalty.											
2:2	A	SWANSEA	11	W	3-2	3-2	Stewart 11p, 43p, Cottee 13	Parkes	Stewart	Walford	Gale	Martin	Devonshire	Ward	McAvennie*	Dickens	Cottee	Orr	Parris
8/10		*3,584*	*3:22*				*Waddle 6, Randell 23*	*Hughes*	*Sharpe*	*Sullivan*	*Price*	*McHale*	*Harrison*	*Hutchinson*	*Randell*	*Turner*	*Waddle**	*Pascoe*	*Stevenson*
							Ref: R Groves (Hammers win 6-2 on aggregate)	Swansea are facing a winding up order, and desperately need to cause an upset. They take the lead, then come back to 2-2, but are pegged back by two penalties, both conceded by John Sharpe. He hauls down McAvennie for the first and handles Cottee's shot on the line for the second.											
3	A	MANCHESTER U	7	L	0-1	0-0		Parkes	Stewart	Walford	Gale	Martin	Devonshire	Ward	McAvennie	Dickens*	Cottee	Orr	Parris
29/10		*32,057*	*1*				*Whiteside 77*	*Bailey*	*Duxbury**	*Albiston*	*Whiteside*	*Moran*	*Hogg*	*McGrath*	*Olsen*	*Hughes*	*Stapleton*	*Barnes*	*Brazil*
							Ref: F Roberts	The only goal came when Olsen cut inside and laid on a chance to Whiteside. Then Ward's indirect free-kick flew past the diving Gary Bailey. The ref consulted a linesman, agreed that Bailey had not got a touch, and ruled it out. Man U haven't lost to any London side for 27 games.											

FA Cup																			
3	A	CHARLTON	5	W	1-0	0-0	Cottee 88	Parkes	Stewart	Walford	Gale	Martin	Devonshire	Ward	McAvennie	Dickens	Cottee	Parris	
5/1		*13,037*	*2:3*					*Johns*	*Humphrey*	*Reid*	*Curbishley*	*Thompson*	*Pender*	*Gritt*	*Lee*	*Pearson*	*Aizlewood*	*Flanagan*	
							Ref: B Hill	Charlton play home matches at Selhurst Park. This televised Sunday cup-tie was rich in entertainment but short on goals. On a pitch so frozen that Crystal Palace's match on Saturday was called off, McAvennie seized on Humphrey's slice to lob Johns. Cottee got the finishing touch.											
4	H	IPSWICH	5	D	0-0	0-0		Parkes	Stewart	Walford*	Gale	Martin	Devonshire	Ward	McAvennie	Dickens	Cottee	Parris	Goddard
25/1		25,035	*19*					*Cooper*	*Yallop*	*McCall*	*Stockwell**	*Cranson*	*Butcher*	*Putney*	*Brennan*	*D'Avray*	*Wilson*	*Dozzell*	*Zondervan*
							Ref: J Martin	Lucky Hammers. In the second half they fell to pieces. Putney's downward header beat Parkes but reared up off the frozen surface to clear the crossbar. D'Avray and Dozzell also missed good chances for Ipswich. Terry Butcher kept Cottee and McAvennie in his pocket throughout.											
4R	A	IPSWICH	5	D	1-1	0-0	Cottee 106	Parkes	Parris	Walford*	Gale	Martin	Devonshire	Ward	McAvennie	Dickens	Cottee	Pike	Orr
4/2		*25,384*	*19*		*aet*		*Dozzell 93*	*Cooper*	*Yallop*	*McCall*	*Zondervan*	*Cranson*	*Butcher*	*Putney**	*Brennan*	*D'Avray*	*Wilson*	*Dozzell*	*Cole*
							Ref: J Martin	Ipswich are on a high after beating Liverpool three days earlier. Three hours without a goal sends this tie into extra-time. Jason Dozzell, whose earlier header had been brilliantly saved, shrugged off Dickens to put Ipswich in front. Tony Cottee levelled, putting away Parris's square pass.											
4 RR	A	IPSWICH	5	W	1-0	0-0	Cottee 111	Parkes	Stewart	Parris	Gale	Martin	Orr	Ward	McAvennie	Dickens	Cottee	Pike	
6/2		*14,515*	*19*		*aet*			*Cooper*	*Yallop*	*McCall*	*Zondervan*	*Cranson*	*Butcher*	*Putney**	*Brennan*	*D'Avray*	*Wilson*	*Dozzell*	*Baker*
							Ref: K Baker	Lyall lost the toss to decide the venue of this second replay. A red ball is used on an icy pitch. Once again extra-time is needed, and in the 321st minute of this protracted tie Cottee capitalised on Brennan's error. Cottee has now scored in each of his last five games at Portman Road.											
5	H	MANCHESTER U	5	D	1-1	1-0	McAvennie 25	Parkes	Stewart	Parris	Gale	Martin	Devonshire	Ward	McAvennie	Dickens	Cottee	Pike	
5/3		26,441	*2*				*Stapleton 73*	*Turner*	*Duxbury*	*Albiston*	*Whiteside*	*McGrath*	*Moran*	*Robson**	*Strachan*	*Hughes*	*Stapleton*	*Gibson C*	*Olsen*
							Ref: B Stevens	A month has been lost to the weather. After three minutes of this tempestuous tie Bryan Robson dislocates his shoulder when tackling Cottee. Cottee squared for McAvennie to net. Frank Stapleton's super header from Duxbury's cross earned a fourth recent cup-tie at Old Trafford.											
5R	A	MANCHESTER U	5	W	2-0	1-0	Pike 18, Stewart 54p	Parkes	Stewart	Parris	Gale	Martin	Devonshire	Ward	McAvennie	Dickens	Cottee	Pike	
9/3		*30,441*	*2*					*Turner*	*Duxbury*	*Albiston*	*Whiteside*	*McGrath*	*Higgins**	*Olsen*	*Strachan*	*Hughes*	*Stapleton*	*Gibson C*	*Blackmore*
							Ref: B Stevens	Two decisions determined the outcome of this televised Sunday replay and left Man U supporters wild with rage. West Ham were hanging on to Pike's header when Stapleton nudged Martin for a fiercely disputed penalty. Seconds later Stewart shoved Stapleton in the box. No penalty.											
QF	A	SHEFFIELD WED	5	L	1-2	0-2	Cottee 48	Parkes	Stewart	Parris	Gale	Martin	Devonshire	Ward	McAvennie	Dickens	Cottee	Pike	
12/3		*35,522*	*8*				*Worthington 16, Shutt 35*	*Hodge*	*Sterland*	*Morris*	*Smith*	*Shirtliff*	*Worthington*	*Marwood**	*Megson*	*Chapman*	*Shutt*	*Snodin*	*Chamberlain*
							Ref: J Worrall	Three days after beating Man U, West Ham get their come-uppance. Marwood's sixth corner in the first 16 minutes proves fatal. Shutt cuts inside Parris to set up Worthington. West Ham never recover. This is the Owls' first win in nine cup quarter-finals under Howard Wilkinson.											

		Home					Away					
	P	W	D	L	F	A	W	D	L	F	A	Pts
1 Liverpool	42	16	4	1	58	14	10	6	5	31	23	88
2 Everton	42	16	3	2	54	18	10	5	6	33	23	86
3 WEST HAM	42	17	2	2	48	16	9	4	8	26	24	84
4 Manchester U	42	12	5	4	35	12	10	5	6	35	24	76
5 Sheffield Wed	42	13	6	2	36	23	8	4	9	27	31	73
6 Chelsea	42	12	4	5	32	27	8	7	6	25	29	71
7 Arsenal	42	13	5	3	29	15	7	4	10	20	32	69
8 Nott'm Forest	42	11	5	5	38	25	8	6	7	31	28	68
9 Luton	42	12	6	3	37	15	6	6	9	24	29	66
10 Tottenham	42	12	2	7	47	25	7	6	8	27	27	65
11 Newcastle	42	12	5	4	46	31	5	7	9	21	41	63
12 Watford	42	11	6	4	40	22	5	5	11	29	40	59
13 QP Rangers	42	12	3	6	33	20	3	4	14	20	44	52
14 Southampton	42	10	6	5	32	18	2	4	15	19	44	46
15 Manchester C	42	7	7	7	25	26	4	5	12	18	31	45
16 Aston Villa	42	7	6	8	27	28	3	8	10	24	39	44
17 Coventry	42	6	5	10	31	35	5	5	11	17	36	43
18 Oxford	42	7	7	7	34	27	3	5	13	28	53	42
19 Leicester	42	7	8	6	35	35	3	4	14	19	41	42
20 Ipswich	42	8	5	8	20	24	3	3	15	12	31	41
21 Birmingham	42	5	2	14	13	25	3	3	15	17	48	29
22 West Brom	42	3	8	10	21	36	1	4	16	14	53	24
	924	229	110	123	771	517	123	110	229	517	771	1276

Odds & ends

Double wins: (8) QPR, Leicester, Newcastle, Ipswich, Oxford, Watford, Coventry, WBA.
Double losses: (0).

Won from behind: (7) Villa (h), Everton (h), Oxford (h&a), Man U (h), Ipswich (h), Swansea LC (a).
Lost from in front: (2) Villa (a), Chelsea (h).

High spots: Finishing 3rd, West Ham's highest ever position.
Winning nine successive league games from 19 October.

Low spots: Not clinching their first ever league championship.
Losing three of the first four league games.

West Ham faced Manchester U in both cups.
Nine of Ray Stewart's 10 goals were penalties.

Hammer of the Year: Tony Cottee.
Ever-presents: (3) Tony Gale, Phil Parkes, Mark Ward.
Hat-tricks: (1) Alvin Martin.
Leading scorer: (28) Frank McAvennie.

	Appearances						Goals			
	Lge	*Sub*	LC	*Sub*	FAC	*Sub*	**Lge**	LC	FAC	**Tot**
Barnes, Bobby		*1*								
Campbell, Greg	**1**	*2*								
Cottee, Tony	**41**	*1*	3		7		**20**	2	4	**26**
Devonshire, Alan	**38**		3		6		**3**			**3**
Dickens, Alan	**40**	*1*	3		7		**4**			**4**
Gale, Tony	**42**		3		7					
Goddard, Paul	**1**	*5*				*1*	**1**			**1**
Hilton, Paul	**2**									
McAvennie, Frank	**41**		3		7		**26**	1	1	**28**
Martin, Alvin	**40**		3		7		**4**			**4**
Orr, Neil	**33**	*3*	3		1	*1*	**2**			**2**
Parkes, Phil	**42**		3		7					
Parris, George	**23**	*3*		*2*	7		**1**			**1**
Pike, Geoff	**10**				5				1	**1**
Potts, Steve	**0**	*1*								
Stewart, Ray	**39**		3		6		**6**	3	1	**10**
Walford, Steve	**27**		3		3					
Ward, Mark	**42**		3		7		**3**			**3**
(own-goals)							**4**			**4**
(18 players used)	**462**	***17***	**33**	***2***	**77**	***2***	**74**	**6**	**7**	**87**

Frank McAvennie lets fly at Old Trafford

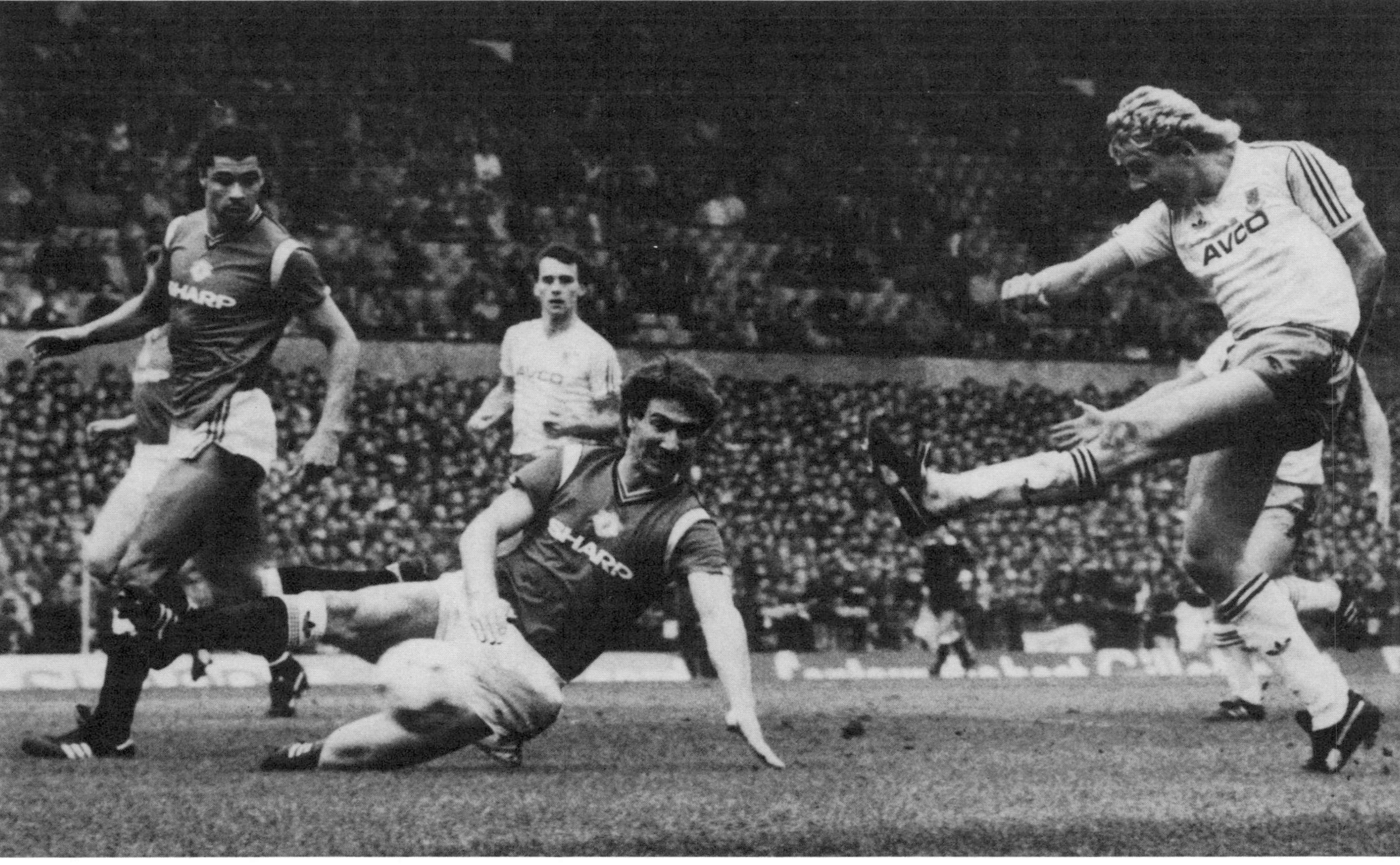

Kevin Keen scores at Stoke in August 1989

No	Date		Att	Pos	Pt		F-A	H-T	Scorers, Times, and Referees	1	2	3	4	5	6	7	8	9	10	11	12 sub used
1	H	COVENTRY				W	1-0	0-0	Gale 83	Parkes	Stewart	Parris	Gale	Martin	Devonshire	Ward	McAvennie	Dickens	Cottee	Orr	
	23/8		21,368		3					*Ogrizovic*	*Borrows*	*Downs*	*McGrath*	*Kilcline*	*Peake*	*Bennett**	*Phillips*	*Regis*	*Houchen*	*Pickering*	*Adams*
									Ref: L Shapter	Tony Gale, his eye bloodied from a collision with Coventry new boy, Keith Houchen, scores his first ever Hammers goal. Peake fouled Devonshire and Gale drove the free-kick past Ogrizovic. Coventry showed no interest in scoring until after they fell behind, and no ideas then.											
2	A	MANCHESTER U				W	3-2	2-1	McAvennie 1, 82, Devonshire 38	Parkes	Stewart	Parris	Hilton	Martin	Devonshire	Ward	McAvennie	Dickens	Cottee	Orr	
	25/8		**43,306**		6				*Stapleton 39, Davenport 46*	*Turner*	*Duxbury*	*Albiston*	*Whiteside*	*McGrath*	*Moran*	*Strachan*	*Blackmore*	*Stapleton*	*Davenport*	*Gibson**	*Olsen*
									Ref: G Tyson	After just 32 seconds Dickens chipped forward for McAvennie to net. Devonshire's lob, following a one-two with Parris, was quickly followed by Stapleton nodding in from Gibson. McAvennie's late header puts extra pressure on Ron Atkinson, whose Old Trafford days are numbered.											
3	A	OXFORD		3		D	0-0	0-0		Parkes	Stewart	Parris	Gale	Martin	Devonshire	Ward	McAvennie	Dickens	Cottee	Orr	
	30/8		*11,684*	*19*	7					*Judge*	*Langan*	*Trewick*	*Phillips*	*Briggs*	*Shotton*	*Houghton*	*Aldridge*	*Charles*	*Hebberd*	*Perryman*	
									Ref: H King	Trevor Hebberd plays a blinder as Oxford's sweeper, snuffing out whatever attacks West Ham muster. Oxford feel aggrieved at not bagging their first win of the season. Shotton's free-kick smashed against Parkes' left post, and Aldridge and Charles both missed gilt-edged chances.											
4	H	NOTT'M FOREST				L	1-2	1-0	McAvennie 19	Parkes	Stewart	Parris	Gale	Martin	Devonshire*	Ward	McAvennie	Dickens	Cottee	Orr	Goddard
	2/9		21,305		7				*Clough 62, Webb 64*	*Sutton*	*Fleming*	*Pearce*	*Walker*	*Metgod*	*Bowyer*	*Carr*	*Webb*	*Clough*	*Birtles*	*Campbell*	
									Ref: D Axcell	Dickens supplied McAvennie, who – angered by being left out of Roxburgh's Scottish squad – sprinted through to finish with a precise shot. In the space of three minutes Webb set up Nigel Clough's equaliser, then scored himself to transform the Boleyn into a ghostly, silent morgue.											
5	H	LIVERPOOL		12		L	2-5	1-1	Stewart 8p, Cottee 55 *[Rush 70]*	Parkes	Stewart	Parris	Gale	Martin	Pike*	Ward	McAvennie	Dickens	Cottee	Orr	**Keen**
	6/9		**29,807**	*2*	7				*Whelan 25, Johnston 50, Dalglish 66, 90,*	*Hooper*	*Venison*	*Beglin*	*Gillespie*	*Whelan*	*Hansen**	*McDonald*	*Johnston*	*Rush*	*Lawrenson*	*McMahon*	*Dalglish*
									Ref: J Martin	The double winners see less of Dalglish on the pitch these days, but Hansen's torn hamstring brings him on early. West Ham's penalty came when Gillespie tripped Cottee. It was all-square after an hour. Dalglish's two goals were both deflected. He admitted: 'the margin flattered us'.											
6	A	QP RANGERS		6		W	3-2	2-0	Cottee 6, 10, 80	Parkes	Stewart	Parris	Gale	Martin	Walford	Keen	McAvennie	Dickens	Cottee	Orr	
	13/9		*19,257*	*7*	10				*James 70, Byrne 85*	*Seaman*	*Neill*	*Dawes*	*Allen*	*McDonald*	*Chivers*	*Lee*	*James*	*Rosenior*	*Byrne*	*Fereday**	*Robinson*
									Ref: B Stevens	Cottee has won his first England cap as a substitute in Sweden and celebrates with a hat-trick in this rain-drenched thriller, though two goals were deflected. His first goal was a free-kick; his second from McAvennie' cross. Byrne rounded Walford near the end to set nerves on edge.											
7	H	LUTON		4		W	2-0	1-0	Parris 41, Gale 57	Parkes	Stewart	Walford	Gale	Martin !	Parris	Keen	McAvennie	Dickens*	Cottee	Orr	Pike
	20/9		19,133	*13*	13					*Sealey*	*Johnston*	*Grimes*	*Nicholas*	*Foster*	*Donaghy*	*Hill*	*Stein B !*	*Newell**	*Wilson*	*Preece*	*Stein M*
									Ref: J Deakin	England boss Bobby Robson watches from the stand as Alvin Martin and Brian Stein swap punches 10 minutes from time and both are sent off. Martin fears for his England place, with an automatic two-match ban to come, and knowing that Mark Wright is coming back to fitness.											
8	A	SHEFFIELD WED		7		D	2-2	0-1	Martin 60, Orr 78	Parkes	Stewart	Parris	Gale	Martin	Walford	Ward	McAvennie	Dickens	Cottee	Orr	
	27/9		*25,715*	*8*	14				*Madden 18, Megson 89*	*Hodge*	*Sterland*	*Worthington*	*Madden*	*Knight*	*Chamberlain*	*Marwood*	*Megson*	*Chapman*	*Shutt*	*Shelton*	
									Ref: N Ashley	FA Chairman Bert Millichip stays in the same hotel as West Ham. He has publicly advised Bobby Robson to drop Alvin Martin for being sent off against Luton. Neil Orr, whose wife's baby is overdue, put West Ham 2-1 ahead in this fixture against Howard Wilkinson's Wednesday.											
9	A	WATFORD		8		D	2-2	2-1	Dickens 16, McAvennie 23	Parkes	Stewart	Parris	Gale	Hilton	Walford	Ward	McAvennie	Dickens	Cottee	Orr*	Keen
	4/10		*17,120*	*14*	15				*Callaghan 35, Blissett 70*	*Coton*	*Bardsley*	*Sinnott*	*Richardson*	*Terry*	*McClelland*	*Callaghan*	*Blissett*	*Roberts**	*Jackett*	*Barnes*	*Porter*
									Ref: B Hamer	For the fourth time this season West Ham fail to protect a lead. Luther Blissett rescues a point for Graham Taylor's Watford after a tactical switch pairs him up front with John Barnes. Lyall is furious that his team sat back to protect their lead rather than search for further goals.											
10	H	CHELSEA		4		W	5-3	2-1	McAv 32, Stew'rt 34p,79p, C'ttee 85,87	Parkes	Stewart	Parris	Gale	Hilton	Keen	Ward	McAvennie*	Dickens	Cottee	Orr	Bonds
	11/10		26,859	*19*	18				*Jones 24p, Dixon 58, Bumstead 62*	*Godden*	*Wood*	*Rougvie*	*Pates*	*Wicks*	*Bumstead*	*Nevin*	*Jones*	*Dixon*	*McAllister*	*McNaught*	
									Ref: M Reed	John Hollins' Chelsea are in turmoil on and off the pitch. Both sides enjoy iffy penalties, Chelsea when Nevin fell over Gale's leg; West Ham when Godden collided with Keen. Chelsea led 3-2 after an hour, then collapsed. 'Pulsating' said Lyall. 'Backsides need kicking' said Hollins.											

11	A	NORWICH	5	D	1-1	0-0	Goddard 75	Parkes	Stewart	Parris	Gale	Hilton	Keen	Ward*	Goddard	Dickens	Cottee	Orr	Bonds
18/10		*22,884*	*2*	19			*Drinkell 58*	*Benstead*	*Culverhouse*	*Spearing*	*Bruce*	*Phelan*	*Elliott*	*Crook*	*Drinkell*	*Biggins*	*Barham*	*Gordon**	*Hodgson*
							Ref: A Seville	Ken Brown's enterprising Norwich are knocked off the top, conceding their first goal in six matches. The scorer was Paul Goddard, starting his first game in 14 months. He netted off Barham's shoulder, after the ball was headed on by Hilton. Biggins provided the equaliser for Drinkell.											
12	H	CHARLTON	8	L	1-3	1-2	Cottee 44	Parkes	Stewart	Parris	Gale	Hilton	Devonshire*	Ward	Goddard	Dickens	Cottee	Orr	Keen
25/10		24,141	*12*	19			*Melrose 1, Walsh 37, Pearson 76*	*Johns*	*Humphrey*	*Reid*	*Peake*	*Thompson*	*Shirtliff*	*Lee*	*Stuart*	*Melrose*	*Aizlewood*	*Walsh**	*Pearson*
							Ref: R Milford	Homeless Charlton win their fourth league game in a row, helped by a goal within nine seconds. Lee's through-ball enabled Melrose to chip over Parkes. At 0-2 Ward's deep cross was met by Tony Cottee's volley, but Pearson rounded Phil Parkes to eclipse hopes of a fight-back.											
13	H	EVERTON	8	W	1-0	0-0	Dickens 48	Parkes	Stewart	Parris	Gale	Hilton	Devonshire	Ward	Goddard	Dickens	Cottee	Orr	
2/11		19,094	*3*	22				*Southall*	*Harper*	*Power*	*Ratcliffe*	*Mountfield*	*Langley**	*Steven*	*Heath*	*Sharp*	*Wilkinson*	*Sheedy*	*Aspinall*
							Ref: P Vanes	This live Sunday match produced a TV thriller. Howard Kendall's Everton have now won just one out of six visits to London opponents. Alan Dickens' header from Devonshire's corner loops over Southall and under the bar, and West Ham somehow survive Everton's furious late rally.											
14	A	ARSENAL	7	D	0-0	0-0		Parkes	Stewart	Parris	Gale	Hilton	Devonshire	Ward	McAvennie	Dickens	Cottee	Walford	
8/11		*36,084*	*3*	23				*Lukic*	*Anderson*	*Sansom*	*Williams*	*O'Leary*	*Adams*	*Rocastle*	*Davis*	*Quinn*	*Groves*	*Hayes*	
							Ref: J Martin	Paul Goddard has been sold to Newcastle, but Cottee's partnership with McAvennie looks more penetrating than Arsenal's endless supply of high balls to Niall Quinn. West Ham might have had six, and had two efforts disallowed. Graham said: 'West Ham are much better than us'.											
15	A	WIMBLEDON	5	W	1-0	0-0	Cottee 55	Parkes	Stewart	Parris	Gale	Hilton	Devonshire*	Ward	McAvennie	Dickens	Cottee	Orr	Walford
15/11		*10,342*	*13*	26				*Beasant*	*Kay*	*Winterburn*	*Galliers**	*Gayle*	*Thorn*	*Clement*	*Cork*	*Fashanu*	*Downes*	*Fairweather*	*Gage*
							Ref: J Moules	Dave Bassett's promoted Wimbledon were top in September but are now spinning down the table. Bobby Robson looks on from Plough Lane's rickety stand as Cottee bags another all-important goal that maintains West Ham's unbeaten away record. Wimbledon were taught a lesson.											
16	H	ASTON VILLA	4	D	1-1	1-0	Cottee 9	Parkes	Walford	Parris	Gale	Hilton	Devonshire	Ward	McAvennie	Dickens	Cottee	Keen*	Bonds
22/11		21,959	*16*	27			*Thompson 63*	*Spink*	*Williams*	*Dorigo*	*Evans*	*Elliott*	*Keown*	*Norton*	*Kerr*	*Thompson*	*Hunt**	*Hodge*	*Daley*
							Ref: A Gunn	Villa boss Billy McNeill admits this was a great advert for football. Norton's wayward corner left all Villa's tall defenders at the wrong end of the pitch, leaving Cottee to waltz round Williams. Thompson's free header rescued a point for a Villa team that did not earn a single booking.											
17	A	NEWCASTLE	7	L	**0-4**	0-2	*[Jackson D 66]*	Parkes	Stewart	Parris	Gale	Hilton	Devonshire	Ward	McAvennie	Dickens*	Cottee	Orr	**Ince**
30/11		*22,077*	*22*	27			*McDonald 29, Thomas A 33, 80,*	*Thomas M*	*Anderson*	*Wharton*	*McCreery*	*Jackson P*	*Roeder*	*McDonald*	*Thomas A*	*Goddard**	*Beardsley*	*Stephenson*	*Jackson D*
							Ref: K Hackett	This Sunday TV match tore up West Ham's unbeaten away record and threw up an oddity. McDonald's opener was the first Newcastle goal seen on live TV since 1955. All four goals came from crosses pulled back from the byline. Willie McFaul's team pull out of the bottom three.											
18	H	SOUTHAMPTON	5	W	3-1	2-1	Ince 15, Devonshire 42, Cottee 61p	Parkes	Potts	Parris	Gale	Martin	Devonshire	Ward	McAvennie	Ince	Cottee	Orr	
6/12		18,111	*14*	30			*Clarke 19*	*Shilton*	*Forrest*	*Tankard*	*Case*	*Blake*	*Bond*	*Lawrence*	*Cockerill*	*Clarke*	*Hobson*	*Wallace*	
							Ref: M James	With Dickens injured, teenager Paul Ince steps in and plays a stormer. His uncompromising battle with veteran Jimmy Case in midfield made onlookers flinch. Ince opens the scoring with a diving header and later wins a penalty, when fouled by Blake, which is converted by Cottee.											
19	A	MANCHESTER C	6	L	1-3	0-1	Martin 46	Parkes	Potts	Parris	Gale	Martin	Devonshire	Ward	McAvennie	Ince	Cottee	Orr*	Dickens
13/12		*19,067*	*20*	30			*White 17, Varadi 59, 86*	*Suckling*	*Gidman*	*Wilson*	*Clements*	*McCarthy*	*Grealish**	*White*	*McNab*	*Varadi*	*Moulden*	*Simpson*	*Redmond*
							Ref: C Seel	Another bad defeat to a lowly northern team has Lyall complaining about slow build-ups. Jimmy Frizzell's City climb off the bottom thanks to sparkling displays from young wingers White and Simpson. Mick McCarthy easily snuffed out the combined threat of Cottee and McAvennie.											
20	H	QP RANGERS	7	D	1-1	1-0	Cottee 24p	Parkes	Potts	Parris	Gale	Martin	Devonshire	Ward	McAvennie	Dickens	Cottee	Orr	
20/12		17,290	*17*	31			*Fenwick 80p*	*Seaman*	*Neill*	*James*	*Allen*	*McDonald*	*Fenwick*	*Lee*	*Robinson*	*Bannister*	*Byrne**	*Peacock*	*Fillery*
							Ref: M Dimblebee	The offside tactics of Jim Smith's QPR don't endear the visitors to Upton Park. McDonald's duff challenge on Dickens brought the first penalty; Martin's foul on Gavin Peacock the second. Drained of confidence, Cottee spurns four great chances to add to his penalty-kick.											
21	A	TOTTENHAM	9	L	**0-4**	0-1		Parkes	Potts	Parris	Walford*	Martin	Devonshire	Ward	McAvennie	Dickens	Cottee	Orr	Hilton
26/12		*39,019*	5	31			*Allen C 13, 88, Hodge 53, Waddle 54*	*Clemence*	*Thomas D*	*Thomas M**	*Hodge*	*Gough*	*Mabbutt*	*Allen C*	*Allen P*	*Waddle*	*Hoddle*	*Galvin*	*Ardiles*
							Ref: R Lewis	Steve Hodge makes his Spurs debut in this rout, West Ham's heaviest defeat against Tottenham in 19 years. Hoddle made three goals for David Pleat's side. Cottee, McAvennie and Devonshire were invisible. Yet again Lyall locks the dressing room door behind his demoralised players.											

No	Date		Att	Pos	Pt	F-A	H-T	Scorers, Times, and Referees	1	2	3	4	5	6	7	8	9	10	11	12 sub used
22	H	WIMBLEDON		12	L	2-3	2-2	Cottee 3, Hilton 35	Parkes	Potts	Parris	Hilton	Martin	Ince	Ward	McAvennie	Keen*	Cottee	Pike	Dickens
	27/12		19,122	*10*	31			*Fashanu 12, Sayer 37, Fairweather 64*	*Beasant*	*Kay*	*Winterburn*	*Sanchez*	*Gayle*	*Thorn*	*Fairweather*	*Sayer*	*Fashanu*	*Downes*	*Hodges*	
								Ref: B Hill	Lyall drops his entire midfield, but that cannot prevent the loss of seven goals in 24 hours. Only three teams in the division have now conceded fewer. Confidence has drained from the entire team, not least Phil Parkes, who makes a complete hash of saving Carlton Fairweather's winner.											
23	H	LEICESTER		8	W	**4-1**	3-0	Cottee 9, 20, Dickens 25, McAvennie 90	Parkes	Walford	Parris	Hilton	Martin	Devonshire	Ward	McAvennie	Dickens	Cottee	Pike	
	1/1		16,625	22	34			*Moran 87*	*Andrews*	*Morgan*	*Venus*	*Feeley*	*O'Neill*	*McAllister*	*Lynex*	*Moran*	*Smith*	*Ramsey*	*Kelly**	*Alleyne*
								Ref: G Ashby	Bottom-placed Leicester are no match even for shell-shocked Hammers, whose first goal on a rain-soaked pitch is a thing of beauty. The ball was played rapidly from defence to attack, where Tony Cottee chests it down to score. Frank McAvennie's goal is his first for two months.											
24	A	LIVERPOOL		10	L	0-1	0-0		Parkes	Walford	Parris	Hilton	Martin	Devonshire	Orr	McAvennie	Dickens*	Cottee	Pike	Ince
	3/1		*41,286*	*3*	34			*McMahon 84*	*Grobbelaar*	*Gillespie*	*Beglin*	*Lawrenson*	*Whelan*	*Hansen*	*Walsh*	*Johnston*	*Rush*	*Molby*	*McMahon*	
								Ref: M Peck	Liverpool press from the start, but never lose their patience in the face of resolute defending. Phil Parkes touched Molby's free-kick onto a post and then saved when Paul Walsh was put clear. With time running out Steve McMahon seized on Ian Rush's header to drive in the winner.											
25	A	COVENTRY		9	W	3-1	2-0	Cottee 15, 45, 58	Parkes	Walford	Parris	Hilton	Martin	Devonshire	Ward	McAvennie	Dickens	Cottee	**Robson**	
	24/1		*14,191*	*8*	37			*Borrows 87p*	*Ogrizovic*	*Borrows*	*Downs*	*Emerson*	*Kilcline**	*Peake*	*McGrath*	*Houchen*	*Regis*	*Gynn*	*Phillips*	*Painter*
								Ref: D Allison	Cottee bags his third hat-trick of the season and Italian clubs are said to be queuing for his signature. West Ham have now done the double over Coventry for four seasons in a row. Cottee has helped himself to 10 goals. Stewart Robson, a £700,000 buy from Arsenal, has a fine debut.											
26	H	OXFORD		9	L	0-1	0-1		Parkes	Stewart	Parris	Gale	Hilton	Devonshire	Ward	McAvennie	Dickens*	Cottee	Robson	Bonds
	7/2		15,220	*15*	37			*Leworthy 3*	*Hardwick*	*Langan*	*Dreyer*	*Trewick*	*Briggs*	*Caton*	*Houghton*	*Leworthy*	*Whitehurst*	*Hebberd*	*Brock*	
								Ref: K Baker	Maurice Evans' Oxford record their first away win in five months. Leworthy finds himself unopposed to score a quick goal, and thereafter much-maligned keeper Steve Hardwick – under even greater pressure now Peter Hucker has been signed from QPR – keeps Cottee at bay.											
27	A	NOTT'M FOREST		9	D	1-1	0-1	Stewart 65p	Parkes	Stewart	Parris	Gale	Bonds	Walford	Ward	McAvennie	Pike	Cottee	Robson	
	14/2		*19,373*	*4*	38			*Birtles 42p*	*Sutton*	*Fleming*	*Williams*	*Walker*	*Fairclough*	*Bowyer*	*Carr*	*Webb*	*Clough*	*Birtles*	*Mills*	
								Ref: G Tyson	Forest extend their unbeaten run to seven, but their fans are fuming at the penalty which denied them a win. Fleming barely touched Parris, but the West Ham man went down and Ray Stewart levelled from the spot. Forest's own penalty – Robson fouling Webb – was no less dubious.											
28	A	LUTON		13	L	1-2	1-1	Cottee 8	Parkes	Stewart	Walford*	Gale	Bonds	Dickens	Ward	McAvennie	Pike	Cottee	Robson	Ince
	28/2		*11,101*	*4*	38			*Nicholas 40, Grimes 70*	*Sealey*	*Johnston*	*Grimes*	*Nicholas*	*Foster*	*Donaghy*	*Hill*	*Stein B*	*Newell*	*Harford*	*Wilson*	
								Ref: B Hill	Luton are an unexpected fourth, five points behind leaders Everton. They have lost just once at home, and when Cottee turns in McAvennie's centre it is only the eighth goal conceded at Kenilworth Road. Luton turn the screw following Peter Nicholas's equaliser from 25 yards.											
29	A	CHARLTON		14	L	1-2	0-1	Robson 68	Parkes	Stewart	Walford	Gale	Bonds	Dickens	Ward	McAvennie*	Pike	Cottee	Robson	Parris
	7/3		***10,100***	*18*	38			*Melrose 5, 47*	*Bolder*	*Humphrey*	*Reid*	*Peake*	*Thompson*	*Miller*	*Bennett**	*Lee*	*Melrose*	*Shipley*	*Walsh*	*Stuart*
								Ref: P Don	Charlton's first league win of 1987 is achieved against a West Ham defence which plays like strangers. Charlton were helped by an early goal, when Robert Lee eluded Walford to cross for Melrose's glancing header. Three Charlton players lined up for Melrose's cross for No 2.											
30	H	NORWICH		14	L	0-2	0-1		Parkes	Stewart	Parris	Gale	Bonds	Dickens	**Brady**	Ince	Pike*	Cottee	Robson	Keen
	14/3		21,531	5	38			*Bruce 2, Drinkell 89*	*Gunn*	*Brown*	*Spearing*	*Bruce*	*Phelan*	*Butterworth*	*Crook*	*Drinkell*	*Rosario*	*Putney*	*Gordon*	
								Ref: M Bailey	31-year-old Liam Brady signs for West Ham instead of Celtic for a nominal fee. His arrival boosts the gate but is unable to prevent a fourth successive defeat. Norwich played slick football, in the mould of West Ham. Kevin Drinkell's neat right-footer sealed the points near the end.											
31	A	CHELSEA		15	L	0-1	0-1		Parkes	Stewart	Parris	Gale	**Strodder**	Brady	Ward	McAvennie	Pike	Cottee	Robson	
	21/3		*25,386*	*20*	38			*Nevin 20*	*Godden*	*Clarke*	*Dublin*	*Wicks*	*McLaughlin*	*Wood*	*Nevin*	*Hazard*	*Durie*	*West*	*Jones**	*Dixon*
								Ref: J Key	Bottom of the table at Christmas, Chelsea have hauled themselves above West Ham. Hazard's rushed volley breaks kindly to Nevin. West Ham enjoyed much second-half possession, but threatened little. Cottee 'scored' through the side-netting, which was repaired by Chelsea's physio.											

No	Venue	Opponent	Pos	Res	F-A	H-T	Scorers, Times, Referees	1	2	3	4	5	6	7	8	9	10	11	12 sub used
32	H	SHEFFIELD WED	15	L	0-2	0-1		Parkes	Stewart*	Parris	Gale	Strodder	Brady	Ward	McAvennie !	Dickens	Cottee	Robson	Keen
24/3		**13,514**	*14*	38			*Chapman 6, Shutt 58*	*Hodge*	*Sterland*	*Snodin*	*Smith !*	*Madden*	*Worthington*	*Marwood*	*Megson*	*Chapman*	*Shutt**	*Shelton*	*Hirst*
							Ref: J Ashworth	Upton Park sees its lowest gate of the season as despondency sets in. The Hammers' sixth successive defeat was made worse by the expulsion of McAvennie for a reckless lunge at Smith, who retaliated and was also sent off. Lee Chapman found himself unmarked for the early goal.											
33	H	WATFORD	15	W	1-0	0-0	Parris 90	Parkes	Bonds	**McQueen**	Gale	Strodder	Brady	Ward	McAvennie	Parris	Cottee	Robson*	Dickens
28/3		16,485	*10*	41				*Coton*	*Gibbs*	*Rostron*	*Richardson*	*Sims*	*McClelland*	*Bardsley*	*Blissett*	*Falco*	*Jackett*	*Porter*	
							Ref: I Borrett	Tommy McQueen is the third new boy, following the arrival of Brady and Strodder. Parris is shunted from left-back to midfield. He asks the referee how long is left, is told one minute, and lets fly. It brings West Ham's first win since 1 January and first clean sheet since November.											
34	H	ARSENAL	14	W	3-1	1-1	Cottee 4p, 56, Brady 79	McAlister	Bonds	McQueen	Gale	Strodder	Brady	Ward	Dickens	Parris	Cottee	Robson	
8/4		26,174	*4*	44			*Hayes 12p*	*Wilmot*	*Anderson*	*Thomas*	*O'Leary*	*Adams*	*Williams*	*Rocastle*	*Davis*	*Groves*	*Nicholas*	*Hayes**	*Rix*
							Ref: D Hedges	Arsenal have won the Littlewoods Cup. Hayes' penalty was twice-taken, after Parris fouled Rocastle. The second half is delayed due to crowd trouble – the players led from the pitch. The trouble was exacerbated by Brady's inflammatory gesture following his goal. He was cautioned.											
35	A	EVERTON	14	L	**0-4**	0-4	*[Watson 39]*	McAlister	Bonds	McQueen	Gale*	Strodder	Brady	Pike	Dickens	Parris	Cottee	Robson	Orr
11/4		*35,731*	*1*	44			*Clarke 20, Reid 25, Stevens 33,*	*Southall*	*Stevens*	*Power*	*Ratcliffe*	*Watson*	*Reid*	*Steven*	*Heath*	*Clarke*	*Harper*	*Sheedy*	
							Ref: D Hutchinson	West Ham's injury-ravaged team are no match for Kendall's champions-elect. The Hammers were growing in confidence, being on level terms after 20 minutes, but Wayne Clarke scores off a post and Reid bends a 20-yarder. Before they know it West Ham are 0-4 down by half-time.											
36	H	MANCHESTER U	14	D	0-0	0-0		McAlister	Parris	McQueen	Bonds	Strodder	Brady	Ward	McAvennie	Dickens	Cottee	Robson	
14/4		23,486	*11*	45				*Walsh*	*Duxbury*	*Gibson C*	*Moses*	*McGrath*	*Moran*	*Robson**	*Strachan*	*Stapleton*	*Gibson T*	*Davenport*	*Albiston*
							Ref: J Martin	This was a frantic encounter for the first hour, but as it dawned on the players that no one was going to score it fizzled out. Four players were booked, including both Robsons – Bryan and Stewart. Bryan Robson eventually limped off, slowed by Dickens' crunching tackle early on.											
37	A	LEICESTER	14	L	0-2	0-0		McAlister	Bonds	McQueen	Gale	Strodder	Brady	Ward	McAvennie	Parris*	Cottee	Robson	Dickens
18/4		*10,434*	*10*	45			*Smith 50, O'Neil 75*	*Andrews*	*Morgan*	*Venus*	*Osman*	*O'Neill*	*McAllister*	*Russell**	*Mauchlen*	*Smith*	*Ramsey*	*Wilson*	*Buckley*
							Ref: B Nixon	Leicester are one of those struggling teams desperate to drag West Ham further into the mire. Alan Smith's goals will later see him transferred to Arsenal, and his effort five minutes after half-time does wonders for Leicester's confidence. But they fail to win another match and go down.											
38	H	TOTTENHAM	14	W	2-1	1-0	McAvennie 43, Cottee 63p	McAlister	Bonds	McQueen	Gale	Strodder	Devonshire	Ward	McAvennie	Brady	Cottee	Robson	
20/4		23,972	*3*	48			*Allen C 59*	*Clemence*	*Hughton*	*Thomas M*	*Hodge*	*Gough*	*Polston*	*Allen C*	*Allen P*	*Waddle*	*Hoddle*	*Galvin**	*Claesen*
							Ref: J Deakin	Spurs have thrashed West Ham twice this season, so revenge is sweet, especially as it ends Spurs' hopes of the championship. Not that the win was uncontested. Following Clive Allen's 47th goal of this extraordinary season Robson appeared to run straight into Richard Gough. Penalty!											
39	A	ASTON VILLA	14	L	**0-4**	0-2		McAlister	Bonds*	McQueen	Gale	Strodder	Devonshire	Ward	McAvennie	Brady	Cottee	Robson	Dickens
25/4		*13,584*	*21*	48			*Hunt 15, Aspinall 35, 56, Stainrod 57*	*Poole*	*Williams*	*Dorigo*	*Keown*	*Elliott*	*Stainrod*	*Birch*	*Aspinall*	*Gray*	*Hunt*	*Daley**	*Walters*
							Ref: J Lloyd	Doomed Villa record their biggest win in two years. Robson should have scored at 0-0 but was dispossessed by Steve Hunt, who scored when Tom McAlister fumbled a corner. Warren Aspinall's goal was his first for Villa. West Ham have now conceded four or more goals six times.											
40	H	NEWCASTLE	15	D	1-1	0-1	Ward 84	McAlister	Potts	McQueen*	Bonds	Strodder	Ince	Ward	McAvennie	Dickens	Cottee	Robson	Keen
2/5		17,844	*17*	49			*McDonald 7p*	*Thomas M*	*McDonald*	*Wharton*	*Jackson P*	*Roeder*	*McCreery*	*Jackson D*	*Gascoigne*	*Goddard*	*Cunningham*	*Anderson**	*Thomas A*
							Ref: M James	Newcastle were bottom in early March, but have now taken 25 points from 12 games. Paul Goddard can't stop scoring for the Magpies, though he fires blanks against his former club. Newcastle's winning run also coincided with the return of young Gascoigne, to link up with Beardsley.											
41	A	SOUTHAMPTON	16	L	0-1	0-0		McAlister	Bonds	McQueen	Potts	Strodder	Ince	Ward	McAvennie	Brady	Cottee	Robson	
4/5		*16,810*	*13*	49			*Clarke 81*	*Flowers*	*Forrest*	*Armstrong*	*Case*	*Wright*	*Bond*	*Lawrence**	*Cockerill*	*Clarke*	*Hobson*	*Le Tissier*	*Maskell*
							Ref: M Reed	Yet another defeat, this time brought about by Northern Ireland's World Cup striker Colin Clarke, who headed his 22nd goal from David Armstrong's left-wing cross. Clarke had earlier hit a post from three yards out. At the death Cottee shrugged off Kevin Bond but shot wide.											
42	H	MANCHESTER C	15	W	2-0	1-0	Cottee 34, Brady 51	McAlister	Potts	Orr	Keen	Strodder	Brady	Ward*	McAvennie	Robson	Cottee	Ince	**Dolan**
9/5		18,413	*21*	52				*Nixon*	*Clements*	*Wilson*	*Redmond*	*McCarthy**	*Langley*	*May*	*McNab*	*Moulden*	*Stewart*	*Simpson*	*White*
	Home	Away					Ref: B Stevens	Tony Cottee has handed in a transfer request. He deflects Ward's shot past Nixon for his 29th goal of the season. City would have been relegated even had they won, which did not look likely. Eamonn Dolan makes his debut as a sub, having scored 21 goals for the reserves.											
Average	20,545	22,121																	

Littlewoods Cup					F-A	H-T	Scorers, Times, and Referees	1	2	3	4	5	6	7	8	9	10	11	12 sub used
2:1	A	PRESTON	4	D	1-1	1-0	Ward 34	Parkes	Stewart	Parris	Gale	Martin	Walford	Ward	McAvennie	Pike	Cottee	Orr	
	23/9	*13,153*	*4:2*				*Allardyce 62*	*Brown*	*Bulmer*	*McAteer*	*Atkins*	*Jones*	*Allardyce*	*Williams*	*Clark*	*Thomas*	*Hildersley*	*Brazil*	
							Ref: T Mills	Preston, from the soccer basement, dictated play from the start. Ward's breakaway goal, following an exchange of passes with McAvennie, prompted West Ham to fall back to protect their lead. Allardyce's header from Hildersley's cross was the least that Preston deserved.											
2:2	H	PRESTON	8	W	4-1	1-1	Cottee 12, 75, 84, Dickens 59	Parkes	Stewart	Parris	Keen	Hilton	Walford	Ward	McAvennie	Dickens*	Cottee	Orr	Bonds
	7/10	12,742	*4:7*				*Williams 27*	*Kelly*	*McNeil*	*Bennett*	*Chapman**	*Jones*	*Atkins*	*Williams*	*McAteer*	*Thomas^*	*Hildersley*	*Brazil*	*Saunders/Allatt*
							Ref: V Callow (Hammers win 5-2 on aggregate)	The first goal of Cottee's hat-trick came when Kelly failed to hold Stewart's shot. Williams' equaliser looked ominous until Alan Dickens' header restored the lead, McAvennie nodding across goal. Five minutes from time Billy Bonds comes on, having been out for more than a year.											
3	A	WATFORD	8	W	3-2	1-0	Goddard 12, Dickens 52, Ward 61	Parkes	Stewart	Parris	Gale	Hilton*	Devonshire	Ward	Goddard	Dickens	Cottee	Orr	Walford
	29/10	*17,523*	*17*				*Jackett 48p, Bardsley 83*	*Sherwood*	*Bardsley*	*Rostron*	*Richardson*	*Terry*	*McClelland*	*Sterling*	*Sinnott*	*Allen*	*Jackett*	*Barnes*	
							Ref: J Bray	A thrilling cup-tie. Paul Goddard's ferocious opener was neutralised from the spot when Tony Gale held down McClelland. Dickens restored the lead with a slow-motion shot. After Bardsley's diving header made it 3-2, John Barnes missed a glorious chance to earn Watford a replay.											
4	H	OXFORD	5	W	1-0	0-0	Cottee 81p	Parkes	Walford*	Parris	Gale	Hilton	Devonshire	Ward	McAvennie	Dickens	Cottee	Keen	Bonds
	18/11	20,530	*11*					*Hardwick*	*Langan*	*Slatter*	*Phillips !*	*Briggs**	*Shotton*	*Houghton*	*Aldridge*	*Leworthy*	*Reck*	*Brock*	*Dreyer*
							Ref: H Taylor	The Milk Cup holders don't go out without a fight. Four Oxford players are booked and Phillips' second yellow card sees him sent off for dissent. Shotton felled McAvennie in the box for the crucial penalty, described by Maurice Evans as a 'total joke'. Brock hit Parkes' crossbar.											
QF	H	TOTTENHAM	9	D	1-1	0-1	Cottee 48	Parkes	Walford	Parris	Hilton	Martin	Devonshire	Ward	McAvennie	Dickens	Cottee	Robson	
	27/1	29,477	*5*				*Allen C 39*	*Clemence*	*Thomas D*	*Thomas M*	*Ardiles*	*Gough*	*Mabbutt*	*Allen C*	*Allen P*	*Waddle*	*Hoddle*	*Galvin*	
							Ref: B Stevens	Spurs were no less superior than when winning 4-0 on Boxing Day. Clive Allen turned in cousin Paul Allen's cross, but missed a string of easier chances. West Ham's equaliser was unexpected and fluky. Danny Thomas blocked Dickens' run, but the ball flew in off Cottee's knee.											
QF	A	TOTTENHAM	9	L	0-5	0-1		Parkes	Bonds	Parris*	Gale	Martin	Devonshire	Ward	McAvennie	Orr	Cottee	Robson	Hilton
R	2/2	*41,995*	*5*				*Claesen 5, Hoddle 71, Allen C 80,86p, 89*	*Clemence*	*Thomas D*	*Thomas M*	*Ardiles*	*Gough*	*Mabbutt*	*Allen C*	*Allen P*	*Waddle*	*Hoddle*	*Claesen*	
							Ref: V Callow	Billy Bonds' first start in 18 months cannot prevent another thrashing by David Pleat's Spurs. The nightmare began early, when Ardiles on the halfway line sent Claeson through. Clive Allen's late hat-trick included one penalty, when Martin felled Paul Allen. Spurs now meet Arsenal.											

FA Cup																			
3	A	ORIENT	10	D	1-1	1-0	Hilton 31	Parkes	Walford	Parris	Hilton	Martin	Devonshire	Ward	McAvennie	Ince	Cottee	Pike	
	10/1	*19,225*	*4:21*				*Castle 90p*	*Wells*	*Cornwell*	*Dickenson*	*Foster*	*Hales**	*Cunningham*	*Castle*	*Brooks*	*Jones*	*Godfrey**	*John*	*Comfort*
							Ref: N Midgley	The Public Address System echoes to the *Eastenders* theme. Frank Clark's Orient are 79 league places below West Ham and have lost their last three home games. Hilton's header from Ward's free-kick looked to have brought victory, until Steve Castle converts his first ever penalty.											
3R	H	ORIENT	9	W	4-1	1-0	Parris 27, Keen 79, McAv' 81, Cottee 90	Parkes	Walford*	Parris	Hilton	Gale	Keen	Dickens	McAvennie	Dickens	Cottee	Orr	Bonds
	31/1	19,424	*4:19*				*Brooks 57*	*Wells*	*Cornwell*	*Dickenson*	*Foster*	*Hales*	*Cunningham**	*Castle*	*Brooks*	*Jones*	*Godfrey*	*John*	*Comfort*
							Ref: R Milford	Dickenson levelled for Orient, only for the referee to give them a free-kick instead, which Brooks blasts in from 25 yards. Parkes then makes a flying save from Jones. It took the arrival of Billy Bonds to turn the tie. Wells parried from Cottee and Kevin Keen turned in the loose ball.											
4	H	SHEFFIELD UTD	9	W	4-0	1-0	McAvennie 18, 54, Robson 52, Gale 67	Parkes	Bonds	Parris	Gale	Stewart	Devonshire*	Ward	McAvennie	Pike	Cottee	Robson	Keen
	9/2	17,194	*2:13*					*Burridge*	*Wilder*	*Pike*	*Arnott*	*Stancliffe*	*Barnsley*	*Smith*	*Foley*	*Withe*	*Daws**	*Beagrie*	*Dempsey*
							Ref: D Hedges	The winners know they face Sheffield Wednesday in Round 5, which is a perfect incentive for the Blades. It was an untidy cup-tie. John Burridge entertained Upton Park with his warm-up routine, and entertained them again when spilling Cottee's cross for Robson to make it 2-0.											

Rd	H/A	Opponent	Pos	Res	F-A	H-T	Scorers, Times, and Referees	1	2	3	4	5	6	7	8	9	10	11	subs used
5	A	SHEFFIELD WED	9	D	1-1	1-1	McAvennie 10	Parkes	Stewart	Parris	Gale	Bonds	Walford	Ward	McAvennie	Pike	Cottee	Robson	
21/2		*30,257*	*14*				*Shelton 40*	*Hodge*	*Sterland**	*Snodin*	*Smith*	*Madden*	*Worthington*	*Marwood*	*Megson*	*Bradshaw*	*Hirst^*	*Shelton*	*Morris/Shutt*
							Ref: H Taylor	Bonds was a pro before his opponent David Hirst was born. Wednesday preserve their 14-year unbeaten home record in the FA Cup through a four-man move finished by Shelton. Fortune had earlier smiled on West Ham. Cottee's shot turned into a cross which went in off McAvennie.											
5R	H	SHEFFIELD WED	9	L	0-2	0-2		Parkes	Stewart	Parris*	Gale	Bonds	Devonshire	Ward	McAvennie	Pike	Cottee	Robson	Dickens
25/2		30,257	*14*				*Chapman 34, Bradshaw 43*	*Hodge*	*Sterland**	*Snodin*	*Smith*	*Madden*	*Worthington*	*Marwood*	*Megson*	*Chapman*	*Bradshaw^*	*Shelton*	*Morris/Chamb'lain*
							Ref: H Taylor	Wednesday had won away from home only twice all season. Lee Chapman returns from suspension and turns the ball in from Marwood's corner. Gale and Bonds left the ball to each other, allowing Bradshaw to add a second. The Owls also beat West Ham in the FA Cup last year.											

	P	Home W	D	L	F	A	Away W	D	L	F	A	Pts
1 Everton	42	16	4	1	49	11	10	4	7	27	20	86
2 Liverpool	42	15	3	3	43	16	8	5	8	29	26	77
3 Tottenham	42	14	3	4	40	14	7	5	9	28	29	71
4 Arsenal	42	12	5	4	31	12	8	5	8	27	23	70
5 Norwich	42	9	10	2	27	20	8	7	6	26	31	68
6 Wimbledon	42	11	5	5	32	22	8	4	9	25	28	66
7 Luton	42	14	5	2	29	13	4	7	10	18	32	66
8 Nott'm Forest	42	12	8	1	36	14	6	3	12	28	37	65
9 Watford	42	12	5	4	38	20	6	4	11	29	34	63
10 Coventry	42	14	4	3	35	17	3	8	10	15	28	63
11 Manchester U	42	13	3	5	38	18	1	11	9	14	27	56
12 Southampton	42	11	5	5	44	24	3	5	13	25	44	52
13 Sheffield Wed	42	9	7	5	39	24	4	6	11	19	35	52
14 Chelsea	42	8	6	7	30	30	5	7	9	23	34	52
15 WEST HAM	42	10	4	7	33	28	4	6	11	19	39	52
16 QP Rangers	42	9	7	5	31	27	4	4	13	17	37	50
17 Newcastle	42	10	4	7	33	29	2	7	12	14	36	47
18 Oxford	42	8	8	5	30	25	3	5	13	14	44	46
19 Charlton*	42	7	7	7	26	22	4	4	13	19	33	44
20 Leicester	42	9	7	5	39	24	2	2	17	15	52	42
21 Manchester C	42	8	6	7	28	24	0	9	12	8	33	39
22 Aston Villa	42	7	7	7	25	25	1	5	15	20	54	36
	924	238	123	101	756	459	101	123	238	459	756	1263

* stay up after play-offs

Odds & ends

Double wins: (1) Coventry.
Double losses: (2) Liverpool, Charlton.

Won from behind: (1) Chelsea (h).
Lost from in front: (4) Forest (h), Liverpool (h), Wimbledon (h), Luton (a).

High spots: Winning the first two league games.
Six unbeaten league games from 13 September, up to 5th.

Low spots: Five successive league defeats from 28 February.
Anti-climactic season after finishing 3rd one year earlier.

Hammer of the Year: Billy Bonds.
Ever-presents: (1) Tony Cottee.
Hat-tricks: (3) Tony Cottee (3).
Leading scorer: (28) Tony Cottee.

	Appearances Lge	*Sub*	LC	*Sub*	FAC	*Sub*	Goals Lge	LC	FAC	Tot
Bonds, Billy	**13**	*4*	1	*2*	3	*1*				
Brady, Liam	**12**						**2**			**2**
Cottee, Tony	**42**		6		5		**22**	5	1	**28**
Devonshire, Alan	**20**		4		3		**2**			**2**
Dickens, Alan	**31**	*5*	4		2	*1*	**3**	2		**5**
Dolan, Eamonn		*1*								
Gale, Tony	**32**		4		4		**2**		1	**3**
Goddard, Paul	**3**	*1*	1				**1**	1		**2**
Hilton, Paul	**15**	*1*	4	*1*	2		**1**		1	**2**
Ince, Paul	**7**	*3*			1		**1**			**1**
Keen, Kevin	**7**	*6*	2		1	*1*			1	**1**
McAlister, Tom	**9**									
McAvennie, Frank	**36**		5		4		**7**		4	**11**
McQueen, Tom	**9**									
Martin, Alvin	**16**		3		1		**2**			**2**
Orr, Neil	**21**	*1*	4		1		**1**			**1**
Parkes, Phil	**33**		6		5					
Parris, George	**35**	*1*	6		5		**1**		1	**2**
Pike, Geoff	**10**	*1*	1		4					
Potts, Steve	**8**									
Robson, Stewart	**18**		2		3		**2**		1	**3**
Stewart, Ray	**23**		3		3		**4**			**4**
Strodder, Gary	**12**									
Walford, Steve	**13**	*1*	4	*1*	3					
Ward, Mark	**37**		6		5		**1**	2		**3**
25 players used	**462**	***25***	**66**	***4***	**55**	***3***	**52**	**10**	**10**	**72**

BARCLAYS LEAGUE DIVISION 1 | Manager: John Lyall | SEASON 1987-88

No	Date		Att	Pos	Pt	F-A	H-T	Scorers, Times, and Referees	1	2	3	4	5	6	7	8	9	10	11	subs used
1	H	QP RANGERS			L	0-3	0-3		McAlister	Stewart^	McQueen	Orr	Martin	Devonshire*	Ward	McAvennie	Brady	Cottee	Robson	Dickens/Strodder
	15/8		22,881		–			*Stewart 13 (og), Bannister 38, Brock 44*	*Seaman*	*Brock*	*Dennis*	*Parker*	*McDonald*	*Fenwick*	*Allen*	*Byrne*	*Coney*	*Bannister*	*Brock*	
								Ref: M Peck	QPR boss Jim Smith has spent £1 million of chairman David Bulstrode's money on four new players. Ray Stewart headed Fereday's cross into his own net. Fereday's cross provided No 2 and Brock's 25-yarder a third before half-time. Paul Parker tracked Tony Cottee wherever he went.											
2	A	LUTON		18	D	2-2	2-1	Brady 20, Stewart 30p	McAlister	Stewart	McQueen	Strodder	Martin	Brady	Ward	McAvennie	Ince	Cottee	Robson	
	22/8		*18,073*		1			*Harford 5, 51*	*Sealey*	*Breacker*	*Grimes*	*Hill*	*Foster*	*McDonough*	*Wilson D*	*Wilson R**	*Harford*	*Newell*	*Preece*	*Nwajiobi*
								Ref: J Martin	Both teams score their first goals and pick up their first point. Mick Harford headed in Tim Breacker's cross. Brady levelled on the volley after Sealey parried from McAvennie. McDonough whipped away Cottee's legs for the penalty. When Ricky Hill hit the bar, Harford made it 2-2.											
3	H	NORWICH		14	W	2-0	0-0	Cottee 51, 65	McAlister	Stewart	McQueen	Strodder	Martin	Brady	Ward	McAvennie	Ince	Cottee	Robson	
	29/8		16,394	*17*	4				*Gunn*	*Culverhouse*	*Spearing*	*Bruce*	*Phelan*	*Butterworth*	*Fox*	*Drinkell*	*Biggins*	*Crook*	*Bowen**	*Gordon*
								Ref: M Reed	West Ham are on song and Norwich take it on the chin. Cottee looked sharp throughout, prompting suggestions that England manager Bobby Robson must be considering him. Ward set up Cottee's first-time opener. Stewart's whipped cross was then met with a spectacular volley.											
4	A	PORTSMOUTH		14	L	1-2	1-1	Strodder 11	McAlister	Stewart*	McQueen	Strodder	Martin	Brady	Ward	McAvennie	Ince	Cottee	Robson	Parris
	31/8		*16,104*	*20*	4			*Dillon 15p, 69*	*Knight*	*Swain*	*Horne*	*Dillon*	*Shotton*	*Gilbert*	*Fillery*	*Kennedy*	*Baird*	*Mariner*	*Hilaire*	
								Ref: J Deakin	Winless Pompey have just been crushed 0-6 by Arsenal. Strodder heads his first goal for West Ham since his £100,000 transfer from Lincoln. McAlister felled Vince Hilaire for Pompey's equalising penalty. Dillon's second goal, from Fillery's cross, won the match for Portsmouth.											
5	H	LIVERPOOL		15	D	1-1	0-0	Cottee 73	McAlister	Stewart	McQueen*	Strodder	Martin	Brady	Ward	McAvennie	Ince	Cottee	Robson	Parris
	5/9		**29,865**	*9*	5			*Aldridge 51p*	*Grobbelaar*	*Gillespie*	*Venison*	*Nicol*	*Whelan*	*Hansen*	*Beardsley*	*Aldridge*	*Spackman*	*Barnes*	*McMahon*	
								Ref: A Gunn	A collapsed sewer at Anfield means Liverpool have yet to play at home. Dalglish has added Barnes and Beardsley to an already strong squad. Aldridge nets from the spot after Parris fells McMahon. Hansen's silly back-pass let in Cottee. Liverpool, on top throughout, hit the post twice.											
6	A	WIMBLEDON		16	D	1-1	0-1	Cottee 62	McAlister	Stewart	Parris	Strodder	Martin	Brady	Ward !	McAvennie	Ince	Cottee	Robson	
	12/9		*8,507*	*4*	6			*Wise 20*	*Beasant*	*Scales*	*Phelan*	*Ryan*	*Young**	*Thorn*	*Wise*	*Sayer^*	*Fashanu*	*Sanchez*	*Cork*	*Gayle/Gibson*
								Ref: A Buksh	10 minutes after scoring for the Dons, Dennis Wise gets involved with Mark Ward, who strikes Wise in the face and is shown the red card. 10-man West Ham should have had little chance to recover against obdurate opponents, but George Parris crosses for Cottee's headed equaliser.											
7	H	TOTTENHAM		18	L	0-1	0-1		McAlister	Stewart	Parris	Strodder*	Martin	Brady	Ward	McAvennie	Ince	Cottee	Robson	Hilton
	19/9		27,750	*2*	6			*Fairclough 38*	*Clemence*	*Stevens*	*Thomas*	*Gough*	*Fairclough*	*Moran^*	*Allen C**	*Allen P*	*Ardiles*	*Hodge*	*Claesen*	*Metgod/Samways*
								Ref: R Lewis	Spurs' boss David Pleat relishes the performance of 35-year-old Ardiles, who becomes so agitated that he is eventually booked. Fairclough's volley from Moran's cross is small reward for Spurs' first-half dominance. Fairclough's professional foul on Ince provoked a late free-for-all.											
8	A	ARSENAL		19	L	0-1	0-0		McAlister	Stewart	Parris	Strodder	Martin	Brady	Keen	McAvennie	Ince	Cottee	Robson	
	26/9		*40,127*	*7*	6			*Sansom 80*	*Lukic*	*Thomas*	*Sansom*	*Williams*	*O'Leary*	*Adams*	*Rocastle**	*Davis*	*Smith*	*Groves*	*Rix*	*Hayes*
								Ref: D Elleray	Liam Brady returns to Highbury for the first time since leaving for Italy seven years earlier. He is visibly choked and plays poorly. Afterwards he castigates George Graham's direct style, but admits it was effective. Full-back Sansom scores his first goal in two years, on his birthday.											
9	H	DERBY		17	D	1-1	1-0	Brady 24	McAlister	Stewart*	McQueen^	Strodder	Martin	Brady	Keen	Parris	Ince	Cottee	Robson	Hilton/**Slater**
	3/10		17,226	*12*	7			*Gee 63*	*Shilton*	*Sage*	*Forsyth*	*Williams*	*Wright*	*MacLaren*	*Callaghan*	*Gee*	*Davison*	*Gregory*	*Cross*	
								Ref: B Hill	Frank McAvennie has signed for Celtic for £800,000. West Ham deserved more for their first-half dominance than Liam Brady's blasted free-kick, touched to him by Robson. Phil Gee's simple equaliser left the Hammers hanging on desperately by the end. West Ham need a striker.											
10	H	CHARLTON		17	D	1-1	1-1	Ince 7	McAlister	Stewart	Parris	Keen	Martin	Brady	Ward	Dickens	Ince	Cottee	Robson	
	10/10		15,757	*21*	8			*Crooks 30*	*Bolder*	*Humphrey*	*Reid*	*Peake*	*Shirtliff*	*Thompson*	*Stuart*	*Lee*	*Jones*	*Campbell*	*Crooks*	
								Ref: R Groves	The search for a striker canvases the following names: Colin Clarke, Paul Walsh, Kerry Dixon, Mick Harford, Kevin Drinkell. Charlton are bottom, and looked up against it once Dickens made a quick goal for Ince. Steve Thompson's header was knocked over the line by Crooks.											

No	Venue	Opponent / Date	Att	Pos	Res	Pts	F-A	H-T	Scorers, Times, and Referees	1	2	3	4	5	6	7	8	9	10	11	subs used
11	A	OXFORD		16	W		2-1	2-1	Caton 6 (og), Cottee 25	McAlister	Stewart	Parris	Dickens	Martin	Brady	Keen	Ward	Ince	Cottee	Robson	
		17/10	*9,092*	*10*		11			*Saunders 34*	*Hucker*	*Bardsley*	*Dreyer*	*Shelton*	*Slatter*	*Caton*	*Houghton**	*Foyle^*	*Saunders*	*Phillips*	*Hebberd*	*Hill/Whitehurst*
									Ref: J Worrall	A great start, when Caton steers Mark Ward's cross into his own net. West Ham were helped again when Dreyer dives in rashly on Cottee, who cuts inside to score from a tight angle. But after Dean Saunders heads his first goal of the season it is all hands to the West Ham pump.											
12	H	MANCHESTER U		15	D		1-1	0-1	Stewart 68p	McAlister	Stewart	Parris	Keen	Martin	Brady	Ward	Dickens	Ince	Cottee	McQueen	
		25/10	19,863	*4*		12			*Gibson 45*	*Walsh*	*Anderson*	*Gibson*	*McGrath*	*Moran*	*Duxbury*	*Robson*	*Strachan**	*McClair*	*Davenport*	*Olsen*	*Blackmore*
									Ref: B Stevens	This Sunday match failed to ignite, other than through Alex Ferguson's inflammatory post-match comments, suggesting that Stewart should have been sent off following a clash with Bryan Robson. Gibson's free-kick was deflected in. McGrath felled Ward for the disputed penalty.											
13	A	WATFORD		14	W		2-1	1-0	Dickens 15, Cottee 69	McAlister	Stewart	Parris	Keen	Martin	Brady	Ward	Dickens	Ince	Cottee	Robson	
		31/10	*14,427*	*20*		15			*Allen 89*	*Coton*	*Gibbs*	*Rostron*	*Jackett*	*Morris*	*McClelland*	*Agana**	*Allen*	*Senior*	*Porter*	*Hodges*	*Sherwood*
									Ref: P Don	Dave Bassett's Watford slump to their fifth successive league defeat, though they had trounced Darlington 8-0 in the Littlewoods Cup. Dickens' header from Keen's centre went in off a post. Ince then set up Cottee. Allen's late reply was Watford's first league goal in six games.											
14	H	SHEFFIELD WED		15	L		0-1	0-1		McAlister	Stewart	Parris	Keen*	Martin	Brady	Ward	Dickens	Ince	Cottee	Robson	Dolan
		7/11	16,277	*16*		15			*Bradshaw 22*	*Hodge*	*Jacobs*	*Worthington*	*Pearson*	*Madden*	*Proctor*	*Chamberlain**	*Megson*	*West*	*Bradshaw^*	*Galvin*	*Owen/Fee*
									Ref: K Cooper	'A thousand apologies,' says Ron Atkinson afterwards, as the Owls win their fourth successive game with their one and only shot on target. McAlister parried Galvin's volley but Bradshaw tapped in. This is Wednesday's third win at Upton Park in a year, following wins in both cups.											
15	A	EVERTON		15	L		1-3	0-3	Hilton 81	McAlister	Bonds	Parris*	Hilton	Martin^	Brady	Ward	Dickens	Ince	Cottee	Robson	Strodder/Keen
		14/11	*29,405*	*5*		15			*Watson 34, Reid 37, Sharp 45*	*Southall*	*Stevens*	*v d Hauwe*	*Ratcliffe*	*Watson*	*Reid*	*Steven**	*Heath*	*Sharp*	*Snodin*	*Sheedy^*	*Harper/Wilson*
									Ref: R Milford	Everton's Sharp is just the sort of target man Lyall covets, but of course he is unavailable. Colin Harvey's defending champions won as they pleased after Dave Watson headed Sheedy's free-kick in off a post. Bonds marked his first game of the season with a back-pass to Peter Reid.											
16	H	NOTT'M FOREST		13	W		3-2	1-1	Cottee 13, 52, Stewart 50p	McAlister	Bonds	Parris	Hilton	Stewart	Keen	Ward	Dickens	Ince	Cottee	Robson	
		21/11	17,216	*4*		18			*Webb 32, Clough 70*	*Sutton*	*Chettle*	*Pearce*	*Walker*	*Foster*	*Wilson*	*Carr**	*Webb*	*Clough*	*Wilkinson^*	*Rice*	*Starbuck/Gaynor*
									Ref: G Courtney	Forest were unbeaten in the league in two months before this jewel of a match. Stewart's penalty had to be retaken as Sutton moved too soon. Cottee's second goal, a Brazilian-style scissors-kick volley, had the crowd in raptures. Referee Courtney said 'it was a pleasure to be involved.'											
17	A	COVENTRY		14	D		0-0	0-0		McAlister	Bonds	Parris	Hilton	Stewart	Keen	Ward	Dickens	Ince	Cottee	Robson	
		28/11	*16,740*	*15*		19				*Ogrizovic*	*Borrows*	*Pickering*	*Emerson*	*Smith K*	*Downs*	*Bennett*	*Phillips*	*Houchen*	*Speedie*	*Gynn*	
									Ref: R Nixon	England manager Bobby Robson runs his eye over Tony Cottee, who had scored eight goals in five previous matches on this lucky ground. This time he was repeatedly denied by Ogrizovic. Stewart's professional foul on Houchen earned a yellow card. Today it would have been red.											
18	H	SOUTHAMPTON		11	W		2-1	1-1	Keen 13, Dickens 75	McAlister	Bonds	Parris	Strodder	Stewart	Keen	Ward !	Dickens	Ince	Cottee	Robson	
		5/12	**14,975**	*10*		22			*Wallace D 42*	*Burridge*	*Forrest*	*Statham*	*Case*	*Moore*	*Bond*	*Townsend*	*Cockerill*	*Clarke*	*Baker G*	*Wallace D*	
									Ref: R Hamer	Mark Ward is sent off for the second time this season. His first yellow card was for dissent, his second in injury time for not retreating 10 yards at a free-kick. West Ham won through Keen's first league goal and Dickens' neat effort, which erased memories of Robson's awful back-pass.											
19	A	CHELSEA		12	D		1-1	1-0	Parris 26	McAlister	Bonds	Parris	Strodder	Stewart	Keen	Ward	Dickens	Hilton	Cottee	Robson	
		12/12	*22,850*	*7*		23			*Wilson K 83*	*Freestone*	*Clarke*	*Dorigo*	*Pates*	*McLaughlin*	*Wood*	*Nevin**	*Hazard*	*Dixon*	*Wilson K*	*Wilson C*	*Wegerle*
									Ref: D Hedges	Pre-match drama when Paul Ince collapses watching TV and is rushed to hospital. John Hollins' Chelsea maintain their unbeaten home record when Kevin Wilson – deputising for the injured Durie – scores his first ever Chelsea goal. West Ham have now lost just two out of 11 games.											
20	H	NEWCASTLE		10	W		2-1	0-0	Robson 47, Ince 82	McAlister	Bonds*	Parris	Strodder	Stewart	Keen	Brady	Dickens	Ince	Cottee	Robson	Hilton
		19/12	18,679	*14*		26			*Mirandhina 78*	*Kelly*	*Anderson*	*Tinnion**	*McCreery*	*Jackson P^*	*Roeder*	*McDonald*	*Gascoigne*	*Goddard*	*Mirandhina*	*Cornwell*	*Jackson D*
									Ref: P Vanes	What a battle between 41-year-old Bonds and whipper-snapper Gascoigne, who says Bonds kept saying 'calm down'. Brady set up Robson's goal, which was cancelled out by the Brazilian Mirandhina's fifth goal in six games. Ince won the match with a 25-yarder into the top corner.											
21	H	WIMBLEDON		10	L		1-2	0-2	Stewart 58p	McAlister	Bonds	Parris*	Strodder	Stewart	Keen	Ward	Dickens^	Ince	Cottee	Robson	Hilton/Brady
		26/12	18,605	*7*		26			*Sanchez 15, Fashanu 45*	*Beasant*	*Goodyear*	*Scales*	*Jones*	*Young*	*Thorn*	*Fairweather*	*Cork**	*Fashanu*	*Sanchez*	*Wise*	*Turner*
									Ref: A Gunn	Vinnie Jones is booked inside four seconds for a foul on Ince, but then shows his creative side by manufacturing both Dons' goals – Sanchez's side-footer and Fashanu's hook. When Wise and Robson tumbled in the box the ref gave a penalty but might have given a free-kick to Wise.											

BARCLAYS LEAGUE DIVISION 1 Manager: John Lyall SEASON 1987-88

No	Date		Att	Pos	Pt	F-A	H-T	Scorers, Times, and Referees	1	2	3	4	5	6	7	8	9	10	11	subs used
22	A	TOTTENHAM		13	L	1-2	0-1	Hilton 66	McAlister	Bonds	Parris	Hilton	Stewart	Keen	Ward*	Brady	Ince	Cottee	Robson	Strodder
	28/12		*39,456*	*12*	26			*Waddle 31, Fairclough 70*	*Parks*	*Hughton*	*Thomas*	*Hodge*	*Fairclough*	*Stevens**	*Moran^*	*Allen P*	*Waddle*	*Ardiles*	*Howells*	*Statham/Close*
								Ref: J Martin	David Pleat has resigned. Spurs' second victory under new manager Terry Venables comes when Fairclough heads in Chris Waddle's cross. Earlier Waddle scored from a free-kick after Ray Stewart fouled Paul Moran, and Hilton levelled after a bout of head tennis with Tony Cottee.											
23	A	NORWICH		14	L	**1-4**	1-0	Cottee 27 *[Rosario 85]*	McAlister	Bonds	Parris	Hilton	Stewart	Keen^	Ward	Dickens	Ince*	Cottee	Robson	Gale/Dolan
	1/1		*20,069*	*15*	26			*Gordon 47, Drinkell 67, Bowen 79,*	*Gunn*	*Culverhouse*	*Bowen*	*Putney*	*Phelan*	*Butterworth*	*Fox*	*Drinkell*	*Rosario*	*Gloss*	*Gordon*	
								Ref: B Hill	The festive season continues to backfire as West Ham succumb to their third quick defeat and their heaviest of the season. Norwich started the season dreadfully, but despite selling Steve Bruce to Man U, have won all three holiday fixtures. They are poised to climb above West Ham.											
24	H	LUTON		14	D	1-1	0-0	Ince 60	McAlister	Bonds	Parris*	Strodder	Stewart	Potts	Ward	Gale	Hilton	Cottee	Robson	Ince
	2/1		16,716	*8*	27			*Stein M 76*	*Sealey*	*Breacker*	*Johnson*	*McDonough*	*Foster*	*Donaghy*	*Wilson D*	*Stein B*	*Harford*	*Stein M*	*Allinson*	
								Ref: P Foakes	The storm that burst before kick-off ruins the pitch. West Ham's dismal luck continues when they lose Parris with a broken ankle. Defender Hilton partners Cottee in attack and misses the chances that come his way. Ince's goal was half-saved. Harford headed down to Mark Stein.											
25	A	QP RANGERS		12	W	1-0	0-0	Dickens 75	McAlister	Stewart	McQueen	Bonds	Strodder	Gale	Ward	Brady	Dickens	Cottee	Robson	
	16/1		*14,509*	*7*	30				*Johns*	*Dawes*	*Dennis*	*Parker*	*McDonald*	*Maguire*	*Allen*	*Falco*	*Bannister*	*Fereday**	*Brock^*	*Byrne/Kerslake*
								Ref: J Key	Potts and Ince were hurt in a car crash on their way to training at Basildon. West Ham won on the Omniturf pitch despite Falco hitting the underside of the bar and Bannister missing two sitters. Brady's precise pass let Dickens in on goal. The sides now meet again in the FA Cup.											
26	A	LIVERPOOL		14	D	0-0	0-0		McAlister	Stewart	Ince	Bonds	Strodder	Gale	Ward	Brady	Dickens*	Cottee	Robson	McQueen
	6/2		***42,049***	*1*	31				*Grobbelaar*	*Ablett*	*Venison*	*Nicol*	*Spackman*	*Hansen*	*Beardsley*	*Aldridge**	*Houghton*	*Barnes*	*McMahon*	*Johnston*
								Ref: J McAulay	A 0-0 on the day that Luton beat Oxford 7-4 was never going to grab headlines, even though West Ham became the first team to avoid defeat at Anfield this season. McAlister was the star. Five players were booked, two from Liverpool, who had totted up only four cautions all season.											
27	H	PORTSMOUTH		13	D	1-1	0-0	Cottee 67	McAlister	Stewart	Ince	Bonds	Strodder	Gale	Ward	Brady	Dickens	Cottee	Robson	
	13/2		18,639	*15*	32			*Connor 78*	*Knight*	*Whitehead*	*Hardyman*	*Dillon*	*Daish*	*Ball*	*Horne*	*Sandford**	*Baird^*	*Connor*	*Hilaire*	*Kelly/Gilbert*
								Ref: J Worrall	Alan Dickens sports two black eyes, donated by Liverpool players at Anfield. Cottee's 25-yarder, in off the bar, looked like earning three vital points. But McAlister left his goal-line to take Dillon's cross by the corner flag and the ball swerved behind him. It was touched in by Connor.											
28	A	DERBY		13	L	0-1	0-0		McAlister	Stewart	Ince	Bonds	Strodder	Gale	Ward	Brady*	Dickens^	Cottee	Robson	Keen/McQueen
	27/2		*16,301*	*18*	32			*Callaghan 46*	*Shilton*	*Blades**	*Forsyth*	*Williams*	*Wright*	*Hindmarch*	*McMinn^*	*Lewis*	*Gee*	*Gregory*	*Callaghan*	*MacLaren/Garner*
								Ref: K Lupton	Only Brady stood out among the dross, but he caught his studs and was stretchered off after 39 minutes, his season over. Stodder fouled Gee in the box but McMinn's penalty hit a post. A headed goal gave Derby their first win since November. Lyall locks his team in the dressing room.											
29	H	OXFORD		13	D	1-1	0-0	Ward 71	McAlister	Stewart	McQueen	Bonds	Strodder	Gale	Ward	Keen	Ince*	Cottee	Robson	Dolan
	5/3		14,980	*19*	33			Phillips 69	*Judge*	*Bardsley*	*Dreyer*	*Shelton*	*Briggs*	*Greenhall**	*Whitehurst*	*Foyle*	*Saunders*	*Phillips*	*Hill*	*Rhoades-Brown*
								Ref: R Milford	Lyall hopes to sign Kerry Dixon for £1.2 million, with Dickens going to Chelsea in part-exchange. Dickens is left out of the team. McAlister couldn't hold Phillips' effort, but West Ham levelled from Robson's long throw. Biggest cheer came when a fan thumped the ball into the net.											
30	A	CHARLTON		15	L	0-3	0-2		McAlister	Stewart	McQueen	Bonds	Strodder	Gale	Ward	Dickens*	Dolan	Cottee	Robson	Keen
	12/3		***8,118***	*19*	33			*Crooks 29, 68, Stuart 31*	*Bolder*	*Humphrey*	*Reid*	*Mackenzie*	*Shirtliff*	*Miller*	*Stuart*	*Leaburn*	*Gritt*	*Lee*	*Crooks*	
								Ref: J Martin	Dixon and Harford have both rejected moves to West Ham. Lowly Charlton won with embarrassing ease and Lyall wisely stays away from the press conference. Without injured Brady, West Ham were lacking in midfield. Charlton went 3-0 up when Crooks was left totally unmarked.											
31	H	WATFORD		15	W	1-0	0-0	Rosenior 61	McAlister	Stewart	Potts	Bonds	Strodder	Gale	Ward	Keen	**Rosenior**	Cottee	Robson*	Dickens
	19/3		16,051	*21*	36				*Coton*	*Gibbs*	*Rostron*	*Sherwood*	*Terry*	*McClelland*	*Sterling*	*Allen**	*Blissett*	*Porter*	*Jackett*	*Roberts*
								Ref: R Lewis	Leroy Rosenior, who had rejected Watford, signs for £250,000 from Fulham and is an instant hit. He won his battle with Terry and also chased a long pass to score, earning West Ham their second win in 11 games. It might have been different had Watford taken any of their chances.											

No	Venue	Opponent	Pos	Res	F-A	H-T	Scorers, Times, and Referees	1	2	3	4	5	6	7	8	9	10	11	subs used
32	A	MANCHESTER U	15	L	1-3	0-0	Rosenior 81	McAlister	Stewart	Potts	Bonds	Strodder	Gale	Ward	Keen*	Rosenior	Cottee	Dickens	Parris
26/3		*37,269*	*2*	36			*Strachan 58, Anderson 83, Robson 89*	*Turner*	*Anderson*	*Blackmore*	*Bruce*	*McGrath*	*Duxbury*	*Strachan*	*Robson**	*McClair*	*Davenport*	*Gibson*	*Olsen*
							Ref: G Ashby	Man U might be second, but Liverpool are so far out in front that the title is as good as theirs. Strachan orchestrated this win, scoring first by skipping round Stewart to net from 15 yards. West Ham's only grievance was the corner-kick which paved the way for Viv Anderson's goal.											
33	A	SHEFFIELD WED	15	L	1-2	0-1	Rosenior 65	McAlister	Stewart	**Dicks**	Bonds*	Strodder^	Gale	Ward	Parris	Rosenior	Cottee	Robson	Dickens/Potts
2/4		*18,435*	*8*	36			*Hurst 37, Chamberlain 50*	*Pressman*	*Sterland*	*Worthington*	*Madden*	*Cranson*	*Proctor*	*Chamberlain**	*Megson*	*Chapman*	*Hirst^*	*Jonsson*	*Bradshaw/Fee*
							Ref: B Hill	Julian Dicks makes his debut in this defeat, which saw Billy Bonds limp off at half-time with a wrenched knee. Leroy Rosenior scores his third goal in as many games, and late pressure almost earned West Ham a draw. Wednesday's third win in a row follows five straight defeats.											
34	H	EVERTON	17	D	0-0	0-0		McAlister	Stewart*	Dicks	Parris	Strodder	Gale	Ward	Dickens	Rosenior	Cottee	Robson	Ince
4/4		21,195	*4*	37				*Southall*	*Stevens*	*Pointon*	*v d Hauwe*	*Mountfield*	*Reid*	*Steven*	*Clarke**	*Heath*	*Harper*	*Sheedy*	*Snodin*
							Ref: J Ashworth	Cottee sprinted out at Upton Park as if to endear himself to the club poised to sign him. West Ham were denied a win by the reflexes of Neville Southall, whose saves from Robson and Rosenior's header earned applause. Van den Hauwe's late back-header was disallowed for pushing.											
35	H	ARSENAL	17	L	0-1	0-0		Parkes	Potts*	Dicks	Bonds	Strodder	Gale	Ward	Parris	Rosenior	Cottee	Robson	Keen
12/4		26,746	*6*	37			*Thomas 77*	*Lukic*	*Winterburn*	*Sansom*	*Thomas*	*Caesar*	*Adams*	*Rocastle*	*Davis*	*Smith*	*Merson*	*Richardson**	*Rix*
							Ref: R Gifford	Arsenal players are competing for places in the Littlewoods Cup final, and five bookings tells its own story. Mark Ward was the first, when he tried to kick Michael Thomas into the stand. Rocastle freed Thomas to score past Phil Parkes, who was playing his first game in over a year.											
36	A	NOTT'M FOREST	18	D	0-0	0-0		McAlister	Parris	Dicks	Bonds	Strodder	Gale	Ward	Dickens	Rosenior	Cottee	Robson	
20/4		*15,775*	*5*	38				*Sutton*	*Fleming*	*Pearce*	*Chettle*	*Foster*	*Wilson*	*Crosby*	*Webb*	*Clough*	*Carr*	*Rice*	
							Ref: H King	Twice Cottee was clean through on Sutton, and twice he failed to capitalise. It is his ninth game without a goal, and West Ham could do with one. Forest exerted much pressure but created few chances. West Ham could have won it at the death, but Rosenior blazed over the crossbar.											
37	H	COVENTRY	16	D	1-1	0-0	Cottee 78	McAlister	Parris	Dicks	Keen^	Strodder	Gale	Ward	Dickens	Ince*	Cottee	Robson	Hilton/Slater
23/4		17,733	*9*	39			*Regis 56*	*Ogrizovic*	*Borrows*	*Pickering*	*Sedgley*	*Kilcline*	*Peake*	*Emerson*	*Phillips*	*Regis*	*Speedie*	*Smith D*	
							Ref: M James	Lyall lost Bonds and Rosenior before kick-off. Ogrizovic's long punt sets up Regis's swivelling goal. Cottee's first goal in 10 games comes when Oggy and Peake get in a tizzy. Three super saves by McAlister earn a point that keeps West Ham one place above the play-off position.											
38	A	SOUTHAMPTON	18	L	1-2	0-0	Cottee 57	McAlister	Potts	Dicks	Bonds	Strodder	Gale	Ward	Dickens	Rosenior	Cottee	Parris	
30/4		*15,652*	*11*	39			*Bond 72, 84*	*Burridge*	*Forrest*	*Statham*	*Case**	*Moore*	*Bond*	*Wallace R*	*Baker G*	*Clarke*	*Townsend*	*Shearer*	*Le Tissier*
							Ref: D Hedges	Saints end the season with a flourish, losing just once in their last eight games. West Ham could have done with less fired-up opponents, and lose to two late goals by central defender Kevin Bond, who had only scored once all season. Hammers now face a crisis match with Chelsea.											
39	H	CHELSEA	16	W	**4-1**	2-0	Rosenior 14, 36, Hilton 56, Cottee 89	McAlister	Parris	Dicks	Potts	Hilton	Gale	Ward	Dickens	Rosenior !	Cottee	Robson	
2/5		28,521	*17*	42			*West 85*	*Digweed*	*Hall*	*Dorigo*	*Wicks*	*McLaughlin*	*Clarke*	*Nevin*	*Hazard**	*Dixon*	*Durie*	*Bumstead*	*West*
							Ref: D Scott	7th in December, Chelsea have collapsed with one win in 25 games. Two right-footed shots by Rosenior put West Ham in command, but he is later sent off for the first time ever for throttling Clarke. West Ham are safe as Chelsea must play Charlton. Both cannot overtake West Ham.											
40	A	NEWCASTLE	16	L	1-2	1-0	Robson 11	McAlister	Parris	Dicks	Potts	Hilton	Gale	Ward	Dickens	Rosenior	Cottee	Robson	
7/5		*23,731*	*8*	42			*O'Neill 56, Dicks 67 (og)*	*Kelly*	*McDonald*	*Cornwell*	*McCreery*	*Anderson*	*Scott*	*Jackson D*	*Gascoigne*	*Goddard*	*O'Neill**	*Lormor*	*Bogie*
	Home	Away					Ref: K Walmsley	Nothing rides on this match, so Julian Dicks' embarrassment at scoring his first Hammers goal – at the wrong end – does not have tragic consequences. Chelsea's draw with Charlton means that all three clubs finish on 42 points. Chelsea lose the play-off final with Middlesbrough.											
Average	20,725	21,334																	

Littlewoods Cup				F-A	H-T	Scorers, Times, and Referees	1	2	3	4	5	6	7	8	9	10	11	subs used
2:1 A BARNSLEY	18	D		0-0	0-0		McAlister	Potts*	Parris	Strodder	Martin	Brady	Ward	McAvennie	Ince	Cottee	Robson	McQueen
22/9	*10,330*	*2:4*					*Baker*	*Joyce*	*Cross*	*Thomas*	*Gray*	*Futcher*	*Wylde*	*Agnew*	*Lowndes*	*MacDonald*	*Clarke**	*Beresford*
						Ref: A Seville	Barnsley are just seven places below West Ham in the Football League, and there is no discernible gap in status. West Ham retreated for much of the time behind a five-man defence, with Ince sweeping up. Thomas hit McAllister's post. Manager Allan Clarke was booked for coaching.											
2:2 H BARNSLEY	17	L		2-5	2-0	Keen 3, Robson 31 *[MacDonald 112]*	McAlister	Parris*	McQueen^	Strodder	Martin	Brady	Ward	Keen	Ince	Cottee	Robson	Dickens/Hilton
6/10	12,403	*2:13*		*aet*		*Agnew 55p, 72, B'ford 102, L'ndes 104,*	*Baker*	*Joyce*	*Cross*	*Thomas*	*Gray*	*Futcher*	*Beresford*	*Agnew*	*Lowndes*	*MacDonald*	*Broddle*	
						Ref: K Morton (Hammers lose 2-5 on aggregate)	Fans call for Lyall's head. Barnsley had scored once in six games but hardly deserved to go 0-2 down when Cottee's penalty was pushed out to Robson. Martin's push on Gray and Agnew's bullet free-kick put Barnsley ahead on away goals. Beresford's free-kick in extra-time settled it.											

FA Cup				F-A	H-T													
3 H CHARLTON	14	W		2-0	0-0	Brady 75, Cottee 87	McAlister	Potts	Stewart	Bonds	Strodder	Gale	Ward	Brady*	Hilton	Cottee	Robson	Ince
9/1	22,043	*20*					*Bolder*	*Humphrey*	*Reid*	*Mackenzie*	*Shirtliff*	*Thompson*	*Bennett*	*Campbell*	*Jones**	*Lee^*	*Mortimer*	*Williams/Crooks*
						Ref: V Callow	Billy Bonds, shortly to get his MBE, plays a blinder, and sets up the second, decisive goal for Cottee. The breakthrough had come when Shirtliff fouled Cottee, and Brady's free-kick flew into the net. Charlton never tested McAlister. West Ham will lose here 0-3 in the league.											
4 A QP RANGERS	12	L		1-3	0-0	Cottee 51	McAlister	Stewart	McQueen*	Bonds	Strodder	Gale	Ward	Brady	Dickens	Cottee	Robson	Hilton
30/1	*23,651*	*1:7*				*Pizanti 49, Bannister 64, Allen 83*	*Johns*	*Dawes*	*Pizanti*	*Parker*	*McDonald*	*Maguire*	*Allen*	*Falco*	*Bannister*	*Fereday**	*Brock*	*Byrne*
						Ref: H King	West Ham have won on their three previous games on QPR's plastic pitch. Kick-off was delayed one hour after Hammers' fans spilled onto the touchlines. Cottee's close-range equaliser counted for nothing when Bannister, with his back to goal, restored the lead with a curling shot.											

		Home					Away					
	P	W	D	L	F	A	W	D	L	F	A	Pts
1 Liverpool	40	15	5	0	49	9	11	7	2	38	15	90
2 Manchester U	40	14	5	1	41	17	9	7	4	30	21	81
3 Nott'm Forest	40	11	7	2	40	17	9	6	5	27	22	73
4 Everton	40	14	4	2	34	11	5	9	6	19	16	70
5 QP Rangers	40	12	4	4	30	14	7	6	7	18	24	67
6 Arsenal	40	11	4	5	35	16	7	8	5	23	23	66
7 Wimbledon	40	8	9	3	32	20	6	6	8	26	27	57
8 Newcastle	40	9	6	5	32	23	5	8	7	23	30	56
9 Luton	40	11	6	3	40	21	3	5	12	17	37	53
10 Coventry	40	6	8	6	23	25	7	6	7	23	28	53
11 Sheffield Wed	40	10	2	8	27	30	5	6	9	25	36	53
12 Southampton	40	6	8	6	27	26	6	6	8	22	27	50
13 Tottenham	40	9	5	6	26	23	3	6	11	12	25	47
14 Norwich	40	7	5	8	26	26	5	4	11	14	26	45
15 Derby	40	6	7	7	18	17	4	6	10	17	28	43
16 WEST HAM	40	6	9	5	23	21	3	6	11	17	31	42
17 Charlton	40	7	7	6	23	21	2	8	10	15	31	42
18 Chelsea*	40	7	11	2	24	17	2	4	14	26	51	42
19 Portsmouth	40	4	8	8	21	27	3	6	11	15	39	35
20 Watford	40	4	5	11	15	24	3	6	11	12	27	32
21 Oxford	40	5	7	8	24	34	1	6	13	20	46	31
	840	182	132	106	610	439	106	132	182	439	610	1128

* relegated after play-offs

Odds & ends

Double wins: (1) Watford.
Double losses: (3) Spurs, Arsenal, Sheff Wed.

Won from behind: (0)
Lost from in front: (5) Portsmouth (a), Norwich (a), Southampton (a), Newcastle (a), Barnsley LC (h).

High spots: Five unbeaten games, winning three, from 16 November.
Five unbeaten games, winning two, from 3 October.

Low spots: Seven league games without a win from 26 March.
Catastrophic defeat by Second Division Barnsley in Littlewoods Cup.

Hammer of the Year: Stewart Robson.
Ever-presents: (1) Tony Cottee.
Hat-tricks: (0).
Leading scorer: (15) Tony Cottee.

	Appearances						Goals			
	Lge	*Sub*	LC	*Sub*	FAC	*Sub*	**Lge**	LC	FAC	**Tot**
Bonds, Billy	**22**				2					
Brady, Liam	**21**	*1*	2		2		**2**		1	**3**
Cottee, Tony	**40**		2		2		**13**		2	**15**
Devonshire, Alan	**1**									
Dickens, Alan	**25**	*3*		*1*	1		**3**			**3**
Dicks, Julian	**8**									
Dolan, Eamonn	**1**	*3*								
Gale, Tony	**17**	*1*			2					
Hilton, Paul	**9**	*5*		*1*	1	*1*	**3**			**3**
Ince, Paul	**26**	*2*	2			*1*	**3**			**3**
Keen, Kevin	**19**	*4*	1				**1**	1		**2**
McAlister, Tom	**39**		2		2					
McAvennie, Frank	**8**		1							
McQueen, Tom	**10**	*2*	1	*1*	1					
Martin, Alvin	**15**		2							
Orr, Neil	**1**									
Parkes, Phil	**1**									
Parris, George	**27**	*3*	2				**1**			**1**
Potts, Steve	**7**	*1*	1		1					
Robson, Stewart	**37**		2		2		**2**	1		**3**
Rosenior, Leroy	**9**						**5**			**5**
Slater, Stuart		*2*								
Stewart, Ray	**33**				2		**4**			**4**
Strodder, Gary	**27**	*3*	2		2		**1**			**1**
Ward, Mark	**37**		2		2		**1**			**1**
(own-goals)							**1**			**1**
25 players used	**440**	***30***	**22**	***3***	**22**	***2***	**40**	**2**	**3**	**45**

BARCLAYS LEAGUE DIVISION 1 Manager: John Lyall SEASON 1988-89

No	Date		Att	Pos	Pt	F-A	H-T	Scorers, Times, and Referees	1	2	3	4	5	6	7	8	9	10	11	subs used
1	A	SOUTHAMPTON			L	0-4	0-2	*[Le Tissier 87]*	McAlister	Potts	Dicks	Gale*	Martin	Keen	Ward	Parris	Slater^	**Kelly**	Robson	Hilton/Dickens
	27/8		*18,407*		–			*Rideout 37, 60, Cockerill 44,*	*Burridge*	*Forrest*	*Statham*	*Case*	*Moore*	*Osman*	*Wallace Rod*	*Cockerill*	*Clarke*	*Rideout*	*Wallace D**	*Le Tissier*
								Ref: B Hill	Pre-season had gone well, but after this disaster John Lyall summons his players back for Bank Holiday punishment training. West Ham were not helped by losing Stuart Slater concussed in the first minute, or Gale, who limped off at half-time. £600,000 David Kelly had a tough debut.											
2	H	CHARLTON		20	L	1-3	0-1	Keen 53p	McAlister	Potts*	Dicks	Dickens	Martin	Keen^	Ward	Parris	Slater	Kelly	Robson	Ince/Devonshire
	3/9		19,566	*10*	–			*Williams 23, 48, Robson 56 (og)*	*Bolder*	*Humphrey*	*Reid*	*MacKenzie*	*Shirtliff*	*Miller*	*Lee R*	*Williams*	*Gritt*	*Leaburn*	*Stuart*	
								Ref: D Axcell	A horror show against opponents West Ham expect to beat. Paul Williams capitalised on an almighty cock-up between Robson and McAlister for Charlton's first, and was unmarked to head the second. Kelly was impeded for the penalty, but Robson then headed into his own net.											
3	A	WIMBLEDON		13	W	1-0	1-0	Ward 20	**McKnight**	Parris	Dicks	Hilton	Martin	Ince	Ward	Kelly*	Rosenior	Dickens	Robson	Devonshire
	10/9		***7,730***	*18*	3				*Green*	*Joseph*	*Phelan*	*Ryan**	*Young*	*Scales*	*Gibson*	*Fairweather*	*Fashanu*	*Cork*	*Wise*	*Brooke*
								Ref: R Lewis	Lyall, sober-suited and chain smoking, enjoys West Ham's first goal and first points. They also picked up four bookings against the FA Cup-holders, managed by Lyall's former player, Bobby Gould. Ward won the game with a curling free-kick. Five bookings in the last five minutes.											
4	H	ASTON VILLA		13	D	2-2	0-2	Mountfield 63 (og), Kelly 66	McKnight	Parris	Dicks	Strodder*	Martin	Ince	Ward	Kelly	Rosenior	Dickens	Robson	Devonshire
	17/9		19,186	*10*	4			*McInally 31, 36*	*Spink*	*Price*	*Mountfield*	*Gray A*	*Evans**	*Keown*	*Daley*	*Platt*	*McInally*	*Cownas*	*Gray S*	*Gage*
								Ref: R Gifford	Alan McInally's two first-half goals appear to have ended the contest, but sub Alan Devonshire's arrival sparks West Ham into life. His lob hits a post but goes in off Mountfield. Allan Evans then fluffed a back-pass, which let in David Kelly for his first league goal for his new club.											
5	A	MANCHESTER U		17	L	0-2	0-1		McKnight	Parris	Dicks	Strodder*	Hilton	Ince	Ward	Kelly	Rosenior	Dickens	Robson	Devonshire
	24/9		*39,941*	*5*	4			*Davenport 37, Hughes 69*	*Leighton*	*Blackmore*	*Sharpe**	*Bruce*	*Garton^*	*Duxbury*	*Robson*	*Strachan*	*McClair*	*Hughes*	*Davenport*	*Olsen/Beardsmore*
								Ref: G Tyson	This result was hard on West Ham. Alex Ferguson brought Mark Hughes back from Barcelona, and Hughes comes up with his first goal since his return. Peter Davenport had exchanged passes with McClair to score the opener. Dickens and Robson both missed good early openings.											
6	H	ARSENAL		20	L	1-4	1-2	Dickens 30	McKnight	Parris*	Dicks	Hilton	Martin	Ince	Ward	Kelly	Rosenior^	Dickens	Robson	Strodder/Devonshire
	1/10		27,658	*7*	4			*Smith 17, 19, Thomas 82, Rocastle 90*	*Lukic*	*Dixon*	*Winterburn*	*Thomas*	*Bould*	*Adams*	*Rocastle*	*Davis*	*Smith*	*Groves**	*Marwood*	*Hayes*
								Ref: R Hamer	West Ham never recovered from presenting Alan Smith with two gift goals, taking his tally to nine from six games. Both were the result of crosses that should have been cleared. Dickens' goal flattered to deceive. Lyall raged at his players for an hour afterwards in the dressing room.											
7	A	MIDDLESBROUGH		20	L	0-1	0-1		McKnight	Potts*	Dicks	Gale	Hilton	Devonshire	Ward	Kelly	Parris	Dickens	Ince	Keen
	8/10		*19,608*	*10*	4			*Pallister 40*	*Pears*	*Parkinson*	*Cooper*	*Mowbray*	*Hamilton*	*Pallister*	*Slaven*	*Brennan*	*Burke**	*Kerr^*	*Ripley*	*Glover/Kernaghan*
								Ref: K Breen	David Kelly plays alone up front, and keeps goalkeeper Steve Pears on his toes. But Kelly's cheeky dummy is cut out by Gary Pallister, who strides the length of the pitch and plays a one-two with Bernie Slaven to score a fine goal. Paul Ince gets his fourth yellow card of the season.											
8	A	QP RANGERS		20	L	1-2	1-0	Kelly 30	McKnight	Potts	Dicks	Gale	Hilton	Devonshire*	Ward	Kelly	Rosenior	Dickens	Ince	Keen
	15/10		*14,566*	*9*	4			*Stein 55, Maddix 67*	*Johns*	*Barker*	*Allen*	*Parker*	*McDonald*	*Maddix*	*Falco*	*Francis*	*Fereday*	*Stein**	*Brock^*	*Coney/Kerslake*
								Ref: K Barratt	A super match that brought Loftus Road to its feet at the end. West Ham's first-half superiority was threatened after 34 minutes when Dicks brought down Stein, only for Trevor Francis to shoot wide from the spot. But Francis inspires QPR in the second half, crossing for both goals.											
9	H	NEWCASTLE		18	W	2-0	0-0	Dickens 55, Stewart 81p	McKnight	Stewart	Dicks	Gale	Martin	Devonshire*	Ward	Kelly	Slater	Dickens	Ince	Keen
	22/10		17,765	*20*	7				*Beasant*	*Anderson*	*Tinnion*	*McCreery**	*Scott*	*Thorn^*	*Stephenson*	*Hendrie*	*Mirandinha*	*Jackson*	*O'Neill*	*Robertson/Bogie*
								Ref: A Gunn	The two bottom teams meet in this six-pointer. West Ham played above themselves at times. Dickens nets from Devonshire's quick free-kick, and Beasant flattens Slater for a late penalty. Drama at the end, when O'Neill is led from the pitch with a broken nose. No one saw nothing!											
10	H	LIVERPOOL		18	L	0-2	0-0		McKnight	Stewart	Dicks	Gale	Martin	Devonshire	Ward	Kelly*	Slater	Dickens	Ince	Rosenior
	29/10		**30,188**	*4*	7			*Rush 69, Beardsley 80*	*Hooper*	*Ablett*	*Venison*	*Nicol*	*Whelan**	*Burrows*	*Beardsley*	*Aldridge*	*Rush*	*Barnes*	*Houghton*	*Spackman*
								Ref: R Milford	Liverpool always looked more likely, but it took a long time for them to stamp their authority. Rush broke the deadlock, killing the ball with his right foot and scoring with his left. 'There's only one Ian Rush,' sang Reds' fans. Burrows then enabled Beardsley to tuck away the second.											

11 A COVENTRY		18	D	1-1	1-0	Kelly 32	McKnight	Potts	Dicks	Gale	Martin	Keen	Ward	Kelly	Rosenior	Dickens	Ince	
5/11	14,651	7	8			Thompson 82	Ogrizovic	Borrows	Downs	Sedgley	Emerson*	Rodger	Clark	Speedie	Regis	Bannister^	Smith	Thompson/Houchen
						Ref: E Parker	Kelly nets the rebound after Alan Dickens' shot hits a post. Thereafter Allen McKnight pulls out the stops as injury-ravaged City pile forward. Time is running out when he turns aside Speedie's left-foot shot. But from the ensuing corner substitute Keith Thompson nets the equaliser.											
12 H NOTT'M FOREST		17	D	3-3	2-3	Kelly 2, 42, Rosenior 57	McKnight	Potts	Dicks	Gale	Martin	Keen	Ward	Kelly*	Rosenior	Dickens	Ince^	Brady/Parris
12/11	21,583	9	9			Clough 7, 21, Hodge 41	Sutton	Chettle	Pearce*	Walker	Foster	Hodge	Starbuck	Wilson	Clough	Chapman^	Rice	Laws/Crosby
						Ref: I Hemsley	David Kelly sprained an ankle after scoring two goals and will miss Ireland's vital World Cup-tie in Spain. He was actually on the ground when scoring his second. After a thrill-a-minute first half, Leroy Rosenior earned a point for West Ham with a wonderful diving header.											
13 A LUTON		19	L	1-4	0-3	Martin 63	McKnight	Potts	Dicks	Gale	Martin	Keen*	Ward	Brady	Rosenior	Dickens^	Ince	Parris/Hilton
19/11	9,308	16	9			Black 15, 38, Wegerle 19, Wilson 67	Sealey	Johnson R	Grimes	Preece	Foster	Johnson M	Wilson	Wegerle	Harford	Oldfield	Black	
						Ref: V Callow	West Ham are brought down by two athletic goals by Kingsley Black, the first of which arrived when Johnson's cross eluded the Hammers' defence. Goal of the match was Danny Wilson's belter from 20 yards. Paul Ince was one of the few Hammers to distinguish himself.											
14 H EVERTON		19	L	0-1	0-0		McKnight	Potts	Dicks	Gale	Martin	Keen	Ward*	Brady	Rosenior	Dickens	Ince	Devonshire
26/11	22,176	10	9			Steven 53	Southall	Snodin	v d Hauwe	Ratcliffe	Watson	Reid	Steven	McCall	Sharp	Cottee	Wilson	
						Ref: P Durkin	Cottee was sold to Everton for £2 million in the summer and his first visit back provokes dreadful hostility. The crowd were further incensed by Colin Harvey's team's offside trap and constant passing back to Southall. Cottee almost scored in 30 seconds and set up Steven's winner.											
15 A MILLWALL		19	W	1-0	1-0	Ince 17	McKnight	Potts	Dicks	Gale	Martin	Devonshire	Brady	Kelly	Rosenior	Dickens	Ince	
3/12	20,105	3	12				Horne	Stevens	Dawes	Hurlock	Wood	McLeary	Stephenson	Briley	Sheringham	Cascarino	O'Callaghan	
						Ref: R Wiseman	West Ham are on a high after their crushing cup win over Liverpool, and their achievement in ending the last undefeated home record in the division provokes an avalanche of coins. Dawes' misdirected back-pass presented Hammers with a gift goal. They endured a second-half siege.											
16 H SHEFFIELD WED		19	D	0-0	0-0		McKnight	Potts	Parris	Gale	Martin	Devonshire	Brady	Kelly	Rosenior	Dickens	Ince	
10/12	16,676	12	13				Pressman	Sterland*	Worthington	Cranson	Pearson	Jonsson	Megson	Hirst	Hodgson	Harper	Proctor	Varadi
						Ref: L Shapter	A dreadful, tedious match that had supporters streaming for the exits long before the end. Brady hit the bar in the first minute; David Hodgson hit the wood for Wednesday. Parris, Martin and Kelly squandered half-chances near the end. Just one goal keeps West Ham off the bottom.											
17 H TOTTENHAM		20	L	0-2	0-1		McKnight	Potts	Parris	Gale	Martin	Devonshire*	Brady	Kelly	Rosenior	Dickens	Ince	Keen
17/12	28,365	11	13			Mabbutt 23, Thomas 70	Mimms	Butters	Thomas	Fenwick	Fairclough	Mabbutt	Walsh*	Gascoigne^	Waddle	Stewart	Allen	Robson/Polston
						Ref: D Reeves	Gary Mabbutt starts and finishes the move that sends West Ham to the bottom. Gascoigne tormented the visitors through the first half, before retiring through injury. Mimms is barracked by Spurs fans, but he foils Dickens' 25-yarder. Mitchell Thomas's intended cross sails in for 0-2.											
18 A NORWICH		20	L	1-2	0-0	Stewart 71p	McKnight	Potts	Parris	Gale	Martin*	Devonshire	Brady	Kelly	Rosenior	Dickens^	Ince	Stewart/Keen
27/12	17,491	1	13			Gordon 53, Townsend 61	Gunn	Culverhouse	Bowen	Crook	Linighan	Townsend*	Gordon	Fleck	Rosario	Phelan	Putney	Butterworth
						Ref: M Bailey	Norwich top the table, despite not winning at Carrow Road since October. In this televised match Gordon burst down the right to open the scoring. Fleck squares to Townsend for the second. Phelan barges over David Kelly for the penalty, but West Ham are now three points adrift.											
19 A CHARLTON		20	D	0-0	0-0		McKnight	Potts	Dicks	Gale	Martin	Stewart	Brady*	Kelly	Rosenior	Dickens	Keen	Parris
31/12	11,084	18	14				Bolder	Humphrey	Reid	Shirtliff	Pates	Gritt*	Campbell	Mackenzie	Lee R	Leaburn^	Mortimer	Williams/Peake
						Ref: J Moules	The two bottom sides produce a predictable draw. Lennie Lawrence's team had not won in 11 games. Happiest man was keeper Bob Bolder: it was his 100th match. Liam Brady did his best, and when he was subbed after 83 minutes the crowd booed, not realising he had a groin injury.											
20 H WIMBLEDON		20	L	1-2	1-1	Rosenior 39	McKnight	Potts	Dicks	Gale	Martin	Stewart	Brady	Kelly	Rosenior	Dickens	Keen	
2/1	18,346	17	14			Wise 14, 84	Segers	Scales	Phelan	Jones	Young	Curle	Fairweather	Gibson*	Fashanu	Sanchez	Wise^	Cork/Kruszynski
						Ref: R Milford	Uncompromising Dons are too tough for fragile Hammers. Dennis Wise featured in everything, blasting in Curle's centre and restoring the Dons' lead with a deflected free-kick. Wise was later carried off after a clash with Dicks. Rosenior's goal was his first since November.											
21 A DERBY		19	W	2-1	2-1	Kelly 12, Brady 45	McKnight	Stewart*	Dicks	Gale	Potts	Devonshire	Brady^	Kelly	Rosenior	Dickens	Ince	Strodder/Keen
14/1	16,796	8	17			Saunders 1	Shilton	Blades	Forsyth	Williams	Wright	Hindmarch	McMinn*	Saunders	Gee^	Hebberd	Callaghan	Cross/Penney
						Ref: A Dawson	Dean Saunders' first-minute header was cancelled out by David Kelly's looping header. Kelly knew little about it, as Peter Shilton injured himself colliding with the goal-scorer. With half-time looming Liam Brady fired an exquisite 25-yarder in off the junction of post and bar.											

BARCLAYS LEAGUE DIVISION 1 Manager: John Lyall SEASON 1988-89

No	Date		Att	Pos	Pt	F-A	H-T	Scorers, Times, and Referees	1	2	3	4	5	6	7	8	9	10	11	subs used
22	H	MANCHESTER U		19	L	1-3	1-1	Brady 22p	McKnight	Potts	Dicks	Gale	Martin	Devonshire^	Brady	Kelly*	Rosenior	Ward	Ince	Strodder/Keen
	21/1		**29,822**	*6*	17			*Strachan 28, Martin 54, McClair 60*	*Leighton*	*Gill*	*Martin*	*Bruce*	*Blackmore*	*Donaghy*	*Robson*	*Strachan**	*McClair*	*Hughes*	*Milne*	*Sharpe*
								Ref: A Gunn	Man U's first win at Upton Park since winning the European Cup in 1968 looked unlikely when Kelly twice spurned one-on-one chances against Leighton. Bruce fouled Rosenior for Brady's penalty. Once McKnight failed to hold Robson's shot, to let in Strachan, the tide turned.											
23	A	ARSENAL		20	L	1-2	0-0	Dicks 84	McKnight	Potts	Dicks	Gale	Strodder	Devonshire*	Ward	Dickens	Rosenior	Brady	Ince	Kelly
	4/2		*40,139*	*1*	17			*Groves 58, Smith 61*	*Lukic*	*Dixon*	*Winterburn*	*Thomas*	*O'Leary**	*Adams*	*Rocastle*	*Richardson*	*Smith*	*Merson^*	*Groves*	*Bould/Hayes*
								Ref: J Worrall	Arsenal avenge their FA Cup defeat, though measured on chances created West Ham could consider themselves hard done by. McKnight's confidence is draining away. The keeper was at fault with both goals – Groves' looping header and a shot from Smith that squeezed under him.											
24	H	QP RANGERS		20	D	0-0	0-0		Parkes	Potts	Dicks	Gale	Martin	Devonshire	Ward	Dickens*	Slater	Brady	Ince	Parris
	25/2		17,371	*16*	18				*Seaman*	*Channing*	*Dennis**	*Reid*	*McDonald*	*Spackman*	*Barker*	*Gray*	*Falco^*	*Maddix*	*Stein*	*Pisanti/Coney*
								Ref: K Hackett	Both sets of supporters rise to acclaim Phil Parkes, who has served both clubs well. West Ham have not won at home for four months, while QPR have scored just once – a penalty – in their last six games. A goalless draw was therefore predictable, though Rangers had the edge.											
25	H	COVENTRY		20	D	1-1	0-1	Ince 81	Parkes	Potts	Dicks	Gale	Martin	Devonshire	Kelly	Dickens	Slater	Brady	Ince	
	11/3		15,205	*6*	19			*Kilcline 13p*	*Ogrizovic*	*Borrows*	*Dobson*	*Phillips*	*Kilcline*	*Peake*	*Bennett*	*Speedie*	*Regis**	*Bannister*	*Smith*	*Clark*
								Ref: B Stevens	Brady's dreadful back-pass, which led to Parkes bringing down Bennett, looked like costing West Ham the match until the inspirational Ince skirted Kilcline to equalise with a low drive. Three times Ogrizovic thwarted Dickens. At the death Oggy saved from Dicks in the top corner.											
26	A	ASTON VILLA		20	W	1-0	1-0	Ince 10	Parkes	Parris	Dicks	Gale	Hilton	Devonshire*	Ward	McAvennie	Slater	Brady	Ince	Dickens
	25/3		*22,471*	*14*	22				*Butler*	*Price*	*Gray S*	*Platt*	*Sims*	*Keown*	*Callaghan*	*Daley*	*McInally**	*Cownas^*	*Williams*	*Olney/Mountfield*
								Ref: D Scott	Frank McAvennie has re-signed from Celtic for £1.25 million, £400,000 more than Celtic paid for him 18 months previously. West Ham have just been knocked out of the FA Cup by Norwich, and Paul Ince's sensational goal – running 60 yards and scoring from 30 – was just the tonic.											
27	H	NORWICH		20	L	0-2	0-0		Parkes	Parris	Dicks	Gale	Hilton	Dickens	Ward	McAvennie	Slater	Brady*	Ince	Rosenior
	27/3		27,265	*2*	22			*Linighan 70, Allen 86*	*Gunn*	*Culverhouse*	*Bowen*	*Butterworth*	*Linighan*	*Townsend*	*Gordon*	*Fleck**	*Allen*	*Phelan^*	*Putney*	*Coney/Crook*
								Ref: J Deakin	Norwich's title hopes have been jolted by a home defeat by Newcastle, and they could have been 0-3 down to West Ham. The turning point was when Phelan pushed Ince in the box. The ref waved play on and Ince was booked for dissent. 10 minutes later Linighan had a free header.											
28	A	TOTTENHAM		20	L	0-3	0-1		Parkes	Parris	Dicks	Gale	Strodder*	Potts	Ward	McAvennie	Slater	Brady	Ince	Dickens
	1/4		*28,376*	*6*	22			*Nayim 41, Fenwick 82p, Stewart 88*	*Thorstvedt*	*Butters*	*Hughton*	*Fenwick*	*Nayim**	*Mabbutt*	*Walshs*	*Gascoigne*	*Waddle*	*Stewart*	*Allen*	*Howells*
								Ref: R Lewis	It is 20 years to the day since Parkes made his league debut with Walsall. Spurs were flattered by the score, and were indebted to Thorstvedt's 48th-minute save from McAvennie's header. When Parkes brought down Stewart, Fenwick scored twice from the spot after encroachment.											
29	H	DERBY		20	D	1-1	1-1	Rosenior 23	Parkes	Parris	Dicks	Gale*	Martin	Dickens	Ward	McAvennie	Rosenior	Brady^	Ince	Potts/Slater
	8/4		16,560	*9*	23			*Micklewhite 11*	*Shilton*	*Blades*	*Forsyth*	*Williams*	*Wright*	*Hindmarch*	*McMinn*	*Saunders*	*Goddard**	*Hebberd*	*Micklewhite*	*Cross*
								Ref: B Hill	Gary Micklewhite cannot believe his luck as he is allowed to saunter through a static Hammers defence to score with a feeble shot. Leroy Rosenior levelled with a far-post header, and Mark Ward missed the chance of securing a rare win when shooting into the side-netting.											
30	H	MIDDLESBROUGH		20	L	1-2	1-0	Keen 21	Parkes	Parris	Dicks	Potts	Hilton	Dickens	Ward	McAvennie	Rosenior	Brady	Keen	
	11/4		16,217	*15*	23			*Slaven 84, 86*	*Poole*	*Parkinson*	*Cooper*	*Mowbray*	*Proctor*	*Pallister*	*Slaven*	*Kernaghan*	*Ripley**	*Burke*	*Hamilton*	*Kerr*
								Ref: B Hamer	A killer defeat by a team which had not won in 11 games. Parris hit the bar from 30 yards before Keen exchanged passes with McAvennie to score. Bernie Slaven's late scrambled equaliser saw the scorer booked for excessive celebrations. Two minutes later Slaven headed the winner.											
31	H	SOUTHAMPTON		20	L	1-2	1-1	Brady 25p	Parkes	Parris	Keen	Potts	Hilton	Dickens^	Ward	McAvennie	Rosenior	Brady*	Ince	Slater/McQueen
	15/4		**14,766**	*16*	23			*Wallace Rod 1, Rideout 51*	*Burridge*	*Wallace Ray*	*Adams*	*Case*	*Moore*	*Osman*	*Wallace Rod*	*Cockerill*	*Rideout*	*Horne*	*Wallace D*	
								Ref: K Cooper	This was the day of the Hillsborough disaster. Chris Nichol's Saints ease their relegation fears with their second win in 24 games. Rod Wallace put away Cockerill's through ball in 33 seconds. Russell Osman needlessly handled for the penalty. Rideout headed in from Horne's cross.											

No	Venue	Opponent	Pos	Res	F-A	H-T	Scorers, Times, and Referees	1	2	3	4	5	6	7	8	9	10	11	subs used
32	H	MILLWALL	20	W	**3-0**	3-0	Dicks 20, Dickens 23, Parris 43	Parkes	Parris	Dicks	Gale	Potts	Dickens	Ward	McAvennie	Slater	Keen	Ince*	McQueen
22/4		16,603	*7*	26				*Horne*	*Stevens*	*Dawes*	*Carter**	*Wood*	*McLeary*	*Salman*	*Briley^*	*Horrix*	*Cascarino*	*O'Callaghan*	*Lawrence/Thompson*
							Ref: A Seville	The minute's silence for the victims of Hillsborough is sullied by obscenities that leaves Millwall chairman Reg Burr feeling ashamed. Horne fumbled Dicks' shot through a crowd of players. The goal of the match belonged to Parris, following a slick build-up with Ince and Slater.											
33	A	NEWCASTLE	20	W	2-1	1-1	Keen 7, Ward 79	Parkes	Parris	Dicks	Gale	Martin	Dickens	Ward	McAvennie^	Slater	Keen	Ince	Kelly
3/5		*14,202*	*19*	29			*Lormer 1*	*Wright*	*Anderson**	*Sansom*	*McCreery*	*Scott*	*Roeder*	*Lormor*	*Sweeney*	*Thorn*	*Pinge^*	*Brock*	*Kristensen/McDonald*
							Ref: J Key	Newcastle have played more games, so though they remain above West Ham this defeat relegates the Magpies. Gayle's error let in Lormor in the first minute. Slater's shot was then pushed out to Keen. Ward's angled winner provoked irate Geordies to menace the directors' box.											
34	H	LUTON	19	W	1-0	1-0	Dickens 17	Parkes	Parris	Dicks	Gale*	Martin	Dickens	Ward	Slater	Rosenior^	Keen	Ince	Potts/Kelly
6/5		18,606	*17*	32				*Chamberlain*	*Breacker*	*Dreyer*	*Preece*	*Foster*	*Beaumont*	*Wilson*	*Wegerle*	*Harford*	*Hill*	*Black**	*Cooke*
							Ref: L Shapter	West Ham gain revenge over their Littlewoods Cup executioners with their third successive win. The Hammers are still six points from safety, but have played three games fewer than vanquished Luton. Their survival is now in their own hands, but all four remaining games are away.											
35	A	SHEFFIELD WED	19	W	2-0	0-0	Dickens 50, Rosenior 76	Parkes	Parris	Dicks	Gale*	Martin	Dickens	Ward	Slater	Rosenior	Keen	Ince	Potts^
9/5		*19,905*	*18*	35				*Turner*	*Harper*	*Worthington**	*Palmer*	*Pearson*	*Madden*	*Bennett^*	*Fee*	*Whitton*	*Hirst*	*Barrick*	*Galvin/Reeves*
							Ref: P Tyldesley	This is Ron Atkinson's Wednesday's first home match since the Hillsborough disaster. The Leppings Lane end is closed. With both teams in the drop zone, this is another critical six-pointer. Alan Dickens skipped between two defenders to lob a super goal. Rosenior headed a second.											
36	A	EVERTON	19	L	1-3	1-1	Slater 15	Parkes	Parris	Dicks	Gale	Martin	Dickens	Ward	Slater	Rosenior	Keen^	Ince*	Potts/Kelly
13/5		*21,694*	*11*	*35*			*Sheedy 27, Watson 54, Bracewell 83*	*Southall*	*McDonald*	*Pointon*	*Ratcliffe*	*Watson*	*Bracewell*	*Nevin*	*Steven*	*Sharp*	*Cottee*	*Sheedy**	*Wilson*
							Ref: H Taylor	Everton have lost at home just twice, but when Slater capitalised on Pointon's error West Ham's fifth straight win looked on the cards. The bubble burst when Parkes carried the ball outside the box and Sheedy fired the free-kick into the top corner. Both Luton and Wednesday won.											
37	A	NOTT'M FOREST	19	W	2-1	2-1	Rosenior 1, 18	McKnight	Parris	Dicks	Gale	Martin	Dickens	Ward	Slater	Rosenior	Keen	Brady*	Potts
18/5		*20,943*	*3*	38			*Chapman 31*	*Sutton*	*Laws*	*Pearce*	*Walker*	*Chettle*	*Hodge*	*Gaynor*	*Webb*	*Clough*	*Chapman*	*Parker*	
							Ref: D Phillips	Rosenior puts away Brady's cross in 19 seconds, the fastest goal of the season. West Ham's second goal is a duplicate of the first. But Lee Chapman heads in Tommy Gaynor's centre and Gaynor later hits the bar as the Hammers hang on defiantly to register five wins in six games.											
38	A	LIVERPOOL	19	L	**1-5**	1-1	Rosenior 29 *[Barnes 90]*	McKnight	Parris	Dicks	Gale	Martin	Dickens	Ward	Slater	Rosenior	Brady*	Ince^	McAvennie/Keen
23/5		***41,855***	*1*	*38*			*Aldridge 20, Houghton 63, 80, Rush 84,*	*Grobbelaar*	*Ablett*	*Venison*	*Nicol*	*Whelan*	*Hansen**	*Houghton*	*Aldridge^*	*Rush*	*Barnes*	*McMahon*	*Burrows/Beardsley*
	Home	Away					Ref: S Lodge	Liverpool have already won the FA Cup and have won 16 out of their last 17 games. Aldridge's header from Barnes' cross is cancelled out by Rosenior's from Ward. Ray Houghton, once given away by West Ham, skirts Gale to make it 2-1. Liverpool will lose the decider to Arsenal.											
Average	20,743	21,014																	

Littlewoods Cup

No	Venue	Opponent	Pos	Res	F-A	H-T	Scorers, Times, and Referees	1	2	3	4	5	6	7	8	9	10	11	subs used
2:1	A	SUNDERLAND	17	W	3-0	1-0	Kelly 6, 65, Rosenior 48	McKnight	Parris	Dicks	Hilton	Martin*	Ince	Ward	Kelly	Rosenior	Dickens	Robson	Potts
27/9		*13,691*	*2:18*					*Hesford*	*Kay*	*Agboola*	*Bennett**	*MacPhail*	*Doyle*	*Owers*	*Armstrong*	*Gates*	*Gabbiadini*	*Pascoe*	*Gray*
							Ref: G Aplin	Sunderland have yet to win in Division 2 since promotion. They are so bad they make West Ham look good. Kelly was at the heart of all West Ham's best moments, scoring first with a chip and then converting Rosenior's cross to the far post. In between, his back-heel set up Rosenior.											
2:2	H	SUNDERLAND	20	W	2-1	1-0	Kelly 43, Dickens 59	McKnight	Potts	Dicks	Gale	Hilton	Devonshire*	Ward	Kelly	Parris	Dickens	Ince	Keen
12/10		10,558	*2:16*				*Gabbiadini 74*	*Hesford*	*Gray*	*Agboola*	*Ord*	*MacPhail*	*Doyle**	*Owers*	*Armstrong*	*Gates*	*Gabbiadini*	*Pascoe^*	*Lemon/Ogilvie*
							Ref: A Seville (Hammers win 5-1 on aggregate)	A meaningless cup-tie played on a rain-sodden pitch before a paltry attendance. Sunderland face a reprimand for arriving late after their coach was held up. Midway through the first half, play was halted due to floodlight failure. Dickens' short pass to Kelly made it 4-0 before half-time.											
3	H	DERBY	18	W	5-0	1-0	Martin 44, 79, Stewart 53p, [Rosenior 69, Keen 89]	McKnight	Stewart	Dicks	Gale	Martin	Keen	Ward	Kelly*	Rosenior	Dickens	Ince	Brady
1/11		14,226	*13*					*Shilton*	*Sage*	*Forsyth*	*Williams*	*Hindmarch*	*Blades*	*McMinn*	*Gee**	*Goddard*	*Hebberd*	*Callaghan^*	*Micklewhite/Cross*
							Ref: K Morton	Derby have the meanest defence, just five goals conceded in nine games. They miss cup-tied Saunders and suspended Wright. The second goal was odd. Ince headed in but the ref gave a penalty. Later Ward blasted the ball at the head of the prostrate Callaghan. No action was taken.											

Littlewoods Cup					F-A	H-T	Scorers, Times, and Referees	1	2	3	4	5	6	7	8	9	10	11	subs used
4	H	LIVERPOOL	19	W	4-1	2-1	Ince 21,24, Staunton 56 (og), Gale 76	McKnight	Potts	Dicks	Gale	Martin	Devonshire	Brady	Kelly	Rosenior	Dickens	Ince	
30/11		26,971	*4*				*Aldridge 34p*	*Hooper*	*Ablett*	*Venison*	*Nicol**	*Whelan*	*Spackman*	*Beardsley*	*Aldridge*	*Saunders*	*Houghton*	*McMahon^*	*Watson/Durnin*
							Ref: J Ashworth	This is heaviest defeat – on grass – of Dalglish's managerial career and Liverpool's heaviest cup defeat since before the War. Magnificent Ince threatens to win it on his own with a volley and a header. Pool's only bright moment came when Martin climbed all over Aldridge in the box.											
QF	H	ASTON VILLA	19	W	2-1	1-0	Ince 14, Kelly 85	McKnight	Potts	Dicks	Gale	Strodder	Devonshire	Brady	Kelly	Rosenior	Dickens*	Ince	Ward
18/1		30,110	*12*				*Platt 90*	*Spink*	*Price*	*Gray S*	*Gage*	*Mountfield*	*Keown*	*Gray A*	*Platt*	*McInally*	*Cowans*	*Daley**	*Olney*
							Ref: J Martin	Gale is acting captain for this emphatic win, which is distorted by David Platt's late overhead-kick. After eight minutes Price toppled Rosenior, but Spink saved Brady's penalty. Ince scored when the ball spun off Mountfield. When Keown flattened Rosenior, Kelly fired in the free-kick.											
SF	H	LUTON	20	L	0-3	0-1		McKnight	Potts	Dicks	Gale	Martin	Devonshire	Ward	Dickens	Rosenior	Brady*	Ince	Kelly
1 12/2		24,602	*14*				*Harford 45, Wegerle 55, Wilson 75p*	*Sealey*	*Breacker*	*Grimes*	*Preece*	*Foster*	*Beaumont*	*Wilson*	*Wegerle*	*Harford*	*Hill*	*Black*	
							Ref: G Courtney	McKnight cements West Ham's elimination by gifting Luton their two first goals, which beat him at his near post. Dicks' upended Wegerle for the penalty that put the seal on West Ham's defeat. Poor McKnight was cheered whenever he held a back-pass; he now makes way for Parkes.											
SF	A	LUTON	20	L	0-2	0-1		Parkes	Potts	Dicks	Gale	Martin	Kelly	Ward	Parris	Slater	Brady	Ince	
2 1/3		*12,020*	*14*				*Harford 43, Wegerle 55*	*Sealey*	*Breacker*	*Grimes*	*Preece*	*Foster*	*Beaumont*	*Wilson*	*Wegerle*	*Harford*	*Hill*	*Black*	
							Ref: D Axcell (Hammers lose 0-5 on aggregate)	Without the injured Rosenior, West Ham never look like recouping the deficit, which means John Lyall tastes defeat for the first time in five semi-finals. Luton had not lost in 20 cup-ties played on their plastic pitch. Once Harford had been set up by Preece, everyone went to sleep.											

FA Cup																			
3	H	ARSENAL	20	D	2-2	2-1	Dickens 18, Bould 41 (og)	McKnight	Stewart	Dicks	Potts	Martin	Devonshire*	Brady	Kelly	Rosenior	Dickens	Ince	Keen
8/1		22,017	*1*				*Merson 44, 65*	*Lukic*	*O'Leary*	*Winterburn*	*Thomas*	*Bould**	*Adams*	*Rocastle*	*Richardson*	*Smith*	*Merson*	*Marwood^*	*Davis/Groves*
							Ref: N Midgley	Top plays bottom, and bottom nearly wins. When Lukic and Bould get into a tizzy, trying to deal with Potts' high ball, West Ham lead 2-0. They need to hold out till half-time, but are pegged back when Merson beats McKnight with ease. A bout of head tennis precedes the equaliser.											
3R	A	ARSENAL	20	W	1-0	0-0	Rosenior 77	McKnight	Stewart	Dicks	Potts	Martin*	Devonshire	Brady^	Kelly	Rosenior	Dickens	Ince	Strodder/Keen
11/1		*44,124*	*1*					*Lukic*	*Dixon*	*Winterburn*	*Thomas*	*O'Leary*	*Adams*	*Rocastle**	*Richardson*	*Smith*	*Merson*	*Marwood^*	*Davis/Groves*
							Ref: N Midgley	26 league points separate the sides. Arsenal are the division's top scorers. Smith, Merson and Marwood have bagged 36 between them, but fail to put McKnight under any pressure. Rosenior's header wins it. On three out of four previous Cup meetings, the victors have gone on to win it.											
4	A	SWINDON	19	D	0-0	0-0		McKnight	Potts	Dicks	Gale	Martin	Devonshire*	Ward	Kelly	Rosenior	Brady	Ince	Dickens
28/1		*18,627*	*2:16*					*Digby*	*McLoughlin*	*Bodin*	*Jones*	*Calderwood*	*Gittens*	*Foley*	*Cornwell*	*Henry*	*MacLaren*	*Geddis**	*Hockaday*
							Ref: M Peck	An undistinguished cup-tie. After four minutes Rosenior fastened on to a poor back-pass but his effort was saved by Fraser Digby. After 48 minutes Digby saves from the same player. David Kelly hit the bar in the second half. Paul Ince had his name taken for excessive protests.											
4R	H	SWINDON	19	W	1-0	0-0	Rosenior 61	McKnight	Potts	Dicks	Gale	Martin*	Devonshire	Ward	Kelly^	Rosenior	Brady	Ince	Strodder/Dickens
1/2		24,723	*2:16*					*Digby*	*McLoughlin*	*Bodin*	*Jones*	*Calderwood*	*Gittens*	*Foley*	*Cornwell*	*Hockaday**	*MacLaren*	*Geddis*	*Henry*
							Ref: M Peck	Lou Macari's Swindon are denied the victory their enterprise warranted, leaving West Ham to slink away unable to believe their luck. Dicks' cross was missed by Kelly and Ince, but not by Rosenior. Twice West Ham have won the Cup after beating Swindon. Macari has left his mark!											
5	A	CHARLTON	20	W	1-0	0-0	Slater 53	Parkes	Potts	Parris	Gale	Martin	Devonshire*	Ward !	Dickens	Slater	Brady	Ince	Keen
18/2		*18,785*	*17*					*Bolder*	*Humphrey*	*Reid*	*Shirtliff*	*Pates*	*Peake**	*Lee R^*	*Mortimer*	*MacKenzie*	*Williams*	*Crooks*	*Leaburn/Campbell*
							Ref: J Ashworth	38-year-old Phil Parkes is recalled in goal, 10 years after he first signed for the Hammers. Charlton have not reached the last eight of the FA Cup for 42 years, but must have fancied their chances after Ward was sent off following a clash with Pates. Slater converts Devonshire's cross.											

QF	H	NORWICH	20	D	0-0	0-0	
	18/3	29,119	*2*				Ref: L Shapter
QF	A	NORWICH	20	L	1-3	0-2	Ince 74
R	22/3	*25,785*	*2*				*Allen 25, 27, Gordon 85*
							Ref: L Shapter

QF H NORWICH (18/3):
Parkes, Potts, Dicks, Gale, Strodder, Devonshire*, Kelly, Dickens, Slater, Brady, Ince, Keen
Gunn, Culverhouse, Bowen, Butterworth, Linighan, Townsend, Gordon, Rosario, Allen, Phelan, Putney, Fox*

Norwich are still chasing the double. The tie was played in a cold wind. *The Times* wrote of West Ham's attack: 'Kelly and Slater were as effective as anaesthetised flies'. Strodder hit the post for West Ham and Gordon for Norwich. Twice Linighan wasted free headers at corners.

QF R A NORWICH (22/3):
Parkes, Potts, Dicks, Gale, Strodder, Devonshire*, Kelly^, Dickens, Slater, Brady, Ince, Hilton/Keen
Gunn, Culverhouse, Bowen, Butterworth, Linighan, Townsend, Gordon, Rosario, Allen, Phelan, Putney, Crook*

Malcolm Allen bags two pickpocket goals for Norwich to leave West Ham chasing the improbable. They could never get a grip on City's 6ft 3in striker, Rosario, though they battled manfully to the end. There is nothing left in West Ham's season, other than near-inevitable relegation.

		Home					Away					
	P	W	D	L	F	A	W	D	L	F	A	Pts
1 Arsenal	38	10	6	3	35	19	12	4	3	38	17	76
2 Liverpool	38	11	5	3	33	11	11	5	3	32	17	76
3 Nott'm Forest	38	8	7	4	31	16	9	6	4	33	27	64
4 Norwich	38	8	7	4	23	20	9	4	6	25	25	62
5 Derby	38	9	3	7	23	18	8	4	7	17	20	58
6 Tottenham	38	8	6	5	31	24	7	6	6	29	22	57
7 Coventry	38	9	4	6	28	23	5	9	5	19	19	55
8 Everton	38	10	7	2	33	18	4	5	10	17	27	54
9 QP Rangers	38	9	5	5	23	16	5	6	8	20	21	53
10 Millwall	38	10	3	6	27	21	4	8	7	20	31	53
11 Manchester U	38	10	5	4	27	13	3	7	9	18	22	51
12 Wimbledon	38	10	3	6	30	19	4	6	9	20	27	51
13 Southampton	38	6	7	6	25	26	4	8	7	27	40	45
14 Charlton	38	6	7	6	25	24	4	5	10	19	34	42
15 Sheffield Wed	38	6	6	7	21	25	4	6	9	13	26	42
16 Luton	38	8	6	5	32	21	2	5	12	10	31	41
17 Aston Villa	38	7	6	6	25	22	2	7	10	20	34	40
18 Middlesbro'	38	6	7	6	28	30	3	5	11	16	31	39
19 WEST HAM	38	3	6	10	19	30	7	2	10	18	32	38
20 Newcastle	38	3	6	10	19	28	4	4	11	13	35	31
	760	157	112	111	538	424	111	112	157	424	538	1028

Odds & ends

Double wins: (2) Newcastle, Millwall.
Double losses: (8) Southampton, Man U, Arsenal, Middlesbrough, Liverpool, Everton, Spurs, Norwich.

Won from behind: (2) Derby (h), Newcastle (a).
Lost from in front: (4) QPR (a), Man U (h), Middlesbrough (h), Everton (a).

High spots: Four successive league wins from 22 April to give a fighting chance of avoiding relegation.
Reaching semi-final of Littlewoods Cup.

Low spots: Relegation.
The anguish of having to wait several days after the last match to have relegation confirmed.

Hammer of the Year Paul Ince.
Ever-presents: (0).
Hat-tricks: (0).
Leading scorer: (11) Leroy Rosenior.

	Appearances						Goals			
	Lge	*Sub*	LC	*Sub*	FAC	*Sub*	Lge	LC	FAC	Tot
Brady, Liam	**21**	*1*	4	*1*	7		**3**			**3**
Devonshire, Alan	**14**	*6*	4		7					
Dickens, Alan	**34**	*3*	6		5	*2*	**5**	1	1	**7**
Dicks, Julian	**34**		7		6		**2**			**2**
Gale, Tony	**31**		6		5			1		**1**
Hilton, Paul	**9**	*2*	2			*1*				
Ince, Paul	**32**	*1*	7		7		**3**	3	1	**7**
Keen, Kevin	**16**	*8*	1	*1*		*5*	**3**	1		**4**
Kelly, David	**21**	*4*	6	*1*	6		**6**	4		**10**
McAlister, Tom	**2**									
McAvennie, Frank	**8**	*1*								
McKnight, Allen	**23**		6		4					
McQueen, Tom		*2*								
Martin, Alvin	**27**		5		5		**1**	2		**3**
Parkes, Phil	**13**		1		3					
Parris, George	**23**	*4*	3		1		**1**			**1**
Potts, Steve	**23**	*5*	5	*1*	7					
Rosenior, Leroy	**26**	*2*	5		4		**7**	2	2	**11**
Robson, Stewart	**6**		1							
Slater, Stuart	**16**	*2*	1		3		**1**		1	**2**
Stewart, Ray	**5**	*1*	1		2		**2**	1		**3**
Strodder, Gary	**4**	*3*	1		2	*2*				
Ward, Mark	**30**		5	*1*	3		**2**			**2**
(own-goals)							**1**	1	1	**3**
23 players used	**418**	***45***	**77**	***5***	**77**	***10***	**37**	**16**	**6**	**59**

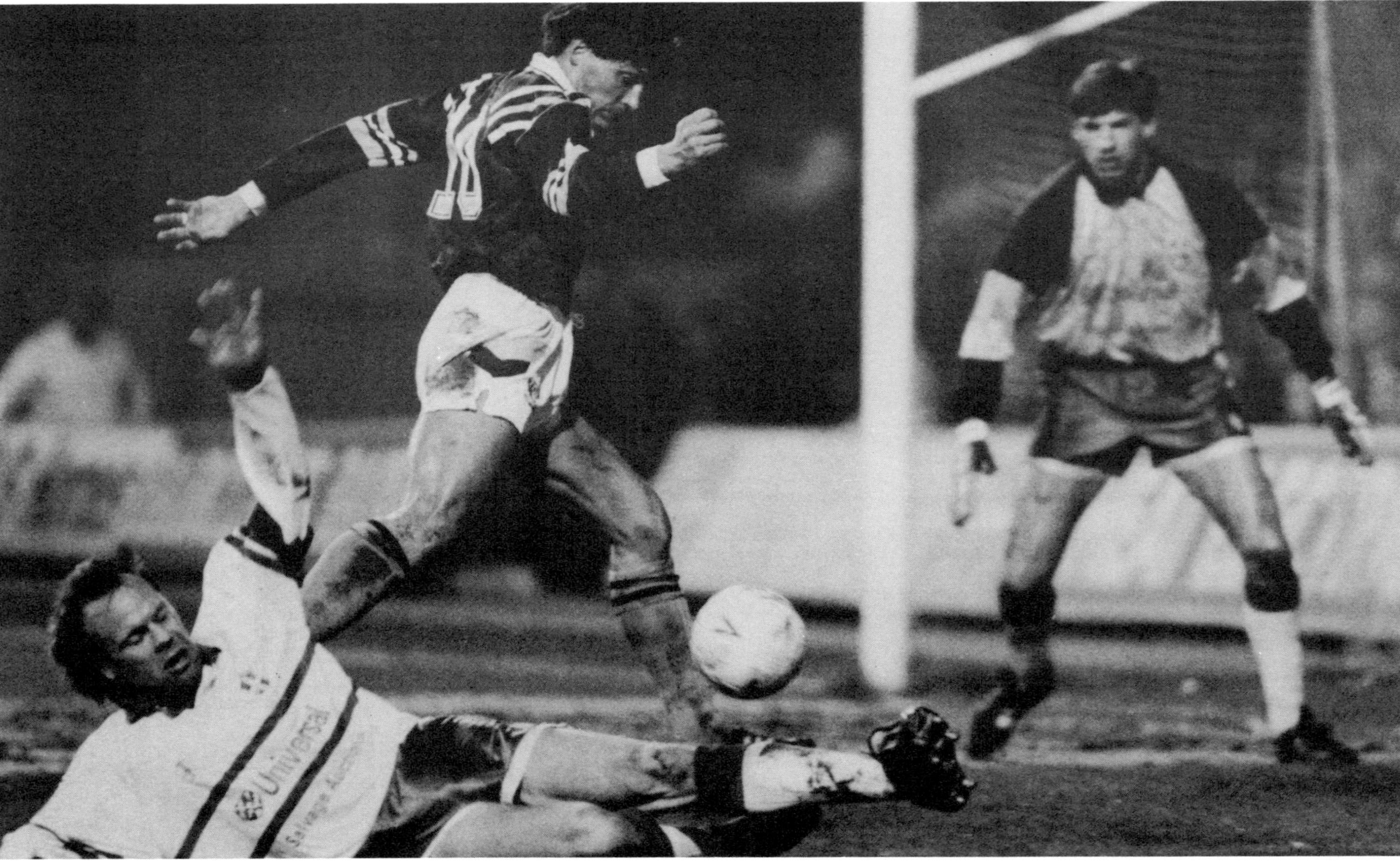

Trevor Morley in action at Luton

Tony Cottee scores at Upton Park

BARCLAYS LEAGUE DIVISION 2

Manager: Lou Macari ⇨ Billy Bonds

SEASON 1989-90

No	Date		Att	Pos	Pt	F-A	H-T	Scorers, Times, and Referees	1	2	3	4	5	6	7	8	9	10	11	subs used
1	A	STOKE			D	1-1	1-0	Keen 32	Parkes	Potts	Parris	Gale	Martin	Keen	Ward	McAvennie*	Slater	Brady	Ince	Kelly
	19/8		16,058		1			Biggins 85	Fox	Butler	Statham	Kamara	Cranson	Beeston	Hackett	Scott*	Bamber	Biggins	Beagrie	Saunders
								Ref: G Aplin	Motorway roadworks delayed kick-off by 17 minutes. New boss Macari sees record buy Frank McAvennie break a leg in a 55th-minute clash with Chris Kamara. Hammers were ahead through Keen's goal, against the run of play. Beagrie's cross was glanced in by Wayne Biggins.											
2	H	BRADFORD C			W	2-0	2-0	Slater 32, 33	Parkes	Potts	Dicks	Gale	Martin	Keen	Ward	Kelly	Slater	Brady	Parris	
	23/8		19,914		4				Tomlinson	Abbott	Tinnion	Aizlewood	Sinnott	Evans	Duxbury	Davies	Jewell	Quinn	Ellis*	Chapman
								Ref: B Hill	With Rosenior and McAvennie injured, Macari is short of strikers. Talk of Ince about to sign for Man U has the crowd chanting: 'We hate Paul Ince.' Slater's cheeky solo goal, when he skipped round Mark Aizlewood, was capped seconds later when he was unmarked for Ward's cross.											
3	H	PLYMOUTH		1	W	3-2	1-0	Kelly 20, Allen 50, Keen 75	Parkes	Potts	Dicks	Gale	Martin	Keen	Ward	Kelly	**Allen M**	Brady	Parris	
	26/8		20,231		7			Stuart 54, 77	Wilmot	Brown	Brimcombe	Marker	Burrows	Smith	Byrne	McCarthy	Tynan	Thomas	Stuart	
								Ref: T Holbrook	Martin Allen has signed from QPR for £675,000, having had a bust-up with Trevor Francis over attending the birth of his child. His header makes it 2-0. It was 3-1 when Ward's shot was blocked but Keen followed up. When Stuart fired inside the near post it set up a nervy climax.											
4	A	HULL		1	D	1-1	1-0	Ward 5	Parkes	Potts	Dicks	Gale	Martin	Keen	Ward	Kelly !	Allen	Brady*	Slater	Devonshire
	2/9		9,235		8			Swan 64	Kelly	Murray*	Jacobs	Swan	Terry	Jobson^	Askew	Roberts	Brown	McParland	Doyle !	de Mange/Jenkinson
								Ref: J Ashworth	Kelly's cross is turned in by Mark Ward for the perfect start. Hull's makeshift striker Peter Swan levelled at the second attempt. Four minutes from time Dicks' free-kick cannons off the wall and a free-for-all ensues. Kelly and Doyle are sent off. Suspension will claim another striker.											
5	H	SWINDON		3	D	1-1	1-0	Allen 16	Parkes	Potts	Dicks	Gale	Martin	Keen	Ward	Kelly*	Allen	Brady^	Parris	Dolan/Devonshire
	9/9		21,469	14	9			Gittens 53	Digby	Barnard	King	McLoughlin	Calderwood	Gittens	Jones	Close	White	MacLaren	Galvin*	Cornwall
								Ref: A Seville	Stuart Slater missed this match, having run into a goal-post in training. Ward combined with Liam Brady down the left for the first goal; John Gittens flicked over Parkes' head for the equaliser. Dicks and Galvin were booked for dissent in a match that at times threatened to boil over.											
6	A	BRIGHTON		8	L	**0-3**	0-3		Parkes	Potts	Dicks	Gale	Martin	Keen	Ward	Slater	Allen	Brady	Parris	
	16/9		12,689	2	9			Bremner 4, Codner 15, Nelson 18	Keeley	Chivers	Chapman*	Curbishley	Bissett	Gatting	Trusson	Wood	Bremner	Codner	Wilkins	Owers
								Ref: R Wiseman	A cold wet day, and West Ham trail 0-3 after just 18 minutes. The crucial first goal was a deflected header. West Ham might have clawed their way back, but when Bissett felled Ward on 53 mins, Brady's penalty was saved. Macari kept his players behind locked doors for over an hour.											
7	H	WATFORD		5	W	1-0	1-0	Dicks 17p	Parkes	Potts	Dicks	Gale	Martin	Keen	Allen	Slater	Dolan*	**Foster**	Parris	Rosenior
	23/9		20,728	9	12				Coton	Gibbins	Jackett	Richardson*	Holdsworth	Roeder	Thomas	Wilkinson	Roberts^	Porter	Hodges	Henry/Falconer
								Ref: K Morton	21-year-old Dicks is made skipper in place of Alvin Martin, who had held the honour for five years. When Gary Porter tugged Slater's shirt, Dicks obliged from the spot. Watford boss Steve Harrison complained that Potts twice handled in the box, but got away with it each time.											
8	A	PORTSMOUTH		2	W	1-0	0-0	Rosenior 89	Parkes	Potts	Dicks	Gale	Martin	Keen	Allen	Slater	Rosenior	Foster	Parris	
	26/9		12,632	21	15				Knight	Maguire	Beresford	Fillery	Sandford	Ball	Wigley*	Kuhl	Whittingham	Chamberlain	Black	Neill
								Ref: D Hutchinson	Pompey are on a high following good results against Man U in the Littlewoods Cup and Middlesbrough in the league. Though still unfit, and having had two operations this year, Leroy Rosenior wants to play. He bags a precious late winner when George Parris cuts the ball back.											
9	H	WEST BROM		7	L	2-3	0-2	Dolan 68, Parris 70	Parkes	Potts	Dicks	Gale	Martin	Keen	Allen	Slater	Kelly*	Foster	Parris	Dolan
	30/9		19,842	12	15			Ford 14, McNally 33, 73p	Naylor	Bradley	Burgess	Robson*	Whyte	North	Ford	Goodman	Thomas	McNally	Anderson	Talbot
								Ref: M Bodenham	George Parris made one goal and scored another – nutmegging Burgess and chipping Naylor – to haul West Ham back on level terms. Foster completed a wretched match by pushing Whyte for the decisive penalty. Foster had also been at fault when Goodman's cross made it 2-0.											
10	H	LEEDS		10	L	0-1	0-1		Parkes	Potts	Dicks	Gale*	Martin	Keen	Allen	Slater	Ward	Foster	Parris	Brady
	7/10		23,539	3	15			Jones 22	Day	Sterland	Whitlow	Jones	Fairclough	Haddock	Strachan	Barry	Baird	Davison*	Williams	Shutt
								Ref: R Groves	An aimless match, settled by Vinnie Jones, who turned in Michael Whitlow's low cross. Stuart Slater was caught offside five times in the first seven minutes. Gale collided with Batty and went off with knee trouble. West Ham hardly ever threatened ex-Hammer Mervyn Day in goal.											
11	A	SHEFFIELD UTD		8	W	2-0	1-0	Ward 38, 71p	Parkes	Potts	Dicks	Strodder	Martin	Keen	Ward	Slater	Dolan	Foster	Parris	
	14/10		20,822	1	18				Tracey	Hill*	Rostron	Booker	Stancliffe	Morris	Bradshaw	Gannon	Agana	Deane	Bryson^	Todd/Francis
								Ref: K Redfern	United lose their unbeaten record but retain their top position. Hammers' hero is Mark Ward, signed from Oldham for £250,000 in 1985, but unsettled at Upton Park. At 0-0 Tracey fouled Slater but Dicks' penalty hit the bar. When Jones felled Dolan, Ward took the kick himself.											

No	Venue	Opponent	Att	Pos	Res	FT	HT	Scorers, Times, and Referees												subs used
12	H	SUNDERLAND		7	W	**5-0**	3-0	Allen 9, Slater 16, Keen 41, Dolan 85, 86	Parkes	Potts	Dicks*	Strodder	Martin	Keen	Ward	Slater	Dolan	Allen	Parris	Brady
18/10			20,901	*8*	21				*Carter*	*Kay*	*Hardyman*	*Bennett*	*MacPhail*	*Owers*	*Bracewell*	*Armstrong*	*Gates**	*Gabbiadini*	*Pascoe^*	*Cullen/Hauser*
								Ref: J Martin	It takes Parris just 15 seconds to be booked and just nine minutes for Allen to curl the opening goal. When Slater chested down and volleyed No 2 you knew it wouldn't be Sunderland's day. Said boss Denis Smith: 'God knows what a full-strength Hammers would have done to us.'											
13	A	PORT VALE		4	D	2-2	1-0	Keen 43, Slater 64	Parkes	Potts	Dicks	Strodder	Martin	Keen	Ward	Slater	Dolan	Allen	Parris	
21/10			*8,899*	*16*	22			*Martin 51 (og), Futcher 87*	*Grew*	*Webb*	*Hughes*	*Walker**	*Aspin*	*Glover*	*Miller^*	*Earle*	*Cross*	*Beckford*	*Mills*	*Jeffers/Futcher*
								Ref: J Hendrick	Wet and blustery, and motorway hold-ups delays the kick-off. Keen sprints from the halfway line to make it 1-0, only for Martin to head into his own net. Dolan's header hit a post before Slater restored the lead. Beckford headed down Webb's cross for Ron Futcher to make it 2-2.											
14	H	OXFORD		5	W	3-2	1-1	Parris 18, Slater 55, Dicks 69	Parkes	Potts	Dicks	Strodder	Martin	Keen	Brady	Slater	Dolan	Allen	Parris	
28/10			19,177	*20*	25			*Stein 16, Mustoe 57*	*Judge*	*Smart*	*Phillips*	*Lewis*	*Foster*	*Greenall*	*Mustoe*	*Ford*	*Durin*	*Stein*	*Heath**	*Simpson*
								Ref: D Axcell	Liam Brady is the architect of this exciting win, which is remembered largely for two thunderbolts. George Parris's bullet from outside the area was a quick riposte to Marke Stein's opener. After Robbie Mustoe's equaliser Keen's short free-kick enabled Dicks' to fire a 30-yard screamer.											
15	A	BOURNEMOUTH		5	D	1-1	1-1	Strodder 33	Parkes	Potts	Dicks	Strodder	Martin	Keen*	Brady	Slater	Dolan	Allen	Parris	Ward
1/11			*9,979*	*14*	26			*Blissett 21*	*Peyton*	*Bond*	*Coleman*	*Teale*	*Shearer*	*Peacock*	*O'Connor*	*Moulden*	*O'Driscoll*	*Brooks*	*Blissett*	
								Ref: H King	West Ham have never beaten the Cherries, but might have done had Keen's 71st-minute effort bounced in, rather than off the post. Ref Howard King gave Macari a lift home afterwards, and one wonders whether they discussed Luther Blisset's chipped goal, which looked to be offside.											
16	A	WOLVES		5	L	0-1	0-0		Parkes	Potts	Dicks	Strodder	Martin	Keen*	Brady	Slater	Dolan^	Allen	Parris	Ward/Foster
4/11			*22,231*	*11*	26			*Bull 66*	*Kendall*	*Bennett*	*Venus*	*Bellamy*	*Westley*	*Downing*	*Thompson*	*Cook*	*Bull*	*Mutch*	*Dennison*	
								Ref: W Flood	West Ham managed just two shots on target – from Strodder and Allen – so they can have few complaints. Steve Bull had been sent off in midweek against Leicester. But now he took a delicate pass from Mutch, swept past Strodder, and scored coolly. Parkes was the busier keeper.											
17	H	NEWCASTLE		7	D	0-0	0-0		Parkes	Potts	Dicks	Strodder	Martin	Keen	Brady*	Slater	Dolan^	Ward	Parris	Devonshire/Kelly
11/11			**25,892**	*3*	27				*Burridge*	*Ranson*	*Stimson*	*Dillon*	*Scott*	*Kristensen*	*Brazil**	*Brock^*	*Quinn*	*McGhee*	*O'Brien*	*Gallagher/Anderson*
								Ref: D Hedges	This was a no-holds-barred encounter that conjured up few memorable moments. Brady's 25-yard free-kick was turned aside by John Burridge, and sub David Kelly was off-target with a bicycle-kick. Jim Smith was the happier manager. Police had to go into the crowd to eject hooligans.											
18	H	MIDDLESBROUGH		5	W	2-0	1-0	Slater 8, Dicks 59p	Parkes	Potts	Dicks	Foster	Martin	Keen	Brady	Slater	Allen	Ward	Parris	
18/11			18,720	*21*	30				*Poole*	*Parkinson*	*Mohan*	*Mowbray*	*Coleman*	*Putney*	*Slaven*	*Proctor*	*Burke**	*Brennan*	*Davenport*	*Kernaghan*
								Ref: K Cooper	Slater fears for his place now that Justin Fashanu has signed on loan, and scores with a low, angled shot. The lead was doubled when Parris was toppled by Simon Coleman in the box. The score looks comfortable but is deceptive. Slaven and Kernaghan both hit the wood late on.											
19	A	BLACKBURN		7	L	4-5	1-4	Brady 38, Dicks 47p, Slater 64, Ward 87	Parkes	Potts	Dicks	Strodder	Martin	Devonshire	Brady	Slater	Allen	Ward	**Fashanu**	
25/11			*10,215*	*5*	30			*Sellars 4,9, Garner 29, Stap' 34, Johnrose 46*	*Collier*	*Atkins*	*Sulley*	*Reid*	*Hill*	*May*	*Irvine*	*Johnrose*	*Stapleton*	*Garner**	*Sellars*	*Kennedy*
								Ref: T Holbrook	The score sounds close until it is realised that West Ham were 0-4 down after 33 minutes and 1-5 after 46 minutes. Brady had pulled one back for West Ham when chesting down and turning to score. Keith Hill handled for Dicks' penalty. Devonshire plays his first game of the season.											
20	H	STOKE		7	D	0-0	0-0		Parkes	Potts	Dicks	Strodder	Martin	Devonshire*	Brady	Slater	Keen	Ward	Fashanu^	Kelly/Foster
2/12			17,704	*23*	31				*Fox*	*Butler*	*Carr*	*Kamara*	*Higgins*	*Berry*	*Hackett*	*Beeston*	*Saunders*	*Biggins*	*Hilaire*	
								Ref: B Hill	Stoke's Chris Kamara was booed constantly for the tackle which broke McAvennie's leg on the opening day. Alan Ball's team relied on the offside trap, but should have lost when Butler tripped Ward after 55 mins. Dicks had already scored 7 penalties, but this one was saved by Fox.											
21	A	BRADFORD C		7	L	1-2	1-1	Ward 29	Parkes	Potts	McQueen	Strodder	Martin	Gale	Brady	Slater	Keen	Ward	Allen	
9/12			*9,257*	*19*	31			*Leonard 15, Quinn 90*	*Tomlinson*	*Mitchell*	*Tinnion**	*Aizlewood*	*Oliver*	*Abbott*	*Megson*	*Evans*	*Leonard*	*Quinn*	*Campbell*	*Davies*
								Ref: A Wilkie	Hammers missed chances galore and cannot believe they lost. Brady had set up Ward's equaliser, after Leonard's header had put City in front. Thereafter there was only one team in it, but nearly three minutes into stoppage-time Jimmy Quinn was left unmarked on the edge of the box.											
22	H	OLDHAM		8	L	0-2	0-2		**Suckling**	Potts	Dicks	Strodder*	Martin	Gale	Brady	Slater	Foster^	Ward	Allen	Keen/Devonshire
16/12			**14,960**	*4*	31			*Milligan 3, Ritchie 20*	*Rhodes*	*Irwin*	*Barlow*	*Henry*	*Barratt*	*Warhurst**	*Marshall*	*Ritchie*	*Bunn*	*Milligan*	*Holden R*	*Palmer*
								Ref: B Hamer	With Parkes having crocked knees and Miklosko's work permit being delayed, Perry Suckling is signed on loan from Palace. He is quickly beaten by Mike Milligan's header into the top corner. Irwin's cross was then turned in by Foster and Ritchie. Irwin's free-kick also hit the post.											
23	A	IPSWICH		10	L	0-1	0-1		Suckling	Potts	Dicks	Strodder	Martin	Gale	Brady*	Slater^	Keen	Ward	Allen	Parris/Kelly
26/12			*24,365*	*5*	31			*Stockwell 40*	*Forrest*	*Stockwell*	*Thompson*	*Zondervan**	*Yallop*	*Linighan*	*Donowa*	*Dozzell*	*Wark*	*Kiwomya^*	*Milton*	*Humes/D'Avray*
								Ref: J Ashworth	West Ham have been beaten 3-4 by Chelsea in the Zenith-Data Cup. This Boxing Day fixture brings out Portman Road's biggest gate in four years. Louis Donowa's cross to Mick Stockwell earns three more points for John Duncan's young side. Bonds played Tony Gale in midfield.											

No	Date	Att	Pos	Pt	F-A	H-T	Scorers, Times, and Referees	1	2	3	4	5	6	7	8	9	10	11	subs used
24	A LEICESTER		11	L	0-1	0-0		Suckling	Potts	Dicks	Strodder	Martin	Gale	Allen	**Bishop**	**Morley**	Kelly	Parris	
	30/12	*16,925*	*13*	31			*Mauchlen 88*	*Hodge*	*Mauchlen*	*Spearing**	*Mills*	*Walsh*	*Paris*	*Reid^*	*Moran*	*Campbell*	*McAllister*	*Wright*	*James/North*
							Ref: J Deakin	West Ham's dreadful run – one point from six games – continues, this time against David Pleat's resurgent Leicester. City were bottom of the league in October, but have now won five of their last six. Mauchlen's late strike is his first and last goal of the season. 1989 ends on a downer.											
25	H BARNSLEY		11	W	4-2	3-0	Allen 4, Keen 23, 42, Dicks 50p	Suckling	Potts	Dicks	Parris	Martin	Gale	**Quinn**	Bishop	Keen*	Morley	Allen	Kelly
	1/1	18,391	*21*	34			*Dobbin 75, Archdeacon 88*	*Baker*	*Dobbin*	*Cross*	*Futcher*	*Sholton*	*Smith**	*Broddle^*	*Agnew*	*Foreman*	*Currie*	*Archdeacon*	*Cooper/Tiler*
							Ref: M James	Jimmy Quinn is the latest addition to West Ham's ranks. None of the three new buys gets on the scoresheet, but Trevor Morley comes closest – twice hitting the woodwork. Morley was also fouled for the penalty. Strangest goal was Keen's first, a cross which floated in off the far post.											
26	A PLYMOUTH		10	D	1-1	0-1	Quinn 56	Suckling	Potts	Dicks	Gale	Martin	Devonshire*	Allen	Bishop	Keen^	Morley	Quinn	Brady/Parris
	13/1	*11,671*	*16*	35			*Tynan 2*	*Wilmot*	*Brown*	*Broddle*	*Marker*	*Burrows*	*Hodges*	*Summerfield*	*McCarthy**	*Tynan*	*Thomas*	*Robson*	*Campbell*
							Ref: M Reed	West Ham have been knocked out of the FA Cup by Torquay, and they are equally dreadful against these other west country opponents, who had not won at home in six attempts. Lou Macari refused to face the press afterwards over rumours of financial irregularities while at Swindon.											
27	H HULL		11	L	1-2	1-1	Morley 17	Suckling	Potts*	McQueen	Strodder^	Martin	Gale	Brady	Bishop	Quinn	Morley	Keen	**Kelly P**/Kelly D
	20/1	16,847	*19*	35			*Buckley 34, Payton 60*	*Hesford*	*Brown*	*Jacobs*	*Jobson*	*Buckley*	*de Mange*	*Roberts*	*Payton**	*Whitehurst*	*Askew*	*Doyle*	*Agata*
							Ref: R Nixon	Paul Kelly makes his second-half debut but cannot prevent struggling Hull deepening Macari's wounds. West Ham looked punchless in attack, despite scoring first when Quinn's shot bounced off a defender to Morley. Buckley headed Hull level, then Payton converted de Mange's cross.											
28	H BRIGHTON		11	W	3-1	0-1	Quinn 60, 84, Dicks 78	Parkes	Robson	Dicks	Parris*	Martin	Gale	Brady	Bishop	Kelly	Slater	Keen	Quinn
	10/2	19,101	*22*	38			*Nelson 14*	*Keeley*	*Chivers*	*Chapman*	*Curbishley*	*Gatting*	*Dublin*	*Nelson*	*Barham*	*Bissett*	*Codner*	*Wilkins*	
							Ref: P Danson	Quinn's half-time arrival transformed the match. Gary Nelson's close-range header had put lowly Brighton in front. Steve Gatting's comical lob over his own keeper set up the equaliser. Dicks then uncorked one of his 30-yard scorchers, before Quinn headed in Keen's free-kick.											
29	A SWINDON		12	D	2-2	1-1	Quinn 29, 70	**Miklosko**	Robson	Dicks	Parris	Martin	Gale	Brady	Allen	Quinn	Slater*	Keen^	Bishop/Kelly
	18/2	*16,105*	*3*	39			*White 42, MacLaren 66*	*Digby*	*Kerslake*	*Bodin*	*McLoughlin*	*Calderwood*	*Gittens*	*Jones*	*Shearer*	*White*	*MacLaren*	*Foley*	
							Ref: V Callow	A Sunday match. Macari was absent, rather than face his ex-club, and Bonds takes charge. Not the most promising time for Miklosko to make his debut after his £300,000 transfer, but two saves from Tom Jones secures a point. Quinn's header equalised MacLaren's deflected free-kick.											
30	H BLACKBURN		14	D	1-1	1-0	Quinn 23	Miklosko	Robson*	Dicks	Parris	Martin	Gale	Brady^	Allen	Quinn	Slater	Keen	Kelly/Bishop
	24/2	20,054	*6*	40			*Sellars 78*	*Gennoe*	*Atkins*	*Sulley*	*Reid*	*Moran*	*Mail*	*Kennedy*	*Millar*	*Stapleton*	*Garner**	*Sellars*	*Gayle*
							Ref: M Bodenham	Billy Bonds has been installed as manager, having played almost 800 games for the club, and he receives a rapturous welcome. Quinn's diving header is the least West Ham deserve for their first-half dominance, but Scott Sellars poached an equaliser from Howard Gayle's cross.											
31	A MIDDLESBROUGH		10	W	1-0	0-0	Allen 86	Miklosko	Robson	Dicks	Parris	Martin	Gale	Brady*	Allen	Quinn^	Slater	Keen	Bishop/Morley
	3/3	*23,617*	*21*	43				*Pears*	*Parkinson*	*McGee*	*Kernaghan*	*Coleman*	*Proctor*	*Slaven*	*Kerr**	*Baird*	*Brennan*	*Ripley*	*Davenport*
							Ref: J Kirkby	Dicks announces: 'It is better now Lou Macari has gone.' Perhaps Dicks was on Cloud Nine after Pears failed to hold his shot and Martin Allen nips in for a late winner. It is Bonds' first win and Hammers' first away win since October. The less said about the rest of the match the better.											
32	H PORTSMOUTH		10	W	2-1	1-0	Allen 32, Dicks 81p	Miklosko	Slater	Dicks	Parris	Foster	Gale	Brady*	Allen	Rosenior^	Keen	Kelly	Quinn/Bishop
	10/3	20,961	*17*	46			*Kuhl 63*	*Knight*	*Neill*	*Sevens*	*Fillery**	*Hogg*	*Ball*	*Wigley*	*Kuhl*	*Whittingham*	*Black*	*Chamberlain*	*Gilligan*
							Ref: D Axcell	West Ham did not perform, and Bonds admits Portsmouth were unlucky to lose to Kevin Ball's Maradona-style handball in his own box. Guy Whittingham had outjumped Foster – playing his first game since December – to draw level. A Dicks raid down the left brought the first goal.											
33	A WATFORD		10	W	1-0	0-0	Morley 61	Miklosko	Slater	Dicks	Parris	Foster	Gale	Bishop	Allen	Quinn	Keen	Morley	
	13/3	*15,683*	*13*	49				*Coton*	*Williams*	*Drysdale*	*Richardson*	*Holdsworth*	*Roeder*	*Thomas*	*Allison**	*Pullan*	*Penrice*	*Ashby*	*Roberts*
							Ref: M Pierce	Watford started at a gallop, but once West Ham had weathered the storm they were always the more likely winners. Gale's free-kick led to Trevor Morley side-footing home at the far post. When Holdsworth felled Morley in the box, Dicks' penalty was turned aside by Tony Coton.											
34	A LEEDS		10	L	2-3	0-2	Morley 51, Chapman 68 (og)	Miklosko	Slater	McQueen	Parris*	Foster	Gale	Bishop	Allen	Quinn	Keen	Morley	Brady
	17/3	***32,536***	*1*	49			*Chapman 18, 42, Strachan 64*	*Day*	*Sterland*	*Snodin*	*Jones*	*Fairclough*	*Haddock*	*Strachan*	*Speed*	*Chapman*	*Varadi**	*Hendrie*	*Shutt*
							Ref: K Redfern	Wilkinson's Leeds are unbeaten at home and heading for the championship. Gordon Strachan plays a blinder, setting up Lee Chapman's goals with a back-heel and a lob, before scoring himself. Chapman netted three times, but the third was at the wrong end, diverting Foster's header.											

No	Venue / Date	Opponent	Att	Pos	Pts	Res	FT	HT	Scorers, Times, and Referees	1	2	3	4	5	6	7	8	9	10	11	subs used
35	H	SHEFFIELD UTD		9		W	5-0	1-0	Morley 4, Quinn 53p, 57, 80, Allen 72	Miklosko	Slater	McQueen	Parris	Foster	Gale	Bishop	Allen	Quinn	Keen	Morley	
	21/3		21,629	2	52					Tracey	Wilder	Rostron	Booker	Morris	Todd*	Wood^	Gannon	Whitehurst	Deane	Bryson	Hill/Bradshaw
									Ref: G Ashby	Blades' first league defeat since 1 January is a humiliating affair for manager Bassett. Man-of-the-match Slater pulled the strings, tormenting full-back Wilder and setting up goals for Morley and Quinn, who has scored six goals in five games. Tracey fouled Morley for the penalty.											
36	A	SUNDERLAND		10		L	3-4	1-1	Quinn 15, 58, Morley 80 [Gabbiadini 77]	Miklosko	Slater	McQueen	Parris	Strodder	Gale	Bishop	Allen	Quinn	Keen*	Morley	Brady
	24/3		13,896	9	52				Brady 24, Hardyman 60p, Owers 70,	Norman	Kay	Hardyman*	Heathcote	MacPhail	Owers	Bracewell	Armstrong	Brady	Gabbiadini	Pascoe	Agboola
									Ref: T Mills	Dicks was eligible, but injured a thigh in training. With Martin out with tonsillitis, and Foster also injured, Bonds has little option choosing his defence. Pick of the goals was Kieron Brady's overhead kick. When Hardyman made it 2-2 from the spot, Sunderland began to take control.											
37	H	PORT VALE		10		D	2-2	0-0	Morley 53, Gale 58	Miklosko	Slater	Dicks	Parris	Foster	Gale	Bishop	Allen	Quinn*	Keen^	Morley	McAvennie/Brady
	31/3		20,507	11	53				Beckford 54, Cross 75	Grew	Mills	Hughes	Walker	Parkin	Glover	Porter	Earle	Millar*	Beckford	Jeffers	Cross
									Ref: K Barratt	This match produced a rarity – two separate penalties saved by two different players. Mark Grew was Vale's hero, saving from Dicks at 0-0 and from Quinn at 2-1, after Gale's header had restored the lead. The misses proved costly when sub Nicky Cross equalised for the Valiants.											
38	A	WEST BROM		10		W	3-1	2-1	Quinn 6, Bishop 28, Keen 69	Miklosko	Slater	Dicks	Parris	Strodder	Gale	Bishop	Allen	Quinn	Keen	Morley	
	4/4		11,556	16	56				Goodman 30	Naylor	Bradley	Harbey	Shakespeare	North	Whyte	Ford	Goodman	Bannister	Cartwright	Hackett*	Foster
									Ref: C Trussell	15 goals in five games sounds good, but West Ham have also let in 10, which is not so good. When Stacey North handled outside the box, Quinn's free-kick was deflected in. Quinn's far-post header made No 2 for Bishop. Goodman pulled one back after a corner was nodded on.											
39	A	OXFORD		8		W	2-0	0-0	Morley 69, Quinn 80	Miklosko	Slater	Dicks	Parris	Foster	Gale	Bishop	Allen	Quinn	Keen*	Morley	McQueen
	7/4		8,371	14	59					Kee	Smart	Ford	Lewis	Foster	Evans	Heath*	Mustoe	Durin	Stein	Simpson	Foyle
									Ref: P Vanes	'We didn't play: it is as simple as that,' is Bonds' frank assessment of West Ham's flattering win over Brian Horton's Oxford. Goal No 1 came when Paul Kee failed to gather Bishop's corner. Quinn's 30-yard daisy-trimmer made the points safe but Miklosko played his best game so far.											
40	H	BOURNEMOUTH		8		W	4-1	2-1	Miller 20 (og), Bishop 21, Dicks 64p, [Allen 74]	Miklosko	Slater	Dicks	Parris*	Foster	Gale	Bishop	Allen	Quinn	Keen	Morley^	Potts/McAvennie
	11/4		20,202	19	62				Coleman 37	Peyton	Slatter*	Coleman	Shearer	Miller	Peacock	O'Driscoll	Redknapp	Aylott^	Holmes	Blissett	Mundee/Cadette
									Ref: R Hamer	Cherries' manager Harry Redknapp has nothing but praise for the Hammers. This is the third game in a row in which Quinn scores a deflected goal, but this time the deviation is so great he cannot claim it. Miller's foul on Quinn earned the penalty. Quinn then nodded on for Allen.											
41	A	BARNSLEY		8		D	1-1	1-1	Morley 24	Miklosko	Slater	Dicks	Parris	Foster	Gale	Keen	Allen	Quinn	Morley	Brady	
	14/4		10,344	18	63				Taggart 11	Baker	Fleming	Taggart	Tiler	Cross	Smith	McCord*	Banks	Saville	Agnew	Cooper^	Lowndes/O'Connell
									Ref: M Peck	This Easter fixture brought a rousing performance from West Ham, but the two dropped points suggest the play-offs may be beyond Billy Bonds' team. Barnsley's needs are of a different order. They are now unbeaten in six, and their late-season rally will stave off relegation.											
42	H	IPSWICH		7		W	2-0	2-0	Allen 27, Keen 36	Miklosko	Slater	Dicks	Parris	Foster	Gale	Brady^	Allen	Quinn	Keen	Morley*	McAvennie/Potts
	17/4		25,178	10	66					Forrest	Yallop	Thompson	Zondervan	Gayle	Linighan	Kiwomya*	Stuart	Wark	Dozzell	Milton^	Donowa/Humes
									Ref: K Burge	Kevin Keen steals the show in this, his 100th senior appearance for the Hammers. His slide-rule pass makes the first goal for Martin Allen, and he scores the second with a thumping volley. John Duncan's Ipswich pressed hard, and Miklosko saved well from Linighan and Dozzell.											
43	A	OLDHAM		7		L	0-3	0-0		Miklosko	Slater	Dicks	Parris	Foster	Gale	Brady	Allen	Quinn	Keen	Morley*	McQueen
	21/4		12,190	9	66				Ritchie 52p, Bunn 55, 85	Rhodes	Irwin	Barlow	Henry	Barrett	Warhurst	Redfearn	Ritchie	Bunn	Milligan	Holden R	
									Ref: K Barratt	Oldham haunt West Ham's season, inflicting their heaviest cup and league defeats. West Ham were faring well until the 52nd minute when Miklosko brought down Redfearn, but insisted he had played the ball first. Once Ritchie had converted from the spot, West Ham fell apart.											
44	A	NEWCASTLE		7		L	1-2	1-0	Dicks 35p	Miklosko	Slater	Dicks	Potts	Foster	Gale	Robson	Allen	Quinn*	Keen	Morley^	McAvennie/Parris
	28/4		31,496	3	66				Kristensen 52, Quinn 56	Burridge	Scott	Stimpson	Aitken	Anderson	Ranson	Brown	Dillon*	Quinn	McGhee	Kristensen	O'Brien
									Ref: V Callow	Dicks' penalty, when Martin Allen was knocked off the ball, was just reward for West Ham's first-half dominance. The Magpies took control after the break, taking all three points when Mick Quinn netted his 36th goal of the season. Frank McAvennie came on for the last 30 minutes.											
45	H	LEICESTER		7		W	3-1	2-0	Rosenior 28, Keen 36, Morley 48	Miklosko	Slater	Dicks	Potts	Foster	Gale	Robson	Allen	Rosenior	Keen*	Morley	Brady
	2/5		17,939	12	69				Ramsey 61	Hodge	Mills	Linton*	Ramsey	Oldfield^	James	Reid	North	Kelly	McAllister	Wright	Oakes/Smith
									Ref: M Reed	Leroy Rosenior celebrates his surprise recall with a fine header from Dicks' cross. When Morley was tripped in the box, Dicks' penalty was saved by Martin Hodge, but Keen followed up. Leicester's Tommy Wright missed two late chances that might have turned the game around.											
46	H	WOLVES		7		W	4-0	2-0	Keen 18, Morley 39, Robson 47, Brady 88	Miklosko	Slater	Dicks	Potts	Foster	Gale	Robson	Allen	Rosenior	Keen*	Morley^	Brady/Quinn
	5/5		22,509	10	72					Kendall	Bennett	Thompson	Venus	Westley	Bellamy	Cook*	Downing^	Bull	Paskin	Dennison	Jones/McLoughlin
	Home		Away						Ref: D Allison	Liam Brady bids farewell on a sun-kissed afternoon with a late goal that prompts the friendliest of pitch invasions. When play restarted, the ref let discretion rule and immediately blew for time. Fingers crossed that the FA will ban Swindon, and let West Ham take their play-off place.											
	Average 20,278		15,686																		

LEAGUE DIVISION 2 (CUP-TIES) Manager: Lou Macari ⇨ Billy Bonds SEASON 1989-90

Littlewoods Cup			F-A	H-T	Scorers, Times, and Referees	1	2	3	4	5	6	7	8	9	10	11	subs used
2:1 A BIRMINGHAM	8	W	2-1	1-0	Allen 37, Slater 87	Parkes	Potts	Dicks	Gale	Martin	Keen	Ward*	Slater	Allen	Dolan	Parris	Brady
19/9 *10,987*	*3:9*				*Sproson 86*	*Thomas*	*Ashley*	*Matthewson*	*Atkins*	*Sproson*	*Overson*	*Peer*	*Bailey*	*Gordon**	*Gleghorn*	*Hopkins*	*Sturridge*
					Ref: D Allison	The introduction of Brady for the hamstrung Ward on 27 minutes slowed the pace of the game and turned it West Ham's way. In a furious climax Hopkins' shot was charged down for Sproson. Almost from the kick-off Slater fired goalwards and Thomas failed to hold the shot.											
2:2 H BIRMINGHAM	7	D	1-1	0-0	Dicks 53	Parkes	Potts	Dicks	Gale	Martin	Keen	Allen	Slater	Dolan*	Ward^	Parris	Kelly/Brady
4/10 12,187	*3:4*				*Atkins 70*	*Thomas*	*Ashley*	*Matthewson*	*Atkins*	*Sproson*	*Overson*	*Tait**	*Bailey*	*Sturridge^*	*Gleghorn*	*Hopkins*	*Peer/Roberts*
					Ref: A Gunn (Hammers win 3-1 on aggregate)	The tie could have swung either way during an eventful first half, which might have finished 3-3. But Dicks' thunderbolt meant City needed to score twice. On another day Dennis Bailey might have grabbed a hat-trick, though Mark Ward's shot hit the Birmingham bar from 35 yards.											
3 A ASTON VILLA	4	D	0-0	0-0		Parkes	Potts	Dicks	Strodder	Martin	Keen	Brady*	Slater	Dolan	Allen	Parris	Kelly
25/10 *20,989*	*1:9*					*Spink*	*Price*	*Gage*	*Birch**	*Mountfield*	*Nielsen*	*Daley^*	*Platt*	*Olney*	*Cowans*	*Gray*	*Ormondroyd/Blake*
					Ref: G Courtney	West Ham beat Villa in the quarter-finals last season, and following this defiant draw are favourites to get past them again. Trouble is brewing off the pitch. Mark Ward arrives at the team bus but words are exchanged and he refuses to board it. His absence allowed a rare start for Brady.											
3R H ASTON VILLA	5	W	1-0	1-0	Dicks 31	Parkes	Potts	Dicks	Strodder	Martin	Keen	Brady	Slater	Dolan	Ward	Parris	
8/11 23,833	*1:4*					*Spink*	*Price*	*Gage**	*McGrath*	*Mountfield*	*Nielsen*	*Daley^*	*Platt*	*Olney*	*Cowans*	*Ormondroyd*	*Comyn/Callaghan*
					Ref: D Hutchinson	Graham Taylor's Villa hit six past Everton last Sunday, but they have no answer to the inspirational Brady. The goal came when Paul McGrath fouled Slater. Kevin Keen rolled the free-kick to Dicks. England new boy David Platt had the ball in the net but it was scrubbed off for offside.											
4 H WIMBLEDON	5	W	1-0	0-0	Allen 81	Parkes	Potts	Dicks !	Strodder	Martin	Keen*	Brady	Slater	Allen	Ward	Parris^	Fashanu/Devonshire
22/11 24,746	*1:14*					*Segers*	*Joseph*	*Phelan*	*Ryan*	*Young*	*Curle*	*Fairweather*	*Miller**	*Cotterill*	*Sanchez^*	*Wise*	*Cork/Scales*
					Ref: A Buksh	A blood-curdling match, with five booked and Dicks sent off for a late tackle on Wise. Keen cleared Eric Young's header off the line as West Ham withstood early pressure. Ward's cross set up Martin Allen's sizzling volley, but there was still time for Alan Cork to miss an open goal.											
QF H DERBY	10	D	1-1	1-0	Dicks 37	Parkes	Potts	Dicks	Parris	Martin	Gale	Brady	Kelly	Rosenior*	Allen !	Keen	Slater
17/1 25,035	*1:7*				*Saunders 78*	*Shilton*	*Sage*	*Forsyth*	*Williams*	*Wright*	*Hindmarch*	*Pickering*	*Saunders*	*Ramage**	*Hebberd*	*Cross^*	*PattersonFrancis*
					Ref: V Callow	When Hindmarch fouled Leroy Rosenior, Liam Brady touched the free-kick to Julian Dicks. Gayle's frightful back-pass let in Dean Saunders for the equaliser. Martin Allen was sent off for an airborne tackle on Mark Patterson, at which point 10-man Hammers shut up shop.											
QF A DERBY	11	D	0-0	0-0		Parkes	Strodder	McQueen	Parris	Martin	Gale	Brady*	Kelly	Slater	Robson^	Keen	Milne/Devonshire
R 24/1 *22,510*	*1:9*		*aet*			*Taylor*	*Sage*	*Forsyth*	*Williams*	*Wright*	*Hindmarch*	*Patterson*	*Saunders*	*Harford**	*Hebberd*	*McCord^*	*Francis/Briscoe*
					Ref: J Worrall	This cup-tie was all elbow grease and no skill. With Peter Shilton injured, Derby fielded rookie keeper Martin Taylor. Stewart Robson played his first West Ham match in 16 months. Liam Brady went down without earning a penalty, and a Kevin Keen effort was ruled out for offside.											
QF H DERBY	11	W	2-1	1-0	Slater 34, Keen 49	Parkes	Potts*	Dicks	Parris	Martin	Gale	Brady	Kelly	Slater	Robson	Keen	McQueen
RR 31/1 25,166	*1:9*				*Saunders 57*	*Taylor*	*Sage*	*Forsyth*	*Williams*	*Patterson*	*Davidson*	*Francis**	*Saunders*	*Harford*	*Hebberd*	*Briscoe*	*Ramage*
					Ref: K Barratt	Derby are missing the England pair Peter Shilton and Mark Wright, and in driving rain fall behind to Stuart Slater, who banged in Dicks' free-kick. After Keen's goal, Saunders' bullet made it 2-1. Brady cleared Forsyth's header off the line to send West Ham through after five hours.											
SF A OLDHAM	11	L	0-6	0-3	*[Holden 46, Palmer 69]*	Parkes	Robson	Dicks	Parris	Martin	Gale	Brady	Slater	Strodder*	Kelly	Keen	Devonshire
1 14/2 *19,263*	*4*				*Adams 11, Ritchie 19, 78, Barrett 33,*	*Hallworth*	*Irwin*	*Barlow*	*Henry*	*Marshall*	*Barrett*	*Adams*	*Ritchie*	*Palmer*	*Milligan*	*Holden R*	
					Ref: L Shapter	Lou Macari refuses to blame Oldham's plastic pitch for this nightmare defeat. He concedes that West Ham were 'outpaced, outworked, and outclassed'. Kick-off was delayed 15 minutes as trains were delayed. Hammers' only moment of ill-fortune came when Slater hit a post at 0-1.											
SF H OLDHAM	10	W	3-0	1-0	Martin 13, Dicks 46p, Kelly 65	Miklosko	Slater	Dicks	Parris	Martin	Gale	Brady*	Allen	Rosenior	Kelly	Keen	McQueen
2 7/3 15,431	*4*					*Hallworth*	*Irwin*	*Barlow*	*Henry*	*Barrett*	*Warhurst*	*Adams*	*Palmer*	*Marshall*	*Milligan*	*Holden R*	
					Ref: T Holbrook (Hammers lose 3-6 on aggregate)	It is all academic of course, though had the goals come earlier who knows what might have happened. Bonds uses this match to allow Rosenior his comeback. Hallworth hauled down Keen for Dicks' penalty. At 3-0 Dicks hit the bar. Had it gone in, Oldham's defence may have cracked.											

FA Cup

3	A	TORQUAY	11	L	0-1	0-0		Parkes, Potts, Dicks, Parris*, Martin, Gale, Quinn, Bishop, Keen, Morley, Allen, Rosenior
	6/1		*5,342 4:19*				*Hirons 77*	*Veysey, Holmes, Lloyd, Matthews, Elliott, Uzell, Smith P, Edwards, Taylor, Caldwell*, Weston, Hirons*
							Ref: G Ashby	Ex-Southend boss Dave Smith masterminds this humiliating defeat. On a quagmire pitch, Paul Smith crosses for 18-year-old sub Paul Hirons to score with his first touch. Coach Mick McGiven walked out on the Hammers 24 hours before the game, as the Swindon scandal deepens.

		Home					Away					
	P	W	D	L	F	A	W	D	L	F	A	Pts
1 Leeds	46	16	6	1	46	18	8	7	8	33	34	85
2 Sheffield Utd	46	14	5	4	43	27	10	8	5	35	31	85
3 Newcastle	46	17	4	2	51	26	5	10	8	29	29	80
4 Swindon †	46	12	6	5	49	29	8	8	7	30	30	74
5 Blackburn	46	10	9	4	43	30	9	8	6	31	29	74
6 Sunderland *	46	10	8	5	41	32	10	6	7	29	32	74
7 WEST HAM	46	14	5	4	50	22	6	7	10	30	35	72
8 Oldham	46	15	7	1	50	23	4	7	12	20	34	71
9 Ipswich	46	13	7	3	38	22	6	5	12	29	44	69
10 Wolves	46	12	5	6	37	20	6	8	9	30	40	67
11 Port Vale	46	11	9	3	37	20	4	7	12	25	37	61
12 Portsmouth	46	9	8	6	40	34	6	8	9	22	31	61
13 Leicester	46	10	8	5	34	29	5	6	12	33	50	59
14 Hull	46	7	8	8	27	31	7	8	8	31	34	58
15 Watford	46	11	6	6	41	28	3	9	11	17	32	57
16 Plymouth	46	9	8	6	30	23	5	5	13	28	40	55
17 Oxford	46	8	7	8	35	31	7	2	14	22	36	54
18 Brighton	46	10	6	7	28	27	5	3	15	28	45	54
19 Barnsley	46	7	9	7	22	23	6	6	11	27	48	54
20 West Brom	46	6	8	9	35	37	6	7	10	32	34	51
21 Middlesbro	46	10	3	10	33	29	3	8	12	19	34	50
22 Bournemouth	46	8	6	9	30	31	4	6	13	27	44	48
23 Bradford C	46	9	6	8	26	24	0	8	15	18	44	41
24 Stoke	46	4	11	8	20	24	2	8	13	15	39	37
	1104	252	165	135	886	640	135	165	252	640	886	1491

* promoted after play-offs
† promotion not accepted

Odds & ends

Double wins: (5) Watford, Portsmouth, Sheff U, Oxford, Middlesbrough.
Double losses: (2) Leeds, Oldham.

Won from behind: (2) Oxford (h), Brighton (h).
Lost from in front: (3) Hull (h), Sunderland (a), Newcastle (a).

High spots: Two unbeaten runs of six games, winning four, beginning 10 February and 31 March.
Reaching semi-final of Littlewoods Cup.

Low spots: Four successive league defeats in December that effectively put paid to hopes of promotion.
Being crushed 0-6 by Oldham in Littlewoods Cup semi-final.
Losing to Fourth Division Torquay in FA Cup.

Hammer of the Year Julian Dicks.
Ever-presents: (0).
Hat-tricks: (1) Jimmy Quinn.
Leading scorer: (13) Jimmy Quinn, Julian Dicks.

	Appearances						Goals			
	Lge	*Sub*	LC	*Sub*	FAC	*Sub*	Lge	LC	FAC	Tot
Allen, Martin	**39**		6		1		**9**	2		**11**
Bishop, Ian	**13**	*4*			1		**2**			**2**
Brady, Liam	**25**	*8*	8	*2*			**2**			**2**
Devonshire, Alan	**3**	*4*		*3*						
Dicks, Julian	**40**		9		1		**9**	4		**13**
Dolan, Eammon	**8**	*2*	4				**3**			**3**
Fashanu, Justin	**2**			*1*						
Foster, Colin	**20**	*2*								
Gale, Tony	**36**		7		1		**1**			**1**
Ince, Paul	**1**									
Keen, Kevin	**43**	*1*	10		1		**10**	1		**11**
Kelly, David	**8**	*8*	5	*2*			**1**	1		**2**
Kelly Paul		*1*								
McAvennie, Frank	**1**	*4*								
McQueen, Tom	**5**	*2*	1	*2*						
Martin, Alvin	**31**		10		1			1		**1**
Miklosko, Ludo	**18**		1							
Milne, Ralph				*1*						
Morley, Trevor	**18**	*1*			1		**10**			**10**
Parkes, Phil	**22**		9		1					
Parris, George	**35**	*3*	9		1		**2**			**2**
Potts, Steve	**30**	*2*	8		1					
Quinn, Jimmy	**18**	*3*			1		**13**			**13**
Rosenior, Leroy	**4**	*1*	2			*1*	**2**			**2**
Robson, Stewart	**7**		3				**1**			**1**
Slater, Stuart	**40**		9	*1*			**7**	2		**9**
Strodder, Gary	**16**		5				**1**			**1**
Suckling, Perry	**6**									
Ward, Mark	**17**	*2*	4				**5**			**5**
(own-goals)							**2**			**2**
29 players used	**506**	***48***	**110**	***12***	**11**	***1***	**80**	**11**		**91**

Potts and Miklosko guard the goal

John Hartson celebrates a goal

David Unsworth skips over Liverpool's Robbie Fowler

No	Date		Att	Pos	Pt	F-A	H-T	Scorers, Times, and Referees	1	2	3	4	5	6	7	8	9	10	11	subs used
1	A	MIDDLESBROUGH			D	0-0	0-0		Miklosko	Potts	Dicks	Foster	Martin	Keen	Bishop	McAvennie	Slater	Allen	Morley	
	25/8		*20,680*		1				*Pears*	*Cooper*	*Phillips*	*Mowbray*	*Kernaghan*	*Wark*	*Slaven*	*Mustoe*	*Baird*	*Proctor*	*Hendrie*	
								Ref: J Worrall	Boro just escaped relegation in May, but would have got off to a winning start but for super saves from Miklosko, just back from the World Cup. Slaven was twice denied, first a 20-yard volley, then when Ludo dived at his feet. McAvennie returns after missing a year through injury.											
2	H	PORTSMOUTH	20,835	14	D	1-1	1-1	McAvennie 23	Miklosko	Potts	Dicks	Foster	Martin	Keen	Bishop	McAvennie	Slater	Allen	Morley	
	29/8			*13*	2			*Whittingham 20*	*Knight*	*Neill*	*Beresford*	*Finney*	*Kuhl*	*Maguire*	*Wigley*	*Stevens*	*Clarke*	*Whittingham*	*Chamberlain*	
								Ref: J Barratt	In an atmosphere of thunder and lightning, Frank McAvennie scores his first Hammers goal in three years. He swooped when Knight fumbled Morley's shot. Whittingham had put Pompey ahead from the edge of the box, after playing a one-two with Clarke. Pompey also hit the post.											
3	H	WATFORD	19,872	7	W	1-0	0-0	Dicks 83p	Miklosko	Potts	Dicks	Foster	Martin	Keen	Bishop	McAvennie	Slater	Allen^	Morley*	Quinn/Parris
	1/9			*22*	5				*James*	*Williams !*	*Dublin*	*Porter*	*McLaughlin*	*Holdsworth*	*Thomas*	*Wilkinson*	*Kennedy*	*Falconer*	*Bazeley**	*Drysdale*
								Ref: J Ashworth	West Ham's first win does not mean they played well. On the contrary, according to Bonds: 'We don't chase back when we lose the ball'. Williams was sent off in the second half for fouling Slater. With the game looking goalless, three Watford players seemed to drag down Keen.											
4	A	LEICESTER	*14,605*	4	W	2-1	1-0	James 38 (og), Morley 49	Miklosko	Potts	Dicks	Foster	Martin	Keen	Bishop	McAvennie*	Slater^	Allen	Morley	Quinn/Parris
	8/9			*20*	8			*Mills 63*	*Muggleton*	*Mills*	*Johnson*	*Mauchlen**	*Walsh*	*James*	*Hill^*	*North*	*Kitson*	*Davies*	*Kelly*	*Reid/Ramsey*
								Ref: R Milford	David Pleat's lightweight Leicester – spearheaded by former Hammer David Kelly – lose their third game in a row. They were not helped by losing Paul Kitson in the first half, following a collision with Slater. City's Tony James lobbed an intended back-pass over his own keeper.											
5	H	WOLVES	23,241	6	D	1-1	1-0	Martin 2	Miklosko	Potts	Dicks	Foster	Martin	Keen	Bishop	McAvennie	**Livett***	Allen	Morley	Parris
	15/9			*13*	9			*Bull 72*	*Stowell*	*Roberts**	*Venus*	*Bellamy*	*Hindmarch*	*Downing*	*Thompson*	*Cook*	*Bull*	*Mutch*	*Dennison^*	*Ashley/McLoughlin*
								Ref: P Danson	Wolves' Steve Bull played in the World Cup in Italy in the summer, but is kept at bay for 72 minutes, when he manages to shake off Foster to equalise. Alvin Martin had blasted a rare goal after just 90 seconds. Right at the end Trevor Morley crashed a shot against the crossbar.											
6	H	IPSWICH	18,764	3	W	3-1	0-1	Bishop 62, Quinn 81, Morley 90	Miklosko	Potts^	Dicks	Foster	Martin	Keen	Bishop	McAvennie*	Slater	Allen	Morley	Quinn/Parris
	19/9			*15*	12			*Milton 11*	*Forrest*	*Yallop*	*Hill*	*Stockwell*	*Gayle*	*Linighan**	*Gregory*	*Redford*	*Zondervan*	*Kiwomya*	*Milton*	*Thompson !*
								Ref: G Ashby	John Lyall, sacked by West Ham, makes a quick return to his former home. Inside 20 seconds Dicks clears off the line. Redford crosses for Kiwomya to score; then Allen sets up Bishop. On 78 minutes Neil Thompson is sent off for toppling Morley, whereupon Quinn chips Forrest.											
7	A	NEWCASTLE	*25,462*	3	D	1-1	1-1	Morley 45	Miklosko	Potts	Dicks	Foster	Martin	Keen	Bishop	Quinn*	Slater^	Allen	Morley	McAvennie/Parris
	22/9			*7*	13			*McGhee 15*	*Burridge*	*Scott*	*Anderson**	*Aitken*	*Kristensen*	*Ranson*	*Dillon*	*Brock^*	*Quinn*	*McGhee*	*Fereday*	*Simpson/O'Brien*
								Ref: T Fitzharris	Jim Smith's Newcastle missed promotion via the play-offs and are now struggling. Billy Bonds disputed the goal that put the Magpies ahead, claiming that all the world saw skipper Roy Aitken handle during the build-up. Slater's cross to Morley maintained West Ham's unbeaten start.											
8	A	SHEFFIELD WED	***28,786***	4	D	1-1	0-1	Dicks 76	Miklosko	Potts	Dicks	Foster	Martin^	Keen	Bishop	Quinn*	Slater	Allen	Morley	McAvennie/Parris
	29/9			*2*	14			*Hirst 2*	*Pressman*	*Nilsson*	*King*	*Palmer*	*Shirtliff*	*Pearson*	*Wilson**	*Sheridan*	*Hirst*	*Williams*	*Worthington*	*Francis*
								Ref: E Parker	Two unbeaten teams, but West Ham were lucky. At half-time Bonds moaned: 'They outfought us, outran us, out-passed us.' Hirst had turned Martin to convert Sheridan's cross, after which Ludo kept the Owls at bay. Bishop squared a free-kick to Dicks, whose shot was deflected in.											
9	H	OXFORD	**18,125**	4	W	2-0	2-0	Foster 12, Morley 43	Miklosko	Potts	Dicks	Foster	Martin	Keen	Bishop	Quinn	Slater*	Allen	Morley	Parris
	3/10			*23*	17				*Walker*	*Robinson*	*Ford*	*Phillips*	*Jackson*	*Melville*	*Magilton*	*Lewis**	*Foyle*	*Stein*	*Simpson*	*Penney*
								Ref: K Morton	Two points from seven games for luckless Oxford, but Bonds is not deceived by this result. Miklosko made three fine saves from Martin Foyle, and Oxford also wasted a 34th-minute penalty when Martin bundled Foyle. Simpson shot wide. Quinn netted after Foster headed onto the bar.											
10	H	HULL	19,472	3	W	**7-1**	2-1	Quinn 8, 62, Potts 31, Dicks 46p, 81, [Parris 58, Morley 70]	Miklosko	Potts	Dicks	Foster	Martin	Keen*	Bishop	Quinn^	Parris	Allen	Morley	McAvennie/**Rush**
	6/10			*17*	20			*Hockaday 30*	*Hesford*	*Hockaday**	*Doyle*	*Mail^*	*Buckley*	*Wilcox*	*Thomas*	*Peyton*	*Swan*	*Palin*	*Finnigan*	*Ngata/McParland*
								Ref: B Stevens	Hull were unbeaten in seven. Men of the match were Parris and Potts, who restored Hammers' lead with his first ever goal, Hesford fumbling seconds after Hockaday had headed an equaliser. Mail brought down Morley for the penalty. Best goal was Quinn's second, a fierce volley.											
11	A	BRISTOL CITY	*16,838*	3	D	1-1	0-0	McAvennie 61	Miklosko	Potts	Dicks	Foster	Martin	Parris	Bishop	Quinn	Slater*	Allen	Morley	McAvennie
	13/10			*13*	21			*Morgan 64*	*Leaning*	*Llewellyn*	*Bailey*	*Aizlewood*	*Shelton*	*Rennie*	*May*	*Newman*	*Taylor*	*Morgan*	*Smith*	
								Ref: J Deakin	McAvennie, a £1.2 million signing, does not like being dropped in favour of Jimmy Quinn. He comes on for Slater and almost immediately puts away Morley's through-ball. Hammers' reject Nicky Morgan levelled with a far-post header. Dicks, promoted to captain, is booked again.											

12	A	SWINDON	3	W	1-0	0-0	McAvennie 82	Miklosko	Potts	Dicks^	Foster	Martin	Parris	Bishop	Quinn*	Gale	Allen	Morley	McAvennie/**Breacker**
20/10		*13,658*	*13*	24				*Digby*	*Kerslake*	*Bodin*	*Hazard**	*Tanner*	*Gittens*	*Jones*	*Simpson*	*White*	*MacLaren*	*Foley*	*Close*
							Ref: R Gifford	Swindon had the edge when McAvennie comes off the bench after 71 minutes. 11 minutes later Morley plays the ball into his path and the sub wins the game. McAvennie is so fed up with being sub that he is said to be signing for QPR for £400,000. Breacker comes on after 37 mins.											
13	H	BLACKBURN	3	W	1-0	1-0	Bishop 19	Miklosko	Breacker	Dicks^	Foster	Martin	Parris	Bishop	Quinn*	Gale	Allen	Morley	McAvennie/Slater
24/10		20,003	*20*	27				*Grew*	*Duxbury**	*Beglin*	*Reid*	*Dewhurst*	*Moran*	*Gayle*	*Millar*	*Stapleton*	*Garner*	*Atkins*	*Richardson*
							Ref: J Martin	Pre-Dalglish, Rovers are managed by Don Mackay and playing badly. Bishop wins the ball off Moran in the centre circle, advances, and fires a right-footer from 20 yards. Morley later hit the underside of the bar with a floater. It's 15 without defeat, but Dicks faces surgery on his knee.											
14	H	CHARLTON	2	W	2-1	0-0	Allen 53, 70	Miklosko	Breacker	Keen	Foster	Martin	Parris	Bishop	McAvennie	Slater*	Allen	Morley	Rush
27/10		24,019	*23*	30			*Dyer 81*	*Bolder*	*Pitcher*	*Reid*	*Peake*	*Webster*	*Balmer*	*Lee R*	*Mackenzie*	*Dyer*	*Watson*	*Minto*	
							Ref: L Shapter	Relegated Charlton play their home matches at Selhurst Park, pending restoration of their Valley stadium. Lennie Lawrence's team played bright football, but are beaten by two thunderous strikes by Allen. Miklosko made some great saves before Alex Dyer scored from close range.											
15	A	NOTTS CO	2	W	1-0	0-0	Morley 57	Miklosko	Breacker	Parris	Foster	Martin	**Hughton**	Bishop	Keen	Rush	Allen	Morley	
3/11		*10,871*	*8*	33				*Cherry*	*Palmer*	*Harding*	*Short, Craig*	*Yates*	*O'Riordan**	*Thomas*	*Turner*	*Bartlett*	*Regis*	*Draper*	*Johnson*
							Ref: J Watson	Fortune favours the Hammers as County miss chances galore. With both McAvennie and Quinn injured, Trevor Morley plays as a lone striker, spinning to volley the only goal over the keeper from 20 yards. Chris Hughton makes his first appearance, signed on loan from Tottenham.											
16	A	MILLWALL	2	D	1-1	0-0	McAvennie 73	Miklosko	Breacker	Parris	Foster	Martin	Hughton	Bishop	Keen	McAvennie	Allen*	Morley	Rush
10/11		*20,591*	*6*	34			*Stephenson 47*	*Horne*	*Stevens*	*Dawes*	*Waddock*	*Wood*	*McLeary*	*Carter*	*Allen**	*Sheringham*	*Rae*	*Stephenson*	*Goddard*
							Ref: K Cooper	Bruce Rioch's Millwall play their part in this thrilling derby. Stephenson's rocket deserved to give Millwall the lead. Bishop then opens up the left side of the Lions' defence and Keen's cross eludes everyone except McAvennie. Bonds admits West Ham enjoyed a Houdini-like escape.											
17	H	BRIGHTON	2	W	2-1	0-1	Slater 56, Foster 72	Miklosko	Breacker	Parris	Foster	Martin	Hughton	Bishop	McAvennie	Rush*	Keen	Morley	Slater
17/11		23,082	*9*	37			*Small 39*	*Digweed*	*Crumplin*	*Chapman*	*Wilkins*	*Gatting*	*Chivers*	*Barham*	*Byrne*	*Small*	*Codner*	*Walker*	
							Ref: H King	So superior are Brighton that at half-time manager-of-the-month Bonds admits he would be delighted with a draw. Barham's cross had put the Seagulls ahead, but in rain and thunder Slater cuts in to fire into the top corner and Foster heads in Keen's corner. Oldham lose at Port Vale.											
18	A	PLYMOUTH	1	W	1-0	0-0	McAvennie 62	Miklosko	Breacker	Parris	Foster	Martin	Hughton	Bishop	McAvennie	Slater	Keen	Morley	
24/11		*11,490*	*12*	40				*Wilmot*	*Brown*	*Morgan*	*Marker*	*Burrows*	*Salman*	*Barlow*	*Fiore*	*Robinson**	*Ampadu^*	*Hodges*	*Morrison/Adcock*
							Ref: R Hamer	Two goalkeeping moments determine this result, which sends West Ham top for the first time, unbeaten in 18 league games. Argyle's Wilmot cannot hold Morley's shot, which bounces out of his arms. In injury-time sub Morrison looked to have levelled, but Miklosko saves brilliantly.											
19	H	WEST BROM	1	W	3-1	2-0	Parris 20, Morley 24, McAvennie 59	Miklosko	Breacker	Parris	Foster	Martin	Hughton	Bishop	McAvennie	Slater	Keen*	Morley	Allen
1/12		24,753	*17*	43			*Ford 60*	*Naylor*	*Robson*	*Harbey*	*Roberts*	*Bradley*	*Strodder*	*Ford*	*West*	*Bannister*	*Parkin*	*Anderson**	*Goodman*
							Ref: M Bailey	So fragile are the Hammers that even when 3-0 up they could easily have lost. Parris scores No 1 from 25 yards. Seconds after McAvennie's dipping volley, Ford nets at the far post. Miklosko pulled off save after save, and four minutes from time Colin West blazes wide from the spot.											
20	A	PORTSMOUTH	1	W	1-0	0-0	Morley 59	Miklosko	Breacker	Parris	Foster	Martin^	Hughton	Bishop	McAvennie*	Slater	Allen	Morley	Quinn/ Gale
8/12		*12,045*	*22*	46				*Knight*	*Neill*	*Beresford*	*Aspinall*	*Butters*	*Awford*	*Anderton**	*Stevens*	*Clarke*	*Whittingham*	*Chamberlain*	*Wigley*
							Ref: R Bigger	Miklosko saves the day and the points. On a cold windy day, Ludo pulls off a super save from Whittingham to keep yet another clean sheet. Pompey boss Frank Burrows is glad to see the back of West Ham for this season. With Oldham's match off, West Ham are five points clear.											
21	H	MIDDLESBROUGH	1	D	0-0	0-0		Miklosko	Breacker	Parris	Gale	Potts	Hughton	Keen	McAvennie	Slater	Allen	Morley*	Quinn
15/12		23,705	*4*	47				*Pears*	*Cooper*	*McGee*	*Mowbray*	*Coleman*	*Wark*	*Slaven*	*Mustoe*	*Baird*	*Kerr*	*Hendrie**	*Ripley*
							Ref: A Gunn	The second 0-0 with Boro. For once it is West Ham who bemoan the run of the ball, as Stephen Pears in Boro's goal defies everything thrown at him. Both sides had penalty claims denied. With Breacker's arrival, Potts is switched to central defence, and the move may be permanent.											
22	A	BARNSLEY	2	L	0-1	0-1		Miklosko	Breacker	Parris	Gale	Potts	Hughton	Keen	McAvennie*	Slater	Allen	Morley	Quinn
22/12		*10,348*	*8*	47			*Smith 20*	*Baker*	*Banks**	*Taggart*	*Fleming*	*Smith*	*Tiler*	*O'Connell*	*Rammell^*	*Saville*	*Agnew*	*Archdeacon*	*Connolly/Deehan*
							Ref: D Allison	Hammered 1-5 by Luton in midweek in the Zenith-Data Cup, West Ham now surrender their unbeaten league record. O'Connell's miskick fell to Smith for the only goal. Morley's 'goal' was controversially ruled offside. Arsenal now boast the only unbeaten record in all four divisions.											
23	H	OLDHAM	1	W	2-0	1-0	Morley 10, Slater 46	Miklosko	Breacker	Parris	Gale	Foster	Hughton	Keen	Quinn	Slater	Allen	Morley	
26/12		24,950	*2*	50				*Hallworth*	*Warhurst*	*Barlow*	*Henry*	*Barrett*	*Jobson*	*Donachie**	*Palmer*	*Marshall*	*Redfearn*	*Holden*	*Currie*
							Ref: J Carter	A top of the table clash played in a blustery wind. Agony as Morley is toppled by Earl Barrett, but John Hallworth saves Quinn's penalty. All was put right when Foster flicked on for Morley to make it 1-0. West Ham go back to the top but have played one game more than Oldham.											

No	Date	Att	Pos	Pt	F-A	H-T	Scorers, Times, and Referees	1	2	3	4	5	6	7	8	9	10	11	subs used
24	H PORT VALE		1	D	0-0	0-0		Miklosko	Breacker	Parris	Gale	Foster	Hughton	Keen	Quinn	Slater	Allen*	Morley	Potts
	29/12	23,603	*12*	51				*Wood*	*Aspin*	*Agboola*	*Walker*	*Parkin*	*Glover*	*Porter*	*Earle*	*Jepson*	*Beckford*	*Jeffers*	
							Ref: G Singh	In treacherous wet conditions Vale looked stronger in the first half but were under the hammer afterwards. At the end Darren Beckford rounded Gale and Miklosko but fired into the side netting. Vale boss John Rudge said: 'I don't think West Ham have had a harder game all season'.											
25	A BRISTOL ROV		1	W	1-0	0-0	Quinn 48	Miklosko	Breacker	Parris	Gale	Foster	Hughton	Keen	Potts	Quinn	Slater	Morley	
	1/1	*7,932*	*10*	54				*Parkin*	*Bloomer*	*Twentyman*	*Yates*	*Mehew**	*Jones*	*Holloway*	*Reece*	*White*	*Saunders*	*Pounder*	*Nixon*
							Ref: K Burge	Under Gerry Francis - once linked with West Ham - Rovers were unbeaten in nine games. That run comes to an end at tiny Twerton Park when Quinn finishes off Keen's cross with a mighty header. 20 minutes from time Breacker brought down Holloway, whose spot-kick was saved.											
26	A WATFORD		1	W	1-0	0-0	Morley 66	Miklosko	Breacker	Parris	Gale	Foster^	Hughton	Keen	Slater	Quinn*	Potts	Morley	**Clarke**/Robson
	12/1	*17,172*	*22*	57				*James*	*Gibbs*	*Williams*	*Ashby*	*McLaughlin*	*Devonshire*	*Thomas**	*Wilkinson*	*Penrice*	*Porter*	*Falconer*	*Gavin*
							Ref: I Hemley	Jack Petchey bought Watford from Elton John in the summer, and under Steve Perryman they are unbeaten in eight. The goal stemmed from Miklosko's huge punt downfield. Watford's best player was former Hammers star Alan Devonshire. Stewart Robson returns after long injury.											
27	H LEICESTER		1	W	1-0	1-0	Parris 37	Miklosko	Breacker	Parris	Gale	Bishop	Hughton	Keen	Slater*	Quinn	Potts	Morley	McAvennie
	19/1	21,652	*20*	60				*Muggleton*	*Mauchlen*	*Gibson*	*North*	*Madden*	*James*	*Peake**	*Reid^*	*Oldfield*	*Mills*	*Kelly*	*Wright/Smith*
							Ref: P Durkin	The only goal was down to Leicester's Ally Mauchlen, who was caught day-dreaming as Parris blasted past Muggleton. But this was no fluke: both Parris and Quinn hit the bar. The result keeps West Ham five points ahead of second-placed Oldham. David Pleat's Leicester will survive.											
28	A WOLVES		1	L	1-2	0-1	McAvennie 57	Miklosko	Breacker	Parris^	Gale	Bishop	Hughton	Keen	McAvennie	Slater*	Potts	Morley	Allen/Quinn
	2/2	*19,454*	*8*	60			*Birch 44, Bull 48*	*Stowell*	*Bennett*	*Thompson*	*Hindmarch*	*Stancliffe*	*Blake*	*Birch*	*Cook*	*Bull*	*Mutch*	*Dennison**	*Steele*
							Ref: B Hill	Having beaten Luton 5-0 in the FA Cup, West Ham are rudely brought back to earth. Paul Birch scores on his Wolves' debut. Then Bishop's short pass is cut out, setting up a second. It is the first time Ludo has been beaten twice in the league all season. Oldham lose 1-5 at Oxford.											
29	H MILLWALL		1	W	3-1	1-1	McAvennie 16, 48, Morley 61	Miklosko	Breacker	Parris	Gale*	Bishop	Hughton	Keen	McAvennie	Slater	Potts	Morley	Allen
	24/2	20,503	*7*	63			*Goodman 44*	*Horne*	*Cunningham*	*Dawes*	*Waddock**	*Thompson*	*McLeary*	*Stephenson*	*Goodman*	*Sheringham*	*Rae*	*McGlashan*	*Allen*
							Ref: M Peck	This Sunday match was sparked into life by McAvennie's far-post header, which was shortly cancelled out by John Goodman's snap-shot. The lead was restored when Horne saved at Slater's feet, but the ball fell to McAvennie. Gale broke his nose in a collision with Teddy Sheringham.											
30	A WEST BROM		1	D	0-0	0-0		Miklosko	Breacker	Parris	Gale	Bishop	Hughton	Keen*	McAvennie	Slater	Potts	Morley	Allen
	2/3	*16,089*	*18*	64				*Rees*	*Hodson*	*Shakespeare*	*Roberts*	*Bradley*	*Burgess*	*Ford*	*Parkin*	*Bannister*	*Robson*	*Anderson*	
							Ref: M Bodenham	Bobby Gould takes charge of his first game for Albion. Despite being at home he plays just one up front and packs his defence. West Ham's best chance came when Bradley cleared off the line from Morley. The Tannoy man gave the time as 17:10, then said 'that means 10 past 5.'											
31	H PLYMOUTH		1	D	2-2	1-0	Marker 18 (og), Breacker 77	Miklosko	Breacker	Parris	Foster	Bishop	Hughton*	Keen	McAvennie	Slater	Potts	Quinn	Allen
	5/3	18,933	*17*	65			*Turner 50, 75*	*Wilmot*	*Brown*	*Morgan*	*Marker*	*Burrows*	*Salman*	*Barlow*	*Hodges*	*Turner*	*Clement*	*Fiore*	
							Ref: A Gunn	Howard Kendall watches Everton's next FA Cup opponents. 6ft 4in Robbie Turner outjumped Foster to put Plymouth ahead, Breacker scores his first Hammers goal, and Wilmot saves Parris's penalty – the first he'd ever taken. Trevor Morley is in hospital after his wife stabbed him.											
32	A OXFORD		2	L	1-2	0-1	Quinn 54	Miklosko	Breacker*	Parris	Gale	Foster	Hughton	Bishop	McAvennie	**Carr**^	Potts	Quinn	Keen/Slater
	13/3	*8,225*	*14*	65			*Simpson 10, Durnin 47*	*Veysey*	*Robinson*	*Ford*	*Foyle*	*Foster*	*Melville*	*Magilton*	*Phillips*	*Lewis*	*Durnin*	*Simpson*	
							Ref: A Seville	It is just 48 hours since the famous win over Everton, and West Ham suffer a hangover. Franz Carr has signed on loan from Forest. Simpson, from a corner, and Durnin, after Foster's hesitancy, put Oxford two up. Quinn pounces after McAvennie hits a post. Oldham reclaim top spot.											
33	H SHEFFIELD WED		2	L	1-3	0-1	Quinn 51	Miklosko	Potts	Parris	Gale	Foster	Hughton*	Bishop	McAvennie	Slater	Keen	Quinn^	Allen/Carr
	16/3	26,182	*3*	65			*Hirst 30, Williams 61, 81*	*Turner*	*Anderson*	*King*	*Palmer*	*Shirtliff*	*Pearson*	*Wilson**	*Sheridan*	*Hirst^*	*Williams*	*McCall*	*MacKenzie/Francis*
							Ref: K Redfearn	Ron Atkinson's Owls inflict Bonds' first home defeat since he took charge. It is the first time Ludo concedes three league goals, and the first time any of Big Ron's sides have won at Upton Park. It is Wednesday's 10th away win, but West Ham are still 10 points clear of the play-offs.											
34	H BRISTOL CITY		2	W	1-0	0-0	Gale 67	Miklosko	Potts	Parris	Gale	Foster	Hughton	Bishop	McAvennie !	Slater*	Keen	Quinn^	Allen/Rosenior
	20/3	22,951	*7*	68				*Leaning*	*Llewellyn !*	*Scott*	*May*	*Bryant*	*Aizlewood*	*Shelton*	*Newman*	*Taylor*	*Morgan*	*Donowa**	*Allison*
							Ref: P Alcock	Tony Gale's Brazilian style free-kick won the points and brought West Ham back to winning ways, but the match ended two men short after McAvennie tussled with Andy Llewellyn and both were expelled. Leroy Rosenior returns from Fulham to play his first game of the season.											

No	Venue	Opponent	Pos	Res	F-A	H-T	Scorers, Times, and Referees	1	2	3	4	5	6	7	8	9	10	11	12 subs used
35	A	HULL	2	D	0-0	0-0		Miklosko	Potts	Parris	Gale	Foster	Hughton	Bishop	McAvennie*	**Dowie**	Keen^	Allen	Carr/Rosenior
23/3		*9,558*	23	69				*Butler*	*Norton*	*Thompson*	*Buckley*	*Mail*	*Shotton*	*Hockaday*	*Peyton*	*Swan*	*Atkinson*	*Warren**	*Jenkinson*
							Ref: J Kirkby	Hull lost 1-7 in October and have the most leaky defence in the division, so this result takes some explaining. Yet Hull beat leaders Oldham in midweek and have now conceded just two goals in six games. Iain Dowie makes his league debut after his £500,000 signing from Luton.											
36	A	OLDHAM	2	D	1-1	0-0	Bishop 58p	Miklosko	Potts	Parris	Gale	Foster	Hughton	Bishop	McAvennie	Dowie	Slater	Allen	
29/3		*16,932*	*1*	70			*Ritchie 87p*	*Hallworth*	*Halle*	*Barlow*	*Henry*	*Barrett*	*Jobson*	*Adams*	*Ritchie*	*Palmer**	*Redfearn^*	*Holden*	*Currie/Warhurst*
							Ref: G Alpin	A Friday afternoon crunch game. Dowie had played for Northern Ireland in Yugoslavia on Wednesday and looked half fit. Oldham shaded the first half, but after Ritchie handled Dowie's header West Ham had the chances to clinch the win. Instead, Bishop pulled down Halle in the box.											
37	H	BARNSLEY	2	W	3-2	0-2	McAvennie 56, Dowie 83, Foster 88	Miklosko	Potts	Parris	Gale	Foster	Hughton*	Bishop	McAvennie	Dowie	Slater	Allen	Keen
1/4		24,607	*9*	73			*Saville 13, O'Connell 31*	*Baker*	*Dobbin**	*Fleming*	*Robinson*	*Smith*	*Tiler*	*O'Connell*	*Rammell^*	*Saville*	*Agnew*	*Archdeacon*	*Rimmer/Deehan*
							Ref: P Vanes	Iain Dowie's home debut sees him wearing bicycle shorts to cover the dreadful burns suffered on Oldham's plastic pitch. Mel Machin's Barnsley are so close to completing the double, but substitute Keen supplies crosses for two of the three headers that turn the game around.											
38	A	PORT VALE	1	W	1-0	0-0	Bishop 71	Miklosko	Potts	Parris	Gale	Foster	Hughton	Bishop	Slater	Dowie	Keen	Allen	
6/4		*9,658*	*15*	76				*Grew*	*Mills*	*Platnauer*	*Walker*	*Parkin*	*Glover*	*Kent*	*Earle*	*van der Laan*	*Beckford*	*Porter**	*Millar*
							Ref: K Cooper	Vale had lost just one of their previous six games. West Ham's 12th 1-0 win of the season is due to Bishop's thunderous drive from out of the blue. A swirling wind detracted from the match as a spectacle, but the result means West Ham are 13 points clear of the play-off positions.											
39	A	BRIGHTON	1	L	0-1	0-1		Miklosko	Potts	Parris	Stewart	Foster	Hughton^	Bishop	Keen	Dowie*	Morley	Slater	Allen/Quinn
10/4		*11,904*	*6*	76			*Byrne 44*	*Digweed*	*Crumplin*	*Gatting*	*Wilkins*	*Pates*	*Chivers*	*Barham**	*Byrne*	*Small*	*Codner*	*Walker*	*Nelson*
							Ref: M Pierce	West Ham's smash and grab tactics on their travels were rudely copied by Brighton, who won despite taking a territorial hammering by West Ham for much of the game. John Byrne's cruel goal bounced over Ludo's head. Ray Stewart plays his first league game in 2½ years.											
40	A	IPSWICH	1	W	1-0	1-0	Morley 29	Miklosko	Potts	Parris	Gale	Foster^	Hughton	Bishop	Slater	Dowie*	Keen	Morley	McAvennie/Allen
17/4		*20,290*	*16*	79				*Forrest*	*Humes**	*Thompson*	*Stockwell*	*Gayle*	*Linighan*	*Zondervan*	*Goddard*	*Houghton*	*Dozzell*	*Kiwomya^*	*Yallop/Milton*
							Ref: P Foakes	It is just three days since West Ham were thumped by Nottingham Forest in the FA Cup. They post a double over John Lyall's Ipswich, thanks to Trevor Morley's interception of Tony Hume's back-pass. But Foster goes off with hamstring trouble and will miss the next four games.											
41	H	SWINDON	1	W	2-0	1-0	Parris 21, Dowie 88	Miklosko	Potts	Parris	Gale	Stewart	Hughton	Bishop	Slater	Dowie	Keen*	Morley	Allen
20/4		25,944	*19*	82				*Digby*	*Kerslake*	*Viveash*	*Hazard*	*Simpson*	*Calderwood*	*Jones*	*Shearer*	*Rideout**	*MacLaren*	*Foley*	*White*
							Ref: J Martin	This result guarantees promotion with five games still to play. West Ham enjoyed some luck, and Glenn Hoddle's Swindon dominated the second half. Many a Hammers supporters' finger nail was chewed down until Dowie's late strike settled the matter. Now for the championship.											
42	H	NEWCASTLE	1	D	1-1	0-1	Dowie 62	Miklosko	Potts	Parris	Gale	Stewart*	Hughton	Bishop	Slater	Dowie	Keen	Morley	Allen
24/4		24,195	*12*	83			*Peacock 16*	*Srnicek*	*Watson*	*Elliott*	*O'Brien*	*Scott*	*Kristensen*	*Clark*	*Peacock*	*Quinn*	*Hunt*	*Brock*	
							Ref: R Milford	Ossie Ardiles' Newcastle, free from tension, run the show for the first half, when they had the chances to seal up the points. West Ham have no answer to their fluid tactic of playing on the ground through the middle. George Parris's cross on to Iain Dowie's head deflated the Magpies.											
43	A	BLACKBURN	1	L	**1-3**	1-3	Dowie 43	Miklosko	Potts	Parris	Gale	Stewart	Hughton	Bishop	Keen	Dowie	Slater*	Morley^	Allen/Quinn
27/4		*10,808*	*17*	83			*Richardson 2, Atkins 4, Sellars 14*	*Mimms*	*Atkins*	*Sulley*	*Reid*	*Moran*	*Dobson*	*Irvine*	*Richardson*	*Livingstone*	*Stapleton*	*Sellars**	*Shepstone*
							Ref: J Key	This dreadful result was made worse by Oldham's win at Ipswich. Last season West Ham lost 4-5 at Ewood, and at half-time a repeat scoreline looked on the cards. Three rat-a-tat-tat Rovers goals looked to have killed off the contest until Keen's corner enabled Dowie to pull one back.											
44	A	CHARLTON	1	D	1-1	1-1	Allen 15	Miklosko	Potts	Parris	Breacker	Stewart	Hughton	Bishop	Allen	Dowie*	Slater	Morley	Quinn
4/5		*16,137*	*14*	84			*Minto 32*	*Bolder*	*Pitcher*	*Reid*	*Peake*	*Webster**	*Balmer*	*Lee R*	*Dyer*	*Grant^*	*Mortimer*	*Minto*	*Curbishley/Leaburn*
							Ref: R Wiseman	Homeless Charlton are tenants at Selhurst Park, and this match entices their biggest home gate of the season. Tony Gale misses the rest of the season through suspension, and with Foster still out with hamstring problems, Billy Bonds has to send out a makeshift central defence.											
45	H	BRISTOL ROV	1	W	1-0	1-0	Slater 36	Miklosko	Breacker	Parris	Potts	Foster	Hughton	Bishop	Slater	Dowie*	Allen^	Morley	McAvennie/Keen
8/5		23,054	*12*	87				*Parkin*	*Alexander*	*Twentyman*	*Yates*	*Boothroyd**	*Jones*	*Holloway*	*Reece*	*White*	*Saunders*	*Pounder*	*Hazel*
							Ref: T Holbrook	Gerry Francis' mid-table Rovers created nothing to threaten West Ham's defence, in which Foster returns after injury. The atmosphere is rather subdued, given the importance of the game, which brings the Hammers' 14th 1-0 win of the season. Everything is set up for the championship.											
46	H	NOTTS CO	2	L	1-2	0-2	Parris 77	Miklosko	Potts	Parris	Breacker	Foster	Hughton^	Bishop	Slater	Dowie*	Allen	Morley	McAvennie/Keen
11/5		**26,551**	*4*	87			*Draper 17, 27*	*Cherry*	*Palmer*	*Paris*	*Short, Craig**	*Short, Chris*	*O'Riordan*	*Harding*	*Turner*	*Regis*	*Draper*	*Johnson*	*Davis*
Home		Away					Ref: B Hill	Two Paris's play at No 3. West Ham need to match Oldham's result at home to third-place Sheffield Wednesday to seal the title. After an hour Oldham are losing 0-2 and Upton Park starts celebrating. But Oldham hit back, and Redfearn's injury-time winner shatters West Ham's dream.											
Average 22,565		15,193																	

Rumbelows Cup					F-A	H-T	Scorers, Times, and Referees	1	2	3	4	5	6	7	8	9	10	11	subs used
2:1	H	STOKE	3	W	3-0	1-0	Dicks 43p, Keen 64, Quinn 86	Miklosko	Potts	Dicks	Foster	Martin	Keen	Bishop	Quinn	Slater	Allen*	Morley	Parris
26/9		15,870 *3:7*						*Fox*	*Butler*	*Statham**	*Beeston*	*Blake*	*Sandford*	*Kennedy*	*Evans*	*Kelly^*	*Biggins*	*Ware*	*Fowler/Thomas*
							Ref: B Hill	Sandford brings down Morley in the box. Dicks blasts the penalty and foolish Fox almost gets his fingers cut off. Slater sets up Keen for No 2. Morley's cheeky backheel brought a third goal, for Quinn. Stoke boss Alan Ball knows his team can't score four goals at the Victoria Ground.											
2:2	A	STOKE	3	W	2-1	0-1	Allen 64, 79	Miklosko	Potts	Dicks	Foster	Martin	Keen*	Bishop	Parris	Quinn^	Allen	Morley	Gale/McAvennie
10/10		*8,411* *3:4*					*Evans 37*	*Fox*	*Butler*	*Carr*	*Ware*	*Blake*	*Sandford*	*Scott*	*Ellis*	*Evans*	*Biggins*	*Kevan**	*Boughey*
							Ref: N Midgeley (Hammers win 5-1 on aggregate)	Tim Breacker has signed from Luton for £600,000, Bonds' first signing since taking over from Lou Macari in February 1990. But Bonds keeps faith with Potts and Breacker does not play. Dicks' dreadful back-header lets in Evans to lift Stoke's spirits. Allen's header settles the outcome.											
3	A	OXFORD	2	L	1-2	1-1	Morley 10	Miklosko	Rush	Keen	Foster	Martin	Parris	Bishop	Quinn	Slater	Allen	Morley	
31/10		*7,528* *22*					*Foyle 18, Magilton 90*	*Kee*	*Robinson*	*Evans*	*Lewis*	*Foster*	*Melville*	*Magilton*	*Stein**	*Foyle*	*Nogan*	*Simpson*	*Penney*
							Ref: V Callow	A four-hour hold up on the M25 delays supporters. West Ham's first defeat in any competition comes when Paul Simpson sets up Magilton. Morley had driven in Keen's cross. When Foster brought down Stein, Simpson's penalty hit the post. He had also missed in the league fixture.											

FA Cup																			
3	A	ALDERSHOT	1	D	0-0	0-0		Miklosko	Breacker	Parris	Gale	Foster*	Hughton	Keen	Slater	Quinn	Potts	Morley	Livett
5/1		*22,929* *4:19*						*Hucker*	*Brown*	*Cooper*	*Randall*	*Ogley*	*Flower*	*Burvill*	*Puckett*	*Williams*	*Henry*	*Stewart*	
							Ref: H King (At Upton Park)	The team-sheets handed out wrongly listed this as a Division 2 match, though it aptly summed up a shambles of a cup-tie. Aldershot had been drawn at home but switched the venue to reap the rewards. Morley came nearest to a goal, but was thwarted by Peter Hucker's double save.											
3R	H	ALDERSHOT	1	W	6-1	4-1	Morley 14, 82, Slater 28, Parris 35, [Bishop 39, Quinn 87]	Miklosko	Breacker	Parris	Gale	Robson*	Hughton	Keen	Slater	Quinn	Potts	Morley	Bishop
16/1		21,484 *4:20*					*Randall 45*	*Hucker*	*Brown*	*Cooper*	*Randall*	*Ogley*	*Flower !*	*Burvill*	*Puckett**	*Williams*	*Henry*	*Stewart*	*Whitlock*
							Ref: H King	Aldershot manager Len Walker can at least count the reward of 44,000 spectators and the sale of TV rights to BSkyB. The leakiest defence in the division was not helped by having John Flower sent off for earning his second yellow card when fouling Slater. Parris fed Morley for No 1.											
4	A	LUTON	1	D	1-1	1-0	Parris 42	Miklosko	Breacker	Parris	Gale	Bishop	Hughton	Keen*	Slater	Allen	Potts	Morley	McAvennie
26/1		*12,087* *1:16*					*Black 70*	*Chamberlain*	*James*	*Harvey*	*Williams*	*McDonough*	*Dreyer*	*Elstrup*	*Preece**	*Farrell^*	*Pembridge*	*Black*	*Rees/Dowie*
							Ref: R Groves	Having lost 1-5 here in the Zenith-Data Cup, West Ham lead until Keen fouls Preece on the edge of the box, and Williams' free-kick is turned in by Black. After the final whistle the teams hear that Crewe await the winners. The police normally need 10 days for a reply; not this time.											
4R	H	LUTON	1	W	5-0	1-0	Parris 45, Bishop 53, McAvennie 54, [Morley 68, 83]	Miklosko	Breacker	Parris	Gale	Bishop	Hughton	Keen	McAvennie	Slater	Potts	Morley	
30/1		25,659 *1:16*						*Chamberlain*	*James**	*Harvey*	*Williams*	*McDonough*	*Dreyer*	*Elstrup^*	*Preece*	*Dowie*	*Pembridge*	*Black*	*Johnson/Farrell*
							Ref: R Groves	The loss of Lars Elstrup after 18 minutes disrupted Luton. They hold out till the stroke of half-time when George Parris - who might have had a first-half hat-trick - scores his fourth goal in four games. Morley's two goals make him Hammers' top scorer with 15. Now for lowly Crewe.											
5	H	CREWE	1	W	1-0	0-0	Quinn 75	Miklosko	Breacker	Parris	Gale	Bishop	Hughton	Keen	McAvennie*	Slater	Potts	Morley	Quinn
16/2		25,298 *3:21*						*Edwards P*	*Swain*	*McKearney*	*Smart*	*Carr*	*Lennon*	*Jasper**	*Hignett^*	*Sussex*	*Gardiner*	*Doyle*	*Edwards R/Murphy*
							Ref: G Ashby	West Ham have never played Crewe before. Two minutes after coming off the bench Jimmy Quinn - who used to support Crewe as a boy - slips Keen's cross past Paul Edwards. Crewe's reserve keeper had done his best to improve upon the worst defensive record in Division 3.											
QF	H	EVERTON	1	W	2-1	1-0	Foster 33, Slater 59	Miklosko	Breacker	Parris	Gale	Foster	Hughton	Bishop	McAvennie	Slater	Potts	Quinn*	Keen
11/3		28,161 *1:11*					*Watson 86*	*Southall*	*McDonald**	*Hinchcliffe*	*Ratcliffe*	*Watson*	*Keown*	*Nevin*	*McCall*	*Sharp*	*Milligan^*	*Ebbrell*	*Cottee/Newell*
							Ref: M Reed	A Monday night thriller. Everton line up with just Graeme Sharp up front. Foster finds himself upfield as a cross comes over. He ignores cries of 'leave it' and volleys past Southall. Ebbrell and Keown were booked for fouling Slater. Only when Cottee came on did Everton threaten.											
SF	N	NOTT'M FOREST	1	L	0-4	0-0	*[Charles 80]*	Miklosko	Potts	Parris	Gale !	Foster	Hughton	Bishop	Slater	Allen*	Keen	Morley^	Stewart/Quinn
14/4		*40,041* *1:14*					*Crosby 49, Keane 58, Pearce 70,*	*Crossley*	*Charles*	*Pearce*	*Walker*	*Chettle*	*Parker*	*Crosby*	*Keane**	*Clough*	*Glover*	*Woan*	*Laws*
		(At Villa Park)					Ref: K Hackett	Who knows what might have happened had referee Hackett taken a different view of Gale's collision with Gary Crosby as both players chased a through ball. Gale was judged guilty of a professional foul and sent off for the first time in his career. In the second half Forest ran rampant.											

		Home					Away					
	P	W	D	L	F	A	W	D	L	F	A	Pts
1 Oldham	46	17	5	1	55	21	8	8	7	28	32	88
2 WEST HAM	46	15	6	2	41	18	9	9	5	19	16	87
3 Sheffield Wed	46	12	10	1	43	23	10	6	7	37	28	82
4 Notts Co*	46	14	4	5	45	28	9	7	7	31	27	80
5 Millwall	46	11	6	6	43	28	9	7	7	27	23	73
6 Brighton	46	12	4	7	37	31	9	3	11	26	38	70
7 Middlesbro	46	12	4	7	36	17	8	5	10	30	30	69
8 Barnsley	46	13	7	3	39	16	6	5	12	24	32	69
9 Bristol City	46	14	5	4	44	28	6	2	15	24	43	67
10 Oxford	46	10	9	4	41	29	4	10	9	28	37	61
11 Newcastle	46	8	10	5	24	22	6	7	10	25	34	59
12 Wolves	46	11	6	6	45	35	2	13	8	18	28	58
13 Bristol Rov	46	11	7	5	29	20	4	6	13	27	39	58
14 Ipswich	46	9	8	6	32	28	4	10	9	28	40	57
15 Port Vale	46	10	4	9	32	24	5	8	10	24	40	57
16 Charlton	46	8	7	8	27	25	5	10	8	30	36	56
17 Portsmouth	46	10	6	7	34	27	4	5	14	24	43	53
18 Plymouth	46	10	10	3	36	20	2	7	14	18	48	53
19 Blackburn	46	8	6	9	26	27	6	4	13	25	39	52
20 Watford	46	5	8	10	24	32	7	7	9	21	27	51
21 Swindon	46	8	6	9	31	30	4	8	11	34	43	50
22 Leicester	46	12	4	7	41	33	2	4	17	19	50	50
23 West Brom	46	7	11	5	26	21	3	7	13	26	40	48
24 Hull	46	6	10	7	35	32	4	5	14	22	53	45
	1104	253	163	136	866	615	136	163	253	615	866	1493

* promoted after play-offs

Odds & ends

Double wins: (5) Watford, Leicester, Ipswich, Swindon, Bristol Rov.
Double losses: (0).

Won from behind: (4) Ipswich (h), Brighton (h), Barnsley (h), Stoke RC (a).
Lost from in front: (1) Oxford RC (a).

High spots: Promotion.
Not losing until 22 December in the league, a run of 21 games.
Reaching semi-final of Rumbelows Cup.

Low spots: Four league games without a win from 2 March.
Losing so heavily in Rumbelows Cup semi-final.
Losing the Second Division championship on the final day of the season.

Hammer of the Year: Ludek Miklosko.
Ever-presents: (1) Ludek Miklosko.
Hat-tricks: (0).
Leading scorer: (17) Trevor Morley.

	Appearances						Goals			
	Lge	*Sub*	LC	*Sub*	FAC	*Sub*	Lge	LC	FAC	Tot
Allan, Martin	**28**	*12*	3		2		**3**	2		**5**
Bishop, Ian	**40**		3		5	*1*	**4**		2	**6**
Breacker, Tim	**23**	*1*			6		**1**			**1**
Carr, Franz	**1**	*2*								
Clarke, Simon		*1*								
Dicks, Julian	**13**		2				**4**	1		**5**
Dowie, Iain	**12**						**4**			**4**
Foster, Colin	**36**		3		3		**3**		1	**4**
Gale, Tony	**23**	*1*		*1*	7		**1**			**1**
Hughton, Chris	**32**				7					
Kevin, Kevin	**36**	*4*	3		6	*1*		1		**1**
Livett, Simon	**1**					*1*				
McAvennie, Frank	**24**	*10*		*1*	3	*1*	**10**		1	**11**
Martin, Alvin	**20**		3				**1**			**1**
Miklosko, Ludek	**46**		3		7					
Morley, Trevor	**38**		3		6		**12**	1	4	**17**
Parris, George	**37**	*7*	2	*1*	7		**5**		3	**8**
Potts, Steve	**36**	*1*	2		7		**1**			**1**
Quinn, Jimmy	**16**	*10*	3		3	*2*	**6**	1	2	**9**
Robson, Stewart		*1*			1					
Rosenior, Leroy		*2*								
Rush, Matthew	**2**	*3*	1							
Slater, Stuart	**37**	*3*	2		7		**3**		2	**5**
Stewart, Ray	**5**					*1*				
(own-goals)							**2**			**2**
24 players used	**506**	***58***	**33**	***3***	**77**	***7***	**60**	**6**	**15**	**81**

No	Date	Att	Pos	Pt	F-A	H-T	Scorers, Times, and Referees	1	2	3	4	5	6	7	8	9	10	11	subs used
1	H LUTON			D	0-0	0-0		Miklosko	**Brown**	**Thomas**	Breacker	Foster	Parris	Bishop*	Slater	**Small**	Rosenior	Allen M	Keen
	17/8	25,079		1				*Chamberlain*	*Beaumont*	*Harvey*	*McDonough*	*Ridger*	*Dreyer*	*Farrell**	*Preece*	*Stein*	*Pembridge*	*Black*	*Gray*
							Ref: M Bodenham	Division 1 has been expanded from 20 teams to 22. West Ham are among the favourites for the drop, so manager David Pleat is happy with this opening day point. Bonds prefers Rosenior to Morley, and gives debuts to three players - Mike Small, Kenny Brown and Mitchell Thomas.											
2	A SHEFFIELD UTD			D	1-1	0-0	Small 47	Miklosko	Brown	Thomas	Breacker	Foster	Parris	Bishop	Slater	Small	Rosenior*	Allen M^	Morley/Keen
	20/8	*21,463*		2			*Beesley 49*	*Tracey*	*Pemberton*	*Cowan*	*Jones*	*Beesley*	*Hill*	*Hoyland*	*Booker*	*Agana*	*Deane**	*Hodges^*	*Bryson/Whitehouse*
							Ref: I Hendrick	The Blades had a great run after Christmas. A grim match that produced seven bookings, just about par for Dave Bassett. The first half was extended by five minutes, not for injuries but for bookings. After Small swivelled to fire the opener, Beesley thundered an equaliser on the run.											
3	A WIMBLEDON			L	0-2	0-1		Miklosko	Brown	Thomas	Breacker	Foster	Parris	Bishop	Slater^	Small	Rosenior	Allen M*	Morley/Rush
	24/8	***10,801***		2			*Earle 31, Fashanu 70*	*Segers*	*Joseph*	*Phelan*	*Barton*	*Scales*	*Fitzgerald*	*Clarke**	*Earle*	*Fashanu !*	*Ryan*	*Fairweather^*	*Cork/Elkins*
							Ref: I Wiseman	The match centred on Dons' new captain John Fashanu. First he broke Foster's nose, accusing the Hammer of racist abuse. Fashanu is booked, then booked again – and sent off – for clattering Miklosko with his foot up. Said Dons' boss Ray Harford: 'He showed a lack of intelligence.'											
4	H ASTON VILLA			W	3-1	0-0	Small 66, Rosenior 68, Brown 87	Miklosko	Brown	Thomas	Breacker	Foster	Parris	Bishop	Slater	Small	Rosenior	Allen M*	Rush
	28/8	23,644	*9*	5			*Daley 50*	*Spink*	*Ehiogu*	*Price**	*Teale*	*McGrath*	*Richardson*	*Daley*	*Penrice*	*Regis*	*Cowans*	*Mortimer*	*Yorke*
							Ref: A Gunn	The pairing of Small and Rosenior – combined cost £700,000 – transformed this match to bring about Villa's first defeat. Daley's pacey opener was cancelled out when Small turned Ehiogu inside out. Thomas' flick set up Rosenior before Brown uncorked a spectacular 25-yarder											
5	H NOTTS CO		16	L	0-2	0-0		**Parks**	Brown	Thomas	Breacker	Foster	Parris	Bishop	Slater	Small	Rosenior*	Rush^	Morley/Hughton
	31/8	20,093		5			*Bartlett 64, 67*	*Cherry*	*Palmer*	*Paris*	*Short, Craig*	*Yates*	*Draper*	*Thomas*	*Dryden*	*Regis**	*Bartlett*	*Johnson*	*Turner*
							Ref: J Deakin	The last meeting of these sides saw West Ham robbed of the Division 2 Championship. Iain Dowie has gone to Southampton for a small profit. Miklosko is out with an injured ankle, making way for Tony Parks, on loan from Spurs. Lax defending brought two goals for Kevin Bartlett.											
6	A QP RANGERS		13	D	0-0	0-0		Parks	Brown	Thomas	Breacker	Foster	Parris	Bishop	Slater	Small*	Potts	Morley^	Rush/Rosenior
	4/9	*16,616*	*21*	6				*Stejskal*	*Bardsley*	*Brevett*	*Holloway**	*Peacock*	*Maddix*	*Bailey*	*Barker*	*Thompson*	*Wegerle*	*Wilson*	*Ferdinand*
							Ref: P Don	Gerry Francis' team are still looking for their first win. Miklosko is on international duty with Czechoslovakia. This was an enterprising 0-0 draw that earned a standing ovation at the end. The better chances fell to QPR. Skipper Ian Bishop was booked after a clash with Thompson.											
7	H CHELSEA		17	D	1-1	0-0	Small 48	Miklosko	Brown	Thomas	Breacker	Foster	Parris	Bishop	Slater	Small	Potts	Morley	
	7/9	18,875	*5*	7			*Dixon 56*	*Hitchcock*	*Clarke*	*Boyd*	*Jones*	*Elliott*	*Monkou*	*Le Saux*	*Townsend*	*Dixon*	*Wilson**	*Wise*	*Allon*
							Ref: J Carter	A vital Hammers win tossed away through bad luck, wasted chances and inspired goalkeeping by Hitchcock. West Ham hit the woodwork three times in the space of a few minutes. The third time, Small pounced to score. Le Saux crossed to the far post for Dixon's headed equaliser.											
8	A NORWICH		18	L	1-2	1-2	Small 15	Miklosko	Brown	Thomas	Breacker	Foster	Parris*	Bishop	Slater	Small	Potts	Morley^	Rush/Rosenior
	14/9	*15,348*	*14*	7			*Fox 13, Gordon 39*	*Gunn*	*Culverhouse*	*Bowen*	*Butterworth*	*Blades*	*Crook*	*Gordon*	*Fleck*	*Newman*	*Fox*	*Ullathorne**	*Goss*
							Ref: T West	West Ham fans are growing restless. The sweeper system that looked effective against Chelsea back-fired, so the players reverted to 4-4-2 during the game. Kenny Brown returns to his former club. Gordon's winner was a fluke, the ball taking a deflection to wrong-foot Miklosko.											
9	A CRYS PALACE		16	W	3-2	0-1	Thomas 52, Morley 56, Small 75	Miklosko	Brown	Parris	Thomas	Foster	Breacker	Bishop	Slater	Small	Potts	Morley	
	17/9	*21,363*	*15*	10			*Salako 12, Wright 61*	*Suckling*	*Humphrey*	*Sinton*	*Gray*	*Young*	*Thorn*	*McGoldrick**	*Pardew*	*Bright*	*Wright*	*Salako*	*Collymore*
							Ref: R Milford	Palace are besieged by the media following alleged racist remarks by chairman Ron Noades. Manager Steve Coppell said he felt punch-drunk by it all. West Ham's second goal was a fluke, Ludo's huge punt going in off Morley's heel. Small headed the winner from Breacker's cross.											
10	H MANCHESTER C		18	L	1-2	0-0	Brown 83	Miklosko	Brown	Thomas	Breacker	Foster !	Parris	Bishop	Slater	Small	Potts	Morley*	Rosenior
	21/9	**25,558**	*6*	10			*Redmond 76p, Hendry 90*	*Coton*	*Hill*	*Pointon*	*Brightwell*	*Curle*	*Redmond*	*White*	*Heath*	*Quinn*	*Megson*	*Hughes**	*Hendry*
							Ref: K Barratt	After an awful first half things had to improve. Foster unintentionally handles Quinn's shot and is sent off. Redmond stumbles while taking the penalty but the ball still goes in. Slater's cross set up the equaliser, but at the death Coton's clearance bounced in the area for Hendry's winner.											

No	Date	Opponent	Att	Pos	Pt	F-A	H-T	Scorers, Times, and Referees	1	2	3	4	5	6	7	8	9	10	11	subs used
11	A	NOTT'M FOREST		18	D	2-2	2-1	Small 16, 43	Miklosko	Breacker	Thomas	Gale	Foster	Parris	Bishop	Slater	Small*	Potts	Morley	Rosenior
	28/9		*25,613*	*14*	11			*Woan 4, Sheringham 77*	*Crossley*	*Charles*	*Pearce*	*Chettle*	*Tiler*	*Keane*	*Black*	*Parker*	*Gaynor**	*Sheringham*	*Woan*	*Walker*
								Ref: J Watson	Last season West Ham lost 0-4 to Forest in the FA Cup. Tony Gale plays his first full match of the season. Bishop plays a blinder. Hammers' first goal climaxed dazzling interplay between six players. Near the end Forest's centre-half Des Walker came on as a makeshift striker.											
12	H	COVENTRY		18	L	0-1	0-0		Miklosko	Breacker	Thomas*	Gale	Brown	Parris	Bishop	Slater	Small	Potts	Morley^	Allen M/Keen
	5/10		21,817	*5*	11			*Gallacher 78*	*Ogrizovic*	*Borrows*	*Billing*	*Robson*	*Pearce*	*Atherton*	*McGrath*	*Gynn*	*Furlong**	*Gallacher*	*Ndlovu^*	*Rosario/Emerson*
								Ref: P Foakes	Coventry are riding high and ex-Hammer Stewart Robson revels as their skipper. After 25 minutes Morley collides with keeper Ogrizovic and goes off shortly after with a gashed eye. West Ham looked the stronger team and came so close when Parris lobbed the keeper but hit a post.											
13	A	OLDHAM		18	D	2-2	1-2	Small 35, McAvennie 82	Miklosko	Breacker	Thomas	Gale	Potts	Parris	Bishop	Slater*	Small	Keen	Morley^	Allen M/McAvennie
	19/10		*14,365*	*16*	12			*McDonald 6, Breacker 40 (og)*	*Hallworth*	*Fleming*	*Barlow*	*Henry*	*Barrett*	*Jobson*	*McDonald*	*Marshall*	*Sharp*	*Milligan*	*Holden*	
								Ref: P Vanes	A meeting between the top two promoted clubs. Morley squandered two great chances before McAvennie came off the bench to replace him. Oldham boss Joe Royle complained about his defenders, even though two of them – Jobson and Barrett – were in last week's England squad.											
14	H	TOTTENHAM		17	W	2-1	2-1	Small 12, Thomas 28	Miklosko	Breacker	Thomas	Gale	Potts	Parris	Bishop	McAvennie	Small	Keen*	Slater	Allen M
	26/10		23,946	*13*	15			*Lineker 5*	*Thorstvedt*	*Edinburgh*	*v d Hauwe**	*Nayim^*	*Sedgley*	*Mabbutt*	*Stewart*	*Durie !*	*Samways*	*Lineker*	*Allen P*	*Bergsson/Houghton*
								Ref: D Elleray	The sting came in the tail. Breacker pushed Durie who claimed a penalty, not given. Durie took out his frustration on tiny Slater and provokes a brawl that even sucked in saintly Lineker. Durie was expelled. Small and McAvennie both hit a post, which denied West Ham an easier win.											
15	A	ARSENAL		14	W	1-0	0-0	Small 76	Miklosko	Breacker	Thomas	Gale	Potts	Parris	Bishop	McAvennie	Small	Keen	Slater	
	2/11		*33,539*	*5*	18				*Seaman*	*Dixon*	*Winterburn*	*Thomas**	*Pates*	*Linighan*	*Rocastle*	*Wright*	*Smith*	*Merson*	*Limpar*	*Groves*
								Ref: J Martin	Arsenal are distracted at the prospect of playing Benfica on Wednesday. They rest Tony Adams and look perfectly dreadful. Benfica spies dare not believe their eyes. West Ham hit Arsenal on the break with devastating effect. Mike Small's wonder strike had his team-mates in ecstasy.											
16	H	LIVERPOOL		15	D	0-0	0-0		Miklosko	Breacker	Thomas	Gale	Potts	Parris	Bishop	McAvennie	Small	Keen	Slater	
	17/11		23,569	*11*	19				*Grobbelaar*	*Jones*	*Burrows*	*Nicol*	*Molby*	*Tanner*	*McManam'n*	*Marsh*	*Rush*	*Walters*	*McMahon*	
								Ref: G Ashby	This Sunday match shown on TV was a wonderful advert for what is generally a dismal league. The result extends the Hammers' unbeaten run to seven games. Mike Small plays just 10 days after a cartilage operation. Ron Greenwood has returned to Upton Park as a 'consultant'.											
17	A	MANCHESTER U		16	L	1-2	0-2	McAvennie 76	Miklosko	Breacker	Thomas	Gale	Potts	Parris	Bishop	McAvennie	Small	Keen*	Slater	Allen M
	23/11		***47,185***	*1*	19			*Giggs 15, Robson 42*	*Schmeichel*	*Parker**	*Irwin*	*Bruce*	*Webb*	*Pallister*	*Robson*	*Kanchelskis*	*McClair*	*Hughes*	*Giggs*	*Blackmore*
								Ref: D Elleray	A ridiculous score, which greatly flattered the Hammers. Man U go back to the top with a wonder display. 'We could have had 10,' moaned Ferguson. Giggs scored with a super volley, and he and Kanchelskis were unstoppable, yet Schmeichel saved from McAvennie at the death.											
18	H	SHEFFIELD WED		17	L	1-2	0-1	Breacker 84	Miklosko	Breacker	Thomas	Gale	Potts	Parris	Bishop	McAvennie	Small	Keen*	Slater	Allen M
	30/11		24,116	*4*	19			*Harkes 24, Jemson 85*	*Woods*	*Harkes*	*King*	*Palmer**	*Warhurst*	*Pearson*	*B't-Williams*	*Sheridan*	*Hirst*	*Jemson*	*Worthington*	*Anderson*
								Ref: C Wilkes	Martin Allen comes off the bench and within seconds goes over the top on Carlton Palmer, who is stretchered off. Owls' boss Trevor Francis is angry that Allen isn't sent off. Friction between Frances and Allen dates from QPR, when Allen insisted on attending the birth of his first child.											
19	A	EVERTON		18	L	**0-4**	0-3	*[Johnston 53]*	Miklosko	Breacker !	Thomas	Gale	Potts	Parris*	Bishop	McAvennie	Small	Allen M	Slater	Keen
	7/12		*21,563*	*7*	19			*Cottee 8, Beagrie 10, Beardsley 37,*	*Southall*	*Jackson*	*Hinchcliffe*	*Ebbrell*	*Watson*	*Keown*	*Ward**	*Beardsley*	*Johnston*	*Cottee*	*Beagrie*	*Warzycha*
								Ref: A Wilkie	Everton were thrashed 1-4 by Leeds in the Rumbelows Cup in midweek, and West Ham feel the backlash. Breacker is booked for fouling Hinchcliffe and booked again for hacking Beagrie. So off he goes. Ian Bishop tried hard to impress Howard Kendall, who had twice sold him.											
20	H	SHEFFIELD UTD		18	D	1-1	0-0	Dicks 87p	Miklosko	Brown	Dicks	Gale	Potts	Foster	Bishop	McAvennie	Small*	Allen M	Slater	Keen
	21/12		19,287	*19*	20			*Deane 84*	*Tracey*	*Gage*	*Cowan*	*Gannon*	*Gayle !*	*Beesley*	*Bryson**	*Hoyland*	*Littlejohn*	*Deane*	*Whitehouse*	*Hodges*
								Ref: M Pierce	Julian Dicks makes his comeback after four months out injured, but is to blame for the first goal when he fails to control the ball. West Ham revert to the sweeper system. After 70 minutes Gayle is sent off for swearing, which seems harsh. Dicks rescues a point with a vicious penalty.											
21	A	ASTON VILLA		19	L	1-3	0-2	McAvennie 64	Miklosko	Breacker	Dicks	Gale	Potts	Parris	Bishop	McAvennie	Small*	Keen	Slater	Morley
	26/12		*31,959*	*6*	20			*Yorke 34, Daley 35, Richardson 89*	*Sealey*	*Kubicki*	*Staunton*	*Teale*	*McGrath*	*Richardson*	*Daley*	*Blake*	*Regis*	*Parker*	*Yorke**	*Froggatt*
								Ref: L Dilkes	Villa enjoyed so much possession against lightweight West Ham that it was surprising they had to wait so long to seal this win. Yorke opened with a close-range header; Daley's shot went in off Potts; McAvennie headed in Dicks' chipped pass; Richardson turned in Yorke's cross.											

No	Date	Att	Pos	Pt	F-A	H-T	Scorers, Times, and Referees	1	2	3	4	5	6	7	8	9	10	11	subs used
22	A NOTTS CO		21	L	0-3	0-0		Miklosko	Breacker	Dicks	Gale	Potts	Foster	Bishop	McAvennie	Small	Keen	Slater	
	28/12	*11,163*	*18*	20			*Turner 51, Harding 62, Agana 69*	*Cherry*	*Palmer*	*Paris*	*Short, Craig*	*Yates*	*Short, Chris*	*Thomas*	*Turner*	*Harding*	*Agana**	*Johnson^*	*Rideout/Slawson*
							Ref: J Worrall	West Ham are on a slippery slope now. They held their heads up through the first half, but once County took the lead the Hammers folded. Only skipper Ian Bishop acquitted himself adequately. With this result Luton climb above West Ham, who have taken just 2 points out of 21.											
23	H LEEDS		21	L	1-3	1-2	Dicks 24p	Miklosko	Breacker	Dicks	Gale	Potts	Thomas	Bishop	McAvennie	Small*	Keen	Slater	Morley
	1/1	21,766	*1*	20			*Chapman 11, 85, McAllister 38*	*Lukic*	*Sterland*	*Dorigo*	*Batty*	*Fairclough*	*Whyte*	*Strachan*	*Wallace, Rod*	*Chapman*	*McAllister*	*Speed*	
							Ref: R Groves	From Farnborough to table-topping Leeds. West Ham's best moment came when Dorigo fouled Keen for the penalty which made it 1-1. But then luck deserted the Hammers. But for John Lukic's heroics Leeds might well have lost. David Batty admitted: 'We were lucky to hold out.'											
24	H WIMBLEDON		21	D	1-1	0-0	Morley 89	Miklosko	Breacker	Dicks	Gale	Foster	Thomas*	Bishop	McAvennie	Brown	Keen^	Slater	Morley/Small
	11/1	18,485	*17*	21			*Sanchez 52*	*Segers*	*McGee*	*Phelan*	*Barton*	*Scales*	*Fitzgerald*	*Newhouse**	*Earle*	*Fashanu*	*Sanchez*	*Anthrobus*	*Clarke*
							Ref: R Gifford	The ill-fated debenture bond scheme for redeveloping Upton Park has enraged fans, who begin a series of demonstrations. Sanchez's powerful header gives the Dons a well-merited lead. Barton then fouled Bishop, Segers blocked Dicks' penalty, but Morley stooped to head into goal.											
25	A LUTON		20	W	1-0	0-0	Small 69	Miklosko	Breacker	Dicks	Potts	Foster	Thomas	Bishop	McAvennie^	Brown	Morley	Slater*	Keen/Small
	18/1	*11,088*	*22*	24				*Sutton*	*James*	*Harvey*	*Kamara*	*Dreyer*	*Peake*	*Telfer**	*Stein*	*Nogan^*	*Pembridge*	*Preece*	*Campbell/Oakes*
							Ref: R Bigger	The two bottom teams swap places as a result of Mike Small's fortuitous goal. His shot deflected off Peake's right foot for the winner. Peake was lucky to be still on the pitch, having head-butted Morley in the first half. David Pleat admitted that Luton were never going to score.											
26	H OLDHAM		20	W	1-0	1-0	Thomas 33	Parks	Breacker	Dicks	Potts	Foster	Thomas	Keen	McAvennie	Brown	Morley*	Slater	Small
	1/2	19,012	*16*	27				*Hallworth*	*Barrett*	*Barlow*	*Henry*	*Jobson*	*Marshall*	*Adams*	*Bernard*	*Sharp*	*Milligan**	*Holden^*	*Fleming/Palmer*
							Ref: K Cooper	Six points in two games and two clean sheets. But it was another dodgy goal that won this game. Mitchell Thomas, a £500,000 summer buy, sliced his shot badly, but the ball somehow beat Hallworth. Parks played instead of the calf-strained Miklosko, and saved well from Barlow.											
27	A SHEFFIELD WED		21	L	1-2	1-0	Small 14	Parks	Breacker	Dicks	Potts	Foster	**Atteveld**	Bishop	Keen*	Small	Allen M	Slater	Brown
	22/2	*24,150*	*4*	27			*Palmer 80, Anderson 88*	*Woods*	*Nilsson*	*Worthington*	*Palmer*	*Anderson*	*Shirtliff*	*Wilson*	*Hyde**	*Hirst*	*Johnson^*	*Harkes*	*B'tWilliams/Williams*
							Ref: T Fitzharris	A grudge match, fuelled by memories of Martin Allen's crippling lunge at Palmer at Upton Park. Small heads in after the ball comes back off a post. The Owls force 17 second-half corners, but their winner comes from a disputed free-kick. Tony Parks was cautioned by police at the end.											
28	H EVERTON		21	L	0-2	0-1		Parks	Breacker^	Dicks	Potts	Foster	Thomas	Bishop	Brown	Small	Allen M	Slater*	Morley/Rush
	29/2	20,976	*9*	27			*Johnston 6, Ablett 64*	*Southall*	*Jackson**	*Ablett*	*Ebbrell*	*Watson*	*Keown*	*Ward*	*Beardsley*	*Johnston*	*Cottee^*	*Hinchcliffe*	*Beagrie/Harper*
							Ref: A Smith	Out of the Cup, headed for the drop, and a pitch invasion to protest at the board. These are bad times for West Ham. Angry fans held up play by releasing thousands of balloons. One fan also planted the corner flag in the centre-circle. Martin Allen admitted later: 'we did not play well.'											
29	A SOUTHAMPTON		22	L	0-1	0-0		Parks	Potts	Dicks	Gale^	Foster	Thomas*	Bishop	Brown	Small	Allen M	Slater	Morley/Rush
	3/3	*14,548*	*21*	27			*Dowie 62*	*Flowers*	*Dodd*	*Benali*	*Horne*	*Moore*	*Ruddock*	*Le Tissier*	*Cockerill*	*Shearer*	*Dowie*	*Hurlock*	
							Ref: R Lewis	The two bottom teams swap places, thanks to former Hammer Iain Dowie's header from Horne's deep cross. The game was dreadfully scrappy, ruled by fear, with highly promising Alan Shearer as anonymous as everyone else. Hammers find themselves bottom for the first time.											
30	A LIVERPOOL		22	L	0-1	0-1		Miklosko	Brown	Dicks	Gale	Potts	Thomas*	Bishop	Keen	Small	Allen M	Slater	Rush
	11/3	*30,821*	*5*	27			*Saunders 3*	*Grobbelaar*	*Jones*	*Venison*	*Nicol*	*Redknapp*	*Wright*	*Saunders*	*Houghton**	*Thomas*	*Barnes^*	*McManam'n*	*Marsh/Rosenthal*
							Ref: J Rushton	Draws won't save West Ham, so Bonds instructs his players to go out to win. Jamie Redknapp's fierce 30-yarder took everyone by surprise and was spilled by Miklosko. That gave West Ham little option but to attack. Graeme Souness's tight-marking instructions stifled West Ham.											
31	H ARSENAL		22	L	0-2	0-1		Miklosko	Brown	Dicks	Gale	Foster	Keen	Bishop	McAvennie*	Small	Allen M^	Slater	Morley/Parris
	14/3	22,640	*6*	27			*Wright 13, 51*	*Seaman*	*Dixon*	*Winterburn*	*Hillier*	*Bould*	*Adams*	*Rocastle*	*Wright*	*Smith**	*Merson*	*Groves^*	*Campbell/O'Leary*
							Ref: B Hill	Dicks spent the match kicking Perry Groves up in the air, in one spell committing five fouls on the winger in 11 minutes. The ref booked both players, Groves for over-protesting. Like West Ham, Arsenal fans are up in arms over redevelopment plans and release a barrage of balloons.											

32	H	QP RANGERS	22	D	2-2	1-0	Small 28, Breacker 75	Miklosko	Brown	Dicks	Gale	Foster	Keen^	Bishop*	McAvennie	Small	Allen M	Slater	Thomas/Breacker
21/3		20,401	*9*	28			*Allen 50, 70*	*Stejskal*	*Bardsley*	*Wilson*	*Impey*	*Peacock*	*McDonald*	*Wilkins*	*Holloway*	*Ferdinand*	*Allen B**	*Sinton*	*Barker*
							Ref: D Allison	A tale of two Allens. Martin Allen's strike is disallowed, owing to Small being offside. West Ham could have been 2-0 up, but within seconds cousin Bradley Allen beat three defenders to equalise. After the game Dicks was called into Taylor's England squad to visit Czechoslovakia.											
33	A	LEEDS	22	D	0-0	0-0		Miklosko	Brown	Dicks	Breacker	Foster	Potts	Bishop	Thomas	Small	Allen M^	Slater*	McAvennie /Gale
28/3		*31,101*	*1*	29				*Lukic*	*Cantona*	*Dorigo*	*Batty*	*Fairclough*	*Newsome*	*Strachan*	*Wallace, Rd**	*Chapman*	*McAllister*	*Speed*	*Wetherall*
							Ref: K Barratt	Lee Chapman's unbelievable misses in this game threaten Leeds' championship hopes. The worst boob came after 20 minutes, when Cantona's wonderful reverse pass sent Batty clear down the right. Batty's cross was missed in front of the posts. Miklosko made some good saves too.											
34	A	TOTTENHAM	22	L	0-3	0-1		Miklosko	Brown*	Dicks	Gale	Foster	Breacker^	Bishop	Thomas	Small	Potts	Slater	McAvennie /Keen
1/4		*31,809*	*17*	29			*Lineker 16, 53, 60p*	*Walker*	*v d Hauwe**	*Edinburgh*	*Gray^*	*Dundy*	*Mabbutt*	*Stewart*	*Durie*	*Nayim*	*Lineker*	*Allen P*	*Sedgley/Walsh*
							Ref: D Gallagher	Three strikes from the right boot of Gary Lineker earn three points for the team with the worst home record in the division. Ex-Hammer Paul Allen rolled the ball into his path for 1-0. Breacker fouled Durie for the decisive penalty. At the end of the season Lineker will be off to Japan.											
35	A	CHELSEA	22	L	1-2	1-1	Allen C 27	Miklosko	Brown	Dicks	Gale	Foster	Potts	Bishop	McAvennie	Thomas	**Allen C**	Keen*	Morley
4/4		*20,684*	*9*	29			*Wise 26, Cascarino 48*	*Beasant*	*Clarke*	*Myers*	*Jones**	*Elliott*	*Monkou*	*Le Saux*	*Bailey*	*Stuart*	*Cascarino*	*Wise*	*Barnard*
							Ref: P Jones	Chelsea had won at home just once in 1992, and they too are immersed in off-pitch troubles over the future of their stadium. West Ham did not win their first corner till the 79th minute. Billy Bonds kept his players behind locked doors afterwards for an inquest into their lack of passion.											
36	H	NORWICH	22	W	**4-0**	2-0	Rush 14, 36, Dicks 71p, Bishop 79	Miklosko	Breacker	Dicks	Potts	Martin A	Thomas	Bishop	Rush	Small*	Allen C	Slater	Keen
11/4		**16,896**	*17*	32				*Walton*	*Bowen*	*Ullathorne*	*Butterworth*	*Polston*	*Goss*	*Fox*	*Power**	*Newman*	*Beckford*	*Smith*	*Sutton^/Sutch*
							Ref: P Foakes	John Major has just won the General Election. Bonds drops five players. Matthew Rush plays his first full 90 minutes, and is rewarded with two headers from Bishop corners. When Thomas was brought down for a penalty, Dicks had no intention of letting Rush claim his hat-trick.											
37	H	SOUTHAMPTON	22	L	0-1	0-0		Miklosko	Breacker	Gale	Hughton	Martin A	Morley	Bishop	Rush*	Small	Allen C	Slater	Keen
14/4		18,298	*17*	32			*Adams 88*	*Flowers*	*Kenna*	*Adams*	*Horne*	*Moore*	*Ruddock*	*Le Tissier*	*Cockerill*	*Shearer*	*Dowie**	*Benali*	*Widdrington*
							Ref: R Hamer	Two minutes from time Le Tissier crosses and Mickey Adams volleys in at the far post. This is Saints' seventh win in eight games, a superb run that hauls them out of the relegation mire. The Hammers crowd had threatened to walk out after 50 minutes in protest, but they stayed put.											
38	A	MANCHESTER C	22	L	0-2	0-1		Miklosko	Breacker	Dicks	Potts	Martin A	Keen	Bishop	Gale	Small*	Morley	Slater	Clarke
18/4		*25,601*	*5*	32			*Pointon 1, Clarke 77*	*Coton*	*Hill**	*Pointon*	*Brightwell*	*Curle*	*Vonk*	*White*	*Sheron*	*Hughes*	*Simpson*	*McMahon*	*Clarke*
							Ref: M Peck	In the first minute the ball rebounded into the path of City's Neil Pointon, who obliged with his first goal of the season. With West Ham having to press forward in a vain attempt to save the game, Wayne Clarke found himself with time and space to tuck the ball under Miklosko.											
39	H	CRYS PALACE	22	L	0-2	0-1		Miklosko	Breacker*	Dicks	Potts	Martin A	Thomas	Bishop	Keen	Morley	Allen C	Slater	Brown
20/4		17,710	*10*	32			*Bright 26, Coleman 53*	*Martyn*	*Humphrey*	*Sinnott*	*Southgate*	*Young*	*Thorn*	*Gordon**	*Thomas*	*Bright*	*Coleman*	*McGoldrick*	*Moralee*
							Ref: A Buksch	This is West Ham's first ever defeat by Palace, and it means only mathematical improbabilities can save them now. Tim Breacker's crazy back-pass set up Bright's 21st goal of the season. Palace's up-and-under tactics presented too many questions for West Ham to answer.											
40	H	MANCHESTER U	22	W	1-0	0-0	Brown 66	Miklosko	Potts	Dicks	Gale	Martin A	Thomas	Bishop	Keen	Small	Brown	Slater	
22/4		24,197	*2*	35				*Schmeichel*	*Irwin*	*Donaghy**	*Bruce*	*Phelan*	*Pallister*	*Giggs*	*Blackmore^*	*McClair*	*Hughes*	*Sharpe*	*Ferguson/Kanchel's*
							Ref: J Deakin	Having lost at home to Forest two days earlier, this is a crippling defeat for title chasing Man U. Ferguson's team played cautiously and with little rhythm, and managed no shots at all by half-time. Pallister inadvertently steered Slater's cross to Brown, whose father was in the stand.											
41	A	COVENTRY	22	L	0-1	0-1		Miklosko	Potts	Dicks	Gale	Martin A	Thomas	Bishop^	Keen	Small	Brown*	Slater	Morley/**Martin D**
25/4		*15,398*	*19*	35			*Gynn 44*	*Ogrizovic*	*McGrath*	*Sansom**	*Robson*	*Billing*	*Atherton*	*Flynn*	*Gynn*	*Ndlovu*	*Gallacher*	*Smith*	*Borrows*
							Ref: P Wright	This result sends West Ham down. Ironically, the only team they could in theory have overtaken was Don Howe's Coventry, who had failed to score in their last five games. Ludo made a hash of Kevin Gallacher's cross, and Gynn swept home. Dicks had West Ham's only shot on target.											
42	H	NOTTINGHAM F	22	W	3-0	0-0	McAvennie 60, 81, 85	Miklosko	Potts	Dicks	Gale	Martin A	Thomas*	Bishop	Allen M	Small	Martin D	Slater	McAvennie
2/5		20,629	*8*	38				*Crossley*	*Chettle*	*Williams*	*Walker*	*Crosby*	*Wilson**	*Black*	*Gemmill*	*Clough*	*Sheringham*	*Woan^*	*Stone/Glover*
Home		Away					Ref: N Midgley	Frank McAvennie comes on as a second-half substitute and records a hat-trick in his farewell appearance in claret and blue. He was assisted by Brian Clough playing his son Nigel at centre-half. Alvin Martin set up Dean Martin to 'score' on his full debut, but the effort was disallowed.											
Average 21,285		22,641																	

Rumbelows Cup					F-A	H-T	Scorers, Times, and Referees	1	2	3	4	5	6	7	8	9	10	11	subs used
2:1	A	BRADFORD C	18	W	1-1	1-1	Small 12	Miklosko	Brown	Parris	Thomas	Foster	Breacker	Bishop	Slater	Small	Potts	Morley*	Gale
24/9		*7,034 3:10*					*Leonard 5*	*Tomlinson*	*Mitchell*	*Dowson*	*James*	*Leonard*	*Gardner*	*Babb*	*Duxbury*	*Torpey*	*Tinnion*	*Reid*	
							Ref: R Nixon	City have suffered only one defeat in eight and tackle the Hammers with gusto. Leonard scored off a post to put them in front, and had he paid proper attention Mitchell would have made it 2-0. Morley's cross drifted over the entire home defence for Small's downward header.											
2:2	H	BRADFORD C	18	W	4-0	2-0	Keen 9, Morley 36, Parris 56, Small 73	Miklosko	Breacker	Thomas	Gale	Foster	Parris	Bishop	Slater	Small*	Keen	Morley	McAvennie
9/10		17,232 *3:13*						*Tomlinson*	*Mitchell*	*Dowson*	*James*	*Oliver*	*Gardner*	*Babb*	*Duxbury*	*Torpey**	*Tinnion*	*Morgan^*	*Leonard/McCarthy*
							Ref: M James (Hammers win 5-1 on aggregate)	A huge ovation after 87 minutes greets Frank McAvennie's first appearance of the season, though the contest was over long before then. West Ham went in front when Slater's cross came off a defender for Keen. Morley and Small added headers, and Parris rounded keeper Tomlinson.											
3	A	SHEFFIELD UTD	17	W	2-0	1-0	McAvennie 44, Small 54p	Miklosko	Breacker	Thomas	Gale*	Potts	Parris	Bishop	McAvennie	Small	Keen	Slater	Allen M
29/10		*11,144 22*						*Kite*	*Pemberton*	*Cowan*	*Gannon*	*Gayle*	*Beesley*	*Bryson**	*Holroyd*	*Agana*	*Bradshaw^*	*Whitehouse*	*Mendonca/Lake*
							Ref: G Courtney	McAvennie's header from Slater's cross gives West Ham the edge they never surrender. The 4-4-2 system looks solid. When John Pemberton hacked down Slater in the box it extended West Ham's unbeaten run to five. The Blades didn't have the best of luck, hitting a post in each half.											
4	A	NORWICH	17	L	1-2	0-0	Small 73	Miklosko	Breacker	Thomas	Gale	Potts	Parris	Bishop	McAvennie	Small	Allen M	Slater	
4/12		*16,325 8*					*Fleck 65, 89p*	*Gunn*	*Phillips*	*Bowen*	*Sutton*	*Blades**	*Goss*	*Ullathorne*	*Fleck*	*Newman*	*Sherwood*	*Beckford^*	*Crook/Fox*
							Ref: K Morton	Robert Fleck sinks West Ham single handed. His first was a swivelling volley from 20 yards, his second – the late winner – a penalty when Thomas needlessly pushed Bowen in the area. McAvennie's flick on to Small had made it 1-1. Beckford missed numerous chances for City.											

FA Cup																			
3	A	FARNBOROUGH	21	D	1-1	0-0	Dicks 66	Miklosko	Breacker	Dicks	Gale	Potts*	Thomas	Bishop	McAvennie	Small	Keen	Slater	Morley
4/1		*23,449*					*Coney 86p*	*Power*	*Stemp*	*Baker**	*Broome*	*Bye*	*Wigmore*	*Doherty^*	*Holmes*	*Coney*	*Read*	*Fleming*	*Horton/Rogers*
							Ref: R Groves (At Upton Park)	Farnborough switch the tie to the Boleyn. New skipper Dicks plays a one-two with Small to put West Ham in front, but with time running out he handles in the box. Regular taker Mick Doherty had been subbed, so Dagenham-based Hammers' fan Dean Coney did the business instead.											
3R	H	FARNBOROUGH	21	W	1-0	0-0	Morley 88	Miklosko	Breacker	Dicks	Gale	Foster	Thomas	Bishop	McAvennie	Brown	Morley	Slater	
14/1		23,869						*Power*	*Stemp*	*Baker**	*Broome*	*Bye*	*Wigmore*	*Doherty*	*Holmes*	*Coney*	*Read*	*Fleming*	*Rogers*
							Ref: R Groves	West Ham look bewildered in the face of the GM Vauxhall Conference side's fluent play. Breacker's late cross set up the Hammers' totally ill-merited win. Power tried to fist clear, but the ball fell to Morley. Farnborough had had the best chance, but Ludo spread himself to deny Read.											
4	H	WREXHAM	20	D	2-2	1-0	Dicks 27, Morley 74	Miklosko	Breacker	Dicks	Potts	Foster	Thomas	Keen	McAvennie*	Brown	Morley	Slater	Small
25/1		24,712 *4:19*					*Phillips 60, Jones L 80*	*O'Keefe*	*Thackeray*	*Hardy*	*Taylor*	*Thomas*	*Sertori*	*Davies**	*Owen*	*Connolly*	*Watkin*	*Phillips*	*Jones L*
							Ref: C Trussell	Hammers fans stage a stand-up, sit-down demo before kick-off. Wrexham had beaten Arsenal in Round 3. Dicks and Morley both scored with headers from set pieces. Wrexham earned a replay when Miklosko could only get a faint touch to 18-year-old substitute, Lee Jones', effort.											
4R	A	WREXHAM	20	W	1-0	1-0	Foster 27	Parks	Breacker	Dicks	Potts	Foster	Thomas	Keen	McAvennie*	Brown	Small^	Slater	Martin D/Morley
4/2		*17,995 4:19*						*O'Keefe*	*Thackeray*	*Hardy*	*Taylor*	*Thomas*	*Seroti*	*Davies*	*Owen*	*Connolly*	*Watkin*	*Phillips**	*Jones L*
							Ref: C Trussell	Wrexham are near the foot of Division 4, and ex-Man U winger Mickey Thomas faces charges of counterfeiting. O'Keefe is stranded at Kean's corner: Foster's looping header is his first goal of the season. Breacker scythes Connolly, who has burst clear, but escapes with a yellow card.											
5	A	SUNDERLAND	20	D	1-1	0-0	Small 48	Parks	Breacker	Dicks	Potts	Foster	Atteveld	Keen	Brown	Small	Allen M	Slater	
15/2		*25,475 2:12*					*Byrne 64*	*Norman*	*Kay*	*Rogan*	*Bennett**	*Hardyman*	*Davenport*	*Bracewell*	*Ballk*	*Armstrong*	*Byrne*	*Atkinson*	*Pascoe*
							Ref: R Nixon	West Ham live to fight another day after a cup-tie played in an icy Roker wind, against a team with a caretaker manager – Malcolm Crosby. Martin Allen tried to claim Mike Small's goal. John Byrne miskicked Sunderland's equaliser. The winners will play Chelsea in the last eight.											
5R	H	SUNDERLAND	21	L	2-3	1-2	Allen 38, 56	Parks	Breacker	Dicks	Potts	Foster	Atteveld*	Bishop	Keen	Small	Allen M	Slater	Morley
26/2		25,830 *2:12*					*Byrne 6, 24, Rush 78*	*Norman*	*Kay*	*Rogan*	*Rush*	*Hardyman*	*Davenport**	*Bracewell*	*Ball*	*Armstrong*	*Byrne*	*Atkinson*	*Brady*
							Ref: R Nixon	Sunderland had not beaten a top division side in the FA Cup for 13 years. They were helped in this replay by on-loan Atteveld's ludicrous early back-pass from the halfway line. The result is West Ham's first home defeat under floodlights in three years. Sunderland will reach Wembley.											

		Home					Away					
	P	W	D	L	F	A	W	D	L	F	A	Pts
1 Leeds	42	13	8	0	38	13	9	8	4	36	24	82
2 Manchester U	42	12	7	2	34	13	9	8	4	29	20	78
3 Sheffield Wed	42	13	5	3	39	24	8	7	6	23	25	75
4 Arsenal	42	12	7	2	51	22	7	8	6	30	24	72
5 Manchester C	42	13	4	4	32	14	7	6	8	29	34	70
6 Liverpool	42	13	5	3	34	17	3	11	7	13	23	64
7 Aston Villa	42	13	3	5	31	16	4	6	11	17	28	60
8 Nott'm Forest	42	10	7	4	36	27	6	4	11	24	31	59
9 Sheffield Utd	42	9	6	6	29	23	7	3	11	36	40	57
10 Crys Palace	42	7	8	6	24	25	7	7	7	29	36	57
11 QP Rangers	42	6	10	5	25	21	6	8	7	23	26	54
12 Everton	42	8	8	5	28	19	5	6	10	24	32	53
13 Wimbledon	42	10	5	6	32	20	3	9	9	21	33	53
14 Chelsea	42	7	8	6	31	30	6	6	9	19	30	53
15 Tottenham	42	7	3	11	33	35	8	4	9	25	28	52
16 Southampton	42	7	5	9	17	28	7	5	9	22	27	52
17 Oldham	42	11	5	5	46	36	3	4	14	17	31	51
18 Norwich	42	8	6	7	29	28	3	6	12	18	35	45
19 Coventry	42	6	7	8	18	15	5	4	12	17	29	44
20 Luton	42	10	7	4	25	17	0	5	16	13	54	42
21 Notts Co	42	7	5	9	24	29	3	5	13	16	33	40
22 WEST HAM	42	6	6	9	22	24	3	5	13	15	35	38
	924	208	135	119	678	496	119	135	208	496	678	1251

Odds & ends

Double wins: (0).
Double losses: (6) Notts Co, Man C, Coventry, Sheff W, Everton, Southampton.

Won from behind: (3) Villa (h), Palace (a), Spurs (h).
Lost from in front: (1) Sheff W (a).

High spots: Four unbeaten league games from 18 October.

Low spots: Relegation, and the humiliation of finishing last.
Five successive league defeats from 22 February.

Hammer of the Year: Julian Dicks.
Ever-presents: (0).
Hat-tricks: (1) Frank McAvennie.
Leading scorer: (18) Mike Small.

	Appearances						Goals			
	Lge	*Sub*	LC	*Sub*	FAC	*Sub*	**Lge**	LC	FAC	**Tot**
Allen, Clive	**4**						**1**			**1**
Allen, Martin	**14**	*5*	1	*1*	2				2	**2**
Atteveld, Ray	**1**				2					
Bishop, Ian	**41**		4		3		**1**			**1**
Breacker, Tim	**33**	*1*	4		6		**2**			**2**
Brown, Kenny	**25**	*2*	1		4		**3**			**3**
Clarke, Simon		*1*								
Dicks, Julian	**23**				6		**3**		2	**5**
Foster, Colin	**24**		2		5				1	**1**
Gale, Tony	**24**	*1*	3	*1*	2					
Hughton, Chris		*1*								
Keen, Kevin	**20**	*9*	2		5			1		**1**
Martin, Alvin	**7**									
Martin, Dean	**1**	*1*				*1*				
Miklosko, Ludek	**36**		4		3					
McAvennie, Frank	**16**	*4*	2	*1*	4		**6**	1		**7**
Morley, Trevor	**13**	*11*	2		2	*3*	**2**	1	2	**5**
Parks, Tony	**6**				3					
Parris, George	**20**	*1*	4					1		**1**
Potts, Steve	**34**		3		5					
Rosenior, Leroy	**5**	*4*					**1**			**1**
Rush, Matthew	**3**	*7*					**2**			**2**
Slater, Stuart	**41**		4		6					
Small, Mike	**37**	*3*	4		4	*1*	**13**	4	1	**18**
Thomas, Mitchell	**34**	*1*	4		4		**3**			**3**
25 players used	**462**	***52***	**44**	***3***	**66**	***5***	**37**	**8**	**8**	**53**

No	Date		Att	Pos	Pt	F-A	H-T	Scorers, Times, and Referees	1	2	3	4	5	6	7	8	9	10	11	subs used
1	A	BARNSLEY			W	1-0	1-0	Allen C 21	Miklosko	Breacker	Dicks	Potts	Martin	Parris^	Bishop	**Butler**	Small !	Allen C*	Keen	Gale/**Robson**
	16/8		*6,761*		3				*Butler*	*Robinson*	*Bishop*	*Fleming*	*Taggart*	*Archdeacon*	*Redfearn*	*Bullimore*	*Pearson*	*Currie*	*Rammell**	*Liddell*
								Ref: R Nixon	Supporters saddened by the sale of Stuart Slater to Celtic are cheered by this win, secured after Clive Allen played a one-two with Keen. West Ham hung on grimly after half-time and survived two strong penalty shouts. On 83 mins Small was expelled for foul language to a linesman.											
2	H	CHARLTON		17	L	0-1	0-1		Miklosko	Breacker	Dicks	Potts	Martin	Parris	Bishop*	Butler	Small	Allen C	Keen	Robson
	22/8		17,054	*1*	3			*Pardew 31*	*Bolder*	*Pitcher**	*Barness*	*Pardew*	*Webster*	*Gatting*	*Lee^*	*Bumstead*	*Dyer*	*Nelson*	*Walsh*	*Balmer/Grant*
								Ref: P Durkin	Bonds had watched Robert Lee, whose cross set up a simple goal for Alan Pardew. Small hit a post, Keen's lob was disallowed, and Martin's header was cleared off the line. Mark Robson, a free-transfer from Spurs, comes off the bench. Alan Curbishley is co-manager of Charlton.											
3	A	NEWCASTLE		19	L	0-2	0-2		Miklosko	Breacker	Dicks !	Potts	Martin	**Holmes***	Bishop	Butler	Allen M	Allen C	Keen	Small
	29/8		***29,855***	*4*	3			*Peacock 44, Kelly 45*	*Wright*	*Venison*	*Ranson*	*O'Brien*	*Scott*	*Howey*	*Carr*	*Peacock*	*Kelly*	*Clark*	*Sheedy*	
								Ref: W Burns	The Keegan revival at St James' Park is under way. 15 minutes from time Dicks, already booked, was sent off for elbowing Franz Carr, who had played for Hammers on loan. New signing Matt Holmes also had to go off concussed. One Hammers goal in three games tells the story.											
4	H	WATFORD		13	W	2-1	0-0	Allen M 52, Allen C 84	Miklosko	Breacker	Dicks	Potts	Martin	Allen M	Robson*	Butler	Morley	Allen C	Keen	Parris
	5/9		11,921	*8*	6			*Furlong 82*	*Suckling*	*Gibbs*	*Drysdale*	*Dublin*	*Holdsworth*	*Ashby*	*Hessenthaler*	*Nogan*	*Furlong*	*Butler**	*Soloman^*	*Bazeley/Putney*
								Ref: R Lewis	Watford boss Steve Perryman admitted: 'We didn't deserve a point.' But when Paul Furlong pushed Alvin Martin off the ball to score from a tight angle, it looked like they would get one. The new back-pass law saw a free-kick given against Ludo, after the ball spun to him off Dicks.											
5	A	PETERBOROUGH		7	W	3-1	3-1	Morley 25, Allen M 28, Keen 41	Miklosko	Breacker	Thomas	Potts	Martin	Allen M	Robson	Butler	Morley	Allen C*	Keen	Small
	12/9		*10,657*	*17*	9			*Adcock 19*	*Bennett*	*Luke*	*Robinson*	*Halsall*	*Howarth*	*Welsh*	*Sterling*	*Ebdon*	*Adcock*	*Charlery*	*Barnes**	*Costello*
								Ref: J Rushton	The first ever competitive match with The Posh. Morley and Keen's goals were both aided by deflections. Martin Allen, who had missed badly earlier on, made amends by springing the offside trap to put West Ham 2-1 ahead. Bonds is rumoured to be about to enter the transfer market.											
6	A	BRISTOL CITY		5	W	5-1	3-0	Robson 6, Allen C 44, 85, Morley 27, 89	Miklosko	Breacker	Thomas	Potts	Martin	Allen M	Robson*	Butler	Morley	Allen C	Keen	Small
	15/9		*14,130*	*9*	12			*Scott 54*	*Welch*	*Llewellyn*	*Scott*	*Thompson*	*Bryant*	*Edwards*	*Harrison*	*Dziek'owski**	*Rosenior*	*Cole^*	*Shelton*	*Allison/Connor*
								Ref: J Martin	Coach Harry Redknapp was interviewed by police for gestures allegedly aimed at the Ashton Gate crowd. The game looked over by half-time, but Scott's free-kick encouraged Andy Cole to spark a second-half onslaught. Clive Allen's second goal took the sting out of City's revival.											
7	H	DERBY		5	D	1-1	0-1	Morley 47	Miklosko	Breacker	Thomas	Potts	Martin	Allen M	Robson*	Butler	Morley	Allen C	Keen	Small
	20/9		11,493	*24*	13			*Thomas 41 (og)*	*Taylor*	*Comyn*	*Forsyth*	*Short*	*Wassall*	*Pembridge*	*Johnson*	*Kitson*	*Gabbiadini**	*Williams^*	*Simpson*	*Sturridge/Coleman*
								Ref: I Hemsley	Rock-bottom Derby have equalled the British record transfer fee for a defender, signing Craig Short from Notts Co for £2.5 million. Morley, who has signed a new one-year contract, was marked by Short but escaped to equalise. Thomas' own-goal went in off Miklosko. Kitson plays.											
8	A	PORTSMOUTH		4	W	1-0	1-0	Allen C 45	Miklosko	Breacker	Dicks	Potts	Martin	Allen M	Robson*	Butler	Morley	Allen C	Keen	Holmes
	27/9		*12,158*	*15*	16				*Knight*	*Awford*	*Daniel*	*McLoughlin*	*Symons*	*Aspinall*	*Neill**	*Dolling*	*Clarke*	*Whittingham*	*Murray^*	*Walsh/Powell*
								Ref: K Cooper	Dicks' suspension is over, but he was not immediately restored to the side. Friction with Bonds intensifies, though Dicks says: 'Me and Billy get on fine.' Morley is denied a goal by the inside of a post and by super saves from Knight. Bonds says: 'We played some great football.'											
9	A	WOLVES		7	D	0-0	0-0		Miklosko	Breacker	Dicks !	Potts	Martin	Allen M	Robson*	Butler	Morley	Allen C^	Keen	Holmes/Gale
	4/10		*14,391*	*3*	17				*Stowell*	*Ashley*	*Edwards*	*Downing*	*Mountfield*	*Blades*	*Birch*	*Cook*	*Bull*	*Roberts**	*Rankine*	*Mutch*
								Ref: D Allison	Dicks is sent off yet again, this time for series of running clashes with Steve Bull. With both players having been booked, Dicks lunges at the England striker and gets his second yellow card. Bull was accused of feigning injury. A game which started brightly quickly degenerated.											
10	H	SUNDERLAND		5	W	**6-0**	3-0	Keen 25, Morley 28, Allen M 39, [Martin 48, Robson 62, 89]	Miklosko	Breacker	Dicks	Potts	Martin	Allen M	Robson	Butler	Morley	Allen C	Keen	
	11/10		**10,326**	*15*	20				*Carter*	*Kay*	*Rogan*	*Owers*	*Bennett*	*Ball*	*Cunningham**	*Goodman*	*Davenport*	*Gray, Martin*	*Armstong^*	*Atkinson/Rush*
								Ref: R Milford	Having lost to Crewe, this is a timely pick-me-up in front of a TV audience. The Hammers' record win, in 1968, was against Sunderland, when Geoff Hurst scored six. At 0-0 Don Goodman cleared the West Ham offside trap, but missed. The Boleyn's lowest league crowd for 30 years.											
11	A	BRISTOL ROV		2	W	4-0	3-0	Morley 17, Dicks 35p, Keen 41, Allen C 83	Miklosko	Breacker	Dicks	Potts	Martin	Allen M	Robson	Butler	Morley	Allen C	Keen	
	17/10		***6,189***	*24*	23				*Kelly*	*Alexander*	*Clark*	*Yates*	*Hardyman*	*Skinner*	*Mehew*	*Reece*	*Taylor*	*Stewart*	*Cross*	
								Ref: G Ashby	The Hammers started slowly but gradually upped the tempo. Morley held his nerve to put them in front. Dicks' thunderbolt penalty marked his temporary farewell, as he commences a five-match ban and is fined one week's wages. Clive Allen added No 4 when Butler's shot hit a post.											

No	Date	Opponent	Att	Pos	Pt	Res	F-A	H-T	Scorers, Times, and Referees	1	2	3	4	5	6	7	8	9	10	11	subs used
12	H	SWINDON		3		L	0-1	0-0		Miklosko	Breacker	Parris !	Potts	Martin	Allen M	Robson	Butler	Morley	Allen C	Keen	
	24/10		17,842	*2*	23				*Maskell 84*	*Hammond*	*Kerslake*	*Horlock*	*Hoddle*	*Calderwood*	*Taylor*	*Hazard*	*Moncur**	*Maskell*	*Ling*	*Mitchell*	*White*
									Ref: I Borrett	West Ham deserved better than this, losing to a disputed free-kick which led to a deflected goal. George Parris had brought down Martin Ling for which he was sent off. The healthy-sized crowd was a response to lowered ticket prices and the prospect of seeing Glenn Hoddle in action.											
13	A	CAMBRIDGE		4		L	1-2	0-1	Morley 50	Miklosko	Breacker	Parris	Potts	Martin	Allen M	Robson	Butler	Morley	Allen C	Keen	
	31/10		*7,214*	*17*	23				*Norbury 36, White 72*	*Dennis*	*Fensome*	*Kimble*	*Raynor*	*Heathcote*	*O'Shea*	*Rowett*	*Norbury**	*White*	*Clayton*	*Philpott^*	*Ainsworth/Danzey*
									Ref: G Pooley	Managerless Cambridge, who reached last season's play-offs, are the arch-exponents of up-and-under football. At 1-1 Devon White capitalised when West Ham failed to clear their lines. So convinced were the Hammers that White was offside that Martin Allen was booked for dissent.											
14	A	GRIMSBY		4		D	1-1	0-0	Morley 74	Miklosko	Breacker	Parris	Potts	Martin	Allen M	Robson*	Butler	Morley	Allen C	Keen	Holmes
	3/11		*9,119*	*13*	24				*Mendonca 54*	*Beasant*	*McDermott*	*Croft*	*Futcher*	*Lever*	*Dobbin*	*Watson*	*Gilbert*	*Groves*	*Mendonca*	*Rees**	*Smith*
									Ref: W Burns	West Ham are unchanged despite having lost their last two. Two super goals enlivened this match. Mendonca's 25-yard stunner was answered by Trevor Morley's drive, set up by Matt Holmes. For the second game in a row Clive Allen is one-on-one with the goalkeeper, and misses.											
15	H	NOTTS CO		4		W	2-0	1-0	Allen C 42, Morley 60	Miklosko	Breacker	Brown	Potts	Martin	Allen M	Robson	Butler	Morley	Allen C	Keen	
	7/11		12,345	*21*	27					*Cherry*	*Short, Chris*	*Thomas*	*Palmer*	*Johnson*	*Williams*	*Devlin*	*Turner**	*Lund*	*Draper*	*Slawson*	*Bartlett*
									Ref: A Gunn	Upton Park is strangely subdued, perhaps by County's spoiling tactics. Mark Robson set Clive Allen away to curl the first goal. Trevor Morley added a second after Steve Potts' shot was parried. County manager Neil Warnock had the grace to say afterwards 'the score flattered us.'											
16	A	MILLWALL		5		L	1-2	0-1	Robson 77	Miklosko	Breacker	Brown	Potts	Martin	Parris	Robson	Holmes	Morley	Allen C	Keen*	Clarke
	15/11		*12,445*	*4*	27				*Allen M 41p, Barber 55*	*Keller*	*Cunningham*	*Dawes*	*May*	*Cooper*	*Stevens*	*Rae*	*Moralee**	*Allen M^*	*Byrne*	*Barber*	*Dolby/Goodman*
									Ref: K Morton	Both teams have an M Allen, so it is as well for commentators that West Ham's 'Martin' is suspended. Millwall's 'Malcolm' scored from the spot after Robson felled Cunningham. At 2-0, Robson chipped Keller and Alvin Martin hit a post. Lions' Mick McCarthy was mighty relieved.											
17	H	OXFORD		4		W	5-3	3-1	Allen C 4, B'ker 38, Dicks 42, 50, Morley 86	Miklosko	Breacker	Dicks	Potts	Martin	Parris	Robson	Holmes	Morley	Allen C	Keen*	Brown
	21/11		11,842	*13*	30				*Durnin 1, Magilton 51, Melville 53*	*Reece*	*Smart*	*Ford*	*Lewis*	*Evans*	*Melville*	*Magilton*	*Beauchamp*	*Penney*	*Durnin**	*Allen C*	*Cusack*
									Ref: R Wiseman	A wonderful game, agreed Oxford boss Brian Horton, which earned a standing ovation at the end. Before kick-off Oxford boasted the meanest away defence in the division. A corner inside 45 seconds brought Durnin's goal. It was nip and tuck until Morley glanced in a late free-kick.											
18	H	BIRMINGHAM		3		W	3-1	1-1	Allen C 21, 86, Morley 85	Miklosko	Breacker	Dicks	Potts	Foster	Parris	Robson	Holmes	Morley	Allen C	Keen*	Bishop
	28/11		15,004	*19*	33				*Rodgerson 12*	*Sealey*	*Holmes**	*Potter*	*Tait*	*Rogers*	*Matthewson*	*Rodgerson*	*Gayle*	*Speedie*	*Frain*	*Donowa*	*Sturridge*
									Ref: R Pawley	Trevor Morley was sent off in Reggiani in midweek in the Anglo-Italian Cup. With club captain Dicks suspended, and deputy Alvin Martin also missing, the armband passes to Steve Potts. Clive Allen equalised for the Hammers with a glancing header from Mark Robson's cross.											
19	A	TRANMERE		3		L	**2-5**	1-1	Morley 20, Allen C 79	Miklosko	Breacker	Dicks	Potts	Martin	Allen M^	Robson	Parris*	Morley	Allen C	Keen	Bishop/Foster
	4/12		*11,782*	*2*	33				*Aldridge 17, 71, 89, Irons 48, Malkin 90*	*Nixon*	*Higgins*	*Brannan*	*Irons*	*Mungall*	*Vickers*	*Morrissey*	*Aldridge*	*Malkin*	*McNab**	*Nevin*	*Martindale*
									Ref: P Harrison	Tranmere stay on Newcastle's heels thanks to veteran John Aldridge's latest hat-trick. For his first he skipped round Miklosko; for his third he exploited Ludo's hashed clearance. Bonds: 'You could have driven a double decker bus through our defence.' Now off to Cozenza in Italy.											
20	H	SOUTHEND		3		W	2-0	1-0	Morley 37, Allen C 67	Miklosko	Breacker	Dicks	Potts	Martin	Parris*	Robson	Allen M	Morley	Allen C	Keen	Bishop
	12/12		15,739	*24*	36					*Sansome*	*Edwards*	*Powell*	*Cornwall*	*Scully*	*Prior*	*Locke*	*Sussex*	*Brown*	*Collymore*	*Tilson*	
									Ref: W Burge	Hammers on half-throttle were still far too good for dreadful Southend, for whom only recent signing Stan Collymore made any impact. Keen and Robson out wide repeatedly opened up the visiting defence. Both goals were headers. Southend boss Colin Murphy had no poems to recite.											
21	A	BRENTFORD		3		D	0-0	0-0		Miklosko	Breacker	Dicks	Potts	Martin	Allen M	Robson*	Bishop	Morley	Allen C	Keen	**Bunbury**
	20/12		*11,912*	*12*	37					*Benstead*	*Statham*	*Manuel*	*Millen*	*Westley*	*Ratcliffe*	*Bennett**	*Luscombe^*	*Allon*	*Blissett*	*Gayle*	*Smillie/Godfrey*
									Ref: M James	Trevor Morley won most of his aerial battles against a 6ft 4in centre-half. Keeper Graham Benstead did well to save from Clive Allen and Bishop, but West Ham might easily have lost at the death when substitute Neil Smillie was denied by Miklosko. Brentford's slide now begins.											
22	A	CHARLTON		3		D	1-1	1-0	Dicks 10	Miklosko	Breacker	Dicks	Potts	Martin	Allen M	Robson	Bishop*	Morley	Allen C	Keen	Bunbury
	26/12		*8,337*	*11*	38				*Bumstead 79*	*Bolder*	*Pitcher*	*Minto*	*Bumstead*	*Webster*	*Balmer*	*Robinson*	*Power*	*Leaburn**	*Nelson*	*Walsh*	*Garland*
									Ref: I Hemley	The capacity of the restored Valley is so small that West Ham supporters are restricted to just 400 tickets. Julian Dicks' free-kick is deflected past Bob Bolder and the Hammers lead for over an hour, but when John Bumstead hits the post he is also quickest to pounce on the loose ball.											
23	H	LUTON		3		D	2-2	0-0	Dicks 52p, Breacker 67	Miklosko	Breacker	Dicks	Potts	Martin	Allen M	Robson	Butler	Morley	Allen C	Keen	
	28/12		18,786	*20*	39				*Hughes 68, Dreyer 70*	*Chamberlain*	*Dreyer*	*James*	*Johnson*	*Hughes*	*Peake*	*Williams**	*Telfer*	*Rees^*	*Gray*	*Preece*	*Benjamin/Oakes*
									Ref: M Pierce	David Pleat thought his side were in control till half-time. When Robson was nudged off the ball by Hughes, Dicks obliged from the spot. Tim Breacker then scored from 25 yards against his former club. Hughes' instant reply was capped when a scrambled corner just crossed the line.											

No	Date		Att	Pos	Pt	F-A	H-T	Scorers, Times, and Referees	1	2	3	4	5	6	7	8	9	10	11	subs used
24	A	DERBY		2	W	2-0	2-0	Robson 9, Morley 15	Miklosko	Breacker	Dicks !	Potts	Martin^	Allen M	Robson*	Butler	Morley	Allen C	Keen	Foster/Parris
	10/1		13,737	11	42				Sutton	Kavanagh	Forsyth	Short	Coleman	Pembridge	McMinn	Kuhl	Kitson	Johnson*	Simpson	Gabbiadini
								Ref: A Wilkie	Dicks is in the news again, this time for his late lunge at Ted McMinn which earned a second yellow card. It's his third dismissal of the season, and Bonds has no sympathy with him. Fortunately, West Ham were 2-0 up at the time, so Dicks' loss was not vital. Best Hammer was Morley.											
25	H	PORTSMOUTH		3	W	2-0	1-0	Morley 26, Foster 55	Miklosko	Breacker	Dicks	Potts	Foster	Allen M	Robson^	Butler	Morley	Allen C*	Keen	Holmes/Parris
	16/1		18,127	6	45				Knight	Awford	Daniel	McLoughlin	Symons	Burns*	Neill^	Chamberlain	Walsh	Whittingham	Aspinall	Powell/Maguire
								Ref: R Gifford	Morley's brave flying header required treatment for a gashed lip. Foster's goal was also a header. Pompey boss Jim Smith said: 'West Ham are the best team we have played this season'. Pompey will shortly start their surge. Had they lost this game 0-1, they would have won promotion.											
26	H	BRISTOL CITY		2	W	2-0	0-0	Morley 66, Robson 73	Miklosko	Breacker	Brown	Potts	Gale	Allen M	Robson^	Butler	Morley	Bunbury*	Keen	Holmes/Parris
	27/1		12,118	18	48				Welch	Atteveld*	Scott	Aizlewood	Bryant	Osman	Shelton	Harrison	Allison	Cole	Gavin^	Rosenior/Dziek'owski
								Ref: B Hill	Yet another 2-0 win. Russell Osman takes charge of City for the first time, and Canadian international Alex Bunbury starts a game for the first time. The break came when Welch failed to hold Keen's shot. Atteveld, formerly at Upton Park, escaped expulsion for a late foul on M Allen.											
27	A	LEICESTER		2	W	2-1	1-1	Robson 19, Gale 53	Miklosko	Breacker	Brown	Potts	Gale	Allen M	Robson*	Butler	Morley	Holmes	Keen^	Parris/**Jones**
	30/1		18,838	6	51			Lowe 6	Hoult	Mills	Gibson	Smith	Walsh	Hill*	Oldfield	Thompson	Joachim^	Lowe	Philpott	James/Gee
								Ref: K Redfearn	Signed back in November, Billericay's Steve Jones makes his long-awaited debut. Mind you, he does not come on till the 88th minute. Gale's looping header was the transfer-listed player's first goal for two years. The result leaves third-placed Tranmere six points behind the Hammers.											
28	H	BARNSLEY		2	D	1-1	1-1	Jones 10	Miklosko	Breacker	Dicks	Potts	Gale	Allen M	Robson	Butler	Morley	Jones	Keen	
	6/2		14,101	16	52			Rammell 42	Butler	Robinson	Taggart	Fleming	Bishop	Archdeacon	O'Connell	Redfearn	Pearson	Currie*	Rammell	Liddell
								Ref: S Dunn	Two weeks earlier Barnsley dumped West Ham from the FA Cup. Steve Jones starts his first game and scores his first goal, after Robson's shot fell to him. Martin Allen then hit a dipper against the bar. Rammell's equaliser came when a Barnsley corner was headed back across goal.											
29	H	PETERBOROUGH		2	W	2-1	2-1	Butler 4, Jones 13	Miklosko	Breacker	Dicks	Potts	Gale	Allen M	Robson	Butler	Morley	Jones	Keen*	Holmes
	9/2		12,537	11	55			Ebdon 36	Bennett	Luke	Spearing	Halsall	Bradshaw	Welsh*	Sterling	McGlashan	Adcock	Philliskirk	Curtis^	Howarth/Iorfa
								Ref: G Pooley	Peter Butler scores his first Hammers goal, after Keen's header came back off a post. Steve Jones swivels to connect with Morley's header for his second goal in 72 hours. Ebdon made it 2-1 with a half-volley. Early in the second half Jones was fouled but Dicks' penalty was saved.											
30	A	WATFORD		2	W	2-1	1-0	Robson 21, Keen 68	Miklosko	Breacker	Dicks	Potts	Gale	Allen M	Robson*	Butler	Morley	Jones^	Keen	Holmes/Bishop
	13/2		13,115	14	58			Charley 52	Suckling	Lavin*	Drysdale	Dublin	Holdsworth	Willis	Hessenthaler	Nogan^	Furlong	Charlery	Soloman	Holdsworth/Porter
								Ref: K Leach	Kevin Keen's father once managed, and was sacked by, Watford. Robson's diving header from Dicks' cross was cancelled out by Hessenthaler's low shot, turned in by Ken Charlery. Keen then fires a ballistic winner. This win leaves Hammers four points behind leaders Newcastle.											
31	H	NEWCASTLE		2	D	0-0	0-0		Miklosko	Brown	Dicks	Potts	Gale	Allen M	Robson	Butler	Morley	Bishop	Keen*	Jones
	21/2		24,159	1	59				Srnicek	Venison	Beresford	O'Brien	Scott	Howey	Lee	Peacock	Kelly	Clark	Sheedy	
								Ref: K Cooper	A Sunday TV stalemate. Keegan may be building a reputation for gung-ho football, but he knows the importance of not losing and packs his midfield. Bonds does the same, with the result that chances are few. Ex-Hammer David Kelly was rudely barracked on his return to Upton Pk.											
32	A	SUNDERLAND		2	D	0-0	0-0		Miklosko	Brown	Dicks	Potts	Gale	Bishop	Robson^	Butler	Morley	Bunbury*	Keen	Parris/Holmes
	27/2		19,068	16	60				Norman	Kay	Ord	Atkinson	Butcher	Ball	Mooney*	Goodman	Colquhoun	Gray, Michael	Armstrong	Davenport
								Ref: J Worrall	Bobby Moore died in midweek and the football world is in mourning. Wreathes are laid by both sets of supporters and the minute's silence was scrupulously observed. With Martin Allen suspended, it falls to Ian Bishop to wear Moore's No 6 shirt. The game itself was forgettable.											
33	H	WOLVES		2	W	3-1	0-0	Morley 58, Dicks 61p, Holmes 87	Miklosko	Brown	Dicks	Potts	Gale	Bishop	Robson	Butler	Morley	Small	Keen^	Holmes
	6/3		24,679	11	63			Bull 57	Stowell	Blades	Venus	Burke	Mountfield	Madden	Rankine*	Cook	Bull	Thompson	Dennison	Mutch
								Ref: R Bigger	Upton Park is awash with wreathes. Hurst and Peters place a floral No 6 in the centre-circle. Bishop wears No 12, not 6. Bull volleys in against the run of play. It is quickly levelled when Morley converts Robson's cross. Madden fouled Keen for the penalty, but it looked outside the box.											
34	H	GRIMSBY		2	W	2-1	2-0	Dicks 6, 11	Miklosko	Brown	Dicks	Potts	Gale	Allen M	Robson	Butler	Morley	Small*	Keen	Bishop
	9/3		13,170	9	66			Groves 61	Wilmott	McDermott	Croft	Futcher	Lever	Jobling	Ford	Gilbert*	Groves	Rees	Woods^	Mendonca/Agnew
								Ref: A Gunn	Hammers' unbeaten league run is now 15 games. Dicks headed in Keen's corner, then blasted a second after a corner had been cleared. A post then denied him a hat-trick. But Dicks' hand also conceded a penalty, which Gilbert fired against the bar. Groves' goal was a fantastic volley.											

No	Venue	Opponent	Att	Pos	Res	F-A	H-T	Scorers, Times, and Referees	1	2	3	4	5	6	7	8	9	10	11	subs used
35	A	NOTTS CO		2	L	0-1	0-0		Miklosko	Brown	Dicks	Potts	Gale	Allen M	Robson*	Butler	Morley	Small	Keen	Bishop
	13/3		10,272	17	66			Walker 70	Cherry	Short, Chris	Johnson	Thomas	Cox	Walker	Lund	Draper	Wilson	Williams*	Smith	Devlin
								Ref: I Cruickshanks	County have a plush new stadium and a new manager, Michael Walker. Richard Walker scores on his debut to inflict on West Ham their first league defeat since 4 December. Home keeper Steve Cherry was untroubled apart from Robson's cheeky back-heel. Dicks was booked again.											
36	H	TRANMERE		2	W	2-0	0-0	Dicks 54p, 82p	Miklosko	Brown	Dicks	Potts	Gale	Allen M	Robson*	Butler	**Speedie**	Morley	Keen	Holmes
	20/3		16,369	7	69				Nixon	Higgins	Mungall	Irons	Proctor	Vickers	Morrissey	Coyne	Malkin*	Nevin	Thomas	Branch
								Ref: M Read	Dicks is rumoured to be about to sign for Chelsea. Perhaps they want his spot-kick expertise, for he blazed two penalties past Nixon, both for fouls against Morley. The first was questionable, as he and Vickers chased a through ball. Much-travelled David Speedie has arrived on loan.											
37	A	OXFORD		2	L	0-1	0-0		Miklosko	Brown	Dicks	Potts	Gale	Allen M	Holmes	Butler	Speedie	Morley	Keen*	Robson
	23/3		9,506	15	69			Melville 85	Reece	Robinson	Ford	Lewis	Evans	Melville	Phillips	Beauchamp	Cusack	Durnin	Narbett	
								Ref: K Burge	Oxford had taken just one point from their previous six games, so this is a mighty upset, watched by Oxford's biggest gate of the season. After half-time the home side were attacking at will down the Manor's slope. Near the end Cusack's cross was met by the unmarked Andy Melville.											
38	H	MILLWALL		2	D	2-2	2-1	Keen 12, Morley 13	Miklosko	Breacker	Brown	Potts	Gale	Bishop	Robson	Butler	Speedie	Morley	Keen	
	28/3		15,723	5	70			Moralee 1, Stevens 77	Keller	Cunningham	Dawes	Roberts	Cooper	Stevens	Maguire*	Bogie	Allen M^	Moralee	Barber	Kerr/Gaynor
								Ref: M Bailey	A mid-day kick-off, after the clocks have been changed, seems to leave West Ham sluggish. Jamie Moralee's sensational start for Millwall was pegged back by Keen's flying volley and Morley's side-step. Stevens restored parity with a brave header, though Gale's free-kick hit a post.											
39	A	BIRMINGHAM		2	W	2-1	0-1	Brown 87, Bishop 89	Miklosko	Breacker	Brown	Potts	Gale	Bishop	Robson*	Butler	Speedie	Jones^	Keen	Holmes/Foster
	3/4		19,053	21	73			Saville 12	Catlin	Clarkson	Frain	Parris	Dryden	Matthewson	Moulden*	Rodgerson	Saville	Peer	Smith	Sturridge
								Ref: M Peck	What a finish! Andy Saville had been playing for Hartlepool earlier in the season but his goal spelled gloom for Hammers until Kenny Brown's pile-driver and Ian Bishop's dipping winner sends the Boleyn into raptures. Colin Foster had come off the bench to play as a makeshift striker.											
40	A	SOUTHEND		3	L	0-1	0-1		Miklosko	Breacker	Dicks	Potts	Gale	Bishop	Robson	Butler	Speedie	Foster	Keen	
	7/4		12,813	23	73			Angell 32	Royce	Edwards	Powell	Jones	Scully	Prior	Ansah	Smith	Tilson	Collymore	Angell	
								Ref: I Borrett	Barry Fry has only been at Southend a few days but Roots Hall is a frenzy of excitement. West Ham played well, but the goal that beat them was a gem. Keith Jones freed Stan Collymore down the left. Potts was turned inside out and the cross was smashed in off the bar by Angell.											
41	H	LEICESTER		3	W	3-0	2-0	Speedie 10, 29, Keen 47	Miklosko	Breacker	Dicks	Potts	Gale	Bishop	Robson	Butler	Speedie	Morley	Keen	
	11/4		13,951		76				Poole	Coatsworth*	Mills	Smith	Walsh	Hill	Oldfield	Thompson	Joachim	Lowe	Philpott^	Whitlow/James
								Ref: G Poll	33-year-old David Speedie has already played for four clubs this season. West Ham fans have not taken to him. He waits for this TV Sunday match to score his first Hammers goals. He bagged two but should have had five. Portsmouth's win the previous day keeps West Ham third.											
42	A	LUTON		3	L	0-2	0-0		Miklosko	Breacker	Dicks	Potts	Gale	Bishop	Allen M*	Butler	Speedie	Morley	Keen	Holmes
	13/4		10,959	16	76			Gray 84p, Williams 88	Chamberlain	Dreyer	Telfer^	Johnson	James	Peake	Hughes*	Kamara	Dixon	Gray	Preece	Oakes/Williams
								Ref: G Singh	A calamitous defeat, which turned on a ferociously contested late penalty. Dicks was shoved off the ball by Kerry Dixon and in the subsequent melee handled the ball. Dicks should have been sent off. Phil Gray despatched the penalty. Williams then caught West Ham on the break.											
43	H	BRENTFORD		3	W	4-0	1-0	Butler 17, Keen 67, Morley 72, Allen M 89	Miklosko	Breacker	Dicks	Potts	Gale	Allen M	Robson	Butler	Speedie	Morley	Keen	
	17/4		16,522	20	79				Peyton	Statham	Sansom	Westley	Evans	Manuel	Stephenson*	Dickens	Gayle	Blissett	Bennett	Smillie
								Ref: P Foakes	Peter Butler's son was born on the Monday and he celebrates with his second goal of the season – a glancing header from Dicks' cross. The Bees are on a dreadful slide and will go down. Speedie appeared to throw a punch but escaped. Portsmouth have won 10 out of their last 11.											
44	H	BRISTOL ROV		3	W	2-1	0-0	Dicks 55p, Speedie 58	Miklosko	Breacker	Dicks	Potts	Gale	Allen M	Robson*	Butler	Speedie	Morley	Keen	Bishop
	24/4		16,682	24	82			Clark 49	Kelly	Maddison	Tillson	Yates	Clark	Mehew*	Channing^	Evans	Taylor	Saunders	Waddock	Stewart/Reece
								Ref: A Smith	Bottom-placed Rovers are already down, and Clark's goal is too much for some Hammers fans to stomach. Speedie is the butt of their abuse. But it is his cross which was handled for the penalty. His courageous headed winner, which left him semi-conscious, earned standing applause.											
45	A	SWINDON		2	W	3-1	1-0	Morley 42, Allen C 57, Brown 82	Miklosko	Breacker	Dicks	Potts	Gale	Bishop	Robson*	Butler	Speedie	Morley^	Keen	Allen C/Brown
	2/5		17,004	5	85			Hazard 61	Digby	Summerbee	Viveash	Hoddle	Calderwood	Taylor	Hazard	MacLaren	Mitchell	Ling	White*	Marwood
								Ref: T Holbrook	This match was played on Sunday. On Saturday Portsmouth lost 1-4 at Sunderland, their first defeat in 12. Morley, recovered from flu, evades the offside trap for No 1. Clive Allen returns after three months out with a calf injury and adds No 2. Ludo then lets a shot go through his legs.											
46	H	CAMBRIDGE		2	W	2-0	0-0	Speedie 47, Allen C 90	Miklosko	Breacker	Dicks	Potts	Gale	Bishop	Robson*	Butler	Speedie^	Morley	Keen	Allen C/Allen M
	8/5		**27,399**	23	88				Filan	Heathcote	Kimble*	Raynor	Chapple	O'Shea	Sheffield^	Claridge	Butler	Clayton	Leadbitter	Fensome/Bartlett
	Home	Away						Ref: D Elleray	Cambridge must win to stay up. Manager Ian Atkins has pinned up Bishop's quote: 'Cambridge ought to be a formality.' Portsmouth must beat Grimsby by more than West Ham beat Cambridge. Leadbitter's equaliser is disallowed for offside. Pompey lead 2-1 when Clive Allen seals it.											
Average	15,984	13,014																		

Coca-Cola Cup					F-A	H-T	Scorers, Times, and Referees	1	2	3	4	5	6	7	8	9	10	11	subs used
2:1 H	CREWE		5	D	0-0	0-0		Miklosko	Breacker	Thomas	Potts	Martin	Allen M	Robson	Butler	Morley	Allen C	Keen*	Small
23/9		6,981	*3:4*					*Greygoose*	*McKearney*	*Whalley*	*Wilson*	*Carr*	*Macauley*	*Gardiner*	*Garvey*	*Clarkson**	*Harvey^*	*Walters*	*Naylor/Hughes*
							Ref: A Maile	A small crowd. Under Dario, Crewe are renowned for playing enterprising football, whoever the opposition. Using a sweeper, and spraying passes about, Crewe constantly frustrated the Hammers, though Graygoose saved well from Morley and Martin Allen. Bonds leaves out Dicks.											
2:2 A	CREWE		7	L	0-2	0-0		Miklosko	Breacker	Dicks	Potts	Martin	Allen M	Robson	Butler	Morley	Allen C	Keen	
7/10		*5,427*	*3:4*				*Naylor 72, Hignett 79*	*Greygoose*	*McKearney*	*Whalley*	*Wilson*	*Carr*	*Macauley*	*Hignett*	*Naylor*	*Clarkson**	*Harvey^*	*Walters*	*Garvey/Gardiner*
							Ref: T Lunt (Hammers lose 0-2 on aggregate)	The unbeaten run comes to an abrupt end. Hammers blunted their swords against the inspired goalkeeping of Dean Graygoose – whose save from Dicks' volley was breathtaking – and were exposed to devastating counter-attacks. Crewe got behind West Ham's defence far too often.											
FA Cup																			
3 A	WEST BROM		3	W	2-0	2-0	Allen C 33, Robson 42	Miklosko	Breacker	Dicks	Potts	Martin	Allen M	Robson	Butler	Morley	Allen C	Keen	
2/1		*25,896*	*2:2*					*Naylor*	*Shakesp're**	*Lilwall*	*Bradley*	*Raven*	*Strodder*	*Garner*	*Hamilton*	*Taylor*	*McNally*	*Donovan^*	*Fereday/Hackett*
							Ref: A Gunn	Freezing weather and thickening fog, which did more to threaten West Ham's cup progress than could Ardiles' WBA. Martin Allen's through ball set up cousin Clive; and Dick's dummy made No 2. Both Morley and Bradley hit the woodwork. Bobby Moore does radio commentary.											
4 A	BARNSLEY		3	L	1-4	0-2	Morley 52p	Miklosko	Breacker	Brown	Potts	Foster	Allen M	Robson*	Butler	Morley	Holmes	Keen	Bunbury
24/1		*13,716*	*12*				*Rammell 32, 34, 77, Redfearn 71*	*Butler*	*Gridlet*	*Taggart*	*Fleming*	*Bishop*	*Archdeacon*	*Redfearn*	*O'Connell*	*Currie*	*Biggins**	*Rammell*	*Pearson*
							Ref: C Trussell	The squally wind was with West Ham in the first half but they could not capitalise. Instead Wayne Biggins made two goals for Andy Rammell. Hammers' only hope came when Fleming shoved Allen in the back. Penalty! Holmes later hit the bar. Rammell's hat-trick goal was deflected.											

	Home						Away					
	P	W	D	L	F	A	W	D	L	F	A	Pts
1 Newcastle	46	16	6	1	58	15	13	3	7	34	23	96
2 WEST HAM	46	16	5	2	50	17	10	5	8	31	24	88
3 Portsmouth	46	19	2	2	48	9	7	8	8	32	37	88
4 Tranmere	46	15	4	4	48	24	8	6	9	24	32	79
5 Swindon *	46	15	5	3	41	23	6	8	9	33	36	76
6 Leicester	46	14	5	4	43	24	8	5	10	28	40	76
7 Millwall	46	14	6	3	46	21	4	10	9	19	32	70
8 Derby	46	11	2	10	40	33	8	7	8	28	24	66
9 Grimsby	46	12	6	5	33	25	7	1	15	25	32	64
10 Peterborough	46	7	11	5	30	26	9	3	11	25	37	62
11 Wolves	46	11	6	6	37	26	5	7	11	20	30	61
12 Charlton	46	10	8	5	28	19	6	5	12	21	27	61
13 Barnsley	46	12	4	7	29	19	5	5	13	27	41	60
14 Oxford	46	8	7	8	29	21	6	7	10	24	35	56
15 Bristol City	46	10	7	6	29	25	4	7	12	20	42	56
16 Watford	46	8	7	8	27	30	6	6	11	30	41	55
17 Notts Co	46	10	7	6	33	21	2	9	12	22	49	52
18 Southend	46	9	8	6	33	22	4	5	14	21	42	52
19 Birmingham	46	10	4	9	30	32	3	8	12	20	40	51
20 Luton	46	6	13	4	26	26	4	8	11	22	36	51
21 Sunderland	46	9	6	8	34	28	4	5	14	16	36	50
22 Brentford	46	7	6	10	28	30	6	4	13	24	41	49
23 Cambridge	46	8	6	9	29	32	3	10	10	19	37	49
24 Bristol Rov	46	6	6	11	30	42	4	5	14	25	45	41
	1104	263	147	142	859	590	142	147	263	590	859	1509

* promoted after play-offs

Odds & ends

Double wins: (7) Watford, Peterborough, Bristol C, Portsmouth, Bristol R, Birmingham, Leicester.

Double losses: (0).

Won from behind: (7) Peterborough (a), Oxford (h), Birmingham (h&a), Leicester (a), Wolves (h), Bristol R (h).

Lost from in front: (0).

High spots: Promotion.

Four successive league wins in January and again in April-May.

Unbeaten run of 15 league games, from 20 December.

Low spots: Picking up just one point from three games beginning 24 October.

An embarrassing Coca-Cola Cup exit at Third Division Crewe.

Hammer of the Year: Steve Potts.

Ever-presents: (3) Ludek Miklosko, Steve Potts, Kevin Keen.

Hat-tricks: (0).

Leading scorer: (21) Trevor Morley.

	Appearances						Goals			
	Lge	*Sub*	LC	*Sub*	FAC	*Sub*	Lge	LC	FAC	Tot
Allen, Clive	**25**	*2*	2		1		**14**		1	**15**
Allen, Martin	**33**	*1*	2		2		**4**			**4**
Bishop, Ian	**15**	*7*					**1**			**1**
Breacker, Tim	**39**		2		2		**2**			**2**
Brown, Kenny	**13**	*2*			1		**2**			**2**
Bunbury, Alex	**2**	*2*				*1*				
Butler, Peter	**39**		2		2		**2**			**2**
Clarke, Simon		*1*								
Dicks, Julian	**34**		1		1		**11**			**11**
Foster, Colin	**3**	*3*			1		**1**			**1**
Gale, Tony	**21**	*2*					**1**			**1**
Holmes, Matt	**6**	*12*			1					
Jones, Steve	**4**	*2*					**2**			**2**
Keen, Kevin	**46**		2		2		**7**			**7**
Martin, Alvin	**23**		2		1		**1**			**1**
Miklosko, Ludek	**46**		2		2					
Morley, Trevor	**41**		2		2		**20**		1	**21**
Parris, George	**10**	*6*								
Potts, Steve	**46**		2		2					
Robson, Mark	**41**	*3*	2		2		**8**		1	**9**
Small, Mike	**5**	*4*		*1*						
Speedie, David	**11**						**4**			**4**
Thomas, Mitchell	**3**		1							
(own-goals)							**1**			**1**
23 players used	**506**	***47***	**22**	***1***	**22**	***1***	**81**		**3**	**84**

No	Date		Att	Pos	Pt	F-A	H-T	Scorers, Times, and Referees	SQUAD	NUMBERS	IN	USE								subs used
1	H	WIMBLEDON			L	0-2	0-0		Miklosko	Breacker	Dicks	Potts	Gale	Allen M	**Gordon**	Butler	Morley	Allen C	Holmes*	**Rowland**
	14/8		20,369		–			*Fashanu 63, Sanchez 72*	*Segers*	*Joseph*	*Kimble*	*Sanchez*	*Scales*	*Fitzgerald*	*Clarke^*	*Earle*	*Fashanu*	*Holdsworth*	*Fear**	*Blackwell/Barton*
								Ref: K Burge	Squad numbers are in, with Dons' Alan Kimble wearing shirt No 35. Upton Park resembles a building site for this first match back in the big time. Wimbledon cruise to a second-half victory, but Sam Hammam was reported to the FA for scrawling graffiti on the changing room walls.											
2	A	LEEDS			L	0-1	0-0		Miklosko	Breacker	Dicks	Potts^	Foster	Gale	Gordon	Butler	Morley	Allen C*	Allen M	Rowland/Robson
	17/8		*34,588*		–			*Speed 61*	*Lukic*	*Kelly*	*Dorigo*	*Batty*	*Fairclough*	*O'Leary*	*Strachan^*	*Whelan**	*Deane*	*McAllister*	*Speed*	*Wallace/Newsome*
								Ref: R Dilkes	Champions in 1992, Leeds barely survived the drop the following season. Nor are they firing on all cylinders this time, for this will be their only win in their first five games. Hammers are used to losing at Elland Road; once they fell behind they hadn't the firepower to fight back.											
3	A	COVENTRY		19	D	1-1	1-0	Gordon 45	Miklosko	Breacker	Dicks	Potts	Foster	Allen M	Gordon	Butler	Morley	Allen C	Rowland	
	21/8		*12,864*	*4*	1			*Wegerle 57*	*Gould*	*Sheridan^*	*Babb*	*Atherton*	*Rennie*	*Morgan*	*Williams**	*Ndlovu*	*Wegerle*	*Quinn*	*Flynn*	*Williams/Boland*
								Ref: S Lodge	Dale Gordon scores West Ham's first goal of 1993-94 at just the right moment, on the stroke of half-time, but not even that tonic can prompt a first victory. Off the field all the talk surrounds Julian Dicks, who Bonds seems set to sell to raise much-needed cash. But Dicks wants to stay.											
4	H	SHEFFIELD WED		15	W	2-0	0-0	Allen C 79, 84	Miklosko	Breacker	Dicks	Potts	Foster	Allen M	Gordon*	Butler	Morley	Allen C	Rowland	Holmes
	25/8		19,441	*21*	4				*Woods*	*Nilsson*	*Worthington*	*Palmer*	*Warhurst**	*Walker*	*Hyde*	*Waddle*	*Hirst^*	*Bt-Williams*	*Sinton*	*Bright/Pearson*
								Ref: J Worrall	Trevor Francis' Wednesday go into this game with no goals and just one point, so West Ham were looking to win this one. Upton Park is not impressed by Hammers' efforts, but Clive Allen then pops up with a double strike. They will stand as his only Hammers goals of the season.											
5	H	QP RANGERS		17	L	0-4	0-1	*[Penrice 53]*	Miklosko	Breacker	Dicks	Potts	Foster	Allen M	Robson	Butler	Morley	Allen C	Rowland	
	28/8		18,084	*13*	4			*Peacock 12, Ferdinand 47, 71,*	*Roberts*	*Bardsley*	*Wilson*	*Wilkins^*	*Peacock*	*McDonald*	*Impey*	*Sinclair*	*Ferdinand*	*Penrice**	*Barker*	*Allen/Ready*
								Ref: V Callow	Rangers have a defence like a sieve, and have conceded 10 goals in their first four games, so their first clean-sheet speaks volumes for West Ham's lack of enterprise. On the transfer front, Southampton boss Ian Branfoot has failed to sign the Hammers' Tim Breacker and Ian Bishop.											
6	A	MANCHESTER U		19	L	0-3	0-2		Miklosko	Breacker	Dicks	Potts	Foster	Allen M*	Gordon^	Holmes	Morley	Allen C	Rowland	Gale/Robson
	1/9		***44,613***	*1*	4			*Sharpe 17, Cantona 44p, Bruce 88*	*Schmeichel*	*Parker*	*Irwin*	*Bruce*	*Sharpe*	*Pallister*	*Cantona*	*Ince**	*Keane*	*Kanchelskis^*	*Giggs*	*McClair/Robson*
								Ref: R Milford	The defending champions will lead the table from August to May, and only Keegan's Newcastle have done so much as draw with them so far. Lee Sharpe is on fire, scoring his fourth goal in three games. Cantona's penalty just before half-time effectively settled the game's outcome.											
7	H	SWINDON		19	D	0-0	0-0		Miklosko	Breacker	Dicks	Potts	Gale	Bishop	Gordon*	Holmes	Morley	Jones	Rowland	Rush
	11/9		**15,777**	*22*	5				*Digby*	*Summerbee*	*Nijholt*	*Moncur*	*Whitbread*	*Taylor*	*Hazard*	*Mutch*	*Fjortoft**	*Ling*	*Horlock^*	*White/Fenwick*
								Ref: A Gunn	The play-offs brought promotion to Swindon, at which point Glenn Hoddle decamped to Chelsea. John Gorman's winless team have already been hit for five by Liverpool and Southampton, so this is yet another dismal result. Neither side looks good enough for the Premiership.											
8	A	BLACKBURN		18	W	2-0	1-0	Chapman 33, Morley 71	Miklosko	Rowland	**Burrows**	Potts	Gale	Bishop	Gordon	Holmes	**Chapman**	**Marsh***	Morley	Allen M
	18/9		*14,437*	*7*	8				*Mimms*	*May*	*Le Saux*	*Sherwood*	*Moran**	*Warhurst*	*Ripley*	*Berg*	*Newell*	*Gallacher*	*Wilcox^*	*Marker/Shearer*
								Ref: K Hackett	Rovers, unbeaten away, and victors at Anfield last time out, are proving vulnerable at Ewood. Dicks has gone to Liverpool, in exchange for Burrows and Marsh. Lee Chapman arrives from Portsmouth and scores with his one and only chance, after Mimms and Berg get in a dither.											
9	A	NEWCASTLE		18	L	0-2	0-0		Miklosko	Brown*	Burrows	Potts	Gale	Bishop	Gordon	Morley^	Chapman	Marsh	Holmes	Allen M/**Boere** !
	25/9		*34,179*	*11*	8			*Cole 51, 84*	*Hooper*	*Venison*	*Beresford*	*Bracewell*	*Scott*	*Watson*	*Lee*	*Beardsley*	*Cole*	*Clark*	*Allen*	
								Ref: M Reed	No one can stop Andy Cole scoring, least of all porous Hammers. Jeroen Boere signed from Go Ahead Eagles in midweek, comes on as sub after Cole's first goal and gets sent off after Cole's second for clashing with Kevin Scott and Barry Venison. Newcastle are unbeaten in eight.											
10	H	CHELSEA		17	W	1-0	1-0	Morley 41	Miklosko	Breacker	Burrows	Potts	Gale	Bishop	Butler	Morley	Chapman	Marsh*	Holmes	Allen M
	2/10		18,917	*14*	11				*Kharin*	*Clarke^*	*Sinclair*	*Kjeldbjerg*	*Dow**	*Donaghy*	*Hoddle*	*Newton*	*Shipperley*	*Peacock*	*Wise !*	*Spencer/Hall*
								Ref: R Hart	Rebuilding at Upton Park meant this match started at 2.15. Trevor Morley's neat goal did much to beat Chelsea, but so did Wise's dismissal for giving 12 studs to Burrows. Inspired by player-manager Hoddle, 10-man Chelsea pressed forward, leaving gaps that Chapman failed to exploit.											

No	Date	Venue	Opponent	Att	Pos	Res	Pts	F-A	H-T	Scorers, Times, and Referees	1	2	3	4	5	6	7	8	9	10	11	subs used
11		H	ASTON VILLA		17	D		0-0	0-0		Miklosko	Breacker	Burrows	Potts	Gale	Bishop	Butler	Morley	Chapman	Marsh	Holmes	
	16/10			20,416	*7*		12				*Bosnich*	*Cox*	*Small*	*Teale*	*McGrath*	*Richardson*	*Houghton*	*Townsend*	*Saunders*	*Atkinson*	*Daley*	
										Ref: S Lodge	Atkinson's Villa preserve their unbeaten away record but maintain his own Boleyn jinx, where none of his teams have ever won. Ron is being talked of as the next England boss. The best chance in this physical clash fell to Chapman, when Bosnich tried and failed to dribble round him.											
12		A	NORWICH		17	D		0-0	0-0		Miklosko	Breacker	Burrows	Potts	Gale*	Bishop	Butler	Morley	Chapman	Marsh	Holmes	Rowland
	23/10			*20,175*	*2*		13				*Gunn*	*Culverhouse*	*Bowen*	*Butterworth*	*Newman*	*Goss*	*Crook*	*Megson*	*Sutch**	*Fox*	*Sutton*	*Eadie*
										Ref: J Worrall	These are heady times for Mike Walker's Norwich. They have beaten Inter Milan in the UEFA Cup, lie second in the league, and stretch their unbeaten run to seven with this draw. Their Achilles heel is their inability to score at home, just two goals in six games at Carrow Road.											
13		H	MANCHESTER C		14	W		3-1	2-0	Burrows 3, Chapman 29, Holmes 69	Miklosko	Breacker	Burrows	Potts	Martin	Bishop	Butler	Morley	Chapman	Marsh	Holmes*	Rowland
	1/11			16,605	*16*		16			*Curle 85p*	*Coton*	*Edghill*	*Phelan*	*McMahon*	*Curle*	*Kernaghan*	*White*	*Sheron^*	*Quinn*	*Flitcroft*	*Lomas**	*Vonk/Griffiths*
										Ref: K Morton	Beforehand West Ham boasted the feeblest Premier goal-tally. Brian Horton had been pulling City up the table, but they flounder on the rock of Alvin Martin, who had a tooth extracted hours earlier. The third-minute breakthrough came when keeper Coton picked up Curle's back-pass.											
14		A	LIVERPOOL		15	L		0-2	0-0		Miklosko	Breacker	Burrows	Potts	Martin	Bishop	Butler	Morley	Chapman	Marsh	Holmes	
	6/11			*42,254*	*5*		16			*Clough 67, Martin 83 (og)*	*Grobbelaar*	*Jones**	*Harkness*	*Nicol^*	*Wright*	*Ruddock*	*Clough*	*Stewart*	*Rush*	*Matteo*	*Fowler*	*Redknapp/Bjornebye*
										Ref: K Barratt	It is 30 years since Hammers won at Anfield, but they were holding up against Souness's revamped team until Clough dribbled through. Martin then deflected Matteo's effort. Dicks was out of Liverpool's team with knee trouble, but Anfield applauded the return of Marsh and Burrows.											
15		H	OLDHAM		14	W		2-0	1-0	Martin 43, Morley 74	Miklosko	Breacker	Burrows	Potts	Martin	Bishop	Butler	Morley	Chapman	Marsh	Holmes	
	20/11			17,211	*21*		19				*Walsh*	*Fleming*	*Makin !*	*Brennan^*	*Jobson*	*Redmond*	*Halle*	*Olney**	*Sharp*	*Milligan*	*Bernard*	*Ritchie/Pointon*
										Ref: D Allison	Martin returns from Achilles injury to score his first goal in 14 months. Oldham's cause was not helped by the dismissal of Makin, booked for fouling Breacker in the first half, then repeating the offence in the second. Not to be outdone by Martin, Morley's own header was just as good.											
16		H	ARSENAL		14	D		0-0	0-0		Miklosko	Breacker	Burrows	Potts	Gale	Bishop	Butler	Morley	Chapman	Marsh	Holmes	
	24/11			20,279	*7*		20				*Seaman !*	*Dixon*	*Winterburn*	*Morrow*	*Linighan*	*Bould*	*Keown*	*Wright^*	*Smith*	*Merson*	*Limpar**	*Campbell/Miller*
										Ref: P Durkin	Arsenal have conceded two goals in eight away games. They would have lost a third in the 85th minute had not Seaman body-checked Morley, who was through on goal, for which he was sent off for the first time. A bad week for Seaman, beaten by an eight-second goal by San Marino.											
17		A	SOUTHAMPTON		10	W		2-0	2-0	Morley 30, Chapman 36	Miklosko	Breacker	Burrows	Potts	Gale	Bishop	Butler	Morley	Chapman	Allen M	Holmes	
	29/11			*13,258*	*20*		23				*Andrews*	*Kenna*	*Benali*	*Charlton**	*Wood*	*Monkou*	*Le Tissier*	*Cockerill^*	*Dowie*	*Maddison*	*Allen*	*Adams/Bennett*
										Ref: M Bodenham	West Ham's eighth clean sheet in 11 league games lifts them to 10th, their highest position for seven years. Holmes' crosses made both West Ham goals, a downward header by Morley and a deflected volley by Chapman. Saints looked to Le Tissier, but he fired nothing but blanks.											
18		A	WIMBLEDON		10	W		2-1	1-0	Chapman 44,78	Miklosko	Breacker	Burrows	Potts	Gale	Bishop	Butler	Morley	Chapman	Allen M	Holmes	
	4/12			*10,903*	*15*		26			*Holdsworth 83*	*Segers*	*Barton*	*McAllister*	*Jones*	*Scales*	*Fitzgerald*	*Clarke*	*Earle*	*Berry**	*Holdsworth*	*Ardley*	*Talboys*
										Ref: D Gallagher	Dons leave out Fashanu, following the horrific injury to Spurs' Gary Mabbutt. Lee Chapman capitalises on Route 1 for his second goal, when Morley helped on Miklosko's long punt. Over the years Chapman has been a bogey-man to the Dons. Fashanu should have played centre-half.											
19		H	LEEDS		10	L		0-1	0-0		Miklosko	Breacker	Burrows	Potts	Gale	Bishop	Butler	Morley*	Chapman	Marsh	Holmes	Boere
	8/12			20,468	*2*		26			*Wallace Rod 84*	*Beaney*	*Kelly*	*Dorigo*	*Sharp*	*Fairclough*	*Wetherall*	*Strachan*	*Wallace Rod*	*Deane*	*McAllister*	*Speed**	*Pemberton*
										Ref: I Borrett	Leeds secure second place with their 14th unbeaten game. Dorigo's clever pass allowed Rod Wallace to sidefoot the winner, his seventh goal in seven matches. Had the Hammers won, they would have been just three points behind Leeds but Man U's lead at the top is a huge 12 points.											
20		H	COVENTRY		9	W		3-2	2-1	Breacker 11, Butler 40, Morley 59p	Miklosko	Breacker	Burrows	Potts	Gale	Bishop*	Butler	Morley	Chapman	Marsh	Holmes	Allen M
	11/12			17,243	*16*		29			*Darby 41, 77*	*Ogrizovic*	*Atherton*	*Morgan*	*Flynn*	*Babb*	*Rennie*	*Darby*	*Ndlovu*	*Wegerle**	*Quinn*	*Boland^*	*Williams/Marsden*
										Ref: K Cooper	West Ham climb to dizzy ninth, a mere 20 points behind Man U. Butler killed the ball to set up Breacker, then linked with Marsh and Morley for his first of the season. Ndlovu shoved Marsh for the penalty. Gale felled Williams but West Ham were lucky. It should have been a penalty.											
21		A	SHEFFIELD WED		11	L		**0-5**	0-1	*[Jemson 73, Palmer 88]*	Miklosko	Breacker	Burrows	Potts	Gale	Bishop*	Butler	Morley	Chapman	Marsh	Holmes^	Allen M/Boere
	18/12			*26,350*	*13*		29			*Marsh 35 (og), Bright 48, Waddle 51,*	*Pressman*	*Nilsson*	*Worthington*	*Palmer*	*Pearce*	*Walker*	*Jemson*	*Waddle*	*Bright*	*Hyde*	*Bt-Williams*	
										Ref: D Frampton	Until Mike Marsh, standing on the goal-line, helped in Pearce's header that had come down off the bar, there was little sign of this debacle to come. But 33-year-old, flu-stricken Chris Waddle was at his mesmerising best, scoring from 25 yards and engineering three Wednesday goals.											

No	Date		Att	Pos	Pt	F-A	H-T	Scorers, Times, and Referees	SQUAD	NUMBERS	IN	USE								subs used
22	A	IPSWICH		12	D	1-1	0-1	Chapman 77	Miklosko	Breacker	Burrows	Potts	Gale	Bishop	Butler	Morley	Chapman	Marsh	Holmes*	Rowland
	27/12		*20,988*	*11*	30			*Linighan 36*	*Forrest*	*Youds*	*Thompson*	*Stockwell*	*Wark**	*Linighan*	*Williams*	*Slater*	*Palmer*	*Whelan*	*Kiwomya*	*Marshall*
								Ref: G Poll	Ipswich are unbeaten in eight but needed to win before their season's biggest gate to leap-frog the Hammers. Linighan headed Ipswich in front from Thompson's free-kick, but Chapman headed an equaliser from Burrows' centre, which Forrest spilled when he should have gathered.											
23	H	TOTTENHAM		13	L	1-3	1-2	Holmes 11	Miklosko	Breacker	Burrows	Potts	Gale	Bishop	Butler	Morley	Chapman	Marsh	Holmes*	Jones
	28/12		20,787	*11*	30			*Dozzell 34, Hazard 42, Anderton 77*	*Thorstvedt*	*Kerslake*	*Edinburgh*	*Samways*	*Calderwood*	*Sedgley*	*Caskey*	*Barmby**	*Anderton*	*Dozzell*	*Hazard*	*Campbell*
								Ref: G Ashby	Both teams are unchanged after their exertions 24 hours earlier. Ardiles' Spurs are disrupted by the facial injury to Mabbutt, but show their mettle after falling behind to Holmes' cool finish. Best moment of the match came when Anderton lobbed onto the top netting from 45 yards.											
24	A	EVERTON		11	W	1-0	1-0	Breacker 5	Miklosko	Breacker	Burrows	Potts	Gale	Bishop	Butler	Morley	Chapman	Marsh	Holmes*	Rowland
	1/1		*19,602*	*16*	33				*Southall*	*Holmes*	*Snodin*	*Ebbrell*	*Jackson*	*Ablett*	*Ward^*	*Horne*	*Cottee**	*Rideout*	*Beagrie*	*Barlow/Stuart*
								Ref: J Lloyd	Howard Kendall's resignation has not stopped Everton plunging down the table; this is their sixth game without a goal. West Ham won with a neatly executed header during one of their few attacks. Tim Breacker threaded his way through the defence to meet Marsh's clipped pass.											
25	H	SHEFFIELD UTD		11	D	0-0	0-0		Miklosko	Breacker	Burrows	Potts	Gale	Bishop	Butler	Morley*	Chapman	Marsh	Rowland	Jones
	3/1		20,365	*18*	34				*Kelly*	*Bradshaw*	*Beesley*	*Kamara*	*Tuttle*	*Hoyland*	*Hodges*	*Ward*	*Flo*	*Davison**	*Whitehouse*	*Littlejohn*
								Ref: M Reed	The Blades hardly ever score, so their 'nil' was predictable. They wanted a point and in a swirling wind competed for each tackle as if Dave Bassett's life depended on it. The best of West Ham's few chances fell to Marsh, but his low shot was smothered. The crowd booed at the end.											
26	A	ASTON VILLA		12	L	1-3	1-2	Allen M 30	Miklosko	Breacker	Rowland	Potts	Gale	Bishop	Allen M	Morley*	Chapman	Marsh	Holmes	Jones
	15/1		*28,869*	*9*	34			*Richardson 15, Atkinson 43, 68*	*Bosnich*	*Barrett*	*Staunton**	*Teale*	*McGrath*	*Richardson*	*Houghton*	*Townsend*	*Saunders*	*Atkinson*	*Daley*	*Cox*
								Ref: S Lodge	Some sublime goals here. Richardson scores low and hard from 30 yards. Rowland's cross was perfectly headed in by Martin Allen to level. Dalian Atkinson's second goal was a contender for goal-of-the month when sprinting forward to fire a bullet high into the net past Miklosko.											
27	H	NORWICH		12	D	3-3	1-1	Sutton 37 (og), Jones 46, Morley 84	Miklosko	Breacker	Rowland	Potts	Gale^	Bishop	Allen M	Jones	Chapman*	Marsh	Holmes	Morley/Brown
	24/1		20,738	*7*	35			*Sutton 4, 57, Fox 78*	*Gunn*	*Culverhouse*	*Bowen*	*Butterworth*	*Woodthorpe*	*Megson**	*Crook*	*Newman*	*Sutton*	*Fox*	*Goss*	*Ekoku*
								Ref: J Worrall	Having lost manager Mike Walker to Everton, Norwich are bereft of leadership and will eventually sink from second into the bottom half. John Deehan had them playing beautifully in this match, and their intricate passing is a joy. Martin Allen tried to claim West Ham's first goal.											
28	A	MANCHESTER C		12	D	0-0	0-0		Miklosko	Breacker	Rowland	Potts	Brown	Bishop	Allen M	Marsh^	Chapman	Allen C*	Holmes	Morley/**Marquis**
	12/2		*29,118*	*19*	36				*Coton*	*Edghill*	*Phelan*	*McMahon*	*Curle**	*Vonk*	*Rocastle*	*Sheron*	*Griffiths*	*Flitcroft*	*Shutt^*	*Kernaghan/Lomas*
								Ref: V Callow	Francis Lee returns as Messiah to Maine Road, and manager Brian Horton will soon be shown the door. West Ham owe their point largely to Miklosko, who denied Shutt and Sheron with hands, feet, and body. Clive Allan started a game for Hammers for the first time in five months											
29	H	MANCHESTER U		12	D	2-2	0-1	Chapman 69, Morley 72	Miklosko	Breacker	Burrows	Potts	Martin	Bishop	Allen M	Morley	Chapman	Marsh	Holmes	
	26/2		**28,832**	*1*	37			*Hughes 6, Ince 87*	*Schmeichel*	*Parker*	*Irwin^*	*Bruce*	*Kanchelskis**	*Pallister*	*Cantona*	*Ince*	*McClair*	*Hughes*	*Keane*	*Dublin/Thornley*
								Ref: A Wilkie	Since moving to Old Trafford, Paul Ince has restricted his Upton Park appearances. He was cat-called and pelted with bananas before thumping home Keane's cross to level. Chapman's goal from Holmes' cross, followed by Pallister's lax back pass, had set up a deserved Hammers win.											
30	A	SWINDON		13	D	1-1	0-0	Morley 47	Miklosko	Breacker	Burrows	Potts	Martin	Bishop	Allen M	Morley	Chapman	Marsh	Holmes*	Rowland
	5/3		*15,929*	*22*	38			*Fjortoft 88*	*Digby*	*Summerbee*	*Nijholt*	*Horlock*	*Whitbread*	*Taylor*	*Moncur*	*Mutch**	*Fjortoft*	*Ling*	*McAvennie^*	*Scott/Gooden*
								Ref: R Milford	Swindon will concede 100 league goals this season, which means each club averages five against them. West Ham manage just one, Morley putting away Chapman's header. Swindon include former Hammer Frank McAvennie, on loan from Celtic. Fjortoft heads in off a post for 1-1.											
31	H	NEWCASTLE		14	L	2-4	0-1	Breacker 56, Martin 81	Miklosko	Breacker	Rowland	Potts	Martin	Bishop	Butler	Morley*	Chapman	Marsh	Holmes	Boere
	19/3		23,132	*3*	38			*Lee 34, 73, Cole 69, Mathie 90*	*Srnicek*	*Robinson*	*Beresford*	*Venison*	*Elliott*	*Watson^*	*Lee*	*Beardsley*	*Cole*	*Fox**	*Sellars*	*Mathie/Neilson*
								Ref: K Morton	This was one of those games that could have ended 10-10, wonderful for fans, awful for managers. Andy Cole seemed to score everywhere but in London, but he rectified that with his 35th of the season. For all Chapman's aerial dominance, both West Ham's goals came from defenders.											

32	A	CHELSEA	15	L	0-2	0-1		Miklosko	Breacker	Burrows^	Potts	Gale	Bishop	Allen M*	Butler	Chapman	Marsh	Rowland	Morley/Jones
26/3		19,545	14	38			Barnard 39, Hoddle 79	Kharin	Clarke	Barnard	Kjeldbjerg	Johnsen	Burley*	Spencer	Newton	Shipperley^	Peacock	Wise	Hoddle/Donaghy
							Ref: M Bodenham	Hours after Cambridge win the Boat Race, Chelsea keep the Thames celebrations in full voice. It was a game of firsts – Barnards's first goal of the season and Hoddle's first for Chelsea. Bonds, who let two strikers go on transfer deadline day, experimented with playing one up front.											
33	A	SHEFFIELD UTD	15	L	2-3	2-1	Bishop 7, Holmes 31	Miklosko	Breacker	Rowland	Potts	Gale	Bishop	Butler	Morley	Chapman	Marsh^	Holmes*	Allen M/Brown
28/3		13,646	20	38			Whitehouse 39, Gayle 47, Rogers 72	Kelly^	Bradshaw	Nilsen	Gannon*	Tutte	Gayle	Carr	Rogers	Flo	Littlejohn	Whitehouse	Hodges/Tracey
							Ref: P Durkin	Bassett's Blades will lose just two of their last 13, but will be relegated in the last minute of the last match. Three defeats in five days have left West Ham looking over their shoulder. Bishop had scored from 30 yards for the first goal; Miklosko fumbled one of many crosses for the fifth.											
34	H	IPSWICH	14	W	2-1	1-0	Rush 17, Morley 75	Miklosko	Breacker	Rowland	Potts	Gale	Bishop	Butler	Rush*	Morley	Marsh	Holmes	Brown
2/4		18,307	15	41			Mason 87	Baker	Stockwell	Johnson	Williams	Linighan	Whelan	Durrant^	Slater	Palmer	Guentchev	Kiwomya*	Mason/Youds
							Ref: D Elleray	Despite being leading scorer, Chapman is unpopular among the Upton Park faithfuls and is dropped. His replacement, the highly promising Matthew Rush, fired in a half-volley from 25 yards to set up this much-needed win. It was a foul on Rush that earned the free-kick for No 2.											
35	A	TOTTENHAM	13	W	4-1	1-0	Jones 37, Morley 60p, 72, Marsh 80	Miklosko	Breacker	Rowland	Potts	Gale	Bishop	Butler*	Rush	Morley	Marsh	Holmes	Jones
4/4		**31,502**	16	44			Sheringham 66p	Walker	Kerslake	Campbell	Samways	Scott	Mabbutt	Sedgley	Barmby	Anderton	Dozzell^	Rosenthal*	Sheringham/Howells
							Ref: P Don	As Spurs had won just three out of 18 games at home, the last of which was in October, this result is hardly a shock. Kevin Scott brought down Morley for the first penalty; Morley floored Mabbutt for the second. When Marsh angled West Ham's fourth, Spurs completely disintegrated.											
36	H	EVERTON	13	L	0-1	0-0		Miklosko	Breacker	Rowland*	Potts	Gale	Bishop	Jones	Rush	Morley	Marsh	Holmes	Martin
9/4		20,243	17	44			Cottee 72	Southall	Jackson	Snodin	Ebbrell	Watson	Abblett	Stuart	Horne	Cottee	Angell*	Limpar	Rideout
							Ref: P Foakes	Everton arrived with one point and one goal from six games, and a looming destiny with relegation. West Ham had all the play, most of the chances but lost when Cottee took the only chance to fall his way. Man of the match was undeniably Neville Southall for a succession of saves.											
37	A	OLDHAM	13	W	2-1	2-1	Allen M 1, Morley 29	Miklosko	Breacker	Burrows	Brown	Gale	Bishop	Allen M	Rush	Morley	Marsh	Holmes	
16/4		11,669	20	47			Holden 43p	Hallworth	Makin	Pointon*	Henry	Jobson	Fleming	Bernard	Sharp	McCarthy	Milligan	Holden	Beckford
							Ref: K Barratt	Oldham have just lost an FA Cup semi-final replay to Man U and their season comes crashing about their ears. Richard Jobson had just been called into the England squad by Venables, but was partially responsible for both Hammers' goals. Burrows shoved McCarthy for the penalty.											
38	H	LIVERPOOL	13	L	1-2	1-1	Allen M 1	Miklosko	Breacker	Burrows	Potts	Gale	Bishop*	Allen M	Rush	Morley	Marsh	Holmes	Chapman
23/4		26,106	7	47			Fowler 13, Rush 87	James	Harkness	Dicks	Hutchison	Nicol	Ruddock	Clough	Redknapp	Rush	Barnes	Fowler	
							Ref: S Lodge	Julian Dicks returns to the Boleyn in Liverpool red and the stadium rises to acclaim him. Inside a minute Allen lobs David James from the edge of the box. Fowler pounces after John Barnes' shot comes back off a post. Tony Gale's miscued back-pass lets in Ian Rush for the late winner.											
39	H	BLACKBURN	13	L	1-2	0-1	Allen M 64	Miklosko	Breacker	Brown	Potts	Gale	Bishop	Allen M	Rush*	Morley	Marsh	Holmes^	Chapman/**Mitchell**
27/4		22,186	2	47			Berg 12, Pearce 75	Flowers	May	Le Saux	Sherwood	Hendry	Berg	Ripley^	Atkins	Shearer	Wright*	Wilcox	Pearce/Morrison
							Ref: T Holbrook	Rovers have hauled back Man U's lead to two points. Ian Pearce comes off the bench, controls Shearer's 40-yard pass with his first touch and scores with his second. It is their first win at Upton Park since 1964, when they won 8-2. Allen scored with a 25-yard deflected free-kick.											
40	A	ARSENAL	12	W	2-0	0-0	Morley 77, Allen M 88	Miklosko	Breacker	Burrows*	Potts	Gale	Bishop	Allen M	Rush	Morley	Marsh	Brown	**Williamson**
30/4		33,700	4	50				Miller	McGoldrick*	Winterburn	Davis	Bould	Linighan	Parlour	Wright	Campbell	Merson^	Selley	Morrow/Dickov
							Ref: R Milford	Arsenal play Parma in the final of the Cup-Winners' Cup on Wednesday. This, their first league defeat in 20 games, is the worst preparation. Graham rested Seaman and Adams. Miller did well before getting into a tangle with Linighan for the first goal. Allen hit a screamer for No 2.											
41	A	QP RANGERS	13	D	0-0	0-0		Miklosko	Breacker	Brown	Potts	Gale	Bishop	Allen M	Rush*	Morley	Marsh	Williamson	Chapman
3/5		**10,850**	9	51				Roberts	McCarthy	Wilson	Wilkins	Ready	Yates	Holloway^	Barker	Ferdinand	Penrice*	Sinclair	Allen/Brevett
							Ref: R Dilkes	Ray Wilkins' QPR, aided by a surprisingly muscular approach, will finish in the top half of the table. They have won just one of their last nine, but by avoiding defeat by the Hammers ensure that they will finish higher than their London rivals. QPR had won 4-0 at Upton Park in August.											
42	H	SOUTHAMPTON	13	D	3-3	1-1	Will'mson 11, Allen 62, Monkou 89 (og)	Miklosko	Breacker	Burrows	Potts	Gale	Bishop*	Allen M	Rush	Morley	Marsh	Williamson	Chapman
7/5		26,952	18	52			Le Tissier 45, 65p, Maddison 52	Beasant	Kenna	Benali	Charlton	Widdrington	Monkou	Le Tissier	Magilton	Dowie	Maddison	Allen	
	Home	Away					Ref: G Ashby	Two dead-ball strikes takes Le Tissier's tally to 25. The first came when Potts rashly fouled Dowie 20 yards out. That equalised Williamson's 11th-minute goal on his home debut, shooting under Beasant. Player-of-the-Year Morley made it 2-2, before Gale felled Dowie in the box.											
Average	20,574	23,288																	

Coca-Cola Cup					F-A	H-T	Scorers, Times, and Referees	SQUAD	NUMBERS	IN	USE								subs used
2:1	H	CHESTERFIELD	18	W	5-1	3-0	Morley 6p, 69, Chapman 14, 65,	Miklosko	Rowland	Burrows	Potts	Gale	Bishop	Gordon	Morley	Chapman	Holmes	Marsh	
	22/9	12,823 *3:16*					*Norris 55* [Burrows 33]	*Leonard*	*Hebberd*	*Carr C*	*Brien*	*Carr D*	*McGugan*	*Dyche*	*Norris*	*Jules**	*Cash^*	*Curtis*	*Davies/Knowles*
							Ref: I Borrett	John Duncan's Chesterfield are on a losing run in their own division, and their lack of confidence is all too obvious. Conceding a penalty after just six minutes drained away what little confidence they had to begin with. With a four-goal aggregate advantage, the second leg is pointless.											
2:2	A	CHESTERFIELD	17	W	2-0	0-0	Allen M 64, Boere 82	Miklosko	Breacker	Burrows	Potts	Gale	Bishop	Butler*	Morley	Chapman^	Marsh	Holmes	Allen M/Boere
	5/10	*4,890 3:19*						*Marples*	*Hebberd*	*Carr C*	*Brien*	*Madden*	*Dennis*	*Dyche**	*Norris^*	*Davies*	*Curtis*	*Jules*	*Bettney/Taylor*
							Ref: G Singh (Hammers win 7-1 on aggregate)	The deficit is so big that even devoted Spirites are dispirited enough to stay away in droves. The longer the second leg went on without a home goal the more aimless the fixture became. All 22 players were looking forward to a bath by the time Martin Allen extinguished all worries.											
3	A	NOTT'M FOREST	17	L	1-2	0-1	Morley 82	Miklosko	Breacker	Burrows	Potts	Martin	Bishop	Butler*	Morley	Chapman	Marsh	Holmes	Allen M
	27/10	*17,857 1:20*					*Black 28, Collymore 55*	*Wright*	*Laws*	*Pearce*	*Crosby*	*Chettle*	*Stone*	*Phillips*	*Gemmell*	*Glover**	*Collymore*	*Black*	*Webb*
							Ref: G Pooley	Forest fear relegation to Division 2. They also have the Indian sign over the Hammers in the League Cup, winning for the fourth time in four ties. Forest are unbeaten at home in this competition for 44 games, dating back to 1976. Super Stan Collymore headed in at the far post.											

FA Cup																			
3	H	WATFORD	11	W	2-1	0-1	Allen M 64, Marsh 84	Miklosko	Breacker	Burrows*	Potts	Gale	Bishop	Allen M	Morley^	Chapman	Marsh	Rowland	Brown/Jones
	8/1	19,802 *1:21*					*Porter 27p*	*Sheppard*	*Lavin*	*Dublin*	*Hessenthaler*	*Holdsworth*	*Watson*	*Dyer*	*Johnston*	*Furlong*	*Porter*	*Nogan*	
							Ref: D Gallagher	Miklosko brings down Bruce Dyer for a hotly-argued penalty, whereupon the First Division side threaten to extend their lead. Martin Allen's header wiped away the blushes, but Watford still looked to be holding out comfortably. Mike Marsh, unmarked, won the tie at the far post.											
4	A	NOTTS CO	11	D	1-1	1-1	Jones 40	Miklosko	Breacker	Rowland	Potts	Brown	Bishop	Allen M	Jones	Chapman	Marsh	Holmes	
	29/1	*14,952 1:14*					*Lund 38*	*Cherry*	*Palmer*	*Sherlock*	*Turner P*	*Murphy*	*Dijkstra*	*Devlin*	*Draper**	*Lund*	*Legg^*	*Agana*	*Cox/McSwegan*
							Ref: D Pierce	Gary Lund volleys the First Division side ahead, as Miklosko strays into no-man's land. The Hammers' former Billericay marksman and soap-factory worker, Steve Jones, hooks an immediate equaliser on the turn. It is his second goal in a week and his hustle and bustle look promising.											
4R	H	NOTTS CO	11	W	1-0	0-0	Chapman 110	Miklosko	Breacker	Rowland	Potts	Brown	Bishop	Allen M	Jones*	Chapman	Marsh	Holmes	Allen C
	9/2	23,373 *1:14*			*aet*			*Cherry*	*Palmer*	*Sherlock*	*Turner P*	*Johnson*	*Dijkstra*	*Devlin*	*Draper*	*Lund**	*Legg*	*McSwegan*	*Matthews*
							Ref: D Pierce	Upton Park is in mean mood at Lee Chapman's uncoordinated display, when everything he tried went wrong, and urged Bonds to pull him off. Bonds resisted, and with County playing for a shoot-out in extra-time, had his faith vindicated when Chapman headed in Tim Breacker's cross.											
5	A	KIDDERMINSTER	11	W	1-0	0-0	Chapman 69	Miklosko	Breacker	Rowland	Potts	Martin	Bishop	Allen M	Marsh	Chapman	Allan C*	Holmes	Morley
	19/2	*8,000 VC:1*						*Rose*	*Hodson*	*Bancroft*	*Weir*	*Brindley*	*Cartwright**	*Grainger*	*Forsyth*	*Humphreys*	*Davies*	*Purdie*	*Deakin*
							Ref: G Pooley	Kidderminster top the GM Vauxhall Conference. Having seen off Birmingham and Preston, many judges concur that the Harriers can cause an even bigger upset. But the sole remaining non-league team are well beaten. Keeper Rose missed a simple cross, giving Chapman a free header.											
QF	H	LUTON	13	D	0-0	0-0		Miklosko	Breacker	Burrows	Potts	Martin	Bishop	Allen M	Morley	Chapman*	Marsh	Holmes	Allen C
	14/3	27,331 *1:15*						*Sommer*	*Linton*	*James*	*Harper*	*Greene*	*Dreyer*	*Telfer*	*Oakes**	*Dixon^*	*Hughes*	*Preece*	*Burke/Hartson*
							Ref: B Hill	This Monday night cup-tie gave West Ham the perfect opportunity to reach the semi-finals. David Pleat's Luton – two defeats in 17 games – beat Kevin Keegan's Newcastle in Round 4, after drawing at St James' Park, so are not at all overawed. West Ham will not relish the replay.											
QF	A	LUTON	14	L	2-3	1-1	Allen M 30, Bishop 57	Miklosko	Breacker	Burrows	Potts	Martin	Bishop	Butler	Morley	Chapman	Marsh*	Allen M	Jones
R	23/3	*13,166 1:18*					*Oakes 34, 47, 74*	*Sommer*	*Linton*	*James*	*Harper*	*Peake*	*Dreyer*	*Telfer*	*Oakes*	*Dixon*	*Hughes*	*Preece*	
							Ref: B Hill	The name of Scott Oakes will haunt West Ham for years to come, after he single-handedly dumps them on their Premier backsides to win this thrilling cup replay. He had scored against Newcastle in Round 4, Cardiff in Round 5, and now pitches Luton into a semi-final with Chelsea.											

	P	W	D	L	F	A	W	D	L	F	A	Pts
		Home					Away					
1 Manchester U	42	14	6	1	39	13	13	5	3	41	25	92
2 Blackburn	42	14	5	2	31	11	11	4	6	32	25	84
3 Newcastle	42	14	4	3	51	14	9	4	8	31	27	77
4 Arsenal	42	10	8	3	25	15	8	9	4	28	13	71
5 Leeds	42	13	6	2	37	18	5	10	6	28	21	70
6 Wimbledon	42	12	5	4	35	21	6	6	9	21	32	65
7 Sheffield Wed	42	10	7	4	48	24	6	9	6	28	30	64
8 Liverpool	42	12	4	5	33	23	5	5	11	26	32	60
9 QP Rangers	42	8	7	6	32	29	8	5	8	30	32	60
10 Aston Villa	42	8	5	8	23	18	7	7	7	23	32	57
11 Coventry	42	9	7	5	23	17	5	7	9	20	28	56
12 Norwich	42	4	9	8	26	29	8	8	5	39	32	53
13 WEST HAM	42	6	7	8	26	31	7	6	8	21	27	52
14 Chelsea	42	11	5	5	31	20	2	7	12	18	33	51
15 Tottenham	42	4	8	9	29	33	7	4	10	25	26	45
16 Manchester C	42	6	10	5	24	22	3	8	10	14	27	45
17 Everton	42	8	4	9	26	30	4	4	13	16	33	44
18 Southampton	42	9	2	10	30	31	3	5	13	19	35	43
19 Ipswich	42	5	8	8	21	32	4	8	9	14	26	43
20 Sheffield Utd	42	6	10	5	24	23	2	8	11	18	37	42
21 Oldham	42	5	8	8	24	33	4	5	12	18	35	40
22 Swindon	42	4	7	10	25	45	1	8	12	22	55	30
	924	192	142	128	663	532	128	142	192	532	663	1244

Odds & ends

Double wins: (1) Oldham.

Double losses: (3) Leeds, Newcastle, Liverpool.

Won from behind: (1) Watford FAC (h).

Lost from in front: (4) Spurs (h), Sheff U (a), Liverpool (h), Luton FAC (a).

High spots: Nine league games with only one defeat from 2 October.

Low spots: Defeat in the FA Cup at First Division Luton.

Losing the first two league fixtures.

Nine league games without a win from 3 January.

Hammer of the Year: Trevor Morley.

Ever-presents: (1) Ludek Miklosko.

Hat-tricks: (0).

Leading scorer: (16) Trevor Morley.

	Appearances						Goals			
	Lge	*Sub*	LC	*Sub*	FAC	*Sub*	Lge	LC	FAC	Tot
Allen, Clive	7				1	*2*	**2**			**2**
Allen, Martin	20	*6*		*2*	6		**7**	1	2	**10**
Bishop, Ian	36		3		6		**1**		1	**2**
Boere, Jeroen		*4*		*1*				1		**1**
Breacker, Tim	40		2		6		**3**			**3**
Brown, Kenny	6	*3*			2	*1*				
Burrows, David	25		3		3		**1**	1		**2**
Butler, Peter	26		2		1		**1**			**1**
Chapman, Lee	26	*4*	3		6		**7**	2	2	**11**
Dicks, Julian	7									
Foster, Colin	5									
Gale, Tony	31	*1*	2		1					
Gordon, Dale	8		1				**1**			**1**
Holmes, Matt	33	*1*	3		4		**3**			**3**
Jones, Steve	3	*5*			2	*2*	**2**		1	**3**
Marquis, Paul		*1*								
Marsh, Mike	33		3		6		**1**		1	**2**
Martin, Alvin	6	*1*	1		3		**2**			**2**
Miklosko, Ludek	42		3		6					
Mitchell, Paul		*1*								
Morley, Trevor	39	*3*	3		3	*1*	**13**	3		**16**
Potts, Steve	41		3		6					
Rowland, Keith	16	*7*	1		4					
Robson, Marc	1	*2*								
Rush, Matthew	9	*1*					**1**			**1**
Williamson, Danny	2	*1*					**1**			**1**
(own-goals)							**1**			**1**
26 players used	**462**	***41***	**33**	***3***	**66**	***6***	**47**	**8**	**7**	**62**

Rio Ferdinand stretches against Liverpool's Robbie Fowler

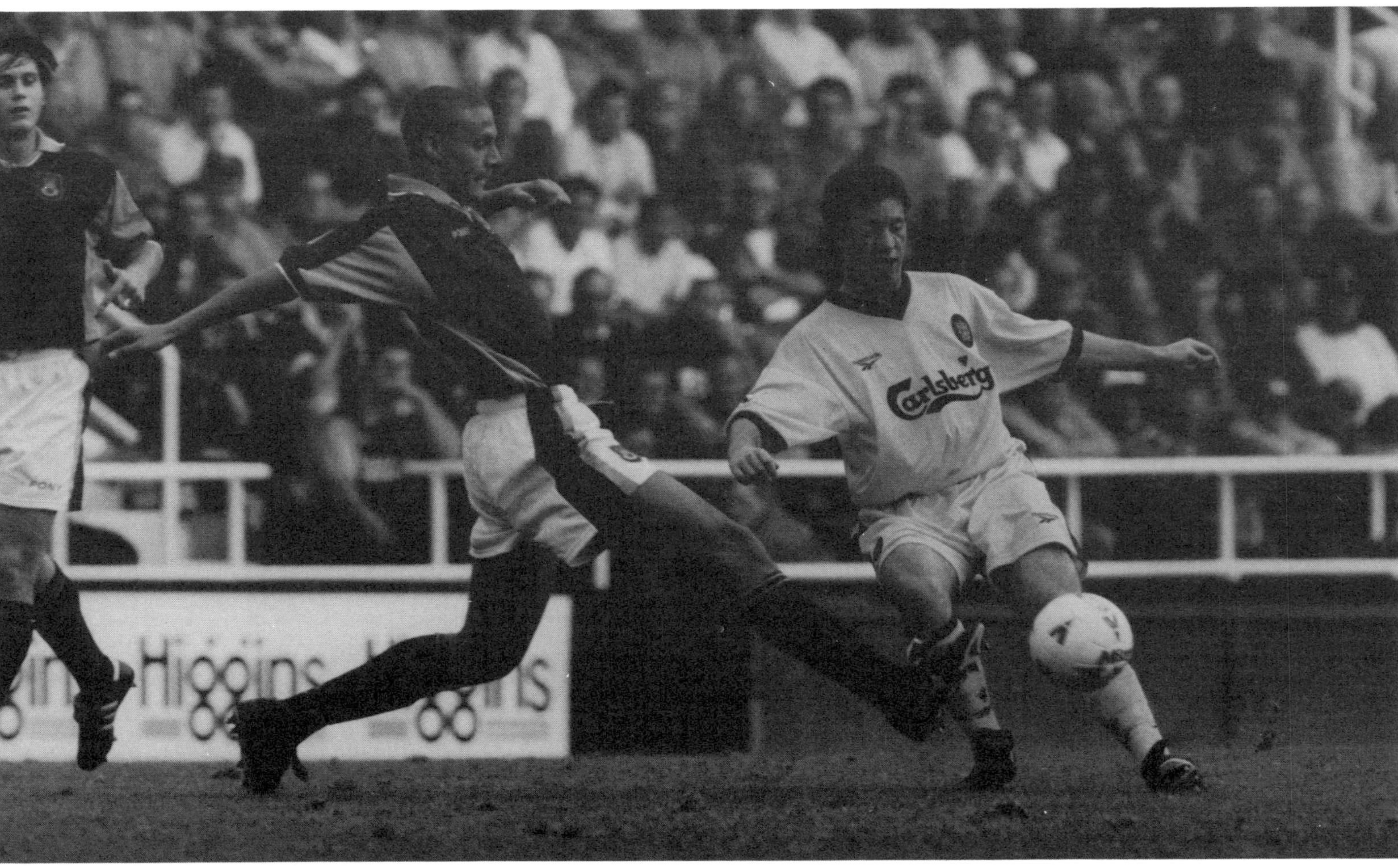

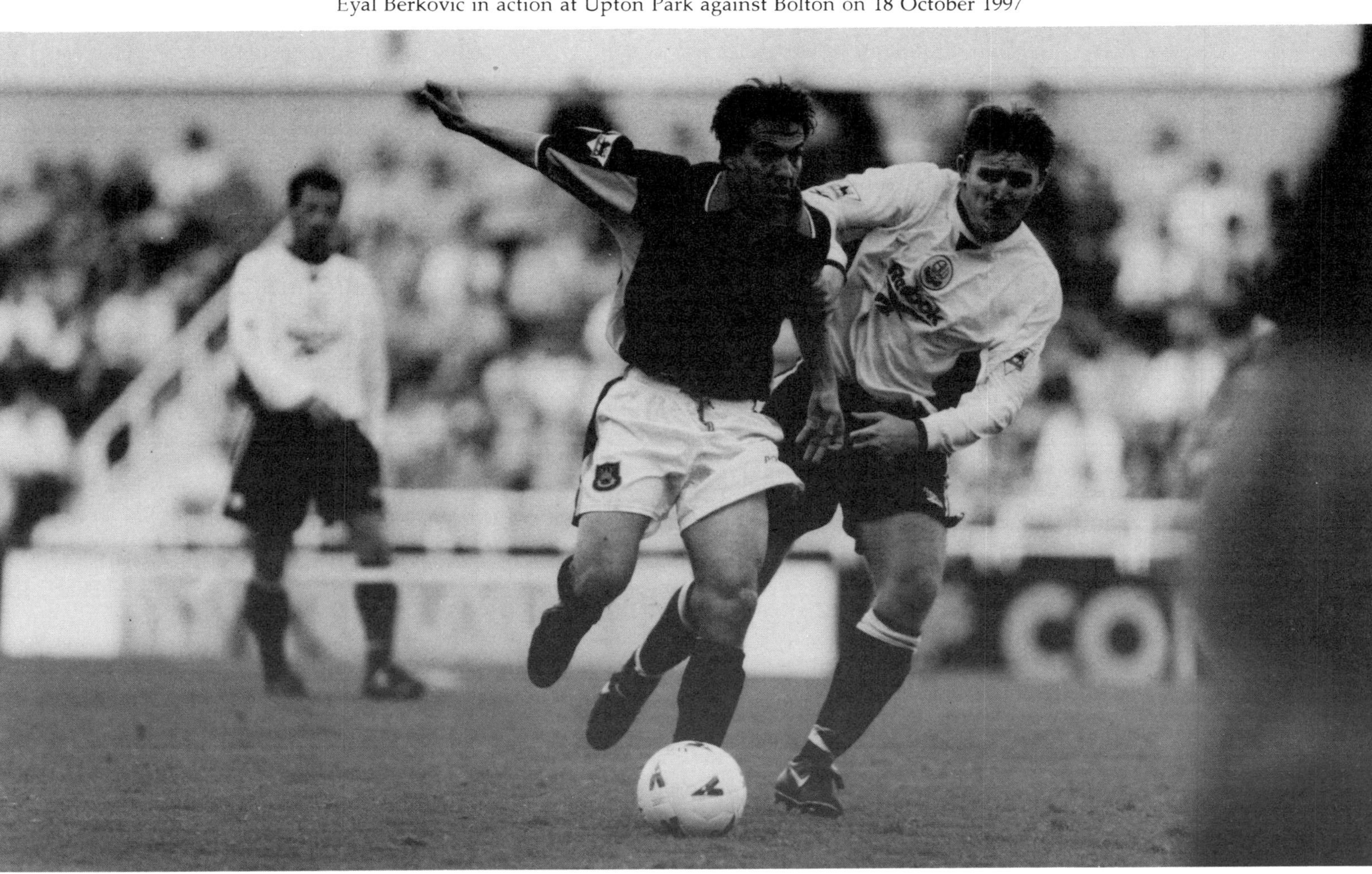

Eyal Berkovic in action at Upton Park against Bolton on 18 October 1997

No		Date	Att	Pos	Pt	F-A	H-T	Scorers, Times, and Referees	SQUAD	NUMBERS	IN	USE								subs used
1	H	LEEDS			D	0-0	0-0		Miklosko	Breacker	Burrows	Potts*	Martin	Allen	Bishop	Butler	Morley	Chapman	Holmes^	**Whitbread**/Marsh
	20/8		18,610		1				*Lukic*	*Kelly*	*Worthington*	*White*	*Palmer*	*Wetherall*	*Strachan*	*Wallace R**	*Deane*	*McAllister*	*Speed*	*Masinga*
								Ref: K Burge	Harry Redknapp takes over from Billy Bonds on the eve of the season, and watches Howard Wilkinson's Leeds dominate this goalless draw. Brian Deane wasted most of Leeds' chances. The Hammers created just one opportunity, when Martin Allen's shot was saved by John Lukic.											
2	A	MANCHESTER C	17		L	**0-3**	0-2		Miklosko	Breacker	Burrows	Potts	Martin	Allen	Bishop	Butler^	Morley	Chapman*	Holmes	Marsh/Whitbread
	24/8		*19,150*	*10*	1			*Walsh 14, Beagrie 42, Rosler 56*	*Coton*	*Phelan**	*McMahon*	*Curle*	*Vonk*	*Summerbee*	*Walsh*	*Rosler^*	*Flitcroft*	*Beagrie*	*Brightwell I*	*Lomas/Quinn*
								Ref: R Hart	Paul Walsh's header from Beagrie's cross knocked the stuffing out of West Ham. Beagrie cut in from the left to make it 2-0 from 20 yards. To suffer such a defeat against a team which barely escaped relegation, and lost their opening match 0-3 at Arsenal, augurs ill for the future.											
3	A	NORWICH	18		L	0-1	0-0		Miklosko	Breacker	Burrows	Potts	Martin	Allen	Bishop	Marsh^	**Moncur**	Jones	Rowland*	Chapman/Whitbread
	27/8		*19,110*	*10*	1			*Robins 65*	*Gunn*	*Bradshaw*	*Bowen*	*Crook*	*Newsome*	*Polson*	*Ekoku**	*Robins^*	*Goss*	*Ullathorne*	*Adams*	*Akinbiyi/Newman*
								Ref: P Jones	Neither side had scored a goal beforehand, so this was always likely to be a low-scoring affair. John Moncur, signed from Swindon for £1 million, made an unspectacular debut. Sub Akinbiyi had been on just three minutes before crossing for Robins to score at the second attempt.											
4	H	NEWCASTLE	21		L	1-3	0-2	Hutchison 87p	Miklosko	Breacker	Burrows	Potts	Martin	Allen*	**Hutchison**	Marsh	Moncur	Butler	Holmes	Jones
	31/8		18,580	*1*	1			*Potts 32 (og), Lee 35, Mathie 88*	*Srnicek*	*Venison*	*Beresford*	*Lee**	*Hottiger*	*Peacock*	*Watson*	*Sellars*	*Albert*	*Cole*	*Mathie*	*Elliott*
								Ref: B Hill	Keegan's Newcastle maintain their 100% record and take their tally to 15 goals in four games. Hammers hung on until Cole's angled shot went in off Potts. Don Hutchison, Hammers' £1.5 million record signing from Liverpool, opened the season's account after John Beresford handled.											
5	A	LIVERPOOL	19		D	0-0	0-0		Miklosko	Breacker	Rowland	Potts	Martin	Allen	Butler	Marsh	Moncur	Rush	Cottee !	
	10/9		*30,907*	*4*	2				*James*	*Jones*	*Ruddock*	*Barnes*	*Scales*	*Molby*	*Redknapp*	*McManam'n*	*Bjornebye*	*Fowler*	*Rush*	
								Ref: P Danson	Roy Evans' Liverpool relinquish their 100% record. Fowler hit the bar, John Barnes the post. Hammers nearly won it at the death when James saved from Moncur. Cottee returns after his six-year stay at Everton and gets sent off after 55 minutes for a two-footed lunge at Rob Jones.											
6	H	ASTON VILLA	17		W	1-0	0-0	Cottee 86	Miklosko	Breacker	Rowland	Potts	Martin	Allen	Butler*	Marsh	Moncur	Rush	Cottee	Chapman
	17/9		18,326	*8*	5				*Bosnich*	*Staunton*	*Richardson*	*Houghton*	*Townsend*	*Ehiogu*	*Barrett*	*Teale*	*Yorke**	*Saunders*	*Fashanu*	*Atkinson*
								Ref: S Lodge	Hammers were without a win, Ron Atkinson's Villa without a defeat, so Cottee's late swivel put paid to both records. Villa looked tired, having played at Internazionale 48 hours earlier, but still had the chances to win. How West Ham reached half-time still level was a mystery.											
7	H	ARSENAL	19		L	0-2	0-1		Miklosko	Breacker	Rowland	Potts	Martin	Allen	Hutchison	Marsh	Moncur	Chapman	Holmes*	Rush
	25/9		18,498	*14*	5			*Adams 18, Wright 54*	*Seaman*	*Dixon*	*Winterburn*	*Adams*	*Keown**	*Merson*	*Schwarz*	*Davis*	*Selley*	*Wright*	*Smith*	*Linighan*
								Ref: K Cooper	Both teams are locked on five points before start of play. Arsenal were still without an away league goal when Smith nodded Davis' free-kick on to Adams. Lee Chapman laboured alone up front for much of the game. Hutchison's two-footed lunge at Smith earned only a yellow card.											
8	A	CHELSEA	15		W	2-1	0-0	Allen 53, Moncur 66	Miklosko	Breacker	Rowland	Potts	Martin	Allen	Hutchison	Marsh	Moncur	Chapman	Rush	
	2/10		*18,696*	*7*	8			*Furlong 62*	*Kharin*	*Clarke !*	*Kjeldbjerg*	*Johnsen*	*Sinclair*	*Rocastle^*	*Peacock*	*Newton*	*Barness**	*Furlong*	*Spencer*	*Shipperley/Lee*
								Ref: P Don	At last West Ham score twice in a game and win away. World Cup ref Philip Don gave 12 fouls in the first four minutes, booked seven players and sent off Steve Clarke for an 87th-minute lunge at Allen. Moncur's corner led to the first goal. His first Hammers goal then won the game.											
9	H	CRYS PALACE	13		W	1-0	0-0	Hutchison 72	Miklosko	Breacker	Rowland	Potts	Martin	Allen	Hutchison	Marsh	Moncur	Chapman*	Cottee	Rush
	8/10		16,959	*18*	11				*Martyn*	*Patterson**	*Gorden*	*Southgate*	*Shaw*	*Coleman*	*Bowey*	*Newman*	*Armstrong*	*Ndah^*	*Salako*	*Dyer/Launders*
								Ref: G Poll	Three wins in a week for buoyant Hammers, inflicting a first away loss on struggling Palace. Three points had looked unlikely when Don Hutchison, pushed up front, stooped to head in Breacker's cross. The best chance for Alan Smith's side came when George Ndah hit a post.											
10	A	MANCHESTER U	14		L	0-1	0-1		Miklosko	Breacker	Rowland	Potts	Martin	Allen	Hutchison	Marsh	Moncur	Rush	Cottee	
	15/10		***43,795***	*4*	11			*Cantona 45*	*Schmeichel*	*Bruce*	*Sharpe*	*Pallister*	*May*	*Ince*	*Cantona*	*Kanchelskis*	*Hughes**	*Irwin*	*Keane*	*McClair*
								Ref: R Gifford	Five home wins out of five for Man U, without the loss of a single goal. But this was a good time for West Ham to play them, with Barcelona due at Old Trafford on Wednesday. In first-half injury-time Giggs set up Cantona for the only goal, but West Ham wasted precious chances.											

No	Venue	Opponent	Pos	Res	FT	HT	Scorers, Times, and Referees	1	2	3	4	5	6	7	8	9	10	11	subs used
11	H	SOUTHAMPTON	12	W	2-0	0-0	Allen 49, Rush 61	Miklosko	Breacker	Dicks	Potts	Martin	Allen	Bishop	Marsh	Rush	Chapman	Cottee	
22/10		18,853	*10*	14				*Beasant*	*Kenna*	*Hall*	*Charlton**	*Allen*	*Magilton*	*Maddison^*	*Le Tissier*	*Monkou*	*Dowie*	*Ekelund*	*Benali/Hughes*
							Ref: J Worray	Inspired by the sight of a gorgeous rainbow, Julian Dicks returns from his unhappy time at Anfield to play a stormer and get booked. Matthew Rush is attracting admiring reviews at Upton Park, and having set up Allen's opener scores the second. Alan Ball bemoans Saints' defence.											
12	A	TOTTENHAM	13	L	1-3	1-1	Rush 42	Miklosko	Rowland	Dicks	Potts	Martin	Allen^	Bishop*	Marsh	Hutchison	Rush	Cottee	Whitbread/Chapman
29/10		*24,271*	*12*	14			*Klinsmann 18, Sheri'm 49, Barmby 63*	*Thorstvedt*	*Edinburgh**	*Popescu*	*Mabbutt*	*Barmby*	*Dumitrescu*	*Dozzell*	*Hazard^*	*Klinsmann*	*Kerslake*	*Campbell*	*Sheringham/Hill*
							Ref: K Morton	Spurs have now conceded 24 league goals, and have the threat of a 6-point deduction hanging over them. This is only Spurs' sixth home league win in 16 months under Ardiles. At 1-1 Cottee heads wide. Four minutes after coming on Sheringham turns the game by firing into the corner.											
13	A	EVERTON	13	L	0-1	0-0		Miklosko	Whitbread	Dicks	Potts	Martin	Rush	Bishop	Marsh	Hutchison	Chapman	Cottee	
1/11		*28,338*	*22*	14			*Ablett 54*	*Southall*	*Jackson*	*Watson*	*Ablett*	*Stuart**	*Parkinson*	*Burrows*	*Amokachi^*	*Durrant*	*Horne*	*Ferguson*	*Limpar/Rideout*
							Ref: K Bodenham	Without a win all season Mike Walker's Everton are in a terrible mess. After Ablett stooped to head them in front, Everton were forced on their heels. In a furious finale Martin's shot is cleared off the line and Chapman's volley hits the bar. Goodison exploded with relief at the end.											
14	H	LEICESTER	14	W	1-0	0-0	Dicks 77p	Miklosko	Whitbread	Dicks	Potts	Martin	Morley	Bishop	Moncur	Hutchison !	Rush	Cottee*	Brown
5/11		18,780	*21*	17				*Ward*	*Grayson*	*Whitlow*	*Mohan*	*Blake*	*Draper*	*Roberts*	*Philott*	*Lowe*	*Lewis*	*Carr*	
							Ref: R Dilkes	Having lost to the bottom team, West Ham dare not slip up against next-to-bottom Leicester. Things did not look bright until Mohan tripped Moncur and Dicks blasted the penalty. Don Hutchison's reputation is clouding his future. He kicked Lee Philpot twice and was expelled.											
15	A	SHEFFIELD WED	17	L	0-1	0-1		Miklosko	Brown	Dicks	Potts	Martin	Allen*	Bishop	Moncur	Morley	Rush	Cottee	Marsh
19/11		*25,300*	*16*	17			*Petrescu 29*	*Pressman*	*Petrescu**	*Nolan*	*Wacker*	*Atherton*	*Sinton*	*Sheridan*	*Bt-Williams^*	*Bright*	*Hyde*	*Pearce*	*Taylor/Watson*
							Ref: G Ashby	Trevor Francis' Wednesday are winning few friends, and nor to tell the truth are the Hammers. The goal that separated the two sides had an element of doubt about it. Chris Bart-Williams chipped the ball forward to Petrescu, who might have been offside. West Ham did not protest.											
16	H	COVENTRY	17	L	0-1	0-0		Miklosko	Brown	Dicks	Potts	Whitbread	Holmes	Bishop*	Marsh	Moncur	Morley	Cottee	Rush
26/11		17,251	*10*	17			*Busst 58*	*Ogrizovic*	*Burrows*	*Busst*	*Morgan*	*Darby*	*Flynn*	*Cook*	*Jones*	*Pressley*	*Ndlovu**	*Dublin*	*Jenkinson*
							Ref: M Reed	Cottee used to love playing Coventry, with 10 goals in six games against them before signing for Everton. Now he can't score against anyone, having a close-in header saved by Ogrizovic. Coventry's late arrival delayed the kick-off. David Busst's unmarked header wins the game.											
17	A	QP RANGERS	17	L	1-2	0-2	Boere 89	Miklosko	Brown	Dicks	Potts	Rowland	Rush	**Hughes**	Marsh	Moncur	Boere	Cottee	
4/12		*12,780*	*16*	17			*Ferdinand 2, Sinclair 37*	*Dykstra*	*Wilson*	*Yates*	*McDonald*	*Impey*	*Sinclair*	*Barker**	*Ferdinand*	*Gallen*	*Maddix*	*Hodge*	*Holloway*
							Ref: P Don	How West Ham envy QPR manager Ray Wilkins the talents of Les Ferdinand and Trevor Sinclair, who scored, respectively, with a prodigious leap and an astonishing burst of acceleration. QPR sat on their lead and were punished by Boere's header – West Ham's 10th goal in 17 games.											
18	A	LEEDS	19	D	2-2	1-2	Boere 45, 79	Miklosko	Brown	Dicks	Potts	**Rieper**	Rowland*	Bishop	Holmes	Rush	Boere	Cottee	Hughes
10/12		*28,987*	*7*	18			*Worthington 3, Deane 25*	*Lukic*	*Kelly*	*Worthingt'n**	*Palmer*	*Wetherall*	*Strachan*	*Deane*	*McAllister*	*Whelan*	*Tinkler*	*Dorigo*	*White*
							Ref: R Hart	Loan signings Rieper and Hughes are shaking things up. Leeds sliced open West Ham's defence twice by 25 minutes. Had it stayed 0-2 at half-time, when Ludo had stitches above an eye, West Ham may have been finished, but the first of Boere's two super headers revitalised the game.											
19	H	MANCHESTER C	17	W	**3-0**	2-0	Cottee 6, 9, 57	Miklosko	Breacker	Dicks	Potts	Martin	Holmes	Bishop	Hughes	Rush	Boere	Cottee	
17/12		17,286	*8*	21				*Dibble*	*Summerbee*	*Walsh*	*Rosler*	*Flitcroft*	*Brightwell I*	*Quinn*	*Lomas*	*Kerr**	*Brightwell D^*	*Kernaghan*	*Vonk/Foster*
							Ref: T Holbrook	City present West Ham with their biggest win of the season and Cottee with his first Hammers hat-trick for eight years – the first with his left, the second with his right, the third a belter from 15 yards. City boss Brian Horton: 'No disrespect, we made them look better than they were.'											
20	H	IPSWICH	18	D	1-1	1-0	Cottee 16	Miklosko	Breacker	Dicks	Potts*	Martin	Holmes	Bishop	Hughes	Rush	Boere	Cottee	Rieper
26/12		20,562	*22*	22			*Thomson 71*	*Forrest*	*Yallop*	*Mason*	*Wark*	*Williams*	*Milton*	*Kiwomya*	*Sedgley**	*Thomsen*	*Vaughan*	*Whelan*	*Slater*
							Ref: P Durkin	Former Hammers are playing a major role in present-day Ipswich. John Lyall resigned three weeks ago, and caretaker boss Paul Goddard takes charge. Ipswich may be bottom, but Claus Thomsen's equalising header was deserved. Tony Cottee had earlier sprung Ipswich's offside trap.											
21	A	WIMBLEDON	18	L	0-1	0-0		Miklosko	Brown	Dicks	Potts	Martin	Rieper*	Bishop	Hughes	Holmes	Boere	Cottee	Rush
28/12		***11,212***	*12*	22			*Fear 55*	*Segers*	*Barton*	*Elkins**	*Jones^*	*Kimble*	*Perry*	*Thorn*	*Cunningham*	*Ekoku*	*Harford*	*Holdsworth*	*Clarke/Fear*
							Ref: P Don	A turgid match, settled by Peter Fear's right-footed half-volley. He had come on as a half-time substitute. 10 minutes later Tony Cottee blazed against the underside of the bar from close range. Redknapp appeared to become involved in an altercation with supporters at the final whistle.											

No	Date	Att	Pos	Pt	F-A	H-T	Scorers, Times, and Referees	SQUAD	NUMBERS	IN	USE								subs used
22	H	NOTTINGHAM F	16	W	3-1	3-0	Cottee 24, Bishop 26, Hughes 44	Miklosko	Breacker	Dicks	Potts	Martin	Holmes	Bishop	Hughes	Moncur^	Boere*	Cottee	Rush/Rieper
	31/12	20,644	4	25			*McGregor 89*	*Crossley*	*Lyttle*	*Chettle*	*Cooper**	*Pearce*	*Woan*	*Stone*	*Bohinen^*	*Haaland*	*Roy*	*Collymore*	*McGregor/Black*
							Ref: D Gallagher	The key battle was between evergreen Alvin Martin and Stan-the-Man Collymore, talked about as an England striker. The balding Martin won hands down. Other Hammers heroes were Moncur in midfield and Michael Hughes, who scored the goal of the game with a superb solo effort.											
23	A	BLACKBURN	16	L	2-4	1-1	Cottee 32, Dicks 58	Miklosko	Breacker	Dicks	Potts	Rieper	Holmes*	Bishop	Hughes	Moncur	Boere	Cottee	Rush
	2/1	*25,503*	*1*	25			*Shearer 14p, 75, 79p, Le Saux 61*	*Flowers*	*Berg*	*Gale*	*Hendry*	*Le Saux*	*Sherwood*	*Atkins**	*Ripley*	*Wilcox*	*Sutton*	*Shearer^*	*Warhurst/Newell*
							Ref: K Morton	Champions-elect Blackburn have won all but one match at Ewood, and go six points clear of Man U. West Ham led 2-1 after an hour, but were exposed by Le Saux's 25-yard free-kick. Alan Shearer's two penalties were conceded by Ludo Miklosko on Shearer, and Rieper on Wilcox.											
24	H	TOTTENHAM	19	L	1-2	1-0	Boere 10	Miklosko	Breacker	Brown	Potts	Martin	Holmes^	Bishop	Hughes*	Moncur	Boere	Cottee	Allen/Morley
	14/1	24,573	*6*	25			*Sheringham 58, Klinsmann 80*	*Walker*	*Austin*	*Calderwood*	*Mabbutt*	*Campbell**	*Popescu*	*Howells*	*Barmby*	*Anderton*	*Sheringham*	*Klinsmann*	*Edinburgh*
							Ref: B Hill	Gerry Francis has replaced Ardiles and masterminded Spurs' sixth successive clean sheet. Boere denied them a seventh, heading in Hughes' corner. Anderton then fouled Holmes inside the box, but the kick was given outside. Miklosko flapped at the free-kick which made it 1-1.											
25	H	SHEFFIELD WED	19	L	0-2	0-1		Miklosko	Breacker !	Brown	Potts	Martin !	Holmes^	Bishop	Hughes*	Moncur	Boere	Cottee	Rieper/Allen
	23/1	**14,554**	*7*	25			*Waddle 33, Bright 83*	*Pressman*	*Nolan*	*Wacker*	*Atherton*	*Bart-Williams*	*Bright*	*Hyde*	*Pearce*	*Ingesson*	*Waddle^*	*Whittingh'm**	*Watson/Petrescu*
							Ref: P Danson	Two red cards for the Irons, the first on 10 minutes when Martin stumbles across Mark Bright on the halfway line. It looked like a rugby tackle but is annulled. Waddle's exquisite angled chip deserved to win any game. Breacker went off on 73 mins, felling Hyde. That ended the contest.											
26	A	LEICESTER	20	W	2-1	2-1	Cottee 29, Dicks 43p	Miklosko	Breacker	Dicks	Potts	Martin	Allen	Moncur	Hughes	Hutchison*	Williamson	Cottee	Boere
	4/2	*20,375*	*22*	28			*Robins 45*	*Poole*	*Grayson*	*Smith**	*Hill*	*Mohan*	*Draper*	*Thompson*	*Roberts*	*Poole*	*Philott*	*Galloway*	*Lawrence*
							Ref: J Worray	Leicester are bottom and doomed, so three points are a must for West Ham. Dicks laid on Cottee's 100th Hammers goal, and when Cottee was fouled in the box Dicks smote home the penalty. Leicester's £1 million signing Mark Robins' goal on half-time ensured a nervy second period.											
27	H	EVERTON	20	D	2-2	1-1	Cottee 22, 60	Miklosko	Brown	Dicks	Potts	Martin	Allen	Moncur	Hughes*	Hutchison	Williamson	Cottee	Boere
	13/2	21,081	*17*	29			*Rideout 43, Limpar 79*	*Southall*	*Watson*	*Unsworth*	*Ablett**	*Stuart*	*Ebrell*	*Hinchcliffe*	*Barrett*	*Horne*	*Rideout*	*Ferguson*	*Limpar*
							Ref: M Reed	The classic six-pointer. Royle's Everton had scored only four goals in 13 away games, so when Cottee scored his second in the mud to make it 2-1, it should have been all over. Two swinging left-footed crosses from Hinchliffe brought two Everton goals, the second deflected by Potts.											
28	A	COVENTRY	20	L	0-2	0-1		Miklosko	Breacker	Dicks	Potts	Martin*	Allen	Holmes^	Moncur	Hutchison	Williamson	Cottee	Rieper/Boere
	18/2	*17,554*	*14*	29			*Ndlovu 25, Marsh 67*	*Ogrizovic*	*Burrows*	*Morgan*	*Rennie*	*Flynn*	*Cook*	*Pickering*	*Marsh*	*Richardson*	*Ndlovu*	*Dublin*	
							Ref: R Dilkes	Ron Atkinson has just taken charge at Highfield Road – his eighth club. The formidable Dion Dublin made both goals, the second for former-Hammer Mike Marsh. Redknapp complained that his team tried to play 'too much football'. Coventry are now five points ahead of West Ham.											
29	H	CHELSEA	20	L	1-2	1-0	Hutchison 11	Miklosko	Breacker	Dicks	Potts	Rieper	Allen	Bishop	Moncur	Hutchison	Morley	Cottee	
	25/2	21,500	*13*	29			*Burley 67, Stein 75*	*Kharin^*	*Clarke*	*Johnsen*	*Newton*	*Minto*	*Briley*	*Rocastle**	*Peacock*	*Spencer*	*Lee*	*Stein*	*Furlong/Hitchock*
							Ref: G Ashby	Chelsea have a date with FC Bruges and were there to be beaten. They should have been, too, as they fell behind to Hutchison's thumping half-volley. West Ham also bit bar and post. But Burley levelled, then set up Stein's terrific volley. Kharin had to be subbed 10 minutes from time.											
30	A	ARSENAL	19	W	1-0	1-0	Hutchison 20	Miklosko	Breacker	Dicks	Potts	Rieper	Allen	Bishop	Moncur	Hutchison	Morley*	Cottee	Rush
	5/3	*34,295*	*11*	32				*Bartram*	*Dixon*	*Winterburn*	*Linighan*	*Bould*	*Jensen**	*Merson*	*Schwarz*	*Parlour*	*Wright*	*Helder^*	*Morrow/Kiwomya*
							Ref: B Hill	George Graham has been 'bunged' into touch, and Stewart Houston is caretaker. Few could have expected this result, settled by Hutchison's sixth goal so far, as Winterburn fluffed a clearance. Seaman has a long-term injury. Moncur and Hutchison were booked as tension mounted.											
31	A	NEWCASTLE	19	L	0-2	0-1		Miklosko	Breacker	Dicks	Potts	Rieper	Allen	Bishop	Hughes	Hutchison	Rush*	Cottee	Morley
	8/3	*34,595*	*3*	32			*Clark 17, Kitson 52*	*Srnicek*	*Venison*	*Beresford*	*Fox**	*Howey^*	*Lee*	*Clark*	*Hottiger*	*Peacock*	*Gillespie*	*Kitson^*	*Watson/Bracewell*
							Ref: T Holbrook	Newcastle are still unbeaten at St James', so this result is hardly unexpected, and leaves West Ham entrenched in the four relegation places. In truth, they got off lightly, and could have been 0-4 down instead of 0-1 at the break. £2.2 million Paul Kitson scored with a sweet left-footer.											

No	Venue/Date	Opponent/Att	Pos	Res/Pts	F-A	H-T	Scorers, Times, and Referees	1	2	3	4	5	6	7	8	9	10	11	subs used
32	H	NORWICH	18	D	2-2	0-1	Cottee 82, 88	Miklosko	Breacker	Dicks	Potts	Rieper	Williamson	Bishop	Moncur*	Hutchison	Morley	Cottee	Hughes
	11/3	21,464	*14*	33			*Eadie 22, Ullathorne 53*	*Marshall*	*Newman*	*Newsome*	*Polston*	*Ullathorne*	*Sutch*	*Eadie^*	*Johnson!*	*Prior*	*Cureton**	*Ward*	*Adams/Akinbiyi*
							Ref: A Wilkie / M Sims	Norwich are on a terrible slide. 7th at New Year, they have not won since. They even have the wrong player sent off – Johnson when it should have been Prior – for fouling Cottee. Substitute ref Sims had just replaced hamstrung Alan Wilkie. Cottee's goals extend Norwich's bad run.											
33	A	SOUTHAMPTON	19	D	1-1	1-0	Hutchison 39	Miklosko	Breacker	Dicks	Potts	Rieper	Rush*	Bishop	Moncur	Hutchison	Holmes	Cottee	Boere
	15/3	*15,178*	*18*	34			*Shipperley 48*	*Beasant*	*Hall*	*Widdrington*	*Benali*	*Magilton*	*Maddison^*	*Le Tissier*	*Heaney**	*Monkou*	*Dodd*	*Shipperley*	*Hughes/Ekelund*
							Ref: K Burge	Bruce Grobbelaar was arrested this morning on charges of match-fixing. Southampton's recent record is earning a fortune for someone – this is their ninth draw in 10 games. Hutchison's header, helped in by Widdrington, was cancelled out by Shipperley's first league goal for the Saints.											
34	A	ASTON VILLA	18	W	2-0	1-0	Moncur 11, Hutchison 49	Miklosko	Breacker	Dicks	Potts	Rieper	Allen	Bishop	Moncur	Hutchison^	Holmes*	Cottee	Rowland/Boere
	18/3	*28,682*	*15*	37				*Bosnich*	*Staunton*	*McGrath*	*Teale*	*Townsend*	*Taylor*	*Charles*	*Johnson**	*Saunders*	*Yorke^*	*Wright*	*Houghton/Ehiogu*
							Ref: M Bodenham	Villa have been reeling since losing a 4-1 lead over Leicester with 11 minutes left, and Brian Little's team are spiralling downwards. Moncur's 25-yarder drains Villa of what little confidence they have. Shaun Teale boobs for the second goal. Few away victories come as easy as this.											
35	A	NOTTINGHAM F	19	D	1-1	0-0	Dicks 65	Miklosko	Brown	Dicks	Potts	Rieper	Allen	Bishop	Hughes	Holmes*	Boere	Cottee	Whitbread
	8/4	*28,361*	*4*	38			*Collymore 78*	*Crossley*	*Lyttle*	*Chettle*	*Cooper*	*Pearce*	*Woan^*	*Stone*	*Phillips*	*Bohinen**	*Roy*	*Collymore*	*Lee/McGregor*
							Ref: G Poll	Three weeks without a fixture. Forest are going well, five wins on the trot, the last a 7-1 drubbing of Sheffield Wednesday at Hillsborough. But Dicks thumped in a free-kick. The equaliser was farcical. Potts and Ludo collided in mid-air, and Collymore rammed in the ensuing corner.											
36	H	WIMBLEDON	17	W	**3-0**	1-0	Dicks 41p, Boere 76, Cottee 78	Miklosko	Breacker	Dicks	Potts	Rieper	Allen	Bishop	Hughes	Holmes	Boere	Cottee	
	13/4	21,084	*9*	41				*Sullivan*	*Barton*	*Elkins*	*Jones*	*Reeves*	*Thorn*	*Cunningham*	*Leonhardsen*	*Gayle**	*Harford*	*Holdsworth*	*Clarke*
							Ref: M Reed	A rare Thursday night game. West Ham are unbeaten in five, beating the Dons at home in the league for the first time. The result also relegates Ipswich and Leicester. Barton fouled Holmes for the penalty, but West Ham were hanging on grimly until Boere's super header settled matters.											
37	A	IPSWICH	18	D	1-1	0-1	Boere 90	Miklosko	Breacker	Dicks	Potts	Rieper	Allen*	Bishop	Moncur	Holmes	Boere	Cottee	Hutchison
	17/4	*19,099*	*22*	42			*Thomson 11*	*Baker*	*Stockwell*	*Yallop*	*Wark*	*Williams*	*Milton**	*Marshall^*	*Mathie*	*Slater*	*Linighan*	*Thomsen*	*Mason/Chapman*
							Ref: M Bodenham	An unreal result. Ipswich had lost their last eight, scored just one goal, and suffered a 0-9 humiliation at Man U. West Ham might have had nine themselves. Instead they needed four minutes stoppage time to get a draw. Ipswich fans were singing 'We're s*** and we're beating you'.											
38	H	BLACKBURN	16	W	2-0	0-0	Rieper 50, Hutchison 83	Miklosko	Breacker	Dicks	Potts	Rieper	Allen	Bishop	Moncur	Hutchison^	Boere*	Holmes	Rush/**Webster**
	30/4	24,202	*1*	45				*Flowers*	*Berg*	*Hendry*	*Le Saux*	*Kenna*	*Sherwood*	*Batty*	*Ripley**	*Witschge*	*Sutton*	*Shearer*	*Newell*
							Ref: K Morton	Man U fans love West Ham as a result of this shock win. Shearer and Sutton, Rovers' 56-goal SAS, were well shackled by Potts and Rieper. Batty should have been expelled for a thigh-high lunge at Bishop. Rieper headed in Moncur's corner. Boere and Hutchison had broken noses.											
39	H	QP RANGERS	15	D	0-0	0-0		Miklosko	Breacker	Dicks	Potts	Rieper	Allen !	Bishop	Moncur	Hutchison^	Boere*	Holmes	Morley/Webster
	3/5	22,923	*8*	46				*Roberts*	*Bardsley*	*Wilson**	*McDonald*	*Impey*	*Holloway*	*Sinclair*	*Barker*	*Ferdinand*	*Penrice^*	*Maddix*	*Brevitt/Gallen*
							Ref: G Willard	Martin Allen was sent off on the hour, retaliating against a foul by Rufus Brevitt, who was one of seven Rangers booked. West Ham carved out few scoring chances and Ludo made a super double save to earn a point, but Palace's defeat at the Dell improves West Ham's survival chances.											
40	A	CRYS PALACE	16	L	0-1	0-0		Miklosko	Breacker	Dicks	Potts	Rieper	Allen^	Bishop	Moncur	Hutchison*	Boere	Holmes	Morley/Webster
	6/5	*18,224*	*19*	46			*Armstrong 50*	*Martyn*	*Humphrey*	*Gorden*	*Southgate*	*Shaw*	*Young*	*Pitcher*	*Houghton*	*Armstrong*	*Dowie*	*Salako*	
							Ref: S Lodge	Palace inflict West Ham's first defeat in nine games, to plunge them back in the mire. The first half was abject. The second had no sooner begun than Chris Armstrong finished off a fluid Palace move. Without the sprightly Cottee, West Ham seldom looked likely to salvage a point.											
41	H	LIVERPOOL	13	W	**3-0**	1-0	Holmes 29, Hutchison 60, 61	Miklosko	Breacker	Dicks*	Potts	Rieper	Moncur	Bishop	Hughes	Hutchison	Morley	Holmes	Webster
	10/5	22,446	*4*	49				*James*	*Babb*	*Scales*	*Matteo**	*Clough*	*Barnes*	*Redknapp*	*Thomas*	*McManam'n*	*Harkness*	*Fowler^*	*Kennedy/Walters*
							Ref: P Durkin	Two matches against Liverpool and Man U stand between West Ham and relegation. With Cottee and Boere out for the season, Hutchison is pushed up front and scores twice in a minute against his former club. Palace are four points behind with one game left, so West Ham are safe.											
42	H	MANCHESTER U	14	D	1-1	1-0	Hughes 31	Miklosko	Breacker	Rowland	Potts	Rieper	Moncur	Bishop	Hughes^	Hutchison*	Morley	Holmes	Allen/Webster
	14/5	**24,783**	*2*	50			*McClair 52*	*Schmeichel*	*Neville G*	*Bruce*	*Pallister*	*Irwin*	*Butt**	*Keane^*	*Ince*	*Sharpe*	*McClair*	*Cole*	*Hughes/Scholes*
	Home	Away					Ref: A Wilkie	Man U must win and Blackburn must lose. Had West Ham needed points themselves the tension would have been unbearable. Mark Hughes was left on the bench till the break, by which time the damage had been done. Two late saves by Miklosko from Cole send the title to Ewood.											
Average	19,730	24020																	

Coca-Cola Cup

Rd		Opponent			F-A	H-T	Scorers, Times, and Referees	SQUAD	NUMBERS	IN	USE								subs used
2:1	A	WALSALL	17	L	1-2	1-1	Ntamark 42 (og)	Miklosko	Breacker	Rowland	Potts	Martin	Allen^	Moncur	Marsh	Hutchison	Rush*	Cottee	Chapman/Whitbread
20/9		*5,994*	*2:11*				*Watkiss 25, Potts 74 (og)*	*Wood*	*Evans*	*Rogers*	*Watkiss*	*Marsh*	*Palmer**	*O'Connor*	*Peer*	*Lightbourne*	*Wilson*	*Ntamark^*	*Ryder/Mehew*
							Ref: P Harrison	Chris Nicholl takes charge of Walsall for the first time in this famous win. Watkiss headed in the far post for Walsall before Ntamark ran the ball inadvertently past his own keeper to make it 1-1. The second own-goal of the night came when Potts miscued a clearance past Miklosko.											
2:2	H	WALSALL	15	W	2-0	0-0	Hutchison 62, Moncur 94	Miklosko	Breacker	Rowland	Potts	Moncur*	Allen	Bishop	Marsh	Hutchison	Whitbread	Chapman	Brown
5/10		13,553	*2:7*		*aet*			*Woods*	*Rider*	*Rogers*	*Watkiss*	*Marsh**	*Palmer*	*O'Connor^*	*Peer*	*Lightbourne*	*Wilson*	*Mehew*	*Ntamark/Evans*
							Ref: J Holbrook (Hammers win 3-2 on aggregate)	With an hour gone West Ham were staring elimination in the face. Without the suspended Cottee, Hutchison played up front, scoring close in following Moncur and Allen's build-up. Mehew wasted the chance to win it for Walsall. In extra-time Moncur drove in a rebound off the post.											
3	H	CHELSEA	12	W	1-0	1-0	Hutchison 2	Miklosko	Breacker	Dicks	Potts	Martin	Allen	Bishop	Marsh	Hutchison	Rush	Cottee	
26/10		18,815	*7*					*Kharin*	*Kjeldberg*	*Johnsen*	*Spackman*	*Newton*	*Barness*	*Hall^*	*Rocastle*	*Peacock**	*Wise*	*Shipperley*	*Hopkin/Lee*
							Ref: K Cooper / J Norbury	Hutchison's sweet curler from 20 yards gave West Ham the perfect start. At half-time the ref's injured Achilles tendon forced a linesman to take over. Glenn Hoddle's injury-racked team made the running after the break, but two headers were kept out by super saves from Miklosko.											
4	H	BOLTON	17	L	1-3	0-1	Cottee 83	Miklosko	Brown	Dicks	Potts	Whitbread	Rush	Bishop	Holmes*	Moncur	Boere	Cottee	Morley
30/11		18,190	*1:4*				*McGinlay 16, 76p, Whitbread 53 (og)*	*Branagan*	*Green*	*Phillips*	*McAteer*	*Coleman*	*Stubbs*	*Lee**	*Sneakes*	*Paatelainen*	*McGinlay*	*Thompson*	*Patterson*
							Ref: P Durkin	First Division Bolton do to West Ham what they had done to Liverpool, Everton, Arsenal and Ipswich in the past two years – winning cup-ties away from home. West Ham's miserable night was sealed when Dicks needlessly handled Thompson's corner. The penalty made it 0-3.											

FA Cup

Rd		Opponent			F-A	H-T	Scorers, Times, and Referees												subs used
3	A	WYCOMBE WAN	16	W	2-0	0-0	Cottee 47, Brown 78	Miklosko	Breacker	Dicks	Potts	Martin	Moncur	Bishop	Hughes	Holmes*	Boere^	Cottee	Brown/Morley
7/1		*9,007*	*2:3*					*Hyde*	*Cousins*	*Brown*	*Crossley*	*Evans*	*Ryan*	*Carroll*	*Bell*	*Regis^*	*Garner*	*Thompson**	*Stapleton/Hemmings*
							Ref: G Willard	Wycombe – with FA Cup-winner Cyrille Regis in their ranks – had not lost at home since September, but could not contain Hughes' crosses. These led to both goals. Alan Hansen on *Match of the Day* had predicted an upset. Hammers fans sang 'There's only one Trevor Brooking'.											
4	A	QP RANGERS	19	L	0-1	0-1		Miklosko	Breacker	Dicks	Potts	Martin	Moncur	Bishop*	Hughes	Allen	Boere	Cottee	Hutchison
28/1		*17,694*	*17*				*Impey 20*	*Roberts*	*Bardsley*	*Yates*	*McDonald*	*Impey*	*Holloway*	*Sinclair*	*Barker*	*Gallen*	*Maddix*	*Dichio*	
							Ref: D Elleray	Ray Wilkins was not associated with robust play as a player, but his QPR side take no prisoners. Four Rangers are booked. Without the injured Ferdinand, Rangers had to find an alternative source of goals. Ian Holloway set up Andrew Impey. England boss Venables watched the game.											

		Home					Away					
	P	W	D	L	F	A	W	D	L	F	A	Pts
1 Blackburn	42	17	2	2	54	21	10	6	5	26	18	89
2 Manchester U	42	16	4	1	42	4	10	6	5	35	24	88
3 Nottingham F	42	12	6	3	36	18	10	5	6	36	25	77
4 Liverpool	42	13	5	3	38	13	8	6	7	27	24	74
5 Leeds	42	13	5	3	35	15	7	8	6	24	23	73
6 Newcastle	42	14	6	1	46	20	6	6	9	21	27	72
7 Tottenham	42	10	5	6	32	25	6	9	6	34	33	62
8 QP Rangers	42	11	3	7	36	26	6	6	9	25	33	60
9 Wimbledon	42	9	5	7	26	26	6	6	9	22	39	56
10 Southampton	42	8	9	4	33	27	4	9	8	28	36	54
11 Chelsea	42	7	7	7	25	22	6	8	7	25	33	54
12 Arsenal	42	6	9	6	27	21	7	3	11	25	28	51
13 Sheffield Wed	42	7	7	7	26	26	6	5	10	23	31	51
14 WEST HAM	42	9	6	6	28	19	4	5	12	16	29	50
15 Everton	42	8	9	4	31	23	3	8	10	13	28	50
16 Coventry	42	7	7	7	23	25	5	7	9	21	37	50
17 Manchester C	42	8	7	6	37	28	4	6	11	16	36	49
18 Aston Villa	42	6	9	6	27	24	5	6	10	24	32	48
19 Crys Palace	42	6	6	9	16	23	5	6	10	18	26	45
20 Norwich	42	8	8	5	27	21	2	5	14	10	33	43
21 Leicester	42	5	6	10	28	37	1	5	15	17	43	29
22 Ipswich	42	5	3	13	24	34	2	3	16	12	59	27
	924	205	134	123	697	498	123	134	205	498	697	1252

Odds & ends

Double wins: (2) Villa, Leicester.
Double losses: (4) Newcastle, Spurs, Sheff Wed, Coventry.

Won from behind: (0).
Lost from in front: (3) Blackburn (a), Spurs (h), Chelsea (h).

High spots: Undefeated run of eight league games from 11 March.

Low spots: Losing to First Division Bolton in Coca-Cola-Cup.
Terrible start to the league, just two points from first five games.
Five league defeats in six games from 29 October.

Hammer of the Year: Steve Potts.
Ever-presents: (2) Ludek Miklosko, Steve Potts.
Hat-tricks: (1) Tony Cottee.
Leading scorer: (15) Tony Cottee.

	Appearances						Goals			
	Lge	*Sub*	LC	*Sub*	FAC	*Sub*	Lge	LC	FAC	Tot
Allen, Martin	**26**	*3*	3		1		**2**			**2**
Bishop, Ian	**31**		3		2		**1**			**1**
Boere, Jeroen	**15**	*5*	1		2		**6**			**6**
Breacker, Tim	**33**		3		2					
Brown, Kenny	**8**	*1*	1	*1*		*1*			1	**1**
Burrows, David	**4**									
Butler, Peter	**5**									
Chapman, Lee	**7**	*3*	1	*1*						
Cottee, Tony	**31**		3		2		**13**	1	1	**15**
Dicks, Julian	**29**		2		2		**5**			**5**
Holmes, Matthew	**24**		1		1		**1**			**1**
Hughes, Michael	**15**	*2*			2		**2**			**2**
Hutchison, Don	**22**	*1*	3			*1*	**9**	2		**11**
Jones, Steve	**1**	*1*								
Marsh, Mike	**13**	*3*	3							
Martin, Alvin	**24**		2		2					
Miklosko, Ludek	**42**		4		2					
Moncur, John	**30**		3		2		**2**	1		**3**
Morley, Trevor	**10**	*4*		*1*		*1*				
Potts, Steve	**42**		4		2					
Rieper, Marc	**17**	*4*					**1**			**1**
Rowland, Keith	**11**	*1*	2							
Rush, Matthew	**15**	*8*	3				**2**			**2**
Webster, Simon		*5*								
Whitbread, Adrian	**3**	*5*	2	*1*						
Williamson, Danny	**4**									
(own-goals)								1		**1**
26 players used	**462**	***46***	**44**	***4***	**22**	***3***	**44**	**5**	**2**	**51**

No		Date	Att	Pos	Pt	F-A	H-T	Scorers, Times, and Referees	SQUAD	NUMBERS	IN	USE								subs used
1	H	LEEDS			L	1-2	1-0	Williamson 5	Miklosko	Breacker	Dicks	Potts	Rieper	Williamson*	Moncur	Bishop	Cottee	Hutchison	Rowland^	Martin/**Boogers**
		19/8	22,901		–			Yeboah 48, 57	Lukic	Kelly	Dorigo^	Palmer"	Wetherall	Pemberton	Yeboah	Wallace*	Deane	McAllister	Speed	Whelan/Worthington/
								Ref: K Burge (Leeds' 3rd sub Beasley)	Tony Yeboah came to Leeds on loan from Eintracht Frankfurt. He has now signed permanently, and he sinks the Hammers with a fierce header and a ferocious volley. It had all started so brightly, Williamson tucking away Rowland's cross. Alvin Martin came on as substitute striker.											
2	A	MANCHESTER U	19	L		1-2	0-0	Bruce 56 og	Miklosko	Breacker	Dicks	Potts	Rieper	Allen	Moncur	Bishop	Cottee	Hutchison	Williamson*	Boogers !
		23/8	31,966	10	–			Scholes 50, Keane 68	Schmeichel	Neville G	Irwin	Bruce	Sharpe	Pallister	Butt	Keane	McClair^	Scholes*	Beckham	Cole/Thornley
								Ref: D Gallagher	Rebuilding has turned Old Trafford into a three-sided ground. United lost their opening match 1-3 at Villa, and might have lost this one too. Hammers' cause was not helped by the dismissal of sub Marco Boogers for a nasty lunge at Gary Neville. 10 men could not rescue a point.											
3	A	NOTT'M FOREST	17	D		1-1	1-1	Allen 14	Miklosko	Breacker	Dicks	Potts	Rieper	Allen	Moncur	Bishop	Cottee*	Hutchison	Slater	Martin
		26/8	26,645	2	1			Pearce 38p	Crossley	Lyttle	Pearce	Cooper	Chettle	Stone	Phillips	Roy*	Bohinen^	Campbell	Woan	Lee/Gemmill
								Ref: G Ashby	Three players took part in the corresponding fixture 10 years previously – Cottee, Martin, and Stuart Pearce. Hammers went in front when Dicks pumped a high ball onto Martin Allen's head. Tugging by Don Hutchison gave away the equaliser. Colin Cooper's header hit the bar.											
4	H	TOTTENHAM	17	D		1-1	1-0	Hutchison 24	Miklosko	Breacker	Dicks	Potts	Rieper	Allen	Moncur	Bishop	Cottee	Hutchison*	Slater	Boere
		30/8	23,516	18	2			Rosenthal 54	Walker	Austin	Wilson	Howells	Calderwood	Mabbutt	McMahon*	Dozzell	Armstrong	Sheringham	Rosenthal	Anderton
								Ref: M Reed	Both sides are left still looking for their first win. Spurs are still mourning the departure of Klinsmann. Don Hutchison speared a 25-yard free-kick into the top corner, but that was cancelled out by Rosenthal, who turned Potts to level. Redknapp needs to find new strikers quickly.											
5	H	CHELSEA	19	L		1-3	0-2	Hutchison 73	Miklosko	Breacker	Dicks	Potts	Rieper	Bishop*	Moncur	Dowie	Cottee	Hutchison	Slater	**Lazaridis**
		11/9	19,228	11	2			Wise 31, Spencer 33, 80	Kharine	Clarke	Minto	Gullit	Johnsen	Sinclair	Newton	Hughes	Spencer	Peacock*	Wise	Lee
								Ref: R Hart	Chelsea's John Spencer celebrates his 25th birthday with Julian Dicks' studs down his head. Dicks earns a yellow card, rather than red, but will face an FA disciplinary hearing. Iain Dowie re-signs after four years away. At 1-2 Miklosko saves Wise's penalty, following Breacker's foul.											
6	A	ARSENAL	19	L		0-1	0-0		Miklosko	Breacker	Dicks !	Potts	Rieper	Bishop	Moncur"	Dowie	Cottee*	Hutchison^	Slater	Martin/Laz/**Sealey**
		16/9	38,065	5	2			Wright 75p	Seaman	Dixon	Winterburn	Parlour	Bould	Adams	Jensen	Wright	Merson	Bergkamp	Helder	
								Ref: A Wilkie	One for the scrapbook. Dicks is booked for fouling Helder, concedes a penalty which Wright missed, and is sent off when fouling Wright once more. When Potts toppled Bergkamp, Wright's aim was more accurate. Hammers employed sub goalkeeper Les Sealey as a makeshift striker.											
7	H	EVERTON	17	W		2-1	2-1	Dicks 7p, 43p	Miklosko	Breacker	Dicks	Potts*	Martin	Bishop	Moncur	Dowie	Cottee^	Lazaridis	Slater	Rieper/Williamson
		23/9	21,085	14	5			Samways 40	Southall	Barrett	Hinchcliffe	Parkinson	Watson	Short	Samways	Horne	Amokachi	Rideout^	Grant*	Limpar/Stuart
								Ref: P Durkin	An ugly match, settled by two nerveless penalties by Julian Dicks, who was at the heart of most that was good and bad. His strikes sandwiched a well-executed reply by Samways, and earned a belated first Hammers win. Alvin Martin creaked like an old tree at times, but did not break.											
8	A	SOUTHAMPTON	16	D		0-0	0-0		Miklosko	Breacker	Rowland	Potts	Martin	Bishop	Moncur	Lazaridis*	Dowie	Hutchison	Slater	Cottee
		2/10	13,568	17	6				Beasant	Dodd	Benali	Magilton	Hall	Monkou	Charlton*	Shipperley	Le Tissier	Maddison	Widdrington	Bennett
								Ref: G Poll	Matt Le Tissier, dropped by England, fathers a daughter before this, his 300th league game for Saints. Dicks is suspended, following recent misdemeanours. In a game of few chances, Le Tissier fired wide, and Widdrington cleared off the line from Dowie, all on his own up front.											
9	A	WIMBLEDON	13	W		1-0	1-0	Cottee 18	Miklosko	Potts	Dicks	Rieper	Martin	Bishop	Moncur	Dowie	Cottee	Slater	Hughes	[Fitzgerald]
		16/10	**9,411**	12	9				Heald	Cunningham	Perry	Jones	McAllister	Thorn"	Goodman	Earle	Skinner^	Holdsworth	Leonhard'n*	Gayle/Clarke/
								Ref: D Gallagher	Tony Cottee scores his first league goal for six months – also against Wimbledon – to defeat a Dons side plunging down the table. His sweet half-volley when the ball looped up off Paul Heald was threatened only by Andy Clarke's bicycle kick which hit the bar. Dicks had a stormer.											
10	H	BLACKBURN	13	D		1-1	1-0	Dowie 25	Miklosko	Potts	Dicks	Rieper	Martin	Bishop	Moncur	Dowie	Cottee	Slater*	Hughes	Hutchison
		21/10	21,776	11	10			Shearer 89	Flowers	Berg	Kenna	Batty	Hendry	Pearce	Ripley	Sherwood^	Shearer	Sutton*	Bohinen	Newell/McKinlay
								Ref: S Lodge	The defending champions had lost all four previous away fixtures and were seconds away from losing this. Iain Dowie's first goal for the Hammers since his return – a sharp downward header – had looked to earn three deserved points, until Shearer headed in Bohinen's centre.											

No Date		Opponent Att	Pos	Res Pts	F-A	H-T	Scorers, Times, and Referees	1	2	3	4	5	6	7	8	9	10	11	subs used
11	A	SHEFFIELD WED	12	W	1-0	1-0	Dowie 40	Miklosko	Potts	Dicks	Rieper	Martin	Bishop	Moncur*	Dowie	Cottee	Slater^	Hughes	Hutchison/**Harkes**
28/10		*23,917*	*13*	13				*Pressman*	*Williams^*	*Nolan*	*Ingesson*	*Atherton*	*Hyde*	*Pembridge*	*Waddle*	*Hirst*	*Whittingh'm**	*Sinton*	*Bright/Degryse*
							Ref: K Cooper	Twice Wednesday hit the bar, and that made all the difference. The goal was too low for them. Dowie's conversion of Slater's cross – the ball being palmed in by Pressman – did not really reflect the balance of play. Fortified by the goal, Dowie almost scored another. He too hit the bar.											
12	H	ASTON VILLA	12	L	**1-4**	0-1	Dicks 85p	Miklosko	Potts	Dicks	Rieper	Martin	Bishop	Slater^	Dowie	Cottee	Hutchison*	Hughes	Boogers/Harkes
4/11		23,637	*5*	13			*Milosevic 33, 89, Johnson 49, Yorke 54*	*Bosnich*	*Charles*	*Wright*	*Southgate*	*McGrath*	*Ehiogu*	*Taylor*	*Draper*	*Milosevic*	*Townsend**	*Yorke*	*Johnson*
							Ref: P Jones	Hammers' heaviest home defeat follows on the heels of an unbeaten October. It was Villa's first win at the Boleyn for 10 years. West Ham had started brightly and twice hit the wood, but Villa missed easier chances than the four they scored. Dicks' fourth penalty makes him top scorer.											
13	A	BOLTON	11	W	**3-0**	0-0	Bishop 46, Cottee 68, Williamson 89	Miklosko	Potts	Rowland	Rieper	Martin	Bishop	Harkes	Dowie	Cottee	Williamson	Hughes	
18/11		19,047	*18*	16				*Branagan*	*McAnespie^*	*Phillips*	*Curcic*	*Bergsson*	*Fairclough*	*Lee**	*Sneekes*	*Patterson !*	*McGinlay*	*Thompson*	*Green/Todd*
							Ref: P Durkin	Newcomers Bolton are heading back whence they came. Ian Bishop marked his 200th league game with a dipping 25-yarder. Bolton responded by collecting cards. Two yellows for skipper Mark Patterson and off he went. The Irons went for the kill. Bolton fans' frustration boiled over.											
14	H	LIVERPOOL	13	D	0-0	0-0		Miklosko	Potts	Rowland	Rieper	Martin	Bishop	Harkes	Dowie	Cottee	Williamson	Hughes	
22/11		**24,324**	*6*	17				*James*	*Jones*	*Harkness*	*Babb*	*Wright*	*Ruddock*	*McManam'n*	*McAteer*	*Collymore*	*Barnes*	*Fowler*	
							Ref: J Winter	Liverpool had lost their last three and recall the sulking Collymore in place of the injured Ian Rush. Lack of goals did not mean lack of thrills. Potts had only scored once in 350 games, but nearly doubled his tally with a 30-yarder. Liverpool's best chances were wasted by Stan the Man.											
15	H	QP RANGERS	10	W	1-0	0-0	Cottee 84	Miklosko	Potts	Rowland*	Rieper	Martin	Bishop	Harkes^	Dowie	Cottee	Williamson	Hughes	Breacker/Slater
25/11		21,504	*18*	20				*Sommer*	*Ready !*	*Brazier*	*Barker*	*Yeats*	*McDonald*	*Impey^*	*Holloway*	*Dichio*	*Gallen*	*Wilkins**	*Maddix/Charles*
							Ref: P Alcock	Boring for neutrals; ecstasy for Hammers as they poke their heads into the top half of the table. Cottee had twisted and turned to tuck away Potts' throw-in for the only goal. QPR's Karl Ready, five bookings in 10 games, body-checked Slater to earn his second yellow of the game.											
16	A	BLACKBURN	13	L	2-4	0-3	Dicks 75p, Slater 86	Miklosko	Breacker	Dicks	Potts	Rieper	Bishop*	Harkes^	Dowie	Cottee"	Williamson	Hughes	Hutch/Slater/Boogers
2/12		*26,638*	*10*	20			*Shearer 3, 17, 65p, Newell 32*	*Flowers*	*Kenna*	*Le Saux*	*Batty*	*Hendry**	*Berg*	*Ripley*	*Sherwood*	*Shearer*	*Newell*	*Bohinen*	*Warhurst*
							Ref: K Burge	They love West Ham at Ewood. The Hammers always lose there, and they also defied Man U last May. Dicks returns from suspension. So careful is he not to get booked that Stuart Ripley enjoys more room than he could have expected, and is the source of all four Rovers goals.											
17	A	EVERTON	13	L	0-3	0-2		Miklosko !	Breacker	Dicks	Potts	Rieper	Bishop	Slater	Dowie	Cottee*	Williamson	Hughes	Rowland
11/12		*31,778*	*11*	20			*Stuart 33, Unsworth 43p, Ebbrell 68*	*Southall*	*Jackson*	*Unsworth*	*Ebbrell*	*Watson*	*Short*	*Kanchelskis*	*Parkinson*	*Amokachi*	*Stuart*	*Limpar**	*Ferguson*
							Ref: M Reed	Miklosko is sent off for smashing Amokachi. Julian Dicks takes his jersey but can't save Unsworth's penalty. It was a day of returns. Cottee returned to the club for whom he scored 99 goals, and Duncan Ferguson returned to Everton from Barlinnie Prison. Dicks denied him a goal.											
18	H	SOUTHAMPTON	13	W	2-1	0-1	Cottee 80, Dowie 82	Miklosko	Potts	Dicks	Rieper	Martin*	Bishop	Moncur^	Dowie	Cottee	Williamson	Hughes	Breacker/Slater
16/12		**18,501**	*15*	23			*Bishop 22 (og)*	*Beasant*	*Dodd*	*Benali*	*Magilton**	*Hall*	*Monkou*	*Le Tissier*	*Venison*	*Shipperley*	*Charlton*	*Oakley^*	*Maddison/Hughes*
							Ref: A Wilkie	It all seemed to be going wrong. Bishop had put through his own goal and Hammers still trailed with 10 minutes left. Foolish Saints had opted to protect their ill-gotten gains by surrendering possession outside their box. Dave Beasant kept out everything until the Hammers' final salvo.											
19	A	MIDDLESBROUGH	13	L	2-4	0-3	Cottee 80, Dicks 86 *[Hendrie 82]*	Miklosko	Breacker`	Dicks	Potts	Rieper	Bishop	Moncur*	Dowie	Cottee	Williamson	Hughes^	Rowland/Slater
23/12		*28,640*	*5*	23			*Fjortoft 20, Cox 21, Morris 28,*	*Walsh*	*Cox*	*Morris*	*Vickers*	*Pearson*	*Whyte*	*Robson*	*Pollock*	*Fjortoft*	*Juninho*	*Hendrie*	
							Ref: S Dunn	High-flying Middlesbrough turn on the style and leave Hammers battered and demoralised. Juninho has set Teesside alight. The contest is over after half an hour, and Hammers are thankful Boro step off the gas. This is Boro's last win for three months, as they plummet down the league.											
20	A	MANCHESTER C	14	L	1-2	0-1	Dowie 74	**Finn**	Harkes	Dicks	Potts	Rieper	Bishop	Moncur	Slater	Dowie	Williamson*	Hughes	Hutchison
1/1		*26,024*	*17*	23			*Quinn 21, 78*	*Immel*	*Summerbee*	*Brightwell*	*Curle*	*Symons*	*Brown*	*Lomas*	*Quinn*	*Rosler^*	*Flitcroft**	*Kinkladze*	*Ekelund/Phillips*
							Ref: M Reed	With Miklosko suspended and Sealey injured, Redknapp has to pitch in YTS signing Neil Finn, at 17 years and three days the Premiership's youngest ever player. Finn himself had hamstring trouble and was not to blame for City scoring twice in a match for the first time this season.											
21	A	LEEDS	14	L	0-2	0-1		Miklosko	Potts	Rowland*	Williamson	Rieper	Dicks	Moncur	Bishop	Cottee	Dowie	Hughes	Slater
13/1		*30,472*	*9*	23			*Brolin 25, 62*	*Beaney*	*Kelly*	*Dorigo**	*Palmer*	*Wetherall*	*Ford*	*Brolin"*	*Wallace^*	*Chapman !*	*McAllister*	*Speed*	*Couzens/Gray/Harte*
							Ref: P Danson	Defeats are coming thick and fast, five from six games. A minute after disgruntled Tomas Brolin had put Leeds in front, Lee Chapman – back at Leeds after three years – clattered Rieper with his elbow and was expelled. Hammers last won at Leeds in 1978, on Alvin Martin's debut.											

No	Date	Opponent	Att	Pos	Pt	F-A	H-T	Scorers, Times, and Referees	SQUAD	NUMBERS	IN	USE								subs used
22	H	MANCHESTER U		16	L	0-1	0-1		Miklosko	Brown	Dicks	Potts	Rieper	Bishop	Moncur	Dowie	Cottee	Williamson	Slater*	Rowland
	22/1		24,197	*2*	23			*Cantona 8*	*Schmeichel*	*Neville G*	*Irwin*	*Bruce*	*Sharpe*	*Neville P*	*Cantona*	*Keane*	*Cole**	*Butt !*	*Giggs*	*Beckham*
								Ref: S Lodge	In retrospect, this fiery match – with Nicky Butt expelled following a Dicks-Cole clash – enables United to reel in Newcastle. Alex Ferguson's team have won just twice in nine league games. Cantona's exquisite goal from an near-impossible angle sparks a six-game winning streak.											
23	H	COVENTRY		14	W	3-2	0-0	Rieper 46, Cottee 59, Dowie 85	Miklosko	Brown	Dicks	Potts	Rieper	Bishop	Moncur^	Dowie	Cottee*	Williamson	Hughes	Whitbread/**Lampard**
	31/1		18,884	*18*	26			*Dublin 62, Whelan 82*	*Ogrizovic*	*Pickering*	*Hall*	*Richardson**	*Shaw*	*Borrows*	*Telfer*	*Williams^*	*Dublin*	*Whelan*	*Salako*	*Ndlovu/Strachan*
								Ref: G Poll	The number of 'oohs' on the new video screen underlined a thrilling second half. Frank Lampard Jnr made his first appearance in Hammers' colours, and Gordon Strachan looked the best player on the pitch when he belatedly came on. Dowie won the game from Williamson's cross.											
24	H	NOTT'M FOREST		13	W	1-0	1-0	Slater 19	Miklosko	Brown	Dicks	Potts	Rieper	Bishop	Slater*	Dowie	Cottee^	Williamson	Hughes	Whitbread/**Dani**
	3/2		21,651	*9*	29				*Crossley*	*Lyttle*	*Phillips*	*Cooper*	*Chettle*	*B'rt-Williams*	*Campbell*	*Gemmill**	*Silenzi*	*Roy*	*Woan*	*Haaland*
								Ref: K Burge	Hectic end-to-end stuff that the purists hate but British fans love. The goal was as messy as the play. Williamson crossed, Cooper slashed and missed, and Slater shot past Crossley. Portuguese heart-throb Dani came on and tried to score from the halfway line. It was that kind of game.											
25	A	TOTTENHAM			W	1-0	1-0	Dani 4	Miklosko	Potts	Dicks	**Bilic**	Rieper	Bishop	Hughes^	Dowie	Dani*	Williamson	Rowland	Cottee/Harkes
	12/2		*29,781*		32				*Walker*	*Austin*	*Wilson*	*Campbell*	*Calderwood*	*Mabbutt*	*Fox*	*Dozzell*	*Armstrong*	*Sheringham*	*Rosenthal**	*Sinton*
								Ref: J Winter	Dean Austin needlessly concedes a corner from which Dani scores – a header from yards out. The chief puzzle was the dearth of goals, since both sides missed chances a-plenty. Dani will flatter to deceive, though Bilic was outstanding on his debut and will maintain his high standard.											
26	A	CHELSEA		12	W	2-1	0-1	Dicks 62, Williamson 72	Miklosko	Potts	Dicks	Bilic	Rieper	Bishop	Hughes	Dowie	Dani*	Williamson	Rowland	Cottee
	17/2		*25,252*	*10*	35			*Peacock 13*	*Hitchcock*	*Petrescu*	*Phelan*	*Duberry*	*Clarke*	*Lee*	*Gullit*	*Newton**	*Furlong*	*Peacock*	*Wise*	*Sinclair*
								Ref: G Willard	Julian Dicks is relishing his nice-boy image. He has not been booked for nine games and plays a stormer in central defence in Redknapp's revamped side. He even headed the equaliser. Chelsea's cause was not helped by losing Eddie Newton after five minutes with a broken leg.											
27	H	NEWCASTLE		13	W	2-0	1-0	Williamson 7, Cottee 82	Miklosko	Potts	Dicks	Bilic*	Rieper	Bishop	Hughes	Dowie	Cottee^	Williamson	Rowland	Harkes/Gordon
	21/2		23,843	*1*	38				*Srnicek*	*Barton*	*Beresford*	*Albert*	*Peacock*	*Howey*	*Asprilla*	*Beardsley*	*Ferdinand*	*Clark*	*Gillespie**	*Kitson*
								Ref: P Alcock	Newcastle start the match nine points clear of Man U, plus a game in hand. They have signed the Colombian Asprilla and he takes centre stage in this epic. He and Ferdinand hit a post, Newcastle dazzle throughout, but West Ham win their fifth game in a row with two fine breakaways.											
28	H	ARSENAL		11	L	0-1	0-1		Miklosko	Harkes*	Dicks	Potts	Rieper	Bishop	Hughes	Dowie	Cottee	Williamson	Rowland	Dani
	24/2		24,217	*6*	38			*Hartson 2*	*Seaman*	*Dixon*	*Winterburn*	*Hillier**	*Keown*	*Linighan*	*Parlour*	*Hartson*	*Merson*	*Bergkamp*	*Morrow*	*Platt*
								Ref: D Elleray	Hammers' winning run comes to a predictable end against Arsenal, who have a habit of winning at the Boleyn. John Harkes' errant back-pass fell to Merson, who set up John Hartson. Dicks then missed a penalty. Suffering from double-vision, his spot-kick lacked his usual venom.											
29	A	COVENTRY		11	D	2-2	2-2	Cottee 2, Rieper 22	Miklosko	Potts	Dicks	Bilic	Rieper	Bishop	Hughes	Dowie	Cottee*	Williamson	Rowland	Harkes
	2/3		*17,448*	*13*	39			*Salako 7, Whelan 15*	*Ogrizovic*	*Borrows*	*Burrows**	*Richardson*	*Shaw*	*Daish*	*Jess*	*Ndlovu*	*Dublin*	*Whelan*	*Salako*	*Williams*
								Ref: M Bodenham	Ron Atkinson has spent £13 million on his team. The game could have been 5-5 at half-time, and both managers made half-time changes to stem the haemorrhaging. Cottee's header was his 13th Hammers goal against Coventry. West Ham wasted three one-on-one opportunities.											
30	H	MIDDLESBROUGH		11	W	2-0	1-0	Dowie 2, Dicks 62p	Miklosko	Breacker	Dicks	Potts	Bilic	Bishop	Hughes	Dowie	Cottee*	Williamson	Rowland	**Dumitrescu**
	9/3		23,850	*13*	42				*Walsh*	*Morris"*	*Fleming*	*Cox*	*Pearson*	*Whyte*	*Hignett**	*Barmby*	*Fjortoft^*	*Mustoe*	*Kavanagh*	*Hendrie/Juninho/*
								Ref: M Reed (Boro's 3rd sub Branco)	Juninho was on the bench, jet-lagged from playing for Brazil. It took Dowie 67 seconds to tap in from six inches, after Gary Walsh botched a clearance. Cox inadvertently handled for a harsh penalty. Since beating West Ham on 23 December, Boro have taken one point from 11 games.											
31	A	NEWCASTLE		11	L	0-3	0-1		Miklosko	Potts	Dicks	Bilic	Rieper	Bishop*	Hughes	Dowie	Dumitrescu^	Williamson	Rowland	Breacker/Dani
	18/3		*36,331*	*1*	42			*Albert 21, Asprilla 55, Ferdinand 65*	*Srnicek*	*Barton**	*Beresford*	*Batty*	*Albert*	*Howie*	*Lee*	*Beardsey*	*Ferdinand*	*Ginola*	*Asprilla*	*Watson*
								Ref: S Lodge	Newcastle are irresistible, and Redknapp is brave and honest enough to admit it. But it is Keegan's first win in four games. Newcastle will lose their next two, and clearly they are there to be taken. West Ham are the only team not to score against Newcastle in this jittery six-game spell.											

No	Date	Opponent	Att	Pos	Pts	F-A	H-T	Scorers, Times, and Referees	1	2	3	4	5	6	7	8	9	10	11	12 subs used
32 H	23/3	MANCHESTER C	24,017	11 *16*	W 45	4-2	1-0	Dowie 21, 53, Dicks 83, Dani 84 / *Quinn 76, 90* / Ref: K Cooper	Miklosko / *Immel*	Breacker / *Summerbee"*	Dicks / *Frontzeck^*	Bilic / *Curle*	Rieper / *Symons*	Bishop / *Brightwell*	Hughes / *Brown*	Dowie / *Clough*	Dumitrescu* / *Rosler**	Williamson / *Lomas !*	Rowland / *Kinkladze*	Dani *[Mazzarelli]* / *Quinn/Hiley/*
									Both team-sheets were packed with foreigners, but the match was frenetically English. The match turned on 42 minutes, when Miklosko saved Curle's penalty. Dowie fired in two thumping headers from corners, Rosler missed open goals, and Lomas was sent off for two yellow cards.											
33 H	6/4	WIMBLEDON	20,462	11 *15*	D 46	1-1	1-1	Dicks 6 / *Jones 9* / Ref: P Durkin	Miklosko / *Sullivan*	Breacker / *Ardley*	Dicks / *Kimble*	Bilic / *Jones*	Rieper / *Blackwell*	Bishop / *Perry*	Hughes / *Gayle**	Dowie / *Earle*	Dani / *Ekoku*	Williamson / *Holdsworth*	Rowland* / *Clarke^*	Slater / *Goodman/Castledine*
									A power failure on the Underground delays kick-off. This is the first season since 1985-86 that West Ham will finish above Wimbledon in the league. Holdsworth forces two sharp shaves by Miklosko. Joe Kinnear summed up the game: 'West Ham's best player was 'wot's 'is name.'											
34 A	8/4	LIVERPOOL	***40,326***	11 *3*	L 46	0-2	0-2	*Collymore 22, Barnes 38* / Ref: P Alcock	Miklosko / *James*	Breacker / *McAteer*	Dicks / *Bjornebye*	Bilic / *Scales*	Rieper / *Matteo*	Bishop / *Thomas*	Hughes* / *McManam'n*	Dowie / *Redknapp*	Slater / *Collymore*	Williamson / *Barnes*	Rowland / *Fowler*	Dani
									Defeat at Coventry on Saturday has all but wrecked Liverpool's title chances, though that does not prevent the largest crowd to watch West Ham turning out. The previous Anfield game brought a 4-3 win over Newcastle, whose defeat at Blackburn tonight presents the title to Man U.											
35 H	13/4	BOLTON	23,086	11 *20*	W 49	1-0	1-0	Cottee 28 / Ref: A Wilkie	Miklosko / *Ward*	Breacker / *Bergsson*	Dicks / *Phillips*	Bilic / *Curcic*	Rieper / *Fairclough*	Bishop / *Coleman*	Slater^ / *Sellars*	Dowie / *Stubbs*	Cottee / *Blake**	Williamson / *McGinlay*	Hughes* / *Thompson*	Moncur/Rowland / *De Freitas*
									Bolton have staged a late rally to avoid the drop, but this defeat makes it all but inevitable. They deserved better on the day. Bishop headed on to his own crossbar and Miklosko made two vital saves when strikers were clear. But Cottee's goal from Williamson's assist proved decisive.											
36 A	17/4	ASTON VILLA	*26,768*	11 *4*	D 50	1-1	0-1	Cottee 84 / *McGrath 27* / Ref: S Dunn	Miklosko / *Bosnich*	Breacker / *Charles**	Dicks / *Wright*	Potts* / *Townsend*	Rieper / *McGrath*	Bilic / *Ehiogu*	Moncur / *Taylor*	Dowie / *Draper*	Cottee / *Milosevic*	Williamson / *Johnson*	Rowland / *Yorke^*	Dani / *Scimeca/Joachim*
									Villa's Coca-Cola Cup win assure their place in Europe. West Ham have staved off the drop, so there was a lack of oomph in this match. Paul McGrath's superb volley was cancelled in the dying minutes when sub Dani's second touch set up Cottee. Villa's Gary Charles broke an ankle.											
37 A	27/4	QP RANGERS	*18,828*	11 *19*	L 50	0-3	0-0	*Ready 60, Gallen 70, 79* / Ref: G Willard	Miklosko / *Sommer*	Breacker / *Ready*	Dicks / *Brevett*	Potts / *Barker*	Rieper / *Yeats*	Bilic / *McDonald*	Hughes / *Dichio*	Moncur* / *Wilkins*	Cottee / *Hateley**	Williamson / *Gallen*	Rowland / *Sinclair*	**Watson** / *Charles*
									Ray Wilkins' team had to win and hope other strugglers lost. Cottee wasted three early chances. Karl Ready's first league goal of the season opened the flood-gates but could not prevent QPR's relegation after 13 years in the top flight. Dani had failed to turn up for training and is out.											
38 H	5/5	SHEFFIELD WED	23,790	10 *15*	D 51	1-1	0-0	Dicks 72 / *Newsome 89* / Ref: R Dilkes	Miklosko / *Pressman*	Breacker / *Atherton*	Dicks / *Briscoe*	Potts / *Pembridge*	Rieper / *Newsome*	Bilic / *Walker*	Hughes / *Degryse^*	Dowie* / *Blinker**	Cottee" / *Hirst*	Williamson / *Hyde*	Rowland^ / *Whittingham*	Martin/L'pard/**Ferd"** / *Waddle/Humphreys*
									Results elsewhere could still send Wednesday down unless they drew. Dicks' diving header was neutralised by Newsome's late header from Whittingham's cross, but it proved to be unnecessary. West Ham finish in the top half for the first time in 10 years. Alvin Martin's final match.											
	Average	Home 22,340	Away 26,449																	

Coca-Cola Cup					F-A	H-T	Scorers, Times, and Referees	SQUAD	NUMBERS	IN	USE								subs used
2:1	A	BRISTOL ROV	19	W	1-0	1-0	Moncur 34	Miklosko	Breacker	Dicks	Potts	Martin	Bishop	Moncur	Dowie*	Cottee	Lazaridis	Slater^	Rieper/Williamson
20/9		*7,103*	*2:11*					*Parkin*	*Pritchard*	*Gurney*	*Browning*	*Wright*	*Tilson*	*Skinner*	*Miller*	*Stewart*	*Channing**	*Taylor*	*Wyatt*
							Ref: K Cooper	Rovers had lost two home games on the trot and showed little inner belief. Slater touched a short free-kick to Moncur, whose shot swerved into the top corner from 30 yards. Dicks – facing a disrepute charge – twice had headers cleared off the line. Still, the second leg looks comfortable.											
2:2	H	BRISTOL ROV	16	W	3-0	0-0	Dicks 47p, Bishop 49, Cottee 75	Miklosko	Breacker	Dicks	Potts	Rieper	Bishop	Moncur	Dowie	Cottee	Slater	Hughes	
4/10		15,375	*2:11*					*Parkin*	*Pritchard*	*Gurney*	*Browning*	*Wright*	*Tilson*	*Sterling*	*Paul*	*Stewart*	*Skinner*	*Channing**	*Davis*
							Ref: R Gifford (Hammers win 4-0 on aggregate)	The longer this tie went on the less likelihood of Rovers springing an upset. Five minutes after half-time the outcome is effectively settled with two further Hammers goals. You can't keep Julian Dicks out of the news at the moment. He is either collecting cards or blasting penalties.											
3	A	SOUTHAMPTON	13	L	1-2	1-1	Cottee 33	Miklosko	Potts	Dicks	Rieper	Martin	Bishop	Moncur	Dowie	Cottee	Slater	Hughes	
25/10		*11,059*	*17*				*Watson 4, Shipperley 79*	*Beasant*	*Dodd*	*Benali*	*Venison*	*Hall*	*Monkou*	*Le Tissier*	*Watson*	*Shipperley*	*Hughes*	*Heaney*	
							Ref: P Danson	Barry Venison has added steel to Dave Merrington's midfield. Four minutes into his Saints debut his wayward shot strikes Watson on the heel and wrong-foots Miklosko. Cottee spun to level from close in, but Neil Shipperley scuttled Hammers' hopes by heading in Jason Dodd's cross.											

FA Cup																			
3	H	SOUTHEND	14	W	2-0	0-0	Moncur 58, Hughes 87	Miklosko	Harkes	Dicks	Potts	Rieper	Bishop	Moncur	Dowie	Cottee	Williamson	Hughes	
6/1		23,284	*1:7*					*Royce*	*Dublin*	*Powell*	*McNally*	*Bodley*	*Gridelet*	*Marsh*	*Byrne*	*Regis*	*Jones**	*Hails*	*Thomson*
							Ref: R Dilkes	Just 13 league places separated these teams, so well were Southend going in Div 1. But the Seasiders, with ex-Hammer Mike Marsh, created nothing and it was just a matter of time. Man of the match was young keeper Simon Royce. Dowie's effort was blocked and fell to Moncur.											
4	H	GRIMSBY	10	D	1-1	1-1	Dowie 35	Miklosko	Potts	Dicks	Rieper	Whitbread	Bishop	Slater*	Dowie	Cottee	Williamson	Hughes	Lazaridis^/Rowland
7/2		22,030	*1:13*				*Laws 24*	*Crichton*	*McDermott*	*Croft*	*Laws*	*Lever*	*Groves*	*Childs*	*Shakespeare*	*Forrester*	*Woods**	*Bonetti^*	*Livingstone/Southall*
							Ref: G Willard	Grimsby, with just one win in 10, made a better fist of it than Southend. Former Italian star Ivano Benetto set up player-manager Brian Laws for a breakaway goal. Dowie's header from Williamson's cross earned a replay, but fixture congestion is threatening West Ham's season.											
4R	A	GRIMSBY	10	L	0-3	0-1		Miklosko	Potts	Dicks	Rieper	Martin*	Bishop	Hughes	Dowie	Cottee	Williamson	Rowland^	Gordon/Harkes
14/2		*8,382*	*1:14*				*Childs 24, Woods 63, Forrester 89*	*Crichton*	*McDermott*	*Croft*	*Fickling*	*Lever*	*Groves*	*Childs**	*Shakespeare*	*Woods*	*Forrrester*	*Southall*	*Livingstone*
							Ref: R Hart	Chelsea await the winners, but not even that prospect can fire the Hammers into life. Bonetti was out with a black eye from a plate flung at him by Brian Laws. At 0-2 Dale Gordon made his first appearance for two years. Grimsby's first home win over a top division team since 1936.											

		Home						Away					
	P	W	D	L	F	A	W	D	L	F	A	Pts
1 Manchester U	38	15	4	0	36	9	10	3	6	37	26	82
2 Newcastle	38	17	1	1	38	9	7	5	7	28	28	78
3 Liverpool	38	14	4	1	46	13	6	7	6	24	21	71
4 Aston Villa	38	11	5	3	32	15	7	4	8	20	20	63
5 Arsenal	38	10	7	2	30	16	7	5	7	19	16	63
6 Everton	38	10	5	4	35	19	7	5	7	29	25	61
7 Blackburn	38	14	2	3	44	19	4	5	10	17	28	61
8 Tottenham	38	9	5	5	26	19	7	8	4	24	19	61
9 Nottingham F	38	11	6	2	29	17	4	7	8	21	37	58
10 WEST HAM	38	9	5	5	25	21	5	4	10	18	31	51
11 Chelsea	38	7	7	5	30	22	5	7	7	16	22	50
12 Middlesbrough	38	8	3	8	27	27	3	7	9	8	23	43
13 Leeds	38	8	3	8	21	21	4	4	11	19	36	43
14 Wimbledon	38	5	6	8	27	33	5	5	9	28	37	41
15 Sheffield Wed	38	7	5	7	30	31	3	5	11	18	30	40
16 Coventry	38	6	7	6	21	23	2	7	10	21	37	38
17 Southampton	38	7	7	5	21	18	2	4	13	13	34	38
18 Manchester C	38	7	7	5	21	19	2	4	13	12	39	38
19 QP Rangers	38	6	5	8	25	26	3	1	15	13	31	33
20 Bolton	38	5	4	10	16	31	3	1	15	23	40	29
	760	186	98	96	580	408	96	98	186	408	580	1042

Odds & ends

Double wins: (1) Bolton.
Double losses: (3) Leeds, Manchester U, Arsenal.

Won from behind: (3) Leeds (h), Southampton (h), Chelsea (a).
Lost from in front: (0).

High spots: Five successive league wins from 31 January.
Just one defeat in nine league games from 23 September.

Low spots: Terrible start, no wins in the first six league games.
Six defeats out of seven league games from 2 December.
Losing at First Division Grimsby in FA Cup.

Hammer of the Year: Julian Dicks.
Ever-presents: (0).
Hat-tricks: (0).
Leading scorer: (12) Tony Cottee.

	Appearances						Goals			
	Lge	*Sub*	LC	*Sub*	FAC	*Sub*	**Lge**	LC	FAC	**Tot**
Allen, Martin	3						**1**			**1**
Bilic, Slaven	13									
Bishop, Ian	35		3		3		**1**	1		**2**
Boere, Jeroen		*1*								
Boogers, Marco		*4*								
Breacker, Tim	19	*3*	2							
Brown, Kenny	3									
Cottee, Tony	3	*3*	3		3		**1**	2		**12**
Dani	3	*6*					**2**			**2**
Dicks, Julian	34		3		3		**1**	1		**11**
Dowie, Iain	33		3		3		**8**		1	**9**
Dumitrescu, Ilie	2	*1*								
Ferdinand, Rio		*1*								
Finn, Neil	1									
Gordon, Dale		*1*				*1*				
Harkes, John	6	*5*			1	*1*				
Hughes, Michael	28		2		3				1	**1**
Hutchison, Don	8	*4*					**2**			**2**
Lampard, Frank		*2*								
Lazaridis, Stan	2	*2*	1			*1*				
Martin, Alvin	1	*4*	2		1					
Miklosko, Ludek	36		3		3					
Moncur, John	19	*1*	3		1			1	1	**2**
Potts, Steve	34		3		3					
Rieper, Marc	35	*1*	2	*1*	3		**2**			**2**
Rowland, Keith	19	*4*			1	*1*				
Sealey, Les	1	*1*								
Slater, Robbie	16	*6*	3		1		**2**			**2**
Watson, Mark		*1*								
Whitbread, Adrian		*2*			1					
Williamson, Danny	28	*1*		*1*	3		**4**			**4**
(own-goals)							**1**			**1**
31 players used	**418**	***54***	**33**	***2***	**33**	***4***	**43**	**5**	**3**	**51**

No	Date		Att	Pos	Pt	F-A	H-T	Scorers, Times, and Referees	SQUAD	NUMBERS	IN	USE								subs used
1	A	ARSENAL			L	0-2	0-2		Miklosko	Breacker	Dicks	Rieper	Bilic*	Williamson	Hughes	Rowland^	Lampard"	Dowie	Jones	Ferdinand/Laz/Slater
	17/8		*38,056*		–			*Hartson 27, Bergkamp 40p*	*Seaman*	*Dixon*	*Winterburn*	*Bould*	*Merson*	*Bergkamp**	*Linighan*	*Keown*	*Parlour*	*Hartson^*	*Morrow*	*Wright/Dickov*
								Ref: P Durkin	Super weather; super pitch; tedious game. Bruce Rioch has left Highbury; Arsene Wenger is coming, and caretaker boss Stewart Houston enjoys a quick win. Rieper handled Dixon's cross for the penalty. Steve Jones, back from Bournemouth, squandered three second-half chances.											
2	H	COVENTRY			D	1-1	0-1	Rieper 74	Miklosko	Breacker*	Dicks	Rieper	Bilic	Williamson	Hughes	Lazaridis	Slater	Dowie	Jones^	**Futre/Bowen**
	21/8		21,680		1			*McAllister 12*	*Ogrizovic*	*Shaw*	*Burrows*	*Daish*	*Jess**	*McAllister*	*Salako*	*Telfer*	*Genaux^*	*Dublin*	*Ducros*	*Williams/Borrows*
								Ref: S Dunn	Paulo Futre made his long-awaited entrance after 53 minutes and lit the fuse for the Hammers' revival. Dicks' free-kick was half-cleared for Rieper to level. Earlier, Regis Genaux had crossed for £3 million Gary McAllister to head his first Coventry goal since signing from Leeds.											
3	H	SOUTHAMPTON		11	W	2-1	0-1	Hughes 73, Dicks 81p	Miklosko	Slater*	Dicks	Rieper^	Bilic	Williamson	Hughes	Lazaridis"	Futre	Dowie	Bowen	Braeck/**Radu/Dumit**
	24/8		21,227	*17*	4			*Heaney 19*	*Beasant*	*Dodd*	*Magilton*	*Le Tissier*	*Shipperley**	*Maddison^*	*Heaney"*	*Charlton*	*Neilson*	*Oakley*	*Dryden*	*Potter/Benali!/Wats'n*
								Ref: D Elleray	Man of the match is referee David Elleray. First he gives the Hammers a penalty when Dryden topples Dumitrescu. Seconds later, he sends off Benali for mowing down Futre, who looked a class apart. Hammers had fallen behind when Bilic and Dicks got in a tizzy. A priceless first win.											
4	A	MIDDLESBROUGH		15	L	**1-4**	0-2	Hughes 57 *[Stamp 81]*	Miklosko	Breacker	Dicks	Potts*	Bilic	Williamson	Hughes	Lazaridis^	Futre	Raducioiu"	Bowen	Dowie/Dumit/L'pard
	4/9		*30,060*	*9*	4			*Emerson 12, Mustoe 28, Ravanelli 52,*	*Miller*	*Whyte*	*Vickers*	*Whelan*	*Cox*	*Emerson*	*Mustoe*	*Fleming*	*Juninho**	*Ravanelli*	*Barmby^*	*Stamp/Moore*
								Ref: P Jones	West Ham are overwhelmed at the Riverside by the dazzling talents of Emerson, Juninho and Fabrizio Ravanelli, who kept up his goal-a-match sequence since his arrival. But West Ham's goal was as good as any, Michael Hughes ramming the ball into the top corner from 25 yards.											
5	A	SUNDERLAND		16	D	0-0	0-0		Miklosko	Breacker	Dicks	Rieper	Bilic	Williamson	Hughes	Dumitrescu*	Futre^	Raducioiu"	Bowen	Rowland/Ferd/Jones
	8/9		*18,642*	*10*	5				*Coton*	*Kubicki*	*Ord*	*Melville*	*Scott*	*Agnew**	*Bracewell*	*Ball*	*Gray*	*Quinn*	*Stewart*	*Russell*
								Ref: G Poll	An apology of a Sunday football match, with Hammers mostly to blame. Redknapp knows who to blame, for he hauls off all three of his Latin forwards, none of whom showed appetite for a scrap. The only bonus was the point earned, following the hiding at the Riverside in midweek.											
6	H	WIMBLEDON		17	L	0-2	0-0		Miklosko	Breacker*	Dicks	Rieper	Bilic	Williamson	Hughes	Dumitrescu^	Futre"	Dowie	Bowen	Laz/Moncur/Cottee
	14/9		21,294	*8*	5			*Clarke 59, Ekoku 86*	*Sullivan*	*Cunningham*	*Perry*	*McAllister*	*Thatcher*	*Ardley*	*Jones*	*Earle*	*Gayle*	*Ekoku*	*Goodman**	*Clarke*
								Ref: R Dilkes	The Dons are on the march. Three losses are followed by three wins. This match opened Harry's eyes to the futility of fancy foreigners coming up against home-grown talents like Perry and Thatcher. 'I want my defenders to defend like they do,' he sighed. Clarke miscued the first goal.											
7	A	NOTT'M FOREST		13	W	2-0	1-0	Bowen 45, Hughes 54	**Mautone**	Bowen	Dicks	Rieper !	Bilic	Lazaridis	Hughes	Bishop*	Moncur	Dowie	Cottee	Lampard
	21/9		*23,352*	*16*	8				*Crossley*	*Lyttle*	*Pearce*	*Cooper*	*Phillips*	*Saunders*	*Woan*	*Jerkan**	*Allen*	*Haarland*	*Roy*	*Lee*
								Ref: G Willard	Before kick-off both teams had won just once. Mark Bowen heads in Lazaridis' cross at the far post. The game ignites early in the second half. Rieper goes off for a professional foul on Brian Roy. Within seconds Cottee – making his first start of the season – shoots and Hughes scores.											
8	H	LIVERPOOL		15	L	1-2	1-1	Bilic 15	Miklosko	Breacker	Dicks	Rieper	Bilic	Bowen*	Hughes	Bishop	Moncur	Dowie	Cottee^	Porfirio/Dumitrescu
	29/9		**25,064**	*1*	8			*Collymore 3, Thomas 55*	*James*	*Scales**	*Matteo*	*Babb*	*McAteer*	*McManam'n*	*Thomas*	*Barnes*	*Bjornebye*	*Berger^*	*Collymore"*	*R'uddock/Jones/*
								Ref: K Burge (Liverpool's 3rd sub Redknapp)	Unbeaten Liverpool stretch their winning sequence to seven, despite the absence of the injured Fowler and the withdrawal after 20 minutes of Collymore. He had turned Rieper to score after 135 seconds. Bilic headed in Hughes's corner. McAteer and Jamie Redknapp set up the winner.											
9	A	EVERTON		16	L	1-2	0-1	Dicks 86p	Miklosko	Bowen	Dicks	Potts*	Bilic	Rowland	Hughes	Bishop^	Moncur	Dowie	Porfirio	Raducioiu/Dumitres
	12/10		*36,571*	*9*	8			*Stuart 14, Speed 78*	*Southall*	*Barrett*	*Short*	*Unsworth*	*Hinchcliffe*	*Kanchelskis*	*Ebbrell**	*Parkinson^*	*Speed*	*Stuart*	*Branch*	*Hottiger/Grant*
								Ref: G Barber	Not a good advert for the Premiership. The first half offered little apart from Hinchcliffe's daisy-cutter and Stuart's conversion. Hammers only got to grips once they were two down. Hinchcliffe felled Porfirio for Dicks to smite a penalty. Afterwards, the gods kept Everton's goal intact.											
10	H	LEICESTER		13	W	1-0	0-0	Moncur 78	Miklosko	Bowen*	Dicks	Rieper	Bilic	Porfirio	Hughes	Bishop	Moncur	Dowie	Raducioiu^	Breacker/Lazaridis
	19/10		22,285	*14*	11				*Keller*	*Grayson*	*Whitlow*	*Watts*	*Walsh!*	*Izzet*	*Lennon*	*Taylor**	*Heskey*	*Prior*	*Marshall^*	*Parker/Claridge*
								Ref: M Riley	'I thought my team desperately unlucky' groaned Martin O'Neill. City had shown plenty of pluck. Walsh's 87th-minute dismissal (his 12th overall) for upending Miklosko, didn't help either. Porfirio's acceleration set up Moncur's side-footed winner. Cottee has gone to Malaysia.											

No	Venue	Opponent	Att	Pos	Res	F-A	H-T	Scorers, Times, and Referees	1	2	3	4	5	6	7	8	9	10	11	subs used
11	H	BLACKBURN		10	W	2-1	0-1	Porfirio 77, Berg 85 (og)	Miklosko	Bowen*	Dicks	Rieper	Bilic	Lazaridis	Hughes	Bishop	Moncur^	Dowie	Porfirio"	Braeck/Futre/L'pard
	26/10		23,947	*20*	14			*Berg 9*	*Flowers*	*Kenna*	*Sherwood*	*Le Saux**	*Wilcox*	*Marker*	*Fenton*	*McKinlay*	*Berg*	*Donis^*	*Flitcroft*	*Croft/Ripley*
								Ref: M Reed	Manager Ray Harford had quit in midweek, but Rovers welcomed back Le Saux after a long injury. They comfortably held their lead for over an hour. But then Futre came on to lift spirits. Dowie laid on the equaliser for Porfirio. Berg deflected Lazaridis' cross for a flattering winner.											
12	A	TOTTENHAM		12	L	0-1	0-0		Miklosko	Breacker	Dicks	Rieper	Bilic	Lazaridis	Hughes	Bishop	Moncur*	Dowie	Porfirio	Futre
	2/11		*32,999*	*8*	14			*Armstrong 67*	*Walker*	*Edinburgh*	*Howells*	*Calderwood*	*Nielsen*	*Sheringham*	*Armstrong*	*Wilson*	*Campbell*	*Carr*	*Allen**	*Rosenthal*
								Ref: J Winter	Spurs contrived just one chance throughout the 90 minutes, and with the unwitting intervention of Bilic – letting Neilsen's pass roll through his legs – they would have been denied that. Bilic nearly atoned, striking the post in the last minute. Redknapp: 'I don't know how we lost.'											
13	A	NEWCASTLE		13	D	1-1	1-0	Rowland 23	Miklosko	Breacker	Dicks	Potts	Bilic	Rowland	Hughes	Bishop	Moncur	Dowie	Raducioiu*	Futre
	16/11		*36,552*	*1*	15			*Beardsley 83*	*Srnicek*	*Elliott**	*Albert*	*Peacock*	*Gillespie^*	*Lee*	*Batty*	*Beardsley*	*Ginola*	*Ferdinand"*	*Asprilla*	*Beresford/Watson/*
								Ref: P Danson (Newcastle's 3rd sub Clark)	Newcastle lead the table, but consider two points were tossed away following Hammers' stubborn rearguard action. It could have been three. Breacker dispossessed Ginola to cross for Rowland at the far post. Beardsley shimmied past defenders before scoring his 200th league goal.											
14	H	DERBY		13	D	1-1	1-1	Bishop 17	Miklosko	Breacker	Dicks	Potts	Bilic	Lazaridis*	Hughes	Bishop	Moncur	Dowie	Porfirio	Futre
	23/11		24,576	*11*	16			*Sturridge 43*	*Hoult*	*Yates*	*McGrath*	*Rowett*	*Laursen**	*Flynn*	*Asanovic*	*Powell D*	*Powell C*	*Ward*	*Sturridge*	*Carsley*
								Ref: S Lodge	Two of the Premiership's lowest scoring teams were seldom likely to bust the net more than once apiece. More graft than skill on show, other than when Porfirio and Asanovic were in possession. Bishop made and scored a cracking opener, but Dean Sturridge's volley flew in off Potts.											
15	A	SHEFFIELD W		14	D	0-0	0-0		Miklosko	Breacker	Dicks	Rieper	Bilic	Lampard	Hughes*	Bishop	Moncur	Dowie	Rowland	Lazaridis
	30/11		*22,321*	*10*	17				*Pressman*	*Nolan**	*Atherton*	*Walker*	*Briscoe^*	*Whittingham*	*Carbone*	*Pembridge*	*Hyde*	*Booth*	*Trustfull"*	*Oakes/Nicol/*
								Ref: P Durkin (Wednesday's 3rd sub Humphreys)	Hammers are still reeling from the Stockport debacle. Hammers supporters aren't too impressed by this dreary performance either. Yet with both Owls full-backs injured and subbed before half-time, West Ham might have chased a rare win. Hughes and Andy Booth each hit the bar.											
16	H	ASTON VILLA		15	:L	0-2	0-1		Miklosko	Breacker*	Dicks	Rieper	Bilic	Rowland^	Hughes	Bishop	Moncur	Dowie	Raducioiu	Bowen/Lazaridis
	4/12		**19,105**	*5*	17			*Ehiogu 38, Yorke 74*	*Oakes*	*Ehiogu*	*Scimeca*	*Staunton*	*Nelson*	*Townsend*	*Taylor*	*Draper*	*Wright*	*Yorke*	*Milosevic*	
								Ref: M Riley	It was in the air that West Ham lost this match. Both Villa goals came from straightforward headers from corner-kicks, and Rieper and Bilic have no excuses. Dwight Yorke's was his eighth goal in nine games. Poor Dowie has not scored in 20 in the league, and was denied by Oakes.											
17	H	MANCHESTER U		14	D	2-2	0-0	Raducioiu 78, Dicks 80p	Miklosko	Bowen	Dicks	Rieper	Bilic*	Rowland^	Hughes	Bishop	Moncur	Dowie	Dumitrescu	Potts/Raducioiu
	8/12		25,045	*6*	18			*Solskjaer 54, Beckham 75*	*Schmeichel*	*Johnsen*	*May*	*Pallister*	*Irwin*	*Poborsky**	*Beckham*	*McClair*	*Giggs*	*Cantona*	*Solskjaer*	*Neville P*
								Ref: P Jones	United are on a high after midweek glory in Vienna. West Ham had fallen 0-2 behind to Beckham's delightful chip and Upton Park was getting restless. Then Raducioiu spun away from Johnsen to pull a goal back. Schmeichel then sent Hughes into orbit and Dicks' penalty was a blur.											
18	A	CHELSEA		15	L	1-3	1-3	Porfirio 11	Miklosko	Bowen	Dicks	Rieper	Bilic	Rowland*	Hughes	Bishop^	Moncur"	Porfirio	**Newell**	Radu/L'pard/W'mson
	21/12		*28,315*	*8*	18			*Hughes 6, 35, Zola 10*	*Grodas*	*Clarke*	*Gullit*	*Duberry*	*Petrescu*	*Burley**	*Newton*	*Di Matteo*	*Clement^*	*Zola*	*Hughes*	*Sinclair/Myers*
								Ref: A Wilkie	Not many players make Julian Dicks look foolish, but Zola's nutmeg *en route* to making it 0-2 did exactly that. Within seconds Porfirio halves the deficit, only for Mark Hughes to hammer No 3. Foolish or not, Dicks was West Ham's best player. His team-mates had nowhere to hide.											
19	H	SUNDERLAND		16	W	2-0	1-0	Bilic 37, Raducioiu 90	Miklosko	Bowen	Dicks	Rieper	Bilic	Williamson	Hughes	Bishop	Moncur*	Porfirio	Newell^	Lampard/Raducioiu
	28/12		24,077	*13*	21				*Perez*	*Hall*	*Melville*	*Ord*	*Kubicki*	*Rae*	*Bracewell*	*Agnew*	*Smith**	*Russell^*	*Kelly*	*Alston/Bridges*
								Ref: R Dilkes	Flu keeps Harry Redknapp in bed and denies him the pleasure of seeing West Ham's first win in two months. Bilic produced the game's two outstanding moments, diving to head the Hammers in front, and forcing the save of the game from Miklosko. Raducioiu scores a farewell goal.											
20	H	NOTT'M FOREST		16	L	0-1	0-1		Miklosko	Bowen*	Dicks	Rieper	Bilic	Williamson	Hughes	Bishop^	Porfirio	Raducioiu	Newell"	Potts/L'pard/Jones
	1/1		22,358	*19*	21			*Campbell 38*	*Crossley*	*Lyttle*	*Blatherwick**	*Chettle*	*Pearce*	*Clough*	*Haaland*	*Cooper*	*Woan*	*Saunders*	*Campbell^*	*Phillips/Gemmill*
								Ref: P Durkin	Having dumped Forest twice this season, Hammers find themselves outplayed on an icy pitch. Half-time was shortened to 10 minutes. Stuart Pearce has taken over from Frank Clark and injected fizz into his team, who won more comfortably than the score suggests and climb to 19th.											
21	A	LIVERPOOL		17	D	0-0	0-0		Miklosko	Breacker	Dicks	Rieper	Bilic	Williamson*	Hughes	Bishop	Moncur	Porfirio^	Jones"	Potts/Newell/Laz'dis
	11/1		*40,102*	*1*	22				*James*	*Matteo*	*Ruddock**	*Babb^*	*McAteer*	*Thomas*	*Bjornebye*	*Barnes"*	*McManam'n*	*Fowler*	*Berger*	*Carragher/Collymore*
								Ref: J Winter (Liverpool's 3rd sub Kennedy)	Liverpool still top the league, but injuries forced them to reshuffle. At one stage Michael Thomas played as centre-half. Though the game died on its feet before the finish, the first half saw the woodwork struck four times. Liverpool won that contest 3-1, Breacker the unlucky Hammer.											

No		Date	Att	Pos	Pt	F-A	H-T	Scorers, Times, and Referees	SQUAD	NUMBERS	IN	USE								subs used
22	H	LEEDS		18	L	0-2	0-0		Miklosko	Breacker	Dicks	Rieper	Bilic	Williamson	Hughes	Bishop	Lazaridis*	Jones	Newell	Porfirio
		20/1	19,441	*11*	22			*Kelly 53, Bowyer 70*	*Martyn*	*Molenaar*	*Wetherall*	*Radebe*	*Kelly*	*Jackson*	*Palmer*	*Bowyer*	*Halle*	*Deane*	*Rush*	
								Ref: G Poll	Lee Bowyer was born three miles from Upton Park, but was snapped up by Charlton. He chested and volleyed Leeds' second, to add to Kelly's free-kick which flew down off the bar and in off Miklosko's head. Hammers seldom created anything, though Bilic hit the bar from 30 yards.											
23	H	ARSENAL		18	L	1-2	0-1	Rose 63 (og)	Miklosko	Breacker	Dicks	Rieper	Bilic	Williamson	Hughes	Rowland*	Moncur^	Porfirio	Newell	Jones/Lampard
		29/1	24,382	*2*	22			*Parlour 8, Wright 67*	*Seaman*	*Dixon*	*Rose"*	*Adams*	*Bould*	*Winterburn*	*Parlour*	*Vieira*	*Hughes**	*Wright^*	*Merson*	*Morrow/Hartson/*
								Ref: M Bodenham (Arsenal's 3rd sub Marshall)	One win in 16 games. Afterwards demonstrators staged a sit-in against the board. West Ham had been overwhelmed, trailing to Parlour's low strike and needing the bar to keep out Merson's sweet chip. No sooner had Michael Rose turned in Bilic's header, than Merson set up Wright.											
24	A	BLACKBURN		18	L	1-2	0-2	Ferdinand 64	Sealey	Breacker	Dicks	Rieper	Bilic	Williamson	Hughes	Bishop	Rowland*	Jones^	Newell	Lazaridis/Ferdinand
		1/2	*21,994*	*13*	22			*Gallacher 36, Sutton 39*	*Flowers*	*Kenna*	*Sherwood*	*Hendry*	*Le Saux*	*Gallacher*	*Sutton*	*Wilcox**	*McKinlay*	*Berg*	*Flitcroft*	*Donis*
								Ref: A Wilkie	The writing is on the wall and West Ham seem to be spiralling out of the Premiership. The score flattered the Hammers, Gallacher scoring from 25 yards and Sutton heading his 11th goal of the season. Rio Ferdinand, on at half-time, struck a beauty out of nothing to bring hope.											
25	A	DERBY		18	L	0-1	0-0		Miklosko	Breacker	Dicks	Rieper*	Potts	Williamson	Rowland^	Bishop	Ferdinand	**Hartson**	**Kitson**	Porfirio/Lampard
		15/2	*18,057*	*13*	22			*Asanovic 53p*	*Hoult*	*Rowett*	*McGrath*	*Stimac*	*Carsley*	*van der Laan*	*Trollope*	*Powell C*	*Dailly*	*Sturridge*	*Asanovic*	
								Ref: G Ashby	Redknapp splashes out £6 million on a new strike force. The result? No goals and a booking for Hartson that brings a suspension. Ferdinand felled Asanovic for the penalty. West Ham were denied two themselves. At half-time a Derby fan proposed to his beloved in the centre circle.											
26	H	TOTTENHAM		17	W	4-3	3-2	Dicks 21, 72p, Kitson 22, Hartson 38	Miklosko	Breacker	Dicks	Ferdinand	Potts	Bowen	Hughes	Bishop	Moncur	Hartson	Kitson*	Dowie
		24/2	23,998	*11*	25			*Sheringh'm 8, Anderton 29, Howells 53*	*Walker*	*Austin*	*Calderwood*	*Campbell*	*Carr*	*Anderton*	*Howells**	*Sinton^*	*Wilson*	*Sheringham*	*Iversen*	*Rosenthal/Nielsen*
								Ref: G Willard	Match of the season, played in howling wind and rain. On form, the two worst teams in the league. Both Hammers new boys leave their mark, as does never-say-die Dicks with the decisive penalty, which Walker wisely evades. Redknapp's verdict on the game: 'No, I did not enjoy it'.											
27	A	LEEDS		18	L	0-1	0-0		Miklosko	Breacker*	Dicks	Ferdinand	Bilic	Bowen^	Hughes !	Bishop"	Moncur	Dowie	Kitson	**Omoy'**/R'land/L'pard
		1/3	*30,575*	*9*	25			*Sharpe 47*	*Martyn*	*Radebe*	*Halle*	*Wetherall*	*Molenaar*	*Bowyer**	*Rush*	*Sharpe*	*Harte*	*Yeboah*	*Deane*	*Palmer*
								Ref: P Jones	George Graham's team have stopped leaking daft goals, but Redknapp's have not. Dicks and Miklosko dither to present Lee Sharpe with the winner. Hughes is sent off after 78 minutes for kicking Radebe. Southampton and Forest both won away, dumping Hammers back in the mire.											
28	H	CHELSEA		17	W	3-2	0-1	Dicks 55p, Kitson 68, 90	Miklosko	Breacker	Dicks	Ferdinand*	Bilic	Potts	Hughes	Bishop^	Moncur	Dowie	Kitson	W'son"/L'pard/P'rfirio
		12/3	24,502	*8*	28			*Vialli 26, Hughes 87*	*Colgan*	*Sinclair*	*Clarke*	*Johnsen*	*Petrescu**	*Burley*	*Wise*	*Hughes P*	*Minto*	*Zola*	*Vialli*	*Hughes M*
								Ref: K Burge	For 45 minutes West Ham were inept, with Gullit's Chelsea leading through Vialli's breakaway goal. An iffy penalty, when Sinclair tackled Porfirio, levels the scores. Super goals by Kitson and Mark Hughes make it 2-2. Then Kitson brushes Dowie's header past debutant Colgan.											
29	A	ASTON VILLA		17	D	0-0	0-0		Miklosko	Breacker	Dicks	Potts	Bilic	Lampard*	Lazaridis	Bishop	Moncur	Hartson	Kitson	Ferdinand
		15/3	*35,992*	*6*	29				*Bosnich*	*Nelson*	*Wright*	*Southgate*	*Ehiogu*	*Hughes*	*Townsend*	*Taylor*	*Draper**	*Yorke*	*Joachim^*	*Hendrie/Johnson*
								Ref: D Elleray	Mark Bosnich is the main reason why the Hammers failed to score, denying both Hartson and Kitson. West Ham also thought they were denied a clear-cut penalty. Frank Lampard Jnr breaks a leg. Julian Dicks is booked for dissent and will miss the crunch match with Middlesbrough.											
30	A	WIMBLEDON		16	D	1-1	0-1	Lazaridis 89	Miklosko	Breacker	Dicks	Rieper	Bilic	Potts*	Ferdinand	Bishop^	Moncur	Hartson	Kitson	Porfirio/Lazaridis
		18/3	*15,771*	*8*	30			*Harford 19*	*Sullivan*	*Cunningham*	*Kimble*	*Perry*	*Blackwell*	*Jones*	*Earle*	*Leonhardsen*	*Ekoku**	*Harford*	*Gayle*	*Holdsworth*
								Ref: J Winter	The new look Hammers are doing the business at home, but were seconds away from a fourth away blank when substitute Lazaridis fired back Gayle's headed clearance. Hartson and Leonhardsen both hit the woodwork, while Vinnie Jones missed a penalty when Breacker held Gayle.											
31	A	COVENTRY		15	W	3-1	2-1	Hartson 27, 49, Ferdinand 34	Miklosko	Breacker*	Dicks	Rieper	Bilic	Potts	Ferdinand^	Bishop"	Moncur	Hartson	Kitson	R'land/Dowie/Porfirio
		22/3	*22,291*	*18*	33			*Rieper 9 (og)*	*Ogrizovic*	*Breen*	*Dublin*	*Shaw*	*Telfer*	*McAllister*	*Williams*	*Richardson*	*Hall**	*Whelan^*	*Huckerby*	*Ndlovu/Burrows*
								Ref: M Reed	Coventry began well, aided by Rieper's inadvertent header into the top corner. But then - to manager Strachan's chagrin - they stop playing the ball down the channels and West Ham wrestle the initiative. Hartson scores two neat goals. It is 11 points from six games. Championship form.											

No	Venue	Date / Opponent / Att	Pos	Res / Pts	FT	HT	Scorers, Times, and Referees	1	2	3	4	5	6	7	8	9	10	11	12 sub used
32	H	MIDDLESBROUGH	16	D	0-0	0-0		Miklosko	Potts	**Hall**	Rieper	Bilic	**Lomas**	Lazaridis*	Bishop	Hughes	Hartson	Kitson	Porfirio
	9/4	23,988	*18*	34				*Schwarzer* Fleming*		*Festa*	*Vickers*	*Kinder*	*Blackmore*	*Emerson*	*Mustoe*	*Moore^*	*Juninho*	*Ravanelli*	*Roberts/Beck*
							Ref: P Jones	Richard Hall and Steve Lomas play their first matches, while the suspended Dicks misses his first of the season. In spite of Boro's galaxy of stars the game splutters but never explodes. The Hammers fail to create a single worthwhile chance. Boro win on points, but not on goals.											
33	A	SOUTHAMPTON	17	L	0-2	0-2		Miklosko	Potts	Hall	Rieper*	Bilic	Lomas	Rowland^	Bishop"	Hughes	Hartson	Kitson	Dowie/Laz/Porfirio
	12/9	***15,244***	*16*	34			*Evans 13, Berkovic 36*	*Taylor*	*Dodd !*	*Lundekvam*	*Van Gobbel*	*Benali*	*Slater*	*Magilton*	*Berkovic**	*Evans*	*Oakley^*	*Ostenstad*	*Neilson/Dryden*
							Ref: S Dunn	First Roker, now the Dell. The press are scathing. The *Sunday Telegraph* says West Ham are disgraceful, contemptible, ignominious, pathetic. Magilton missed a penalty and Dodd was sent off on 44 minutes for a pro foul on Hartson. The result is Saints' first home win since December.											
34	H	EVERTON	18	D	2-2	2-0	Kitson 10, 32	Miklosko	Potts	Hall	Ferdinand	Bilic	Lomas	Porfirio*	Moncur^	Hughes	Hartson	Kitson	Rieper/Bishop
	19/4	24,525	*11*	35			*Branch 78, Ferguson 90*	*Southall*	*Barrett*	*Unsworth*	*Watson*	*Stuart*	*Speed*	*THomsen*	*Ball**	*Dunne*	*Branch*	*Ferguson*	*Barmby*
							Ref: P Alcock	Crisis! Porfirio goes down, but Kitson refuses Hartson's offer to clinch his hat-trick from the spot. Hartson had been nominated. Kitson relents, but his shot is weak. At the death Miklosko misses Barmby's free-kick, Ferguson hooks in. Then a corner flies off a post into Southall's arms.											
35	A	LEICESTER	16	W	1-0	0-0	Moncur 75	Miklosko	Potts	Hall	Ferdinand	Rieper	Lomas	Porfirio*	Moncur	Hughes	Hartson	Kitson^	Rowland/Dowie
	23/4	*20,327*	*14*	38				*Keller*	*Grayson*	*Prior*	*Elliott*	*Walsh*	*Guppy**	*Lennon*	*Parker*	*Izzet^*	*Claridge*	*Heskey*	*Marshall/Campbell*
							Ref: R Dilkes / G Hegley	Little football was played, but that was hardly surprising. Nor were the 10 bookings. Dilkes dished out four in the first half, then collided with Moncur and was replaced. Moncur's goal, at the second attempt, was his second of the season, and his second winning goal against Leicester.											
36	H	SHEFFIELD WED	15	W	**5-1**	3-0	Kitson 5, 13, 89, Hartson 30, 67	Miklosko	Potts	Hall	Ferdinand	Bilic*	Lomas^	Porfirio	Moncur	Lazaridis"	Hartson	Kitson	Rieper/**Boylan**/Bishop
	3/5	24,960	*7*	41			*Carbone 82*	*Pressman*	*Nicol**	*Walker*	*Stefanovic*	*Nolan*	*Whittingh'm^*	*Atherton*	*Pembridge*	*Carbone*	*Booth*	*Hirst !*	*Oakes/Blinker*
							Ref: M Riley	No one was so full of praise for West Ham as Wednesday boss David Pleat. He managed Hartson at Luton and Kitson at Leicester. Hartson's power and Kitson's stealth overwhelm the Owls. On 58 minutes Hirst elbowed Ferdinand and was sent off. Rio got a yellow for retaliation.											
37	H	NEWCASTLE	12	D	0-0	0-0		Miklosko	Potts	Hall	Ferdinand	Bilic	Lomas	Porfirio*	Moncur^	Lazaridis	Hartson	Kitson	Hughes/Bishop
	6/5	24,617	*4*	42				*Srnicek*	*Watson*	*Peacock*	*Albert*	*Beresford*	*Barton*	*Clark*	*Batty*	*Elliott*	*Asprilla**	*Shearer*	*Gillespie*
							Ref: G Poll	Both teams need the points. Dalglish has put the clamps on Newcastle's defence and they are unrecognisable from Keegan's cavaliers. Both sides created one good chance. Hartson cut inside Peacock but shot wide. Then Shearer's header was wonderfully tipped over by Miklokso.											
38	A	MANCHESTER U	14	L	0-2	0-1		Miklosko*	Potts	Hall	Ferdinand^	Bilic	Lomas	Porfirio	Moncur	Lazaridis	Dowie	Kitson	Sealey/Hughes
	11/5	***55,249***	*1*	42			*Solskjaer 11, Cruyff 84*	*Schmeichel*	*Neville P*	*May*	*Johnsen*	*Irwin**	*Poborsky^*	*Beckham*	*Butt*	*Scholes"*	*Cantona*	*Solskjaer*	*Clegg/McClair/Cruyff*
		Home Away					Ref: S Lodge	The fate of both sides had been determined days earlier, denying this fixture significance. Man U's first, second, third and fourth teams all won their respective leagues. Solskjaer netted after Scholes' effort came down off the bar, and Jordi Cruyff scored his first goal since August.											
Average		23,242 28,476																	

Coca-Cola Cup					F-A	H-T	Scorers, Times, and Referees	SQUAD	NUMBERS	IN	USE								subs used
2:1	A	BARNET	17	D	1-1	0-1	Cottee 77	Mautone	Breacker*	Dicks	Rieper	Bilic	Bowen	Hughes	Bishop	Moncur^	Dowie	Cottee	Lazaridis/Lampard
18/9		*3,849 3:17*					*Simpson 13*	*Taylor*	*Primus*	*Pardew*	*Howarth*	*McDonald*	*Wilson*	*Codner*	*Gale*	*Simpson**	*Rattray^*	*Devine*	*Tomlinson/Campbell*
							Ref: M Riley	Steve Mautone is recalled from his loan to Crewe, after Miklosko gets injured, but spills Shaun Gale's effort. Simpson capitalised. Hammers upped the pace kicking downhill after half-time. Cottee headed past lance-corporal Maik Taylor, who Barnet bought out of the Army for £600.											
2:2	H	BARNET	13	W	1-0	0-0	Bilic 48	Mautone	Breacker	Dicks	Rieper	Bilic	Moncur	Lazaridis*	Bishop	Dumitrescu	Dowie	Cottee^	Ferdinand/Jones
25/9		15,264 *3:13*					(Barnet's 3rd sub Tomlinson)	*Taylor*	*Gale**	*McDonald*	*Codner*	*Primus*	*Howarth*	*Rattray^*	*Hardyman"*	*Wilson*	*Devine*	*Pardew*	*Campbell/Hodges/*
							Ref: C Wilkes (Hammers win 2-1 on aggregate)	This had all the makings of a tricky tie. The longer the game went on the greater Barnet's hopes of a famous triumph, but they were sunk by Slaven Bilic's first ever goal for West Ham, heading in Lazaridis' corner. Bilic had been linked with Spurs, but agreed a new deal in midweek.											
3	H	NOTT'M FOREST	13	W	4-1	1-1	Dowie 16, 56, Porfirio 67, Dicks 73p	Miklosko	Bowen	Dicks	Rieper	Bilic	Lazaridis	Hughes	Bishop	Moncur	Dowie	Porfirio	
23/10		19,402 *18*					*Cooper 29*	*Crossley*	*Haarland*	*Cooper*	*Blatherwick*	*Phillips*	*Gemmell*	*Bart-Williams*	*Woan*	*Roy*	*Lee*	*Saunders*	
							Ref: D Elleray	Times are changing at Upton Park, for this team contains just three Englishmen. Hugo Porfirio, on loan from Sporting Lisbon, steals the show with a dazzling display. Forest's only moment to savour came when Cooper headed in Saunders' cross. No substitutes by either side. A rarity.											
4	H	STOCKPORT	13	D	1-1	1-0	Raducioiu 12	Miklosko	Breacker	Dicks	Potts	Bilic	Lazaridis*	Hughes	Bishop	Lampard	Dowie	Raducioiu	Dumitrescu
27/11		20,061 *2:11*					*Cavaco 51*	*Jones*	*Connelly*	*Gannon*	*Flynn*	*Todd*	*Durkan**	*Bennett*	*Marsden*	*Jeffers^*	*Armstrong*	*Angell*	*Dinning/Cavaco*
							Ref: M Bailey	Porfirio is out, leaving the only Portuguese player in Division 2 to grab the headlines. Luis Cavaco came on at half-time and punished Dicks' error. Raducioiu, at £2.6 million the Hammers then record signing, had notched his first goal. But by the end Upton Park was awash with jeers.											
4R	A	STOCKPORT	15	L	1-2	1-2	Dicks 22	Miklosko	Bowen	Dicks	Rieper	Bilic	Moncur	Hughes	Bishop	Dumitrescu	Dowie*	Porfirio	Williamson
18/12		*9,834 2:6*					*Dowie 23 (og), Angell 27*	*Jones*	*Connelly*	*Flynn*	*Gannon*	*Todd*	*Durkan*	*Bennett*	*Marsden*	*Cavaco**	*Armstrong*	*Angell*	*Dinning*
							Ref: U Rennie	Having accounted for Blackburn, Stockport claim another big scalp to reach the last eight for the first time. Heavy rain ruins the pitch. Dicks heads in a corner, only for Dowie to head into his own net and Angell to nod County ahead. Dowie breaks an ankle and Bishop hits the bar.											

FA Cup																			
3	A	WREXHAM	16	D	1-1	1-1	Porfirio 44	Miklosko	Breacker	Dicks	Rieper	Potts	Williamson	Hughes	Bishop	Moncur	Porfirio	Jones	
4/1		*9,747 2:10*					*Hughes 6*	*Marriott*	*McGregor*	*Carey*	*Humes*	*Hardy*	*Chalk*	*Hughes*	*Ward*	*Owen**	*Morris^*	*Watkin*	*Russell/Roberts*
							Ref: M Reed	Snow wipes out most of the Cup programme, but not here, much to Redknapp's displeasure, as the pitch is white and the ball orange. Bryan Hughes headed in Owen's early corner, but Porfirio's miscued lob (genius or fluke?) restored parity. It was his first sight of snow, he insisted.											
3R	H	WREXHAM	18	L	0-1	0-0		Miklosko	Breacker	Dicks	Ferdinand	Bilic	Williamson	Hughes	Bishop	Lampard	Lazaridis*	Jones	Porfirio
25/1		16,763 *2:10*					*Russell 90*	*Mariott*	*McGregor*	*Humes*	*Carey*	*Hardy*	*Chalk*	*Hughes*	*Owen**	*Ward*	*Connelly*	*Watkin*	*Russell*
							Ref: S Lodge	First Stockport, now Wrexham from Division 2 dump the Hammers from a cup. It is as bad as can be for Harry, whose foreign misfits have flown the nest leaving him without a goalscorer. The tie was seconds from extra-time when sub Kevin Russell leathered the ball from 20 yards.											

		Home					Away					
	P	W	D	L	F	A	W	D	L	F	A	Pts
1 Manchester U	38	12	5	2	38	17	9	7	3	38	27	75
2 Newcastle	38	13	3	3	54	20	6	8	5	19	20	68
3 Arsenal	38	10	5	4	36	18	9	6	4	26	14	68
4 Liverpool	38	10	6	3	38	19	9	5	5	24	18	68
5 Aston Villa	38	11	5	3	27	13	6	5	8	20	21	61
6 Chelsea	38	9	8	2	33	22	7	3	9	25	33	59
7 Sheffield Wed	38	8	10	1	25	16	6	5	8	25	35	57
8 Wimbledon	38	9	6	4	28	21	6	5	8	21	25	56
9 Leicester	38	7	5	7	22	26	5	6	8	24	28	47
10 Tottenham	38	8	4	7	19	17	5	3	11	25	34	46
11 Leeds	38	7	7	5	15	13	4	6	9	13	25	46
12 Derby	38	8	6	5	25	22	3	7	9	20	36	46
13 Blackburn	38	8	4	7	28	23	1	11	7	14	20	42
14 WEST HAM	38	7	6	6	27	25	3	6	10	12	23	42
15 Everton	38	7	4	8	24	22	3	8	8	20	35	42
16 Southampton	38	6	7	6	32	24	4	4	11	18	32	41
17 Coventry	38	4	8	7	19	23	5	6	8	19	31	41
18 Sunderland	38	7	6	6	20	18	3	4	12	15	35	40
19 Middlesbro*	38	8	5	6	34	25	2	7	10	17	35	39
20 Nott'm Forest	38	3	9	7	15	27	3	7	9	16	32	34
	760	162	119	99	559	411	99	119	162	411	559	1018

* deducted 3 points

Odds & ends

Double wins: (1) Leicester.
Double losses: (2) Arsenal, Leeds.

Won from behind: (5) Southampton (h), Blackburn (h), Spurs (h), Chelsea (h), Coventry (a).
Lost from in front: (1) Stockport LC (a).

High spots: The arrival of Hartson and Kitson, whose 13 league goals in the last 14 games staved off relegation.
One defeat in 10 games from 12 March.

Low spots: One point from six games prior to the arrival of Hartson and Kitson.
Going out of both cups to Second Division teams.
Calling upon 32 players in 38 league matches.

Hammer of the Year: Julian Dicks.
Ever-presents: (0).
Hat-tricks: (1) Paul Kitson.
Leading scorer: (8) Julian Dicks, Paul Kitson.

	Appearances						Goals			
	Lge	*Sub*	LC	*Sub*	FAC	*Sub*	Lge	LC	FAC	Tot
Bilic, Slaven	**35**		5		1		**2**	1		**3**
Bishop, Ian	**26**	*3*	5		2		**1**			**1**
Bowen, Mark	**15**	*2*	3				**1**			**1**
Boylan, Lee		*1*								
Breacker, Tim	**22**	*4*	3		2					
Cottee, Tony	**2**	*1*	2					1		**1**
Dicks, Julian	**31**		5		2		**6**	2		**8**
Dowie, Iain	**18**	*5*	5					2		**2**
Dumitrescu, Ilie	**3**	*4*	2	*1*						
Ferdinand, Rio	**11**	*4*		*1*	1		**2**			**2**
Futre, Paulo	**4**	*5*								
Hall, Richard	**7**									
Hartson, John	**11**						**5**			**5**
Hughes, Michael	**31**	*2*	4		2		**3**			**3**
Jones, Steve	**5**	*3*		*1*	2					
Kitson, Paul	**14**						**8**			**8**
Lampard, Frank	**3**	*10*	1	*1*	1					
Lazaridis, Stan	**13**	*9*	3	*1*	1		**1**			**1**
Lomas, Steve	**7**									
Mautone, Steve	**1**		2							
Miklosko, Ludek	**36**		3		2					
Moncur, John	**26**	*1*	4		1		**2**			**2**
Newell, Mike	**6**	*1*								
Omoyimni, Emmanuel		*1*								
Potts, Steve	**17**	*3*	1		1					
Porfirio, Hugo	**15**	*8*	2		1	*1*	**2**	1	1	**4**
Raducioiu, Florin	**6**	*5*	1				**2**	1		**3**
Rieper, Marc	**26**	*2*	4		1		**1**			**1**
Rowland, Keith	**11**	*4*					**1**			**1**
Sealey, Les	**1**	*1*								
Slater, Stuart	**2**	*1*								
Williamson, Danny	**13**	*2*		*1*	2					
(own-goals)							**2**			**2**
32 players used	**418**	***82***	**55**	***6***	**22**	***1***	**39**	**8**	**1**	**48**

The 1980 FA Cup winners

List of Subscribers

Votes for the most popular West Ham player 1961-1997

Subscriber	Vote
Alf Allington	Billy Bonds
Ken 'Irons' Ansted	Bobby Moore
Paul Baccarini	Julian Dicks
Steve Bacon	Billy Bonds
Gareth Bailey	Trevor Brooking
Phil Bailey	Billy Bonds
Danny Baldwin	Julian Dicks
Robert Banks	Tony Cottee
Martin Bass	Julian Dicks
Reece Bayliss	Julian Dicks
Antony Beaman	Trevor Brooking
Brian Belton	Alan Sealey
Tim Bennett	Billy Bonds
Jonathan Bill	Geoff Hurst
Chris Bradley	Julian Dicks
Brian Brady	Trevor Brooking
Robert Bragg	Julian Dicks
Paul Brand	Trevor Brooking
Clive Bray	Trevor Brooking
Simon J Bremner	Trevor Brooking
M C Brew	Julian Dicks
Darren Brooks	Trevor Brooking
Steve Broomfield	Trevor Brooking
Helen Brown	Bobby Moore
Mark Brown	Julian Dicks
Roger Browning	Trevor Brooking
Peter Bulley	Trevor Brooking
D R Burack	Billy Bonds
Peter Michael Burch	Bobby Moore
Gary Bush	Bobby Moore
David M Byford	Trevor Brooking
David Carter	Alan Devonshire
Charlie Casey	Trevor Brooking
Robert Charters	Alan Devonshire
Mike Clark	Alan Devonshire
Allan Coles	Bobby Moore
James Colkett	Trevor Brooking
Bob Colley	Bobby Moore
T M Connelly	Johnny Byrne
Shaun Cooke	Julian Dicks
Neil Coombs	Frank McAvennie
Reece Cowan	Julian Dicks
John Crane	Trevor Brooking
Timothy Crane	Trevor Brooking
Charles Leonard Crawley	Bobby Moore
Mark Charles Crawley	Trevor Brooking
Stuart Crowe	Julian Dicks
Mark Cundy	Julian Dicks
Dennis J Curtin	Bobby Moore
Mark Danneau	Bobby Moore
Paul Michael Dodd	Billy Bonds
Ciaran Donegan	Julian Dicks
Dennis Donoghue	Frank McAvennie
Shane Dunbar	Julian Dicks
David A Duncan	Bobby Moore
Clive Dyer	Trevor Brooking
Les Earl	Billy Bonds
J H Eldred	Rio Ferdinand
Craig Ellis	Bryan Robson
Neil Ellis	Steve Potts
Gary Firmager	Alan Devonshire
Jeremy S Fisher	Bobby Moore
Colin Flack	Bobby Moore
Mark Foreman	Trevor Brooking
John Fowler	Trevor Brooking
Tony Fowles	Bobby Moore
Stephen Frearson	Julian Dicks
Geoff Fuller	Bobby Moore
Stuart Fuller	Billy Bonds
Tony Gillham	Bryan Robson
Geoff Goddard	Bobby Moore
John Groombridge	Ray Stewart
Raymond Alan Haggie	Bobby Moore
Glenn W Halffman	Julian Dicks
Shane Hallett	Trevor Brooking
Mark R Harding	Julian Dicks
Don Harrison	Bobby Moore
I C Hawkins	Bobby Moore
Ian Heale	Bobby Moore
Clive Heasman	Trevor Brooking
John Helliar	Bobby Moore
William Hoadley	Martin Allen
Mr Ian Horncastle	Trevor Brooking
Peter Jackson	Billy Bonds
Mr Ian Jacques	Julian Dicks
Daniel James	Julian Dicks
Thomas Jameson	Julian Dicks
Peter Jupp	Geoff Hurst
Mr Alan Kenyon	Bobby Moore
Trevor King	Geoff Hurst

Votes for the most popular West Ham player 1961-1997

Subscriber	Vote
David James Larcombe	Trevor Brooking
Hazel Larking	Steve Potts
Phil S Latchford	Julian Dicks
Vincent Leach	Bobby Moore
John Lennard	Geoff Hurst
Mr Ronald A Liell	Trevor Brooking
John Lowe	Trevor Brooking
David Maddocks	Geoff Hurst
John Markham	Billy Bonds
Kevin Markham	Trevor Brooking
Trevor Markham	Julian Dicks
Steve Marks	Tony Cottee
Chris McMahon	Bobby Moore
Tony Meadway	Billy Bonds
Keith Meredith	Trevor Brooking
Gary Bernard Miller	Bobby Moore
Thomas Minchin	Tony Cottee
Neil Moody	Billy Bonds
Anthony Moore	Trevor Brooking
Lynda Morgan	Paulo Futre
Terry Muzzell	Alan Devonshire
John Northcutt	Billy Bonds
Michael Oliver	David Cross
Geoffrey Peach	Julian Dicks
Stephen Pellicci	Trevor Brooking
Kevin Pendegrass	Trevor Brooking
Angus M Phillips	Trevor Brooking
Danny Phillips	Phil Parkes
Geoff Playle	Frank McAvennie
Mr Michael George Pocock	Frank McAvennie
Steve Poole	Billy Bonds
John Powles	Trevor Brooking
Simon Price	Trevor Brooking
Pauline Rawe	Bobby Moore
John Reynolds	Trevor Brooking
Mr G F Saulter	Bobby Moore
Mark Scallan	Frank McAvennie
Lawrence Segal	Geoff Hurst
Tim Sharman	Frank McAvennie
Roy K Shoesmith	Bobby Moore
Colin J Simpson	Billy Bonds
Bill Sims	Bobby Moore
Fred Sims	Bobby Moore
Alex Smith	Julian Dicks
Darren Bradley Smith	Julian Dicks
Ian Smith	Julian Dicks
Jeff Smith	Frank McAvennie
John Smith	Geoff Hurst
Steve Smith	Julian Dicks
Peter Stewart	Bobby Moore
R Stocken	
Graham & Paul Sturton	Julian Dicks
John Sturton	Brian Dear
Michael Thomas	Mark Robson
Peter Tierney	Trevor Brooking
Mark Todd	Geoff Hurst
Peter Trevillion	Billy Bonds
Kevin Trivett	Bobby Moore
Lawrence & Adam Turner	Trevor Brooking
Martin Tyers	Ian Bishop
Liam Tyrell	Trevor Brooking
Colin Wade	Bobby Moore
Robin John Walsh	Bryan Robson
Sam Walters	Julian Dicks
Sid Walters	Julian Dicks
Simon Ward	Trevor Brooking
Len Warren	Bobby Moore
Helen Watts	Trevor Brooking
Rick Webb	Bobby Moore
Andy Wells	Billy Bonds
John Wells	Trevor Brooking
Shaun West	Ian Bishop
Paul Wheatley	Trevor Brooking
Peter Christopher White	Trevor Brooking
Paul Whitfield	Trevor Brooking
Kevin H Williamson	Billy Bonds
Brad Wilson	Geoff Hurst
Simon Winson	Bobby Moore
Andrew Woolnough	Trevor Brooking
Alan Yard	Julian Dicks

MOST POPULAR WEST HAM PLAYERS
(21 different players received votes)

1st	Trevor Brooking
2nd	Bobby Moore
3rd	Julian Dicks
4th	Billy Bonds
5th	Geoff Hurst
6th	Frank McAvennie